Your Road Map to

BackOffice Expertise

This volume starts with a **"big picture"** view of BackOffice and the way it integrates with an organization's many other facets. People issues are discussed, as well as those pertaining to hardware and software.

Learn the Network Administrator's Role and Common Tasks

Advice on installing and configuring **Windows NT Server** and sharing resources is provided. Implementing and managing **domain security**, and the different domain models that are available, are discussed in detail.

Gain a Thorough Understanding of Windows NT Services

In order to understand BackOffice and its many components, it is essential to begin with a solid foundation—a thorough understanding of **Windows NT services**. You will learn how services differ from standard applications, and how they can be used to control the **security** privileges your BackOffice components have.

Learn the Right Way to Use Networking Protocols

The proper usage of **networking protocols** is critical for the effective use of BackOffice, especially the use of **TCP/IP**. The fundamentals of TCP/IP, and the various utilities to manage IP addressing, receive detailed coverage.

Learn the Benefits of the Remote Access Service (RAS)

Providing **remote dial-up access** is a common requirement for modern networks. Windows NT Server includes the **Remote Access Service (RAS)** to fulfill this need. Study this component carefully if your network users require this capability.

IIS, Active Server Pages (ASP), and FrontPage 97: Taking your Network to the Next Level

The use of the **Internet** has mushroomed, and many organizations are deploying the same tools used on the Internet to create private **intranets**. The BackOffice tools for I-net environments are explored carefully, including both server-based components like **Internet Information Server (IIS)** and **Active Server Pages (ASP)**, but also client-side tools like **FrontPage 97**. Learning this material will dramatically complement your network administration knowledge.

Quench the Rest of Your BackOffice Thirst with Volume II

Special Edition Using Microsoft BackOffice, Volume II (ISBN: 0-7897-1130-3) covers other important BackOffice components, including:

- Exchange Server 5.0
- SQL Server 6.5
- Systems Management Server (SMS) 1.2
- SNA Server 3.0

It also includes information on security and software development in a BackOffice environment.

Special Edition

USING MICROSOFT BACKOFFICE, VOLUME I

Written by Donald M. Benage and Gregory A. Sullivan with

Azam A. Mirza • Larry D. Millett • David O'Leary
Kevin D. Runnels • J. Brad Rhodes • Robert S. Black • Allen Carson
Stephen E. Hayes • Michael W. Lichtenberg • Fred Sebestyen
Jeffrey J. Thurston • David Williams • Gary P. Dzurny • Tim Darby
Daniel Garcia • James D. Marshbank • Joseph P. Lengyel
Sherman D. Cassidy • Robert Bruce Thompson

Special Edition Using Microsoft BackOffice, Volume I

Library of Congress Catalog No.: 97-65021

ISBN: 0-7897-1142-7

99 98 97   6 5 4 3 2 1

Interpretation of the printing code: the rightmost double-digit number is the year of the book's printing; the rightmost single-digit number, the number of the book's printing. For example, a printing code of 97-1 shows that the first printing of the book occurred in 1997.

Screen reproductions in this book were created using Collage Plus from Inner Media, Inc., Hollis, NH.

Contents at a Glance

Volume I

Volume II

Table of Contents

III | Windows NT Server: Enterprise Connectivity

9   Using TCP/IP with Windows NT Server   249

V | Advanced I-Net Development

Credits

PRESIDENT
Roland Elgey

PUBLISHER
Stacy Hiquet

DIRECTOR OF MARKETING
Lynn E. Zingraf

PUBLISHING MANAGER
Fred Slone

SENIOR TITLE MANAGER
Bryan Gambrel

EDITORIAL SERVICES DIRECTOR
Elizabeth Keaffaber

MANAGING EDITOR
Sandy Doell

ACQUISITIONS EDITOR
Jeff Riley

PRODUCT DEVELOPMENT SPECIALIST
Russ Jacobs

PRODUCTION EDITOR
Maureen A. McDaniel

COPY EDITORS
Thomas Cirtin
Matthew B. Cox

PRODUCT MARKETING MANAGER
Kristine R. Ankney

ASSISTANT PRODUCT MARKETING MANAGERS
Karen Hagen
Christy M. Miller

STRATEGIC MARKETING MANAGER
Barry Pruett

TECHNICAL EDITOR
Joel Goodling

TECHNICAL SUPPORT SPECIALIST
Nadeem Muhammed

SOFTWARE SPECIALIST
Brandon K. Penticuff

ACQUISITIONS COORDINATOR
Carmen Krikorian

SOFTWARE RELATIONS COORDINATOR
Susan D. Gallagher

EDITORIAL ASSISTANT
Andrea Duvall

BOOK DESIGNER
Ruth Harvey

COVER DESIGNER
Dan Armstrong

PRODUCTION TEAM
Michael Beaty
Bryan Flores
Jessica Ford
Brian Grossman
Heather Howell
Tony McDonald
Angela Perry
Sossity Smith
Lisa Stumpf

INDEXERS
Ginny Bess
Charlotte Clapp

Composed in *Century Old Style* and *ITC Franklin Gothic* by Que Corporation.

About the Authors

Donald M. Benage

To my wife Diane, my son Andy, and my friends Bob and Steve—thanks for your love and support.

Donald M. Benage is an acknowledged information systems professional and Microsoft Certified Systems Engineer with more than 17 years experience applying leading technologies to complex business solutions. He has provided architecture strategy and technology assessments—as well as detailed systems and network designs—to numerous corporations in many different industries. This, coupled with his vast experience as a network administrator, has uniquely qualified him to work information technology issues with major corporate clients from initial design through implementation, culminating in a valuable transfer of his proactive network management disciplines to client personnel.

Donald began his career as the personal computer burst into the market. He has since achieved vast experience incorporating knowledge in management of computer support operations, hands-on software and hardware evaluation, design of strategic systems for practical implementation, and network administration. Specific Microsoft product expertise was further enhanced by his employment with Microsoft Corporation for more than four years, leaving their ranks as a senior systems engineer to pursue other challenges.

Donald is a frequent speaker in industry seminars and forums dedicated to understanding software development strategies and tools. As a Director with G. A. Sullivan, he manages the day-to-day operations of the Technology Center, its research and development facility. Donald continues in a career filled with recognition for excellence in technical ability and client service.

Gregory A. Sullivan

To my beautiful wife Christine, thanks for allowing me into your heart and your family. To my sister Kari and her husband Troy, thanks for giving us Shane—I know he will make us all proud.

Gregory A. Sullivan, founder and president of G. A. Sullivan, has been an early proponent of many significant advances in software development and, over the years, has amassed an impressive array of credentials.

Motivated by his enthusiasm for the personal computer revolution and how he believed it would ultimately impact the business community, Gregory started G. A. Sullivan in 1982 shortly after receiving his Bachelor's degree in Systems Science and Mathematics from Washington University School of Engineering and Applied Science in St. Louis, Missouri. By taking the simple computer tools available then, he applied them in support of his personal commitment to the short- and long-term success of his clients. As the personal computer revolution exploded into the business community, he focused his energies on rapidly emerging new technologies.

Gregory's recognized participation in the early design and development of new technology advances were critical to establishing and maintaining an industry leadership role. He successfully established formal relationships and partnership agreements with technology leaders such as Microsoft. Additionally, he has established numerous personal affiliations with leading technical forums and organizations. Gregory is a charter member of the Client-Server Round Table and an active member of the Association for Computing Machinery (ACM), the Institute of Electrical and Electronics Engineers (IEEE), and Tau Beta Pi. He is a member of the Washington University School of Engineering and Applied Science National Council, past president of the Alumni Advisory Council, and co-sponsor of the Stifel Jens Scholarship.

Gregory frequently addresses audiences on the topics of software, its application to information technology, and the advancement of the software development profession. By enthusiastically embracing such leadership opportunities within the industry, he has developed a widespread reputation and has positioned G. A. Sullivan as a premier software development and information technology service organization.

Azam A. Mirza

To my lovely wife for her understanding and patience; to my parents for giving me the education, dedication, and work ethic; and to my brother and sisters for providing the moments of laughter that helped me to accomplish my goals. Thank you all for being there.

Azam A. Mirza, a Microsoft Certified Systems Engineer specializing in client-server software development and distributed systems architecture, is a strong proponent of utilizing the Internet to help businesses meet today's challenges while positioning them to better compete in tomorrow's complex business environments. Azam holds a B.S. in Computer Science from Washington University in St. Louis, Missouri, and an M.S. in Engineering Management from the University of Missouri-Rolla. He is an expert in the design, development, implementation, and support of client-server applications in numerous operating system environments and on various hardware platforms. He has extensive software development experience in major software development languages and is well qualified in the field of Internet/intranet technologies. Azam routinely serves as the technical lead analyst and designer for an array of complex system development efforts across a wide range of industry disciplines.

His vast experience with the Internet graphical user interface applications design and development, coupled with his astute awareness of *de facto* standards and widely accepted guidelines for software development, has uniquely qualified him to author numerous standards documents on the consistent development of distributed applications. Azam has published a white paper on the emerging role the Internet is playing in the corporate world, "Intranets and the Internet: An I-Net Introduction." He has also authored a white paper on the Microsoft Active Platform, "Using Active Platform to Enhance Your Web Site." As a consultant for G. A. Sullivan, Azam significantly influences the direction business clients take in applying advanced solutions to their most complex business challenges.

Larry D. Millett

To the further adventures of Mr. Peanut and the Mighty Cosmo!

Larry D. Millett has an M.S. degree in Computer Science from Washington University in St. Louis, Missouri, and a B.A. degree in Philosophy from Harvard University. He has over ten years experience with microcomputer networks including consulting, training, and software development for clients nationwide. He is a member of ACM and a Microsoft Certified Professional. Previous publications include Que's *Special Edition Using Microsoft BackOffice,* white papers, technical articles, and commercial software.

As a G. A. Sullivan consultant, Larry provides technical leadership for distributed, multiplatform software projects. He lives in St. Louis with his wife and two sons, and can be reached by e-mail at **larrym@gasullivan.com**.

David O'Leary

Thanks to my brother Matt and Patrick Barlow for late-night proofreading and insight. Thanks to my parents for everything.

David O'Leary is a senior consultant with G. A. Sullivan specializing in object-oriented analysis, design, and programming. David, who holds a B.S. in Computer Science from Loyola University in New Orleans, Louisiana, gained his intimate knowledge of RAS through his involvement in many client-server and replication-based remote access applications.

Kevin D. Runnels

My work on this book is dedicated to my father, Gary Frederick Runnels (1939-1996), as well as to my grandparents, Mildred and Dealing Runnels.

Kevin D. Runnels is a Microsoft Certified Solution Developer with more than ten years experience in microcomputer programming, networking, and project management. Kevin has developed numerous systems for the accounting and financial services vertical markets and is a strong proponent of using computers as tools to expand business opportunities and markets as well as for traditional transaction processing. He is an expert in the design and development of client-server applications and distributed computing, especially in the Windows NT environment.

Kevin resides in the St. Louis area and has a B.S. in Business Administration from Southeast Missouri State University and an award in accounting from the University of California, Los Angeles. As a consultant for G. A. Sullivan, Kevin continues to leverage his practical business knowledge with his considerable technical expertise to solve complex business problems and to develop new business opportunities for clients nationwide.

J. Brad Rhodes

A special thanks to my wife Renee who has always been loving and patient. Thanks to my daughter Allison for always being a source of inspiration.

J. Brad Rhodes is an experienced developer of client-server systems with an emphasis on systems architecture. Challenged by his involvement in large and medium business solutions, Brad has acquired a thorough understanding of client-server systems development. He has spent the past nine years designing and implementing client-server systems with a special emphasis on open systems technology. His leadership has helped many companies adopt new technologies including relational database management systems, distributed systems, and object-oriented programming and design.

This experience has lead Brad to the position of Vice-President of Technology at Hamilton and Sullivan, a leading provider of client-server solutions for the banking and financial industry. At Hamilton and Sullivan, Brad oversees the development of next generation retail and commercial banking solutions.

Brad holds a B.S in Electrical Engineering from Southern Illinois University at Edwardsville, Illinois, and has nearly completed an M.S. in Electrical Engineering from Washington University in St. Louis, Missouri. Mr. Rhodes is also a Microsoft Certified System Engineer. He lives in the St. Louis area with his wife Renee and daughter Allison.

Robert S. Black

To Mom and Dad for your love, support, and understanding.

Robert S. Black is a graduate of Washington University in St. Louis, Missouri, where he earned a B.S. in both Computer Science and System Science and Engineering. He currently develops software for client-server applications as a software consultant at G. A. Sullivan.

Allen Carson

I dedicate this effort to my parents for putting up with me then, and to my wife Sharon for putting up with me now.

Allen Carson began his career 15 years ago, having spent the majority of those years developing different types of real-time control software. During that time, he participated in several international design projects which produced high-quality medical imaging products that have been distributed throughout the world.

Since joining G. A. Sullivan in 1994, Allen has contributed to numerous client-server software projects. His areas of expertise include database design, OLE server implementation, and GUI design and implementation in Visual C++ working in Windows NT and OS/2 environments. He also provided technical assistance for Que's *Special Edition Using Microsoft BackOffice.*

Allen received a B.E. in Electrical Engineering from Vanderbilt University in Nashville, Tennessee. He continuously pursues educational opportunities to remain current with emerging trends in technology. In preparation for this edition, he received a Certificate Of Excellence in the Official Microsoft Curriculum course, "Managing Webs and Web Content with MS FrontPage." In addition, he has contributed to the development of several Web sites.

Allen and his wife, Sharon Jaffe, reside in the St. Louis area where he is a consultant for G. A. Sullivan.

Stephen E. Hays

To my wife Laura and my children Doug, Sara, and Tom. Thank you for your loving support and understanding. Your encouragement has greatly helped with this project as it does with so many.

Stephen E. Hays is a Microsoft Certified Professional with over 13 years experience in the microcomputer industry. He is involved in all aspects of application development; Internet technology; voice, data, and video network integration; and wide area network implementations. He is responsible for technical review and implementation of the information systems at G. A. Sullivan.

Steve is a point man in hardware and software vendor relationships and partnerships for G. A. Sullivan with involvement in new product review, beta programs, and product implementation.

Steve, a native of St. Louis, resides with his wife Laura and three children, Doug, Sara, and Tom.

Michael W. Lichtenberg

To my wife Kate for all of your love and support.

Michael W. Lichtenberg, a Microsoft Certified Professional and PowerBuilder Certified Developer, holds a B.S. in Computer Science from Washington University in St. Louis, Missouri. He has five years experience in applications programming, focused primarily on client-server business solutions.

Mike's experience in developing client-server applications ranges from single-user solutions created using Xbase programming tools, to advanced solutions created using the most advanced application programming tools and back-end database systems. In various engagements, he has designed and implemented business solutions for a variety of industries, including retail, healthcare, and travel. He has applied his knowledge of application design and development to create business solutions using Microsoft Exchange Client.

Mike works as a consultant for G. A. Sullivan, and resides in Kirkwood, Missouri with his wife Kate.

Fred Sebestyen

Thanks to my wife Nancy for your love and support and my children Sarah and Jacob for your daily inspiration.

Fred Sebestyen earned his B.S. degree in Information Systems Management from Southwest Missouri State University in Springfield, Missouri. After graduation in 1983, he began his career with a local systems integrator in Springfield designing and implementing PC solutions for a variety of businesses.

Relocating back to his home in St. Louis, Fred worked for many years in the defense industry for a major defense contractor implementing and maintaining manufacturing systems. As a consultant, he worked on various classified projects for the defense industry using state-of-the-art technologies.

Advancing his career, he worked at the national service center of a major life insurance company in St. Louis. He established a solid background in information systems for the insurance industry performing many tasks ranging from application development in the DB/2 and IMS mainframe environment to providing technical support and maintenance for PC networks. Fred was also responsible for establishing the initial Web presence for this employer.

His expertise is in problem analysis and resolution using the latest and most appropriate technologies. Fred has maintained a close watch on new and emerging technologies throughout his career. With over 13 years experience in the computer industry, he has a solid background implementing PC networks and PC-based technologies. With the explosion of the World Wide Web, he has brought his knowledge and experience in the industry to the Web, developing Web sites and Web-based applications for a number of clients.

Fred is a consultant with G. S. Sullivan and resides in St. Louis with his wife Nancy and their two children Jacob and Sarah.

Jeffrey J. Thurston

It is to his family that Jeff wishes to dedicate his work and his life, none of which would be possible without their love, support, and patience.

Jeffrey J. Thurston is a Microsoft Certified Professional with more than 12 years of experience in the use and development of systems for microcomputers. Through his experiences with Novell NetWare, Microsoft Windows for Workgroups, and Microsoft Windows NT, he has developed a formidable knowledge of networking principles. Combined with experience in the languages of C and C++, BASIC, and Pascal, he has developed a broad knowledge base, allowing for a big-picture perspective on microcomputer solutions.

Jeff's most recent project involved a sophisticated client-server solution which included a custom SQL Server to Microsoft Access replicated database component. Development included the use of Microsoft Visual C++, Microsoft Visual Basic, Microsoft SQL Server, Windows 95, and Windows NT. Jeff routinely works with virtually all of the Microsoft development tools and operating systems to provide sophisticated solutions to the clients of G. A. Sullivan.

Jeff resides in the St. Louis area with his wife of 12 years, Joy, and their two sons Jonathan and Jeremy.

David Williams

To my wife Wendy and daughter Jennie—your love and understanding have always helped me through. You make everything worthwhile. To Mom and Dad, you taught me the principles by which I have always strived to live. Thank you.

David Williams has been involved in the design and development of leading-edge software systems for the past eight years. These systems range from scientific and engineering applications to information systems based on Internet technologies. He has had extensive development experience in VMS and UNIX as well as MS-DOS, Windows, and Windows NT. He is well-versed with the various TCP/IP protocols, and is a strong advocate for the use of object-oriented technologies in software design and development.

David holds a B.S. in Electrical Engineering from Purdue University in West Lafayette, Indiana and an M.S. in Electrical Engineering from Washington University in St. Louis, Missouri. He currently resides in the St. Louis area with his wife Wendy and daughter Jennifer.

Gary P. Dzurny

To my parents, who have always encouraged me in the things I have chosen to do. Thank you for all of your hard work and support.

Gary P. Dzurny has been programming for over 15 years concentrating mainly in the area of real-time data acquisition and analysis applications. Before arriving in St. Louis, Gary spent several years working as a Senior Software Engineer on the U.S. Army's Kwajalein Missile Range in the Republic of the Marshall Islands providing software and hardware support to a variety of range instrumentation systems including radar, optical tracking, and telemetry systems. It was here that he gained much experience with synchronous and asynchronous communication protocols. Prior to this, Gary was involved in anti-satellite and smart munitions studies.

More recently, he has been involved with developing a client-server-based reporting application used by a consortium comprised of the world's largest travel companies. Gary, who holds a B.S. in Engineering Physics from Murray State University, resides in the St. Louis area with his fiancée Amy and three children, Sydney, Christian, and Kirby. As a consultant for G. A. Sullivan and a microcomputer enthusiast, he is continuously working at keeping abreast of the current information processing and methodology trends.

Tim Darby

To my mother, Alice Darby.

Tim Darby has 15 years experience in information systems design and integration. He is knowledgeable in many areas of computing, including network management, network design, software development, and operating systems. For the past seven years, he has been involved in all aspects of network planning and integration on large client-server projects, including the Automated Patent System for the U. S. Patent Office. He specializes in Windows NT server-based solutions with SMS as the management platform. He is a Microsoft Certified Systems Engineer employed with Integra Technology International, Inc. He holds a B.S. in Electrical Engineering from Rice University.

Daniel Garcia

Daniel Garcia is a consultant at ConnectOS Corporation, which provides consulting and training for Microsoft Technologies and Web hosting. Daniel is a Microsoft Certified Systems Engineer. His specialties include Microsoft Windows NT Workstation, Microsoft Windows NT Server, Microsoft Internet Information Server, and Microsoft SNA Server. Daniel has experience with a wide range of computer systems, including mainframe, AS/400, VAX, Linux, Macintosh, and Wintel. He can be reached at **dgarcia@connectos.com**.

James D. Marshbank

To my wife Debbie, my mother Irene, and my sister Sandy Durham, thanks for all your love and encouragement. I am so blessed by God having made you a part of my life.

James D. Marshbank is a recognized information systems expert and Microsoft Certified Professional with more than 26 years experience in the management of computer facilities and operations, installation projects, software development projects, and major integration plans. Taking advantage of a strong technical and business background, he regularly participates in advanced technical research and authoring on a wide variety of subjects and projects in diverse forms. His vast experience in the mainframe and personal computer environments has allowed him to address specific technologies for interfacing these two environments and to explore strategies for supporting client enterprise networking needs.

Jim holds a B.S. in Applied Science from Miami University in Oxford, Ohio, and an M.A. in Business Management from Webster University in St. Louis, Missouri. He has been a long-standing advocate of applying advanced technologies to systems designed to achieve enterprise business goals. He is knowledgeable in the leading client-server environments and is an expert in analyzing client needs, determining solutions to those needs, and providing management of the software development and hardware integration projects to implement those solutions.

Jim and his wife Debbie reside in the St. Louis area where Jim, as a senior consultant for G. A. Sullivan, eagerly pursues opportunities to advance information technologies in solving intricate business problems.

Joseph P. Lengyel

Dedicated to the administrative staff at G. A. Sullivan.

Joseph P. Lengyel began his career ten years ago as a teacher. He is a well-qualified educator, experienced in teaching business and computer curriculums. With a B.S. in Business Administration from Fontbonne College in St. Louis, Missouri and upon completing an M.S. in Computer Information Systems from Colorado State University in Fort Collins, Colorado, he began pursuing a dual career in teaching and applying technology to business applications.

Joe's technical experience includes contributions in all aspects of the development effort with particular emphasis on Windows NT Server-based applications. These experiences range from participation in business process reengineering engagements and designing detail object and data models, to development tool evaluation and the practical application of technology through various development efforts.

Joe, who resides in the St. Louis area with his wife Rosalie, is a consultant for G. A. Sullivan. He continues to maintain a presence in teaching, capitalizing on first-hand experience in industry and his technical leadership roles in the effective use of information technology.

Sherman D. Cassidy

For my wife Liz, your love and support mean more than you know. For my daughter Irene, you make my life worth living.

Sherman D. Cassidy has an accomplished professional career including ten years in various information systems roles. Sherman's experience ranges from project management and technical leadership to hands-on participation in numerous development efforts.

He is knowledgeable in the leading operating system environments, major microcomputer programming languages, and database management systems. Sherman has particular expertise in all aspects of client-server software applications development. He is a Microsoft Certified Professional and has many acknowledged achievements including expertise in relational database design utilizing Microsoft SQL Server.

Sherman holds a B.S. in Business Administration from the University of Missouri-St. Louis. In addition to his technical background, he has formally taught computer curriculum and authored many diverse forms of articles, newsletters, training materials, and documents associated with systems development.

Sherman, his wife Liz, and daughter Irene reside in the St. Louis area where he is a consultant for G. A. Sullivan.

Robert Bruce Thompson

Robert Bruce Thompson is president of Triad Technology Group, Inc., a network consulting firm in Winston-Salem, North Carolina. He has 24 years experience in programming, systems analysis, microcomputers, data communications, and network administration. Bob is certified by Novell as a Master CNE, by IBM in Advanced Connectivity, by AT&T in Network Systems Design, and is now working on his Microsft CSE. He holds an MBA from Wake Forest University. Bob specializes in network systems design, branch office networking, and the applications of technology to the needs of small businesses. He's the lead author for Que's *Windows NT Workstation 4.0 Internet and Networking Handbook*, and a contributing author for Que's *Upgrading and Repairing Networks*. You can reach him via Internet mail at **rbt@ttgnet.com**.

Acknowledgments

A book of this size is necessarily an undertaking involving the stringent efforts of many people. We would like to thank all the authors, editors, and their families for the hard work and support they contributed. To the many people at Microsoft who helped us along the way, our sincere thanks. To all the people at Que whose professionalism and effort made this book possible, thank you. And to the many other people, friends, and customers of G. A. Sullivan who pitched in with assistance, we extend our sincere gratitude. Thank you all for your help.

In addition, we would like to thank the following people for their special efforts: Joe Ernst, Janine Harrison, Roxanne Hutson, Jim Marshbank, Bill Richardson, and Todd Warren.

We'd Like to Hear from You!

As part of our continuing effort to produce books of the highest possible quality, Que would like to hear your comments. To stay competitive, we *really* want you, as a computer book reader and user, to let us know what you like or dislike most about this book or other Que products.

You can mail comments, ideas, or suggestions for improving future editions to the address below, or send us a fax at (317) 581-4663. Our staff and authors are available for questions and comments through our Internet site at **http://www.quecorp.com** and Macmillan Computer Publishing also has a forum on CompuServe (type **GO QUEBOOKS** at any prompt).

In addition to exploring our forum, please feel free to contact me personally to discuss your opinions of this book: I'm **74671,3710** on CompuServe and **jriley@que.mcp.com** on the Internet.

Thanks in advance—your comments will help us to continue publishing the best books available on new computer technologies in today's market.

Jeff Riley
Acquisitions Editor
Que Corporation
201 W. 103rd Street
Indianapolis, Indiana 46290
USA

N O T E Although we cannot provide general technical support, we're happy to help you resolve problems you encounter related to our books, disks, or other products. If you need such assistance, please contact our Tech Support department at 800-545-5914 ext. 3833.

To order other Que or Macmillan Computer Publishing books or products, please call our Customer Service department at 800-835-3202 ext. 666. ▪

Introduction

Special Edition Using Microsoft BackOffice, a book written by professionals for professionals, is about the Microsoft BackOffice family of products. This book is authored by a team of senior information system consultants and software engineers, all of whom apply their talents for G. A. Sullivan, a premier software development consulting company and Microsoft Solution Provider based in St. Louis, Missouri. Special Edition Using Microsoft BackOffice is designed to guide you through the complex implementation and administration issues associated with BackOffice. As such, it primarily focuses on how to prepare for, install, configure, and administer the various BackOffice products.

One of the most alluring features of this book is its up-to-date information. The authors worked hard to produce a time-critical, technically complete "how-to" book that offers in-depth coverage of the more important elements of the BackOffice family, including the following newest products of BackOffice:

- Exchange Server 5.0
- Microsoft Transaction Server (MTS)
- Active Server Pages
- Content Replication System
- Index Server
- SMS 1.2
- SNA Server 3.0

This book provides thorough coverage of these BackOffice products and includes sufficient Notes, Tips, and Cautions to ensure that you can implement and administer even the most troublesome features and elements of the individual applications.

Microsoft BackOffice, an integrated suite of server-based products that operates under control of the Windows NT Server operating system, is patterned after the success of Microsoft Office, a suite of client-based personal productivity tools designed for the client side of the client-server environment. BackOffice, designed for the server side of the client-server environment, significantly improves network administrator productivity in much the same way that Microsoft Office improves personal productivity. BackOffice was designed to be portable so that it operates on a variety of hardware platforms, and extensible so that new services can easily be added and existing services easily enhanced. Scalability is also a design feature. BackOffice needed to be stable in a growth environment where expansion of application scope could be offset by increasing the hardware's computing capability through additional processors.

Another design goal of BackOffice is that it comply with major open computer standards. Indeed, the BackOffice products do this, in addition to supporting the most popular network protocols. Consistency is also an important design consideration for BackOffice. The various products of BackOffice have a consistent graphical user interface, a consistent set of administrative tools, and a consistent applications programming interface. BackOffice is also designed to be easily integrated with other information system components, applications, and technologies. As such, BackOffice products integrate well with the Internet, UNIX, NetWare, other networks, and desktop computers.

A critical design goal is that BackOffice address the need to control access to and usage of services and resources. BackOffice does an excellent job of this. Primarily through the use of the Windows NT Server operating system—under which the other BackOffice products must operate—abundant security features and tools are available to secure transmissions, control access, and assign authorizations. Attaining a secure BackOffice environment, however, requires not only that these tools and features simply be available, but that they also be applied intelligently, that management of them be disciplined, and that appropriate controls be established. ∎

Who Should Use This Book?

This book is aimed at administrators (of networks, systems, Web servers, databases, file servers, and so on) who are responsible for deploying the BackOffice suite, information systems managers faced with migration issues, and software developers who develop applications and interfaces used with the BackOffice family. The readers of this book will learn how to install, configure, and use BackOffice family components. This book provides excellent advice for administrators who have the task of implementing the BackOffice suite in a client-server environment. It also provides good advice for managers on how to use BackOffice to improve their business footing and leverage their automated information systems to maximize return on investment. Not only will managers learn what to do with BackOffice, they will also find out how to do it and, most importantly, why they should.

With the variety of material presented in *Special Edition Using Microsoft BackOffice*—coupled with its high quality of content, up-to-date material, level of detail, and easy to follow "how-to" format—this will be the all-encompassing book you will quickly come to depend on to supply answers to your BackOffice installation and administration questions. Although each of the products that make up the BackOffice suite is given a separate part within the book, special attention is paid to integration issues and techniques. Additionally, significant portions of the book are devoted to providing background material to enhance your understanding of critical concepts, and advanced topics explain how to really be effective with BackOffice in the enterprise.

How This Book Is Organized

This book is organized in a logical sequence starting in Part I and ending in Part X. Each part generally provides an overview of the BackOffice product, presents detailed instructions on how to install and configure the product, and then covers how the server administrator should use the product on a daily basis. Many parts include chapters explaining related technologies or advanced features of the product.

Volume I

Part I—Exploring Microsoft BackOffice

Part I gives an in-depth discussion of BackOffice and how it fits into an enterprise environment.

Chapter 1, "An Inside Look at BackOffice," describes the products that make up BackOffice and provides an overview of various process models, including the I-net process model. It also describes the role of BackOffice in this Internet-enabled, client-server world; describes how BackOffice moves you beyond client-server; and discusses the added value BackOffice offers to your computing enterprise.

Chapter 2, "Characteristics of BackOffice," details the BackOffice design goals, the role of BackOffice as a network operating system, and the services provided by BackOffice. The chapter concludes with a discussion of why BackOffice is a solid platform for the future and why it is important to you as an administrator, manager, developer, or user.

Chapter 3, "Planning for BackOffice," describes the various steps you should take prior to installing BackOffice. Some of these actions include building the network, establishing the administration team, analyzing the organizational requirements, preparing the facility, establishing policies and procedures, and licensing BackOffice.

Chapter 4, "Enterprise Planning and Implementation," discusses the most important considerations facing an administrator who is involved in creating an enterprise network and setting up servers to operate in such an environment. The chapter attempts to enhance your understanding of how computers on a large network are organized, the basics of network protocols, and Windows NT security.

Part II—Windows NT Server: Installation and Administration

Part II focuses on the base operating system, Windows NT Server, upon which all the other BackOffice products must run. The Windows NT Server part establishes a logical progression of chapters that is paralleled throughout the other parts of the book.

Chapter 5, "Implementing Windows NT Server," covers the installation and use of Windows NT Server. It includes a detailed, step-by-step procedure for installing Windows NT Server. This chapter also describes such related activities as partitioning hard disk space, exploiting the last known good feature, creating the Emergency Repair Disk, logging on and off the server, shutting down and restarting the server, connecting to the network from client workstations, and using Windows NT security.

Chapter 6, "Advanced Windows NT Server Configuration," provides details on using advanced capabilities and features of the operating system such as drive mirroring, and the use of RAID technology to build large disk arrays supporting error detection and recovery.

Chapter 7, "Administering Windows NT Server," outlines the network administrator's server management tasks. It includes a survey of the tools that come with Windows NT Server and discusses typical administrative tasks such as creating user accounts, sharing resources, and changing permissions.

Chapter 8, "Windows NT Server Directory Services," describes the directory services provided by Windows NT including the creation and management of domains, and the major domain models used to organize servers and networks. It also discusses the future of Windows NT directory services.

Part III—Windows NT Server: Enterprise Connectivity

Part III continues with advanced coverage of Windows NT Server. It includes information on using TCP/IP protocols, how to configure and use the remote dial-up component of Windows NT—the Remote Access Service (RAS)—and how to integrate Windows NT with NetWare and UNIX. It also details the protocols and products used to create Wide Area Networks (WANs) and support dial-up connectivity to the network.

Chapter 9, "Using TCP/IP with Windows NT Server," describes the Transmission Control Protocol/Internet Protocol, a network protocol and related applications that have gained wide acceptance and use on the Internet as well as on private networks. The chapter includes a brief tutorial on TCP/IP to help you understand some of the terminology and why things are done the way they are. The use of the Point-to-Point Tunneling Protocol (PPTP) to create Virtual Private Networks (VPNs) is discussed.

Chapter 10, "Name Resolution With TCP/IP," examines the mechanisms used to convert a friendly computer name into a computer's machine address. This basic network service is provided by both Domain Name System (DNS) and Windows Internet Naming System (WINS). The operation of these systems is described.

Chapter 11, "An Inside Look at Remote Access Service (RAS)," examines the basic capabilities of RAS, how to select hardware for dial-up access, and how RAS security is implemented.

Chapter 12, "Implementing Remote Access Service (RAS)," describes how to install and configure RAS using the various protocols available, and how to use the Remote Access administration tool.

Chapter 13, "Implementing Dial-Up Networking Clients," describes how to use RAS with different client configurations. It also shows how to use multilink channel aggregation to combine more than one modem or leased line for greater bandwidth and improved throughput.

Chapter 14, "Windows Integration with NetWare and UNIX," examines the use of Windows NT Server in heterogenous networks with several different operating systems. Novell NetWare issues (including NDS integration) and UNIX interoperability are both given particular attention.

Chapter 15, "Wide Area Network Technologies," describes WANs in more detail, including the strategies required for building WANs, the communication services used to provide WAN connectivity, and protocols.

Part IV—Implementing Intranet and Internet Technologies

After the base operating system—Windows NT Server—is covered, Part IV focuses on the newest additions to the BackOffice product suite, the Internet related products. You learn how this group of products can be used to build servers that allow your organization to have a presence on the Internet, or to create intranets that use Internet tools to deliver information internally.

Chapter 16, "The BackOffice I-Net Toolbox," describes the features of Internet Information Server (IIS) and Microsoft's overall strategy for Internet products. It also discusses third-party add-on products from other vendors.

Chapter 17, "I-Net Tools and Techniques," provides a brief introduction to the Internet and how it has changed the way people think of information technology. It also provides a basic understanding of what it means to your organization to embrace the Internet, and surveys how BackOffice can make your excursion into the Internet world a success.

Chapter 18, "Building a Web with Internet Information Server (IIS)," covers installing and configuring IIS. The use of the Internet Service Manager to control I-net servers is described in detail.

Chapter 19, "Web Browsers," provides an overview of the client-side of the Web—the browser. The two most widely used browsers, Netscape Navigator and Microsoft Internet Explorer, are both described.

Chapter 20, "Using Microsoft FrontPage 97," provides a detailed guide to creating and publishing Web pages with Microsoft's user-friendly Web editior—FrontPage 97. Web server administration and management are also discussed.

Part V—Advanced I-Net Development

Part V covers advanced Internet and intranet (I-net) technologies and products including how to build Web sites that incorporate database information to provide dynamic updates and a survey of Internet security techniques.

Chapter 21, "Implementing Index Server and the Content Replication System," describes two new BackOffice components that can play an important role in Web server management. Index Server provides powerful search capabilities to users who visit your Web site. CRS allows you to quickly and securely move Web content from server to server, across the Internet, or within your own site, at prescheduled times.

Chapter 22, "Implementing Microsoft Proxy Server," details the steps required to set up and manage a proxy server to control access to the Internet and provide enhanced access to your user community.

Chapter 23, "Using Active Platform to Enhance Your Web Site," discusses the very latest Microsoft tools to build state-of-the-art Web sites. The components of Active Platform, and its use of ActiveX technology, are described in detail.

Chapter 24, "Dynamic Content with IIS Using dbWeb and IDC," describes two tools that can be used to include database information in your Web pages. The products discussed allow you to build dynamic pages that provide the specific information your Web users want.

Chapter 25, "Implementing Internet Security," outlines the rapidly changing field of Internet security. Several major technologies and tools are discussed, including Microsoft's Internet Security Framework.

Volume II

Part VI—Exchange Server

Part VI is devoted to the latest version of Microsoft Exchange Server—version 5.0. It describes how to set up the groupware and messaging subsystem of BackOffice, surveys the features of Exchange Server including integration with the Internet, and provides an overview of the various Exchange Server elements. It also describes how to install and configure Exchange Server, and how to install the client software to manage your personal messaging and scheduling needs. In addition, it describes how to implement, use, and replicate public folders, and how to install and use the advanced security features that complement the security already provided by Windows NT.

Chapter 26, "An Inside Look at Exchange Server," explores the capabilities of Exchange Server. Discussion focuses on what Exchange Server really is and what you should do with it.

The chapter also surveys the features of Exchange Server and provides an overview of the various Exchange Server elements.

Chapter 27, "Implementing Exchange Server," looks at how to size your server, install Exchange Server using the Exchange Setup program, use the Exchange Administrator program to configure your site and set up the mailboxes, and use the Exchange Server security features.

Chapter 28, "Using Exchange Client Applications," explores the client applications that come with Exchange Server, describes how to install the client software and use it to manage your personal messaging and scheduling needs, surveys the features of the Exchange Client that are particularly suited for remote users, and discusses the newest client application—Outlook.

Chapter 29, "Distributing Information with Exchange Server," explores the techniques used to create public folders, discusses the basics of implementing and using public folders, describes how to replicate them to other servers to balance the user load and make best use of available network bandwidth, and details how to replicate directory information across all servers in your organization. Internet integration techniques are also discussed.

Chapter 30, "Document Management with Exchange Server," describes how Exchange Server can be used to manage the flow of, storage of, and access to documents of many types. The creation of public folder applications is also discussed.

Chapter 31, "Exchange Server Advanced Topics," details how to install and use the Advanced Security features that complement the security already provided by Windows NT, how to install and use connectors for sending and receiving messages with Microsoft Mail (PC) users and the vast community attached to the Internet, and how to migrate mailboxes from a Microsoft Mail system.

Part VII—SQL Server

In-depth coverage of SQL Server 6.5 comes in Part VII. Included in the SQL Server chapters are discussions on relational database management systems, the role of the database administrator, designing databases, SQL Server management tools, selecting appropriate server hardware, recommended installation options, using SQL Enterprise Manager, proactively monitoring SQL Server, data replication, and the new Distributed Transaction Coordinator. The use of the Distributed Transaction Coordinator (DTC) and Microsoft Transaction Server (MTS) to build distributed applications has been added to this edition.

Chapter 32, "An Inside Look at Relational Databases," provides background information on SQL Server, relational database management systems (RDBMS), the role of the database administrator (DBA), and designing databases. This background information will form a critical foundation as you install SQL Server, create databases, and begin to use SQL Server as an important product for building client-server applications.

Chapter 33, "An Inside Look at SQL Server," describes the basic SQL Server environment, and explores the tools provided to manage SQL Server.

Chapter 34, "Building Your SQL Server," provides guidance on selecting appropriate server hardware; describes how SQL Server allocates and uses disk storage; discusses the installation options you must decide on for your installation to be a success; and details procedures for installing SQL Server, defining devices, defining databases, defining various database objects, and using the SQL Enterprise Manager to create login IDs and usernames.

Chapter 35, "Maintaining SQL Server," discusses the various things you need to know to keep SQL Server running properly. Included in the discussion are some techniques for monitoring the health of SQL Server and some proactive steps you can take to ensure that no problems arise. Procedures for importing and exporting data are also discussed.

Chapter 36, "SQL Server Data Replication," explores the reasons data replication is becoming a widely used feature of SQL Server, and how to set up and manage this important capability.

Chapter 37, "Data Warehousing with SQL Server," describes the growing use of SQL Server to build a data warehouse of information that can be queried for analysis and review.

Chapter 38, "An Inside Look at Distributed Transaction Coordinator (DTC) and Microsoft Transaction Server (MTS)," describes two important tools for building distributed applications. The Distributed Transaction Coordinator (DTC), which is included with SQL Server, is described. Then MTS, a new product which was code-named Viper, is described. Although these advanced topics are not required for every SQL Server installation, they can be powerful additions to your SQL Server Administrator knowledge base.

Part VIII—SNA Server

Part VIII launches you into a thorough discussion of the BackOffice product designed to provide personal computer access to IBM mainframes or AS/400 minicomputers—SNA Server. You learn what the IBM System Network Architecture (SNA) is, how SNA Server integrates with the SNA network structure, the critical preinstallation actions that need to be taken when preparing for SNA Server, how to install and configure SNA Server, and the role of the SNA Server administrator in managing the SNA network.

Chapter 39, "SNA Server Preparation and Installation," provides an overview of IBM's SNA and Microsoft's SNA Server to include a brief survey of some of its more important features. It then acquaints you with the recommended installation preparation actions and details the steps necessary to install SNA Server using SNA Server Setup. Finally, the chapter outlines some common post-installation uses of SNA Server Setup.

Chapter 40, "Building SNA Server," covers the concepts and procedures for configuring the SNA Server and also for configuring the SNA Server-to-host connections. It includes detailed step-by-step procedures for configuring Synchronous Data Link (SDLC), 802.2, X.25, and Channel connections. It also explores the concepts and procedures necessary to configure logical units (LUs), group the LUs into pools, assign LU pools to users and groups, and configure downstream connections.

Chapter 41, "The Role of the SNA Server Administrator," explores the SNA Server Explorer features in detail and, where appropriate, outlines the step-by-step procedures necessary to perform specific tasks associated with them. Features covered include managing connectivity-to-host computer resources, managing access to SNA Server and host resources, and diagnosing problems.

Part IX—Systems Management Server (SMS)

The last product of BackOffice, Systems Management Server (SMS), is covered in Part IX. This part enhances your understanding of what SMS is and why it is needed; provides details on remote application installation, metering, and hardware and software inventory management; and explores the key features of Microsoft SMS and how they can be used to address systems management requirements for an enterprise-wide network. This part also describes how to set up SMS on your network and use it to become more productive as an administrator, some of the more advanced features of SMS and how to automate the process of software distribution and installation, and some techniques for monitoring and troubleshooting SMS.

Chapter 42, "Preparing for SMS," discusses what is meant by the term *systems management*, explores the key features of Microsoft SMS, and describes how this product can be used to address systems management requirements for an enterprise-wide network. It also surveys the various roles servers play in an SMS environment and the work they perform.

Chapter 43, "Implementing SMS," describes how to set up SMS on your network and use it to make you more productive as an administrator. Detailed information is provided to help you set up a primary site server for your central site, install other primary site servers and secondary site servers, and implement the site relationships. It also discusses procedures for adding logon servers and clients to a site and provides an overview of the basics of defining packages and jobs.

Chapter 44, "The Role of the SMS Administrator," describes some of the more advanced features of SMS and how to automate the process of software distribution and installation. SMS Security is reviewed, as well as accessing SMS from remote locations using dial-up lines. The Help Desk features of SMS are explored, and the Network Monitor protocol analysis tool is examined. Some techniques for monitoring and troubleshooting SMS are also discussed.

Chapter 45, "SMS Advanced Topics," describes some expert techniques to complement the routine tools that have already been described. The use of the Network Monitor to analyze network traffic is discussed, as well as third-party product integration.

Part X—Applying Microsoft BackOffice Technology

Part X deals with the practical perspective of using BackOffice to get work done. Discussion includes valuable information on evaluating your organization's needs and implementing a security system that meets those needs. Real-world application scenarios are examined to aid information systems managers and administrators in understanding what BackOffice means to application development and deployment. The concept of *proactive* versus *reactive* network administration is also examined. You learn how to develop aggressive network and server management approaches that usually prevent problems from occurring; but when problems do occur, mitigate their severity and correct them before the user community feels any significant impact.

Chapter 46, "Implementing Real-World Security," provides an overview of the field of security, recommends an approach to evaluating your organization's needs, and describes how to implement a system that meets your requirements. It discusses certain types of products and concepts from a broad perspective rather than from a detailed one because products will change and a targeted focus may invite overlooking other important security areas that may be weak.

Chapter 47, "Building BackOffice Applications," examines how BackOffice is applied to real-world situations. It is intended to aid information systems managers and administrators in understanding what BackOffice means to application development and deployment and, with the help of some application scenarios, highlights some important aspects of BackOffice with respect to application implementation.

Chapter 48, "Proactive Network Administration," discusses how to aggressively work as a network administrator to avoid problems. It helps you to develop an approach to network and server management that will catch most problems before the user community has felt any significant impact.

Appendixes

Appendix A, "SNA Server Preparation Forms," provides blank copies of forms that are useful in gathering and organizing SNA Server installation planning data.

Conventions Used In This Book

This book assumes that you are already familiar with the graphical user interface used in Windows-based applications. As such, no attempt has been made to describe "how" to select or choose various options in the dialog boxes discussed throughout this book. Instead, the terms *click*, *select*, *choose*, *highlight*, *activate*, *disable*, and *turn off/on* have been used to describe the process of positioning the cursor over a dialog box element (radio button, check box, command button, drop-down list arrow, and so on) and clicking a mouse button.

Those familiar with using the keyboard to select various dialog box options may relate this selection process to keystrokes instead of mouse clicks. Either method is equally acceptable.

Several type and font conventions are used in this book to help make reading it easier:

- *Italic type* is used to emphasize the author's points or to introduce new terms.
- Screen messages, code listings, and command samples appear in monospace typeface.
- URLs, newsgroups, Internet addresses, and anything you are asked to type appears in **boldface**.
- Keyboard hotkeys are indicated with underlining. For example, if you see the command Tools, Options, pressing Alt and T causes the Tools menu to appear.

At times, you may be required to press keyboard keys in selected combinations to activate a command or cause a selected display window to appear. When these situations occur, you see the key combinations described in a couple of different ways. When two or more keys need to be depressed simultaneously, a plus sign (+) is used to combine the keys. For example, if the

Alt and Tab keys need to be pressed simultaneously, you would see the annotation Alt+Tab. Likewise, if the Ctrl and Y keys needs to be pressed simultaneously, it would be annotated Ctrl+Y. When keys need to be depressed in a certain sequence with no intervening actions, a comma (,) is used as a separator.

 Tips present short advice on a quick or often overlooked procedure.

N O T E Notes provide additional information that may help you avoid problems, or offer advice that relates to the topic.

CAUTION

Cautions warn you about potential problems that a procedure may cause, unexpected results, and mistakes to avoid.

▶ **See** these cross-references for more information on a particular topic.

Sidebar

Longer discussions not integral to the flow of the chapter are set aside as sidebars. Look for these sidebars to find out even more information.

TROUBLESHOOTING

What is a troubleshooting section? Troubleshooting sections anticipate common problems in the form of a question. The response provides you with practical suggestions for solving these problems.

Exploring Microsoft BackOffice

An Inside Look at BackOffice

by Greg Sullivan

Computer users have longed for more efficient and convenient ways to share information, even before the advent of desktop computing devices. The eventual connection of personal computers into computer networks represented an important step in the evolution of computing process models. Since then, the focus of information technology has shifted to the effective management of distributed computers, data, and processes.

Personal computers were accepted in enterprise computing environments because of the information processing power they offered, the personal workgroup empowerment they enabled, and the independence from centralized information systems organizations they accommodated. This claim is supported by the measurable success of such companies as Microsoft, Intel, Novell, and Compaq. Many of the successful software companies took full advantage of this distribution of computing power by creating tools to place into users' hands. The personal productivity tools bundled in Microsoft Office (Excel, Word, PowerPoint, and Access) are good examples.

With power increasingly distributed across the computing enterprise, it became essential to find an effective way to harness the full capability of all computers within the organization. BackOffice is the glue that enables an enterprise to effectively leverage the full power of computer processors while providing the most benefit to information users in a controlled and secure environment. ◼

What Is BackOffice?

BackOffice is a set of server products, based on Windows NT networks, that operate together as a suite and are sold together in a bundle. Building on the market success of Microsoft Office, which is a collection of products for the *client* in client-server, Microsoft decided to offer their *server* products in a single package also—BackOffice. Although each product is available as a stand-alone server application, purchasing and implementing the package as a whole offers many advantages.

Figure 1.1 depicts the BackOffice products and their primary roles in the information technology enterprise.

FIG. 1.1

The BackOffice suite comprises nine stand-alone server applications in an integrated package.

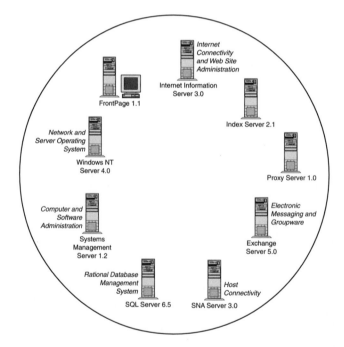

Each product is designed to be competitive on its own in addition to integrating into a heterogeneous computing environment. Consequently, these individual products leverage the synergy of BackOffice as a single package.

BackOffice products contain server-based components as well as software that is installed on client personal computers (PCs). Some of the products include substantial capabilities that are optional or only appropriate in particular environments or networks. In this respect, BackOffice is a much more sophisticated product than a typical desktop application, such as Microsoft Word.

In addition to the individual components, the BackOffice CD includes integrated installation utilities for server and client software components. These utilities will help you select the options you need for your server, and then make recommendations on the type of computer you need to support those options.

This book is about BackOffice 2.5, which is the fourth release of the BackOffice product package. BackOffice 1.0 was first released in the third quarter of 1995. An upgrade was subsequently packaged as BackOffice 1.5 and released in the fourth quarter of 1995. BackOffice 2.0 was released in the first quarter of 1996. BackOffice 2.5 was released in December 1996 and contains the following individual products:

- Windows NT Server 4.0
- Internet Information Server 2.0
- FrontPage 1.1
- Index Server 1.1
- Proxy Server 1.0
- Exchange Server 4.0
- SQL Server 6.5
- SNA Server 3.0
- Systems Management Server 1.2

Related products from Microsoft not included in the BackOffice 2.5 package, but important in BackOffice implementations, are also covered in this book. These include the following:

- Content Replication Server 1.0
- Active Platform

Following is a brief introduction to each of the individual products included in BackOffice 2.5.

Windows NT Server 4.0

Windows NT Server provides the foundation upon which all BackOffice products are built. On the server itself, Windows NT Server provides an open, portable, and scalable operating system. From an enterprise perspective, Windows NT Server also acts as the network operating system, similar to the role of Novell NetWare. As such, it provides the basic file sharing, printing, and workstation connectivity services, and is a platform upon which many other services can be provided. Although Windows NT Server is not as mature as some competitive operating systems, such as UNIX, it has proven to be a secure and reliable product since its introduction.

▶ **See** "A Network Operating System," **p. 53**

Windows NT is sometimes referred to as *industrial-strength Windows*. Two versions of Windows NT are available for purchase. The first is known as Windows NT Workstation. Purchase this version if you choose to use Windows NT on a stand-alone computer. The other version, Windows NT Server, should be purchased if you are using it as a network operating system or need an individual workstation to take advantage of the extra power of Windows NT Server.

Part
I
Ch
1

N O T E   Windows NT Server, not Windows NT Workstation, comes with BackOffice. ■

The differences between Windows NT Workstation and Windows NT Server are significant. The retail version of Windows NT Server supports more processors (up to four) than the retail version of Windows NT Workstation (up to two). This implies that Windows NT Server is suitable for users who require, or prefer, more processors. Windows NT Server is further distinguishable from Windows NT Workstation in that it is designed to share resources with large numbers of users. It provides connectivity to remote networks via Remote Access Server (RAS) as well as connectivity to other networks, such as Novell, Digital Pathworks, and Apple.

▶ **See** "Integration with Other Networks," **p. 51**

Windows NT Workstation contains excellent network client capabilities and peer network server capabilities. Its file and printer sharing abilities are comparable to Windows for Workgroups or Windows 95. Regardless, Windows NT Server is clearly the best choice for a Windows-based network operating system in commercial computing environments.

Internet Information Server 2.0

An important goal of BackOffice 2.5 is to Internet-enable your organization. As such, Microsoft has added to the BackOffice bundle a new product: Internet Information Server (IIS). The first release of IIS was included with BackOffice 2.0. BackOffice 2.5 contains IIS 2.0 even though IIS 3.0 was in beta during the release of BackOffice 2.5. In order to meet customer expectations, Microsoft offers a free upgrade from IIS 2.0 to IIS 3.0 to customers who purchase a BackOffice 2.5 package that contains IIS 2.0.

N O T E   IIS 3.0 is covered in this book even though IIS 2.0 is shipped with BackOffice 2.5. ■

IIS provides the functionality that you would expect from an Internet product, including the following features:

■ The capability to develop and operate World Wide Web servers

■ Support for FTP and Gopher

■ A secure platform

■ Support for the Common Gateway Interface (CGI)

■ Connectivity to other application servers

Many organizations today are gaining a presence on the Internet by creating their own Web pages and exposing them to the Internet via a Web server. Internet Information Server enables organizations to build Web pages in the traditional manner using Hypertext Markup Language (HTML). Additionally, Internet Information Server supports the operation of multiple Web servers on the same physical computer in cases where more than one Web page is appropriate.

▶ **See** "Hypertext Markup Language," **p. 579**

To address security concerns, Microsoft incorporated support for Secure Sockets Layer (SSL), which is based on the widely accepted RSA public-key cryptography system. The Internet Information Server also supports Private Communication Technology (PCT) security. PCT provides the same level of security as SSL, but is more efficient. In addition to SSL and PCT, Microsoft has worked with major credit card companies to develop a secure forum for financial transactions over the Internet. This is known as Secure Transaction Technology (STT) and will be available in a future release of the IIS.

CGI adds functionality to Web pages by enabling developers to build customized modules that can be loaded and executed based on the actions of Web page visitors. This enables Web page creators to enhance a Web page beyond the restrictions of HTML programming. Internet Information Server supports CGI.

▶ **See** "Using CGI," **p. 572**

IIS also comes with Internet Server Application Programming Interface (ISAPI). This is one of the most important features of this product because it enables developers to create dynamic link libraries (DLLs) for execution by the Web server. As such, ISAPI provides much the same functionality as CGI. However, ISAPI is far more efficient because the DLLs load into memory at Web server runtime as opposed to loading on demand. Also, DLL execution is faster because a separate process is not spawned as is the case with CGI. You should also know, however, that because ISAPI runs in the same space as IIS it can cause IIS to hang or crash.

▶ **See** "ISAPI," **p. 1636**

One of the most powerful uses of the Internet is to connect the outside world with internal information. Subject to the appropriate security, this enables an organization to interact with the world via the Internet by providing such functions as taking a customer's order on its Web page and having the order placed directly into the order entry database. ISAPI makes this, as well as connectivity to other application servers, possible.

In addition to the support IIS provides in connecting to the Internet, it is now widely used in support of internal application development. IIS provides a foundation upon which additional Internet-type services can be built and operated. In this manner, IIS is also a useful product for your own networking needs.

▶ **See** "Microsoft Internet Architecture," **p. 483**

FrontPage 97

The most popular use of the Internet today is perusing (or *surfing*) the World Wide Web for interesting information. Until recently, building Web pages for view by Internet users has been a task only possible by programmers familiar with HTML. Although HTML is simple by programming standards, it remains a daunting task to learn enough about HTML to build even a simple Web page.

Building Web pages is greatly simplified with FrontPage. This product provides the capability to create HTML-based Web pages without having to know anything about HTML. Similar to the manner in which such desktop productivity tools as Word and PowerPoint work, FrontPage allows Web pages to be created by manipulating graphical images along with textual data. Of course, if you are familiar with HTML, it is possible to dig deeper with FrontPage and fully exploit its programming interfaces.

Index Server 1.1

Index Server is an add-on product for IIS. It enables Web page authors to index the information contained on a Web page in order to facilitate convenient access to it. Clients can search a Web page for desirable information and expect Index Server to find it quickly due to the manner in which it has organized the data. Index Server is capable of organizing information content within documents as well as properties about the documents—an important capability not shared by all Internet search engines.

Proxy Server 1.0

With so many users in organizations today, it is becoming increasingly difficult to provide high-performance, convenient access to the Internet. Proxy Server is a server product based on Windows NT Server, which enables network administrators to effectively manage Internet access across the entire network. It provides controlled, secure access to the Internet by en-abling administrators to decide who can access the Internet and, to some extent, what they can do while on the Internet.

Exchange Server 4.0

Exchange Server 4.0 is delivered with BackOffice 2.5. Because Exchange Server 5.0 was in beta during the release of BackOffice 2.5, customers are entitled to an upgrade to Exchange Server 5.0 if they purchase a copy of BackOffice that contains Exchange 4.0.

N O T E   Exchange Server 5.0 is covered in this book even though Exchange Server 4.0 is shipped with BackOffice 2.5. ▪

The two primary roles of Exchange Server are electronic messaging and group information sharing and management. As an electronic message tool, Exchange Server provides the means by which messages are sent and received on the enterprise network. This includes electronic mail (e-mail) and information messaging for workgroup applications. Exchange Server is based on the principles of client-server computing and is scalable to accommodate large computing enterprises. You will learn in a following section, "Client-Server Process Model," the principles of client-server computing and its significance to BackOffice.

As a group information management tool, Exchange Server provides basic and powerful groupware capabilities. It is the cornerstone within BackOffice for sharing information across a large network.

▶ **See** "Groupware," **p. 38**

SQL Server 6.5

SQL Server is a full-featured relational database management system (RDBMS). As such, it takes advantage of the principles of client-server computing. As a competitive RDBMS, its capabilities include transaction processing, preservation of referential data integrity, isolation of business rules on the server, execution of stored procedures, distribution of transactions, and data replication. It also comes bundled with a set of graphical administration tools. SQL Server is open, reliable, and scalable—as you would expect from an RDBMS built upon the foundation of Windows NT Server.

SNA Server 3.0

SNA Server provides connection services to IBM AS/400 and IBM mainframe computers. This product enables desktop computers based on MS-DOS, Windows, Windows for Workgroups, Windows NT, Mac OS, UNIX, or OS/2 to "see" host computers. This "visibility" enables computing enterprises to leverage legacy data as the organization makes a transition to more contemporary computing models.

Systems Management Server 1.2

Systems Management Server (SMS) enables network and system administrators to centrally administer the entire network. This includes the administration of each computer on the network and the software on all computers. Specifically, SMS is designed to support the following:

- Hardware and software inventory management
- Automated software installation and distribution (including updates)
- Remote system troubleshooting by enabling an administrator to control the keyboard, mouse, and screen of any computer on the network running MS-DOS or a Windows operating system
- Network application management

SMS simplifies the administrative tasks associated with these important functions.

Perhaps the greatest value of SMS is in the hidden savings to the organization. Today's information systems managers are plagued by many hidden costs associated with managing large networks of PCs. SMS helps reduce costly activities because of its following advantages:

- Users spend less time dealing with file incompatibilities because SMS facilitates the automatic upgrade and associated data conversion of new software packages.
- Help desk personnel spend less time solving user problems because they can see the problem occur directly on the user's desktop without having to leave the help desk.
- Fewer technicians are dispatched to diagnose hardware problems because SMS supports this activity remotely.
- Administrators save time and energy trying to keep up with curious users who are known to tinker with their configurations because SMS tracks user configurations.

BackOffice 2.5 All Together

The BackOffice family of products combined fill a large gap in the computing enterprise. It remains one of the largest bundle of products designed to work together or individually in support of information and network management. Figure 1.2 represents a typical enterprise network with BackOffice providing information-server capabilities and Microsoft Office fulfilling the role of an information client.

FIG. 1.2

Each BackOffice product provides an application service to the users of your enterprise network.

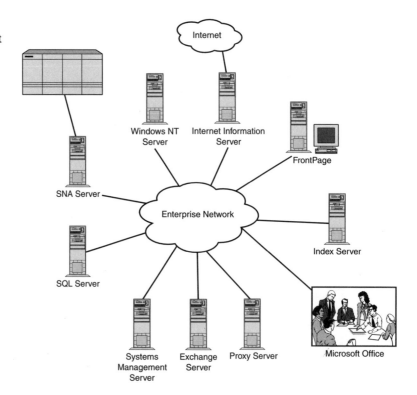

A great deal of synergy exists among the individual BackOffice products; this is, in fact, an important design goal of BackOffice. The individual products are based upon popular, modern computing concepts. Understanding the principles upon which BackOffice is built is essential to successful implementation of the BackOffice components. To this end, it is important to see how BackOffice works in the world of client-server computing and the Internet, the role it plays in an enterprise network, and the value it brings to your computing enterprise.

Understanding Process Models

To understand modern process models, it is important to have an appreciation for how process models have evolved until now. Software applications execute on computer processors. A process model is defined by where the software applications execute in the computing enterprise. A brief history of computing process models will help you understand the positioning of BackOffice with respect to today's computing environments and the future as well.

Host-Based Process Model

The first computers utilized as information management tools were mainframe computers. The proliferation of mainframe computers brought with it the acceptance of the first phase of a computing process model, known as the *host-based process model*. Figure 1.3 is a pictorial representation of host-based computing.

FIG. 1.3
In the host-based process model, all processing occurs on the host.

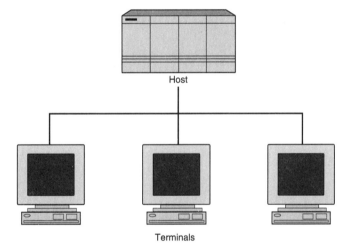

Host

Terminals

Host processing means the mainframe or minicomputer contains all the computing power of the organization. Terminals that connect users to the mainframe or minicomputer are incapable of processing data because these devices do not contain computer processors. Consequently, they became known as *dumb terminals*.

Today, it is common for desktop computer users to connect their PCs to a host computer. Because the PC does contain a processor, it is not referred to as a dumb terminal; however, it can be configured to behave as a dumb terminal by means of a terminal emulation program, which enables computers with processors to perform the duty of a dumb terminal. Consequently, today's PCs can participate in the host-based process model.

Shared-Resource Process Model

In the *shared-resource process model* of computing, nearly all processing occurs on the desktop PC. Figure 1.4 pictorially represents a computer network and the shared-resource process model.

FIG. 1.4

With the advent of microcomputer networks came the shared-resource process model.

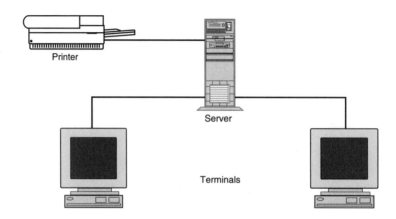

Printer

Server

Terminals

The advantage of the shared resource process model is it enables computer users to share expensive devices. Hardware components, such as printers, disk drives, and modems, become more affordable because their usage can be distributed across a greater number of computer users. Network operating systems, such as Novell NetWare, became popular by exploiting the need to share these devices.

Client-Server Process Model

The proliferation and networking of personal computers resulted in the distribution of computer processing power throughout the organization. Computer processes execute in computing centers, as well as on the desktops of computer users.

Client-server computing is the distribution of processing across the computing enterprise. Software applications are constructed in parts so as to execute a portion on the desktop PC (the *client* of client-server) and the remainder on some sort of powerful computer shared by many users (the *server* of client-server). Figure 1.5 offers a graphical representation of the client-server process model.

True client-server computing is message-based and event-driven. *Message-based* implies that a client sends a request to a server and receives a response. *Event-driven* means an event occurs that triggers the creation and sending of a message (such as a data value changing). Processing can occur on the clients and the servers in this scenario.

Microsoft has long participated in the client-server phase of the process model evolution. Its operating systems enable client PCs to connect with server computers and pass messages back and forth. Microsoft Office applications form the basis for the client side of client-server computing by providing tools that enable desktop processing of enterprise information. Microsoft development tools permit developers to build their own client-server applications. Recently, Microsoft integrated Microsoft Office applications with its development tools. This provides computer users a wide range of possibilities in managing information.

FIG. 1.5
In the client-server process model, processing occurs where it best fits, whether on the client, the server, or both.

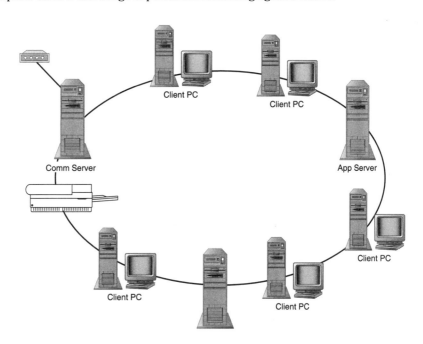

N O T E BackOffice represents state-of-the-art usage of the client-server process model, and provides a solid foundation for the anticipated arrival of distributed computing.

BackOffice products address the server side of client-server, with each product providing a specific set of services. A design goal of BackOffice is to take full advantage of the client-server process model. This has been accomplished in such a way as to provide a smooth transition into subsequent phases of the process model evolution.

I-Net Process Model

The fastest growing segment of the information technology marketplace today is tied to the Internet and its associated technologies. Due to the availability of such sophisticated tools as those provided in BackOffice and other leading vendors, such as Netscape, Internet technologies are now applicable to information systems within an organization.

The application of Internet technologies for internal purposes is referred to as an *intranet*. Building an intranet with Internet technologies for the purposes of serving those only within an organization is fast becoming the predominant way to distribute information to users on a network.

Many organizations are today working on building their own intranets. Where is all of this headed? One of the next logical steps is to extend the information available on an intranet to those people with whom your organization has an interest in sharing information. This can include customers, vendors, potential customers, or others. The extension of an intranet to closely related entities, yet not to the entire Internet, is now referred to by some as an *extranet*.

The Internet, an intranet, and an extranet all use the same technologies and, to a large extent, standards to provide the capability for information to be published and for people and computers to communicate with one another. Because these very different purposes are based on the same concepts, the information technologists have conceived a variety of terms intended to encompass each use of Internet technologies. In this book Internet, intranet, and extranet are collectively referred to as *I-net*.

The application of Internet technologies to application development and internal information publishing has resulted in the creation of an entirely new process model. This new process model is referred to as the *I-net process model*. In addition to its complete support of the client-server process model, BackOffice is designed to support the effective use of the I-net process model as well.

The most important fact to remember about the I-net process model is that it is simply an extension of the client-server process model. Figure 1.6 shows the typical architecture of an application based on the client-server process model. As you can see, there are three levels (or tiers) of interest to the application developer.

FIG. 1.6

A typical client-server application architecture consists of three distinct processing entities, known as tiers.

The data in a client-server application architecture is typically managed by an RDBMS, such as SQL Server. As such, it resides on a server and constitutes a portion of the server side of client-server. In the client-server process model, the presentation—or user interface, as it is often called—resides entirely on the client side of client-server. Rules are commonly placed in either client processes or server processes, but best located in the server processes. SQL Server stored procedures is one manner in which this can be accomplished.

In an application based on the I-net process model, the rules and data reside in server processes, just as in client-server. The only difference in the client-server process model and the I-net process model is the manner in which the presentation is managed. By utilizing the publishing capabilities of the Internet (specifically the Web), it is possible to split apart the user interface from the rules and the data (see Figure 1.7).

FIG. 1.7
An I-net application
architecture splits the
presentation processing
into two components.

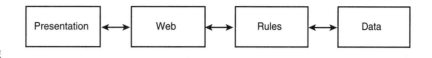

The Web information publishing capabilities of IIS can be used to distribute information managed by applications built upon BackOffice. The beauty of this arrangement is that the information is displayed on the desktop PC with only the use of an Internet browser, such as Microsoft Internet Explorer.

In the I-net application architecture, it is only necessary to build a Web page that users access via a browser, which permits access to the data in accordance with the rules of that particular application. The great problem this solves is that there is no need to develop software to distribute to each desktop PC.

▶ **See** "Building Commercial Applications," **p. 39**

Because software distribution is one of the primary problems plaguing client-server software development, the I-net process model has become an attractive alternative. Nevertheless, client-server software development continues today in greater volume than I-net software development. This is due to the lack of a mature I-net development tool set. Only recently have such I-net development techniques as Microsoft Active Platform and such tools as Java been available for this type of development. As these tools mature and become more widely available, which seems inevitable at this point, more and more commercial applications will be built upon the I-net process model.

▶ **See** "Java," **p. 601**

▶ **See** "Active Platform Features," **p. 710**

An intriguing byproduct of the I-net process model is that desktop computing requirements are significantly reduced because only a browser is needed. Because the desktop needs only a keyboard, monitor, processor, and some memory hardware, vendors have invented a new type of desktop computing device. These Internet-friendly devices are referred to by many names, the most popular being *network computers (NCs)*.

Several leading manufacturers are rushing to build NCs in anticipation of their widespread acceptance due to the forthcoming proliferation of applications based on the I-net process model. It remains to be seen whether or not users will sacrifice the additional capabilities of a PC due to the availability of local storage devices, which are notably missing from NCs (thus resulting in significantly lower costs).

N O T E The I-net process model combines the best of the client-server process model in that distinct computing processes are separated, and the host-based process model in that users are relieved of processing burdens. ▪

The good news for BackOffice environments is that it supports, as well as encourages, the use of either the client-server process model or the I-net process model. In fact, it is possible to build and administer a BackOffice network upon which applications of both types are operated. This is quite common today.

There is little question that the I-net process model is here to stay simply because of the momentum of the Internet and its associated technologies and because of the significant investment being made by the information technology industry's leading vendors. The battle between PCs and NCs may wage on for years to come. Again, BackOffice is designed to accommodate either of the most popular process models today and into the future.

Understanding Information Networks

The process models in use today are merely transitional phases in the evolution of computing and are an important step toward the panacea of distributed computing; that is, information users make decisions at any time from any place. Therefore, the ultimate goal is to be able to process data anywhere on the network (local and remote) with software anywhere on the network. In the world of fully distributed computing, users will be able to transparently share data, processes, and computing power.

Today, we distinguish data from information. Computer users assemble *data* on their desktops for the purpose of making decisions. Data is assembled into meaningful groups to support these thought processes. The assimilation of data from around the network onto the desktop creates *information*. The capability to process information, as opposed to bytes of data, now has become the predominant need of computer users.

Microsoft has addressed the need to assimilate, process, and analyze information by introducing the *document-centric* approach to desktop computing. In this approach, information is retained as an object. These *information objects* are accessed by the appropriate tool or set of tools. An information object can contain sections appropriate for manipulation by a spreadsheet, with other sections accessible by word processors or database management tools.

Although the client-server process model and the I-net process model represent effective ways to distribute processes, BackOffice also facilitates the effective distribution of data, software, and information objects. BackOffice makes possible the effective sharing of data in a computing enterprise across legacy systems, client-server systems, Internet-based systems, and new distributed systems, resulting in the convenient and transparent availability of information objects throughout the organization.

Microsoft refers to the concept of connecting all types of systems for the purpose of processing information (as opposed to data) as *information networking*. This definition of an information network directly maps to the product strategy of BackOffice. Although it may seem a bit self-fulfilling at first, it should not diminish the value of this important concept.

N O T E   The information network is Microsoft's answer to the world of fully distributed computing. ■

Microsoft Office and BackOffice enable Microsoft customers to take full advantage of the information networking revolution. The individual products of BackOffice address information networking as indicated by distributing the following:

- **Data**—Using SQL Server and SNA Server.
- **Processes**—Using Windows NT Server and Internet Information Server.
- **Information objects**—Using Internet Information Server and Exchange Server.
- **Software**—Using System Management Server.

Information networking is based on sound, proven technology principles, such as object-oriented technology. Microsoft supports the distribution of software components with its Common Object Model (COM). COM is the base object model upon which all Microsoft operating systems are built. Furthermore, Microsoft pledges to provide interfaces compliant with industry standards as they emerge.

Built upon COM is Microsoft's object linking and embedding (OLE), which defines how data is combined on the desktop into meaningful information. With OLE, different types of data can be combined into a single document; this is known as *document-centric computing*. Today document-centric computing is limited to the computing desktop. As software and information objects become distributed, OLE will reach across the network.

N O T E   BackOffice is designed and built to fulfill the needs of information networking—today and
into the future. ■

Recently, Microsoft has combined OLE technology with technology of the Internet and created something known as *active technology*. Again, built upon COM, active technologies specify how information objects and software objects will interact in the world of Internet technology. Chapter 23, "Using Active Platform to Enhance Your Web Site," contains a complete description of the various components of Active Platform and how it applies to a BackOffice environment.

The Business Value of BackOffice

How does BackOffice provide value to your organization? The primary basis for the benefit BackOffice provides your computing enterprise lies in the value of the information it manages. The following sections describe the direct and indirect ways in which BackOffice provides advantages to your organization.

Advantageous Pricing Model

Microsoft has bundled several server-based products into BackOffice. Consequently, purchasing BackOffice tends to be financially advantageous as compared to competitive products priced on an individual basis. Volume-based licensing agreements support this concept for organizations of all sizes. Additionally, each BackOffice product is developed from the same foundation, with care taken to ensure consistency across products. This results in reduced learning curves as each new product is encountered during implementation.

The Availability of Enterprise Information

Organizations today strive for more efficient decision making processes in light of business cycles becoming shorter. A good example of this is the shortened product life cycle of Microsoft development tools. Its tools used to exist for nearly 18 months before another version was released. Now the next release appears sometimes as soon as six months later. These accelerated decision making processes rely heavily on the seamless availability of information. Effective movement of data to the desktop is one of the most important roles of BackOffice.

▶ **See** "Publishing and Communication," **p. 37**

The Ease of Administration

As with any server-based product, information systems personnel must be assigned to its administration. BackOffice products come packaged with a consistent set of graphical administration tools, which simplify the complexities of server management. The consistency across server applications yields additional savings through reduced learning curves. Moreover, capacity planning efforts are now consistent throughout the BackOffice product line.

Consistent Development Platform

Application developers enjoy the benefits of BackOffice in many ways. First and foremost is the availability of an open and consistent set of application programming interfaces (APIs). More important, the server application APIs are consistent with those on the client side of Microsoft's information network. These APIs provide developers the capability to conceive, construct, and support distributed applications. Consistency across BackOffice products and into the client side yields significant savings in the development and maintenance of applications.

▶ **See** "Building Commercial Applications," **p. 39**

The Capability to Operate in an Open World

BackOffice is designed to operate in heterogeneous computing environments. To this end, support for a variety of server platforms and client operating systems is available. Each BackOffice server is open to the extent that third-party software developers are encouraged to supply add-on products. Developers can also choose to enhance BackOffice functionality by modifying existing services or developing new ones. New services developed by your own developers can be integrated into BackOffice. Administrators start and stop add-on services just as they do BackOffice services. Knowing a needed service can be purchased or developed adds significant flexibility to BackOffice as a server-based set of solutions.

▶ **See** "A Flexible Set of Services," **p. 54**

The Availability of Skilled Technical Resources

To support the successful implementation of BackOffice, Microsoft has invested heavily in building a network of industry partners. These partners, known as *solution providers,* are located in virtually every major metropolitan area throughout the United States and in most major cities around the world. Solution providers range in size from individual independent contractors to large, international consulting organizations.

The role of a solution provider is to provide expert advice on the use of Microsoft products, including BackOffice. Some solution providers specialize in specific BackOffice products while others service the entire range of BackOffice products. Solution providers are capable of hands-on service as systems engineers in addition to those who provide training services.

Microsoft has worked hard to build the solution provider network in order that its customers can be successful with their products. An important way they assure the customer of high quality service when they engage a solution provider is through the Microsoft Certified Professional program. The Certified Professional program offers four different types of certification, each carrying a different purpose.

Microsoft Certified Systems Engineer (MCSE)   Those who have achieved MCSE status are the best candidates to support you in your BackOffice implementation. MCSE certification involves passing four difficult Windows NT examinations and two elective examinations on BackOffice products. For administrators, this is the most important certification to achieve for BackOffice-related work.

Microsoft Certified Product Specialist (MCPS)   A MCPS is tested on Windows and on a Microsoft desktop product, such as Word or Excel. Because this certification does not include Windows NT or BackOffice products, it is not a certification that adds value to BackOffice assignments.

Microsoft Certified Solution Developer (MCSD)   Software developers can be certified in Microsoft development tools by passing the MCSD examinations. This includes passing two intense examinations on the Windows operating system and services architecture and passing two elective examinations on Microsoft development tools, such as Visual C++ or SQL Server. Because BackOffice is a platform upon which mission-critical applications can be built and operated, MCSD certification is important for software developers working in a BackOffice setting.

▶ **See** "Building Commercial Applications," **p. 39**

Microsoft Certified Trainer (MCT)   Should you seek training in any of the BackOffice family of products, it is important you find a MCT. These people are certified both instructionally and technically in individual BackOffice products. MCTs are available to train you in most Microsoft products, including those in BackOffice.

The Integrated Service Model

All BackOffice components are designed to take full advantage of Windows NT Server as an underlying platform. Each product is designed to leverage the architecture of Windows NT. Consequently, the products integrate closely with Windows NT Server and each other as well. This low level of integration results in a stable and redundant platform upon which information networks can be safely built. The value of stability is further enhanced by the ease with which installation, security, and user logon are integrated. Integration leads to simplified usage, which, in turn, leads to lower administration costs and more satisfied users.

Integrated Installation The unified installation for BackOffice products results in less installation headaches since installation of each BackOffice product can be made from the same set of CDs. The consistency of the installation questions also simplifies the process.

Integrated Security An integrated security model means users have fewer passwords to remember and only log on once to access all BackOffice services. To demonstrate the ease with which users can be administered, Figure 1.8 shows the User Properties dialog box in which user parameters, including security, are set by an administrator.

FIG. 1.8

Users of BackOffice networks are created through the Windows NT Server User Properties dialog box.

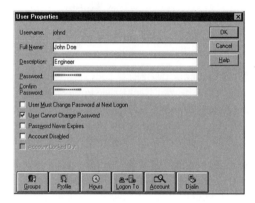

Users can also log on to the information network as a whole, as opposed to having to log on to individual server applications.

Leverage as a Solid Foundation

By implementing more than one of the products in BackOffice, you can leverage the knowledge gained about the Windows NT environment. In general, you will find the subsequent products you implement easier to learn and understand. With each new BackOffice component, there will be new information to learn specific to the component, but there is also similarity in setup options, security, and administration, resulting in time savings.

Most important is the value BackOffice offers in leveraging the future. Microsoft has painted a clear vision in defining information networking as the goal. BackOffice launches the computing world into the future.

The Future of BackOffice

Even though this book covers the use of the current version of BackOffice, it is helpful to understand the direction Microsoft intends to take it. Needless to say, future capabilities of BackOffice are at the discretion of Microsoft, and any ideas presented here can only be taken as speculation. The following list is not intended to be comprehensive, but at least serves as an indication of the commitment Microsoft continues to make to the entire BackOffice family of products:

- **Packaging**—As of this writing, BackOffice comes in a single package under the version number 2.5. It is likely Microsoft will keep the BackOffice family concept intact, but release a variety of BackOffice product bundles. These new product bundles will be targeted at specific markets, such as small business or specific vertical markets. It is even conceivable, given the significant number of new BackOffice and Internet server applications Microsoft will develop, that customized BackOffice bundles can be created. Of course, this pricing model will probably only be available to Microsoft's largest customers.

- **Microsoft Management Console (MMC)**—Each BackOffice product currently comes with its own administration tools. Although there exists many similarities in the administration capabilities of each tool, the fact remains that each product has its own. The MMC is intended to be the single administration tool with which one can administer all of the BackOffice products licensed on a given network. This will be a great step in the history of BackOffice: It will provide a more logical view of the BackOffice services package, as opposed to the current view—which is based on individual BackOffice products. The MMC will fully exploit the underlying BackOffice service model, which is at the heart of its existence.

- **User interface**—The operating system user interfaces that you are accustomed to from Microsoft will change in the near future. A consistent user interface will be available in all Microsoft operating systems whether they are for the desktop, such as Windows 95, or for networking or servers, such as Windows NT. In all cases, the user interface will contain a browser look and feel. Similar to the manner in which today you navigate the Internet with a browser, you will soon be navigating your own computer and your own network with a browser.

- **SQL Server**—The RDBMS component of BackOffice is SQL Server. As it exists today, it adequately serves to support the development and operation of mission-critical commercial applications. The biggest need in the months and years ahead for database management is the capability to build and administer huge data stores for reporting purposes (also known as *data warehouses*). Expect Microsoft to address this need with significant enhancements to future versions of SQL Server expressly for this purpose. In the meantime, it is likely that data warehousing tools will become available from Microsoft as add-on products to SQL Server.

- **Distributed Computing**—Client-server computing and Internet technologies are steps along the way to a world of fully distributed computing. As seen earlier in this chapter in "Understanding Information Networks," fully distributed computing environments encompass seamless distribution of data, software, and processes. Microsoft ensures that new releases of BackOffice and its individual products will continue the move toward fully distributed computing.

- **Distributed File System (DFS)**—DFS enables network administrators and computer users to create logical views of the shared storage devices on the network. Presently, views of storage devices are presented as physical hierarchies. With DFS, it will be possible to organize logical hierarchies regardless of the physical organization of the servers and associated storage devices.

■ **Clustering**—Clustering is a recent development that enables an administrator to treat multiple computers and their associated devices as a single unit. In this manner the devices become easier to administer, become more reliable, and deliver better performance. Today's clustering techniques involve complicated hardware and operating system configurations. Microsoft is contributing to the development of industry-standard clustering methods, and plans to provide these services directly within Windows NT in a future version.

■ **Directory services**—Windows NT Directory Services (NTDS) provides a means by which network resources, such as computers and printers, can be secured and administered. In order to provide a seamless and consistent computing environment for users on the network, it is necessary to have effective directory services. Windows NT has long contained a directory-services facility in NTDS, but many new features are anticipated in the future. A more sophisticated directory-services capability is necessary to administer the forthcoming world of distributed computing.

■ **64-bit**—The most popular processors upon which BackOffice operates are those manufactured by Intel. Even though Intel does not yet offer a 64-bit processor, it is anticipated that Windows NT—and eventually each of the BackOffice products—will appear in 64-bit versions. In the meantime, the 64-bit versions of BackOffice products will be available only on certain 64-bit processors, such as the Digital Alpha AXP.

From Here...

This completes your overview of BackOffice. You have been introduced to each of the BackOffice products, and you have gained important knowledge about the technical foundation of BackOffice: the client-server process model. You also gained an understanding of the business value of BackOffice and what it means to your organization. These important concepts form the foundation of your understanding of BackOffice. For more information about these and related topics, see the following chapters:

■ To further understand the details of BackOffice and the role it can play in your organization, see Chapter 2, "Characteristics of BackOffice."

■ To learn how to prepare for a BackOffice computing environment, see Chapter 3, "Planning for BackOffice."

■ For the details associated with planning your BackOffice implementation, see Chapter 4, "Enterprise Planning and Implementation."

Characteristics of BackOffice

by Greg Sullivan

This chapter presents a brief overview of BackOffice's characteristics. By the end of this chapter, you will have a fundamental knowledge of the purposes for BackOffice, the architecture of BackOffice, and how its design fulfills a variety of needs in modern computing.

Understanding the reasons for the existence of BackOffice, the architecture of BackOffice, and the design principles upon which it is built puts you in the best position to take full advantage of its capabilities. As you learn more about the various roles of BackOffice, keep in mind its place in the evolution of computing. (See Chapter 1, "An Inside Look at BackOffice.")

BackOffice is based on current technologies with an eye toward the future. Microsoft continues to invest heavily in BackOffice as it moves toward an object-based, distributed enterprise computing platform. In fact, the basis for a significant portion of its Internet strategy is BackOffice. This parallels its continued investment in desktop computing tools and platforms.

Interestingly, even though BackOffice is based on current and leading edge concepts, such as object-oriented technology and distributed computing, you will rarely find such a reference in Microsoft marketing materials. Its marketing approach tends to focus on the benefits and value of BackOffice as opposed to its technical underpinnings.

BackOffice roles

Discover the primary purposes for the existence of BackOffice.

BackOffice design goals

Explore the technical underpinnings of BackOffice and learn the foundation of its existence.

How BackOffice serves as a network operating system

Learn the important characteristics of a network operating system and how BackOffice fulfills this need.

What BackOffice services are and how they work

Become acquainted with the most important and basic concept in BackOffice—services.

Why BackOffice is a solid platform for the future

Understand why BackOffice is a safe bet for your organization.

What BackOffice is from your perspective

Learn why BackOffice is important to you as an information systems manager, administrator, developer, or user.

> **N O T E**   Microsoft prefers to avoid technical terms, such as *object-oriented technology* and
> *distributed computing,* when describing BackOffice, even though these concepts form a
> basis for its product strategy. ■

The exception to this, of course, is the marketing leverage Microsoft attempts to gain by aggressively marketing its use of Internet technologies within BackOffice and in support of BackOffice implementations. ■

The Roles of BackOffice

BackOffice means many things to many people. In order to be successful with BackOffice, it is helpful to understand Microsoft's view on the roles it should, and can, play in your organization. According to Microsoft, BackOffice is intended for the following three primary purposes:

- Publishing and communication
- Groupware
- Building commercial applications

Table 2.1 provides an overview of how the individual BackOffice products covered in this book map to each of these roles. In the subsequent sections, each role of BackOffice is covered in detail.

Table 2.1   BackOffice Roles

BackOffice Product	Publishing and Communication	Groupware	Building Commercial Applications
Internet Information Server	✔	✔	✔
Index Server	✔		
Content Replication Server	✔		
Active Platform	✔		
Exchange Server	✔	✔	✔
SQL Server	✔	✔	✔
SNA Server	✔		✔

Notably missing from Table 2.1 are Windows NT and SMS. Windows NT simply serves as the foundation upon which all of the BackOffice applications operate. As such, it is necessary to support all of the aforementioned roles of BackOffice. Most importantly, Windows NT provides the security and service model by which all of these capabilities can be provided.

Regarding SMS, it is an optional BackOffice component and is not necessary in order for BackOffice to fulfill these purposes. If it is implemented, it functions to build and maintain the computing environment within which the stated roles of BackOffice can be delivered.

In the immediately following sections a brief description of each BackOffice role is provided along with an examination of how the pertinent BackOffice products support that purpose.

Publishing and Communication

Since the inception of information systems, computers and software have been created for the purpose of tracking information and making it available, in convenient ways, to interested parties. Also, recent developments and acceptance of the Internet have led to widespread information distribution using the World Wide Web (Web). These, among others, are the two primary manners in which information has been distributed to those interested in receiving it.

Part
I
Ch
2

The capability to publish information by way of stored data and through Internet technologies is an important role BackOffice plays in modern-day information systems. BackOffice forms the foundation upon which systems can publish information, as well as provides the capability to do so. It is arguably the main reason Microsoft has bundled so many products into the BackOffice family.

In order for information to move into the appropriate places, it is necessary for computers to communicate with one another. This capability for computers to communicate is another important role of BackOffice. It supports communication by acting as a network operating system, by accommodating remote access to local networks, by supporting wide area networking, and by enabling seamless connectivity to the Internet. These capabilities of BackOffice are built into Windows NT at the core of BackOffice.

The capability of BackOffice to manage and distribute useful information serves its purpose as a means for publishing and communication. Following is a brief description of the role some BackOffice applications serve in supporting its capability for publishing and communication. Reference to the appropriate section in this book is also provided to further explore each particular product.

Internet Information Server   The primary benefit of Internet Information Server (IIS) in information publishing is its capability to support the creation and operation of Web pages. This vehicle has proven to be a successful way to disseminate information to users across your network (intranet) or to users all over the world (Internet). Chapter 18, "Building a Web with Internet Information Server (IIS)," explains in detail how to use IIS for this purpose. Also notable is that such tools as Microsoft FrontPage 97 have significantly simplified the creation of Web pages.

▶ **See** "Microsoft FrontPage," **p. 491**

Index Server   Index Server supports information publishing by providing a convenient means for organizing documents of unstructured data, such as Word files or Web pages. This enables users of the documents managed by Index Server to quickly search for desirable information and isolate it for viewing purposes. Index Server allows properties to be assigned to binary files and, as importantly, it understands how to use these properties to facilitate convenient access without having to interpret the entire document. See Chapter 21, "Implementing Index Server and the Content Replication System," for a thorough explanation of how to use Index Server for managing published information.

Content Replication Server   The information contained in Web pages is frequently created by more than one author. This often leads to a document management problem in that someone must be responsible for assimilating the information from each author and organizing it for Web page creation and distribution to the target audience. Content Replication Server is provided for this purpose. See Chapter 21, "Implementing Index Server and the Content Replication System," for more information about using Content Replication Server to manage published information.

SQL Server   SQL Server, as you have already seen, is the relational database management component of BackOffice. There are two important ways in which it supports information publishing. First, it is possible to build powerful reporting capabilities (sometimes referred to as *data warehouses*) with SQL Server managed data. Chapter 37, "Data Warehousing with SQL Server," explains how to use SQL Server to enables users access to structured data for reporting purposes or for ad hoc queries.

Secondly, SQL Server now interfaces seamlessly with IIS using a variety of techniques. This enables Web page developers to create dynamic Web pages that are driven by the data in a SQL Server database. To see how SQL Server interfaces with IIS, see Chapter 24, "Dynamic Content with IIS Using dbWeb and IDC." Combined with the data warehousing capabilities of SQL Server, the capability to create dynamic Web pages is a powerful manner in which to distribute information to private users on your intranet or to the public via the Internet.

Exchange Server   The most widely known role of Exchange Server in BackOffice is as the messaging component. Exchange Server also contains a comprehensive document management capability. This capability is delivered through, among other things, Exchange shared folders. These shared folders can be either public or private, and they can contain any type of electronic document desirable. In this manner, Exchange is a powerful publishing tool.

▶ **See** "Document Library," **p. 1039**

SNA Server   There exists to this day in the evolution of information technology a tremendous amount of data on IBM mainframe computers. BackOffice provides the capability to communicate with IBM host computers with SNA Server. This product serves to connect local area networks to the mainframes enabling users and applications to access host data. As such, it provides communication services to computers outside of a traditional BackOffice environment.

▶ **See** "Understanding SNA Server," **p. 1316**

Groupware

Sharing information among many people is a basic capability that we expect from information technology today. The complexities associated with sharing a wide variety of data types have led to the naming of a concept known as *groupware*. Many interpretations exist, but the most popular definition of groupware is software for managing shared documents and for managing electronic discussion groups.

BackOffice, and in particular Exchange Server, is built with this purpose in mind. Following is a brief description of the role some BackOffice applications serve in supporting its capability for groupware. Reference to the appropriate section in this book is also provided to further explore each particular product.

Internet Information Server   IIS supports group activities in numerous ways. Among the most popular is its capability to enable electronic conversations by multiple, simultaneous users on your network or over the Internet. This capability is provided through the use of its bulletin board services.

Part

I

Ch

2

A related way in which IIS supports group activities is through its capability to enable access to discussion databases via browsers. These and several other techniques are explored in detail in Chapter 16, "The BackOffice I-Net Toolbox."

Exchange Server   At the heart of BackOffice groupware capabilities is Exchange Server. The first and most obvious manner in which Exchange Server supports group activities its capability to manage folders of all types of information to users across the entire local area network or wide area network.

▶ **See** "Setting Up the Public Folder Application," **p. 1042**

In addition to its capability to organize published data, it provides the capability to store and route messages. Routing documents throughout a group of people is one of the most important features Exchange Server provides in support of groupware. This includes store and forward document routing and document compilation with security.

▶ **See** "Using Document Routing to Streamline Workflow," **p. 1061**

SQL Server   Although SQL Server does not contribute volumes to the groupware role of BackOffice, it does support some important functions in this regard. Most notably is the capability of SQL Server to protect data with its full transaction processing capability. In addition to data protection services, SQL Server provides transaction audit information. This supports group-type data management activities that are necessary in a groupware environment. Microsoft has also recently added to SQL Server the capability to manage unstructured data, such as Word documents.

▶ **See** "Integrating Exchange Server and SQL Server," **p. 1047**

Building Commercial Applications

BackOffice has become one of the predominant platforms upon which full-scale, mission-critical commercial applications are developed and operated. As Windows NT has gained market acceptance as a server operating system, many companies have converted UNIX-based systems to Windows NT and much of new application development is based on Windows NT. This trend is a direct result of the benefits of BackOffice as an application development and deployment platform. Chapter 47, "Building BackOffice Applications," explores in detail the issues facing developers of BackOffice applications.

The benefits of BackOffice for building commercial applications apply equally to those creating applications for internal use and for those developing applications for sale to other organizations. There are several important reasons why BackOffice is a viable platform for building commercial applications, including the following:

- Windows NT is a powerful and popular server operating system capable of supporting the operation of mission-critical server processes. This includes server applications that can be purchased, such as SQL Server for relational database management, as well as server processes you can choose to develop within your organization as a part of building an application.

  ▶ **See** "Understanding the Server's Role," **p. 109**

- BackOffice supports both of the most widely used process models for application development today: the client-server process model and the I-net process model. Whichever process model is appropriate for your application (or perhaps a combination of the two), BackOffice enables and encourages the effective use of both.

  ▶ **See** "Understanding Process Models," **p. 23**

- The Windows NT service model is open to enable you to develop customized services in support of your own applications. Although these are difficult to develop, this capability is extremely powerful and often necessary. Most importantly, the services you develop can also be administered by the service management capability Windows NT uses to manage its own services. See "A Flexible Set of Services" later in this chapter.

- Each BackOffice product provides an open programming interface known as an *application programming interface (API)*, which enables programmers to take advantage of the inner workings of BackOffice, and incorporate its capabilities directly into custom applications. This is an extremely powerful and important attribute that makes BackOffice an excellent choice for building commercial applications.

  ▶ **See** "Programmatic Interfaces," **p. 1634**

Following is a brief description of the role some BackOffice applications serve in supporting its capability for building commercial applications. Reference to the appropriate section in this book is also provided to further explore each particular product.

Internet Information Server   IIS provides the foundation upon which all types of I-net services can be operated. As with Windows NT server applications, these I-net services can be purchased or built for internal purposes. Content Replication Server and Index Server are good examples of IIS-based server applications available from Microsoft. You can expect Microsoft to continue to develop and sell additional IIS-based server applications.

▶ **See** "Internet Information Server," **p. 480**

This capability to extend the use of Internet technologies yields great benefits when the I-net process model is employed in application development. IIS provides a programming interface known as Internet Server API (ISAPI), which enables application developers to take advantage of this powerful capability to create customized I-net services.

▶ **See** "ISAPI," **p. 1636**

Active Platform   Another form of the extension of Internet technologies in BackOffice is the Active Platform. The Active Platform built into BackOffice provides the capability to build dynamic Web pages. This is an important aspect of developing commercial applications based on the I-net process model. Specifically, the Active Platform consists of the following three primary components, all of which sit atop IIS:

- ActiveX Technologies
- Active Desktop
- Active Server Pages

A complete discussion of the Active Platform can be found in Chapter 23, "Using Active Platform to Enhance Your Web Site."

Part

I

Ch

2

Exchange Server   The messaging component of BackOffice is Exchange Server. Although Exchange Server provides other valuable services in the BackOffice environment, the important one pertinent to building commercial applications is its capability to send and route messages with associated data. The programmatic interface delivered with Exchange Server, Messaging API (MAPI), enables developers to build directly into their applications the capability to send messages when certain conditions arise as automatically detected by the state of the data or based on user action. In both cases, MAPI can be used by the application developer to create a message that contains data from the application and see to it the data is routed to the appropriate recipients.

▶ **See** "MAPI," **p. 1636**

SQL Server   Relational database management within BackOffice is provided by SQL Server. It provides the capability to store, retrieve, and manipulate data in a convenient manner for users and application developers. The most important role SQL Server plays in building commercial applications is that of the relational database management system (RDBMS).

▶ **See** "What Is a Relational Database Management System?" **p. 1110**

Another important aspect of SQL Server is the capability to access it programmatically. SQL Server enables programmatic access through a number of interfaces, including Structured Query Language (SQL); traditional development tools, such as Visual C++; and through specialized interfaces, such as Open Database Connectivity (ODBC).

▶ **See** "Data Definition and Manipulation," **p. 1111**

▶ **See** "ODBC," **p. 1637**

SNA Server   At times, it makes sense to automate the capability for an application built upon BackOffice to access data on a mainframe computer. In order to do this, the application must have access to the host computer and be able to interpret the data to which it has access. SNA Server provides this capability through a programming interface called System Network Architecture API (SNAPI). SNAPI enables developers to code directly into the application the capability to retrieve data from the host by accessing the databases directly or through screen interfaces similar to those viewed by users.

▶ **See** "SNAPI," **p. 1637**

The Design Goals of BackOffice

Now that you understand *why* BackOffice exists, it is helpful to understand its inner-workings. The starting point for *how* BackOffice works is its design goals. Many design goals of BackOffice are based on the need to create value for the product. The BackOffice design goals are shown together in Figure 2.1.

FIG. 2.1

The design goals of BackOffice are important to understand.

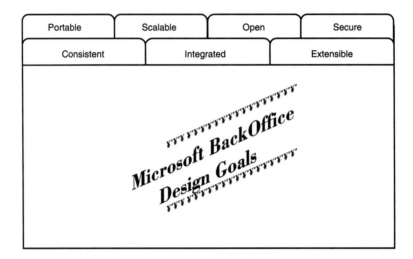

It is important to understand the technical aspects underlying each of these design goals. The following sections describe the important design goals of BackOffice and the technical significance of each.

Portability

The Windows NT operating system is designed to be portable, which implies Windows NT will operate on a variety of hardware platforms. The operating system itself is written primarily in C and C++ to ensure portability of the base source code. The small amount of the operating system written in Assembler also is designed to be portable to other platforms.

This approach makes it possible to port Windows NT to a number of processors relatively easily; consequently, users of Windows NT have choices when acquiring hardware. Windows NT is available for computer systems using the following processors:

- Intel x86, Pentium, and compatibles
- MIPS
- Digital Alpha AXP
- PowerPC

MIPS, Digital Alpha AXP, and PowerPC are examples of reduced instruction set computing (RISC) processors, which Windows NT supports.

As shown in Figure 2.2, Windows NT is written without exploiting any features specific to a particular processor family. It uses only characteristics available on any processor, such as support for virtual memory and 32-bit memory addressing.

FIG. 2.2

One of the design goals of BackOffice is to support portable applications across multiple-processor platforms.

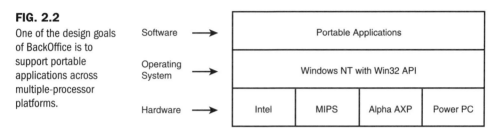

The design of Windows NT and the development tools provided by Microsoft make it possible to write a 32-bit Windows application with source code that is largely the same for all the different processor platforms supported by Windows NT. The application source modules need to be recompiled for the different target platforms, but significant customization for each platform is not required.

In spite of this fact, Microsoft does not offer every BackOffice server application for each processor platform supported by Windows NT. Table 2.2 summarizes the availability of various BackOffice components on each of the supported processors.

Table 2.2   BackOffice Processor Compatibility

Server Application	Intel	MIPS	Digital Alpha AXP	PowerPC
Windows NT	✔	✔	✔	✔
Internet Information Server	✔			
Exchange Server	✔			
SQL Server	✔	✔	✔	
SNA Server	✔			
SMS	✔			

Microsoft claims BackOffice products will be supported on additional platforms as market demand dictates.

Scalability

Scalable operating systems and applications are essential in today's computing world. It is not unusual for application scope to increase suddenly and significantly in a short period of time.

Part

I

Ch

2

Applications must be designed and created such that these spikes can be addressed by straightforward adjustments to the computing hardware. This is more desirable, and typically more affordable, than re-creating an entire business application to accommodate more data.

An operating system is said to be scalable if it automatically takes advantage of additional processors. In other words, an application designed to take advantage of the operating system should receive performance gains, or be able to process additional data without performance degradation, with only a change to the number of processors, and no change to its source code or configuration. Windows NT is a scalable operating system on computers with multiple, identical processors.

There are two ways to "add" processors in the world of BackOffice and Windows NT. Processors can be added in either of the following ways:

- By adding them to the local computer provided it accommodates additional processors
- By enabling a local process to utilize processors of other computers on the network

One common way to increase computing power is to purchase hardware that supports additional processors. Depending on the version of Windows NT you have purchased and installed, and the computer upon which you are running Windows NT, improving performance can be as simple as installing more processors. Before exploring the alternative to plugging in more processors, it is useful to understand exactly how, when, and where Windows NT supports multiple processors (see Figure 2.3).

FIG. 2.3
With the Windows NT Server automatic support for multiple processors, it is possible for an application to access a much larger database—albeit with a sublinear gain in performance—simply by adding more processors.

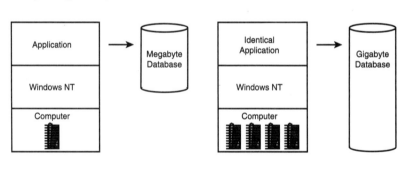

Windows NT will run on computers that have more than one processor. The retail version of Windows NT Workstation uses up to two processors, and Windows NT Server uses up to four. These are the retail versions you will receive if you purchase either product off the shelf.

Some original equipment manufacturers (OEMs) offer versions of Windows NT that support as many as 32 processors.

The capability to execute the operating system and applications on multiple processors at the same time is known as *symmetric multiprocessing* (*SMP*). The SMP capability of Windows NT is designed into its foundation; it is built directly into the operating system kernel to ensure optimal SMP is achieved on each platform Windows NT supports.

In a computer with multiple processors, Windows NT is responsible for distributing processes to be executed on all the available processors (see Figure 2.4). This includes operating system processes, such as service request managers and memory management functions. Microsoft has constructed the operating system such that process overhead is held to the bare minimum to reserve as much processor time as possible for applications.

FIG. 2.4
Windows NT operates under a symmetrical multiprocessing scheme on multiprocessor computers.

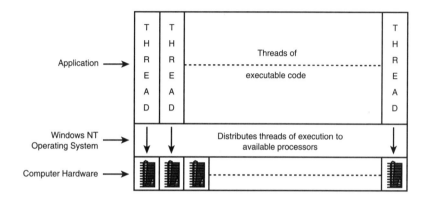

Applications designed to operate on Windows NT or in a BackOffice environment should follow the design recommendations of Microsoft closely. Well-designed applications enjoy the benefits of SMP without undergoing significant overhauls each time processing loads increase.

N O T E All BackOffice products are designed and developed as 32-bit Windows applications that automatically take advantage of the SMP capability of Windows NT. ■

Among the most important of these recommendations is designing applications into separate executable components, known as *threads*. Applications written for 32-bit versions of Windows and Windows NT can break down processes into threads and, therefore, become known as *multithreaded applications*. When Windows NT detects that a multithreaded application is executing and detects the presence of multiple processors, it distributes the application threads among all available processors. Again, operating system threads are also distributed because Windows NT is SMP-based.

N O T E The products included in BackOffice are implemented as multithreaded services that exploit additional processors on a server for performance gains. ■

Currently, Windows NT scales well in the neighborhood of four to eight processors. It has been tested successfully on multiprocessor computers with up to 16 processors. The theoretical limit is 32 processors. Said another way, Windows NT has the capability to work on 32 processors, has been tested on 16 processors, but retains a practical limitation somewhere in the neighborhood of six processors. Figure 2.5 depicts Windows NT processor effectiveness.

Part
I

Ch
2

FIG. 2.5

One way to characterize Windows NT multiprocessor capabilities is by describing its behavior at various numbers of processors.

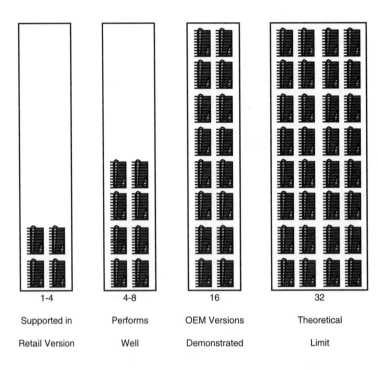

1-4	4-8	16	32
Supported in Retail Version	Performs Well	OEM Versions Demonstrated	Theoretical Limit

N O T E   To say an operating system or application "scales up to *n* processors" implies that after the *n*th processor is added, the operating system or application receives no additional performance improvements. ▪

When additional processors are added to a computer system, there is not necessarily a proportionate gain in performance. In fact, at some point you experience no additional performance improvements. This is due to factors other than processor utilization. For example, on Intel-based personal computers (PCs), the speed with which data is transferred from the processor to memory is fully tapped at four processors. This is why the retail versions of Windows NT only support up to four processors. OEMs design special computers to overcome this problem and offer OEM-specific versions of Windows NT as the base platform.

 T I P   To enable Windows NT to take advantage of additional processors, you need to set it up to use its multiprocessor kernel.

N O T E   Performance results are not necessarily proportionate to the number of processors. ▪

The other way additional processors enable Windows NT to realize performance gains is by providing a means for process execution to be distributed across the network. In other words, processors throughout the network—not just on the local computer—are utilized for process execution (see Figure 2.6). Windows NT and BackOffice rely heavily on a concept known as *remote procedure calls* (*RPCs*) to make this possible.

N O T E Not surprisingly, each BackOffice product uses RPC to interact with client workstations on the network. ■

FIG. 2.6
Windows NT uses remote procedure calls to distribute process execution to other computers on the network as another means for achieving multiprocessing capabilities.

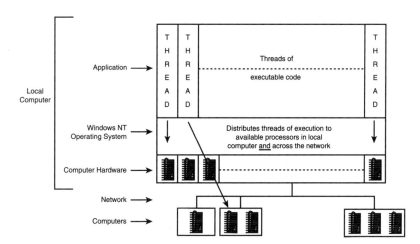

RPC supports the message-based aspect of the client-server and I-net process models. Because RPC enables processes to be executed anywhere on the network, you can optimize overall processor utilization. Consequently, you can take advantage of every available processor on the network. This can be achieved without sacrificing the advantage of multiple processors in any single computer on the network. Moreover, the advantage of RPC does not diminish in a well-designed application as more processors are added to the network.

Applications must be designed specifically to utilize RPC to gain any advantage from the distribution of process execution across the network. Distributed process execution is another way in which Windows NT is scalable.

The Open Concept

There is an ongoing and healthy debate about what constitutes an *open operating system*. Microsoft and Windows NT enthusiasts claim Windows NT is an open operating system. Proponents of rival operating systems frequently disagree. It is accurate to say, however, that Microsoft has supported industry standards. Admittedly, some of these standards were defined by Microsoft. It also offers developer tools, documentation, publications, and conferences aimed at helping information systems professionals develop applications for the BackOffice environment. Whether this constitutes being open is perhaps moot.

N O T E BackOffice integrates with other server applications that may run on the network, including applications competitive with BackOffice products. ■

Microsoft claims each BackOffice product complies with every major open computing standard. Again, some of these standards are established by Microsoft, whereas others are influenced by Microsoft's involvement in the standard-setting organizations. The following describes the most significant interfaces supported by BackOffice:

- **Java**—Developed by Sun Microsystems, Java defines a manner in which Internet-based applications can be developed and accessed by users via an Internet browser. Microsoft has elected to embrace this industry accepted standard and extend it through incorporation into BackOffice.

- **ODBC**—Open Database Connectivity (ODBC) from Microsoft is an industry-standard application programming interface (API) that provides access for client applications to databases. Nearly every leading database vendor supports ODBC interfaces.

- **OLE**—Object Linking and Embedding (OLE) from Microsoft describes how software components work together using object technology. OLE forms the basis for the concept of document-centric computing. It is based on Microsoft's open Common Object Model (COM).

- **SNA**—System Network Architecture (SNA) from IBM is an open standard that describes how PCs, IBM minicomputers, and IBM mainframes communicate with one another. SNA includes an API that enables developers to access data on each type of computer.

- **MAPI**—Messaging API (MAPI) from Microsoft is an open API that provides messaging services for building client-server applications.

- **TAPI**—Telephony API (TAPI) from Microsoft supports the integration of electronic data with voice communication, known as *computer-telephone integration (CTI)*.

- **ISAPI**—Internet Services API (ISAPI) from Microsoft and Process Software exposes the Internet Information Server (IIS) to software developers. This API enables developers to integrate Internet services into their applications.

In addition to supporting these open interfaces, Windows NT Server supports many of the most popular network protocols, including the following:

- Transmission Control Protocol/Internet Protocol (TCP/IP)
- NetBIOS Extended User Interface (NetBEUI)
- Hypertext Transport Protocol (HTTP)
- File Transfer Protocol (FTP)
- Apple File Protocol (AFP)
- Internetwork Packet Exchange/Sequenced Packet Exchange (IPX/SPX)
- Open Data Services (ODS)
- Simple Network Management Protocol (SNMP)
- Simple Mail Transfer Protocol (SMTP)

UNIX interoperability is available through support of the open interfaces and protocols mentioned earlier. X Window system products can execute on Windows NT. Additionally, numerous third-party vendors offer products that bring BackOffice and UNIX closer together. Some of these products are based on the open interfaces, whereas others are based on licensing agreements between Microsoft and the third-party companies. One such example is Microsoft's Windows Interface Source Environment (WISE), which is licensed to a few third parties in the UNIX market. WISE permits Windows-based applications to be supported in UNIX environments while preserving interoperability with BackOffice. See Chapter 14, "Windows Integration with NetWare and UNIX," for a complete discussion on this topic.

Security

In this brave, new world of computing in which data, processes, and information objects are distributed across local area networks (LANs) and wide area networks (WANs), security concerns abound. This is especially true considering the connection many organizations now, or soon will, have to the outside world via the Internet. These physical connections increase the opportunity for security violations.

▶ **See** "Understanding BackOffice Security," **p. 112**

As an information systems professional, you must be serious about securing the information processed by your systems. Secure transmission, controlled access, and assigned authorizations are important aspects of a secure computing environment (see Figure 2.7). Organizations should also construct well-conceived security models and measure their effectiveness through frequent auditing.

FIG. 2.7
BackOffice provides support for addressing the three major aspects of security: access, transmission, and authorization.

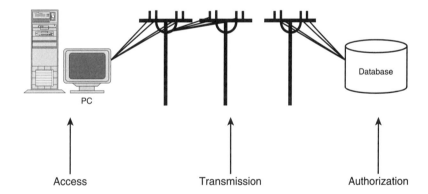

PC

Database

Access   Transmission   Authorization

BackOffice facilitates the implementation of a comprehensive security plan. It addresses the need to control access and usage of services, as well as resources. Securing services and resources protects your processes, computers, peripheral devices, software, and information. Although BackOffice provides the tools for an effective security plan, full security cannot be achieved without the intelligent application of these tools, disciplined management, and the appropriate controls.

The BackOffice security model is fully integrated. This implies users have a single security entry point into the information network with only one username and password to remember. Service and resource access and authorizations are assigned by administrators to each user.

Users have the convenience of easy entry with the comfort of knowing their information is safe.

Robustness

Is BackOffice suitable for mission-critical application deployment? The answer to this question lies in its robustness. Software is said to be robust if it does the following:

- Traps software and hardware exceptions
- Does not harm another application in the event of a failure
- Recovers from errors without loss of data or causing the workstation to be rebooted
- Provides an overall level of stability

Most software products have difficulty laying claim to robustness in their first release. Stability remains elusive regardless of the volume of testing prior to release. However, over a period of time the software developer improves the product based on how it behaves for customers.

Microsoft is no exception to this principle. Many information systems managers await the second release of a software product prior to implementing it in their organization. They receive some additional comfort from the fact that the initial problems with the software have been repaired.

As each new version of the software is released it gets closer to the goal of true robustness. BackOffice is now in its fourth release. As such, it possesses a level of robustness suitable for mission-critical applications.

Consistency

An obvious design goal of BackOffice is the desire for consistency. On the surface, this design goal is observed first as you view the user interfaces for each product and the associated services and administrative tools. A consistent graphical user interface has been achieved among all BackOffice products. This look and feel is also consistent with other Microsoft operating systems and the Microsoft Office family of desktop products.

As important, BackOffice appears consistent to administrators and developers. Administrators are presented with a consistent set of administration tools. Some tools deal with the administration of multiple services at the same time. Ease of administration is a key advantage given the diversity and flexibility of BackOffice services.

N O T E In the future, this consistency will be more obvious as Microsoft releases its Microsoft Management Console. This will become the single interface through which all BackOffice products are administered.

The programming interface available to developers is also constructed in a consistent manner. The Windows NT application programming interface (API) is known as Win32. Win32 is the basis upon which all BackOffice products are developed. Moreover, it is available to you for development of applications or services. Because Win32 is a part of Windows NT, it is available to developers of client applications and server processes. This provides all BackOffice developers the advantage of a consistent programming interface.

Another important way in which Microsoft has achieved consistency is the manner in which Windows NT ports to various processors. It has taken care to use only processor features available on all the processors supported by Windows NT. It is conceivable that Microsoft will never exploit processor-specific features. In this manner, Microsoft will avoid the version fragmentation that has plagued UNIX over the years.

Integration

You have already seen how the BackOffice security model delivers, in part, the design goal of integration. This is but one of the many ways in which integration is accomplished. BackOffice products are designed also to integrate well with the following:

- Windows NT
- Other networks
- The Internet
- Desktop computers

Integration with Windows NT   Windows NT serves as the basis for a complete network operating system. You learn more about BackOffice as a network operating system in the section "A Network Operating System" later in this chapter. With Windows NT as a foundation, BackOffice provides a full set of integrated network services.

BackOffice products also tend to integrate well with each other. An example of this is the dependency SMS has on SQL Server. SQL Server also has built-in integration with Internet Information Server. Curiously though, Exchange Server does not use SQL Server as its database. Instead, it uses an internal Microsoft database engine.

Integration with Other Networks   In addition to the network services provided, BackOffice integrates well with many other popular networks. Connectivity is provided from your computing desktop to Novell NetWare, UNIX, LAN Manager, AppleTalk, DEC PATHWORKS, IBM LAN Server, Network File System (NFS), and Banyan VINES. This level of support for other network operating systems ensures that BackOffice integrates into heterogeneous computing environments. For more information on how BackOffice acts as a network operating system, see "A Network Operating System" later in this chapter.

Integration with the Internet   Perhaps the hottest topic in technology circles today is the Internet. BackOffice comes complete with an Internet Server component, as well as several Internet Server products, such as Proxy Server. This service enables your network and organization to integrate with the world via the Internet. BackOffice also facilitates the delivery of Internet connectivity to the desktops on your network.

▶ **See** "Microsoft Internet Architecture," **p. 483**

Integration with Desktop PCs and NCs   Finally, BackOffice is designed to tightly couple with desktop computers—PCs or network computers (NCs). This, after all, is the sole reason for the existence of BackOffice. Its primary job is to deliver data to the computing desktops in the form of meaningful information. Microsoft has designed BackOffice consistent with desktop design goals to ensure seamless integration of all computers on the network and the Internet, as shown in Figure 2.8.

FIG. 2.8
BackOffice products integrate well with each other, and together they integrate well with other networks, such as Novell and the Internet.

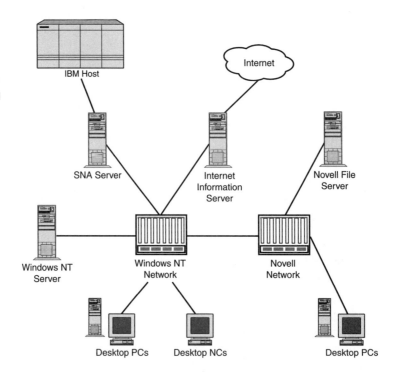

Extensibility

The basic architecture of BackOffice ensures that new services can be added and existing services can be enhanced. The capability to add new services and enhance existing services is known as *extensibility*.

Microsoft continues to invest in the development of new products and services in the BackOffice family. Its many Internet server products, such as Merchant Server and Personalization Server, are a good examples of a recent additions to the product suite. Additionally, Microsoft continues to provide enhanced versions of the core BackOffice products. Exchange Server is a good example of a recent product upgrade.

N O T E   Building your own services is a convenient way to customize BackOffice for your organization. ■

In addition to the products and services available from Microsoft, a market exists for third-party BackOffice products. Microsoft has released a sufficient amount of technical information about the way in which BackOffice services are built and executed to enable developers to create their own services. Consequently, companies have entered into the business of developing and selling BackOffice add-on services. These services can be managed by the same administrative tools used to manage services from Microsoft.

N O T E Microsoft and third parties will continue to build and enhance services. ▦

You can also build your own services or modify existing services. This is the essence of client-server computing and is at the heart of the Internet. A combination of purchased services and home-grown services is typical in today's computing environments. Armed with a consistent set of APIs and an appropriate set of development tools, developers can influence the behavior of existing services. Administrators also possess flexibility in setting the behavioral characteristics of services.

A Network Operating System

BackOffice is used in a networked computing environment. This typically includes desktop PCs and desktop NCs, or *clients*, and larger computers, called *servers*. The servers are shared resources in a network just as other peripheral devices and mainframe computers.

The servers must run a network-capable operating system. Popular network operating systems include UNIX, Novell NetWare, and Windows NT. Client PCs and client NCs can run a wider variety of operating system software including DOS, Windows, Windows for Workgroups, Windows NT Workstation, Windows 95, UNIX, OS/2, and Mac OS.

The various network operating systems offer different sets of network services. Some services are available on all network operating systems; others are not. Network services built in to BackOffice include the following:

- File access
- Print management
- Resource sharing
- Remote administration
- Security
- Dial-up access
- Internet access
- Server-based applications

Some common services are described in the following sections.

Part
I
Ch
2

The Basics: File and Printer Sharing

In a networked environment, it is possible to share resources (such as printers and files) containing important information. This has been the main reason for installing traditional LANs in corporate environments.

Resource Sharing

In addition to file and printer sharing, it is possible to share other resources on a network. It is common, for example, to share a pool of modems so that a group of people can take turns using them to establish a phone link to remote locations. Sharing peripheral devices, such as modems and printers, results in more efficient utilization of hardware. Consequently, computer equipment investments can be leveraged among several users.

Server-Based Applications

In addition to sharing information and peripheral devices, such as printers, a logical next step in the evolution of LAN-based computing is to share processing power. This has been previously described as client-server computing. Network operating systems, such as Windows NT, provide the basis for the client-server process model. RPC is one of the many capabilities of Windows NT that enables client processes to communicate with server processes. These underpinnings permit the creation of server-based applications that are sharable simultaneously among many clients. The same capability of BackOffice as a network operating system supports usage of the I-net process model, as well.

▶ **See** "Understanding Process Models," **p. 23**

A Flexible Set of Services

A key design element of Windows NT is the concept of a service. A *service*, in a Windows NT networking environment, is a special type of server-based application. Service is an appropriate name for this type of application because its typical role is to offer services (the traditional meaning of the word) to users on the network.

BackOffice can be viewed as a set of services made available to computers attached to a network. Typically the consumers, or clients, of these services are desktop computers (either PCs or NCs) in an office environment. The following are some of the services provided by BackOffice:

- Database management
- Inventory of computers connected to the network
- Software installation
- Mainframe and minicomputer connectivity
- Electronic messaging
- Workgroup application support

This represents only a partial list of the available services, but it should give you a flavor of the capabilities of BackOffice. Each component of BackOffice is explored in detail in the chapters to follow. Services have the following characteristics:

- They execute in the background. In other words, they do not generally open a window or update the display in any way while they are running.
- They can be automatically started when the computer is turned on.
- They keep running even as users log on and log off the computer.
- They can be started, stopped, or paused by using standard Windows NT tools. You can control services on the computer using the Services applet in the Control Panel. With the Windows NT Server's administration tool called Server Manager, you can control services on any Windows NT computer for which you are an administrator. See the next section "Starting, Stopping, and Pausing Services" for more information.

Part

I

Ch

2

N O T E Pausing a service enables users who are actively using the service to continue, but no new users can connect to the service. For example, pausing the Server service on a Windows NT server prevents any new users from connecting to shared resources.

- Many services have full-featured administrative programs that enable you to perform advanced configuration and management in addition to the simple start, stop, and pause described earlier. All of BackOffice's components (Internet Information Server, Exchange Server, SQL Server, SNA Server, and SMS) have powerful administrative programs.
- It is possible to create an account specifically for use by a service and give it appropriate security permissions for its work.

The service architecture supported by Windows NT is a powerful, extensible way to develop the server component of client-server applications. Windows NT services are somewhat similar to daemons in UNIX environments or NetWare Loadable Modules (NLMs) in a Novell NetWare environment. You learn the basics of controlling services in the next two sections.

Starting, Stopping, and Pausing Services

In Part II, "Windows NT Server: Installation and Administration," you learn how to use the various administrative applications that enable you to configure and control Windows NT Server and BackOffice. For now, it is useful to understand that some standard administrative utilities come with Windows NT Server that enable you to control Windows NT itself. These utilities also enable you to control applications and services operating on a Windows NT server.

Windows NT Server Manager is shown in Figure 2.9, which is one of the administrative utilities. Server Manager can be used to control services on computers anywhere on the network as long as you have the necessary administrative rights. Server Manager was designed as a tool to let you manage remote servers without having to physically visit a computer and log on.

FIG. 2.9
Use the Windows NT
Server Manager to
select any computer
on the network to
administer.

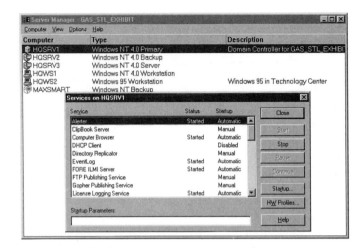

Changing Startup Options for Services

You can also use Server Manager to change the startup options for a service. Most often, services are set to automatically start when the computer is turned on and Windows NT is loaded. Alternatively, you can set the service startup option to Manual. To start the service, an administrator must follow the procedure for starting services (or an equivalent procedure). You can also completely disable a service if you do not want any of its components to be active, or allow it to be started accidentally.

 Use Windows NT Server Manager to stop, start, and configure BackOffice services.

Exploring Further Development

Windows NT and the BackOffice suite of server-based applications create a powerful platform upon which additional product development can take place. It is safe to assume that Microsoft will continue to develop and deliver BackOffice service-based applications. See Chapter 47, "Building BackOffice Applications," for more information.

Many software products have been created to run in a BackOffice environment, and more are being created every day. These products may be shrink-wrapped applications that appeal to a wide audience, or they may be highly customized applications designed to meet specific requirements at a single organization.

In addition to products available through vendors other than Microsoft, Microsoft also continues to develop and sell new BackOffice-based products. In particular, it is amassing a large suite of Internet server products and packaging them in various ways within and separate from BackOffice.

TIP You are strongly encouraged to stay current with BackOffice developments by frequently visiting the BackOffice Web page at **http://www.microsoft.com/backoffice/**.

Additional techniques must be learned to create a service, register it with Windows NT security, and execute it in a network environment. It is beyond the scope of this book to discuss development of BackOffice services. However, it is important to know how the acquisition, development, and administration of these services affect you.

BackOffice from Your Perspective

Now that you are familiar with the roles of BackOffice, the design goals of BackOffice, its role as a network operating system, its flexible set of services, and its basis as a platform for future information processing, what does it all mean to you? This, of course, depends on your role in information systems. If you are an information systems manager, administrator, or developer, you will find that BackOffice offers you many benefits.

As a Manager

Information systems managers, as well as business executives, can realize many benefits from BackOffice. Clearly, the most advantage is gained when the entire BackOffice product suite is implemented. This is true in small, medium, and large organizations due to the economies of scale and product synergy realized as a result of the consistent and integrated foundation BackOffice provides. The benefits that BackOffice provides to managers include the following:

- **Competitive pricing**—By bundling several integrated products into a single package, BackOffice offers a new level of economy to the marketplace for these types of products. The cost advantage is now more available to a larger audience as Microsoft has re-bundled BackOffice into packages targeted at specific audiences.

- **Operational savings**—Consistency and integration yield time and money savings to the organization. This is a result of the reduced cost of learning associated with implementing more than one BackOffice product.

- **Security**—Security is built into the foundation of BackOffice. Coupled with a secure physical environment and secure business processes, BackOffice gives you the comfort of knowing your information and the information of your users is protected.

- **Current technologies**—BackOffice is based on the sound and popular computing trends toward object technology and the Internet. As more software developers accept the object-oriented approach to software development and Internet technologies as a basis for serious software development, it is possible for an organization to realize significant savings in software development costs.

  It is also reasonable to expect the quality of software to be higher. Although some of these savings remain several months or even years away, it is important to know that BackOffice fully supports object technology and the Internet now, and will continue to support them in the future.

■ **Network management**—The cost of administering large networks of PCs, NCs, and servers is rarely understood in detail. This job has been plagued with hidden costs and missed user expectations. BackOffice gives you an excellent means to control the hidden costs associated with large network management through SMS. SMS also addresses the needs of those responsible for asset management by automatically tracking software and hardware inventories.

▶ **See** "Understanding Information Networks," **p. 28**

■ **Standards**—Organizations that set standards for software and hardware usage realize savings in time and money. In large networks, it has been difficult to impose standards due to the complexities associated with tracking user configurations and massive deployment of new versions of software when an upgrade becomes available. SMS now provides a convenient facility for establishing software and hardware standards and monitoring their effectiveness.

■ **User Support**—Many organizations offer internal technical support to their users. SMS provides a convenient facility that enables a help desk person to assist a user on the network by directly manipulating the user's PC or NC. This includes direct control of the keyboard and mouse. A help desk person can observe a user as the problem is experienced and, by taking control of the input devices, demonstrate correct operation while the user watches. This same capability allows hardware problems to be diagnosed remotely. All this leads to reduced costs for supporting the network and its users.

■ **Future**—Industry experts and research organizations frequently discover new ways in which technology can be applied to solve business problems. It is important that your organization is in the best possible position to apply these ideas as the need arises. BackOffice is designed to accommodate the deployment of new ideas in information systems. As a manager, it is comforting to know a BackOffice information network is built to support the next wave of new ideas. The following are examples of current concepts enabled by BackOffice:

- Data warehousing
- Systems and network management
- Consistently distributed objects
- Decision support systems (DSS)
- Executive information systems (EIS)

Overall, you can expect to have a more satisfied user community as a result of a successful BackOffice implementation. Information network users have better information and higher levels of integration. This permits them to make better decisions and be more responsive to the pressures arising from increasingly shorter cycles in the business world (e.g., the product life of a Microsoft product version is now around 6–12 months, while just a year or so ago it was a full 18 months).

As an Administrator

Information systems administration teams require tools to facilitate the delivery of information to the enterprise computing desktops. BackOffice, along with its add-ons and desktop solutions, represent a comprehensive set of tools that facilitate administration. The types of administrators needed and how the team works together are covered in Chapter 3, "Planning for BackOffice." The following explains the benefits that system, network, Internet/intranet, database, and other administrators will derive from BackOffice:

Part
I
Ch
2

- **Consistency**—Each BackOffice product now comes with its own administrative tool, and soon will come with a single administrative tool for all BackOffice products. Administrators faced with the task of managing more than one product are presented with a consistent user interface among all the tools. This results in reduced learning curves as additional products are implemented.

- **Integration**—All BackOffice products share common systems management, registry, performance monitoring, and configuration tools. Again, learning curves are held to a minimum as each new product is introduced into your information network.

- **Overlap**—Microsoft intentionally leverages other BackOffice products in its design. A good example of this is the dependency SMS has on SQL Server. SMS stores its information about your network in a SQL Server database. This reduces the time necessary to administer SMS, as the database administration is already being performed as a part of the SQL Server installation. Microsoft pledges to follow this pattern with future BackOffice products.

- **Tracking**—Each BackOffice product contains an event log to record program execution and client activity. You can configure the event logs to support your specific needs. These event logs can be used, among other things, to troubleshoot problems with the network, applications, or users.

- **Remote access**—Administration can be performed remotely via Remote Access Server (RAS). RAS, which comes with Windows NT Server, enables you to access the network through dial-up connections. Every administrative tool can be executed in this manner.

- **Version control**—Software distribution has become a labor-intensive task. Visiting every user's PC and performing the appropriate action for something as simple as a software version upgrade is now a formidable task in many organizations. BackOffice facilitates the automated management of software version control throughout the network via SMS.

  SMS enables you to control all the software on the network and desktop PCs from a central location. Moreover, BackOffice supports the I-net process model for application deployment, obviating the need for software to be distributed to desktop PCs. In fact, NCs can be used as desktop computing devices in a BackOffice environment provided all applications are developed based on the I-net process model.

  ▶ **See** "I-Net Process Model," **p. 1624**

■ **Hardware inventory**—In addition to managing software distribution, SMS deals with hardware issues. SMS can track hardware inventory, configuration parameters, and assist in diagnosing hardware problems. All this can be done from your administration workstation.

Microsoft understands BackOffice products will only be as successful as the administrators managing the information network. For this reason, it has focused on easing the burden of administration by building a consistent set of graphical administration tools. The strength of the administration tool set will only improve as Microsoft and third-party developers continue to enhance the administrative capabilities of BackOffice.

▶ **See** "Organizing Administration Teams," **p. 73**

As a Developer

Software development is currently undergoing a fundamental transition. The industry is headed toward component-based software derived from the principles of object-oriented technology. This momentum is fueled by the widespread acceptance of the Internet and its associated technologies as a commercial computing environment. Even though you will rarely hear object technology mentioned when discussing BackOffice with Microsoft, it is clearly based on object-oriented concepts. On the other hand, the Internet is typically associated with each new product development effort due to its market visibility.

Software development teams of the future will contain component builders and solution builders. *Component builders* will create the basic software objects that become the building blocks for applications. *Solution builders* will assemble these building blocks into software solutions.

N O T E   BackOffice does not diminish the need for developers to understand the principles of the underlying technologies. ▩

Microsoft has stated its intention to move toward a component-based architecture for all of BackOffice. To the developer, this means BackOffice will appear to you as a large set of building blocks from which you can choose software components when assembling an application. In addition to the many advantages brought about by object technology, BackOffice provides many other benefits to developers, whether you are a component builder or a solution builder. Following is a list of advantages BackOffice offers to developers:

■ **Open API**—As previously mentioned in the section "Consistency," BackOffice is based entirely on the Win32 API. This API is published and available to you for development of your own applications. Moreover, every aspect of BackOffice is based on the same programming model.

■ **Common Object Model**—All of BackOffice is based on the same object model. The COM specification is also available to developers. Understanding these standards will put you in the best possible position to develop stable and sustainable applications. The Active Platform now available in BackOffice is an excellent example of the advantage of COM as an object model.

▶ **See** "Active Platform Features," **p. 710**

- **Consistent**—The same programming model, APIs, and object model apply to client and server development in the worlds of client-server and I-net. Avoiding the cost of relearning any one of these as you shift from client development to server development contributes to more stability in the software and a more effective and efficient development environment.

- **Distributed computing**—BackOffice is a basis for the development of distributed applications. You have already seen in Chapter 1, "An Inside Look at BackOffice," how the information network distributes processes, data, and information objects. Combining BackOffice with any number of sophisticated development tools on the market positions you to design, build, and implement truly distributed applications.

  ▶ **See** "Understanding Information Networks," **p. 28**

- **Object-oriented technology**—Applying the principles of object-oriented technology, it is possible for you to develop applications faster through the planned reuse of software components. Another benefit of software reuse is an increased level of stability in the applications. Applications built for the information network that follow the programming model and object model set forth by Microsoft are assured of measuring up to industry standards. This means your applications will be built by assembling software components originating from Microsoft, third-party vendors, and yourself.

- **Interprocess communication**—The means by which a developer instructs an application to communicate with another application is built into BackOffice. Because the products are so tightly integrated, communicating with one is the same as communicating with any other. The same applies to your own applications. Simplifying interprocess communication significantly reduces the complexities associated with client-server development.

- **Customizable**—BackOffice supports the use of customizable tools, such as Microsoft Visual Basic, Microsoft Visual C++, Microsoft Visual J++, and Microsoft Office. These tools and others similar to them arm you with everything you need to influence the operational characteristics of the information network. Providing this low level of control is a great benefit to developers, whether they are component builders or solution builders.

- **Performance tuning**—In this world of distributed processes, it is often difficult to predict exactly how an application will perform once it is constructed. Some techniques are beginning to appear that enable performance to be modeled in complex computing environments as a part of design work steps. Nevertheless, it will always be necessary to rearrange process models after construction to optimize application performance. This process is often referred to as *performance tuning*. BackOffice has an architecture that permits experimentation with the division of processes.

Even as software development tools have become incredibly powerful, the act of software development remains difficult. Software developers face innumerable complexities with each new application. BackOffice assists developers by simplifying many tasks associated with software development—without sacrificing flexibility. Chapter 47, "Building BackOffice Applications," contains a thorough discussion on the issues facing developers of BackOffice applications.

Part
I
Ch
2

As a Computer User

In addition to being a manager, administrator, or developer, you are also a computer user on the network. What does BackOffice mean to you as a computer user? What does it mean to the users of your network, servers, or applications? Even though this book is not intended for users of BackOffice, it will be helpful for you to understand the many benefits to users, whether you are a manager, administrator, or developer. The advantages of BackOffice to users include the following:

- **Single password**—Users are required to remember only one username and password in a BackOffice environment. Integrated security makes it less frustrating for users in complex information networks.

- **Location independence**—Users can operate their software and manipulate their data on their desktop PCs and desktop NCs at the office, at their homes, or while they're on the road. Remote access appears to the user just as office access. Microsoft has designed all BackOffice products to operate remotely as effectively as they do in the office. This enables traveling personnel to access information regardless of their locations. It also enables companies to establish a telecommuting employment practice on a permanent or temporary basis.

- **Consistent interface**—Client and server applications in the BackOffice environment share the same user interface. This makes it easier for users to move from role to role with minimal impact to their work demands.

- **Desktop integration**—PCs and NCs throughout your organization are equipped with various software packages. Perhaps your organization has selected, and enforces the use of, a standard set of personal productivity tools. BackOffice is designed to integrate with these desktop information utility tools. In fact, the primary purpose of BackOffice is to facilitate information delivery to the PCs and the NCs on the information network. This high level of integration improves accessibility of data throughout the enterprise.

From Here...

The availability of more and better information supports the ultimate goal of any information systems group: to provide users with all the information required to seamlessly support their decision-making processes. Most organizations today are under constant pressure to make better and faster decisions. Facilitating the delivery of information to the decision makers promotes an effective decision-making environment.

To this end, this chapter gave you a first look at the roles BackOffice plays in information systems and the technical foundation upon which BackOffice is designed and built. This includes examining the role of Windows NT Server as a network operating system and gaining an understanding of services—the most basic principle of BackOffice. To bring it all together, you learned what BackOffice means to you as an information systems manager, administrator, developer, or user. For information on related topics, see the following chapters:

- For the final steps in the preparation of your BackOffice implementation, see Chapter 3, "Planning for BackOffice."

- For a thorough discussion of implementation planning, see Chapter 4, "Enterprise Planning and Implementation."

- To get started executing BackOffice, see Chapter 5, "Implementing Windows NT Server."

- To further explore the network implications of Windows NT Server, see Chapter 7, "Administering Windows NT Server."

Part

I

Ch

2

## CHAPTER 3

Planning for BackOffice

by Greg Sullivan and Don Benage

You have learned about the components and purpose of BackOffice. Now it is time to get ready for implementation. Before you actually install BackOffice in your organization, there is much to prepare. In this chapter, you learn the important pieces you must put into place before installing BackOffice.

After you have read this chapter, you will know how to prepare your organization for a successful installation, and you will be ready to implement BackOffice.

There is no significance to the order in which these work steps are presented. All these issues need to be addressed, and the sequence is not important. In fact, several of these activities overlap chronologically. The intent is not to present a detailed work plan, but to identify all the areas that deserve attention. Following these guidelines will enhance the likelihood of a successful BackOffice implementation. ■

Keys to building your network

Gain insight into how to build your network with BackOffice in mind. Discussion centers on the significance of intranet concepts and the Internet to your network.

How to organize an administration team

See how an administration team should be built and organized with attention given to each BackOffice product.

How to select server hardware for BackOffice

Understand the most important aspects of server hardware selection pertaining to each BackOffice product.

How to prepare the facility and set appropriate policies and procedures

These guidelines help you to understand the physical, logistical, and practical aspects of your BackOffice implementation.

How to license BackOffice

Learn the ins and outs of the flexible BackOffice licensing scheme.

Building Your Network

One of the important reasons for the existence of BackOffice is to facilitate the delivery of meaningful information to desktop personal computers (PCs) or desktop network computers (NCs). BackOffice is truly the "glue" that brings together information on the desktop. Whether you are delivering your information to PCs or NCs, you must have a physical network in place for BackOffice to provide this capability.

The network cabling must extend to every desktop PC and NC to which you want to deliver data. The network cabling must also connect to the servers that will run server-based applications, such as the products that make up BackOffice. Each PC, NC, and server must contain a network interface card (NIC) appropriate for the type of network you are using (for example, Ethernet, token-ring, or asynchronous transfer mode).

A representation of a typical network is shown in Figure 3.1. It is important to note that this representation is logical in nature. The network is shown with a hub in the center, even though most modern networks are physically wired in a star configuration with a wire running from each workstation to a multiport hub of some type. In its simplest form, a network consists of network cabling and connectors, communication devices (such as routers and hubs) that propagate data over the cabling, server computers, and client PCs or NCs.

FIG. 3.1
The simplest networks show servers, client PCs, and client NCs logically attached to a central network hub.

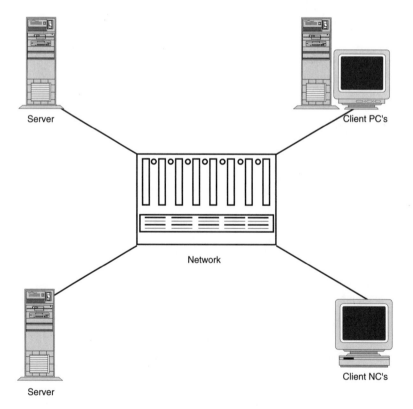

Server

Client PC's

Network

Server

Client NC's

▶ **See** "Understanding Information Networks," **p. 28**

Each network, whether it is a client-server network or an intranet, also requires a network operating system (NOS). The NOS is the software that enables the hardware to act as a network. The NOS for a BackOffice network is Windows NT Server. It provides all the basic NOS services, such as user authentication and controlling access to shared resources (e.g., files and printers). Windows NT Server includes a rich set of graphical administration tools that make it easy to manage your network.

▶ **See** "A Network Operating System," **p. 53**

Before you build a new network for BackOffice, or prepare your existing network, there are some networking fundamentals that you must understand.

Private Network

The basic building block of an enterprise private network is the *local area network* (*LAN*). It is called *local* because all the PCs, NCs, and servers are physically connected via the same cabling. The simple network shown in Figure 3.1 is an example of a LAN.

Many organizations have people located in geographically separate locations. In this situation, it is not convenient, or even possible, to connect everyone to the same LAN cabling system. However, it is still desirable to enable computer systems at different locations to communicate with one another. The solution is to connect multiple LANs together to form a *wide area network* (*WAN*). Figure 3.2 shows a typical representation of a WAN.

FIG. 3.2
Wide area networks typically incorporate multiple local area networks, which are geographically separated into a single, larger network.

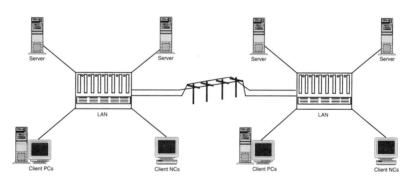

The link that connects the LANs is some type of communication line. These lines are available in many forms from providers of communication transmission services, also known as *carriers*. In addition to the communication lines, which are typically leased, it is necessary to install equipment, such as a router or bridge, to physically connect a LAN to a communication line.

The advantage of a wide area network is that users can interact with one another as if they were connected to the same physical cabling system, as shown in Figure 3.3. The type of connection is usually transparent to a user connected to the network. In some cases, however, the communication lines that connect LANs do not operate at the same rate of speed as local cabling. In these situations, users may experience delays when interacting with a server application, client PC, or client NC on another LAN connected to the WAN.

FIG. 3.3

For simplicity's sake, logical network representations often do not distinguish between the LAN and the WAN because this is usually transparent to the users.

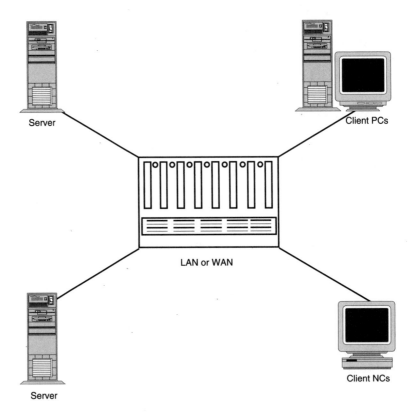

Figure 3.1 through Figure 3.3 depict generic networks. A typical BackOffice network is shown in Figure 3.4. In this figure, each BackOffice product is shown to be installed on a separate server computer. Even though in some situations it is possible to install multiple BackOffice server applications on the same server, they are depicted as individual components in the network diagram. This helps to clarify the role of each server application.

The BackOffice network may also include a connection to an IBM mainframe or minicomputer through the services of SNA Server. You may also notice this network includes remote users that connect to the network through the services of Windows NT Remote Access Service (RAS). In this sense, your private network also includes computers and users that access the network by dialing in from outside the physical location of the network.

FIG. 3.4
A BackOffice network shows the various BackOffice server products attached to the network as logical processes.

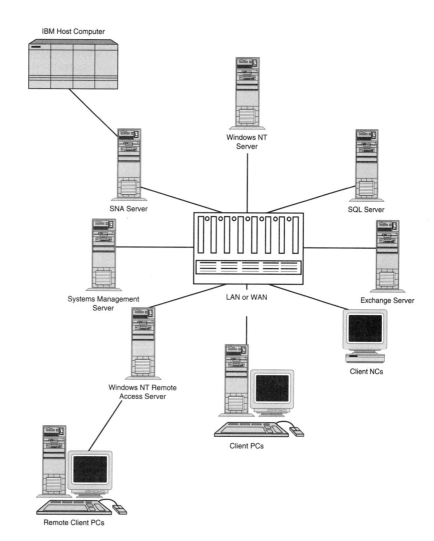

Public Network

You may also desire to connect your organization to the rest of the world. This is possible now due to the proliferation of the Internet. The Internet is a worldwide, wide area network. It was first developed by the United States Department of Defense to facilitate global communication. At its inception, the academic community was included. Academicians throughout the world continue to communicate with one another and share information via the Internet. Therefore, it has become a critical component of educational systems internationally.

▶ **See** "What Is the Internet?," **p. 498**

The network in Figure 3.4 did not depict a connection to the Internet. BackOffice contains a product that enables you to create and maintain a presence on the Internet: the Internet Information Server (IIS). A BackOffice network connected to the Internet is shown in Figure 3.5.

FIG. 3.5

Internet Information Server provides a BackOffice network an Internet presence that allows Internet users to visit your site.

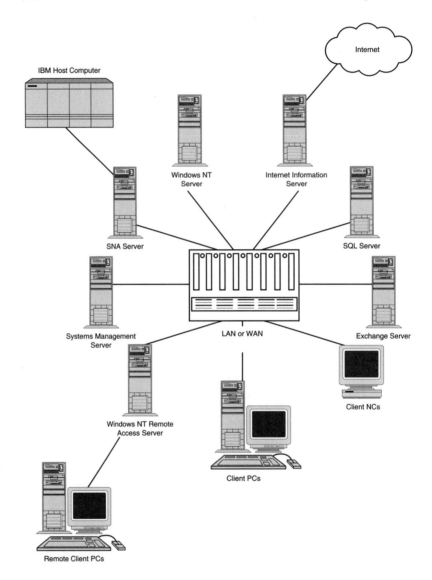

To connect your network to the Internet, you must acquire the services of an Internet service provider (ISP). Most communities now have several companies that provide access to the Internet. These companies will place communication equipment on your premises and connect it to both your network and the Internet. The link to the Internet is made through another communication line, similar to the one you might use to create a wide area network. There are many ways in which to connect to the Internet. Your local ISP will help you understand your options and the associated costs.

▶ **See** "Choosing an Internet Service Provider," **p. 509**

The two primary reasons to connect to a public network, such as the Internet, are to facilitate communication and share information.

BackOffice provides the basic capabilities to communicate and share information with others on both private networks and on the Internet. If you utilize the Internet technologies within BackOffice on your private network, then you have created an *intranet*. As the Internet grows in popularity, the tools used to manage private networks begin to share many similarities with Internet tools; such is the case with most features of BackOffice.

Communication   Internet technology enables people to communicate electronically using their computers. This communication exists in the form of *e-mail*. A user can type a message to anyone else connected to the Internet and send the message as long as the user knows the recipient's Internet e-mail address. This form of communication is quite convenient and has become widely accepted in a short amount of time.

Part

I

Ch

3

BackOffice supports e-mail on an intranet through the services of Exchange Server. This product enables users on the network to electronically communicate with one another. The combination of Exchange Server and Internet Information Server permits users to electronically communicate with not only those on your private network, but also everyone on the global Internet.

Information   Internet technologies can also be used to share information. An intranet or Internet user can publish any information for purposes of sharing it with other interested users on the private or public network. The most popular vehicle for sharing published information on the Internet is referred to as the World Wide Web (Web). Other methods are available as well, with equally colorful monikers. Members of the Internet community have defined how information is to be formatted and placed on the Internet and how other users are to access it.

After you have connected your network to the Internet, a server on your network can be configured to enable access to the information you desire Internet users to see. This computer is usually referred to simply as a *Web server*. You can place the information you want to share on this computer after formatting it using Hypertext Markup Language (HTML). HTML is a collection of formatting codes created by the Internet community. A variety of utilities, including FrontPage (which is covered in Chapter 20, "Using Microsoft FrontPage 97"), make it relatively painless to annotate documents with HTML codes.

▶ **See** "Hypertext Markup Language," **p. 579**

Web servers publish HTML pages using Hypertext Transfer Protocol (HTTP). If you set up your server properly, anyone on the Internet can locate your Web server and view the information. The capability to do this is provided by a software package called a *browser*, or *Web browser*. Browsers for the Web are available from a number of vendors, including Microsoft.

▶ **See** "What Are Web Browsers?," **p. 578**

One of the features available to you with Internet Information Server is this capability to publish information and share it with anyone on the Internet. At times, you may want to publish information only to those within your organization, but still leverage the power and flexibility of the Internet tools. Internet Information Server provides the capability to publish internal information on a *private Web server*. This example illustrates one reason why your private network can be viewed as an intranet.

Because the Web was originally intended for publication purposes, the information was primarily static. Information changed only when the author manually made changes to the published document on the Web server. The need for Web information to be more dynamic has grown, however, because it is more meaningful to present information to users based on their input. This has resulted in more sophisticated Web server and browser products.

▶ **See** "dbWeb," **p. 732**

▶ **See** "The Internet Database Connector," **p. 754**

Many organizations now use, or plan to use, the Internet to interact with their customers. One example of this type of interaction is referred to as *electronic commerce*. Microsoft offers a product known as Merchant Server as a part of its Internet services family of products for this purpose. Supported by the capabilities of dynamic Web information and sophisticated browsers, an organization can sell its products over the Internet.

Electronic commerce is simply the act of enabling a customer connected to the Internet to conduct a secure financial transaction with the organization. For example, a customer can connect to a Web server and place an order for a product. This type of transaction can only be performed if the Web server is capable of dynamically interacting with the user.

N O T E Many other applications are available for the Internet beyond those described here. Chapter 47, "Building BackOffice Applications," explains how you can use BackOffice to build and implement these applications. ■

Significance of Bandwidth

One of the most important characteristics of your network is the rate of speed at which data is transmitted. The cables that make up your network are similar to the plumbing in a building. The pipes carry water, and the network cables carry data. As such, the network cabling is often referred to as the *data pipe*.

If you want the plumbing to carry more water at a faster pace, then a larger pipe is needed or a faster pipe-to-pipe transfer is needed. Similar logic applies in networking except that the pipe is not physically enlarged. Instead, a different kind of cable is used, or the communication equipment that transmits data over the cable is enhanced.

Data traveling across the network is referred to as *network traffic*. The amount of data and the rate of speed with which it moves through the network cables are referred to as *bandwidth*. The more network traffic or the faster the data must be transmitted, the more bandwidth the network requires.

N O T E Network bandwidth is determined by the type of cabling and type of communication equipment used to build the network. These physical aspects define the maximum bandwidth that your network will ever achieve. In some cases, software that implements compression algorithms can be employed to maximize productivity of the existing bandwidth. ▓

Most networks today experience bandwidth limitations. This is due to the nature of the applications that run on the network. Applications based on the client-server and I-net process models are designed specifically to minimize the amount of data transmitted across the network. Therefore, as organizations make increasing use of the client-server and I-net process models, network traffic is reduced. However, networks are still used for many tasks that are bandwidth-intensive, such as file transfers and disk backups. This reinforces the need to proactively plan for an appropriate amount of bandwidth.

> **CAUTION**
>
> You must anticipate the need for more bandwidth when building a network. Your network will likely be transmitting many new types of data in the near future. Some of the unstructured data types, such as full-motion video and audio and other multimedia data, are significantly larger than traditional structured data. It is important that your network can accommodate these volumes and types of data *before* users require additional bandwidth.

It is almost impossible to overbuild your network with respect to bandwidth. If your organization is creating a network with an expected lifetime of over three years, any excess capacity will eventually be needed as new data types and applications are added to the network.

Organizing Administration Teams

Another important aspect of your BackOffice implementation is a team of administrators. The administrators are the individuals responsible for the implementation of BackOffice. After the applications are installed and available to computer users, the administrators are responsible for the ongoing successful operation of the network and BackOffice server applications.

> **CAUTION**
>
> You must have an adequately staffed team of administrators. Many managers underestimate the significance of this issue. Understaffing in this area can be costly to the organization. Many hidden costs are associated with a weak or understaffed administration team because the burden of managing server applications and troubleshooting associated problems falls into the hands of the users. This results in a loss of productivity across the organization.

There is an administrative role for each server application installed on the network. Depending on the size of the organization and the extent of the applications being used, this does not always need to be filled by an additional person. A talented administrator may be able to handle

Part
I

Ch
3

more than one administrative role. This is especially true for BackOffice because the server applications have so many operating similarities.

Conversely, on a very large network with hundreds or thousands of workstations, you will undoubtedly need many people in each role. The key issues are that the tasks and responsibilities associated with each product need to be identified and managed. Watch for signs that an administrator has too much to manage.

Because there is usually overlap in responsibilities across server applications, the administrators should work together as a team. This also provides a built-in means for providing backup administrators. Each server application should have a primary administrator and a backup administrator in case the primary administrator is unavailable in an emergency.

N O T E Administrators should be thoroughly trained in the products for which they are responsible. This training should include not only product training, but also training in the fundamentals of the underlying technology. ■

The roles and responsibilities for each member of a BackOffice administration team are covered in detail in their respective product sections of this book. Following is a brief description of the administration requirements for each BackOffice product and highlights of administrator responsibilities.

Administering Windows NT Server

The primary role of Windows NT Server is to act as the network operating system. The administrator in charge of the network operating system is usually referred to as a *network administrator*, or *LAN administrator.* In addition to managing the network operating system, this individual is typically responsible for the shared resources on the network, such as printers and disk drives on servers. In small organizations, the network administrator may also be responsible for all network connections, as well as the PCs and NCs that connect to the network.

▶ **See** "Understanding the Role of the Network Administrator," **p. 186**

N O T E The network administrator is responsible for the successful implementation of the network and the network operating system. This includes accepting responsibility for those connected to the network and what they can do while they are on it. In most cases, the network administrator's domain of influence includes the other administrators because the network administrator must coordinate all activity on the network. ■

The following list highlights the roles and responsibilities of the network administrator:

- Installing Windows NT Server
- Creating user accounts
- Organizing user groups
- Managing sharable resources
- Setting sharable resource privileges

- Assigning user permissions
- Performing backups of network files
- Monitoring network resource utilization
- Troubleshooting network problems

Administering Windows NT Server with Operators

In addition to the role of network administrator, Windows NT Server gives you the flexibility of assigning a limited set of administrative duties to individuals called *operators*. Operators are frequently chosen from among the personnel of a department to act as a pseudo administrator for the department. An operator cannot perform all the duties of a network administrator, but because operators are usually more accessible to users, they can increase the effectiveness of the administrative team and the satisfaction level of the user community. The four types of operators are as follows:

- Account
- Server
- Print
- Backup

The most commonly used are account and print operators. Account operators can assist users who have forgotten their passwords by giving them new passwords. They can also perform other account related tasks, such as changing a user's name (common after a marriage) or creating an account for a new user. An account operator cannot create or modify an administrator's account.

N O T E Neither an account operator nor an administrator can see a user's password. They can, however, enter a new password for the user if the old one has been forgotten. ■

Print operators assist users having difficulty with documents that have been sent to a network printer. In administrative jargon, these are *jobs* in a *print queue*, and if a job experiences problems, it can create a *log jam effect* for all the print requests sent behind it. For example, if a user sends a print request formatted with the PostScript page description language to a non-PostScript printer, dozens of pages of gibberish are usually the result. If the user who sent the job has left for a meeting or lunch, only a print operator or administrator can pause the printer, delete the faulty job, and restart the printer.

Administering Internet Information Server

The administrator responsible for Internet Information Server is referred to as the *Internet administrator*. Because this often includes responsibility for the information, or *content*, placed on the Web server, the Internet administrator is sometimes referred to as the *Webmaster*. This job overlaps with the database administrator (DBA) in cases where dynamic Web information is driven by SQL Server databases.

▶ **See** "A Guide to Services Provided by the Internet Information Server," **p. 541**

Part I
Ch 3

N O T E The Internet administrator is responsible for the successful operation of Internet Information Server. This includes accepting responsibility for stability and performance of the Internet connection. This can also include accepting responsibility for the information published on the Web server. ▣

The following list highlights the roles and responsibilities of the Internet administrator:

- Installing Internet Information Server
- Providing client software (Web browsers)
- Ensuring that connection to the Internet service provider is constant and stable
- Setting up Web servers—internal and external
- Publishing information on the Web server, if appropriate
- Enabling FTP (File Transfer Protocol) and Gopher, if appropriate
- Monitoring usage
- Setting up security firewalls, if appropriate
- Troubleshooting Internet problems

In addition to these tasks, the Internet administrator will likely also administer related Internet server products. Within BackOffice, this includes Proxy Server, Index Server, and Content Replication Server. Additionally, this may include other Internet server products such as Personalization Server, Merchant Server, and many others. Microsoft will continue to create new server products based on IIS which also must be administered by an administrator. The Internet administrator is the best candidate for administration of these servers.

Administering Exchange Server

The administrator responsible for Exchange Server is referred to as the *Exchange administrator*, or the *mail administrator*.

As organizations become dependent on e-mail, this administrator bears the burden of keeping e-mail flowing all the time. Users expect their e-mail to be received and delivered in a timely fashion just as they are accustomed to reliable voice communication over the telephone. The mail administrator can also lead the organization through an *e-mail culture* transition. Organizations are said to have an e-mail culture if their members rely heavily on electronic messaging.

N O T E The Exchange administrator is responsible for the successful operation of Exchange Server. This includes accepting responsibility for the timely flow of messages throughout the organization and, possibly, to and from external mail systems and the Internet. ▣

The following list highlights the roles and responsibilities of the Exchange administrator:

- Installing Exchange Server
- Distributing client software

- Determining server architecture
- Configuring mail servers
- Setting up user mailboxes
- Setting up auditing
- Enabling Internet mail, if appropriate
- Managing public folders and discussion groups
- Troubleshooting mail problems

Administering SQL Server

The administrator responsible for SQL Server is referred to as the *database administrator*, or *DBA*. The DBA installs and operates SQL Server. The DBA can also be responsible for managing the organization's data stored in SQL Server databases. In some cases, the DBA can also design the databases.

▶ **See** "What Does a DBA Do?," **p. 1117**

N O T E The database administrator is responsible for the successful operation of SQL Server. This can also include accepting responsibility for the data managed by SQL Server. ■

The following list highlights the roles and responsibilities of the database administrator:

- Installing SQL Server
- Establishing standards and procedures for using SQL Server
- Securing the databases
- Selecting related tools and vendors
- Planing for capacity requirements
- Backing up and, if necessary, recovering databases
- Improving performance of database applications
- Designing databases and server processes, if appropriate
- Assisting application developers and database users
- Troubleshooting database problems

Administering SNA Server

The administrator responsible for SNA Server is referred to as the *SNA Server administrator*. The SNA Server administrator is responsible for providing host connectivity to client PCs on the network. The SNA Server administrator determines the maximum number of concurrent users and configures the environment to accommodate their simultaneous connection to the host.

▶ **See** "Managing Connectivity to Host Computer Resources," **p. 1410**

Part I
Ch 3

N O T E   The SNA Server administrator is responsible for the successful operation of SNA Server. This can also include accepting responsibility for assigning user privileges on the mainframe or minicomputers for which SNA Server provides a connection. ◼

The following list highlights the roles and responsibilities of the SNA Server administrator:

- Installing SNA Server
- Distributing client software
- Managing connectivity to host computer resources
- Controlling access to SNA Server
- Setting up auditing
- Monitoring security-related events
- Troubleshooting host communication problems

Administering Systems Management Server

The administrator responsible for Systems Management Server (SMS) is referred to as the *SMS administrator*. Sometimes the SMS administrator is also referred to as the *system administrator*. Regardless of the title, this job is one of the most complex administrator positions. This is consistent with the associated complexities of managing a network to the level of detail supported by SMS. See the section "Understanding the Impact of SMS" later in the chapter for more information.

N O T E   The SMS administrator is responsible for the successful operation of SMS. This can also include accepting responsibility for the software and hardware located across the network. ◼

The following list highlights the roles and responsibilities of the SMS administrator:

- Installing SMS
- Tracking hardware inventory
- Defining packages for software distribution
- Creating jobs for distributing software
- Supporting users with remote diagnostics
- Monitoring network performance
- Tracking user activity and security violations
- Troubleshooting network and system-management problems

Determining Server Configuration

As you think about the size and number of servers you will need, remember that the server is not the place to economize. By the time you have installed LAN cabling and hubs, added desktop computers and NCs, and provided training to the user community, the incremental cost for servers is a small percentage of the overall cost.

The way in which each BackOffice application uses computing resources may guide your decision-making process. For example, the questions of selecting appropriate equipment for a particular server-based task, sizing the server, and performance tuning are challenging issues. The guidelines contained in this section can help you make the best decisions. Finally, validating your decisions with tools like the Windows NT Performance Monitor, and then making adjustments as needed, is an important step in completing the process.

Windows NT Server

Windows NT Server is used as a platform on which to run other applications. It is also responsible on many networks for sharing files and printers unless an alternative NOS (such as NetWare) has been implemented. Sharing files and printers is I/O intensive. Servers upon which Windows NT Server is used exclusively for file and print services will exercise the disk subsystem: disk controllers, disk drives, and drive arrays. Adding more power in the form of additional processors will not usually provide as much performance improvement as adding additional components to the I/O subsystem, such as an additional disk controller.

An exception to this guideline are servers used to operate Windows NT Server as domain controllers. These computers are responsible for validating logon requests. They typically have heavy demands placed on their network adapters and processors, especially during the periods when many users log on to the network, for example, early morning at a typical company. An appropriate choice for a domain controller that was not also used for file and print services, might be a dual processor system with a high-speed network adapter. Current network hub technology can enable a server to have its own high-speed LAN segment to improve network throughput as well.

Internet Information Server

For most organizations, the demands placed on a computer to run Internet Information Server (IIS) will not be too great. There are exceptions, however. The IIS product was used to create the Web server for the 1997 Super Bowl site, **http://www.superbowl.com**. For this type of special situation with thousands of users, the demands can be substantial.

The type of demands depend on the type of Web server you create. A traditional publishing server primarily will tax the disk subsystem and networking components. If you are implementing a server for electronic commerce and interacting with SQL Server, your processing requirements will increase. RAM used for caching information also plays an important role on Web servers.

Whereas the BackOffice family of products now includes numerous current and forthcoming Internet server products, such as Proxy Server, Index Server, and Content Replication Server, similar considerations must be given to the server computers upon which these processes will execute. Care must be taken when incorporating these Internet server processes on top of IIS.

Exchange Server

Exchange Server is a product that, like SQL Server, exercises all subsystems in the computer. It uses a number of server-based services, which places demands on processing power and RAM, and benefits from the addition of one or more additional processors and additional RAM. It manages potentially large user mailboxes with rich data types and can therefore place demands on the disk subsystem. Finally, Exchange uses the network components as its pipeline to the world. Like SQL Server, a large, actively used Exchange Server places balanced demands on all computer subsystems.

SQL Server

Sizing and performance tuning servers running SQL Server are special challenges. How a computer will be utilized by database systems is difficult to anticipate and manage. SQL Server certainly places demands on the disk subsystem, but SQL Server also performs part of the application processing on the server through the use of stored procedures. In addition, it makes good use of additional RAM for procedure and data caching and to manage user data structures.

You could say that it is easy to size a SQL Server—make it big and don't skimp on anything. If you must economize, the disk subsystem is probably the single element that has the biggest impact on performance. It is the area you should invest in first.

SNA Server

The role of SNA Server is to provide connectivity over the network. It is not surprising, therefore, that high-speed network components are important. What is not always recognized is the important role RAM plays for caching of information. Therefore, RAM and networking components are the most important elements of an SNA Server, with the disk subsystem playing a relatively minor role. Processor demands are not exceptional.

Systems Management Server

The distinguishing characteristic of SMS is its use of multiple server-based services. SMS benefits from additional processors and additional RAM. Its disk subsystem requirements vary dramatically depending on the extent to which your organization uses SMS for package distribution. If this feature of SMS is exploited heavily, it will require a lot of storage for package processing.

Redundant Components

The concept of redundancy should be carefully reviewed among the members of the administrative team. Consider implementing redundant sources of important information and equipment to avoid any single points of failure. The use of data replication in SQL Server and the automatic replication of the user account database among domain controllers provided by Windows NT Server are two examples of redundancy. Although redundant components add to the expense of the network, they usually reduce operating costs and expenses associated with downtime. Some of these are hidden costs that can dramatically reduce the effectiveness of your computing infrastructure.

Selecting the Hardware

Now that you have some general guidelines on the way BackOffice components use computing resources, only a few additional considerations remain. In this section, specific types of hardware are discussed.

Of all the advice provided in this book, the discussion on hardware configuration may be the most controversial. Microsoft's own guidelines for the amount of RAM required for servers are frequently dismissed as too little. Certainly, different hardware vendors have different opinions, and they may even produce charts and graphs proving they are right. The information presented in this section will help you determine the specific hardware components that are best for you.

Hardware comes in many shapes and sizes, and it changes constantly. Microsoft includes a Hardware Compatibility List (HCL) in the Windows NT Server (and Windows NT Workstation) box, and provides regular updates to that list on CompuServe, the Microsoft Network online service (MSN), and the Microsoft Web server (**www.microsoft.com**). This is a good starting point when selecting server hardware. If you are considering a computer that doesn't appear on this list, proceed with caution. It need not be completely ruled out, but you should at least ask the hardware vendor for assurances that it is indeed compatible with Windows NT Server. Literally thousands of computers will run Windows NT Server.

After you have found a computer that supports Windows NT Server, you must decide what components and peripherals should be included. Microsoft includes a help file with BackOffice that provides detailed guidelines to assist in determining acceptable minimums for each product, given a user population of a certain size. The preceding discussion about resource utilization by BackOffice products will help you intelligently configure a computer that goes well beyond a minimum configuration.

After reviewing these materials and your own requirements, you should be able to make sound judgments about hardware configurations. The only thing that prevents someone from producing a definitive chart showing exactly what is required is the subjective nature of performance. How fast is fast enough? This is the intangible that you must factor into your decision-making process that depends on the nature of your user community and the type of applications you will provide. Supporting traders on Wall Street is different from using BackOffice to run a monastery print shop. Both are important, but they imply a different level of service.

Processor Type

The selection of processor type is one of the most hotly debated topics in this area. Intel continues to dominate the marketplace, and support for Intel processors is always available first. Because of its market share, the broadest range of products is available on this platform.

Part

I

Ch

3

RISC processors, according to their vendors, provide greater price performance than those from Intel. These claims are difficult to substantiate, although there is evidence indicating that for some types of processing, you can achieve superior performance using these devices. Windows NT Server supports three RISC processor types: MIPS, Alpha AXP, and PowerPC. Unfortunately, not all BackOffice products are available for all processor types. If you want to use RISC processors, check with Microsoft or your software vendor to be certain that all BackOffice components you want to use are available for that processor.

Number of Processors

The use of multiple processors in servers is growing. Although multiple processors have been employed on large computers for years, only in the last few years have they been available in mass-produced computers at a price affordable for small organizations. Multiple processors make sense for processor-intensive applications.

The design of Windows NT Server is such that the operating system does not require extensive tuning—nor do applications need to be rewritten—to take advantage of multiple processors. You can usually just rerun the Setup program to add multiprocessor support while maintaining all your other settings.

Server-based, 32-bit applications written for Windows NT Server (including all BackOffice components) generally employ multiple threads of execution. Windows NT automatically utilizes multiple processors to run these multithreaded applications. The Windows NT Server operating system is itself multithreaded and will benefit from the addition of multiple processors.

If you want to start with a single processor server, you should at least explore the capability to add processors to the machine later. A computer that supports adding processors typically costs more initially. However, by offering you the capability to "snap in" additional power without having to build a new server, this option can save time and money in the long run.

Memory

The guidelines provided by Microsoft with the BackOffice product were created after extensive testing in its computer labs. They can certainly be taken as useful minimums and will serve organizations with low-end to medium expectations well. If your organization uses applications of a particularly demanding nature, consider adding more memory. Under any circumstances, choose computers that support the addition of plenty of RAM, even if you start with a minimal amount.

Because Windows NT supports virtual memory, you will not generally run out of memory if you exceed the available amount. The operating system uses a paging file to move some of the contents of memory temporarily to disk and then swap it back in when needed. You want to avoid a situation in which your server is swapping frequently. Monitoring the use of memory on a server using Performance Monitor (running on another Windows NT machine) is an excellent way to determine whether additional memory is needed on a particular server.

Bus Architecture

An area of the computer sometimes overlooked is the system bus. Several high-speed bus technologies are now available. When selecting a machine for use as a server, make sure that it is based on a high-speed bus architecture.

Size of Disk

At the risk of sounding flippant, a good rule of thumb for sizing disk drives is to start with the amount you think you need, double it, and then double it again. Seriously, it is almost impossible to purchase too much disk space.

With the content and capabilities of software increasing, the use of new and richer data types (especially such multimedia types as video and audio) and the growing use of online help and product manuals, disk space is essential. The price of disk subsystems continues to fall, so the additional requirements are somewhat easier to accept.

Part

I

Ch

3

Type of Disk Subsystem

You must consider a number of important options when selecting disk subsystems. A number of hardware vendors offer RAID (Redundant Array of Inexpensive Disks) technology. RAID level 5, the most commonly used, offers the capability to divide stored data across multiple disks, thereby achieving faster read/write speeds through the use of multiple disk drives and (in some cases) disk controllers. RAID level 5 stores redundant information that enables the automatic re-creation of your data should a single drive fail. This technology is particularly appropriate for SQL Server and situations in which the information is mission critical and high performance is important.

In addition to the RAID capabilities provided by hardware, it is also possible to implement RAID using Windows NT Server. With a premium SCSI adapter and four 2G hard drives, you can implement your own RAID.

To minimize downtime (when a server is unavailable), a number of hardware vendors offer *hot swappable* disk drives. This type of equipment enables you to remove and replace a disk drive while the computer is running. By itself, this technology does not provide any redundancy or backup capability. It simply reduces the amount of time the server is shut down and unavailable and can complement other technologies used for data management.

Peripheral Devices

In addition to the standard components, you usually need some peripheral devices to complete your server. With the size and complexity of modern server-based applications, the compact disc (CD) has become the preferred distribution media for these large applications. Strongly consider at least one CD drive for your server. You may also want to consider sharing a *CD tower* on one of your servers. These devices combine multiple CD drives into a single chassis with shared power and simplified connectivity requirements.

The use of shared laser printers was one of the initial advantages of networking, and it continues to be a widely used feature. It has become common to attach printers directly to the LAN cabling system rather than to a server. Print jobs are still typically sent to a print queue on a server, and then despooled to the network printer. Many options are available for printers including support for color printing, duplexing (printing on both sides of the paper), and different sizes and types of paper.

Making backups of your important information is a critical part of managing your computing resources. Tape backup units are the most practical means of backing up large amounts of information. Some promising new technologies offer large amounts of storage with long shelf life, but tape drives still offer the best balance of features, performance, and cost. If you plan to back up systems over the network, you should recognize the enormous impact this can have on bandwidth utilization, and make every effort to accomplish this task during off-peak periods.

Finally, always provide an *uninterruptible power supply* (*UPS*) for your servers. You can use a large UPS for multiple servers or provide each server with its own smaller unit. Windows NT Server supports the use of a UPS and even automatically warns users and shuts down the server when the backup power is about to be depleted. Of course, unless the user's computers are also provided with backup power supplies, they will have already failed.

The primary benefit of a UPS for a server is to avoid power loss in the midst of disk write activity or other important tasks. By permitting an orderly shutdown of the server, all files will be closed and the integrity of data can be ensured. In addition, a good UPS prevents the server from rebooting during a brief power surge or outage. Split-second power outages are annoying at home because you must reset all your digital clocks, microwaves, VCRs, and so on. In the office, they can cause your data to be lost, or even worse, they may physically damage an active server.

Preparing the Facility

The server computers upon which the BackOffice applications operate should be physically separate from user PCs and NCs. These server computers manage, process, and contain the organization's data. Although means exist for protecting the data electronically, the very best protection available is physical isolation in a locked machine room or wiring closet.

N O T E   Most computer fraud results from access violations. This can be entirely avoided if physical access to the data is restricted.

Confining the server computers to a single location has other advantages, as well. At times when administrators require physical access to the servers, they will find them all conveniently located together. This also enables administrators to more conveniently control the server operating environment by adding features, such as uninterruptible power supplies, to all server computers at once.

In organizations where distributed servers are required, it remains necessary to follow similar guidelines for server management. Server computers located in remote locations outside the main server facility should be placed in physical isolation as well.

Creating a Security Policy

One of the most important issues the administration team should address is the organization's security policy. Hopefully, your organization already has such a policy in place. If so, you can skip this section or review it quickly. If you do not have a visible, actively monitored security policy, then strongly consider the adoption of such a policy immediately.

A complete discussion of appropriate security measures for an organization using computer-based systems is beyond the scope of this book. However, the rudiments of such a policy are outlined in the following list to provide a basic policy upon which further development can be added. Here are some basic, concrete steps that can be taken to improve the security in your organization:

1. Review the physical security of your premises. This includes such things as the door locks, storage of duplicate keys, and locked furniture (desks, file cabinets, and so on) that contain disks, tapes, CDs, and sensitive documents. Without good physical security, there is no security.

2. Review the (existing or proposed) Windows NT user accounts with Administrator access and make sure only those that need to have it are included.

3. Implement a password policy that enforces password aging and keeps a history of at least three passwords. Document the elements of a good password and disseminate this information. Encourage employees to either log off or lock their workstations, especially at the end of the day. Encourage the use of password-protected screen savers with short (five-minute) time-out periods.

Part
I
Ch
3

Choosing a Password

To ensure that good passwords are created, have your users comply with the following guidelines:

- Make it at least six characters long.
- Do not choose a word that appears in any dictionary.
- Include at least one special character.
- Choose one that is easy to remember (which lessens the temptation to write it down).
- Do not choose one that is based on personal attributes, such as a birthday, pet's name, or favorite color.

One way to create acceptable passwords is to use phonetic spelling or replace letters with numerals. For example, Gu3xer&25% is a pretty good password, as is 24%Faers97.

Now that these passwords have appeared in this book, however, they are very poor choices. A well-known tactic used by devious hackers is to employ a *dictionary* attack in which a collection of likely passwords is automatically supplied to attempt access to an account. Example passwords have an uncanny likelihood of ending up in such a dictionary, as do words that beginners think no one would ever guess (but many people do), such as *sex*, *love*, *secret*, and so on.

4. Review all network access permissions periodically. The various servers and shared directories should be documented and published to appropriate employees. You should not use ignorance as an element of security. If employees who should know about resources aren't told about them for fear that the information will be too widely disseminated, you have already been robbed of the complete benefits of that resource. Tell everyone who should know, and use sound security to keep intruders out.

5. Implement auditing and alerts on your network servers and assign personnel to monitor those alerts and take appropriate action. Specifically, it is possible to use the Windows NT Performance Monitor to set alerts on failed logon attempts. Windows NT offers extensive audit and alert capabilities. You should start with a few simple, but important, checkpoints.

6. Publish a written policy that establishes the organization's concern about keeping your information assets secure. The policy must include criteria for valuing and classifying information. This should not be overly complex and may include only two categories: company confidential and public. Guidelines for how this information is handled and destroyed should also be included.

7. Publish a written policy on security issues and clearly state the consequences of noncompliance. The tone of this document should be professional and serious without being threatening.

8. Discuss security issues in an open forum at regular intervals during organizational meetings. These discussions should be held at least annually and perhaps more frequently.

After you have established a security policy, review it carefully with key members of the organization before presenting it to the entire organization. A good security policy is at least a little inconvenient for computer users. For most organizations, however, the threat of being victimized by industrial espionage, malicious hacking, or innocent yet destructive foolishness is real.

Resolving Implementation Issues

In addition to network, hardware, human, and facility issues, there remain several issues to discuss. Windows NT Server contains numerous configuration options and operational characteristics with which it is important to become acquainted, including the following:

- Disk drive partitions
- File systems
- Restart options
- Quota management
- Disaster recovery
- Remote access security
- Network expectations

A brief description of each follows.

Disk Drive Partitions

When you install Windows NT Server, you need to create disk partitions. This deserves some thought. The Windows NT Disk Administrator and the operating system itself provide powerful capabilities to manage storage. Judicious use of partitions can be appropriate. For example, many administrators create a separate partition for the operating system and print spooling information. Others choose to keep all user subdirectories on a separate partition. Using partitions can limit the growth of disk use for some applications and safeguard needed space for the operating system.

File Systems

Windows NT Server supports different file systems. The File Allocation Table (FAT) file system used by MS-DOS is somewhat easier to deal with when responding to hardware problems because you can use MS-DOS-based utilities to do diagnostics and so on. However, the NT File System (NTFS) provides a great deal more security.

Part

I

Ch

3

Restart Options

You can configure Windows NT Server to copy (or dump) the entire contents of RAM to a hard disk in the event of a serious system crash. If you are having serious problems with a server, this can be an important option. It requires, of course, that enough disk space be kept available.

If you have a computer with 128M of RAM, for example, then you must reserve 128M of disk space for the memory dump. You can also set Windows NT Server to restart automatically when such an event occurs, rather than the default behavior of waiting for a manual restart.

Quota Management

Windows NT Server does not (yet) offer the capability to establish per-user disk quotas. This is a feature requested by many users and organizations, and Microsoft has indicated that it may add this feature to future versions of Windows NT Server.

In the meantime, third-party software packages are available that deliver this capability for Windows NT Server. Either use a disk quota package or isolate user directories on a separate partition. If you don't, they will grow to fill the space allowed. They should certainly not be kept on the same drive partition used for the Windows NT paging file.

Disaster Recovery

Backup and recovery are mentioned in several locations in this book, and it is a topic that bears mentioning again. In fact, you should go even one step farther and implement a full disaster recovery plan. There are sad, but true, stories of organizations that simply ceased to exist after a disaster, such as a fire, because all the information about the organization, its personnel, and its constituents was destroyed.

Imagine for a moment that your most important computer systems have crashed, or your entire premises have been destroyed in a fire. Where are your backups? How long will it take to get replacement equipment up and running and reload your backups. Do you have a written plan in place that everyone is aware of and can follow easily? What would you tell the top person in your organization if you were paid a visit immediately following such a disaster? Make a plan, write it down, stage a drill if possible, and be prepared!

Remote Access Security

Windows NT Server includes the Remote Access Service (RAS). This service enables computer users to connect to the network from remote locations through a variety of means. Chapter 12, "Implementing Remote Access Service (RAS)," explores RAS in more detail, but you should already be considering the ramifications to security and other organizational policies that may be caused by adding RAS to your network. Who is authorized to use the service? Can they call from anywhere (a hotel for example), or will the system use a dial-back mechanism for greater security, but limiting them to one location (usually their homes)? If properly managed, it can be a great asset to your organization.

Network Expectations

Your organization should also have a policy on, or at least a general understanding of, the role of the network in general. What is the expected rate of availability? Is it acceptable for the network to be down for an hour? For a day? Must all maintenance be done outside certain peak work hours? These answers can profoundly affect the decisions you make and the amount of money you will have to spend to achieve the desired levels of service.

Understanding the Impact of SMS

Perhaps one of the biggest decisions you will make regarding your BackOffice installation is whether to implement SMS. If you choose to implement SMS, you must also decide at what level to take advantage of its services.

N O T E   Starting your BackOffice environment with SMS will change the course of action taken for preparation and implementation. ▪

Requirements

The bad news is that SMS can be complicated to administer. A full-featured SMS installation should be administered by a full-time professional system administrator, if not a team of administrators. The point here is that it is difficult to take business-minded people with good technical skills and convert them into effective SMS system administrators.

The job of administering SMS should be performed by trained system management experts with a background in computer systems and plenty of experience in network management. Assigning SMS administration responsibilities to anyone else will, at a minimum, create the potential for problems and possibly even lead to a system disaster.

Benefits

Assuming that you put SMS administration in the hands of a trained professional, many benefits are available to you. Many of the topics you learned regarding your preparation for BackOffice become simplified if you choose to implement SMS. For example, SMS does the following:

- Provides useful information for network planning and configuration
- Captures organizational information used in determining server requirements
- Tracks server configurations and disk utilization
- Assists in capacity planning
- Simplifies security administration
- Remotely administers network PCs and NCs
- Aids in hardware and software inventory tracking

Because SMS provides so much support in the implementation of the BackOffice products, incorporating it into the network has an impact on all the other server product installations. Done correctly, SMS will simplify the implementation and administration of the other products. This is good news after you have borne the startup cost associated with a first-time installation of SMS.

For the most part, SMS is a fairly complicated product to install and learn. However, it is possible to implement a limited SMS installation that is administered by someone other than a trained professional. Beginners should have no problem implementing the inventory features of SMS, assuming that they possess adequate networking and general PC skills. At this level, SMS still provides value to the organization.

Finally, SMS yields significant savings with regard to user support. System administrators can use SMS to support users on the network by remotely observing, or controlling, the user's PC. This is a powerful feature of SMS, which offers significant benefits to the organization.

> **N O T E** Preparing for SMS, implementing SMS, the role of the SMS administrator, and several SMS advanced topics are covered entirely in Part IX, "Systems Management Server (SMS)," in Volume II. ▪

Part
I

Ch
3

Licensing BackOffice

At this point, you have learned how to prepare the physical aspects of your BackOffice environment. You have also learned how to build your network and staff your BackOffice administration team to position your organization for a successful implementation. The only remaining item prior to jumping into the details is to purchase the software.

Where and how can BackOffice be purchased? Regardless of the size of your organization, you can only purchase BackOffice from a Microsoft software reseller. Even large organizations that have corporate agreements in place with Microsoft must purchase BackOffice from retail software outlets.

Typically, however, you will not find BackOffice on the shelves of your local software store. This product is targeted at a smaller market than the general public or the population of office PC users. Therefore, retailers are not willing to provide much shelf space for the package. You must ask for BackOffice and, in some cases, it will need to be ordered.

BackOffice server products are licensed independently from the client software components that utilize the server services. This licensing model provides the flexibility to accommodate various uses and configurations in an information network. There are two simple guidelines to remember when licensing BackOffice:

- **Server license**—Each instance of a server product operating on the network must have its own license. In other words, if a BackOffice product is running on a computer, then it requires its own license—regardless of how many instances of the same server application are running elsewhere on the network.

- **Client access license**—Each client PC that connects to a server application and utilizes its services must carry its own license to that particular server. Again, this applies even if multiple computers are running the same BackOffice server application on the network. As you will see in the following sections "Server Licenses" and "Client Licenses," there are two ways to license client PCs and NCs for server access.

In a typical network, as shown in Figure 3.6, server licenses are purchased for BackOffice server applications, and client access licenses are purchased for the client PCs and NCs.

FIG. 3.6

Server applications are licensed separately from client PCs and NCs.

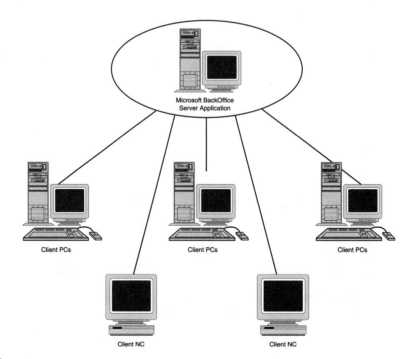

BackOffice networks can contain multiple servers of the same type, multiple servers of different types, or both. A network with varying numbers of the same type of BackOffice server applications can be built by licensing BackOffice as a whole, by licensing individual server application licenses, or both. In some cases, it is advantageous to purchase the entire BackOffice package even though all the products will not be installed. Such is the case when using SMS and SQL Server. The combined license for both of these products is currently more expensive than the single license for BackOffice.

In addition to providing some financial advantage by licensing all the products together for less than the combined individual licenses, Microsoft sometimes offers promotional packages. Some special packages combine server licenses with a fixed number of client access licenses. These types of promotions are offered for your convenience. Other offers include special pricing for upgrading from previous versions of BackOffice or individual BackOffice products. Finally, Microsoft occasionally offers special pricing to those organizations upgrading from a competitive product.

Part
I

Ch
3

Before jumping into a discussion of the type of licenses to purchase, it will help you to know that Windows NT Server contains a small application to assist in implementing the decisions you make regarding client licenses. The application, shown in Figure 3.7, is available on the Control Panel.

FIG. 3.7
Use the Licensing
Control Panel applet to
select which BackOffice
product to license.

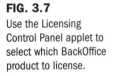

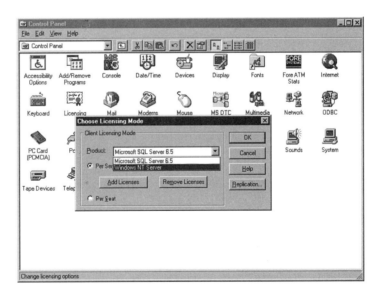

This application is used to set the number of licenses you have acquired. Once set, the number of licenses is monitored by Windows NT Server. If the number of licenses is exceeded, it will record an entry in the Windows NT Server Event Log. These events should be monitored by an appropriate administrator in order that license agreements are honored.

▶ **See** "Viewing Event Logs," **p. 152**

Server Licenses

All BackOffice products are server applications. Each computer running a server application requires a server license. This is true regardless of the number of users that access, or will ever access, the server application. A given computer on the network can run more than one server application at a time. Nevertheless, a separate server license must be purchased for each server application.

N O T E   Each BackOffice server application, regardless of which computer it runs on or how many other servers of the same application exist on the network, must have its own server license. ▓

SMS requires special server licensing. It requires a server license for SQL Server, as well as its own server license. Also, it is common for SMS installations to run SMS on more than one server. Sometimes the primary SMS site server works with other site servers and so-called helper servers. In this case, each server running SMS applications requires its own server license.

N O T E   An SMS server license is not required for Windows NT servers or NetWare servers that share applications installed by SMS for use by client PCs unless the server is also running SMS server components. (This would be possible only on a Windows NT server.) ▓

Client Licenses

You have seen how an information network has application servers (computers that run server software) and user computers (PCs or NCs used by the management and staff of your organization). The user computers are sometimes referred to as *client PCs* or *client NCs* because they receive services from the application servers.

Server computers run software from Microsoft or other software vendors, such as the products included in BackOffice. Additionally, client PCs and client NCs require software that enables them to communicate with server applications. By installing the client software component on a client PC or client NC, the user can access the services of that particular application server on the information network.

Each BackOffice product has a client software component. In most cases, the client software component (but not the client license) is bundled with the server software. One exception to this is the Windows NT Server client software, which is built in to Microsoft desktop operating systems, such as Windows for Workgroups, Windows 95, and Windows NT Workstation. This makes it easier for you to build an information network. Windows for Workgroups and Microsoft networking software for MS-DOS are included on the Windows NT Server CD, but not Windows 95 or Windows NT Workstation.

Regardless of how you obtained the client software, you must purchase a license to use it on every PC or NC that accesses a server. The license you need for the client software component is known as the *client access license*. This license must be purchased regardless of whether the client PC or client NC will be permanently connected to the server.

N O T E   You do not need to acquire a new client software package for each client PC and client NC. You need only purchase the right to use the client software on each client PC and client NC. ▪

There are two ways to purchase client access licenses. You can acquire client access licenses *per server* or *per seat*. Purchasing the per server license implies that the client privileges are granted from the server's perspective. Purchasing the per seat license implies that the client privileges are granted from the clients' perspective. Regardless of whether client access licenses are purchased per server or per client, you must always purchase a server license. Again, the Windows NT license management application will assist you in implementing the client access license type, as shown in Figure 3.8.

FIG. 3.8
Use the Choose Licensing Mode dialog box to select the client access license mode for the BackOffice product selected.

Per Server Client Access License   Licensing client software in per server mode is equivalent to selling *concurrent use licenses*. In this scenario, client access licenses are purchased for the server, as opposed to being purchased for client PCs and client NCs. By purchasing client access licenses for the server, you restrict the number of concurrent users of that particular server application. Again, this applies to every server on the network, regardless of whether the same server product is running on multiple computers.

N O T E   Even in per server licensing, each additional server requires a new set of client access licenses for the total number of concurrent clients that can access it. ▪

In per server licensing, you must purchase as many client access licenses as you expect to have concurrent users of that particular server.

N O T E   Windows NT Server provides a notification if a server application reaches the maximum number of concurrent users. When this occurs, no other users are allowed to connect except for the administrator (unless, of course, some users drop their connections). The administrator can always connect to resolve a lockout. ▪

As you see in the following licensing examples, per server client access licenses are the best way to start as your organization undergoes a gradual implementation of a *complete information network.* In the early stages of the network, it is common for server usage to be less frequent as applications are being tested and implemented throughout the organization. As users become more dependent on the applications built upon the information network, their access to servers approaches constant use. When this occurs, it makes more sense to convert to the per seat mode of licensing clients.

N O T E   There are two special cases for per server client access licenses. The first is that SMS does not allow per server client access licenses. You can purchase client access licenses for SMS only on a per seat basis (explained in the following section). Second, there exists a special client access license option when you purchase BackOffice. This option enables the client PCs and client NCs to access each server application within the BackOffice package. This type of client access license can be purchased only in the per seat mode, as well. ▩

Per Seat Client Access License   Although licensing clients per seat is not necessarily the most economical in the early stages of building your information network, it is the simplest means for licensing clients. This model makes sense when most client PCs and client NCs require constant access to a server. Also, it is required for SMS and the full BackOffice client access license option.

N O T E   Per seat client access licensing is advantageous when you have multiple, similar server applications throughout the network. ▩

In this model, you license client access from the client's perspective. Given a client PC or client NC, determine how many different types of servers the client requires access to. A client access license is then purchased for each type of server that the client desires access to. A client access license is purchased for every server application it will access, but it is only purchased once for each type of server, not for each server. For example, a client with a per seat SQL Server client access license can simultaneously use one, ten, or fifty servers running SQL Server in the organization.

Converting from Per Server to Per Seat Client Licensing   Many organizations start with per server client access licenses because client access to servers is infrequent and not simultaneous. At some point, it is prudent to convert from per server client licensing to per seat client licensing. This occurs when the number of concurrent use (per server) client access licenses equals or exceeds the number of client PCs and client NCs on the network.

N O T E   If you are uncertain about which licensing method to begin with, you should choose per server licensing. Because Microsoft allows a one-time conversion from per server to per seat licensing at no cost, there is little or no disadvantage to begin with per server licensing. ▩

Microsoft recognizes that this situation occurs as organizations build their information networks. Therefore, it provides an opportunity to convert from per server client licensing to per seat client licensing. However, you can convert only once. At the time of the conversion, you need not purchase any additional client software or change any client software configurations.

In fact, you do not even need to notify Microsoft. You need only to convert the server itself. Henceforth, all client access licenses will be purchased in per seat mode.

 TIP The best time to convert from per server to per seat client access licenses is when the number of concurrent use client access licenses equals or exceeds the number of client PCs and client NCs on the network.

For example, if you start with one server and ten per server client access licenses, when you implement a second server of the same type, you can either license it in the same manner as the first or convert the first server to per seat licensing and configure the second server the same. This enables your ten client access licenses to access either server. Of course, the second server will carry its own server license.

Licensing BackOffice versus Licensing Individual Components

As explained in a previous section, "Client Licenses," client access licenses are purchased for each server product a given PC or NC will access. In this sense, *access* implies connecting to the server and utilizing its services. Instead of purchasing client access licenses for each individual server application on each PC and NC, it is possible to equip a PC or NC with a BackOffice client access license.

This entitles the user of this PC or NC to access any or all of the BackOffice server applications installed on the network. The BackOffice client access license can be purchased regardless of whether the server applications were purchased as a part of BackOffice or as individual components.

Licensing Examples

Microsoft provides different ways to license client PCs and client NCs for server access because not every organization uses BackOffice in the same manner. It is helpful to see examples of how the licensing model is applied in some typical situations. In the following examples, SNA Server, SMS, and Internet Information Server are not shown. Nevertheless, the same licenses apply to these products except as noted earlier. These examples provide a basis upon which you can extend the licensing model if more servers or more clients are needed.

Starting with a Simple Windows NT Network Seeing an example can help you understand how a simple Windows NT network should be licensed. This scenario serves as a basis for understanding more complex networks, even though it does not make sense to purchase the entire BackOffice package in this case.

The network shown in Figure 3.9 has one server operating Windows NT Server, two client PCs, and one client NC. Windows NT Server provides basic network operating system services. The server enables the client PCs and client NC to share files, printers, and other resources.

▶ **See** "A Network Operating System," **p. 53**

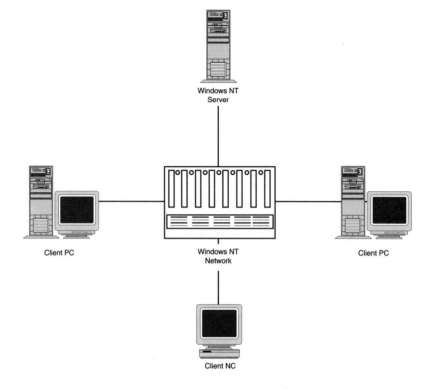

Client PCs may be using different operating systems. If they are using Windows for Workgroups, Windows 95, or Windows NT Workstation, the client software is included in the operating system. Nevertheless, a client access license should be purchased for each client PC.

Client NCs may not be using any operating system at all, even though they may be using different browsers. Regardless of the client NC configuration, a client access license must be purchased for each one. The following licenses should be purchased in this example:

■ One server license for Windows NT Server

■ Three per seat client access licenses for Windows NT Server

In this example, it makes sense to license the client PCs and client NCs per seat because they will be connected to the network at all times during network operation. As such, they will be able to share files and network printers.

Adding One SQL Server   Figure 3.10 shows the same network as Figure 3.9 with the addition of another server computer running SQL Server.

FIG. 3.10
A more sophisticated
Windows NT Network
also contains SQL
Server.

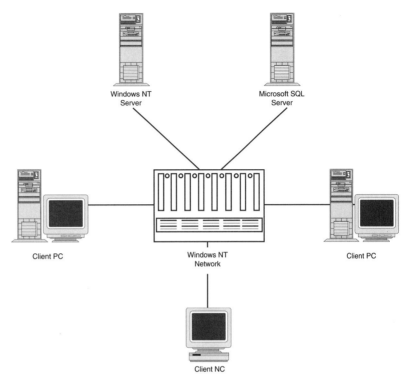

Windows NT
Server

Microsoft SQL
Server

Client PC

Windows NT
Network

Client PC

Client NC

This server computer running SQL Server also requires Windows NT Server. However, the client PCs and client NCs need only purchase client access licenses to the SQL Server on this computer. Additionally, if a Windows NT Server is running a server application on another network operating system, such as Novell NetWare, there is no need to purchase client access licenses for the Windows NT Server. Client access licenses for Windows NT Server need only be purchased if the Windows NT Server provides any of the following services:

- File sharing services
- Printer sharing services
- Macintosh connectivity
- Remote Access Service

Server computers that only run other server applications need not have Windows NT Server client access licenses. Because these services are provided by the other Windows NT Server computer, the SQL Server computer only requires client access licenses for SQL Server. The following licenses should be purchased in this example:

- Two server licenses for Windows NT Server
- One server license for SQL Server

Part

I

Ch

3

- Three per seat client access licenses for Windows NT Server
- Three per seat client access licenses for SQL Server

Because each client PC and client NC requires network services at all times, the Windows NT Server client access licenses should be purchased on a per seat basis. However, the SQL Server client access licenses can be purchased on a per server basis if you do not expect both PCs and the NC to be accessing the SQL Server at the same time. As soon as each client PC and client NC requires a constant connection to the SQL Server, it is time to convert the SQL Server client access licenses to the per seat licensing model.

Adding Remote PCs   Windows NT Server also provides access to the network for remote PCs. This is available through the built-in Remote Access Service (RAS), which is a service that controls remote access to the network via modems. Adding remote PCs to a network highlights the flexibility of the BackOffice licensing model.

▶ **See** "Understanding Dial-Up Access to BackOffice," **p. 114**

Figure 3.11 shows the same network as in Figure 3.10 with the addition of five remote PCs. In this example, the remote PCs are enabled to dial in at any time on the available modems. However, because the RAS computer is equipped with only two modems, a maximum of two remote PCs can be connected at one time. The following licenses should be purchased in this example:

- Three server licenses for Windows NT Server
- One server license for SQL Server
- Five per server client access licenses for Windows NT Server
- Five per server client access licenses for SQL Server
- Two per server client access licenses for the Windows NT Server running Remote Access Service

This example highlights per server client access licenses due to the remote PCs. Because the remote PCs have a limited connection path to the other servers, it is prudent to purchase client access licenses from the servers' perspectives.

These examples serve to illustrate the flexibility of the BackOffice licensing model. Clearly, your networks can be considerably more complex. In such cases, the licensing examples given in this chapter can be extended based on the principles described and demonstrated for each scenario.

FIG. 3.11
Adding remote PCs, which require access to application servers on the Windows NT network, creates a more complex licensing scenario.

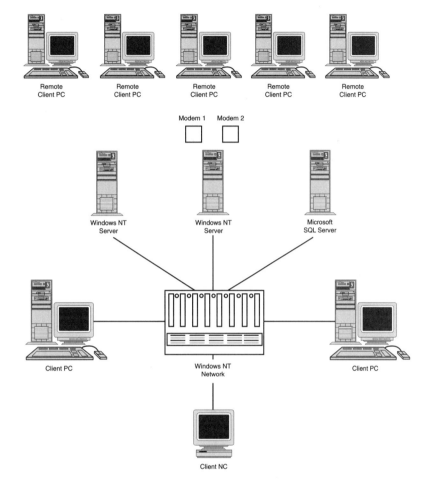

Part
I

Ch
3

From Here...

Prior to this chapter, you gained a general understanding of what BackOffice is and what it can do for you. In this chapter, you learned all the areas that require attention before implementing BackOffice in your organization. This includes information about important aspects of preparation, such as network hardware and server computer configuration, human issues pertaining to the administration of the network and server applications, security and related policies and procedures, facility management, and actually purchasing BackOffice. For more information on these and related topics, see the following chapters:

■ For a thorough discussion of the important steps to take prior to installing BackOffice, see Chapter 4, "Enterprise Planning and Implementation."

■ To begin the physical aspects of your BackOffice installation, see Chapter 5, "Implementing Windows NT Server."

■ For more information on how BackOffice supports wide area networking and why this is important, see Chapter 15, "Wide Area Network Technologies."

■ To develop a better appreciation of administering a BackOffice network, see Chapter 48, "Proactive Network Administration."

## CHAPTER 4

Enterprise Planning and Implementation

by Don Benage

Setting up a single, stand-alone Windows NT computer is a straightforward task. Things become more complicated, however, when you must connect a server to an enterprise-wide network. The need for cooperation with others and coordination with the work they are doing becomes important. Decisions that were previously somewhat arbitrary become critical issues.

This chapter discusses the most important considerations facing an administrator involved in creating an enterprise network and setting up servers to run in such an environment. When you finish this chapter, you will understand how computers on a large network are organized, the basics of network protocols, and Windows NT security. ■

What aspects of your organization make an impact on a Microsoft BackOffice implementation?

Analyze your organization with respect to the number and type of users, their needs, and application server requirements.

How to logically organize your servers

Learn the structures for organizing servers and users with Microsoft BackOffice family products, and learn how to map your organization to fit these structures.

Why network protocols are important

Learn how computers communicate with one another through network communication protocols.

Microsoft BackOffice security basics

Explore the considerations you should give to security in planning your implementation.

How Microsoft BackOffice supports remote access

Learn how Microsoft BackOffice provides built-in access to users not connected directly to the network.

Analyzing Organizational Requirements

Administrators, managers, and users should work together to define the organization's needs with respect to a Microsoft BackOffice network. To determine the requirements, the administration team must perform the following activities at regular intervals (at least annually):

- Identify organizational structure
- Select server applications
- Design server organization
- Determine server configurations
- Choose peripheral devices

Each of these activities is described in the sections that follow.

Organizational Structure

The first area of emphasis in analyzing the organizational requirements is the user community. The administration team should begin with a thorough inventory of the users connected to the network. The following areas should be documented as a basis for making implementation decisions:

- **Number of users**—Determine how many users are on the network and where they are located. It may be helpful to keep this information by geographic location. At a minimum, the number of users should be tracked for each LAN within the enterprise WAN, as well as the total number of users on the WAN. Management should be queried for estimates regarding the rate of growth in the user population over the next one, two, and three years. These estimates should be tracked against the actual number of users as each year passes.

- **Type of users**—It is also necessary to document information about the characteristics of the users and their computers. Records should be kept about the configuration of PCs on the network, PC operating systems, and desktop software. You may also be interested in knowing the various skill levels of the users. This information helps you to group users into categories, which are more manageable for network decision-making purposes. Systems Management Server (SMS) can help to gather this information if it is used in your network.

- **User organization**—Learn how the users are organized. Most organizations are arranged in one or more levels of divisions, departments, or other functional entities. The administration team should "map" the various levels of these groups of users to the Microsoft BackOffice family user models. See "Understanding BackOffice Structures for Organizing Servers" later in this chapter for a thorough discussion of user organization.

Server Applications

After the user characteristics are understood, it is possible to analyze their requirements to determine which network services are needed. The administration team should map user requirements to the available server applications.

Each Microsoft BackOffice family product provides a different set of network services, as follows:

- **Windows NT Server**—Windows NT Server fulfills the most basic of network user requirements. This product is necessary for a network to exist at all because it acts as the network operating system. Windows NT Server also is the operating system upon which all other Microsoft BackOffice family applications operate.

- **Microsoft Internet Information Server**—Microsoft Internet Information Server (IIS) provides a connection to the world via the Internet. IIS is Microsoft's Web server and it provides the major services available on the World Wide Web (WWW). The Microsoft Internet Information Server can also be used to create your own private Internet, commonly referred to as an *intranet*. When used in conjunction with other members of the Microsoft BackOffice family, it can provide the capability to operate a commercial-grade Internet site and to conduct electronic commerce on the Web.

- **Microsoft Index Server**—Microsoft Index Server provides the capability to index the information stored on an Internet Information Server and then enables users to create queries that search for specific information. Forms can be created that make it easy for users to submit queries.

- **Microsoft Proxy Server**—Microsoft Proxy Server provides a secure gateway to the Internet. This product controls the flow of information between a private network and the public Internet network. It can be configured to allow only certain people to access the Internet, control which Internet applications and protocols they can use, and what times it can be used. Furthermore, it will often provide faster access to popular Internet servers through its caching feature, which maintains a regularly updated local copy of information from frequently used remote servers.

- **Microsoft Exchange Server**—Microsoft Exchange Server provides messaging services to the network. The primary application of this product is in providing e-mail services to the users. In addition to e-mail, Microsoft Exchange Server offers other services, sometimes referred to as *groupware* or *workgroup applications,* such as document routing, public discussion forums, and document libraries.

- **Microsoft SQL Server**—Microsoft SQL Server provides relational database management services. This product is the foundation upon which most client-server applications are built. Microsoft SQL Server stores, manages, and protects the organization's data.

- **Microsoft SNA Server**—Microsoft SNA Server provides connectivity services to IBM mainframes and minicomputers. This product enables users to access and manipulate host information from their network PCs.

■ **Microsoft Systems Management Server**—Microsoft SMS provides a number of important network services. This product is the cornerstone of desktop systems management. It can be used to track the inventory of hardware on the network and to manage software distribution. These aspects of network administration can be significant for large networks. Microsoft SMS greatly simplifies the delivery of these services. It can also be used by administrators to remotely troubleshoot problems on the network.

▶ **See** "Building Your Network," **p. 66**

Approaches to Server Size and Placement

Microsoft BackOffice family applications run on a server attached to the network. Deciding how many servers to operate and where to place each server application is the next step in preparing for your Microsoft BackOffice implementation.

Two schools of thought exist on server organization: the *super server* school and the *distributed computing* school. Both approaches have strengths and weaknesses. You must weigh the tradeoffs and decide which approach makes sense in your organization.

The super server approach involves buying one (or few) very large computers with multiple processors and a large amount (for example, 256M or more) of random-access memory (RAM). This concentrated power can be easier to physically secure than multiple smaller machines. It also offers the advantage of letting one application make full use of the super server if other applications are not yet active, or if they experience a reduced load during off-peak hours. By careful scheduling, you can bring a tremendous amount of computing power to bear on your server application.

The distributed computing approach favors multiple, redundant servers each performing a portion of the overall delivery of service. This redundancy reduces the impact of a single machine failure. In a geographically distributed network, it can aid in the placement of server resources on the same fast LAN with client workstations. But, it does make physical security a greater challenge and reduces your ability to easily apply a lot of computing power to one task.

▶ **See** "Building WANs," **p. 457**

Of course, your approach need not be one or the other. You can adopt a largely distributed approach, applying an occasional super server if concentrated power is needed for a very demanding application. There is no single correct approach that fits the needs of all organizations.

Understanding BackOffice Structures for Organizing Servers

It makes sense to provide some logical organization for the network. Microsoft has developed several mechanisms for organizing groups of servers and desktop computers. This not only makes it easier to manage the network, but can also simplify things for the user community by making it easier to find a particular shared resource. These logical network structures can also provide a span of control for a security authority.

Some of these structures are used for only one of the BackOffice family products. An *organization* is only used when setting up Exchange Server, for example. Only Systems Management Server (SMS) uses *machine groups*. SMS and Exchange Server both use *sites*. SQL Server uses *server groups*. In addition, these structures don't necessarily map directly into the domain structures Windows NT uses to manage security. At first, this may seem arbitrary and needlessly complex. After you understand each of the products better, however, you should see the logic behind some of these differences. The products do different things and different structures are appropriate to manage them.

There is one more thing to remember that may help make sense of all this. Don't make things any more complicated than they need to be. The capability to break computers and users into groups makes it easier to manage them. If natural divisions don't suggest themselves, perhaps you don't need to take advantage of these capabilities. On smaller networks (fewer than 100 users) you may only need the following:

- One domain for security
- A single site for SMS
- One server group for SQL Server
- One organization with a single site for Exchange Server

Part

I

Ch

4

Workgroups

The simplest structure you can use to provide some order on a network is the *workgroup*. A workgroup, for the purposes of Microsoft networking, is nothing more than a convenient way to restrict browsing for shared resources to a small group of computers. If you want to use a shared laser printer, for example, you don't need to look at a list of all the printers on your entire network. You can simply check through a much smaller list of computers in your workgroup, which are usually in close physical proximity. Therefore, workgroups perform much the same function for networks as subdirectories (or folders) perform for hard disks. They enable you to logically group related items into smaller, more manageable groups.

A workgroup has no role in authenticating a user's identity or enforcing security. Windows NT Servers in a workgroup each have their own account database. If you want to use resources on two different Windows NT Servers in a workgroup (not a *domain*), you need to have an account on both computers, as shown in Figure 4.1. If you change your password on one server, it does not automatically change on the other.

FIG. 4.1
In a workgroup
environment, Microsoft
BackOffice servers have
separate user accounts
and security policies,
which means no
replication of account
information occurs from
one server to another.

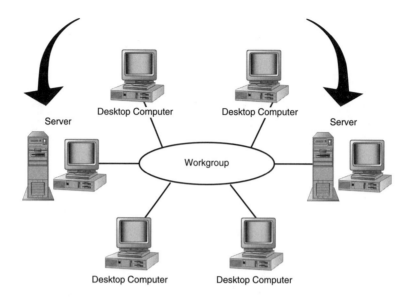

Domains

When you log on to a computer that is part of a domain, you still enjoy all the capabilities of a workgroup. In addition, domains build upon the browsing help offered by workgroups by adding significant security features. All the servers in a domain share the same user account database. As a result, you only need one user account ID and its corresponding password to access shared resources anywhere in the domain.

To establish a domain, you must configure at least one Windows NT Server as a *domain controller*. This computer contains the master copy of the user account database. It is kept in an encrypted form so that it cannot be read by unauthorized persons, and permissions are set such that it cannot be tampered with or accidentally deleted. The domain controller also keeps the master copy of the policy information regarding passwords. It is possible, for example, to require that all passwords be at least six characters long, and a new password be selected every 90 days.

Unless you have a very small network, you will also want one or more additional domain controllers, sometimes referred to as *backup domain controllers*. These computers are automatically updated whenever a user account is added, modified, or deleted. If any changes are made to the security policy of the domain, they are also forwarded to all domain controllers, as shown in Figure 4.2. By default, this occurs approximately every five minutes.

 TIP   A common mistake made by people new to Windows NT Server is to assume that the five-minute interval is too long. In practice, five minutes is usually plenty fast. Try using the network this way for at least a week before going to the trouble to change it. You'll probably find that it is adequate.

FIG. 4.2
In a domain environ-
ment, account and
security policy
information is
automatically
replicated from the
primary domain
controller to all other
domain controllers.

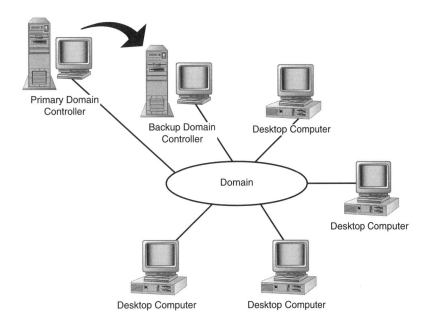

After you establish a domain, you can create user accounts and organize users into groups that reflect their computer needs or departmental affiliation in your organization. For example, you might create a group containing everyone who needs to use a particular application or a group containing everyone in the research department. After you create accounts and groups, you can use them to assign permissions to access shared resources on your network.

 In general, it is a good idea to assign permissions to groups rather than individual accounts. As new users are added, you simply add them to the appropriate groups, and they will inherit the necessary permissions to use the resources they need. A user can belong to many groups.

An additional feature provided by Windows NT Server is the capability to establish *trust relationships* between two domains. A trust relationship is set up by the *domain administrators* for two domains. If domain B trusts domain A, then user accounts and groups from A can be assigned permission to use resources in B. In a very real sense, the administrators of B are trusting the administrators of A to be responsible about security policy and assigning users to particular groups. In Figure 4.3, the domain GAS_STL_EXHIBIT trusts the domain GSULLIVAN.

NOTE It is common for a domain to correspond to a geographic location or an organizational structure, such as a department. ■

A single domain can span geographic locations, if necessary. More complex domain models also can be created, using domain trust, to accommodate large numbers of computers and users. A utility included in the Windows NT Resource Kit offers guidance for domain planning. This is an essential activity that should ideally take place before installing your first server. Although it is possible to reorganize your domain design later, it is not a simple process.

Part

I

Ch

4

FIG. 4.3

Establishing a trust relationship between domains involves an exchange of passwords between administrators for the two domains.

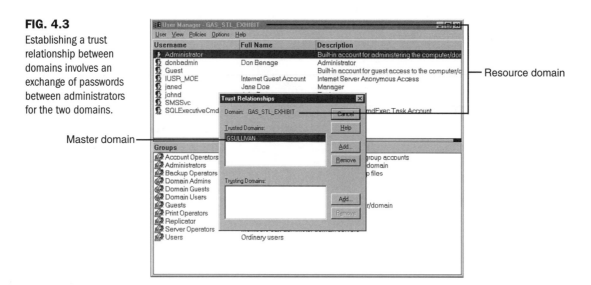

Resource domain

Master domain

N O T E The Windows NT Resource Kit is a separate product available from Microsoft. It does not ship as a part of the Windows NT package or the Microsoft BackOffice package. The Windows NT Resource Kit is a useful product for Windows NT network administrators and should be included as a part of the implementation and administration toolset. ▪

In addition to the workgroups and domains understood by Windows NT, several other structures are used by the other server-based applications in the BackOffice family.

Organizations

Another structure used by one of the BackOffice family products is the *organization*. It is the largest logical entity understood by Exchange Server. An organization usually corresponds to an entire corporation, educational institution, or other similar entity.

Sites

Two of the BackOffice Server products, SMS and Exchange Server, enable you to create *sites*. These do not necessarily correspond to domains, although they can. Sites almost always correspond to a physical site at one geographic location. For Exchange Server, the entire site must be on the same high-speed network; incorporating slower, wide area links into a site causes problems. For SMS, a site corresponds to a group of computers that all report their inventory information to the same *site server*.

Machine Groups

In addition to sites, SMS includes the idea of machine groups. This is a mechanism to form an arbitrary group of computers that need to be managed in the same way. They can be scattered among several sites in disparate geographic areas. Their only relationship is that they are managed together. In a large organization, you might have a single member of the human resources department in each regional office, for example. The computers for these users would all likely require the same applications and would, therefore, be good candidates for inclusion in a machine group.

Server Groups

SQL Server enables you to group servers together for administrative purposes. Database administrators (DBAs) can create their own server groups to organize servers for which they are responsible. These groups are set up only at the computer on which they are created. Other administrators can create their own groups on the computers they use to do their work.

Understanding the Server's Role

When you install Windows NT Server, you configure it to take on a certain role. With version 4.0 of Windows NT Server, the current version, you can either designate a server as a *domain controller* or a *server*. These roles are described in the following sections.

Domain Controller

As previously discussed, each domain has one or more domain controllers. These servers each have a copy of the user account database and security policy for the domain. When a user logs on, a logon request is sent out on the network. Whichever domain controller receives the request first checks its copy of the account database and attempts to validate the user's ID and password.

The exact mechanics of the conversation are somewhat more complicated, and the particulars vary depending on how the network is set up. The important things to remember are the following:

- In general, logons are handled by all domain controllers.
- A natural load balancing occurs. If one server gets busy handling requests, another domain controller responds to a new logon request more quickly. This happens automatically due to the second server's smaller workload and relatively better performance at that moment in time.
- Cleartext (unencrypted) passwords are never passed over the network cable. This is an important consideration given the popularity and availability of network protocol analyzers that can capture and display the contents of network packets.

Server

Although it can be somewhat confusing, there is a role called *server* for a Windows NT server in a domain. So a server, running the operating system called Windows NT Server, can be configured as the *server* role in a domain. With this role, it is possible to configure a computer to participate in domain security without itself validating logons. This role is particularly useful for computers running server-based applications, such as SQL Server. These computers can easily be added to, or removed from, a particular domain because they don't play an active role in account validation. By making a server a member of a domain, you can use accounts from that domain, or any trusted domain, to assign permissions to resources on that server.

Understanding Network Protocols

When two computers communicate on a network, they need to speak the same language. Just as an American and a native of Japan can't understand each other unless they share a common language, so computers must also use the same language, or protocol, if they are to transmit information to one another.

A *network protocol* is a detailed recipe for taking information, breaking it into groups or *packets*, adding some additional control information, and sending it over a wire (or even through the air with some equipment!) to another computer. A variety of network protocols have been developed over the years with different characteristics. The main features of the most widely used protocols supported by Windows NT are outlined in the following sections.

Using a LAN or WAN

An important factor in deciding how to organize your network and what protocol to use is the size of the network. It is relatively simple to communicate with other computers in physical proximity to your computer over cables specifically designed for computer networking. This type of network is referred to as a local area network or LAN.

If you need to be able to communicate with computers at another geographic location—in another city or country for example—you will certainly not be able to run your own cable to the other site. You will probably need to arrange to use a cable owned by a telecommunications company (your local phone company for example) or another service provider. This requires special equipment designed for communication over such lines, and you then have a wide area network or WAN. It is also possible to create a Virtual Private Network (VPN) and connect to your private network over the Internet. See Chapter 9, "Using TCP/IP with Windows NT Server," for more discussion on this topic.

The computer programs implementing a network protocol for a particular operating system are commonly referred to as a *protocol stack*. When LANs were first developed, it was common to have a single program handle all networking issues. This type of program was called a *monolithic stack*. Now it is more common for a protocol stack to have separate program components for the network adapter installed in your computer and the particular type of network protocol (for example, TCP/IP) you are using. These specific network protocols are sometimes referred to as *transport stacks*.

Protocol stacks have the three following significant characteristics:

- Size
- Speed
- Capability to be used on a routed WAN

On computers running DOS or DOS/Windows, the size of the protocol stack is an important issue. DOS-based computers must operate within the constraints of a 640K address space. On more powerful operating systems, such as Windows 95 or Windows NT, this limitation has been eliminated. Therefore, the relative size of a particular protocol stack on Windows NT, for example, is not very important.

The speed of a protocol stack isn't always important, but may be an issue with certain applications where response time is critical. It is difficult to measure the actual speed of a protocol stack because many things affect their performance. Relative performance characteristics are well understood, however, and can help you decide which transport stack to use.

If a transport stack can be used on a WAN to send packets of information across *routers* to remote network segments, the stack is said to be *routable*. Routable stacks generally have better error handling capabilities and are, therefore, more resilient when used over slow lines of poor quality. They also carry additional information indicating which network segment they are bound for and may indicate the best path to get there.

NetBEUI

NetBEUI (NetBIOS Extended User Interface) is a network protocol developed by IBM and Microsoft for use on LANs of 250 nodes or fewer. It is a small, fast stack, but is not routable. Many people confuse NetBIOS and NetBEUI. NetBIOS is a method of writing network aware applications that includes a naming scheme, programmatic interface, and messaging protocols. It can be implemented over any transport protocol and is supported by Microsoft on NetBEUI, IPX/SPX, and TCP/IP.

Part
I

Ch
4

In recent years, NetBIOS based networks have occasionally been criticized for their use of *broadcasts*—network packets that are addressed to essentially all devices on the network. Although many networks that implement support for NetBIOS use broadcasts for name propagation and discovery, the use of NetBIOS naming does not necessarily imply an abundance of broadcast traffic. In particular, Microsoft networks implemented on TCP/IP (see a following section, "Transmission Control Protocol/Internet Protocol (TCP/IP)") can use other methods, such as the Windows Internet Name Service (WINS) and a "browsing" protocol, which dramatically reduce the amount of broadcast traffic on the network.

NetBEUI is NetBIOS based and does use broadcasts rather heavily for name resolution. It is a good choice for small networks, the environment for which it was designed.

Internetwork Packet Exchange/Sequenced Packet Exchange (IPX/SPX)

This transport stack was made popular by Novell with its NetWare network products. In its initial incarnation, it did not meet strict requirements for routability; however, Novell has enhanced the transport over the years. Also, because of NetWare's popularity, many WAN vendors adapted their equipment to work with Novell's IPX/SPX. It can, therefore, be successfully used in many WAN environments.

Microsoft networks can be run exclusively over IPX/SPX if you so desire. Early versions of Windows for Workgroups did not support peer networking over IPX/SPX (they required NetBEUI to share files and printers); but the 3.11 release fixed that limitation, and both Windows 95 and Windows NT can provide full network functionality over IPX/SPX. The network protocol that is outpacing all others in the breadth of its use and the richness of it features is TCP/IP.

Transmission Control Protocol/Internet Protocol (TCP/IP)

TCP/IP is a protocol whose time has come. This protocol was developed through the cooperative efforts of the Internet community over the past ten years. As corporations began connecting the many small LANs they had built to form one large WAN, a routable protocol became essential. With the explosion of interest in the Internet, it was inevitable that TCP/IP would become widely used. Many corporations want to attach their corporate WAN to the Internet, and TCP/IP is the protocol of choice.

In comparison to other transports, TCP/IP is generally bigger and slower. Recently, however, improved stacks have been developed that are not much slower than NetBEUI. As a rule of thumb, the latest stacks included with Windows NT and Windows 95 are on the order of 5 to 20 percent slower than NetBEUI. Perform controlled tests in your own environment if you need more exact performance comparisons.

The real benefit to using TCP/IP is, of course, that it is designed for wide area networking and is routable. It performs as well as possible under poor conditions, using slow lines with a lot of extraneous noise. TCP/IP is essential if you want to connect your computer or your entire network to the Internet. It is also the protocol of choice if you intend to use the rich set of Internet tools (e.g., Web servers, chat servers, and streaming media servers) to create a private intranet. For more information, see Chapter 16, "The BackOffice I-Net Toolbox."

Understanding BackOffice Security

The security provided on a Microsoft BackOffice network is potentially controlled by a number of different sources. Basic user logon validation is provided by the network operating system (NOS). This could be either Windows NT Server, Novell NetWare, or another NOS. There are advantages to using Windows NT Server, and it is the only NOS discussed in this section, but some organizations add Windows NT Server as a platform to run server-based applications and continue to use another NOS for user validation and file and print services. The rest of this section describes different security elements provided by Microsoft BackOffice. For a more thorough discussion of Microsoft BackOffice security, see Chapter 7, "Administering Windows NT Server."

Using a Single User ID for the Enterprise

It is possible, and even desirable, for users to have a single user ID and password for all Windows NT-based services. By using a single domain, or implementing a master domain model using domain trust, a single account can be granted access permissions on any computer in your organization. Planning for and implementing a domain structure is covered in Chapter 8, "Windows NT Server Directory Services." A domain account enables users to do the following:

- Log on to the network at their desktop computers.
- Connect to shared printers and files.
- Use SQL Server databases.
- View local Web servers on the organization's intranet.
- Gain access to the Internet through a proxy server.
- Open their electronic mailboxes to send and receive e-mail.
- Open shared folders of information and participate in bulletin-board-style discussion databases.
- Automatically install new software distributed over the network by Systems Management Server (SMS).
- Attach to a gateway that provides LAN-based connectivity to a mini or mainframe computer (you may still need a separate ID and password to log on to some larger computers).

This list is just a sample of the kinds of Windows NT-based services that can be accessed with a single ID and password. Being able to integrate the security for all these services with the native Windows NT security subsystem is certainly a powerful feature. This capability is very popular with users who quickly get tired of managing and remembering multiple IDs and passwords. There are reasons, however, that you may not want to allow a single ID and password to be used for everything. If a user ID and password combination is discovered and misused, the results are obviously more traumatic if the compromised account has permissions to many resources.

In some organizations, it makes sense to give the authority over database resources to a separate group of people. The database administrators may feel a need to create a separate set of user accounts that are used solely for database access. SQL Server allows either choice.

▶ **See** "Using SQL Server Security," **p. 1227**

N O T E SQL Server also offers the capability, as an option, to encrypt data as it is transmitted over the network. ▪

There are special security considerations for e-mail. The information included in messages may be extremely sensitive. Exchange Server offers powerful capabilities that augment the simple access control provided by an ID and password. It is possible to encrypt your message to another individual using a public key algorithm. It is also possible to digitally sign your message so that the recipient knows the message came from you, and it has not been altered in any way.

▶ **See** "Using Exchange Server Advanced Security," **p. 1074**

Part

I

Ch

4

Special procedures are also required to enforce security in an I-net environment. There are specific products and protocols that have been created to enable you to send information over the public Internet in encrypted form so that only the intended recipient can understand the information. This is very important in electronic commerce applications where credit card numbers must be transmitted. Methods for identifying yourself and authenticating the fact that you are who you claim to be through the use of *certificates* are also available. Certificate technology can also be used by an organization to authenticate the identity of its Web site, its servers, and its content.

Proxy servers play a role in securing the network by controlling access to the Internet. By implementing some controls on who can use the Internet, and what services are available, you can decrease the chances that a virus will be inadvertently downloaded to your private network. See Chapter 22, "Implementing Microsoft Proxy Server," for more information on Microsoft's proxy server. You can also use proxy servers in conjunction with packet filtering (or screening) routers to limit incoming Internet traffic to just the traffic addressed to the proxy server. This focuses any potential intruder's attack on a single machine, and can make the difficult task of securing your private network against outside access somewhat easier.

▶ **See** "Network Security," **p. 1605**

Using Service Accounts

As discussed earlier, a *service* is a special type of program designed to run unattended on a Windows NT server. Every service runs in its own security context. In other words, a service runs in the context of a particular account just as regular users do. You can run services using a special type of account, called a *system account*, or you can define an account specifically for use by a service.

A system account has access privileges only on the computer on which it is defined. This can be a problem if it is a service that needs to communicate with other similar services on other computers. Clearly, in an e-mail system some services need to have access privileges on more than one computer. This is also true in a SQL Server environment where data replication is desired. In addition, some Web site implementations use a member of the BackOffice family called the Content Replication System to move information among I-net servers. In these situations, it is important to define a *service account* that is used as the security context for the service.

If you have a single domain, your service account is a regular domain account. In a master domain environment, you would want to create your service accounts in the master domain, even though most services are likely to be run in a resource domain.

▶ **See** "Creating a Service Account," **p. 195**

Understanding Dial-Up Access to BackOffice

On many networks, it is important to provide access to users who need to connect from their homes or from a hotel as they travel. Windows NT Server includes the Remote Access Service

(RAS). With this service, and the addition of some specialized hardware, you can attach up to 256 modems to a single Windows NT server. Remote users can then use a modem to dial this server and attach to the network. They do not need to have a network adapter in their computer because they will not be attached directly to the network cable plant. A modem connection is slower than typical network speeds, even with high-speed modems using compression technology. You can think of them as full-fledged users attached to the network through a slow line. Users connected in this way are usually able to access all network services.

 TIP To attach 256 modems to a single server, you would need a relatively powerful computer with more than one processor. It makes sense to use two or more computers with fewer modems to provide some redundancy and eliminate single points of failure.

Understanding the Remote Access Service

RAS is a powerful service that can greatly extend the reach, and the usefulness, of your network. By enabling users to connect from remote locations, you can offer them network services almost anywhere. RAS supports connectivity through multiple mechanisms. The most common are as follows:

- X.25 packet switched networks
- Integrated Services Digital Network (ISDN) connections
- Standard telephone-line connections utilizing modems

For more information, see Chapter 11, "An Inside Look at Remote Access Service (RAS)."

By far the most common means of connecting is the third—standard telephone lines. With relatively high-speed modems (14.4K baud or better), you can get very acceptable performance. Many modems now available include the capability to compress and decompress information on-the-fly. This can yield an effective throughput rate that is approximately double the rated speed, or better, depending on the type of information you are transmitting.

RAS access is particularly suited to client-server applications that minimize the amount of information transmitted from one computer to another. For example, in a typical database operation, a small query is sent to the database engine on the server. Only the resultant answer set is sent back over the wire. Large indexes are kept and used on the server and need not be transmitted to the (remote) desktop client.

Another method for providing network connectivity to remote users is available from other vendors. This method enables one computer to remotely control a network-attached computer's mouse, keyboard, and display over a modem connection. An advantage of this configuration is improved speed because only typed keystrokes and the resulting screen changes need to be transferred across the wire. The downside is the need to have two computers dedicated to a single user's activity for the duration of the connection. If you need ten active connections, you must have 20 computers—two for each connection.

Part
I
Ch
4

With the design of RAS, on the other hand, the remote access connection takes the place of the network attachment. No additional locally attached computer is required. All network traffic destined for the client computer is transmitted over the RAS connection. Using RAS to provide ten active connections would require only 11 computers: the server and ten workstations. RAS, therefore, provides a cost-effective method for remote network access.

Using Remote Access to Connect to Your Server

To connect to a RAS server, you must use special RAS client software. You cannot use standard asynchronous communications software. Fortunately, the RAS client software is included with Windows NT, Windows 95, and Windows for Workgroups. RAS software for Windows and DOS-based systems is included on the BackOffice CD.

The procedures for setting up RAS are covered in more detail in Chapter 12, "Implementing Remote Access Service (RAS)," but an overview is presented here to aid in planning, as follows:

1. An administrator configures RAS on one or more servers.
2. An administrator enables one or more accounts to use RAS.
3. A user or administrator configures the client software on a desktop computer or laptop that will be used at the remote site.
4. The user starts the RAS client and connects to the RAS server.
5. The user logs on and is authenticated by the domain controller as a valid user.

After you have made a connection, you can access and use any of the services on the network, including shared resources—such as files and printers and server-based applications like SQL Server databases.

From Here...

You should now have a better picture of the way Windows NT Server can be used to build a large enterprise network and how individual servers participate. You've also learned some important terminology, as well as the basics of Windows NT and BackOffice security. In Chapter 5, "Implementing Windows NT Server," you learn exactly how to set up Windows NT Server on a computer, and how to configure it to perform the tasks you've been learning about. For more information on some of the topics addressed in this chapter, consult the following chapters:

- For advanced setup advice on such features as virtual memory, drive mirroring, and RAID configuration, see Chapter 6, "Advanced Windows NT Server Configuration."
- For basic guidelines on administration of a Windows NT Server, see Chapter 7, "Administering Windows NT Server."
- For a complete understanding of network administration in a multidomain Microsoft BackOffice environment, see Chapter 8, "Windows NT Server Directory Services."

■ To learn about setting up the remote access capability of Windows NT Server, see Chapter 12, "Implementing Remote Access Service (RAS)."

■ To become acquainted with the practical aspects of a secure environment, see Chapter 46, "Implementing Real-World Security."

■ To explore ways to best manage and administer your Microsoft BackOffice network, see Chapter 48, "Proactive Network Administration."

Windows NT Server: Installation and Administration

## CHAPTER 5

Implementing Windows NT Server

by Gary Dzurny and Kevin Runnels

Designed from the ground up as a robust, scaleable, high performance operating system, Windows NT Server represents Microsoft's crown jewel in the family of Windows based operating systems. Since its initial release, Windows NT Server has proven to be a secure and reliable operating system for mission-critical applications. Functioning both as a full-featured, "next generation" desktop operating system, as well as a network operating system, Windows NT Server provides the foundation for the entire family of Microsoft BackOffice solutions. ■

What's new with Windows NT Server?

Discover the new features of Windows NT Server 4.0, including overviews of the new user interface, surprising architectural changes, diagnostics tools, administrative wizards, Domain Name System, communication enhancements, and more.

Minimum hardware requirements and hardware compatibility

Learn about the necessary hardware requirements, and read about suggested hardware for improved performance and reliability.

Shutting down and restarting the server

Obtain an understanding of how to log on, log off, shut down, and restart the server.

How to connect a client workstation to the server

Learn how to connect to the Windows NT server from a variety of different client workstations, enhancing your ability to perform network administrator tasks and support your user community.

Emergency repair process

Create an emergency repair disk so that you can rebuild a server that has suffered a catastrophic failure.

New Features in Windows NT 4.0

Microsoft Windows NT Server introduces several new features with the latest release, including new software tools, as well as changes to the underlying operating system. New software tools included in this version are a new task manager, administrative wizards, a new WinMSD diagnostics tool, Internet Information Server, and FrontPage 97. New changes to the operating system range from a newly designed Windows 95-style user interface, to distributed computing support with the distributed component object model (DCOM) additions. Also new to the operating system is support for multi-protocol routing of network packets, support for the internet compatible Domain Name Systems (DNS) addressing scheme, and new communication protocols.

The Windows 95 User Interface

Although not completely identical, the new user interface (UI) in Windows NT Server is very nearly the same as that used in Microsoft Windows 95. In short, if you have used Windows 95 for any length of time, you will instantly feel at home. The new UI sports the Windows 95 desktop, replete with the dockable taskbar and Start button for menu access to folders and programs. Icons are used on the desktop to represent objects that you have decided to make accessible without looking through menus or folders, along with the standard icons for My Computer, Network Neighborhood, and so on. Differences between the UI on Microsoft Windows NT Server and their counterparts on Windows 95 include the System Properties Sheet and Device Manager Sheet.

The new UI is attractive and easier to use than its predecessors; however, you're likely to only be interacting with the UI for running system monitors and configuring system components and network connections at the server.

Architectural Changes

Though not as immediately apparent as the new user interface, the new architectural changes in Windows NT Server are actually more significant to its utilization as a mission-critical operating system and file server. The fundamental architecture of the operating system is essentially divided into two sections: the *user mode* section and the *kernel mode* section. Windows NT Server has proven itself over the years to be a stable operating system, perhaps at the expense of performance. The stability of the system has been a direct reflection of the architectural division of the operating system into the user and kernel mode sections.

With this newest release, Microsoft has moved portions of the operating system that previously operated in user mode to the kernel mode. One of the more surprising changes is that the graphics device drivers that render output to video cards and printers has been moved to kernel mode. This has resulted in performance improvements, especially with graphics intensive applications. However, because a graphics device driver can now directly access portions of memory that were previously physically impossible for it to access, a tradeoff has been made between graphics performance and the stability of the operating system.

As you will typically be using Windows NT Server to configure and administer your network and Microsoft BackOffice solutions, the speed of the graphics will not be nearly as important to you as the stability of the system. It is important to use only tested and approved graphics device drivers on your server to protect your system from problems with poorly written device drivers.

TIP Use a Microsoft Windows NT Workstation system to administer your servers over a network connection. This enables you to safely take advantage of high resolution displays.

Task Manager

The Windows NT Server Task Manager, shown in Figure 5.1, is available by right-clicking the taskbar to activate the context menu, or by pressing Ctrl+Alt+Delete. The Task Manager offers substantially more functionality than the Windows 95 Task Manager and is more like a hybrid of the Windows 95 task manager and the Windows 95 System Monitor. The Windows NT Task Manager allows for the monitoring and control of applications and tasks running on the server and enables you to kill processes that are not responding. In addition, the Task Manager reports on important performance metrics, such as CPU and memory usage.

FIG. 5.1
The Windows NT Server Task Manager provides unified access to the management of system processes and performance measurements.

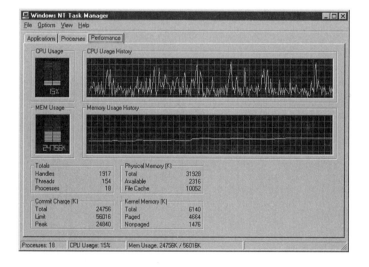

Part

II

Ch

5

WinMSD Diagnostics Utility

WinMSD, or Windows NT Diagnostics, is a diagnostics utility available through the Administrative Tools group. If you have used the diagnostics utility in previous versions of Windows NT Server, you'll find almost the same information available, though perhaps not under the same tab or menu. WinMSD provides information on device drivers, network usage, system resources, IRQ, and I/O address usage. A very welcome feature is WinMSD's capability to remotely examine diagnostic information from other Windows NT computers over the network.

Administrative Wizards

Following the lead of the *wizard* concept introduced in Microsoft's application software, Windows NT Server provides Administrative Wizards in the operating system. These Wizards give you a quick and easy, though somewhat limited, way to handle some of the more common administrative tasks. The available Wizards provide a roadmap for adding a new user account, creating and modifying group accounts, managing file and folder access, adding printers, adding or removing programs, installing new modems, installing or updating network client workstations, and checking license compliance for installed applications (see Figure 5.2). These Wizards will take you, step-by-step, through their specific tasks. Unfortunately, they don't allow for user customization to provide for some of your more difficult or time consuming administrative duties. The tasks they do cover are really pretty easy to perform without using a wizard, but they can be helpful to new administrators.

FIG. 5.2

New Administrative Wizards in Windows NT 4.0 can be accessed through the start menu under Administrative Tools.

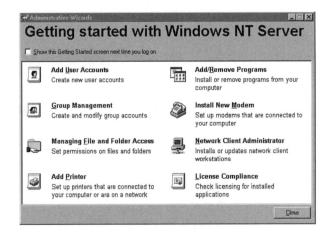

Domain Name System (DNS)

DNS is a distributed database of computer names and IP addresses. This enables your Windows NT Server to resolve such names as gfr.bigco.com to addresses like **155.39.27.8**. DNS is distributed in the sense that DNS systems can query each other for entries they may not contain. If your network consists entirely of Windows NT machines, you don't really need to use DNS. If your network is hooked up to the Internet, you still may not need to maintain your own DNS system if you have access to one through your Internet service provider. However, if you are connected to multiple networks and some of those networks are not Microsoft networks, you may need to configure DNS for internetwork operation.

Windows NT Server still supports the Windows Internet Naming Service (WINS), but this standard never caught on outside of Microsoft operating systems and the NetBEUI protocol. WINS is similar to DNS except that its database of names and corresponding addresses is automatically updated, whereas the traditional DNS system must be manually edited to add or change entries. Windows NT Server, in situations where you need to attach your Windows NT network to a DNS network, enables you to combine the two approaches and eliminate administrative headaches. For an in-depth discussion of name resolution, see Chapter 10, "Name Resolution with TCP/IP."

Multi-Protocol Routers

Routers are typically thought of as stand-alone pieces of hardware that perform the role of a traffic cop in directing network packets from one part of the network to another. Microsoft Windows NT Server has the capability to route network traffic by itself, without the need for a specialized router. For smaller enterprises, this capability serves as a low cost solution for LAN to LAN routing if your network utilizes TCP/IP, IPX/SPX, or even AppleTalk protocols. However, it is advisable to purchase a hardware routing solution to handle large traffic loads for larger enterprises.

Distributed Component Object Model (DCOM)

Object-oriented software is the new paradigm for modern systems. The Windows NT Server Distributed Component Object Model, or DCOM, is distributed in the sense that software objects can use this service to communicate with each other from different machines over a network. Using Access Control Lists, or *shares,* you can specify which users have access to specific object servers. A configuration utility called DCOMCNFG is used to configure the individual software objects (see Figure 5.3). Software that you can purchase that can utilize DCOM should have specific configuration information for that specific software component. DCOM configuration is covered in more detail in Chapter 38, "An Inside Look at Distributed Transaction Coordinator (DTC) and Microsoft Transaction Server (MTS)."

FIG. 5.3
The DCOMCNFG utility can be located in the system directory of your Windows NT installation directory.

Internet Information Server

Riding the wave of Internet connectivity and the World Wide Web phenomenon, Microsoft Windows NT Server provides a host of new Internet specific components, such as Internet Information Server, or IIS. IIS actually incorporates a World Wide Web server, FTP server, and

Gopher server all in one package. Touted as the fastest Web server available today, IIS does offer excellent overall performance, but especially shines when combined with SQL Server to deliver database information via the World Wide Web. IIS supports an API level interface to SQL Server that provides much faster database access through the Web than conventional CGI scripting. Additional information regarding the integration of IIS with SQL Server can be found in Chapter 24, "Dynamic Content with IIS Using dbWeb and IDC." For additional information regarding the setup and configuration of IIS, see Chapter 18, "Building A Web With Internet Information Server (IIS)."

As complements to IIS, Windows NT Server provides Microsoft FrontPage 97, Microsoft Index Server, and Microsoft Proxy Server. FrontPage is used for Web page content creation and includes an HTML editor and wizards to assist in building Web sites that follow a common style, such as the *corporate presence* and *project* Web site styles. FrontPage also includes a Personal Server and server extensions. The Personal Server is a scaled down replacement for IIS and only exists because FrontPage is also marketed through the retail channel as a stand-alone product. Windows 95 users would make use of the Personal Server as the Windows 95 operating system lacks an integrated Web server. The server extensions provide hooks to integrate Web pages created with FrontPage more closely with features provided in IIS. Detailed information about Microsoft FrontPage can be found in Chapter 20, "Using Microsoft FrontPage 97."

The Microsoft Index Server is used for quick indexing and searching of documents for corporate Internet/intranet sites. Index Server searches are not restricted to searching only HTML pages, as do many other search tools. IIS utilizes open standard content filters to search any file type, including Excel and Word formats. Chapter 21, "Implementing Index Server and the Content Replication System," contains detailed information on the administration and use of Index Server.

New Communication Capabilities

Microsoft Windows NT Server has introduced a new TCP/IP based communication protocol in the Point to Point Tunneling Protocol (PPTP). PPTP enables you to "privately" connect to your company network over the Internet, a technique Microsoft refers to as *virtual private networking*. Essentially, PPTP encapsulates your original packet into an encrypted TCP/IP packet, which is then sent over the TCP/IP network. The TCP/IP network could even include the Internet. When the packet arrives at its destination on the network, it is then decrypted, and the original network packet is restored. PPTP is covered in more detail in Chapter 9, "Using TCP/IP with Windows NT Server."

Another new communication technology introduced with Windows NT Server is Multilink Channel Aggregation. Utilized through Dial-Up Networking, Multilink enables computers dialing into Windows NT Server to use more than one dial up line at a time to achieve higher transfer speeds. For example, two 28.8K modems can be used for one network connection, sending packets through both lines simultaneously. This would provide the same throughput as a single 56K leased line. For information on how to set up and configure Multilink, see Chapter 13, "Implementing Dial-Up Networking Clients."

Verifying Hardware Compatibility

A server's performance directly affects the productivity of everyone who uses it. Select hardware carefully to ensure a fast, yet reliable system. There are many bargain basement hardware systems available that advertise blistering performance at a low price. However, if your server is constructed of lower quality components or isn't completely compatible with your operating system, then your perceived cost savings just became a major expense. Invest wisely in hardware. Important decisions include processor type (Intel or RISC), number of processors, speed of processors, memory capacity, and disk storage capacity.

A Hardware Compatibility List is on the installation CD for Windows NT. This list details hardware that the Windows Hardware Quality Labs has tested and found to be compatible with Windows NT. To be as certain as possible you are making a wise hardware investment, you may want to consider purchasing only listed hardware.

 The latest Hardware Compatibility List can be downloaded from the Windows Hardware Quality Labs at **www.microsoft.com/hwtest**.

System Requirements

The minimum system requirements for Windows NT server are described by Microsoft as a 486/33 MHz or higher, or Pentium or Pentium PRO processor with 16M of RAM and 125M of available hard disk space. Never purchase a system that only meets the minimum requirements. It can only be assumed that these "minimum" requirements exist to encourage sales of Windows NT by suggesting that relatively inexpensive hardware can capably run the system. Reasonable performance can be obtained by utilizing a 133 MHz Pentium processor with 32M of RAM and 1 GB of hard disk space. The price of hardware continues to drop at an astonishing rate, and this "reasonable performance" hardware requirement outlined above is not an expensive computer. Other BackOffice solutions will require more disk space, and memory seems to make the biggest performance difference, so consider investing in those areas first.

 The number of users has the biggest impact on the performance of a server. Microsoft publishes a number of worksheets and whitepapers on planning a Windows NT Server Network; these are available from **http://www.microsoft.com/windows/common/aa56.htm**. Use such materials to guide you in your hardware purchases.

Part
II

Ch
5

Intel versus RISC

The Intel architecture dominates the Windows NT Server market. Although it is true that the RISC implementations of Windows NT can outperform competing Intel products in many tests, they always perform Intel emulation slower than the native Intel processor. The fact is that the majority of software available for Windows NT was developed on a machine that has an Intel processor and will perform best on that same architecture. Version 4.0 of Windows NT Server has dropped support for the 386 processor (despite the legacy existence of the /i386 subdirectory on the installation CD). If you intend to run any software on the server besides BackOffice, invest in an Intel based machine.

Symmetric Multiprocessing versus Uniprocessor

The vast majority of desktop computers have a single microprocessor. Windows NT Server is the first Microsoft operating system to support more than one processor. In fact, Windows NT Server 4.0 can support up to four microprocessors in the standard version you purchase over the counter. Support for more than four microprocessors can be obtained by contacting your system hardware manufacturer.

Multiprocessing systems are categorized as being either asymmetric or symmetric. Asymmetric systems typically use one processor for operating system code and other processors for user applications. Symmetric systems, however, can execute operating system code or user code on any available processor. As you can see, symmetric multiprocessing provides a much cleaner way to balance loads on the system and provides for superior throughput. Windows NT Server uses the symmetric processing design.

Multiprocessing systems provide performance advantages when CPU utilization is high. However, as a server, you'll find that your real performance issues will typically be related to the amount of available RAM and hard disk space. A server that has insufficient RAM will page out to the hard disk often and become very sluggish.

 Use Performance Monitor to determine whether your server is I/O bound or CPU bound.

Memory

You can never have too much memory. Start with at least 32 megabytes. Many manufacturers now install non-parity memory in some systems, but an enterprise server requires parity memory. Expect to pay a small premium to get parity memory. Parity memory adds one extra bit to each byte and some extra parity checking circuitry. The parity bit indicates whether the data bit contains an even or odd number of one's. This scheme can detect memory errors.

Modern semiconductor memory is extremely reliable, and many question the value of parity checking. Parity unquestionably adds expense and slows performance. When the system detects a parity error, the only appropriate response is to stop the system. (Error-correcting parity chips are available, but are more expensive.) Opponents of parity say that failures are extremely rare, and the response to errors (system shutdown) is unsatisfactory. On the other hand, undetected system errors can manifest as bizarre, inexplicable problems, or subtle undetected errors in critical applications. The late Seymour Cray once designed a computer with non-parity memory. In production, the machines displayed anomalous behaviors ultimately traced to memory errors. Subsequent Cray designs used parity memory.

Mass Storage

Your Windows NT server will probably include multiple hard disks, a tape drive, and CD-ROM. Windows NT includes excellent support for the Small Computer Systems Interface (SCSI), and the SCSI provides the best support for this variety of mass storage devices. Windows NT Server includes a number of fault tolerance features that work only with SCSI controllers.

Invest in superior performance and reliability. The hard disk subsystem is the hardest working component of a network server, and the component most prone to failure. Invest in a high-end, bus-mastering SCSI controller. Windows NT Server provides software implementation for Redundant Array of Inexpensive Disks (RAID) level 0 (disk striping), level 1 (disk mirroring), or level 5 (disk striping with parity) with ordinary IDE or SCSI drives. However, IDE controllers can only access one drive at a time, whereas SCSI supports parallel access. Windows NT Server also supports sector sparing (hot fixing) on SCSI drives. When the Windows NT Server fault tolerance driver detects imminent failure in a disk sector, it moves the data to a spare sector with no interruption of service.

Note that Windows NT supports only SCSI tape drives. The popular and inexpensive QIC-40 and QIC-80 tape drives, which run from a floppy controller, are not supported. Almost all high-capacity tape drives are SCSI-based; don't invest in anything less than 2G.

You're unlikely to run multimedia applications on your Windows NT Server, so you need not buy the fastest CD-ROM available. An inexpensive double-speed or quad-speed drive will serve nicely. Windows NT prefers SCSI-based CD-ROMs, but a few proprietary semi-SCSI interfaces are supported. A separate CD-ROM interface will use an expansion slot, an IRQ, and a DMA. You might also consider a fast CD-ROM "jukebox" to share as a network resource. This can be particularly valuable to a software development group because so much developers' documentation is now distributed on CD-ROM.

Part
II

Ch
5

Power Conditioning

Most desktop computers are protected with inexpensive surge protectors. This might be better than nothing, but it certainly will not suffice for an enterprise server. Manufacturers exploit fear of lightning to sell surge protectors, but small power glitches cause far more problems. An IBM engineer tells the story of a customer whose mainframe computer kept randomly rebooting. After weeks of troubleshooting, a crack team of IBM engineers began to torture test the system. They attacked the machine with diagnostic software, rubber hammers, and huge electrostatic discharges, but the machine shrugged it all off (as it was designed to do). However, the machine continued to reboot unpredictably. The team finally traced the problem to a faulty contact in an elevator shaft. When the elevator passed this contact, a brief short circuit interrupted power on the high voltage loop that supplied the computer. A team of IBM's best engineers spent weeks tracking down this problem, which could have been prevented by simple power conditioning.

Less dramatically, a simple power outage can wreak havoc with SQL Server or Exchange Server. A good uninterruptible power supply (UPS) will include an RS-232 connection to signal the attached server when power fails. This signal can trigger a script to shut down the server in an orderly fashion while running on battery power. Because most power outages last less than a minute, the shutdown script might be triggered by a low battery signal from the UPS, rather than by power failure.

Expect to spend at least 300 dollars for a UPS with good power filtering and signaling capabilities. A better UPS will enable you to monitor power quality. Widely used brands include American Power Conversion, Tripp Lite, Clary, and Liebert. Purchase the serial cable to interface the UPS to your Windows NT server from the manufacturer. There is no real standard and the cables are usually specific to the brand of UPS that you purchase. You'll find references to UPS Interface Voltages in the UPS applet in the Control Panel. Again, you will need to refer to documentation from the manufacturer to identify the correct positive or negative settings for each signal. Make it a habit to check the battery each time you shut down the server.

Installing Windows NT Server

The fastest way to install Windows NT is to order it pre-installed on your system. Many hardware vendors now offer this service.

The following section describes, in detail, a typical installation from a supported CD-ROM. Subsequent sections discuss differences when installing from a shared network drive, and issues in upgrading or replacing an existing operating system.

Installing from a Supported CD-ROM

The typical Windows NT installation kit includes three floppy disks and a CD-ROM. The floppy disks include just enough of the Windows NT operating system (OS) to boot up, mount a supported CD-ROM drive, and continue installation from the CD-ROM. This method does not require any previously installed OS and generally allows the greatest flexibility.

If an OS is already installed on the server, you can install from a supported CD-ROM without the benefit of floppy disks. Select the drive containing the Windows NT Server CD-ROM, switch to the appropriate directory for your hardware (for example, I386), and run `WINNT /b` (`WINNT32 /b` if your current OS is 32-bit). This can be a convenient option when upgrading a prior version of Windows NT. The process copies all files needed for the installation from the CD-ROM to a local hard drive, updates the system files, and then reboots the computer.

The installation proceeds as an interactive dialog session. The Setup program assesses the availability of necessary system resources. If the process encounters a problem, the installation or upgrade will halt. At certain times in the process, the computer will reboot to establish modifications to the computer's configuration. This is normal. If the computer's hard disk drive was originally formatted using MS-DOS, you will notice that it now has dual boot capability. For the duration of the setup process, choose the Windows NT Server 4.0 option when booting.

Follow these steps to install Windows NT Server from a supported CD-ROM:

1. Insert the setup boot disk in drive A and insert the Windows NT Server CD in the CD-ROM drive. Boot the computer.

2. The setup process begins with hardware detection.

3. A blue screen with white lettering announces Windows NT Setup. When prompted, insert Setup Disk Number 2.

4. Setup switches to 50-line video mode while the Windows NT kernel loads. After another few moments, GUI mode starts with the Welcome to Setup dialog box. Press Enter to continue the process.

5. You will encounter a dialog box concerning mass storage devices not long into the process. These mass storage devices include IDE drives, SCSI drives, CD-ROM drives, or other special disk controllers. If you know other devices are present, but are not listed as mass storage devices, cancel the Setup program at the first opportunity. Check the connections and configuration of these devices. Consult the vendor if necessary.

6. You will find a 12-page License Agreement that you are supposed to read. After you have done this, press F8 to continue.

7. The system will present a list of detected devices, such as your display adapter and your keyboard type. If you want to change any item on the list, press the up or down cursor keys to highlight the item you want to change and press Enter. Otherwise, select No Changes and press the Enter key.

8. The setup process will identify which partitions are available for installation. If you have an existing DOS partition that you want to keep, install Windows NT on a different partition. You will be able to access data on the DOS partition from Windows NT, even if you install with the NTFS option. However, you will not be able to access the NTFS partition from DOS. Unless you have an overwhelming need to access the NTFS partition from DOS, choose the NTFS option for your new server installation. If you have an existing DOS partition that you don't want to keep, the Setup program will convert the partition to NTFS for you.

9. You will be asked for a directory to install your operating system with a suggested default of WINNT. Choose the default directory.

10. Setup will then examine your hard disk for errors. You can choose between performing a quick scan or a more exhaustive and time consuming scan. It is best to take the time to do a full examination of your hard disk. As was stated in the previous section "Mass Storage," the hard disk subsystem is a critical component to your system and you should do all you can to make sure that it is working properly. If you have more than one hard drive, the exhaustive examination will examine all of them. This is a non-destructive examination, so any data on an existing DOS partition will remain unaffected.

11. Setup will copy files to the new drive and partition and reboot to the Windows NT graphical user interface (GUI). A Setup Wizard guides you through the rest of the setup process.

12. You are prompted for your name and the name of your organization.

13. Keep your CD case nearby as you are expected to type in the ten-digit CD key on the back of your CD case.

Part
II

Ch
5

14. Select a licensing mode for this server. The options are licenses per server and licenses per seat. Determine the number of users this server will support in advance. Take into consideration network growth. In either case, you must complete the License Agreement dialog box.

15. The next dialog box asks for a name for your computer. This name must be 15 characters or less. This name must be unique on the network. As you type in your computer name, it will appear as all capitals.

16. You are now asked to specify what type of server you want, and you are presented with the following three choices:

    - Primary domain controller

    - Backup domain controller

    - Stand-alone server

17. You are now prompted to enter a password for the default Administrator account. The password must be 14 characters or less. Write down this password and keep it in a safe place.

18. The Setup program offers to create an emergency disk. Go ahead and make one now, but you can make one later using the RDISK utility if you desire.

19. The next screen enables you to select which components of the operating system you want to install. The components all fall under the following categories:

    - Accessibility options

    - Accessories

    - Communication

    - Games

    - Multimedia

    - Windows messaging

20. The system then begins to install Windows NT Networking and will present the following options regarding how your computer will participate on a network:

    - Do not connect to a network at this time.

    - This computer will participate on a network.

    In addition, the way your computer is physically connected to the network must be identified, as follows:

    - Wired to the network (ISDN or network adapter)

    - Remotely connected to a network using a modem

21. The system enables you to identify your time zone and set the date and time.

22. An auto-detection of your graphics subsystem is performed and a test screen is shown so that you can determine the best display for your needs.

23. Depending on the options you selected earlier in the setup process, the Setup program will install and configure various files, including Windows messaging, shortcuts, and system security.

24. If you chose to create an emergency repair disk, the system prompts for the blank floppy at this point. The disk is formatted and configuration files are copied to it.

 TIP Make a backup of the emergency repair disk and store it in a safe place.

25. Setup cleans up its temporary files and enables you to reboot to your new operating system.

Installing from a Network Drive

Installing from the network requires a DOS-based network and a shared directory that points to the network directory where the Setup program resides. You can run the Setup program from any computer running Windows NT, Windows for Workgroups, LAN Manager, Novell NetWare, or Banyan VINES. After establishing a connection to the shared network directory, copy all files located in the \I386 subdirectories to the computer on which Windows NT is being installed.

After copying all installation files from the network, switch to the local drive and directory containing the installation files and run WINNT /b (WINNT32 /b from Windows NT or Windows 95).

N O T E The network installation procedure can be modified slightly to install from an unsupported CD-ROM. Just copy all files from the \I386 directory on the NT Server CD to a local hard drive and run WINNT /b. ■

Part
II

Ch
5

Using the Hardware Profile/Last Known Good Feature

During startup, right after the hardware detection routine executes, the user is given the option to invoke the Hardware Profile/Last Known Good menu, which can be done by simply pressing the space bar when prompted. This option enables a user to select a hardware profile to be used when Windows NT is started. A hardware profile indicates which drivers are to be loaded during the startup process. This is particularly convenient when using a portable computer because it allows for a boot configuration with different video display and network settings at home or on the road. One can create new hardware profiles via the Hardware Profiles option under the System Properties dialog box (see Figure 5.4).

FIG. 5.4

The Hardware Profiles tab allows for configuring multiple hardware profiles.

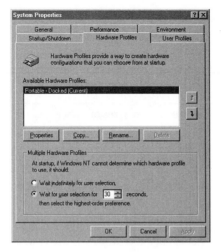

The current hardware profile in use is indicated in the list of profiles available for that system. You can disable a network connection or indicate that the profile is for a docked portable computer via the Properties dialog box (see Figure 5.5). The startup criteria can also be set to select which profile should be used as default.

FIG. 5.5

Portable computer properties for a hardware profile can be set via the property option.

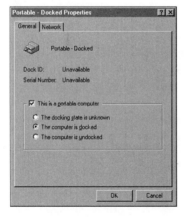

The user can also select the Last Known Good profile within the Hardware Profile/Last Known Good startup menu. This feature can save the day when configuration changes render a server unbootable. Each time the server boots successfully, the current configuration is saved as the last known good profile. Be aware that configuration changes since last successful startup will be lost by using the last known good configuration.

 TIP The configuration is actually saved when the first user successfully logs on after startup. To avoid saving the current startup configuration as the last known good configuration, reset before logging on.

Using the Emergency Repair Disk

In the event your system fails (that is, the system files, boot sector, or BOOT.INI file become corrupted), and you are unable to restart the computer using the Last Known Good option, an emergency repair can be performed to restore system-type files and configuration preferences established prior to the failure. To repair a Windows NT Server installation, Windows NT Setup uses information saved on the emergency repair disk (ERD) or in the Windows subdirectory called REPAIR.

During installation of Windows NT Server, you are provided the option of creating an ERD. Regardless of whether the disk is created at that time, repair information is written to the REPAIR subdirectory. During a repair of the system, you can direct the program to use the ERD, or the information in the REPAIR subdirectory. If the repair process is successful, the computer will be returned to the condition it was in after the last update to the repair information. Refer to "Installing Windows NT Server" earlier in this chapter for more information on creating the emergency repair disk during Windows NT Server installation.

Creating an Updated Emergency Repair Disk

Windows NT Server automatically creates repair information during installation. However, this information is not maintained dynamically. As the complexion of the server changes due to installation of additional software, you should update the ERD.

The repair disk utility updates repair information and creates an ERD in separate steps. You can update repair information in the REPAIR subdirectory without creating a new ERD. If you create an ERD without first updating the repair information, the ERD will reflect an old configuration. Normally, update repair information and then create a new ERD.

Follow these steps to update repair information and create a new ERD:

1. Log on as an administrator.

2. Run the RDISK.EXE program (normally found in the WINNT35\SYSTEM32 directory). The Repair Disk Utility message box appears. It tells you the purpose of the utility and warns you against using it as a backup tool. It also has four buttons: Update Repair Info, Create Repair Disk, Exit, and Help.

3. Click Update Repair Info. The utility updates the repair information stored in the REPAIR directory.

4. Click Create Repair Disk. The program prompts you to insert a floppy disk.

N O T E Make sure that the disk you are using for the emergency repair disk does not contain important files. Creation of the disk erases all files previously saved on it. Also, the emergency repair disk is not a boot disk, so trying to boot your machine with it will not be unsuccessful. ▪

5. The program formats the floppy disk inserted in step 4 and copies repair information onto the disk.

Part

II

Ch

5

6. Click Exit to close the Repair Disk Utility.

When you create the ERD, the following files are copied from the REPAIR subdirectory to the floppy:

- AUTOEXEC.NT
- CONFIG.NT
- DEFAULT._
- NTUSER.DA_
- SAM._
- SECURITY._
- SETUP.LOG
- SOFTWARE._
- SYSTEM._

The ERD is PC specific and should only be used with the PC on which it was created. Make backup copies of the disk in case the original is corrupted. Be sure to store it in a safe place. Place a label, with the date and description, on each disk created.

Understanding the Emergency Repair Process

Before performing an emergency repair, check to make sure that what the process is attempting to fix is the probable cause of the boot failure. Remember, the server is down, and end users are waiting to use its resources. Use your time wisely and economically to determine the source of the problem and eradicate it. If you have been running Windows NT successfully and it fails to boot, you can use the following simple procedure to try to recover:

1. Verify that the problem has not been caused by changes or failures in hardware. Check all cables for loose or bad connections. Verify new settings on existing hardware. Make sure that any new cards or drives are compatible and have been installed correctly. Any of these can be the cause of boot problems.

2. Try using the Last Known Good option at the OSLOADER screen. Obviously, this option is only useful if the machine has no hardware problems.

If the preceding options do not succeed, you will need to perform an emergency repair. It is useful to know what occurs when performing this procedure. The following steps are performed by the emergency repair process:

1. CHKDSK is run on the disk partition containing Windows NT system files. On x86-based computers, CHKDSK also is run on the system partition. This verifies that every file in the installation is good through a checksum algorithm. If files are missing or corrupt, they can be restored from the Windows NT Server installation software.

2. The default system and security registry archives are replaced. Each replacement is contingent upon user confirmation.

3. The boot loader is reinstalled.

The repair process enables you to repair one or more of the following:

- **System files**—Setup checks the Windows NT directory tree against the log file on the emergency repair disk to ensure that all system files are present. If they are missing or corrupt, they can be restored. It also checks the Windows NT files on the system partition and verifies that they are present and in good order.

- **Default system configuration**—Setup checks the Registry for errors. If any configuration errors are found, you will have the option of restoring a setting to what it was when Windows NT was installed. User accounts and file security added since installation will be lost, unless they were backed up in \%SYSTEMROOT%\SYSTEM32\CONFIG or updated on the emergency repair disk using the Repair Disk Utility.

- **Boot variables**—Setup restores the boot variables for a particular installation on the hard disk. You must provide the emergency repair disk for this option.

- **Boot sector (x86-based only)**—Setup writes a new boot sector on the system partition. If any files are missing or corrupt, the repair restores them from the appropriate Windows NT Setup disk or CD. If you have accidentally changed the system partition on your x86-based computer so that Windows NT no longer starts, Repair restores the original boot configuration so that Windows NT can be started.

N O T E The emergency repair disk may be unable to restore some of the Windows NT system files if additional drivers or third-party software were added after the installation. This includes display and printer drivers, network software, audio adapters, and any other software copied to the system after Windows NT Server was installed. The emergency repair disk will have no information on these files and will be unable to verify them. Troubleshooting and restoration of such files must be done manually, rather than with the emergency repair disk. Think about using backup tapes to restore such drivers. ▪

▶ **See** "Making Backups," **p. 211**

Performing an Emergency Repair

To execute a repair on an x86-based computer, perform the following tasks:

1. If you installed Windows NT using the original Setup floppies, CD, or WINNT.EXE, start Setup just as you did originally. That is, insert the first Setup Boot Disk in drive A and start the computer.

2. When prompted, type **R** to indicate that you want to repair Windows NT files.

3. A repairs options screen is presented to the user, which enables the selection of optional tasks to be performed during the repair process. These tasks include the following:

   - Inspect the Registry files.
   - Inspect the startup environment.
   - Verify the Windows NT system files.
   - Inspect the boot sector.

The user can press Enter and accept the default options, which perform each of these optional tasks.

4. Setup asks you for the emergency repair disk. If you do not have one, Setup presents a list of the Windows NT installations that it found on the computer, and you can pick one.

5. Follow the instructions on the screen, inserting the emergency repair disk in drive A and providing any other Windows NT Setup disks as requested. You will be able to choose what should be restored. You can bypass a repair on one or more items, but it is not recommended.

6. When the final message appears, remove the emergency repair disk and restart the computer.

To execute a repair on a RISC-based computer, perform the following tasks:

1. Start the NT setup program as instructed in your manufacturer's supplied documentation.

2. When prompted, type **R** to indicate that you want to repair Windows NT files.

3. Follow the instructions on the screen, inserting the emergency repair disk in drive A and providing other Windows NT Setup disks as requested.

4. When the final message appears, remove the emergency repair disk and press Enter to restart the computer.

Logging On and Off

Normally, Windows NT Server will run with nobody logged on to the local machine. Many remote users may log on for the purpose of accessing services, but a local user typically logs on only for server administration or maintenance.

Follow these steps to log on to the Windows NT Server:

1. Press Ctrl+Alt+Del. The Welcome dialog box appears.

TIP You can customize the Welcome dialog box. Add the keys `LegalNoticeCaption` and `LegalNoticeText` to the registry at `\HKEY_LOCAL_MACHINE\SOFTWARE\Microsoft \Windows NT\Current Version\Winlogon`. The values you enter will appear as the caption and text, respectively, of the Welcome dialog box. The user must click OK in this message box to continue the logon process. Use this feature to provide fair warning of the consequences of unauthorized access attempts.

2. Type a valid user ID in the Username box.

3. If you are logging on to a domain server, select the domain name in the From drop-down list box. Otherwise, select the name of the local machine.

4. In the Password box, type the password for the user ID entered in step 3.

5. Click OK or press Enter.

TROUBLESHOOTING

My logon fails. The password in Windows NT is case-sensitive. Check Caps Lock and retype your password. (The user ID is not case-sensitive.)

Never walk away from a Windows NT Server while logged on locally as an administrator. The intuitive interface makes it easy for any user to make drastic changes to your network configuration (for example, Disk Administrator, delete partition). Even a well-intentioned person can commit an expensive blunder.

After completing administrative tasks, follow these steps to log off the server:

1. Press Ctrl+Alt+Del. The Windows NT Security dialog box appears.
2. Click the Logoff button.
3. A confirmation message box appears. Click Yes.

You can also log off by choosing the Shutdown option from the Start menu.

Shutting Down and Restarting the Server

Occasionally, you will need to shut down the server for routine maintenance or equipment upgrades. Configuration changes often require restarting the server, and a restart begins with a shutdown. It's important to perform an orderly shutdown to avoid data loss.

Because a shutdown disconnects all clients, try to schedule configuration changes for periods of low activity. It's also wise to advise concerned users in advance of any scheduled downtime.

Perform the following steps when restarting the server:

1. Log on as an administrator.
2. Open Control Panel and select the Services icon. Select the Server service and click Pause. Pausing the Server service prevents new users from logging on. Close Control Panel.
3. Use Server Manager to contact active users. Select Computer, Send Message, and compose a message asking them to log off. Wait a few minutes to allow them to comply.
4. Shut down active applications, such as SQL Server and Exchange Server. Shutting down these services may also require disconnecting users.

N O T E   16-bit Windows clients must be running the WinPopup program to receive messages from the Server Manager. ■

5. Use Server Manager to disconnect any users who could not be contacted. Select Computer, Properties and click Users in the Properties dialog box. Click Disconnect All in the User Sessions dialog box.

Part

II

Ch

5

6. Press Ctrl+Alt+Del. The Windows NT Security dialog box appears.

7. Click Shutdown.

8. The Shutdown Computer dialog box appears. To shut down without an immediate restart, click Shutdown and then click OK. To restart the server, click the Shutdown and Restart button, click OK, and continue with step 9.

9. The server restarts.

10. Log on as an administrator.

11. Restart applications and services. Verify successful restart.

12. Notify users that the server is available.

13. Log off.

 Configuration changes often require a restart before becoming effective. Such changes include installing new or updated drivers and installing certain applications. In such cases, a Restart dialog box appears immediately after completing the configuration change. When you know that a configuration change requires a restart, first complete step 1 through step 5 in the preceding list.

Getting Connected from a Client Workstation

Most users will interact with Windows NT Server through client workstations. Client sessions typically involve several activities: logging on, using file and print services, using other application services (SQL Server, Exchange Server, and so on), and logging off. A network administrator must know how to configure a variety of workstations to properly perform these tasks.

DOS

Prior versions of Windows NT used software called the Workgroup Connection for DOS to connect DOS workstations. Windows NT Server 4.0 enables you to generate a client setup disk. The software contained on this disk takes better advantage of the Windows NT Server environment, and the Workgroup Connection for DOS should no longer be used.

Windows workstations use the same client software as DOS workstations. Using the PC on which Windows NT Server has been installed, perform the following steps to create a client setup kit for Windows and DOS workstations:

1. Label two formatted high-density floppy disks as Windows NT Server DOS Client Setup Disks 1 and 2.

2. Insert the Windows NT Server CD-ROM in your CD-ROM drive.

3. Start Network Client Administrator from the Network Administration program group to display the Network Client Administrator dialog box (see Figure 5.6).

FIG. 5.6

The Network Client
main setup menu
enables you to set up
a client workstation
from a DOS prompt.

N O T E Network Client Administrator can create either a single network installation startup disk or a
set of installation disks. The single disk enables a workstation to boot up, connect to a
Windows NT Server, and download the rest of the needed client files. Although this may seem
convenient, there are a number of severe limitations, as follows:

- The disk must boot with the same version of DOS as the target workstation. A different
  disk is required for every DOS version on your network.
- The disk is specific to the type of network interface card (NIC). A different disk is
  required for each type of NIC on your network.
- You must copy all the client setup files to a shared directory on the server.
- If the procedure fails, you will have to use the multidisk setup kit.

For these reasons, it's best to always use the multidisk install set. The only exception would arise if you
have to install many systems of the same type. Then the shortcomings of this method may be offset by
an overall time savings, and the avoidance of swapping disks during each installation. ■

4. Click the Make Installation Disk Set option button to select the option, and then click
   Continue. The Share Network Client Installation Files dialog box appears (see
   Figure 5.7).

FIG. 5.7

The Share Network
Client Installation Files
dialog box enables you
to specify the source of
the client installation
files.

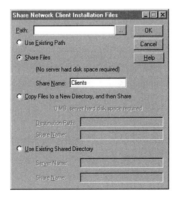

5. Type **D:\CLIENTS** (where D: is the letter for your Windows NT Server CD-ROM) in the
   Path text box.
6. Click Use Existing Path to select the option.

Part

II

Ch

5

7. Click OK to display the Make Installation Disk Set dialog box.

8. Select Network Client v3.0 for MS-DOS and Windows.

9. Select a Destination Drive.

10. Insert the floppy disk labeled Disk 1 in the destination drive and then click OK.

11. Swap disks as prompted.

Follow these steps to install client software at a DOS or Windows 3.1 workstation:

1. Identify the make and model of the workstation's NIC. You also need to know the card's IRQ and I/O port settings.

2. Insert the Windows NT Server DOS Client Setup Disk 1 in the workstation's floppy drive. At the DOS command prompt, type **A:SETUP** (or **B:SETUP**, if appropriate) and press Enter.

3. You will see a typical Microsoft character mode setup screen. Press Enter to proceed.

4. The default directory for installation of the client software is C:\NET. Either accept this default or change it as desired. You cannot install the software in the Windows directory of a Windows 3.1 workstation.

5. The network drivers use memory on the client. Allocating more memory to the drivers can improve performance, but leaves less memory for other applications. At this point, a dialog box enables you to press Enter to maximize performance; press C to conserve memory.

6. Enter a computer name of up to 15 characters consisting of letters, numbers and/or the special characters: {, }, !, #, $, %, ^, &, (,), _, ', and ~. The name must be unique: it cannot match any other computer name or domain name in the network.

7. The main setup menu appears (see Figure 5.8). Choose Change Names to set the user name, workgroup name, and domain name. Enter the appropriate names, and select The Listed Names Are Correct to return to the main setup menu.

FIG. 5.8

The Network Client main setup menu enables you to set up a client workstation from a DOS prompt.

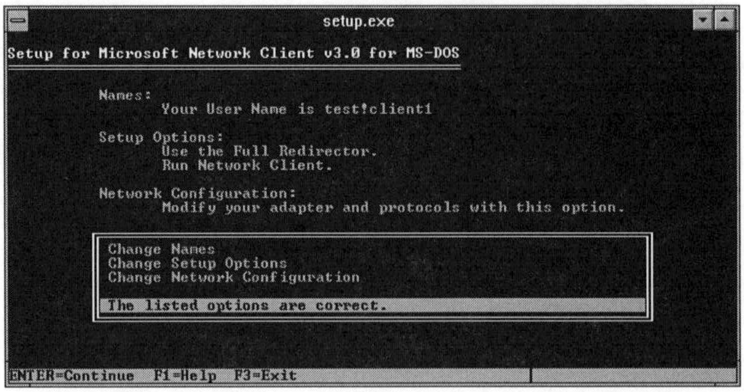

8. Choose Change Setup Options. The Network Client Setup Options screen appears, as shown in Figure 5.9.

FIG. 5.9

The Network Client main setup options screen facilitates a client workstation installation.

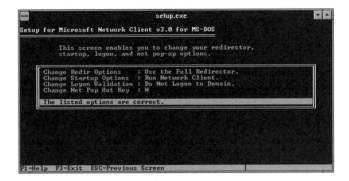

9. Select the Full Redirector or Basic Redirector. The Full Redirector is required for Windows or for dial-in networking. In most other cases, the Basic Redirector is adequate and uses less memory.

10. Decide whether to run the network client and the Net Pop-Up utility at system startup. If you run the network client, you can also decide whether to log on to a domain during startup. If you choose to load the Net Pop-Up, you can change the default hotkey (Alt+N) to another letter. For most users, you will probably want to run the network client, but not the pop-up (which, of course, consumes additional memory), and log on to a domain.

11. Select The Listed Options Are Correct to return to the main setup menu.

12. Choose Change Network Configuration to configure the network adapter and protocols. The Network Client screen appears (see Figure 5.10).

FIG. 5.10

The Network Client screen enables you to specify the network adapter and protocol for the client being installed.

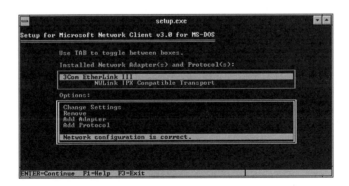

13. Select the correct network adapter for the workstation in the Installed Network Adapters box. Then select Change Settings in the Options box.

14. Verify that the Driver, Interrupt, and I/O settings are correct. Change incorrect settings. Select The Listed Options Are Correct to return to the Network Client screen. Repeat steps 13 and 14 for each network adapter.

15. Use the Tab key to switch between the Protocols box and the Options box. Set up the network protocols appropriate for your network.

16. Select Network Configuration Is Correct to return to the Network Client main setup menu. Choose The Listed Options Are Correct.

17. Remove the installation floppy disks and reboot the machine to activate the network client software.

After the client software is installed and activated, the NET command on the client workstation provides access to all network services. Running NET with no command options loads the Net Pop-Up program. The Net Pop-Up provides an intuitive interface for connecting to network drives and printers, but consumes memory.

The NET command also supports a number of command-line options that can be used in batch files. The following are a few of the options:

- NET LOGON logs a user on to the domain specified during setup. Username and password are optional parameters.

- NET LOGOFF logs the current user off.

- NET USE *<drive> <UNC path>* attaches to a shared drive on the network. For example, NET USE F: \\Moby\Users\Larry maps drive F to the shared directory Larry in the Users shared directory on Moby.

- NET USE *<port> <UNC path>* [/PERSISTENT:YES] attaches to a shared printer on the network. For example, NET USE LPT1: \\Moby\Laser1 /PERSISTENT:YES redirects the local printer to the shared printer Laser1 on Moby. The /PERSISTENT:YES option causes this device to be automatically reattached when the network client starts, and can be used with drives or printers.

- NET PASSWORD changes the user password.

- NET SEND sends a message to a user, domain, or all users on a server. Users must be running the messenger service (or WinPopup) to receive the message. To notify all users that a server will shut down in five minutes, for example, you might use NET SEND /USERS to send the message The server Moby will shut down in five minutes. Please log off. The /USERS option sends the message to all users logged on the server.

- NET HELP displays a summary of available options for the NET command. You can specify a particular option for more detailed information. For example, NET HELP USE displays information about NET USE.

Windows

To set up networking for Windows (versions 3.1 and later, excluding Windows for Workgroups), first complete the DOS setup described previously in this section and then follow these steps:

1. Start Windows.

2. Start the Windows Setup program (usually found in the Main program group).

3. Choose Options, Change System Settings to display the Change System Settings dialog box.

4. Drop down the Network list box. Select Microsoft Network (or 100% Compatible). Click OK.

5. Exit Windows Setup and restart Windows.

To use network drives, you can use the NET USE command from DOS as described earlier. You can also use File Manager to connect to network drives or Print Manager to connect to network printers.

Windows for Workgroups

Windows for Workgroups (WFW) is a network client right out of the box. Typically, you need to make only one small change to set up a WFW workstation as a client in a Windows NT Server domain, as follows:

1. Start WFW.

2. Start Control Panel. Double-click the Network icon. The Microsoft Windows Network dialog box appears.

3. Click the Startup button. The Startup Settings dialog box appears.

4. Under Options for Enterprise Networking, enable Log On to Windows NT or LAN Manager Domain. Enter the Domain Name. Click OK.

5. Click OK in the Microsoft Windows Network dialog box. Close the Control Panel.

6. Restart WFW.

TROUBLESHOOTING

A WFW workstation running only NetBEUI cannot communicate with a Windows NT Workstation running only NWLink. The primary network protocol in Windows NT Server 3.5 is NWLink, Microsoft's implementation of the IPX/SPX protocol used on Novell networks. The primary protocol in WFW is NetBEUI. When two nodes on a Microsoft network cannot communicate, a prevalent cause is the lack of a common protocol. To solve the problem, set up a common protocol by installing IPX/SPX on the WFW client or installing NetBEUI on the server.

Log on and off the network using the Logon/Logoff icon in the Network program group. Once logged on to a network, use WFW's File Manager to connect to network drives and use Print Manager to connect to network printers.

Windows 95

Microsoft designed Windows 95 as a network operating system from the ground up. Many of the most important networking features in this operating system will become apparent when Microsoft delivers network OLE. Until then, users can still appreciate the seamless access to network resources built into the Explorer shell.

To configure a Windows 95 workstation as a client for Windows NT Server, follow these steps:

1. Open Control Panel. Select the Network icon. The Network dialog box shown in Figure 5.11 appears.

FIG. 5.11
The Windows 95 Network dialog box facilitates configuration of a client workstation running Windows 95.

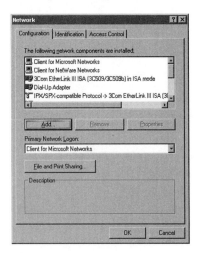

2. Double-click Client for Microsoft Networks. The Client for Microsoft Networks Properties dialog box appears (see Figure 5.12).

FIG. 5.12
The Client for Microsoft Networks Properties dialog box shows the general configurable property options.

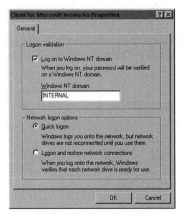

3. Check the Logon to Windows NT Domain check box. Enter the appropriate name for the Windows NT Domain.

4. Click OK. Click OK again in the Windows 95 Network dialog box. Close Control Panel.

5. You must restart the computer before the new setting takes effect.

The fastest way to connect to a network drive in Windows 95 is to right-click the Network Neighborhood icon from the desktop and select Map Network Drive from the pop-up menu. The Map Network Drive dialog box appears so that you can specify a drive letter and UNC share name. This dialog box does not have a Browse button, so you must know the exact UNC name of the resource. The dialog box remembers shares to which you have successfully connected in the past, and these shares can be displayed for selection by clicking the Path dropdown list box.

You can also access network resources by exploring the network neighborhood. To open a Word document on a server, for example, right-click Network Neighborhood and choose Explore from the pop-up menu. In Explorer, open Entire Network, the domain, the machine, and the share where the file resides, and then proceed down into the subdirectories until you can double-click the file. As depicted in Figure 5.13, for example, the Word document named REVIEW2.DOC can be opened simply by double-clicking it.

FIG. 5.13

Explorer can be used to open a network file.

Part

II

Ch

5

Windows 95 can use network printers in a couple of different ways. DOS programs print directly to a printer port, so Windows 95 must capture the printer port and redirect the output across the network. Windows and Windows 95 programs do not need to capture a printer port because they can print to any printer defined in the Printers utility. Follow these steps to set up a network printer for use in Windows 95:

1. Right-click the icon for Network Neighborhood and select Explore from the pop-up menu.

2. Browse until you find the printer you want to use. Then select that printer (see Figure 5.14).

3. Choose File, Install from the Network Neighborhood menu.

4. Follow instructions in the Printer Setup Wizard. You may need a copy of the printer driver.

FIG. 5.14
Selecting a network printer with Explorer is accomplished by finding the desired printer and clicking it.

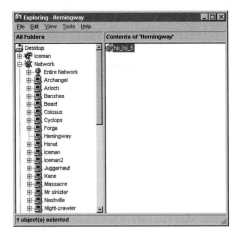

Windows NT Workstation

Not surprisingly, Windows NT is its own best network client. A Windows NT client can remotely administer a server using Server Manager (provided the user is an administrator). A system running Windows NT Server can be a primary domain controller (PDC), a backup domain controller (BDC), or just a server. Each domain has exactly one PDC that is responsible for maintaining the domain's user accounts database and processing domain logons. A BDC maintains an additional copy of the user database and assists with processing logons.

N O T E   A system running Windows NT Server can participate in a Microsoft network only as a member of a domain. A system running Windows NT Workstation can be a member of a workgroup or a member of a domain, but not both at the same time. ■

To map a network drive, choose Map Network Drive under the Tools option in Explorer and select the drive letter. You may also enter a network path for the connection. By default, you are connected using the username you logged in under. If you want to connect using a different account, enter the appropriate username within the Connect As dialog box. To add a network printer, select the My Computer icon on the desktop and open the Printers folder. Within this folder is an Add A Printer wizard application that will assist with installing and connecting to a network printer.

OS/2

To create a network client setup kit for OS/2 workstations, follow the earlier procedure for DOS clients, but in step 6, select LAN Manager 2.2c as the Network Client or Service. This setup kit requires four high-density floppy disks.

After creating the setup kit, insert the first floppy in drive A and run **A:SETUP**. See the Installation Guide supplied with the Windows NT Server software package for guidance on running the Setup program and procedures pertaining to OS/2.

Setting Up Auditing

A thorough security policy includes logging of security events. Different organizations will have different logging requirements, and Windows NT provides good flexibility. Auditing can impose a considerable performance penalty, so monitor only those activities required by your security policy.

Windows NT Server can monitor success and failure for each of the following security events:

■ **Logon and logoff**—Very useful information. Performance penalty usually minimal; depends on volume of logon requests processed by the server.

■ **File and object access**—File access can be audited only for files in NTFS partitions. Auditing for selected files must be enabled in File Manager. Auditing for selected printers must be enabled in Print Manager. Moderate to high performance penalty, depending on objects monitored.

■ **Use of user rights**—Generates mountains of extremely detailed access information. Very high performance penalty.

■ **User and group management**—Vital information. Negligible performance penalty.

■ **Security policy changes**—Vital information. Negligible performance penalty.

■ **Restart, shutdown, and system security**—Vital information. Negligible performance penalty.

■ **Process tracking**—Can be useful for troubleshooting. High performance penalty.

Follow these steps to enable auditing on a Windows NT Server domain:

1. Log on as an administrator.

2. Open the Administrative Tools program group. Double-click User Manager for Domains.

3. Choose User Manager, Policies, and select Audit. The Audit Policy dialog box appears. If the Do Not Audit option button is selected, the Audit These Events area of the dialog box will be grayed, as shown in Figure 5.15.

Part
II

Ch
5

FIG. 5.15
The Audit Policy dialog box is showing that no audit options are selected.

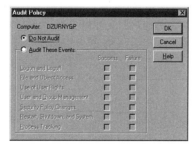

4. Select Audit These Events. Note that this area of the dialog box becomes available for use.

5. Select the list of events you want to audit. Figure 5.16 is a sample of what the Audit Policy dialog box should look like (with the possible exception of event selection) after you have completed this step.

FIG. 5.16

The Audit Policy dialog box allows selecting events to be audited.

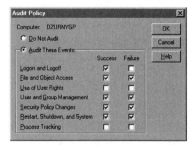

6. Click OK to return to User Manager. Choose User, Exit to close User Manager.

Files are usually the most sensitive network resources. Therefore, it is critical that access to certain files and directories be tightly controlled and managed. This ultimately requires that access be monitored from time to time to validate the effectiveness of management controls and access restrictions on selected files or directories. Auditing access can be a very useful capability when such monitoring needs to be done.

 The audit access can only be used on NTFS partitions.

Perform the following steps to audit access to a selected file or directory:

1. Enable File and Object Access auditing for the domain via the Audit Policy menu.
2. In My Computer or through Explorer, select the file or directory you want to audit.
3. Choose File, Properties.
4. Click the Security tab, and then click Auditing. The Directory Auditing dialog box appears (see Figure 5.17).
5. Set the level at which auditing changes will apply by doing one of the following:
   - To affect only the directory and its files, select Replace Auditing On Existing Files.
   - To affect the directory, its files, subdirectories, and subdirectory files, select both Replace Auditing On Subdirectories and Replace Auditing On Existing Files.
   - To affect only the directory (not the files, subdirectories, or subdirectory files), click to clear both Replace Auditing On Subdirectories and Replace Auditing On Existing Files.
   - To affect only the directory and subdirectories (not files in the directory or subdirectories), select Replace Auditing on Subdirectories and click to clear Replace Auditing on Existing Files.

FIG. 5.17
The Directory Auditing
dialog box is showing
the audit policy for the
selected group.

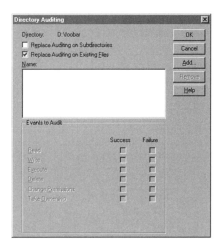

6. To add a user or group to Name, click Add and complete the Add Users and Groups dialog box.

7. Select one or more users or groups in Names.

8. Under Events to Audit, select Success, Failure, or both for each event you want to audit.

Checking the Logs

The Event Log Service is one of the most useful features of Windows NT Server. It provides a common method for capturing information about system startup, configuration errors, security events, and application events. Information captured here is a primary source for troubleshooting and monitoring performance.

Windows NT Server records a variety of events in its three Log files, as follows:

- **System Log**—Records system events, such as system startup, service startup failure, and browser elections. This log can be useful for troubleshooting.

- **Security Log**—Records events selected for auditing. Depending on the audits enabled. This log can grow quite rapidly.

- **Application Log**—Can be used by applications to record important events.

The Logs record five types of events:

- **Information events**—Marked by a letter *i* in a blue circle

- **Warning events**—Marked by an exclamation point in a yellow circle

- **Critical errors**—Marked by a stop sign icon

- **Success audits**—Marked by a key icon

- **Failure audits**—Marked by a padlock icon

The Event Log Service starts automatically at system startup. In the next two sections, learn to view logged events and manage the log files.

Viewing Event Logs

To view a log, Log on as an administrator, and run Event Viewer from the Administrative Tools group. From the Log menu, select the Log you want to view. Figure 5.18 is a view of a System Log.

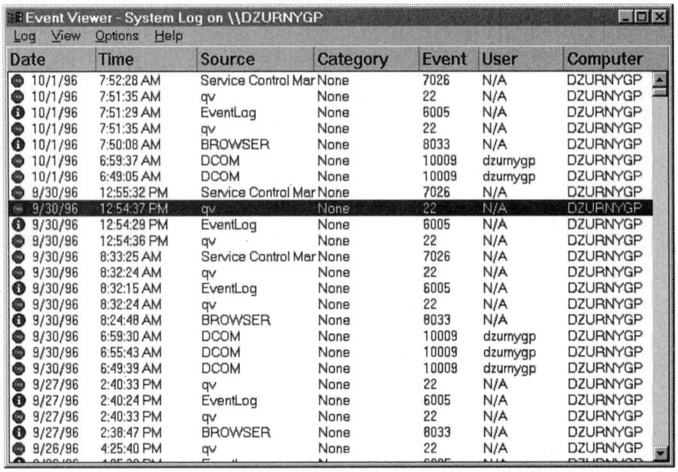

FIG. 5.18
The Event Viewer window is showing detailed audit information for system events.

The Event Viewer displays the date and time and five information columns for each event, as explained in the following table:

Column	Description
Source	Identifies the process that logged the event.
Category	A classification of the event as defined by the source. Applies mainly to the Security Log.
Event	A numeric identifier referring to the source.
User	Identifies the user account under which the event occurred.
Computer	Identifies the computer where the event occurred.

To view additional details for an event, double-click the event. You see the Event Detail dialog box, as shown in Figure 5.19.

In addition to the information from the list view, the detail view presents a description of the event and can include additional data, such as a stack dump.

FIG. 5.19

The Event Detail dialog box provides more information about a selected log event.

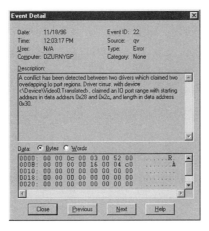

Managing Event Logs

By default, Windows NT Server allocates 512K bytes for each log and overwrites events older than seven days. Each of these parameters can be configured independently for each log. When it's important to save log data for future reference, the overwrite delay should reflect your archiving schedule (seven days with weekly archiving, for example). Perform the following steps to configure these options:

1. Log on as administrator. Start Event Viewer from the Administrative Tools group.

2. Choose Event Viewer, Log, and select Log Settings. The Event Log Settings dialog box appears, as shown in Figure 5.20.

Part

II

Ch

5

FIG. 5.20

The Event Log Settings dialog box enables you to customize the logging of each event type.

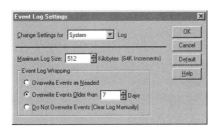

3. Select the Log you want to configure in the Change Settings For Log drop-down list.

4. Set the Maximum Log Size.

5. Configure Event Log Wrapping by choosing particular options. Overwrite Events as Needed grows the log to its maximum size and then overwrites the oldest events with new events. Do Not Overwrite Events retains all log entries so that you must manually purge the log. You might use this option for a sensitive security log, but make sure that the allocated size is adequate.

Logs can be saved (archived) for future reference so that space allocated for the logs can be made available for other uses. Logs can be saved in one of the three following formats:

- **Native log file format (EVT)**—This format can be loaded and viewed later with Event Viewer.
- **Text format (TXT)**—This format can be viewed with a standard text editor browser.
- **Comma delimited text (TXT)**—This format can be imported into other applications.

To save a log, follow these steps:

1. Log on as administrator. Start Event Viewer from the Administrative Tools group.
2. Choose Event Viewer, Log, and select Save As. You see the Windows common file dialog box.
3. Select the format in which to save the file from the Save File as Type drop-down list.
4. Specify the directory and file name in which to save the file. Click the OK button.

To clear a log, choose Event Viewer, Log, and select Clear All Events. Be sure to select the correct log first! Event Viewer asks if you want to save the file first and then warns you that clearing the log is irreversible.

From Here...

This chapter taught you how to install your Windows NT Server. Your server acumen now includes concepts such as system requirements, features new to NT, audit logs, and emergency repair disks. You learned how to connect to the server from a workstation under a variety of operating systems. For more information on the subjects discussed in this chapter, refer to the following chapters:

- To review the goals and strategies of using the suite of BackOffice products, see Chapter 2, "Characteristics of BackOffice."
- To review the role the server will play in your organization, see Chapter 4, "Enterprise Planning and Implementation."
- For information on the day-to-day duties of the network administrator, see Chapter 7, "Administering Windows NT Server."
- To learn about installing, configuring, and using the Remote Access Service, see Chapter 12, "Implementing Remote Access Service (RAS)."
- For information on configuring and using Internet Information Server (IIS), see Chapter 18, "Building A Web With Internet Information Server (IIS)."

## CHAPTER 6

Advanced Windows NT Server Configuration

by Larry Millett

Windows NT Server provides a variety of configuration options to maximize reliability and performance. These include the following:

- Restart options control server restart in the event of a system crash.

- Virtual memory configuration enables you to tune server performance for specific applications.

- Disk Administrator enables you to maximize disk subsystem performance and fault tolerance.

This chapter begins with a discussion of automatic restart options and reviews virtual memory settings. The rest of the chapter puts Disk Administrator through its paces, from basic concepts through redundant arrays of inexpensive drives (RAID). After reading this chapter, you will understand how to configure Windows NT Server for fault tolerance and high performance. ■

System recovery

Software problems may cause NT Server to close all programs and stop the server. Learn to automate Windows NT's response and recovery in the event of a system stop error.

Virtual memory

NT Server uses a scheme called virtual memory to simulate physical memory with disk space. Find out how to configure the size and location of memory swap files.

Disk Administrator

NT's Disk Administrator is a graphical tool for all disk management tasks. Use Disk Administrator to create and format partitions and logical drives, and for more advanced tasks.

Redundant Arrays of Inexpensive Drives (RAID)

Windows NT provides software implementations of RAID level 0 (stripe set) for improved hard disk performance, RAID level 1 (disk mirroring) to recover from a system partition failure, and RAID level 5 (stripe sets with parity) for fault tolerance with high performance and efficient use of disk space.

Configuring Recovery Options

Certain system errors, known as *stop errors,* cause Windows NT Server to stop all processes and shut down. Windows NT Server can perform several optional actions in the event of a stop error, including alerts to system administrators, core dump, and automatic restart.

To configure recovery options for Windows NT Server, perform the following steps:

1. Open Control Panel. Double-click the System icon.

 T I P   For quick access to the System Properties dialog box, right-click the My Computer icon and select Properties from the pop-up menu.

2. Select the Startup/Shutdown tab in the System Properties dialog box, as shown in Figure 6.1.

FIG. 6.1

Configure system recovery options using the Startup/Shutdown property sheet of the System Properties dialog box.

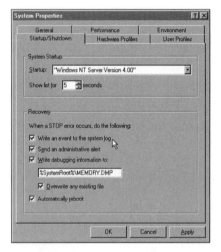

3. Enable the option to Write an Event to the Administrative log. Windows NT Server will record an event describing the stop error in the administrative log where it can be viewed later with Event Viewer.

4. Enable the option to Send an Administrative Alert, if desired. This option will send an alert to specified users.

N O T E   The administrative alert function requires the Windows NT Alerter service. ▨

▶ **See** "Setting and Responding to Alerts," **p. 209**

5. If desired, specify a location to Write Debugging Information To. This causes the contents of RAM to be written to the file you specify (affectionately known as a core

dump). The default file is %SystemRoot%\MEMORY.DMP, where %SystemRoot% is an alias for the Windows NT Server system directory (typically C:\Windows\System32). You can specify whether to Overwrite an existing file.

N O T E The Write debugging information option (when enabled) requires a paging file on the system partition at least as large as the amount of physical memory. When a stop error occurs, Windows NT Server writes the contents of memory to this paging file. When the system restarts, Windows NT Server copies the core dump from the paging file to the specified debugging file before initializing the paging file. ▪

6. Enable the option to Automatically Reboot. This will bring the server back up immediately without intervention by an administrator. However, a recurring stop error will put the server into a shutdown/restart loop, which will require intervention by an administrator.

N O T E For dual boot systems, the Startup section specifies the default operating system (OS) and the delay during boot up when you can select a different OS. The options reflect the contents of BOOT.INI.

When automatic reboot is enabled, the default OS should be Windows NT Server. ▪

Configuring Virtual Memory

Windows NT Server provides a separate 4G logical address space for each application. This means that each program can run as if it were the only program running on a computer with 4G of physical memory. Very few servers have 4G of memory installed. Windows NT Server uses a strategy called *virtual memory* to swap idle portions of a program to and from a hard disk. The total physical memory plus the total size of all swap files determine the total virtual memory available on a server. For example, a server might have 256M of physical memory, and 256M of hard disk space set aside for a total 512M virtual memory. Although this is substantially less than 4G, it's enough for some very heavy duty computing.

Disk swapping can slow down Windows NT Server substantially, so it's best to have plenty of physical memory. On the other hand, reduced performance is better than an out of memory error.

Windows NT Server enables you to specify minimum and maximum sizes for memory swap files, and allows a separate swap file on each physical disk. The OS will dynamically vary the size of the swap files within the specified range. For best performance, Microsoft recommends setting up a separate paging file on each disk.

To configure virtual memory for Windows NT Server, follow these steps (this procedure requires a system restart):

1. Right-click the My Computer icon. Select Properties from the pop-up menu.
2. Select the Performance tab in the System Properties dialog box, as shown in Figure 6.2.

Part
II

Ch
6

FIG. 6.2

Configure virtual
memory at the
Performance tab of the
Windows NT Server 4.0
System Properties
dialog box.

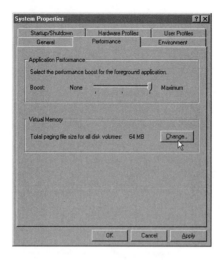

3. Click the Change button in the Virtual Memory section of the dialog box. The Virtual
   Memory dialog box appears (see Figure 6.3).

FIG. 6.3

Set the size and
location of swap files
with the Windows NT
Server 4.0 Virtual
Memory dialog box.

4. The Drive list box shows a list of available volumes and the size of any existing paging
   files on each. To change the size of an existing paging file, or to create a new paging file,
   select the appropriate volume from the Drive list box.

5. Specify an Initial Size and a Maximum Size (in megabytes) for the paging file on the
   selected volume. Click Set to establish the new paging file.

6. The dialog box section labeled Total Paging File Size for All Drives shows minimum size
   (2M), the recommended total size, and the currently allocated total size of all paging
   files.

7. Specify a Maximum Registry Size larger than the current registry size. This sets an upper limit on growth of the Windows NT registry files. These files tend to grow slowly, except when software is first installed on a new server.

8. Click OK to close the dialog box and immediately apply the changes specified.

NOTE The Application Performance setting controls the relative priority of foreground tasks over background tasks in Windows NT Server. Typically, nobody uses a server as a workstation, so it makes little sense to boost foreground performance. For a dedicated server that provides a particular application service (such as SQL Server), foreground performance should be boosted. ▓

Configuring Hard Disk Space

Windows NT Server provides a range of options for configuring disk space. Determine your needs based on three factors: performance, fault tolerance, and efficient use of disk space. For best performance, use a stripe set without parity. For fault tolerance, use a stripe set with parity (better read performance) or a mirror set (better write performance). For the most efficient use of disk space, Windows NT Server 4.0 supports file compression.

> **CAUTION**
>
> You should create an updated emergency repair disk (ERD) after any disk configuration changes.

▶ **See** "Creating an Updated Emergency Repair Disk," **p. 135**

Windows NT Server's Disk Administrator tool makes it easy to get the most from your hard disk subsystem. This tool provides a graphical interface for a variety of functions, as follows:

- ▓ Creating primary and extended partitions
- ▓ Formatting volumes
- ▓ Combining several partitions into a volume set
- ▓ Creating mirror sets for fault tolerance (RAID level 1)
- ▓ Creating stripe sets for improved performance (RAID level 0)
- ▓ Creating stripe sets with parity for fault tolerance (RAID level 5)

NOTE Disk Administrator offers two distinct views of your disk subsystem: the Volumes view and the Disk Configuration view. You can select either view from the View menu. The Volumes view is useful if you have many volumes; otherwise, the Disk Configuration view is kinder and gentler. Instructions in this chapter assume the Disk Configuration view. ▓

Part
II

Ch
6

Disks, Partitions, Volumes, and Free Space

To use Disk Administrator effectively, you must first understand a few basic concepts. A *disk* is a physical hard drive. Windows NT Server does not allow you to work with smaller physical units (platters, heads, cylinders, tracks, or segments). A *partition* is a portion of a disk that the OS treats as an independent logical device. A partition can be *primary* or *extended*. An extended partition can be further subdivided; a primary partition cannot. A primary partition can be formatted, but an extended partition must have additional structures defined before formatting. Each disk can have up to four partitions; only one can be an extended partition.

N O T E   MS-DOS and Windows 95 support only one primary partition per disk. If you create more than one primary partition on a disk, Disk Administrator warns you that the new partition will be inaccessible from MS-DOS or Windows 95.

In order to dual boot Windows NT Server and MS-DOS or Windows 95, the first primary partition on the first physical disk (disk 0) must be large enough to contain all shared files. This shared partition must not be compressed. ▪

Windows NT Server defines two important partitions: *system* and *boot*. The naming is counter-intuitive: the system partition contains platform-specific files necessary to boot Windows NT Server, and the boot partition contains Windows NT Server system files. The system partition must be a primary partition on the first physical disk (disk 0). The boot partition can be the same as the system partition (recommended) or can be separate. Neither the system partition nor the boot partition can be part of a volume set or a stripe set. Disk Administrator cannot modify the system partition.

A *logical drive* is a portion of disk space in an extended partition that can be formatted with a file system. An extended partition might contain several logical drives, no logical drives, or portions of many logical drives. The term *logical drive* never refers to a formatted primary partition.

N O T E   By default, Windows NT Server assigns a drive letter to each primary partition, CD-ROM drive, and logical drive. Disk Administrator can assign drive letters permanently and arbitrarily: Right-click the volume and select Assign Drive Letter from the pop-up menu. Use this feature to add new logical drives and primary partitions without disrupting existing configurations and scripts. ▪

A *volume* is a formatted primary partition or logical drive. *Free space* is hard disk space not assigned to a logical drive or primary partition. It includes unpartitioned space and space in extended partitions not yet assigned to a logical drive.

Creating a Primary Partition

The first partition on the first hard disk must be a primary partition. This partition stores the Windows NT Server startup and system files. If no such partition exists, Windows NT Server creates one automatically during installation. Each disk can contain up to four partitions, but MS-DOS and Windows 95 can access only the first primary partition on a disk.

TIP A primary partition is designed to contain startup files for an operating system; extended partitions offer substantially more flexibility.

Follow these steps to create a primary partition with Disk Administrator:

1. Log on as an administrator. Start Disk Administrator from the Administrative Tools folder. The Disk Administrator main window appears, as shown in Figure 6.4.

FIG. 6.4

Most disk management tasks begin at the Disk Administrator main window.

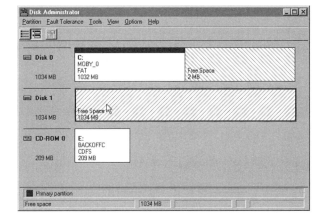

2. Click an area of free space in which to create an extended partition. Make sure that the free space you select is not part of an extended partition.

N O T E Disk Administrator marks free space with diagonal lines. If the lines run upward from left to right, the free space is unpartitioned. If the lines run upward from right to left, the free space is part of an extended partition. ■

3. Right-click the selected free space and select Create from the pop-up menu. If this is not the first primary partition on the disk, you will see a warning that the new partition is not accessible from MS-DOS. Click OK to close the message box.

4. You will see the Create Primary Partition dialog box depicted in Figure 6.5. Specify a size for the new partition and click OK.

Part

II

Ch

6

FIG. 6.5

Specify the size of a new primary partition with the Create Primary Partition dialog box.

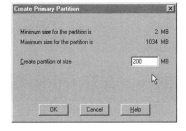

5. Select Partition, Commit Changes Now from the Disk Administrator main menu. When you see a Confirm message box, click Yes to confirm that you want to update your disk configuration and acknowledge the message box advising you to update your ERD.

N O T E   Disk Administrator does not update your hard disk until you commit partition changes. If you exit before committing changes, Disk Administrator will remind you (but not force you) to commit changes before exiting.

Unlike the MS-DOS or Windows 95, Windows NT does not require a system restart after modifying partitions. ■

6. The new primary partition must be formatted before use. See "Formatting Logical Drives and Primary Partitions" later in this chapter.

Creating an Extended Partition

An extended partition provides the best flexibility for configuring Windows NT Server disk space. Windows NT can subdivide an extended partition into many logical drives, while a primary partition can contain only a single volume. Unlike a primary partition, an extended partition can span multiple disks and grow over time.

Follow these steps to create an extended partition with Disk Administrator:

1. Log on as an administrator. Start Disk Administrator from the Administrative Tools folder. You see the Disk Administrator main window (refer to Figure 6.4).

2. Right-click an area of unpartitioned free space in which to create an extended partition. Select Create Extended from the pop-up menu shown in Figure 6.6.

FIG. 6.6

Select Create Extended from the pop-up menu, or choose Partition, Create Extended from the Disk Administrator main menu.

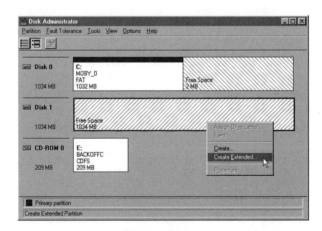

3. You will see a Create Extended Partition dialog box similar to that in Figure 6.7. Specify a size for the new partition and click OK. Usually, you will want to include all available free space in the extended partition.

FIG. 6.7

Specify the size for a new extended partition using the Create Extended Partition dialog box.

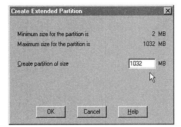

4. Select Partition, Commit Changes Now from the Disk Administrator main menu. When you see a Confirm message box, click Yes to confirm that you want to update your disk configuration and acknowledge the message box advising you to update your ERD.

Creating a Logical Drive on an Extended Partition

The simplest way to use an extended partition is to create a logical drive. A logical drive can be formatted and used just like a primary partition, except that it cannot be the Windows NT system partition.

Follow these steps to create a logical drive on an extended partition:

1. Log on as an administrator. Start Disk Administrator from the Administrative Tools folder. You see the Disk Administrator main window (refer to Figure 6.4).

2. Right-click an extended partition on which to create a logical drive. Select Create from the pop-up menu, as shown in Figure 6.8.

FIG. 6.8

Select Create from the pop-up menu, or choose Partition, Create from the Disk Administrator main menu, to create a new logical drive.

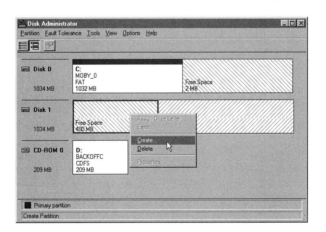

Part

II

Ch

6

3. You will see a Create Logical Drive dialog box similar to that in Figure 6.9. Specify a size for the new partition and click OK. Usually, you will want to include all available free space in the extended partition.

FIG. 6.9

Specify the size of a new logical drive using the Create Logical Drive dialog box.

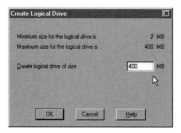

4. Right-click the new logical drive and select Commit Changes Now from the pop-up menu. When you see a Confirm message box, click Yes to confirm that you want to update your disk configuration and acknowledge the message box advising you to update your ERD.

5. The new logical drive must be formatted before use, which is described in the following section.

Formatting Logical Drives and Primary Partitions

Newly created primary partitions and logical drives must be formatted before they can be used. Formatting installs and initializes a file system on the selected disk space. File system choices include File Allocation Table (FAT) or Windows NT File System (NTFS). Only NTFS supports Windows NT Server's advanced security features.

N O T E   Prior versions of Windows NT Server supported the OS/2 High Performance File System (HPFS); version 4.0 drops support for HPFS. ▓

Follow these steps to format a logical drive or primary partition using Disk Administrator:

1. Log on as an administrator. Start Disk Administrator from the Administrative Tools folder. You see the Disk Administrator main window (refer to Figure 6.4).

2. Right-click the primary partition or logical drive you want to format. Select Format from the pop-up menu, as shown in Figure 6.10.

FIG. 6.10

Select Format from the pop-up menu, or choose Tools, Format from the Disk Administrator main menu.

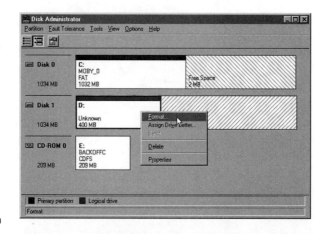

3. You will see a Format dialog box similar to that shown in Figure 6.11.

FIG. 6.11

Specify format options, including file system and allocation unit size, with the Windows NT Server 4.0 Format dialog box.

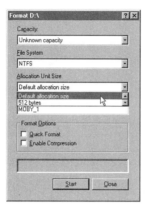

4. Select the File Allocation Table (FAT) file system or the Windows NT File System (NTFS). For best performance, use NTFS wherever possible. Specify a volume label, if desired.

N O T E The Format dialog box includes several other options beyond the file system and volume label. The Capacity setting is useful only for floppy disks. Use the default Allocation Unit Size except in rare instances; if you need a small drive to contain the maximum possible number of very small files (less than 2K), use 512 byte allocation units. The Quick Format option (not available for mirror sets or stripe sets with parity) initializes the file system without scanning the volume for errors. Enable Compression initializes the root directory as a compressed directory so that all new files and folders added to the volume are compressed by default. Compression can be easily enabled or disabled at any time without reformatting. ▪

5. After selecting format options, click OK. Disk Administrator warns you that formatting will destroy the current contents of the volume. Acknowledge the warning and continue. A bar graph shows progress (percentage complete) as the format proceeds.

6. When the formatting is complete, close the Format dialog box. The Disk Administrator main window now shows the volume formatted with the specified file system and volume label.

Implementing Volume Sets

A *volume set* joins two or more areas of free space into a single logical drive. You could use a volume set, for example, to create a single 4G logical drive spanning four 1G disks. A volume set can span up to 32 physical disks, and, once formatted, functions as a single volume.

You can also create a volume set by *extending* an existing volume. Extending appends free space to an existing volume or volume set, a useful way to bring new disk space online. Only volumes formatted with NTFS can be extended; stripe sets, mirror sets, and the system partition can never be extended.

Part
II

Ch
6

> **CAUTION**
>
> If any one disk used by a volume set fails, all data on the volume set will be lost. The likelihood of such a failure increases with the number of disks spanned by a volume set. A logical drive implemented as a volume set spanning four disks is four times as likely to fail as a logical drive residing on a single disk.
>
> A stripe set with parity creates a fault tolerant volume spanning multiple disks, but with less efficient use of disk space.

Creating a Volume Set   Follow these steps to create a volume set (requires a system restart):

1. Log on as an administrator. Start Disk Administrator from the Administrative Tools program group. The Disk Administrator main window appears (refer to Figure 6.4).

2. Hold down Ctrl and click each area of free space to include in the volume set (at least two).

3. Right-click one of the selected areas of free space and select Create Volume Set from the pop-up menu. The Create Volume Set dialog box appears similar to that in Figure 6.12.

FIG. 6.12

Specify the size of a new volume set using the Create Volume Set dialog box.

4. Specify the desired size for the new volume set. Click OK.

5. Right-click any disk and select Partition, Commit Changes Now from the Disk Administrator main menu. When you see a Confirm message box, click Yes to confirm that you want to update your disk configuration. Disk Administrator warns that the system must be restarted. Click Yes to restart the system. Acknowledge the message box advising you to update your ERD.

6. The new logical drive must be formatted before use.

Extending a Volume   Windows NT Server can extend an NTFS formatted volume onto free space on any disk. This results in a larger volume, which can be a useful way to bring new disk space online. Volume sets can grow larger, but never smaller.

Follow these steps to extend an NTFS formatted volume (requires a system restart):

1. Log on as an administrator and start Disk Administrator. The Disk Administrator main window appears (refer to Figure 6.4).

2. Click the volume you want to extend (must be formatted with NTFS). Hold down Ctrl and click one or more areas of free space.

3. Right-click the selected area of free space and select Ex_tend Volume Set from the pop-up menu. You will see the Extend Volume Set dialog box, as shown in Figure 6.13.

FIG. 6.13
Use the Extend Volume dialog box to specify the new size for the extended volume set.

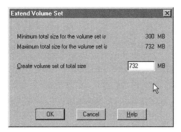

4. Specify the desired size for the extended volume set. Click OK.

5. Select _Partition, C_ommit Changes Now from the Disk Administrator main menu. When you see a Confirm message box, click Yes to confirm that you want to update your disk configuration and acknowledge the message box advising you to update your ERD.

6. Disk Administrator quickly formats the new extension (during which the mouse pointer appears as an hourglass), and prompts you to restart the system.

Software RAID

Windows NT Server provides software support for RAID level 0 (stripe sets), RAID level 1 (mirroring), and RAID level 5 (stripe sets with parity) using ordinary hard disks. RAID became popular in the late 1980s as an alternative to the single large expensive drive (SLED). Beyond the obvious economic disadvantage, a SLED represented a single point of failure for a computer system. RAID provides improved fault tolerance and improved performance. Combining individually unreliable components of mediocre performance into a highly reliable high performance system is a hallmark of engineering excellence.

 For best performance with RAID, use identical disks.

Many vendors offer hardware RAID subsystems with carefully matched and tuned disks and controllers. These subsystems generally outperform the software implementation in Windows NT Server, but also cost substantially more. When using hardware RAID, follow the manufacturer's instructions for managing RAID volume sets. The procedures outlined in this section apply only to RAID sets implemented through NT's software support.

N O T E Although Windows NT Server supports stripe sets and stripe sets with parity for IDE drives, SCSI is a far better choice for a high performance server. The IDE specification provides for only two controllers in a computer and only two drives per controller. Windows NT supports up to four SCSI controllers with up to seven devices on each controller. High performance SCSI controllers support parallel writes to multiple drives or direct writes from one drive to another (via DMA), as well as a much higher base bandwidth. ▪

RAID level 0 provides maximum performance, at the expense of reliability. RAID level 1 and RAID level 5 provide fault tolerance. On most servers, it makes sense to mirror the system partition. A stripe set with parity makes sense for critical online data (such as a SQL Server database).

RAID Level 1: Disk Mirroring

Disk mirroring provides protection against hard disk failure by maintaining an exact copy of a partition on a separate physical drive. If one drive in a mirror set fails, no data will be lost. Disk striping with parity offers a similar degree of fault tolerance; however, mirroring is the only fault tolerance option available for the system partition.

> **CAUTION**
>
> Establishing a mirror for the system partition makes it impossible to dual boot MS-DOS or Windows 95.

 When one component of a mirror set fails, it can be replaced without loss of data. This process (described in the following section) is *much* simpler when the disks containing the mirror contain no other partitions.

For best performance and simplest maintenance, a mirror set should consist of a single partition, including all space on one disk mirrored onto an identical disk.

Establishing a Mirror Set   Follow these steps to establish a mirror set (requires a system restart):

1. Log on as an administrator. Start Disk Administrator from the Administrative Tools folder. You see the Disk Administrator main window (refer to Figure 6.4).

2. Select the partition you want to mirror. Hold down Ctrl and select an equal or larger area of free space on a different disk.

3. Right-click the selected free space and select Establish Mirror from the pop-up menu, as shown in Figure 6.14. If creating a mirror for the Windows NT Server system partition, a message box will advise you to create a fault tolerant boot disk. (This procedure is described in the following section.)

4. Select Partition, Commit Changes Now from the Disk Administrator main menu. Disk Administrator warns that the system must be restarted. Click Yes to confirm and restart the system.

5. After restarting, the new mirror set initializes. This degrades performance temporarily (from a few minutes to several hours, depending on the size of the mirror set) while data replicates.

After creating a new mirror, or if the volumes should get out of synch, Windows NT Server synchronizes the volumes. While synchronization proceeds, Disk Administrator shows the volume description in red text. Once synchronization completes, the volume description reverts to black text.

FIG. 6.14
Select Establish Mirror from the pop-up menu, or choose Fault Tolerance, Establish Mirror from the Disk Administrator main menu.

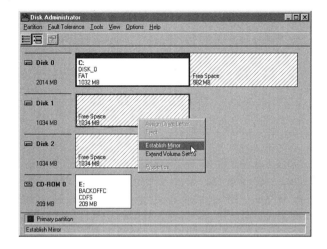

When a component of a mirror set is selected, Disk Administrator shows the status of the mirror set in the status bar (lower-left corner), as shown in Figure 6.15.

FIG. 6.15
Disk Administrator's status bar shows that the mirror set is initializing.

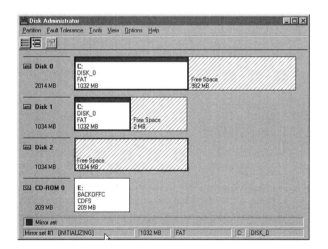

Creating a Fault Tolerant Boot Disk To boot the server after a failure of the disk containing the system partition, you need a fault tolerant boot disk. This disk enables you to start the server from the mirror disk rather than the primary. The boot disk contains an edited version of BOOT.INI identifying the mirror of the system partition as the boot partition. Editing BOOT.INI requires an understanding of the Advanced RISC Computer (ARC) naming convention used in BOOT.INI to identify the system partition. Read the following sidebar "Understanding ARC Names" before creating the fault tolerant boot floppy.

Understanding ARC Names

ARC names uniquely identify a disk partition within a computer. The ARC name includes four parts, identifying the disk controller, the bus, the disk, and the primary partition. An ARC name for the first primary partition on the first disk on the first (only) bus on the first IDE or ESDI controller would look like this:

`multi(0)disk(0)rdisk(0)partition(0)`

The following is a brief discussion of each component of an ARC name:

- **multi(i) or scsi(i)**—This entry identifies a hard disk controller. The entry is `scsi(i)` for SCSI adapters with no BIOS, `multi(i)` otherwise. The i selects a specific controller when the computer contains more than one; for the first controller, i will be 0.

- **disk(j)**—For controllers identified as `scsi(i)`, `disk(j)` specifies the SCSI address of the device. Devices on a SCSI bus are numbered from 0 to 7 (0 to 15 for wide SCSI); 7 is always reserved for the controller. For controllers identified as `multi(i)`, this entry is always `disk(0)`.

- **rdisk(k)**—For IDE or ESDI controllers identified as `multi(i)`, this entry is `rdisk(0)` for the master drive or `rdisk(1)` for the slave drive. For SCSI adapters with BIOS, this entry specifies the SCSI address of the device. For controllers identified as `scsi(i)`, this entry is always `rdisk(0)`.

- **partition(m)**—This entry identifies a partition on a hard disk. Unlike other entries, numbering starts at 1 for the first partition.

The ARC name for the first partition on the master drive on the first IDE controller is as follows:

`multi(0)disk(0)rdisk(0)partition(1)`

Follow these steps to create a fault tolerant boot disk:

1. Format a floppy disk using Windows NT Explorer, Windows NT File Manager, or the Windows NT command line.

2. Copy the following files from the server's boot partition to the floppy disk:
   - `BOOT.INI`
   - `NTLDR`
   - `NTDETECT.COM`
   - `NTBOOTDD.SYS` (if present)

3. Determine the ARC name for the partition that mirrors the system partition (see the sidebar "Understanding ARC Names").

4. Disable the read-only property of `BOOT.INI` on the floppy disk, and edit the file.

5. Replace the ARC names associated with Windows NT Server Version 4.00 and Windows NT Server Version 4.00 [VGA Mode] with the ARC name from step 3. Be sure to change all references in both the [boot loader] and [operating systems] sections of `BOOT.INI`.

6. Save BOOT.INI and close the editor. Re-enable the read-only property of BOOT.INI.

7. Test the new fault tolerant boot disk (see the following sidebar "Testing the Fault Tolerant Boot Disk").

8. Write protect the disk and label it clearly. The label should indicate that the disk is to be used *only* to recover from system partition failure and *only* on the machine where it was created. Store the disk in a safe place.

Testing the Fault Tolerant Boot Disk

The worst time to find that a fault tolerant boot disk doesn't work is after a system partition crash. Take time to test the boot disk right after creating it.

The best way to test is to simulate failure of the disk containing the system partition (replace it, for example, with an unformatted drive) and boot from the disk. If the system boots correctly, the fault tolerant boot disk is good to go. Remount the original disk containing the system partition, label and write-protect the boot disk, and save it in a safe place.

If you simply boot from the disk, without simulating system partition failure, one of two things will happen:

- If BOOT.INI contains an incorrect ARC name, the boot process will be unable to find NTOSKRNL and will halt before displaying the familiar blue text mode startup screen. This indicates that the fault tolerant boot disk is not working.

- If the ARC name is correct, NTOSKRNL will load (you will see the blue text mode startup screen), but the boot will stop with a blue screen full of debug information. This indicates that the fault tolerant boot disk is working. Label and write-protect the disk, and save it in a safe place.

If the boot disk does not seem to be working, you may just need to modify BOOT.INI. If it still doesn't work, reformat the disk and carefully follow the procedure outlined in this section for creating a fault tolerant boot disk.

Breaking a Mirror Set   Breaking a mirror separates the mirror set into two independent partitions. This procedure is required to recover from failure of one partition in a mirror set. Also, if fault tolerance provided by the mirror set is no longer needed, breaking the mirror will free the disk space used for mirroring. Once broken, NT cannot re-establish the mirror (although you can create a new mirror set using the same components).

Follow these steps to break a mirror set (requires a system restart):

1. Log on as an administrator. Start Disk Administrator from the Administrative Tools program group. The Disk Administrator main window appears (refer to Figure 6.4).

2. Right-click one member of the mirror set. Choose Break Mirror from the pop-up menu (see Figure 6.16).

Part

II

Ch

6

FIG. 6.16

Select Break Mirror from the pop-up menu, or choose Fault Tolerance, Break Mirror from the Disk Administrator main menu.

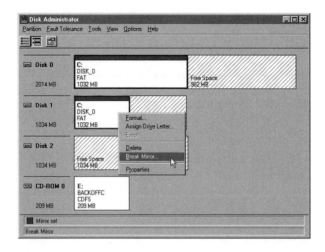

> **CAUTION**
>
> Do not select Delete from the pop-up menu. This will delete the *entire* mirror set.

3. Disk Administrator asks you to confirm that you want to break the mirror set into two independent partitions. Click Yes.

4. You may see a message box warning that the system partition (typically C:) cannot be locked, as shown in Figure 6.17. Click Yes.

FIG. 6.17

The message box indicating that System partition cannot be locked is only a warning.

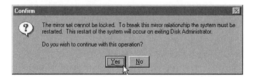

5. Select Partition, Commit Changes Now from the Disk Administrator main menu. Disk Administrator warns that the system must be restarted. Click Yes to confirm and restart the system.

Repairing a Mirror Set When one partition in a mirror set fails, the system continues to operate. Unless you have configured an administrative alert for disk failures, you might not notice the failure until the next time you start Disk Administrator or (if the system partition fails) restart the server. Even though the system continues to run, however, the data previously protected by the mirror is now at risk. A broken mirror must be repaired as soon as possible to minimize risk of data loss.

Repairing a mirror set is straightforward when the failed partition is not the system partition. This includes the case when the failed partition is the mirror of the system partition. Recovery involves three basic steps: replace the failed disk, break the mirror set for the surviving component, and re-establish the mirror onto the replacement disk. Note that the first task (replacing the failed disk) can be quite complicated if the disk contains any other partitions besides the mirror.

Follow this procedure to repair a mirror set when the failed partition is not the system partition (requires multiple system restarts):

1. Shut down the server. Replace the failed disk. Restart the server.

2. Log on as an administrator. Start Disk Administrator from the Administrative Tools program group. The Disk Administrator main window appears (refer to Figure 6.4).

3. Break the mirror set as described in the previous section "Breaking a Mirror Set."

4. Create a new mirror set between the surviving partition of the original mirror set and an area of free space on the replacement disk, as described in a previous section "Establishing a Mirror Set."

Follow these steps to repair a mirror set when the failed partition is the system partition:

1. Shut down the server. Replace the failed disk.

2. Boot the server with the fault tolerant boot disk.

3. Log on as an administrator and start Disk Administrator. You will see the Disk Administrator main window. Select the surviving mirror partition. Disk Administrator's status bar will show that the mirror set is broken (see Figure 6.18).

FIG. 6.18

Disk Administrator status bar shows that the mirror set is broken.

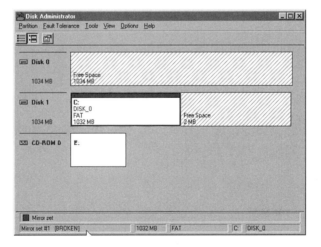

Part

II

Ch

6

4. Right-click the surviving mirror partition and choose <u>B</u>reak Mirror from the pop-up menu, as shown in Figure 6.19. When Disk Administrator displays a confirmation message box, click Yes.

FIG. 6.19

Select Break Mirror from the pop-up menu, or choose Fault Tolerance, Break Mirror from the Disk Administrator main menu.

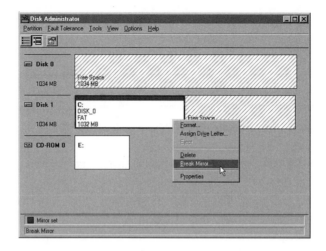

5. Acknowledge Disk Administrator's warning that the system partition cannot be locked by clicking Yes (see Figure 6.20).

FIG. 6.20

The message box indicating that the system partition cannot be locked is only a warning.

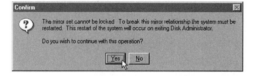

6. Restart using the fault tolerant boot disk. Log on as an administrator and start Disk Administrator.

7. Select the surviving partition and an equal or larger area of unpartitioned free space on the replacement disk. Right-click the surviving partition, and choose Establish Mirror from the pop-up menu, as shown in Figure 6.21.

 The goal of this process is to create a new bootable system partition, which must be a *primary* partition. This means that the mirror must be established on an *unpartitioned* area on the replacement disk. A mirror established on an extended partition will result in a *logical* drive, which cannot be a bootable system partition.

8. Exit Disk Administrator. This will initiate a system restart.

9. Boot again from the fault tolerant boot disk. Log on as an administrator and start Disk Administrator. The system partition will be rebuilt onto the replacement disk from the mirror partition. While the data replicates, Disk Administrator displays partition information in red text for the new member of the mirror set. When one component of the mirror set is selected, the Disk Administrator status bar indicates that the mirror is initializing (see Figure 6.22).

FIG. 6.21

Establish a mirror on the replacement disk.

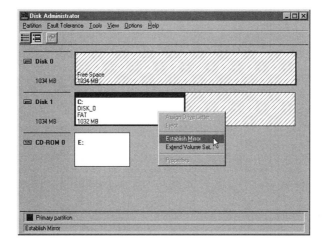

FIG. 6.22

Disk Administrator shows the new mirror initializing.

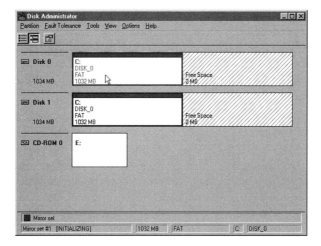

10. Wait until the mirror set initialization completes. When initialization is complete, Disk Administrator displays partition information in normal text for both members of the mirror set. When one component of the mirror set is selected, the Disk Administrator status bar indicates that the mirror is healthy, as shown in Figure 6.23. In order to boot again from the hard drive, the mirror must be broken and re-established from the newly replaced system partition.

11. Restart the system once more using the fault tolerant boot disk. Log on as an administrator and start Disk Administrator.

12. Right-click one member of the mirror set, and choose Break Mirror from the pop-up menu. When Disk Administrator displays a confirmation message box, click Yes. Acknowledge Disk Administrator's warning that the system partition cannot be locked.

FIG. 6.23

Disk Administrator shows that the new mirror set is healthy.

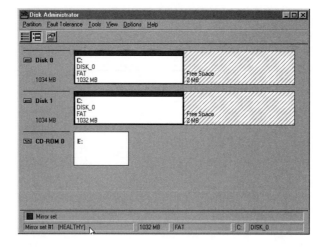

13. If the drive letter assigned to the mirror set is not C:, right-click the volume labeled C: and select Assign Drive Letter from the drop-down list box. Change the assigned drive letter to any other available letter using the Assign Drive Letter dialog box (see Figure 6.24).

FIG. 6.24

Assign drive letters to volumes using the Disk Administrator Assign Drive Letter dialog box.

14. Remove the fault tolerant boot disk from drive A:. Commit changes in Disk Administrator and restart the server.

If Windows NT Server fails to boot from the new system partition, chances are good that you failed to heed the Tip at step 7.

Boot Windows NT Server from the fault tolerant boot disk, log on as an administrator, and check Disk Administrator. Chances are good that the would-be system partition on the replacement disk was built on an extended partition, and is now a logical drive, as shown in Figure 6.25.

To recover from this mistake, you must delete the logical drive and the underlying extended partition from the replacement disk, and begin again with step 6 in this procedure. (See the Tip at step 7.)

Disk Administrator may not allow you to delete the logical drive; on x86 systems, you can just boot MS-DOS from a floppy disk and use `fdisk` to delete the logical drive and extended partition.

FIG. 6.25
A logical drive cannot
be the system partition.

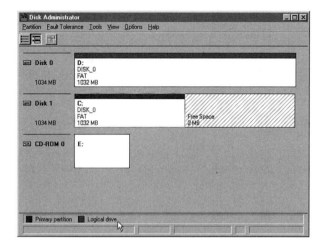

15. Log on as an administrator. Windows NT Server may warn that the system lacks an appropriately sized paging file. Acknowledge the warning and continue (this problem is temporary and should resolve itself).

16. Start Disk Administrator and change the drive letter assigned to the system partition to C:. Commit changes and (you guessed it) restart the server.

17. Create a new mirror set between the new boot partition and the surviving member of the original mirror set, as described above in the section "Establishing a Mirror Set."

RAID Level 0: Stripe Sets

Windows NT Server provides software implementation of RAID level 0, or disk striping. Because disk access is efficiently spread across multiple physical disks, stripe sets offer the best disk performance available under Windows NT. Data is divided into 64K blocks, with consecutive blocks placed on separate disks. This strategy requires that the stripe set occupy equal space on each disk.

N O T E To obtain enhanced performance from a stripe set, the disks must support independent read/write access. A stripe set spanning two hard drives attached to a single IDE controller will not provide enhanced performance because the controller can only access one drive at a time. Even for a system with *two* IDE controllers (the IDE specification allows only two), performance enhancement would be limited. Many SCSI controllers do support multiple independent read/write operations and are therefore a good choice for implementing RAID level 0. ■

RAID level 0 provides no fault tolerance; in fact, stripe sets are more failure prone than simple disk storage. Stripe sets *with parity* offer excellent fault tolerance, and are discussed in a following section "RAID Level 5: Stripe Sets with Parity." Sometimes, however, the performance boost from a RAID level 0 stripe set justifies the increased risk.

Part
II

Ch
6

CAUTION

If any disk in a stripe set fails, all data in the entire stripe set will be lost. The presence of multiple disks actually increases the probability of failure. Do not use stripe sets where the cost of failure is very high. Always maintain a current backup of all data in a stripe set.

Perform the following steps to implement a stripe set. As with volume sets, creating a stripe set requires a system restart:

1. Log on as an administrator. Start Disk Administrator from the Administrative Tools program group. The Disk Administrator main window appears (refer to Figure 6.4).

2. Hold down Ctrl and click one area of free space on each disk to be included in the stripe set (at least two).

3. Right-click one of the selected areas of free space and select Create Stripe Set from the pop-up menu. The Create Stripe Set dialog box appears, similar to that in Figure 6.26.

FIG. 6.26

Specify the size for a new stripe set in the Create Stripe Set dialog box.

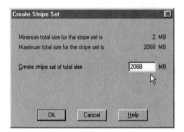

4. Specify the desired size for the new stripe set. The default (and maximum) is *n* times the largest selected area of free space, where *n* is the number of disks selected. The size you select should be an even multiple (in megabytes) of the number of disks in the stripe set. Specify an appropriate size, and click OK.

5. Select Partition, Commit Changes Now from the Disk Administrator main menu. You will see a Confirm message box. Disk Administrator warns that the system must be re-started. Click Yes to confirm the change to your disk configuration and restart the system.

RAID Level 5: Stripe Sets with Parity

Stripe sets with parity (RAID level 5) have become a very popular fault tolerance strategy. The concept is similar to a regular stripe set: data is spread across multiple disks in 64K blocks. However, this method adds redundant data so that if one disk in the set should fail, data can be reconstructed from the remaining disks. The redundant data is called *parity bits*. Parity bits are also spread across all disks in the set, so that the parity information is always on a separate disk from the data it describes.

The disk space required for parity information varies with the number of disks in the stripe set: for three disks, one third; for four disks, one fourth; and for five disks, one fifth. This means that three 1G disks can provide 2G of fault tolerant information storage; four 1G disks can provide 3G, and five 1G disks can provide four fault tolerant gigabytes. Information theory places a lower limit on the amount of parity information required to represent a volume of data, so the 1/n relation only holds for smaller numbers of disks.

A stripe set with parity must span at least three physical disks and can span up to 32. As with regular stripe sets, IDE drives that do not support independent disk access are ill-suited for this purpose.

Creating a Stripe Set with Parity   Follow these steps to set up a stripe set with parity (requires a system restart):

1. Log on as an administrator and start Disk Administrator. The Disk Administrator main window appears (refer to Figure 6.4).
2. Hold down Ctrl and click one area of free space on each disk to be included in the stripe set. You will need to select at least three.
3. Right-click one of the selected areas of free space and select Create Stripe Set with Parity from the pop-up menu. The Create Stripe Set With Parity dialog box appears (see Figure 6.27).

FIG. 6.27

Specify the size for a new stripe set with parity in the Create Stripe Set with Parity dialog box.

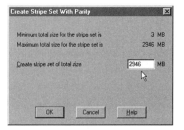

4. Specify the desired size for the new volume. The default is n times the smallest amount of free space on any selected disk, where n is the number of disks in the stripe set. Specify an appropriate size, and click OK.
5. Right-click any disk and choose Commit Changes Now from the pop-up menu. Disk Administrator warns you that the system must be restarted. Click Yes to confirm and restart the system. Acknowledge the warning to update the ERD.
6. After the system restarts, log on as an administrator and start Disk Administrator. Select one component of the new stripe set with parity, and notice the status displayed in the lower-left corner. For several minutes (depending on the size of the stripe set with parity), the status initializes, as shown in Figure 6.28.
7. The new stripe set with parity must be formatted before use. You can begin the format while the stripe set is initializing, or wait for initialization to complete.

Part
II

Ch
6

FIG. 6.28

Disk Administrator shows the stripe set with parity initializing.

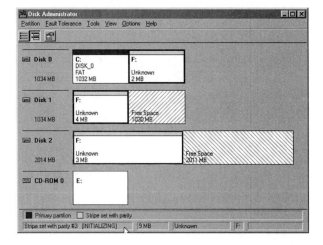

Regenerating a Stripe Set with Parity   If one disk in a stripe set should fail, the stripe set with parity will continue to operate, but with reduced performance. Unless you have configured an administrative alert for disk failures, you might not notice the failure until the next time you start Disk Administrator. Event viewer will show an error, and the event description will read `A stripe set or volume set member listed in the configuration information was missing`, as shown in Figure 6.29.

FIG. 6.29

Event Viewer shows the failure of one disk in a stripe set with parity.

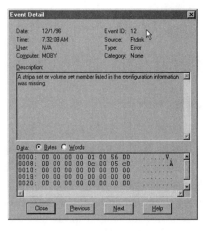

Although the system continues to run, the data previously protected by the stripe set with parity is now at risk. As soon as possible, an administrator should shut down the server, re-place the failed component, and regenerate the stripe set with parity.

Follow these steps to regenerate a stripe set with parity (requires a system restart):

1. Shut down the server and replace the failed disk (this task can be quite complicated if the disk contains any other partitions besides the stripe set with parity).

2. Restart the server. Log on as an administrator and start Disk Administrator. Select any component of the stripe set with parity; the Disk Administrator status bar will indicate that the set is recoverable (see Figure 6.30).

FIG. 6.30

Disk Administrator shows that the stripe set with parity is recoverable.

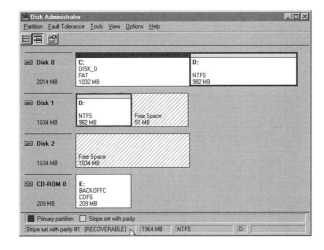

3. Select any component of the stripe set with parity. Hold down Ctrl and click an area of free space on the replacement disk that is at least as large as the individual components of the stripe set with parity.

4. Right-click the stripe set with parity, and choose Regenerate from the pop-up menu (see Figure 6.31).

FIG. 6.31

Select Regenerate from the pop-up menu, or select Fault Tolerance, Regenerate from the Disk Administrator main menu.

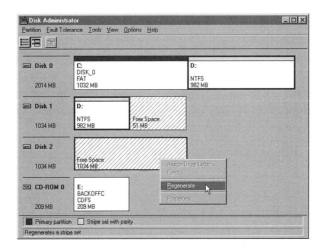

Part

II

Ch

6

5. Right-click any volume in Disk Administrator and select Commit Changes Now from the pop-up menu. Confirm that you do want to save changes now.

6. Windows NT Server will regenerate the stripe set with parity onto the replacement disk. During this process, the system exhibits reduced performance and substantial disk activity. While the stripe set with parity regenerates, Disk Administrator displays partition information in red text for the new member of the set. When one component of the set is selected, the Disk Administrator status bar indicates that the stripe set with parity is initializing, as shown in Figure 6.32.

FIG. 6.32
Disk Administrator
shows the stripe set with
parity regenerating.

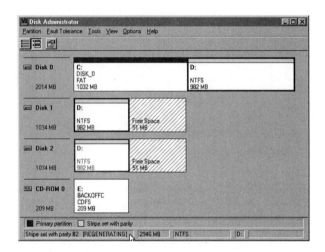

Deleting a Stripe Set with Parity   Follow these steps to delete a stripe set with parity:

1. Log on as an administrator. Start Disk Administrator from the Administrative Tools program group. The Disk Administrator main window appears (refer to Figure 6.4).

2. Right-click any component of the stripe set with parity. Select Delete from the pop-up menu. Acknowledge Disk Administrator's warning that all data on the stripe set with parity will be lost.

3. Choose Partition, Commit Changes Now from the Disk Administrator main menu. Acknowledge Disk Administrator's advice to update your ERD.

From Here...

In this chapter, you learned to configure automatic recovery, virtual memory, and hard disk space. You also learned to use Windows NT Server's support for RAID level 0 (stripe sets), RAID level 1 (mirroring), and RAID level 5 (stripe sets with parity). To learn about related topics, see the following chapters:

■ For ideas about planning network configurations and selecting server hardware, see Chapter 3, "Planning For BackOffice."

■ For information on installing Windows NT Server and instructions for creating an emergency repair disk, see Chapter 5, "Implementing Windows NT Server."

■ For information on managing access to disk resources and backup strategies, see Chapter 7, "Administering Windows NT Server."

Part
II

Ch
6

Administering Windows NT Server

by Larry Millett and Joe Lengyel

Successful deployment of Microsoft BackOffice requires an active and capable network administrator. On an active network with many users, the necessary administrative tasks can require a lot of time. It is nearly impossible for one person to administer the entire BackOffice family. Successful management of each BackOffice component, including Windows NT Server itself, requires a significant level of expertise and knowledge.

After reading this chapter, you will understand how to perform the duties of a network administrator using the tools provided with Windows NT Server. ■

Important tasks in the administration of a Windows NT Server

Learn to administer users and secure resources in a Windows NT Server domain. Learn to configure Windows NT Server for efficient, reliable operation.

Administrative tools provided with Windows NT Server

Learn to use User Manager for Domains, Disk Administrator, and Server Manager. Learn to share resources and implement security through File Manager and Print Manager.

Implementing a security policy

Discover how to manage permissions for shared resources, both within and across domains. Understand the various domain models and the implementation of a trust relationship.

How to back up your Windows NT Server

Review a backup strategy. Learn to use the Windows NT Server Backup utility.

Understanding the Role of the Network Administrator

The network administrator configures and manages the components of a Windows NT server that enable it to attach to a network and communicate with other devices. The administrator's duties include the following:

- Creating user and group accounts
- Sharing resources
- Setting and changing permissions
- Implementing trust relationships between domains
- Monitoring and maximizing server performance
- Configuring appropriate network protocols
- Configuring the server hardware
- Managing network-specific services, such as Schedule and Alerter

Network administrators also usually bear responsibility for establishing an appropriate backup strategy. The actual backups are generally performed by *backup operators*—less experienced people who are trusted to perform this vital administrative task. Network administrators can also formulate and enforce security policies, although larger organizations usually assign this function to a different person or group.

Network administrators may have duties managing additional software components or services that run on the server. A network administrator is often a Systems Management Server (SMS) administrator as well because SMS can play a pivotal role in automating network administration tasks. A network administrator also could administer other BackOffice components, but this is less common. See Chapter 44, "The Role of the SMS Administrator," for more information.

Furthermore, network administrators typically plan and configure servers, and must be thoroughly familiar with the day-to-day operation and use of Windows NT Server.

Surveying the Administrative Tools of Windows NT Server

Windows NT Server includes a rich set of network administration and server management tools. These tools exploit the Windows graphical user interface to make administrative chores simpler to understand and easier to perform. Although some administrative tasks can be performed with command-line utilities, the graphical tools offer equivalent capabilities and are easier to use.

Administrators regularly use seven primary tools, complemented by a handful of tools for occasional use, as follows:

- **User Manager for Domains**—Used for people-specific tasks affecting a user or group of users
- **Server Manager**—Used for server-specific tasks affecting a computer
- **Event Viewer**—Used for troubleshooting, detecting security violations, and verifying the basic status of the server at regular intervals
- **Explorer and Print Manager**—Used for resource sharing and auditing
- **Performance Monitor**—Used for tracking server performance
- **Control Panel**—Used for, among other things, managing user resources and the services available on the computer
- **Backup**—Used for backing up network data to tape

During installation, Windows NT Server automatically adds a folder called Administrative Tools to <u>P</u>rograms on the Start menu, which contains the tools discussed in this chapter. Figure 7.1 depicts a sample Administrative Tools group window. This sample includes the standard Administrative Tools icons loaded during a typical installation, plus several additional ones that have been manually placed there for the convenience of the administrator. You can also install these tools on a Windows NT Workstation client from the Windows NT Server media. Some tools can be run from other versions of Windows as well.

FIG. 7.1

The shortcut to the program group Administrative Tools opens a window containing icons for some of the Windows NT Server administrative tools.

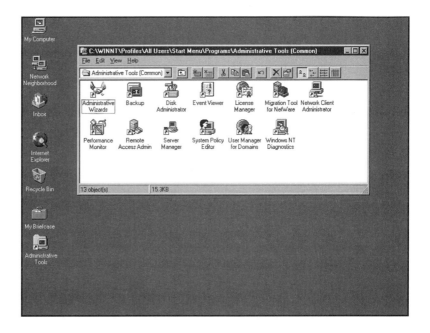

Although all versions of Windows can run some of the tools, only the Windows NT versions (Server and Workstation) include all of the capabilities outlined in this chapter. For example, there are versions of Server Manager and User Manager for Domains that can be run on 16-bit Windows platforms. Quite a number of the administrative tools for the BackOffice family of products are available for Windows 95 (e.g., SQL Server), and the current initiative to create an integrated management tool called the Microsoft Management Console (MMC) will target both Windows 95 and Windows NT 4.0 (and later) platforms. With the current versions of some BackOffice products and some Windows NT Server administration tools, you must use a Windows NT Workstation or Windows NT Server system.

User Manager for Domains

Everyone who uses BackOffice needs a user account in one or more Windows NT domains. These accounts are created and managed with a tool called User Manager for Domains (see Figure 7.2).

▶ **See** "Domains," **p. 227**

FIG. 7.2

With User Manager for Domains, you can create user accounts, assign users to groups, and establish security policies.

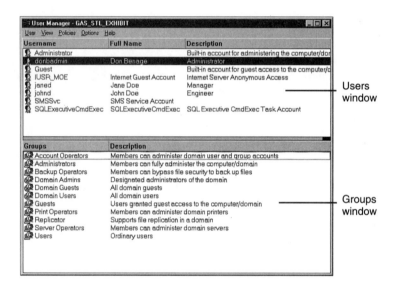

In addition to user account management, User Manager for Domains supports the following tasks:

- Defining a security policy for user accounts
- Creating and managing user groups
- Setting up trust relationships between domains

Versions of User Manager for Domains are available for all versions of Windows. It can also be run effectively from a remote location over a dial-up phone connection. You can probably improve response time when running User Manager for Domains remotely by choosing Options, Low Speed Connection. This reduces the frequency with which User Manager for Domains polls the network for new information and therefore improves its responsiveness over a slow link, such as a dial-up phone connection.

N O T E Windows NT Workstation includes a tool called User Manager (without the "for Domains" designation). This tool enables the creation of local user accounts and groups for use only on the Windows NT computer that is running User Manager. A user who has logged in with such an account will not usually be able to access resources on other computers in a domain.

User Manager for Domains is a much more powerful version of User Manager. It creates accounts that can be used on many computers in the same domain or in domains with trust relationships. ■

Server Manager

You can use the Windows NT Explorer (or the Windows Explorer on Windows 95) to do some of the same things Server Manager does. In particular, Explorer makes it very easy to share directories on a computer's disk drive with other users on a network. The strength of Server Manager is the breadth of different tasks that can be completed with one tool. So although Server Manager isn't the easiest tool to use for sharing directories (e.g., it won't browse directory trees), it can do that job and many others.

Figure 7.3 shows the Server Manager main window. Use Server Manager for the following machine-oriented tasks:

- Sharing server resources
- Setting permissions for shared resources
- Starting and stopping services
- Pausing and continuing services
- Viewing the properties of a Windows NT computer
- Adding a computer to a domain

FIG. 7.3

Views can be manipulated in Server Manager to display servers only, workstations only, or both servers and workstations.

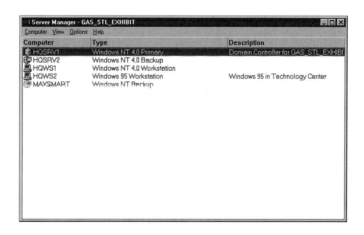

Part

II

Ch

7

Event Log Viewer

The Event Viewer is generally the first tool to use when investigating a problem with a server. Use it to browse the three main logs kept by a Windows NT Server, as follows:

- **System log**—Includes messages about system events, such as service startup and device failures.

- **Security log**—Includes messages about security events, such as user logons and logoffs and unauthorized access attempts. The specific events logged are determined by the audit policy.

- **Application log**—Includes messages generated by applications. The specific messages are determined by the application developer.

  ▶ **See** "Setting Up Auditing," **p. 149**

Windows Explorer (and Windows NT Explorer)

Explorer is familiar to almost anyone who has run any 32-bit version of Windows. It has features especially useful to the administrator because you can use it to create directories on your computer (or on any computer for which you have administrator privileges) and then share these directories with other users or groups on the network.

Print Manager

Print Manager is most often used to manage print queues. However, you can also use Print Manager to share a printer with other network users. Printers can be attached either to a computer or directly to the network cable if they are capable of such an attachment. For example, some of the popular Hewlett Packard (HP) LaserJet printers are capable of being attached directly to a network with the addition of HP's JetDirect interface card.

Performance Monitor

Performance Monitor is a powerful tool that can be used for a variety of tasks. First and foremost, it enables you to monitor the activity on a computer so that you can see exactly what resources (disk, memory, processor, or network connections) are being used. You can graph the activity as it occurs (as depicted in Figure 7.4), write the data to a log file for later analysis, or set alerts that will act as alarms if utilization exceeds a particular threshold for a given resource.

Because of its many capabilities, Performance Monitor can play an important role in trouble-shooting performance problems or determining what to add to a particular server to improve its performance. The Windows NT Resource Kit devotes an entire volume to this important tool.

▶ **See** "Using the Performance Monitor," **p. 1664**

FIG. 7.4
The Performance
Monitor has the
capability of simulta-
neously plotting
multiple variables.

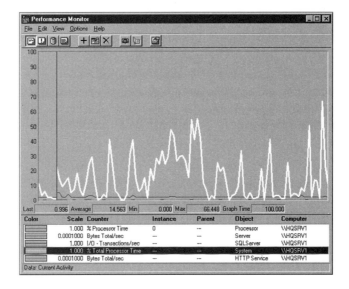

Backup

Backup is a utility for making tape backups of your important information. It works with tape devices listed in the Hardware Compatibility List (HCL). You can find the latest HCL on the Microsoft Network, CompuServe, or at **www.microsoft.com** on the World Wide Web. A copy of the HCL is also included with the Windows NT Server documentation.

Backup enables you to back up not only your data files, but also the registry, which is a hierarchical database of all configuration information for your Windows NT Server. The registry includes the user account database that contains all of your users and groups. In addition, should the need arise, you can use the Backup application to restore information from your tapes to your disk drive. In the event of a total disk failure, you can rebuild your computer with a new disk drive and an appropriate set of tapes.

It is important to use the Backup utility properly to protect yourself against disaster. The process of making backups and tips on creating an appropriate backup regimen are outlined in the section "Developing a Backup Strategy" later in this chapter.

Managing User Accounts

User account management is the most visible activity of a network administrator. All access to Windows NT Server network resources depends on user accounts. Naturally, User Manager for Domains is the tool for most account management tasks. User account management encompasses the following four major tasks (which are covered in detail in the following sections):

■ Defining a security policy for user accounts

■ Creating new accounts and disabling unused accounts

Part
II

Ch
7

- Managing user groups
- Setting user rights

Defining a Security Policy for User Accounts

A user account security policy can control password length, force users to change their passwords at regular intervals, keep a history of passwords to prevent reuse, and set account lockout options. To define a security policy with User Manager for Domains, perform the following steps:

1. Start User Manager for Domains.
2. If the proper domain is not active, choose User, Select Domain. Select the proper domain with the mouse, or type the name of the domain into the Domain text box.
3. Choose Policies, Account. The Account Policy dialog box appears (see Figure 7.5).

FIG. 7.5

Create an account policy by setting options in the Account Policy dialog box. The minimum recommended settings are displayed here.

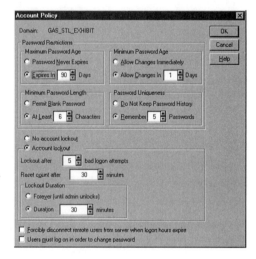

4. Make selections in the dialog box reflecting your company's security policy. Figure 7.5 illustrates a recommended minimum.
5. Click OK.

   ▶ **See** "Creating a Security Policy," **p. 85**

Creating a New User Account

To create a user account with User Manager for Domains, follow these steps:

1. Start User Manager for Domains.
2. If the proper domain is not active, choose User, Select Domain. Select the proper domain with the mouse, or type the name of the domain into the Domain text box.
3. Choose User, New User. You will see the New User dialog box shown in Figure 7.6.

FIG. 7.6

The New User dialog box is used to register new users and to establish group memberships, environmental profiles, logon permissions, and account types.

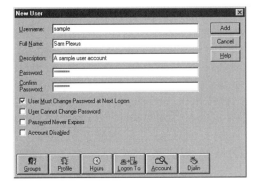

4. Fill out the New User dialog box. You must enter the password twice.

N O T E You cannot see the password or the confirming password as they are entered; you see asterisks instead. This is a security precaution to prevent someone from looking over your shoulder as you type. Because you can't see what you are typing, you must enter the exact same text twice to prevent an accidental keystroke from going unnoticed. Passwords are case-sensitive—that is, capitalization matters. ▨

5. Click Add to add the new user and clear the data from the New User dialog box. Notice that the Cancel button changes to the Close button when the first new user is added. This enables you to continue to add new users (and click Add each time) or click Close to close the dialog box.

Disabling a User Account

Microsoft recommends disabling unused accounts, not deleting them. A disabled account can be easily reactivated, but a deleted account is gone for good. A new account can be created with the same permissions, but that can be a substantial chore on a large network with many shared resources. Perform the following steps to disable a user account:

1. Start User Manager for Domains.
2. If the proper domain is not active, choose User, Select Domain. Select the proper domain with the mouse, or type the name of the domain into the Domain text box.
3. Choose User, Properties. The User Properties dialog box appears. This dialog box is identical to the New User dialog box shown in Figure 7.6 except for the title bar, which says User Properties rather than New User.
4. Click the Account Disabled check box.
5. Click Close.

Managing Group Accounts

Group accounts enable efficient management of security. Although each user may need access to a unique combination of resources, you can identify common needs. For example,

Part

II

Ch

7

accounting personnel might need access to applications, data, and printers on a particular server, whereas marketing personnel need access to different resources.

In this example, you could create one group called Accounting and another called Marketing. You can assign appropriate permissions to the group accounts and then add users to the groups. By assigning a user to the accounting group, you effectively assign that user all permissions held by the group account. If the marketing group should install a new application, you can assign new resource permissions to the marketing group rather than individually to all marketing users.

To create a group with User Manager for Domains, perform the following steps:

1. Start User Manager for Domains.
2. If the proper domain is not active, choose User, Select Domain. Select the proper domain with the mouse, or type the name of the domain into the Domain text box.
3. Choose User, New Global Group, or choose User, New Local Group. The appropriate dialog box appears.

 A *local group* can contain users and groups from the local domain, users from trusted domains, and *global groups* from trusted domains. A global group can only contain users from the local domain.

Use local groups to manage permissions on domain resources. Use global groups to define a set of users who need access to similar resources in other domains.

4. In the New Global Group dialog box, enter a Group Name and Description (see Figure 7.7).

FIG. 7.7
The New Global Group dialog box enables you to enter a name and description for the group as well as select the members for the group.

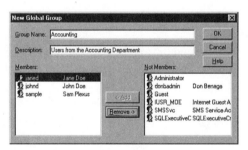

5. Select the users in the Not Members list box that you want to include in the group and click Add. You can select users and click Add multiple times. (If you want, you can also select the users in the Members list box that you want to delete from the group and click Remove.)
6. When the members list is correct, click OK.

▶ **See** "Domains," **p. 227**

Setting User Rights

The user rights policy controls which users can perform certain actions, such as shutting down servers or changing the system time on a computer. Exercise caution when changing Advanced User Rights. They rarely need to be changed. The process is outlined next for those rare occasions when it is necessary. To change user rights, follow these steps:

1. Start User Manager for Domains.

2. If the proper domain is not active, choose User, Select Domain. Select the proper domain with the mouse, or type the name of the domain into the Domain text box.

3. Choose Policies, User Rights. The User Rights Policy dialog box appears (see Figure 7.8).

FIG. 7.8
The User Rights Policy dialog box enables you to add and remove users or groups for selected rights.

4. Make selections in the dialog box reflecting your company's policy. Select a right you want to review or change. If the Grant To scroll box does not contain those users or groups that should have the right shown in the Right drop-down list box, use the Add and Remove buttons to change them.

5. If you click the Show Advanced User Rights check box, you will see many additional rights listed in the Right drop-down list box.

6. Click OK.

Creating a Service Account

All applications running under Windows NT, including server applications (for example, SNA Server), run in a particular account context that controls the rights and permissions of the application. Ordinary applications, such as Microsoft Word, can be executed on both Windows NT Workstation and Windows NT Server. If the current user of the computer logs off, all standard applications will be shut down. A special type of application, known as a *service*, is designed to keep running regardless of who is or is not logged on. Most server-based applications, and all applications in the BackOffice family, are implemented as services.

These services, like standard applications, run in a particular security context. This context may be that of the current user, a special system account, or an account created specifically for this purpose called a *service account*. Service accounts enable the administrator to explicitly control the security privileges that are assigned to a service.

Part
II

Ch
7

In a multiserver environment, for example, it is common for one SNA Server to communicate with other SNA Servers. It is a good idea to create a service account (in a master domain, if you are using a master domain model) that has permissions on multiple servers in the domain. Most of the services in the BackOffice family default to a Local System account that only has privileges on the single computer running the service. You should strongly consider using service accounts for BackOffice family services, especially if you are using multiple domains.

To create a service account with User Manager for Domains, perform the following steps:

1. Start User Manager for Domains.
2. If the proper domain is not active, choose User, Select Domain. Select the proper domain with the mouse, or type the name of the domain into the Domain text box.
3. Choose User, New User. The New User dialog box appears.
4. Enter the new service account information in the New User dialog box. You must enter the password twice.
5. Click Add.
6. Choose Policies, User Rights. The User Rights Policy dialog box appears.
7. Click Show Advanced User Rights, as shown in Figure 7.9.

FIG. 7.9
The User Rights Policy dialog box shows that two service accounts have been granted the right to log on as a service.

8. Select Log On as a Service in the Right drop-down list box (refer to Figure 7.9).
9. Click Add to display the Add Users and Groups dialog box illustrated in Figure 7.10. Click the Show Users button.

FIG. 7.10
Select the new service account and click Add to place it in the Names scroll box.

10. Select the account you created in step 4, and click Add.

11. Click OK in the Add Users and Groups dialog box to close the dialog box and add the account created in step 4 to the Grant To box in the User Rights Policy dialog box.

12. Click OK in the User Rights Policy dialog box.

Other aspects of service management are discussed in the "Understanding Services" section later in this chapter.

Managing Access to Shared Resources

For a few networks, it can make sense to have a single Guest account that provides unlimited access to all resources. In most cases, however, accounts exist to limit network access. A well-defined security policy includes the following four elements:

- Accounts
- Resources
- Permissions
- Logging

Permissions define the ways in which accounts can use resources. *Logging* records access to resources by accounts.

Sharing Directories

Directories can be shared with Server Manager or with Explorer. In this section, the techniques for sharing a local directory through Server Manager and using Explorer to create a server-based shared directory on another computer are presented. To share a directory with Server Manager, complete the following steps:

1. Start Server Manager.

2. If the proper domain is not active, choose Computer, Select Domain. Select the proper domain with the mouse, or type the name of the domain into the Domain text box.

3. Select the computer on which you want to share a directory.

4. Choose Computer, Shared Directories. The Shared Directories dialog box appears (see Figure 7.11).

FIG. 7.11
The Shared Directories dialog box is showing shared directories on the computer named HQSRV2. Available buttons enable new shares to be defined, properties to be modified, and sharing to be terminated on selected directories.

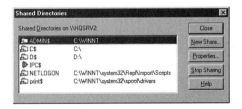

5. Click New Share, and the New Share dialog box appears (see Figure 7.12).

FIG. 7.12

The New Share dialog box enables the share name to be defined and the share properties for the new shared directory to be established.

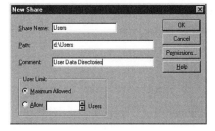

6. Fill in the dialog box with the appropriate information. The path should be a fully qualified path name that refers to the appropriate physical disk drive on the computer that contains the directory (for example, c:\<pathname>). Do not use a logical drive letter you may have connected to the other computer.

7. Click Permissions. The Access Through Share Permissions dialog box appears (see Figure 7.13).

FIG. 7.13

The shared directory Users is set with the group Domain Admins having Full Control permissions.

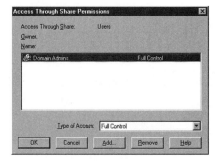

8. The default permissions are for the predefined group Everyone to have Full Control over this resource. This means that everyone on the network can read, write, create, and delete information in this directory. You usually will want to remove that permission and add something more restrictive. Select the Type of Access you want to assign to the selected group for the resource.

9. Click OK in the Access Through Share Permissions dialog box.

10. Click OK in the New Share dialog box.

To create a server-based share for a shared directory on another computer with Explorer, follow these steps:

1. Make a drive connection to the targeted computer. Choose Disk, Connect Network Drive. Connect an available drive letter to the computer and shared directory that contains your new shared directory (for example, \\COMPUTER\C$).

Hidden administrative share names are automatically created for the root directory of each disk drive when you install Windows NT Server. For example, the root directory of C: has a share name of C$. The dollar sign at the end of the name prevents it from showing up in lists when other users are browsing for shared resources. These automatic share names are given permissions for administrators only.

2. Select the directory (probably the root directory) that will contain your new, shared directory.

3. Choose File, Create Directory. The Create Directory dialog box appears.

4. Enter the name of the new directory you would like to create (for example, Public Data).

5. Click OK in the Create Directory dialog box.

6. Now select the newly created directory.

7. Choose Disk, Share As to display the New Share dialog box (refer to Figure 7.12).

8. Enter the appropriate information in the dialog box. The path should be a fully qualified UNC name (for example, \\computer\c$\directory). If you try to use a relative drive letter, Windows NT changes it to a UNC name automatically.

9. Click Permissions. The Access Through Share Permissions dialog box appears (refer to Figure 7.13).

10. The default permissions are for the predefined group Everyone to have Full Control over this resource. This means that everyone on the network can read, write, create, and delete information in this directory. You usually will want to remove that permission and add something more restrictive. Select the Type of Access you want to assign to the selected group for the resource.

11. Click OK in the Access Through Share Permissions dialog box.

12. Click OK in the New Share dialog box.

Sharing Printers

To share a printer using Print Manager, perform the following steps:

1. Start Print Manager. (Look in the Main group, or double-click the printer icon in the Control Panel.)

2. If the printer you would like to share is connected to a computer other than the one you are using, choose Printer, Server Viewer. Select the computer to which the printer is attached.

3. Choose Printer, Create Printer. The Create Printer dialog box appears.

4. Fill out the Create Printer dialog box. The Printer Name is visible to Windows NT users connecting to this printer after it is shared. Select a driver that matches the model of your printer. Enter a description to inform users about the model and capabilities of the printer (for example, Includes Envelope Feeder). Select the Print To destination. Select Share This Printer on the Network. Enter a Share Name and a Location.

5. Click OK in the Create Printer dialog box.

Part
II
Ch
7

Setting Permissions on Shared Resources

Resource permissions can be assigned to a user account or to a group account. Usually, the best way to assign permissions to a user is to add the user to a group, as discussed earlier in the "Managing Group Accounts" section. To use Explorer for setting access permissions, follow these steps:

1. Right-click My Computer and select Explore from the pop-up menu.

2. Select the shared directory for which you want to change permissions.

3. Choose File, Properties to display the Properties dialog box.

4. Select the Sharing tab. In this dialog box, you can edit the default Share Name, enter a descriptive Comment, or limit the number of users that can access this share name concurrently.

5. Click Permissions. The Access Through Share Permissions dialog box appears.

6. The default permissions are for the predefined group Everyone to have Full Control over this resource. This means that everyone on the network can read, write, create, and delete information in this directory. You usually will want to remove that permission and add something more restrictive. Select the Type of Access you want to assign to the selected group for the resource (see Figure 7.14).

FIG. 7.14

The Access Through Share Permissions dialog box is showing different permissions for two groups.

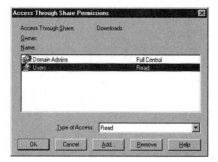

7. You may want to add users or groups to the list that has access to the shared resource. Click Add. The Add Users and Groups dialog box appears.

8. Locate and select the user or group you want to add, and click Add. Repeat this step for all users and groups you want to add.

9. Click OK in the Add Users and Groups dialog box (depicted in Figure 7.15) to close the dialog box and redisplay the Access Through Share Permissions dialog box. Notice that the predefined group Everyone has been removed (by clicking Remove while the group was selected), and additional groups with various types of access have been added.

10. When you are finished adding (and removing) users and groups, click OK in the Access Through Share Permissions dialog box to close the dialog box and redisplay the Properties dialog box.

11. Click OK in the Properties dialog box.

FIG. 7.15

The Add Users and Groups dialog box is showing the user janed from the GAS_STL_EXHIBIT domain being given Full Control access permissions.

Changing Permissions for Local Disk Drive Access

For logical drives formatted with NTFS, Windows NT Server enables you to define file and directory permissions that apply to local users. These permissions apply only to NTFS drives: all local users have full access to FAT and HPFS formatted local drives. This is due to the Windows NT discretionary access control built around the NTFS file system. Each file has security information as an attribute. The FAT file system inherited from MS-DOS has no place to store security attributes in its design.

To use Explorer for changing file and directory access permissions, perform the following steps:

1. Right-click My Computer and select Explore from the pop-up menu.
2. Select the shared directory for which you want to change permissions.
3. Choose File, Properties to display the Downloads Properties dialog box.
4. Select the Security tab (see Figure 7.16).

FIG. 7.16

Permissions are being set directly on the local directory using File Manager.

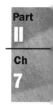

Part

II

Ch

7

N O T E The permissions shown in Figure 7.16 will affect access rights when a user logs on directly at the keyboard of the computer in question. They will also have an impact on the rights when users connect to that computer over the network. The rights a particular user receives will be the most restrictive combination of rights from the Access Through Share permissions and local Directory permissions. For example, if a user is given Full Control on the Access Through Share permissions, but is given Read access on Directory permissions, the user will have only Read access. ■

5. Click Permissions. The Directory Permissions dialog box appears (see Figure 7.17).

FIG. 7.17

The Directory Permissions dialog box displays the access controls applied directly to the files or directories currently selected on an NTFS partition.

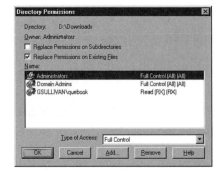

6. Click Add to add new users or groups. The Add Users and Groups dialog box appears.

7. Select the users or groups to whom you would like to assign permissions for this directory, and click Add. You can do this step more than one time for all users and groups that you want to give a particular level of access.

8. Select the Type of Access.

9. Click OK in the Add Users and Groups dialog box.

10. If you want the same permissions to apply to all subdirectories of this directory, select the Replace Permissions on Subdirectories check box.

11. Click OK in the Directory Permissions dialog box.

Logging Account Activities

A complete security policy includes logging of account activities. Windows NT Server provides flexible support for auditing the use of domains, files and directories, and printers. The Windows NT Server Event Log service records specified activities in the security log where they can be browsed with Event Viewer.

You can also establish trust relationships with User Manager for Domains. Trust is a one-way relationship: the *trusting* domain depends on the *trusted* domain to authenticate users. To implement a two-way trust, create a pair of relationships. You need to be a domain administrator for both domains or work with a domain administrator from another domain to create a trust relationship. You can physically go to the domain controllers involved or perform all actions remotely.

To perform the operation remotely, you must either log on with an account that is a domain administrator for both domains, or use the Connect As feature of File Manager in Windows NT. Log on with a domain administrator account from the first domain, and then from the File Manager menubar choose Disk, Connect Network Drive to display the Connect Network Drive dialog box. Then in the Shared Directories drop-down list box, select a shared resource (for example, C$) on the primary domain controller of the second domain. In the Connect As box, enter a domain administrator account from the second domain in the form *<domain>\<user>*. You are prompted to enter the password for this second account. This establishes an administrative account context in the second domain so that you can create the trust relationship.

To create a one-way trust relationship between two domains, complete the following steps:

1. Start User Manager for Domains.

2. If the proper domain is not active, choose User, Select Domain.

3. Select the proper domain with the mouse, or type the name of the domain into the Domain text box. You should select the domain that will be trusted.

4. Choose Policies, Trust Relationships. The Trust Relationships dialog box appears (see Figure 7.18)

FIG. 7.18

The Trust Relationships dialog box is showing the creation of one-way trust relationships.

5. Click Add next to the Trusting Domains list box. The Add Trusting Domain dialog box appears (see Figure 7.19).

FIG. 7.19

The Add Trusting Domain dialog box is used to enter a domain name and password when creating a trust relationship.

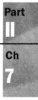

6. Enter the name of the domain you are permitting to trust the first domain.

7. Enter a password and then enter it again to confirm that it was correctly typed. (You will not be able to see the password, as mentioned previously.)

8. Click OK.

9. Select the other domain by choosing <u>U</u>ser, <u>S</u>elect Domain.

10. Select the domain with the mouse, or type the name of the domain into the <u>D</u>omain text box. You should select the domain that will trust the first domain.

11. Choose <u>P</u>olicies, <u>T</u>rust Relationships. The Trust Relationships dialog box appears.

12. Click <u>A</u>dd next to the <u>T</u>rusted Domains list box. The Add Trusted Domain dialog box appears (see Figure 7.20).

FIG. 7.20

The trusted domain and password are supplied in the Add Trusted Domain dialog box.

13. Enter the name of the first domain (the one you are going to trust).

14. Enter the password created in step 7. (You will not be able to see the password.)

15. Click OK in the Add Trusted Domain dialog box. Click OK in the Trust Relationships dialog box.

▶ **See** "Setting Up Auditing," **p. 149**

▶ **See** "Understanding BackOffice Structures for Organizing Servers," **p. 104**

▶ **See** "Domains," **p. 227**

Understanding Services

A *service* is an application running on the server that has the following characteristics:

- It does not depend on anyone being logged on to the computer for its execution. It can be set to start automatically when the server is started, or manually by an administrator.

- It can be set to run in the security context of any account you want. It need not run with the rights and privileges assigned to the user who may currently be logged on.

- A service can perform operations on behalf of a client application. Typically, the client runs in an account context different from that of the service.

- A service runs in the *background*; that is, it need not have an active window with a user interface. A service can be controlled by one or more administrative utilities, but the service itself does not automatically open a window when it starts.

- A service can be started, stopped, paused, or continued. These operations can be performed on the server running the service, or from a remote computer.

All the main programs in the BackOffice family are implemented as one or more services. They also include client components and administrative utilities that are implemented as traditional applications. To control services with Server Manager, complete the following steps:

1. Start Server Manager.
2. If the proper domain is not active, choose Computer, Select Domain.
3. Select the proper domain with the mouse, or type the name of the domain into the Domain text box.
4. Select the computer on which you want to control services.
5. Choose Computer, Services. The Services On dialog box appears (see Figure 7.21).

FIG. 7.21
The services of a Windows NT Server can be started, stopped, or paused using the Server Manager window.

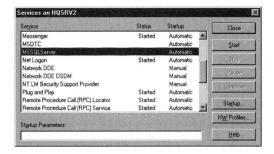

6. At this point, you can select any of the listed services and change their states. If the service is started, you can Stop or Pause it. If it is stopped, you can Start it. If it is paused, you can Continue it.

N O T E Pausing a service enables everyone who is using the service to continue, but no new users are allowed to connect to, or use, the service. Stopping a service disconnects anyone actively using the service and shuts it down.

7. Click the Startup button. The Service On dialog box appears (see Figure 7.22).

FIG. 7.22
The startup options of a Windows NT service are configurable, as shown for the MSSQLServer service on the computer named HQSRV2.

8. The dialog box shown in Figure 7.22 enables you to configure the service to start automatically when the server is started, to be started manually by an administrator, or to be disabled. You can also specify a service account to be used by this service. (See "Creating a Service Account" earlier in this chapter.)

9. Click OK and then Close to close the two dialog boxes.

 T I P   Services on a particular computer can also be configured through the Services icon in the Control Panel for that computer.

Monitoring Server Performance

The performance of an enterprise server has a direct impact on the performance of everybody connected to that server. It's important to take a proactive approach, identifying small issues and potential problems early. Three basic activities are involved in monitoring server performance, as follows:

- Establishing a baseline for normal performance
- Viewing event logs
- Analyzing variations from normal performance

Viewing Event Logs

Windows NT Server enables you to monitor any significant system and application event. The monitoring is configurable. For events that do not necessitate immediate attention, Windows NT Server adds event information to an Event Log file and lets you view this audit trail at a later time.

Windows NT records selected user activities and system events in log files. The System Log records events generated by the Windows NT system components. The failure of a system component to load during startup, such as the Server service, is recorded in the System Log. The Security Log records system security events. This helps track modifications to system security and points out any attempted breaches to security. Attempts to log on to the system may be recorded in the Security Log, depending on the audit settings in User Manager. The Application Log records events generated by applications. For example, a database application might record a data access error. The Event Logs list the following three kinds of messages:

- **Information**—A message to make you aware of a condition or action that is probably not serious
- **Warning**—A message alerting you to a condition or situation that should be investigated and may become more serious if left unchecked
- **Error**—An error message indicating a potentially serious condition (for example, a driver not loading due to a corrupt file)

The Event Viewer enables you to view and monitor these Log files. The Event Viewer is a service that, by default, starts automatically with the system. The Event Viewer startup status can be found in the Services administrator in the Control Panel. It is recommended that you enable the Event Log to start and run on its own. It can be a valuable information source when troubleshooting. To use the Event Viewer, follow these steps:

1. From the Administrative Tools program group, double-click the Event Viewer icon.

2. The Event Viewer window appears (see Figure 7.23). Determine which log file you are viewing.

 T I P There are two ways to determine which log file you are viewing: the title bar and the Log menu. The title bar explicitly specifies the log file type, whereas the Log menu places a check mark next to the log file type you are viewing.

FIG. 7.23

The Event Viewer is showing system type activity written to the System Log.

Date	Time	Source	Category	Event	User	Computer
11/7/96	12:52:24 PM	NETLOGON	None	5711	N/A	HQSRV1
11/7/96	12:47:25 PM	NETLOGON	None	5711	N/A	HQSRV1
11/7/96	12:47:24 PM	NETLOGON	None	5711	N/A	HQSRV1
11/7/96	12:47:24 PM	NETLOGON	None	5711	N/A	HQSRV1
11/7/96	12:47:24 PM	NETLOGON	None	5712	N/A	HQSRV1
11/7/96	12:47:23 PM	BROWSER	None	8035	N/A	HQSRV1
11/7/96	12:46:39 PM	NETLOGON	None	5715	N/A	HQSRV1
11/7/96	12:46:38 PM	NETLOGON	None	5715	N/A	HQSRV1
11/7/96	12:41:38 PM	NETLOGON	None	5715	N/A	HQSRV1
11/7/96	9:13:50 AM	BROWSER	None	8015	N/A	HQSRV1
11/7/96	9:13:50 AM	NETLOGON	None	5715	N/A	HQSRV1
11/7/96	9:13:40 AM	EventLog	None	6005	N/A	HQSRV1
11/7/96	9:01:06 AM	BROWSER	None	8015	N/A	HQSRV1
11/7/96	9:00:38 AM	EventLog	None	6005	N/A	HQSRV1
11/7/96	8:58:17 AM	BROWSER	None	8033	N/A	HQSRV1
11/7/96	8:18:31 AM	DhcpServer	None	1024	N/A	HQSRV1
11/7/96	8:18:03 AM	NETLOGON	None	5719	N/A	HQSRV1
11/7/96	8:18:02 AM	BROWSER	None	8015	N/A	HQSRV1
11/7/96	8:17:48 AM	NETLOGON	None	3096	N/A	HQSRV1
11/7/96	8:17:04 AM	EventLog	None	6005	N/A	HQSRV1
11/7/96	8:15:05 AM	BROWSER	None	8033	N/A	HQSRV1
11/7/96	8:09:33 AM	BROWSER	None	8015	N/A	HQSRV1
11/7/96	8:09:33 AM	NETLOGON	None	5719	N/A	HQSRV1
11/7/96	8:09:18 AM	NETLOGON	None	3096	N/A	HQSRV1
11/7/96	8:08:32 AM	EventLog	None	6005	N/A	HQSRV1

3. Interpret the information displayed in the Event Viewer. The information is displayed in seven columns, as follows:

- **Date**—Indicates the date the event occurred. The icon immediately to the left of the date indicates the status of the event when it occurred.

- **Time**—Indicates the time on the local server that the event occurred.

- **Source**—Indicates the software that logged the event.

- **Category**—Shows the classification of the event as it was defined by the source software.

- **Event**—Indicates a specific number identifying the event.

- **User**—Indicates a user associated with the event.

- **Computer**—Indicates the name of the computer where the event occurred.

 TROUBLESHOOTING

A message tells me that a service won't start. Use the Control Panel Services icon and try to manually start the service. Sometimes you get additional information about why the service won't start, which can aid problem resolution.

Part

II

Ch

7

Managing Event Logs   The Event Viewer is somewhat configurable. Controlling the size of a Log file is useful if you have limited system resources. The log wrapper instructs Windows NT on a course of action should an Event Log be filled. To adjust the settings for a Log file, perform the following tasks:

1. From the Administrative Tools program group, click the Event Viewer icon.

2. Make sure that the active log is the Security Log. If not, choose Log, Security.

3. Choose Log, Log Settings.

4. The Event Log Settings information dialog box appears with default settings (see Figure 7.24). Note that the log type indicates Security.

FIG. 7.24

The Event Log Settings dialog box enables you to manage the capacity of the log.

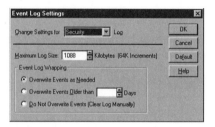

5. Depending on the size of your network, the 512K maximum log size may be sufficient. If you are logging a lot of event detail, however, it could fill up fast. This will probably be a trial and error exercise for you. Initially, you should default to the 512K log size, but change the log wrapping option to Do Not Overwrite Events. When the log fills up, adjust the log wrapping feature, if necessary.

6. Choose OK.

Clearing and Saving Log Files   The Event Logs available in the Event Viewer can be archived for future use. You may find this useful for future troubleshooting or verification. The Log can be saved as a text file or in a file format native to the Event Viewer. The latter format enables you to view the file directly with the Event Viewer.

Archiving the Log saves the entire Log. There are two methods of saving an Event Log: You can choose Log, Save As in the Event Viewer, or you can save the log automatically when prompted after choosing Log, Clear All Events to clear an Event Log as detailed in the next procedure.

To clear the log file, perform the following tasks:

1. From the Administrative Tools program group, click the Event Viewer icon.

2. Choose Log, Clear All Events. The confirmation dialog box shown in Figure 7.25 appears.

3. Obviously, if you have accidentally chosen the Clear option, choose Cancel. If you want to clear the Log and save the contents to a file, choose Yes. At that time, you are asked to supply a file name and path for the file. If you want to clear the Log and not save the contents to a file, choose No.

FIG. 7.25
The Clear Event Log
dialog box forces a
confirmation before
clearing the log.

4. Choose <u>Y</u>es at this time. Note the default file extension EVT. Using this file extension saves the file in an Event Viewer format.

5. If you had not chosen to save the Event Log as a file, you would have received a warning message box. You can choose <u>Y</u>es to clear all events from the Log.

Viewing Remote Log Files   Windows NT Server enables you to look at the Event Log for a user's computer. As an administrator, you will find this useful sometimes. It can assist you in troubleshooting an error situation on that computer. To view a Remote Log file using the Event Viewer, perform the following tasks:

1. From the Administrative Tools program group, double-click the Event Viewer icon.

2. Choose <u>L</u>og, <u>S</u>elect Computer.

3. You are presented with a list of the available computers for which you can view Event Logs (see Figure 7.26).

FIG. 7.26
The Select Computer
dialog box facilitates
the selection of a
computer for viewing
the Remote Log file.

4. Select the computer you want and click OK. If you've done this correctly, the remote computer's Event Log appears on the screen. You will be viewing the same type of Log file as was selected on the server.

5. While attempting to access a Remote Log, you may encounter an access denied message. This can mean that you don't have the correct permissions to view the Event Log, or that the person's computer has been turned off. Verify this before attempting to view the Remote Log again.

Setting and Responding to Alerts

The Alerter service is used to send alert messages to specified users and to users connected to the server. Alert messages warn about many types of problems including security and access issues, printer issues, and user sessions. Administrative alerts are generated by the system as a response to server and resource use. Alert messages are sent as Windows NT messages from the server to a user's computer.

You can determine which computers are notified when alerts occur at the server. For alerts to be sent, the Alerter and Messenger services must be running on the server. For alerts to be received, a Messenger service must be running on the destination computer. If the destination computer is not on, the message eventually will time out. The destination computer must be running Windows for Workgroups, Windows NT, Windows 95, OS/2, or an MS-DOS Messenger driver.

Enabling Administrative Alerts   To enable the Alerter service, perform the following steps:

1. From the Control Panel, choose the Services icon.
2. Locate and select the Alerter service item.
3. Choose the Startup button.
4. Choose Automatic as the Service startup type.
5. Choose OK. The Alerter service now starts automatically with the system.
6. Click Start.

Assigning Administrative Alert Recipients   Use Server Manager to specify the administrators, users, and computers that should receive administrative alerts. To manage the list of administrative alert recipients, perform the following steps:

1. In the Server Manager window, choose Computer, Properties. The Properties dialog box appears, as shown in Figure 7.27.

FIG. 7.27

The Properties for HQSRV1 dialog box enables the administrator to specify the recipients of administrative alerts.

2. In the Properties dialog box, choose Alerts. The Alerts dialog box appears, as shown in Figure 7.28.
3. To add a user or computer to the list of alert recipients, type the username or computer name in the New Computer or Username box, and then choose Add.
4. To remove a user or computer from the list of alert recipients, select the username or computer name from the Send Administrative Alerts To box and then choose Remove.
5. Choose OK to exit.

FIG. 7.28
The Alerts dialog box is showing the addition of the user DONB to receive administrative alerts.

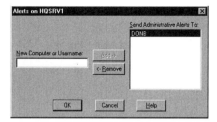

Notifying Users

Sometimes it is important and useful to send a message to a user base. This is especially true following an alert or error message. If the users are sent an alert saying that print services are going down, then it is important to send another message to them when print services are back online. Another important occasion to send a message is when important network resources are going to be down for a period of time. To send a message to a user, perform the following steps:

1. From the Administrative Tools program group, click the Server Manager icon.
2. Choose Computer, Send Message. The Send Message dialog box appears.
3. In the Send Message dialog box, type in the message, as shown in Figure 7.29.

FIG. 7.29
The Send Message dialog box is showing a message that will be sent to specified users or computers.

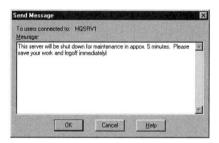

4. Choose OK. The message will be sent to all users currently connected to the selected server that are running the Windows NT Messenger service. Computers running the WinPopUp program will receive the message as well.

N O T E Users will only see messages sent in this fashion if they are running WinPopUp or another utility designed to receive NetBIOS messages. ▦

Making Backups

About the worst thing that can happen to a network administrator is loss of data without adequate backups available. Data stored on your Windows NT Server is critical to your business. It is obvious, then, that a sound backup strategy must be rigorously implemented.

Part
II

Ch
7

This section outlines the tasks that must be carried out by the network administrator to perform backups of the data residing on Windows NT Server. It includes a discussion of backup strategies and methods, Windows NT backup sets, and a step-by-step description of the procedures required to back up and restore data. When you are finished with this section, you will be able to back up and restore data on Windows NT Server in a manner best suited for your network.

The Backup Tool

Windows NT Server includes a backup tool found in the Administrative Tools program group. The program enables you to easily back up and restore important files on NTFS, HPFS, or FAT file systems. You can supply detailed selection criteria for the backup and have the backup verified. The Backup utility enables you to select disks and directories or files to be backed up, including shared directories on other computers.

More complete backup utilities with much richer sets of features are available from various third parties. The Arcada Backup Exec product, for example, enables you to initiate backups from a remote workstation, monitor the progress of the backup in detail, and easily create and manage automated backup schedules. Any large network site should strongly consider purchasing a tool that provides more capabilities than the standard Backup utility combined with the Schedule service. That combination is described here.

Backup Media

The Backup program is designed for use with a tape drive. It is certainly possible to make backups using a fixed disk or floppies, but you may be unable to back up all the system files. We highly recommend that you employ a tape drive. These mass-storage devices make centralized administration of backups more reliable and easier. When storing large amounts of data, it is really the right backup medium choice.

N O T E If you don't have a tape drive, the files REGBACK and REGREST (available with the Windows NT Resource Kit) will enable you to back up and restore the system registry with floppy disks. See the Windows NT Resource Kit for more information on employing this method. ■

Windows NT Server supports high-capacity SCSI tapes for 4mm, 8mm, and 0.25-inch drives, as well as economical mini-cartridge drives. The Backup utility enables you to place multiple backups on a single tape set. You can also span multiple tapes for a single backup. Determine storage needs and objectives prior to purchasing a tape drive. Be sure that the brand and model you intend to purchase is supported and listed on the Hardware Compatibility List.

N O T E Even though you can have numerous tape drives connected to your system, only one can be selected at a time. ■

▶ **See** "Verifying Hardware Compatibility," **p. 127**

Understanding Windows NT Backup Sets

A *backup set* is a collection of files or directories selected for backup. These files or directories can be appended to or replace an existing backup set. A *family set*, or *tape set*, is the group of tapes that make up one backup set. The Backup tool automatically creates a *tape catalog* for each backup set. A tape catalog (stored on the last tape in the tape set) contains information about the backup set.

Backup Methods

File-based backup methods can be broadly categorized as *complete* or *incremental*. A complete backup copies all files from the source. An incremental backup copies only those files that have changed since the last backup. (An archive bit indicates whether each file has changed since last backed up.) Windows NT Backup supports both types of backups, also providing the option to leave the archive bit unchanged. The archive bit is an indication that a file has been archived. Windows NT Server uses the following terms to define backup methods:

- **Daily backup**—This backs up only those files changed that calendar day. The archive bit remains set. These files will be selected for backup during the next normal backup. The daily backup is most often used as an interim backup or to get a copy of working files.

- **Differential backup**—This backs up files flagged as not archived. The archive flag is cleared after backup. This is helpful between full backups because restoring the data only requires restoring the last full backup and the most recent differential backup.

- **Incremental backup**—This backs up files flagged as not archived. They are then flagged as being archived. This is similar to the differential backup.

- **Copy**—All files on the selected disk are backed up, but the archive bit remains set.

- **Normal backup**—This creates a full backup of all files and resets the archive bit for all files successfully backed up. Perform a normal backup periodically for safety.

Developing a Backup Strategy

As with disaster recovery plans, the most critical element of backups is to be sure that they work reliably. This means that the entire backup plan has to be thoroughly designed and periodically tested. An effective backup strategy should provide reliable performance of backups, offsite storage of recent complete backup sets, and reliable restoration when needed.

> **N O T E** Backups provide *disaster recovery*. Do not confuse this with *fault tolerance*, which enables a server to continue operating after a partial failure. Fault tolerance strategies include disk mirroring and stripe sets with parity. Disaster recovery (backup) preserves data after a catastrophic loss, such as the theft of the entire server. ▦

Part

II

Ch

7

Implement your backup plan before beginning network operations. This means that the plan should be fully prepared and exercised prior to the server being put into operation. After the plan is implemented, it must be followed. Consider the following points when developing a backup strategy:

■ Make the backup process someone's job. Assign at least one other person this responsibility in a contingency role.

■ Determine how often you will perform backups. You should base this decision on how much data your organization can afford to lose or rebuild. Most companies implement daily backups.

■ Daily backups can quickly fill a lot of tapes. Most companies have a plan for reusing backup tapes. A popular and straightforward routine is described in "The Child, Parent, Grandparent Method" section later in this chapter.

■ Determine when the backups will occur. Usually, backups occur after hours to spare users the overhead associated with the process. Doing so requires use of the Windows NT Server Schedule Service. Refer to "Scheduling a Backup" later in this chapter for more information. If you decide to perform backups during business hours, determine the impact this will have on your network performance in advance.

■ Regardless of the backup time, devise a plan to verify that the backup occurred completely and without error. Windows NT Backup automatically creates a backup log file. Determine the appropriate level of detail based on the following descriptions:

  • **Full Detail**—Records the name of every file backed up as well as other major backup event information.

  • **Summary Only**—Records major backup event information only.

  • **No Log**—Records nothing.

■ Determine two safe places to store the tapes: one onsite and one offsite. These places need to be secure, yet practical. Store the tapes in a waterproof and fireproof safe or vault, if possible, so that they will be protected in the event that water, smoke, or fire damages the premises. Tapes with data should be stored both onsite and offsite. Tapes with software should be stored offsite.

■ Keep accurate records of the information on each tape. Do this in a binder and on the tape label. This helps you to identify tapes correctly when performing a restore.

■ Create a manual of your backup, restore, and test procedures. When changes in the procedures occur, make these changes to the manual. Keep this manual with other company records. If the backup expert leaves your organization, don't let the knowledge go with him.

The Child, Parent, Grandparent Method

This common backup method keeps daily backups, weekly backups for the past month, and monthly backups for the past year. Daily backups (children) are kept on site; weekly (parent) and monthly (grandparent) backups are kept offsite.

You need enough tapes to perform 16 complete backups plus four daily backups (assuming that backups are performed Monday through Friday only). Daily backups can be complete, incremental, or differential. Tape sets should be labeled for each month (12 sets): Friday1, Friday2, Friday3, Friday4, and Friday5; and Monday, Tuesday, Wednesday, and Thursday.

Monday through Thursday make a daily backup using the tape set labeled for the given week-day. This means that daily backups will be recycled once a week. Each Friday, make a complete backup: Use the Friday1 tape set for the first Friday in a month, Friday2 for the second Friday, and so on. The complete Friday backup sets should be stored offsite. Note that Friday sets get recycled once a month. On the last day of each month, make an extra complete backup using the tape set labeled for that month. Monthly backup sets recycle once a year and should be stored offsite.

Developing a Backup Test

An important component of the backup strategy is the backup test. Every facet of the backup scenario needs to be tested for reliability, validity, timeliness, and security. A test of the backup and restore processes should be periodically performed to make sure that environmental or employment status changes have not rendered the backup process invalid. Consider the follow-ing points when developing a test of the backup and restore procedures:

- Make a list of all the tasks required to perform a backup or restore. Associate people with each task. If any one task is being performed by only one person, there is a danger. On the day when an emergency restore is needed, inevitably that person will be off sick or at lunch. Make it a rule that at least two people are to have access to network adminis-tration, backup tapes, server software, and server hardware and will know how to get the backup job done. Make sure that these people are never on vacation at the same time.

- There is no guarantee that a backup tape will restore. However, if you make a backup and perform a test restore successfully, you can be reasonably assured of a successful restore a second time. Have spare backup tapes available in case a tape goes bad. Perform diagnostics on tapes periodically. Follow the guidelines of the tape manufacturer for replacement tapes.

- Assuming failure, determine how long it will take to restore the last backup. Understand how much downtime your network users can afford. A restore is most valuable if it can speedily bring your network back to normal.

Performing an Interactive Backup

To perform an interactive (user controlled) backup of the C drive, log on as an administrator or backup operator and complete the following tasks:

1. Double-click the Backup program item in the Administrative Tools program group. The Backup window appears.

N O T E The Backup window may be minimized. If so, double-click the icon labeled Drives in the
Backup window. ■

If the tape drive has not been powered on or connected properly, or the correct software driver for your tape drive is missing or improperly installed, you will receive a message. If this message should occur, exit the Backup utility and check both the tape drive connections and the software drivers.

Part
II

Ch
7

TROUBLESHOOTING

Windows NT Server failed to detect the tape drive after system startup. An external SCSI tape drive should be turned on before booting the server. At system startup, the SCSI adapter scans for attached devices, and will not detect a tape drive that has not been turned on. Windows NT Server will be unable to access the drive until it is turned on and the system rebooted.

2. Select the drive you want to back up. You must do this even if there is only one drive in the Drives window. Choose the Backup button in the Backup dialog box. The Backup Information dialog box appears.

TROUBLESHOOTING

The message Tape Drive Error Detected appears. Inserting a tape that has a lower density than the tape drive can cause this error to appear. Click the Backup button in the Backup dialog box to eject the tape.

The Application log in the Event Viewer is filled with the message No tape in drive. Running Backup without a tape can cause this to happen in certain tape drives. You must delete these event messages to free up the Event Log before you can run any other application-associated tasks.

3. Enter a Tape Name. The maximum tape name length is 50 characters or spaces. Only 32 characters are visible, however. Give the tape a descriptive name that will remind you of its contents.

4. Choose the Verify After Backup check box. Although it takes a little longer, the verification helps to ensure that a restore will be complete and accurate. At a minimum, you should include this option when performing a normal backup.

5. Choose the Backup Registry check box if you or others have made changes to the local registry files. These files contain configuration information about the local computer.

6. Select Append to add this backup set to a backup set currently on the tape. Select Replace to have the new backup overwrite the old backup set. Obviously, you need to know what has been archived previously to the tape. For this example, you're performing the first normal backup. Therefore, choose Append.

7. Restrict the access to the backup set by selecting the Restrict Access to Owner or Administrator check box. This limits who can restore backups and institutes a level of security into your backup strategy.

8. Note the drive you have selected. Double-check it for accuracy. If it is not the correct drive, choose Cancel and change the selection.

9. Enter a description for this backup. As with the tape name, give a description that will help you remember the tape contents.

10. Choose Normal from the Backup Type list box.

11. Specify a file that will contain a log of the backup process. A good name is BACKUP.LOG. This file indicates the number of files backed up, how many were not, the amount of time the process consumed, and any errors encountered. You may find it useful to create a special directory in advance to store all log files in.

12. Choose the level of detail you desire for this backup. Consider the following options:

   - **Full Detail**—Records the name of every file backed up as well as other major backup event information.
   - **Summary Only**—Records major backup event information only.
   - **Don't Log**—Records nothing.

   For the first backup, choose Full Detail. Following the backup, review the log. Determine if this level of detail is acceptable or excessive for your needs. Adjust this selection accordingly in the future.

13. Choose OK to complete the Backup Information dialog box and begin the backup operation. The Backup Status dialog box keeps you informed during the entire process.

14. You will probably require the use of multiple backup tapes when backing up the local hard drive. The Windows NT Backup utility makes this easy. When available tape space has been consumed, a dialog box requests an additional tape.

TIP Determine in advance the volume you will be backing up, and have enough tapes available for the entire backup process.

N O T E If you need to terminate the backup process, choose Abort. Any files that were backed up prior to the Abort will be on the tape. Furthermore, any file that was within 1M of completion will be on the tape, but any file that was not within 1M of completion will be corrupted on the tape. ▨

Scheduling a Backup

Backups can be so time-consuming that performing them during business hours can be impractical. The best time for this activity is when it causes the least impact on the use of network resources. This normally would be sometime during the night. The Backup utility included with Windows NT Server does not facilitate scheduling unattended backups. Fortunately, Windows NT Server provides a way to run backups automatically. The command prompt, in conjunction with the Schedule service, enables you to schedule backups (and many other types of activities) while you are away.

Configuring the Schedule Service   The Windows NT Server Schedule service is required to support scheduled backups. Follow these steps to configure the Schedule service to start automatically each time the server restarts:

1. From the Control Panel, select the Services icon.

Part

II

Ch

7

2. Locate and select the Schedule service entry. The default Startup mode for any service is Manual.

3. Choose Startup.

4. Select Automatic as the Startup Type. This enables the Schedule service to start each time the system starts.

5. You need to select an account type. Services need a logon when they start. The default option is system account. Most services log on using the system account. This account will run a service without necessitating a user logon. Some services, however, may need more privileges to perform their programmed actions. The Schedule service is one example.

   If you want to schedule commands that need more than guest privileges on network resources, you will have to assign a network access-permitted account to the service. The system account has only guest privileges on remote shares. Select the system account for now.

6. Choose OK. The Schedule service now has an automatic startup.

7. Choose the Start button. The system attempts to start the Schedule service. If successful, the Schedule service will have a Started status.

8. Click Close.

9. Close the Control Panel.

Setting Up a Scheduled Backup   When the Schedule service is running, you can execute many programs and commands on the server at a specified time and date. Using the command prompt and the AT network command, you can automate the backup process so that it runs after hours.

 The Windows NT Resource Kit includes a GUI alternative to the command prompt for scheduling unattended backups. For a complete description of the AT, NTBACKUP, and BACKUP commands, refer to Windows NT Help in the Main program group.

Naturally, you should determine in advance how often you want to make backups and which files to include. Refer to your backup plan. The following instructions are an example:

1. From the Main program group, click the Command Prompt icon. The session opens to the default directory.

2. Create a text file with the following command line:

   ```
   ntbackup backup C: /D "Daily Backups" /B /L "C:\results.log"
   ```

 Type **edit** at the command prompt to start the text editor, or use Notepad or WordPad.

The components of the command line are defined as follows:

- backup is the operation to be executed.
- C: is the path that will be backed up.

- /D specifies a description of the backup contents.
- /B specifies that the local registry is to be backed up.
- /L specifies the file name and path for the backup log.

The preceding command backs up all files on the C drive. The process replaces any files currently on the tape.

N O T E The NTBACKUP command invokes the Backup tool in the Administrative Tools program group. ▪

3. Save the file as CBACKUP.CMD.
4. Schedule a backup event using the AT command with the following syntax:

```
at [\\computername] time [/every:date[,...] ¦ /next:date[,...]] command
```

The components of the syntax are defined as follows:

- Computername is the computer on which you are scheduling the event to run. If omitted, the event will be scheduled to run on the local system.
- Time is any hour and minute from 00:00 (midnight) to 23:59 (11:59 PM).
- Date is the day of the week or the number representing the day of the week.
- Command is any command, program, or batch file.

N O T E If the command is not an executable file, you must precede the command with cmd /c, for example:

```
at 10:50 "cmd /c c:\users\default\update.bat" ▪
```

 T I P Type **help at** at the command prompt for the AT command syntax.

---

5. Enter an appropriate command to schedule your backups.
6. At the prompt, type **at** by itself to see the scheduled job you just entered. When it executes, the Schedule service performs the instructions specified in CBACKUP.CMD.
7. Type **Exit** and press Enter to close the command prompt.

Restoring Files

The process of restoring files is similar to that for backing them up. To perform a normal restore of the C drive, complete the following tasks:

1. If the backup set spans multiple tapes, insert the last backup tape into the tape drive. If the backup set is contained on only one tape, insert that tape.
2. Click the Backup program item in the Administrative Tools program group. The Backup administration window appears.

Part
II

Ch
7

3. Locate the Tapes window. In all likelihood, the Tapes window will be minimized. If so, double-click the Tapes icon. The Tapes window appears.

4. Select the tape, catalog, or files you want to restore. For this example, select the tape by clicking the check box next to it. This performs a normal restore of the entire tape. Click OK.

5. In the Restore Information dialog box, choose the drive letter to which the tape files should be restored. This is an important step. Be careful to choose the correct drive. For this example, choose drive C.

6. Enable the Verify After Restore check box. This offers assurance that the restore was successful.

7. If your file permissions have changed since the tape backup was made, do not enable the Restore File Permissions check box.

8. If your local registry has changed since the tape backup was made, do not enable the Restore Local Registry check box.

9. Specify a file that will contain a log of the restore process. A good name is RESTORE.LOG. This file will indicate the number of files restored, how many were not, the amount of time the process consumed, and any errors encountered. You may find it useful to create a special directory in advance to store all log files.

10. Choose the level of detail you desire for this restore. Choose Full Detail to record the name of every file restored as well as other major restore information. Choose Summary Only to record major restore information only. Choose Don't Log to record no event information.

11. Click OK.

12. Observe the restore information in the Restore Status information dialog box.

TROUBLESHOOTING

A warning message appears when attempting to restore corrupted files. Windows NT makes a copy of corrupted files during backup. It marks these files appropriately in the backup status field. The corrupted file list is stored in CORRUPT.TXT. As long as these corrupted files exist, you will get a warning any time you attempt to restore one of them. Therefore, these files should be removed before attempting to restore.

Managing Log Files

Windows NT can track selected activities of users by auditing system, security, and application events and then placing entries in respective log files. The System log records events generated by the Windows NT system components. The Security log records system security events. The Application log records events generated by applications. The Event Viewer, which is somewhat configurable, then enables you to view and monitor these log files. It also enables you to control the size of a log file. This is particularly useful if you have limited system resources.

Windows NT can record a wide variety of successful and unsuccessful file access event types. Use the Audit policy in the User Manager for Domains and the Audit policy in the Security menu of File Manager to control the types of security events to be audited as well as file and directory access. This, in turn, determines the types of security events Windows NT records in the log files.

The Event Logs available in the Event Viewer can be archived for future use. You may find this useful for troubleshooting or verification. The Log can be saved as a text file or in a file format native to the Event Viewer. The latter format enables you to view the file directly with the Event Viewer.

▶ **See** "Checking the Logs," **p. 151**

From Here...

This chapter is a survey of the Windows NT Server administrative tools and the typical tasks required of the network administrator. It covered all the basics of sharing resources and setting access permissions, and included important information on making backups. All of the important tools for managing Windows NT servers and its users were described, with how-to information on common actions. For more information on the topics addressed in this chapter, see the following chapters:

- To review basic installation and setup procedures for Windows NT Server, see Chapter 5, "Implementing Windows NT Server."

- To gain a better understanding of the popular TCP/IP transport protocol, see Chapter 9, "Using TCP/IP with Windows NT Server."

- To learn about Windows NT Server Remote Access Service (RAS), see Chapter 11, "An Inside Look at Remote Access Service (RAS)," and Chapter 12, "Implementing Remote Access Service (RAS)."

Part
II

Ch
7

## CHAPTER 8

Windows NT Server Directory Services

by Don Benage

You were introduced to domains in Chapter 4, "Enterprise Planning and Implementation," but the details of the *directory services* provided by Windows NT Server have not yet been presented. This chapter introduces you to the concept of a directory service and the functionality it provides. The specific characteristics of the Windows NT directory services are discussed, along with the different domain models you can implement to best address the needs of your organization. Several ways to configure your organization's servers are presented. These methods all involve the use of multiple domains, and provide different features in terms of security and control.

After a thorough exploration of the current Windows NT Server directory services and the use of domains, this chapter outlines the future development of Active Directory and the Open Directory Services Interface (ODSI). Microsoft has joined with other industry partners and the Internet community in developing solutions to the limitations in current directory services. The current state of that effort and specific product plans are discussed. ■

Why directory services are important

Learn about the features provided by directory services. Find out how Windows NT Server implements directory services, and how to use them.

Microsoft BackOffice security basics

See how security is implemented in Microsoft BackOffice family products, and what considerations you should give to security in planning your implementation.

Implementing domain models and using domain trust

Learn about the primary Windows NT domain models, and find out how to implement an appropriate domain model in your organization.

The future of Windows NT directory services

Learn how Microsoft BackOffice provides built-in access to users not connected directly to the network.

Understanding Directory Services

In a large computer network with many shared resources and users, one of the biggest challenges is finding the resources (printers, shared data, applications, and so on) that you need. It can also be a challenge to find a particular user you would like to communicate with using e-mail or another tool, such as an online chat utility. In the real world, you have many directories to help you find things. The yellow pages and white pages published by telephone companies are probably the most widely used directories, but there are many others. Similar services are provided on computer networks, but as you will learn in this chapter, they are still evolving. The services available today provide the most important features required, but fall short of an *ideal* solution in a number of ways.

The *domain* architecture of Windows NT Server provides the basis for the current directory services on a Windows NT network. The basics of using a single domain have already been outlined in Chapter 4, "Enterprise Planning and Implementation." In that chapter, you learned the difference between a workgroup and a domain, and how domains provided the capability to use a single user ID and password to access resources anywhere in the domain. In addition, you learned how to create a trust relationship between two domains.

By using trust relationships, you can implement a variety of *domain models* that enable you to manage even very large networks effectively. There is not a single correct way to set up a large enterprise. The best choices for you will depend on the nature of your organization, its *culture,* and the type of work environment you want to create. Windows NT Server enables you to configure your domains so that a very rigid structure with tight security controls is present; or you can set up your domains so that a relatively open environment with a few loose controls is provided. You can have a single, centrally located group in control, or delegate a great deal of control to individual departments or locations.

There are a number of features that are provided by a directory service. Some of the features are geared toward the user community and others are targeted at the administrators of the network. The features of a directory service are usually accessed through a variety of applications. Administrators can use specialized tools to add users or other resources to a directory. In addition to logging on to the network (which accesses a directory of valid user IDs and passwords), network users need simple tools that have been *directory enabled.* In other words, the user community should not have to be concerned about the details of a directory service that may be important to administrators.

Authentication

The users of a large network must be authenticated. It is critical to restrict access to network resources to a limited population: only those users who are authorized by the organization that owns and operates the network. Ideally, a single user ID and password provides the credentials needed to access all the resources that the user needs. In the past, it was common for users to need several user IDs and passwords for different systems and, in fact, there are many networks currently in operation for which this is still the case. Older network operating systems (e.g., NetWare 3.x) generally required a separate login for each server that a user accessed. Applications, such as e-mail or databases, can also have separate passwords.

Besides antagonizing users, this can actually lead to reduced security. Because the user community is frustrated with remembering too many passwords, especially if they must regularly be changed, users tend to write them down and leave them in places that are accessible to hackers or other unauthorized users. A centralized directory service that provides single-logon access to a wide range of resources is, therefore, an important component of network security. This feature is provided by Windows NT Server and is one of the strengths of the BackOffice family. The way this is implemented is explored in the next section.

A directory service can sometimes provide authentication for a collection of *heterogeneous resources* in addition to its own native facilities. This kind of integration among products from different vendors was extremely rare in the past, but it is a feature that is becoming more common in response to the demands of network buyers and users.

Locating and Using Resources

Network users also need assistance locating resources. In a large network, it can be difficult to find the printer down the hall or the shareware utilities directory. Some means of quickly and easily locating this type of resource is needed. It is also desirable to facilitate the process of finding a particular user on an e-mail system or other form of electronic communication. Even if you know a person's name, company, street address, and phone number, you cannot send that person e-mail without an e-mail address. The converse situation is also true: an e-mail address is of no use in sending a letter or package via conventional mail or in making a phone call.

A directory service is ideally suited to capture this type of information and provide users with an easily accessible means of looking it up. It can also facilitate sharing this information with coworkers. A sophisticated directory service might even provide a specific subset of its information to the general public. As you will see in the next section, Windows NT Server provides some of this functionality, but benefits from some improvements that are being designed into the next generation of tools and services.

Application Support

A complete directory service also makes its data available to application developers, both as a repository for application-specific information (if appropriate) and as a source for information on people, computers, and other network resources. This use of directory services is an area that everyone agrees is important, but causes the most difficulties in its implementation. To be useful, the information stored by the directory service must have some limitations. It can't become a dumping ground for every piece of *ad hoc* information that arises. On the other hand, it should store information of a generic nature pertaining to a broad range of users. Good judgment is required in deciding what should be added to the directory database.

Windows NT Server Security Overview

Now that you have a feel for the sort of information and features that might be implemented in a directory service, the specific features of Windows NT Server and the other members of the BackOffice family are explored.

The security in a Windows NT Server environment begins with a user logon. This can be done from a desktop computer running a variety of operating systems, as follows:

- MS-DOS
- Windows 3.x
- Windows for Workgroups
- Windows 95
- Windows NT
- Apple's Mac OS
- OS/2
- UNIX

N O T E   The functionality provided for Microsoft's own operating systems is more complete than that which is provided for competitive operating systems. For example, Macintosh clients cannot execute logon scripts stored on a Windows NT server. ■

▶ **See** "Getting Connected from a Client Workstation," **p. 140**
▶ **See** "Integrating Operating Systems," **p. 402**

When a user logs on, the user ID and password are checked against the user account database. A sophisticated protocol is used so that an attacker with the capability to capture the network traffic associated with logging on will not be able to use this information to gain access. If the user ID and password are valid, and if any restrictions regarding time of day, day of the week, or workstations that may be used have been met, the user is authenticated and the logon process is completed. If the ID/password combination is not valid, another opportunity to log on is typically provided. It is possible to disable the account if a set number of invalid logon attempts are made.

Once connected to the network, a user can optionally connect to other shared resources. In this situation, an *access control list (ACL)* for the resource is checked to see if the user has been granted any permissions. Different access levels can be set for different users and groups of users. In fact, it is desirable to use groups wherever possible, and avoid assigning permissions to individual users. This is discussed more fully in the next section.

The basic capability to authenticate users and to regulate access to network resources is the foundation upon which all of the more sophisticated security features are based. This capability is critical in light of the increasing amount of sensitive information that is stored on desktop computers. The next section addresses the use of domains to create a centralized user account database and the use of trust relationships for creating security architectures capable of supporting networks with tens of thousands of users.

Domains

It is possible to set up each Windows NT Server as a stand-alone entity with a completely separate user account database. This creates some obvious problems—especially in a large network environment—and so it is rarely done in practice. Most often, the servers are set up to create a domain.

Each domain has a single *primary domain controller* (*PDC*). There may also be one or more *backup domain controllers* (*BDCs*). In addition, there is a role in the domain known simply as *server*. Each computer running Windows NT Server must take on one of these roles if it is to be included in the domain. The role is determined during installation of the operating system. It is possible to promote a BDC to become the PDC, which automatically demotes the current PDC if it is operational and connected to the network. A BDC can also be promoted if the currently designated PDC has experienced a failure. A repaired PDC that is reconnected to a network with another PDC in operation can be demoted to a BDC. A *server* cannot be converted to a domain controller without reinstalling the operating system.

PDCs and BDCs cannot be added to, or removed from, a domain without reinstalling the operating system. In other words, a domain controller in domain A cannot be moved to domain B. Nor can you take several domain controllers from domain A and rename their domain name to form a new domain. It is, however, possible to rename an *entire* domain. The domain name can be changed on *every* server in the domain, although this can be a difficult task to accomplish and almost always leads to trouble if the domain is larger than two or three servers. For example, when this operation is performed, it usually takes some time before network browsing and searching for network resources function quickly and properly, and some maintenance may need to be done on the Windows Internet Name Service (WINS) database if you are using WINS for name resolution. There is no other scenario in which a domain controller can be moved to a different domain.

A *server*, on the other hand, can be moved from one domain to another with relative ease simply by adding it to the new domain using Server Manager, and changing its domain affiliation in its network properties dialog box. Of course, you should also remove its name from the old domain to avoid confusion. This capability makes the server role ideal for SQL Server database servers and other BackOffice family servers that may need to be moved.

The PDC is the repository of the main copy of the user account database. All changes to the database must be applied to this master copy. Backup copies of the account database are kept on each BDC. As changes are applied to the PDC, they are automatically *replicated* to the BDCs. This is done for two main reasons: to provide a level of fault tolerance (online backup) and to spread the load of authenticating users among multiple servers. Both PDCs and BDCs validate user logons. Computers that are set up as servers do not validate logons, but any shared resources on these computers can be assigned permissions for the users and groups in the domain.

A single domain (set up on appropriate computer hardware) is capable of managing up to 40,000 accounts. These accounts can be individual users, groups, or machine accounts. (See the following Note.) Table 8.1 summarizes Microsoft's recommendations for the required number of BDCs (Intel 486 class machines running at 66 MHz) based on the number of network accounts on the network.

Table 8.1   The Approximate Number of BDCs Required for Different Sizes of Networks

Number of Accounts	Number of BDCs
1–9	0 or 1
10–2,000	1
4,000	2
6,000	3
10,000	5
20,000	10
30,000	15

N O T E   Computers running Windows NT Server or Windows NT Workstation each require a unique machine account in the domain in order to participate in domain security. These must be added to the user and group accounts when calculating the size of the account database. ▪

These numbers should be used only as a guideline. The numbers are based on the following rule of thumb:

> 1 PDC + N BDCs = N×2,000 accounts

When the number of accounts is below 2,000, you should use your judgment and attempt to gauge the activity level and load that will be placed on the servers. For example, do all the users on the network begin work at the same time, or are there groups of users (corresponding to work shifts perhaps) that spread the load more evenly? Are the users on your network power users with a demanding appetite for network resources, or are they occasional users of network resources?

In general, validating logons is an activity that benefits from network bandwidth and domain controllers with fast network adapters, plenty of RAM, and fast processors. Disk space and speed are not very important for this activity.

Security policies are established for an entire domain. Password restrictions (e.g., minimum length, aging, and history) and account lockout settings (e.g., the number of bad logons tolerated before an account is locked) are created and maintained with User Manager for Domains. This security policy information and the user account database are stored on the PDC.

At regular intervals the user account database and the security policy settings are *replicated* to the BDCs. The replication occurs automatically without any setup required on the part of network administrators. The design of the replication process attempts to strike a balance between timeliness of information and keeping the network traffic associated with this process to a minimum. In a network with many BDCs, the replication process targets a configurable number of BDCs rather than all of them at once. Only 2K is required to set up the transmission session, and a maximum of 1K per account is sent during the actual transmission.

Each update transmission is serialized. If a particular BDC is out of service for some time and misses more than 2,000 updates, the entire database will be sent in bulk to the BDC when it is once again on the network. As long as the BDCs are active, only the changes to the database are sent. An administrator can manually initiate a synchronization of the entire domain if necessary using either the Server Manager or by entering the following command from the command line:

```
NET ACCOUNTS /SYNC
```

To use the Server Manager, highlight the PDC and choose Computer, Synchronize Entire Domain.

For the replication process to work effectively, it is important that the system clocks on all servers have the same time. They must be within at least ten minutes of one another, or the process will not function properly. You can cause a BDC to synchronize its clock with the PDC by executing the following command:

```
NET TIME /DOMAIN
```

This command can be run on a regularly scheduled basis using the AT service provided with Windows NT so that the domain controllers are kept on the same time even if there are slight variations in their operation. In order to use this facility, the schedule service must be running on the BDCs. The following command, for example, would cause the NET TIME command to be run every Monday one minute after midnight:

```
AT 00:01 /EVERY:MONDAY "NET TIME /DOMAIN"
```

Trust Relationships

There are reasons why a single domain may not be sufficient for an organization's needs. Some are large enough that 40,000 accounts will not accommodate their entire account database, but there are other reasons as well. By dividing the enterprise into multiple domains, you can delegate the control of account creation and resource management to the people and locations you want to have this control.

Multiple domain environments are created by establishing trust relationships. A trust relationship allows the accounts from one domain to be assigned access permissions for resources in another domain. For example, if domain B trusts domain A, permissions can be assigned allowing users in domain A to use shared data on a server in domain B (see Figure 8.1).

Through the use of trust relationships, a variety of *domain models* can be implemented. The different domain models provide capabilities that match various organizational goals and cultures. For example, you can decide whether control over network user accounts should be in the hands of a single, centralized group or distributed to a number of autonomous groups, each with its own span of control. The primary domain models that are in use are described in the next section.

FIG. 8.1

A simple one-way trust relationship between two domains allows accounts from one domain to be assigned access permissions in the other.

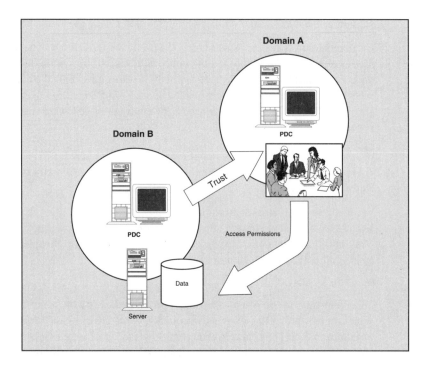

As you review the different domain models and consider the architecture that would best meet the needs of your organization, it is important to remember a few key points about trust relationships, as follows:

- Trust is not transitive. In other words, if domain A trusts domain B, and B trusts C, this does not imply that A trusts C.

- For best results, connect all of the domain controllers in a single domain with reasonably fast links (ISDN or better). It is possible, sometimes even desirable, to place a BDC on the other end of a wide area network (WAN) link; but if the link is too slow, the quality of the network will suffer. See the section "Domain Planning Considerations" later in this chapter for more information on the placement of BDCs.

- Associate a password with each trust relationship. If two domain administrators (one from each domain) are involved in creating the trust relationship, they both need to know the password to complete the operation.

To establish a trust relationship between two domains, you must first decide which is to be the *trusting* domain and which the *trusted* domain. In general, accounts are created in the trusted domain and resources are located in the trusting domain. Review the preceding material if you are still not sure. You must be a Domain Admin of both domains, or have the cooperation of a

Domain Admin for any domains for which you do not have such privileges. If another person is involved, agree beforehand on the password that will be used, and a time by which the first part of the following process (permitting to trust) will have been completed. Then, follow this procedure:

1. Start User Manager for Domains.

2. Choose User, Domain. The Select Domain dialog box appears. Either enter the name of the (soon to be) trusted domain into the Domain text box, or select its name from the list presented in the Select Domain list box. Click OK.

3. Choose Policies, Trust Relationships. The Trust Relationships dialog box appears (see Figure 8.2).

FIG. 8.2

The Trust Relationships dialog box is used to establish trust between two domains.

4. Click the Add button next to the Trusting Domains list box. The Add Trusting Domain dialog box is displayed (see Figure 8.3).

FIG. 8.3

The Add Trusting Domain dialog box is used to permit one domain to trust another.

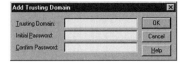

5. Enter the name of the domain that you are permitting to trust this domain in the Trusting Domain text box. Enter the password twice—first in the Initial Password text box, then in the Confirm Password text box.

Now the complimentary procedure must be carried out for the other domain. You must log off and log on using a different workstation that is a member of the new domain, because a single workstation can't simultaneously participate in two domains without a trust relationship. Alternatively, you can use a simple method to establish credentials in the second domain. Using the Explorer, you can map a network drive to an administrative share (e.g., C$) on the PDC in the other domain and use the Connect As text box to enter a Domain Admin user ID from the other domain in the form <domain>/<account>. You will be prompted for the password that corresponds to this account and then a connection will be made establishing you as a Domain Admin for the second domain. You should now be able to choose User, Select Domain from the menu in User Manager for Domains to complete the process.

Domain Models

There are several different domain models from which you can choose. Each has its strengths, and there are particular environments and situations that are best addressed with a certain model. The following are the primary domain models that are often used:

- Single master domain
- Multiple master domain
- Complete trust

The single master domain has the obvious attraction of being simple to understand and implement. As previously mentioned, a single domain is capable of handling up to 40,000 accounts. Unless you need to provide multiple areas of account control or need more accounts than a single domain can accommodate, you should keep things simple and implement a single domain.

A single master domain allows for centralized control of accounts and resources. If you would like to delegate some level of administrative capability, you can use the operator groups to divide responsibilities. There are four main operator groups, as follows:

- Account
- Backup
- Print
- Server

These groups enable you to designate who can help people who have forgotten their passwords, create tape backups, resolve problems with print queues, or reconfigure servers. The exact capabilities of these various groups goes much further than this simple list suggests, but the basic idea is that you divide responsibility by function rather than by geographical area or a physical group of machines.

N O T E You should designate at least two Domain Admins, even on a very small network, to allow for backup in the event of catastrophe. In small organizations, you may have only one active network administrator, but you should still make sure that another person (such as the owner or accountant) has a user ID and password that are in the Domain Admin group. This should not be the account they use every day for normal activity.

On a large network, the number of Domain Admins should be limited to those people who absolutely need to have such privileges. It is a mistake to hand out this capability willy-nilly when a combination of operator roles would generally suffice. ▓

You still need to do some planning if you are implementing on a wide area network (WAN) to make sure that logon validations are handled promptly, and can be accommodated if a WAN link is down. These issues are discussed in the next section, "Domain Planning Considerations."

The single master domain model enables you to further delegate control. The most common implementation uses the one master domain as the repository for all user accounts. Other domains establish a one-way trust relationship with this domain. This provides central control over the creation of user accounts, while allowing the control of resource permissions to be delegated to the area in which those resources are located. These domains are generally referred to as *resource domains.* This model is explored in more detail in the section "The Single Master Domain Model" later in this chapter.

An implementation of the multiple master domain model enables you to establish multiple account domains. For example, in a large manufacturing organization you might have three main operating units of people: Administration, Engineering, and Production. Although you could establish a single master domain and have it managed by a central Information Systems (IS) staff, you might want to separate them. If these operating units are relatively autonomous, it may make sense to have each manage its own user accounts. A master domain can be established for this purpose with one or more resource domains trusting the master. See the section "The Multiple Master Domain Model" later in this chapter for more information.

You should now have a basic understanding of why you might want to create multiple domains, and some of the advantages provided by using different domain models. There are some additional planning issues that should be considered no matter which model is selected. These are outlined in the next section before the master domain models are explored in more detail.

Domain Planning Considerations

When you implement a domain model in the real world, you must make sure that what looked good on paper works in reality. In most diagrams of domain models, the details of WAN links are suppressed. They tend to be *logical* diagrams rather than *physical* diagrams, which correspond to actual components. This section outlines some of the details that must be considered to make sure your plans are successful.

If you are setting up all your servers on a single, high-speed local area network (LAN), then your job is much simpler: the primary planning consideration is ensuring that you select the appropriate number of servers, and they are *sized* properly (i.e., they have the correct components with sufficient speed and capacity to do the job). Sizing issues are discussed in a number of places in this book, and some specifics are offered for different BackOffice family components that make unusual demands on specific hardware elements where this is appropriate. For more information about server sizing, see Chapter 3, "Planning for BackOffice."

Implementations that must span a large geographic area and employ WAN technology require some additional planning. The crux of the matter is a balance of fault tolerance, speed, and expense. Consider for a moment an imaginary company, Fake Corporation, with its headquarters in New York and a branch office in St. Louis. For simplicity, this organization has chosen the single master domain model. A master domain has been established and named FAKE. A resource domain for each office has been established. Their names are NY and STL respectively. Both of these domains trust FAKE (one-way trust). A logical diagram of this scenario is shown in Figure 8.4.

FIG. 8.4

This logical diagram depicts the relationship of the master domain and resource domains for Fake Corporation.

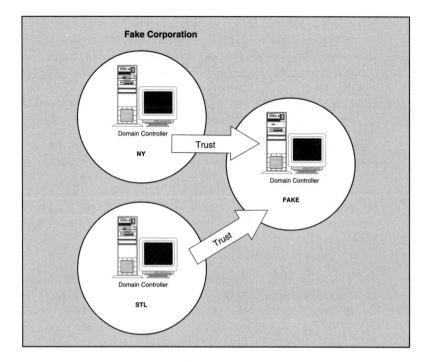

The link between Fake Corporation's New York and St. Louis offices is an ISDN line. It should be reasonably reliable, but may be subject to occasional outages (as is any service). The network traffic between the two offices is anticipated to be only moderate. Most network-based services will be provided by servers located in the same geographic vicinity as the person using them. The WAN link will be used to transfer e-mail from one site to another, perform occasional file transfers, and other *ad hoc* usage.

When it comes time to actually purchase servers and set up the domain structure, some important decisions must be made. It is obvious that at least one server must be established as the PDC for each of the three domains. The PDC for the FAKE domain will *only* be used to validate logons, so a machine with a fast processor (or two) will be selected, and a high-speed network adapter will be used. Now, how many BDCs for FAKE should be created?

Of course, there is no single right answer to this question. It depends on many factors, including some that have not been provided yet in this sample scenario. For example, are there 10 or 10,000 employees in Fake Corporation? Is the organization wildly profitable, or just barely avoiding bankruptcy? Is the organization a cutting-edge-technology firm, or a traditional company using many older and more conservative methods to reach the same ends. Judgment must be used when making these decisions.

Regardless of the answer to these questions, some broad assessments can be made. It is certainly desirable for network operation to be able to continue if the WAN link is temporarily unserviceable. Although the e-mail delivery from one office to another may be interrupted, it would be a more serious problem if users could not log on to the network. To avoid this possibility, a BDC from the master domain is located at each remote location.

As a practical matter in most network environments, a computer workstation can still be started and used even if a domain controller is unavailable. It will be impossible to connect other network resources, but work can continue on the workstation itself. For example, Windows NT Workstation will, by default, cache the last used ID and password locally (in encrypted form). This is obvious to laptop users who have started their computers away from the office. A different user would not be able to use the workstation until the domain controller was available, but the main user of the machine could get some work done until the problem was remedied.

In any case, it is probably undesirable for logon validation traffic to be sent across the WAN link. Again, this is not an absolute rule. Very fast links may well be able to handle this traffic in a timely manner. Although there are some protocol issues that must be addressed (e.g., network logon validation requests can be presented as broadcasts), with proper configuration (typically using WINS) it is possible to log on to a network using a domain controller on the other side of a WAN link. The question is not so much, is it possible, as is it desirable? In most situations, it makes sense to place a BDC at each geographic location for redundancy and logon traffic management. The physical implementation of the Fake Corporation's domain architecture might look like Figure 8.5.

FIG. 8.5
This physical network diagram shows the WAN link and locations of various domain controllers.

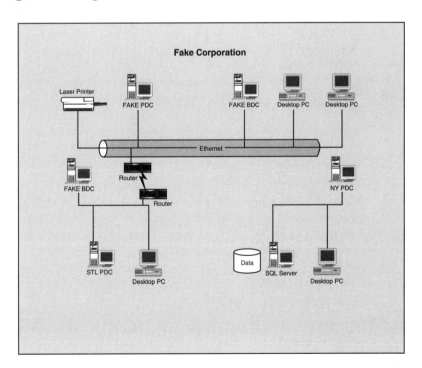

The Single Master Domain Model

The most common domain model used in large enterprises is the single master domain model. This structure uses a single master domain and one or more resource domains. No user accounts are created in the resource domains, but rather, they use accounts from the master domain. In a *pure* implementation of this model, all resources (shared directories, printers, application servers, and so on) would be located in a resource domain. In practice, it is common for some universally used resources (e.g., e-mail servers or remote access servers) to be located in the master domain.

All user accounts and global groups are created in the master domain. This domain is typically administered by the IS department for the organization. As people join the organization, an account is created for them in the master domain. If they leave the organization, that single account can be disabled or deleted, immediately eliminating access to the entire network.

 T I P It is a good idea to disable an account for a short period before deleting it to be absolutely certain that it will never be needed again. Once an account has been deleted, the permissions assigned to that account must be reestablished from scratch, even if a new account with an identical user ID is created. This is due to the fact that permissions are associated with a unique security identifier, or *SID*, which is automatically generated when an account is created.

A master domain typically has at least two domain controllers with fast processors and high-speed network cards. They do not usually need to have a lot of disk storage or RAM (32M to 64M of RAM should be enough) because they are only validating logons. Shared resources and server-based applications run on servers in the resource domains.

N O T E See Chapter 3, "Planning for BackOffice," for more information on selecting appropriate hardware and options for your server. ■

Resource domains are then created by installing one or more domain controllers and establishing a one-way trust relationship. The resource domain *trusts* the master domain. Figure 8.6 depicts a typical master domain with two resource domains—each with a primary domain controller.

The domain controllers and other servers in the resource domain provide the shared resources users need and are the real workhorses of the network. They may have multiple processors and a lot of RAM (128M or more) to support server-based applications. If they exist primarily to support file and printer sharing, you should consider fast disk subsystems with RAID level 5 disk arrays or disk mirroring for high reliability. Windows NT supports RAID up to level 5 as a standard feature.

▶ **See** "Software RAID," **p. 167**

FIG. 8.6
The master domain contains the users and group accounts, while the resource domains contain shared resources.

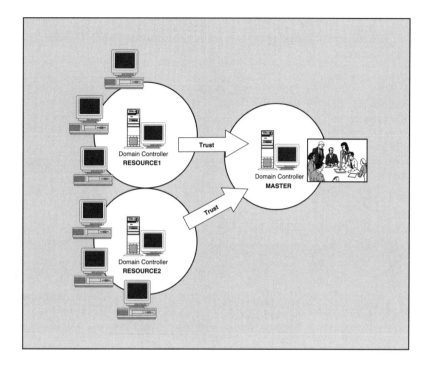

The master domain model yields a very useful environment. The master domain administrators maintain control over who can and cannot log on to the network. But the day-to-day activities of sharing printers and directories and giving users permissions to use them can be controlled by members of the department or organizational unit where the work is being done. By making one or more members of the department administrators of the resource domain, you can delegate some authority and provide an environment responsive to rapid changes. If you want slightly less autonomy with more central control, you can make department members server operators, account operators, printer operators, or backup operators rather than full-fledged administrators.

Administrators and server operators in the resource domain can assign permissions to shared resources. After the trust relationship has been established, the user accounts and global groups from the master domain can be used to assign permissions for resources in the resource domain. Figure 8.7 depicts a typical scenario in which the group Staff from the master domain GSULLIVAN is being given permission to use a shared directory called TechInfo on the server HQSRV1 in the resource domain GAS_STL_EXHIBIT.

Although the administrators of the resource domain control which users and groups are assigned permissions to resources in their domain, they really must *trust* the administrators of the master domain to be responsible about creating user accounts, managing password policies, and assigning group affiliations to user accounts. If zero-length passwords are possible and inappropriate user IDs are included in groups, the permissions on resources will be relatively meaningless. Trust is, therefore, an apt term to describe the relationship between two domains.

FIG. 8.7

Permissions are assigned to a shared directory in a resource domain using master domain accounts and groups.

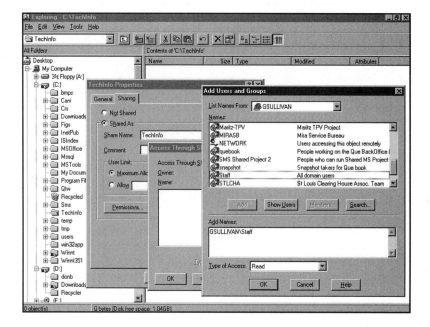

The features of a single master domain model should now make sense. You have learned what its basic features are and how to apply them to actual real-world situations. The next section explores the ramifications of going one step further to the multiple master domain model.

The Multiple Master Domain Model

The multiple master domain model provides additional features and levels of control beyond the single master domain model. It may be selected because of the size of an organization, or to create an architecture that meets the needs of a particular organizational structure.

If the multiple master model has been chosen simply to accommodate the size of a very large organization, the criteria used to break the account population into multiple domains is somewhat arbitrary. It should be chosen to yield a fairly small number of balanced domains. To illustrate with an example, a scheme yielding five well-balanced domains of roughly the same size would be preferable to a method resulting in three large domains and eight very small domains. The criteria used might be based on an alphabetic division based on name, a grouping by department, or other similar method.

In this situation, a trust relationship is set up between all resource domains and each master domain. Because any particular resource domain has a trust relationship with each master domain, permissions can be granted to users from any of those domains based on need.

The user population is thereby broken into smaller, more manageable groups that can be assigned to a particular administrator or an administrative team. Resource domains can still be controlled by a person or group associated with the resource itself, using accounts and groups from the collection of master domains. Figure 8.8 shows the logical design of such a network.

FIG. 8.8

The multiple master domain model allows groups of accounts to be separately managed.

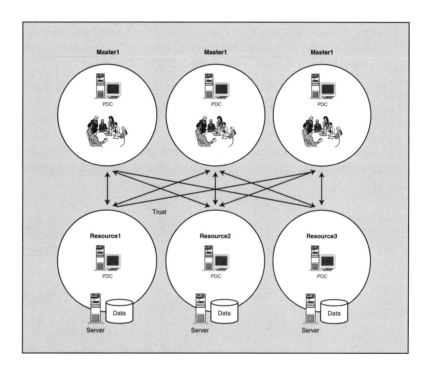

In addition to accommodating a large number of accounts, there may be organizational reasons for creating multiple master domains. The example cited earlier that uses separate and autonomous divisions for Administration, Engineering, and Operations is a good illustration of this type of need. Although the size of the organization may be well within the limits of a single master domain, the management of the Engineering division may not want to depend on the Administration division for network support. If each of these groups wants to be firmly in control of its own destiny, the multiple master domain model is the best fit.

With this situation, it is less important that the various master domains are of equal size. It is important that the domain architecture accurately reflect the organizational needs it was designed to match. Some analysis of the organizational structure may be necessary. For example, do the various entities share any centralized services? This is important in determining where to establish trust relationships and where to locate resources.

Typically, each entity has its own master domain and one or more of its own resource domains. Resources that may require access by the entire organization can be located in a resource domain that trusts all master domains and is managed by a group populated with members of each entity. The rest of the resource domains are dedicated to the needs of the entity that owns them.

A variation of this scheme can accommodate the needs of one or more departments with special security needs. The majority of users are added to a primary master domain, much like the single master model. However, an additional master domain is created for each department that requires especially stringent security (e.g., Human Resources). Standard resources are placed in resource domains that trust all masters. The members of the HR department and any sensitive resources are created in the HR domain.

If any widely used resources are placed in the primary master domain, a one-way trust relationship should be established (e.g., the primary master *trusts* the HR domain) so that users from HR can access these generic resources. In this respect, the HR domain is almost like a standard resource domain, but it contains its own users rather than trusting the primary master. Since it trusts no other domain, only users with a valid HR domain account can access resources contained in that domain. This scenario is depicted in Figure 8.9.

FIG. 8.9

A multiple master domain architecture is showing a special HR domain created to accommodate the tighter security requirements of a particular department.

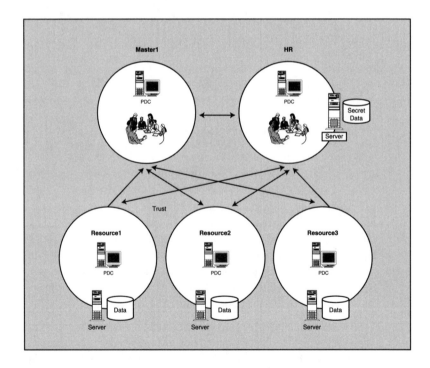

It should be obvious by now that Windows NT domains can be used to create a wide variety of useful architectures with features that match the needs of common organizational needs. By spending some time planning your domain architecture, you can create a design that best fits your organization.

The Future of Windows NT Directory Services

Directory service technology has a long history dating back to the Athena project, the Distributed Computing Environment (DCE), and other such efforts to describe a comprehensive platform for delivering computer-based services. Most recently, the X.500 standard, with its Directory Access Protocol (DAP), has specified a directory service that can be used for a variety of purposes. The recent work by the University of Michigan and the Internet Engineering Task Force (IETF) on the Lightweight Directory Access Protocol (LDAP) promises to alleviate some of the shortcomings of DAP, and has garnered the attention and support of Microsoft, Netscape, Novell, and other important vendors.

Microsoft has announced its intention to improve the current directory service capabilities in Windows NT Server with important new features. The additions will be based on recognized standards (e.g., X.500, LDAP, and DNS) and will be accessible to software developers through a programmatic interface called Open Directory Services Interface (ODSI). This will enable third-party tool and utility vendors to create management and reporting tools that depend on these services. In addition, it will provide application programmers the capability to utilize the information stored in the directory service to make their applications more useful and easier to run.

It is unknown at the time of this writing how this new technology will be packaged. It is likely that it will be a standard component of the next release of Windows NT Server, but it is also likely to be available before then as a plus pack add-on similar to the plus pack offered for Windows 95. The technology was discussed in detail at the Professional Developer's Conference in November of 1996, and the materials from that conference were posted on Microsoft's Web server. This section is based on that information that is subject to change as the technology is completed.

Active Directory

The heart of the new directory service initiative is something called Active Directory. This is a technology that replaces, and is backward-compatible with, the existing domain architecture used to manage these services today. The primary goals of this initiative are the following:

- Make this technology easy to use, or at least easier to use.
- Support multiple *name spaces* (i.e., the naming conventions required by a variety of vendors and technologies). For example, NetBIOS names, Hypertext Transport Protocol (HTTP), Universal Resource Locators (URLs) a.k.a. Web links, X.500 names, and Universal Naming Convention (UNC) names should all be supported.
- Enable the creation of end user applications that depend on directory services that work properly with multiple name spaces. For example, a utility to connect to a print queue should work the same whether the queue is hosted on a Windows NT server, a NetWare server, or a UNIX server. Not only should the user interfaces appear the same to the end user, but the programmatic interfaces should be identical to the tool developer.

■ Enable the creation of administrative tools that work across environments. For example, one tool should enable users to be added to a network, and assign permissions on servers running Windows NT, NetWare, and UNIX.

■ Allow applications and tools to be written in a variety of languages, including C, C++, Java, and Visual Basic. These applications can access directory services using a set of Component Object Model (COM) interfaces knows as ADs, or the LDAP C API.

Some of these goals clearly depend on efforts that must be undertaken outside Microsoft. It remains to be seen how widely adopted this technology will be, but the market is demanding that something be done to alleviate the proprietary nature of directory services and the resulting islands of computing resources that are created. To learn how other vendors' servers might participate in this scheme, see the next section, "The Open Directory Services Interface (ODSI)."

For Windows NT servers, Active Directory creates a hierarchical domain structure that is more flexible and powerful than the flat structure that is currently possible. These new domains have been referred to as NT DS domains to distinguish them from older-style domains as implemented in Windows NT Server version 4.0 and earlier. The new domain structure will support *transitive trust* relationships. In other words, if domain A trusts B, and B trusts C, then A trusts C. This is not the case in current trust relationships, and there are situations when this capability will lead to a cleaner domain architecture that more closely matches the organizational structure.

Transitive trust is a feature of many human organizational structures that are in place in organizations. They are also often, though not always, a characteristic of personal relationships. For example, if I trust Sue, and Sue trusts Joe, I will often trust Joe (based on Sue's trust). In addition to enabling the computer-based domain structure to map human and organizational relationships, transitive trust has the practical effect of reducing the number of individual trust relationships that are required. In a large, multimaster domain architecture, with many resource domains, the number of trust relationships that must be created can be large.

The enterprise network can then be thought of as a hierarchy of NT DS domains (see Figure 8.10). Each domain has its own unique names for each of the name spaces supported. At a minimum, an X.500 name and a DNS name are provided. Objects that are members of the domain also have (a set of) unique names, and should yield a globally unique identifier when used in conjunction with the domain name.

Because the directory service plays a role in authentication and access control, each object that belongs to a domain will have an access control list (ACL) much like those used to secure objects in current Windows NT domains. The ACLs contain individual *access control entries* (*ACE*s) that describe the particular rights granted to a user or group for the object in question. This is probably the single most important feature that a directory service can provide to an application developer—access control in a secure fashion to network-based resources with the same programming conventions, regardless of the network operating system that is managing them.

FIG. 8.10
This figure depicts a hierarchy of domains with transitive trust relationships.

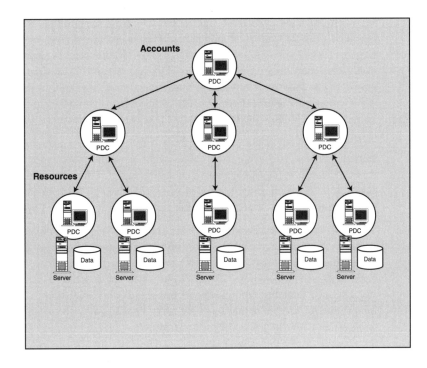

The Open Directory Services Interface (ODSI)

A closely related technology that is critical to the success of future directory services is a uniform method of accessing those services with software. The programmatic interface being promoted by Microsoft is called the *Open Directory Services Interface (ODSI)*. In the same way that Open Database Connectivity (ODBC) drivers have simplified the job of developing database applications, it is hoped that ODSI will simplify directory-enabled or directory-aware applications.

In a manner similar to ODBC, the ODSI initiative involves both client side and server side components. To be successful, both players in a client-server scenario must be involved. Although it is theoretically possible to do all the work on the client, this is not the approach that will ultimately lead to the best performance.

Under the planned initiative, each directory service would implement an ODSI service provider interface that would understand a standard set of requests for directory services. A client can then use a standard, ODSI-based method of requesting directory services from any provider. Clearly, this requires less overhead on the application than under a current scenario. It also makes life much simpler for the application developer, and allows the resulting application to be used much more broadly than before.

Like with ODBC, issues must be addressed. The most straightforward implementation would be to find the least common denominator of services shared by all service providers, and provide this limited subset of features through the ODSI interface. This is probably not good enough to satisfy a wide audience of developers, however. To alleviate this problem, service providers can "inform" the client application about the services they provide, and enable the client to step up to a full range of features if they are available on a particular provider, or scale back to a more limited set available on a less powerful provider.

To become popular, this technology will also have to address the *layering* concern that was, and still is with some, such a big issue. Some members of the development community—though they don't like creating applications that must support different providers or different versions of a program—feel they must provide the absolute best performance possible. This can lead to the desire to use only *native* programming interfaces.

To be successful, ODSI client-side drivers and service providers will need to be implemented in an efficient fashion to alleviate the need for direct use of the native (and proprietary) interfaces. This should be somewhat simpler with directory services than with generic databases because the amount of information requested from, or added to, a directory service is typically much smaller than the potentially huge amount of information that can be transferred to or from a general purpose database. Eventually, service providers can implement the ODSI interface as their native interface if they so desire.

The ODSI initiative offers many powerful features, and it is likely to eventually become a *de facto* standard whether or not it receives the endorsement from a recognized standards body.

From Here...

You should now have a better picture of the way Windows NT Server can be used to build a large enterprise network and how individual servers participate. Also, you learned some important terminology, and the basics of Windows NT and BackOffice security. In Chapter 9, "Using TCP/IP with Windows NT Server," you will learn exactly how to set up Windows NT Server on a computer, and how to configure it to perform the tasks you've been learning about. For more information about some of the topics addressed in this chapter, see the following chapters:

- To begin your Microsoft BackOffice Server implementation, see Chapter 5, "Implementing Windows NT Server."
- For advanced setup advice including virtual memory, drive mirroring, and RAID configuration, see Chapter 6, "Advanced Windows NT Server Configuration."
- For basic guidelines on the administration of a Windows NT Server, including how to share resources and control access by setting permissions, see Chapter 7, "Administering Windows NT Server."
- To learn about setting up the remote access capability of Windows NT Server, see Chapter 12, "Implementing Remote Access Service (RAS)."

- To become acquainted with the practical aspects of a secure environment, see Chapter 46, "Implementing Real-World Security."
- To explore ways to best manage and administer your Microsoft BackOffice network, see Chapter 48, "Proactive Network Administration."

P A R T

III

Windows NT Server: Enterprise Connectivity

## CHAPTER 9

Using TCP/IP with Windows NT Server

by Don Benage and Brad Rhodes

This chapter describes TCP/IP (Transmission Control Protocol/Internet Protocol)—a network protocol—and related applications that have gained wide acceptance and use over the last decade. TCP/IP is the network protocol used on the Internet, which by itself makes the topic worthy of study. It is also very useful in private networks, especially as they grow in size.

The chapter begins with a brief tutorial on TCP/IP. Those familiar with the subject from a background in UNIX networking can skip this section, or at least just skim it. No claims are made of academic rigor—it is intended to be a practical and accessible overview for those interested in a little background material. Nothing presented in the tutorial is essential for installing and using TCP/IP, although it may help you to understand some of the terminology used by TCP/IP aficionados and *why* things are done the way they are. ∎

The importance of TCP/IP

Find out why organizations building large intranets and connecting to the Internet are implementing TCP/IP. Learn about how it works, its advantages, its potential problems, and some solutions to those problems.

How to install and configure TCP/IP

Learn how to install and configure TCP/IP and related components, such as the SNMP Service and the FTP Server Service. Find out how to configure Windows NT Server to use a Hosts file, a DNS, or both.

How to use Dynamic Host Configuration Protocol (DHCP)

Learn how to configure the DHCP Server service using the DHCP Manager administrative utility program. Learn how DHCP automatically leases IP addresses from a pool of available addresses to workstations that connect to the network. Learn how to create static addresses for servers and other key network components and how to manage the IP address pool.

How to use the Windows Internet Name Service (WINS)

Discover how WINS resolves NetBIOS names with dynamically assigned IP addresses.

A Brief TCP/IP Tutorial

TCP/IP is a suite of network protocols that describe precisely how information can be transmitted from one computer to one or more additional computers. It is designed to operate in environments where the conditions are not particularly suitable for this task, and therefore has a strong error detection and correction capability. Most often when the term TCP/IP is used, it is meant to denote not only the protocol suite itself, but also a group of compatible applications and utilities that have been created and used to implement and test the protocols.

TCP/IP has been developed cooperatively by members of the Internet community using a proposal and peer-review process involving documents called *Request for Comments* (*RFCs*). A person or group will propose a design and publish an RFC describing that design. It will be reviewed by other members of the community, some of whom may refine the proposal with additions of their own, again put forth in an RFC. Some of these designs are implemented, tested, and refined even further. Eventually an RFC that describes a set of standards will be developed, and manufacturers will design products that conform to one or more of these RFCs.

This process turns out to be quite effective, over time, at discovering and eliminating problems. The RFC process is ongoing, and existing RFCs are available for public review. You can find them and download them without charge from various locations on the Internet, although average computer users have little use for them. They are primarily intended for individuals and organizations who are designing products and services to be used on the Internet. Some of them include useful information for Internet users, and do not describe standards at all. RFC 1118, The Hitchhikers Guide to the Internet, is an example of this type of RFC.

 You can find RFCs on the Internet by using any of the large search engines on the World Wide Web. For example, use your Web browser to connect to **http://www.yahoo.com**, and search for RFC.

Some of the terminology used in association with TCP/IP may be confusing at first. The term *host* is used to describe a component on a network, such as a computer or router. In some circles, the term host has the connotation of a *large computer system*, such as an IBM mainframe computer. In the context of TCP/IP discussions, a host can be a desktop personal computer or laptop, or a multiprocessor supercomputer.

The term *gateway* is used to describe a piece of equipment commonly referred to as a *router*, which is used to create wide area network (WAN) connections to remote locations. It should not be confused with its other connotation, that of a connection to a computer system using a different operating system or communications protocol. For the purposes of TCP/IP, your *default gateway* is nothing more than the router that connects your local area network (LAN) to the rest of your WAN.

Finally, the term *Internet* itself can be confusing. Internet, with a capital *I,* is generally used to describe the worldwide collection of public and private networks that link educational institutions, research facilities, commercial organizations, government agencies, and military sites. The term *internet*, with a lowercase *i,* refers to any collection of TCP/IP networks linked together with routers. Private internets, or *internetworks*, are increasingly referred to with the term *intranet*. For more extensive coverage of the Internet, see Chapter 17, "I-Net Tools and Techniques."

Why Use TCP/IP?

There are many reasons why the use of TCP/IP is growing. During the last decade, many organizations implemented LANs in offices and sites throughout their facilities. Eventually, they desired to connect these LANs together into WANs. In addition, a growing number of organizations have started to view the WAN as a strategic resource, critical to the success of their efforts. To implement these views, they need a protocol capable of managing large numbers of systems in a routed, WAN environment. This is precisely what TCP/IP was designed to deliver.

TCP/IP is also the protocol used on the Internet and is therefore useful for those individuals and organizations who want to attach directly to the Internet, or access it through a service provider. Furthermore, it allows a high degree of interoperability between dissimilar systems, such as computers running Windows NT and UNIX operating systems. It also provides an environment that supports the development of powerful applications using feature-rich programmatic interfaces. For all these reasons, TCP/IP is a technology whose time has come.

IP Addresses, Host Names, Domain Names, and NetBIOS Names

The central capability provided by TCP/IP, as already mentioned, is a transmission facility—moving information from point A to point B. The transmission of information must be done in a manner that takes into account the involvement of both computers and humans. The computers must be able to send and receive information accurately and quickly, and their human operators must easily be able to specify what actions they desire and understand the results.

The fact that computers and humans require different naming schemes for the elements of a network is the source of much of the difficulty surrounding its operation. Computers need to have a unique *address* for each component on the network to accurately send information to just those components for which it was intended. Humans also need to be able to specify the computer they want to communicate with, and to name their own computer system so that they can describe it to other humans, especially if they are sharing information on the network. But the kind of name appropriate for computer use is much different from that suitable for humans.

This leads to one of the central problems that TCP/IP must solve—name and address resolution. Three types of names are designed for humans, and two addresses are designed primarily for computers and their operating systems and applications. Matching a name with its corresponding address is more difficult than it might at first appear. The types of names involved in a Windows NT network using TCP/IP are the following:

- **Machine address**—Also called *hardware address*. In Ethernet networking, the machine address is a guaranteed unique address that is "hard wired" or manufactured into a computer network product, such as a network adapter for a personal computer. These addresses include a portion that is specific to a particular manufacturer so that two different manufacturers will never create the same address. Within their *private address* *space*, each manufacturer must be sure that they never create two devices with the same address. This is usually done by including a ROM chip or similar element with a unique identifier that becomes part of the address. Machine addresses are expressed as 12 hexadecimal digits (for example, 00 04 AC 26 5E 8E) often written with a space between each two digits for human readability. Other hardware networks, such as ATM and Token Ring networks, will use different schemes to assign machine addresses.

■ **IP address**—An address used by operating systems and networking software on TCP/IP networks. If you create a private network, you must make sure that no two devices have the same IP address. If you want to attach to the Internet, you must request part of the address space from InterNIC (Network Information Center) for use by your organization, and then manage that portion so that no two components use the same address.

N O T E   You can contact InterNIC via e-mail at **info@internic.net** or by phone. In the US, call 1-800-444-4345. In Canada or elsewhere, call 1-619-455-4600. From overseas, you may need to use a country code to access the US when dialing. Or, visit their Web server at **http://rs-internic.com**. ■

IP addresses are written in a form known as *dotted decimal notation*. For example, **123.45.67.89** is a valid IP address. Each of the four parts is called an *octet* and can range from 1 to 254 (0 and 255 are generally reserved for special purposes). This address must be unique for each device on a given network. It is composed of two parts, the *network ID* and the *host ID*. The network ID, the first two octets, must be the same for all devices on a particular network segment or subnetwork, and different from all other subnetworks. The host ID, the last two octets, must be unique within a particular network ID.

■ **Host name**—The "human compatible" name for a computer or device on a TCP/IP network; also called an *FQDN* (*Fully Qualified Domain Name*) or simply a *domain name* when specified in full. A host name for a server might be **dataserver**, and its FQDN might be **dataserver.company.com**. Applications using host names are generally case-sensitive. This name can be used instead of the IP address when entering many commands using TCP/IP-specific applications and utilities. It is not used when entering Windows-based Microsoft networking commands, such as NET USE or NET VIEW, which require the use of a NetBIOS name, explained later in this list.

N O T E   You can use the same name for your host name and NetBIOS name, which can eliminate confusion when entering commands. Each name still retains its own role, however, and the applications that use these names are each designed for a particular type of name (either NetBIOS or host name, but rarely both). ■

■ **Domain name**—Another name for the host name. The last part of this hierarchical name (**company.com** for example) is referred to as a *first-level* (or *top-level*) *name* and is used to uniquely identify your organization to the Internet community. Often a request for a domain name in an application or operating system utility is referring only to the first-level name, not the FQDN.

■ **NetBIOS name**—A name used for Microsoft networking commands, such as NET USE, and automatically used on your behalf when performing networking functions with Windows-based graphical utilities, such as the File Manager or the Windows 95 Network Neighborhood. A NetBIOS name can be 15 characters in length (for example, DATASERVER). Applications using NetBIOS names are not generally case-sensitive.

▶ **See** "Name Resolution in the TCP/IP Environment," **p. 280**

The Problem: Resolving Names and Addresses

During the execution of a network command, the application or operating system must eventually discover the machine address of the devices involved. Because the machine address is almost never entered into an application by users, some means of *resolving* the host name, NetBIOS name, or IP address to machine address must be used. A variety of mechanisms for this purpose have been developed, and they are discussed in this section.

Separate mechanisms exist for each type of name and sometimes more than one process may occur. For example, an application that knows the host name may first resolve this to an IP address and then to a machine address. The mechanisms for resolving each type are presented in the following list and discussed in more detail in the next section. Some of these mechanisms are based upon standards as defined in RFCs or other standards documents, and others are Microsoft-specific methods. IP addresses are resolved to machine addresses using the following methods:

■ Address Resolution Protocol (ARP), defined in RFC 826

■ A search of the corresponding ARP cache in the computer's memory

N O T E There are other approaches for IP address to machine address resolution, but they are not implemented by Windows NT. The use of ARP is the most common method of IP address resolution. ■

Host names are resolved to IP addresses using the methods in the following list. If the computer is configured to use all methods, they will be tried in the following order:

1. HOSTS file
2. Domain Name Server (DNS)
3. Windows Internet Name Service (WINS)
4. A local broadcast
5. LMHOSTS file

NetBIOS names are resolved to IP addresses using the methods presented in the following list. If the computer is configured to use all methods, they will be tried in the following order:

1. A NetBIOS name cache in the computer's memory
2. Windows Internet Name Service (WINS)
3. A local broadcast

4. LMHOSTS file

5. HOSTS file

6. Domain Name Server (DNS)

Name resolution mechanisms for host names and NetBIOS names are similar, but they are carried out in a different order. The mechanisms used can vary depending on how the computer is configured.

Some Solutions to the Problem

This section provides an overview of how the various name and address resolution mechanisms function. Some of these mechanisms include many options and implementation details. This overview presents only the most salient points to assist in a general understanding of the processes involved. Additional information is provided in Volume 2 of the Windows NT Resource Kit, *Windows NT Networking Guide*.

▶ **See** "Name Resolution in the TCP/IP Environment," **p. 280**

ARP   The Address Resolution Protocol is part of the TCP/IP protocol suite. It is only necessary to use ARP on a TCP/IP address that is known to reside on the local physical network. To resolve an IP address for a host on the same local network, the following steps are taken:

▶ **See** "Routing in Windows NT 4.0," **p. 272**

1. The computer checks its own ARP cache, a list of IP addresses, and corresponding hardware addresses that it dynamically manages in memory as it operates.

2. If the address is not found in the ARP cache, an ARP request is broadcast on the local network (broadcasts are not generally forwarded through routers). This request includes its own hardware address and IP address, and the IP address that needs to be resolved. The ARP request is an IP broadcast message. On an Ethernet network, this will map to an Ethernet broadcast.

3. Each computer or host on the local network receives the ARP request. If the IP address does not match its own address, the request is discarded and ignored. If it does match, the host responds with an ARP reply directly (not broadcast) to the original host with its own hardware address. It also updates its own ARP cache with the hardware address of the original host.

4. The original host receives the reply and updates its own ARP cache for future use. A communications link can now be established.

If a destination machine is not on the same physical network as the sending machine, there is no need to resolve the machine address of the destination machine. The packet will be routed at the IP level through an intermediate router. The IP portion of TCP/IP will need to resolve the MAC address of the router so that the packet can be forwarded to the router.

Local Broadcasts   The Microsoft implementation of TCP/IP uses an enhanced version of the *b-node* (broadcast method) of NetBIOS name resolution described in RFC 1001/1002. Broadcasts are used only after first checking the NetBIOS name cache and attempting to contact a WINS server if configured for WINS. (See "Windows Internet Name Service (WINS)" later in the chapter.) Broadcasts use an address that all computers on the local network segment will accept and evaluate. Three broadcasts are sent before the next mechanism is attempted.

 The contents of the NetBIOS cache on a computer can be listed by typing the command **nbtstat -c**. Other uses for the nbtstat command are available by typing **nbtstat -?**.

Part
III

Ch
9

***LMHOSTS* File**   The LMHOSTS file is a text file that lists IP addresses and the corresponding NetBIOS name for remote hosts only (because active local hosts will be discovered by WINS or broadcast first). It is closely related to the HOSTS file described in the following section. The LMHOSTS file is located by default in the \systemroot\SYSTEM32\DRIVERS\ETC directory. It is specifically designed to resolve NetBIOS names and is consulted by traditional TCP/IP utilities (if they accept NetBIOS names) only after trying the NetBIOS name cache, WINS, and b-node broadcasts.

The file is searched sequentially from top to bottom so that frequently used names (such as servers) should generally be listed near the top. By using the #INCLUDE directive in the file, you can load entries from a centralized copy of the LMHOSTS file from a server. A sample LMHOSTS file included with Windows NT Server provides examples of this, and other, directives and describes their usage. Additional information is provided in Volume 2 of the Windows NT Resource Kit, *Windows NT Networking Guide*.

 You can create entries with the #PRE directive in the LMHOSTS file and use the following command to manually preload these entries into your NetBIOS name cache, thereby avoiding the need to perform broadcasts (even without WINS):

nbtstat -R

Be sure that you have enabled LMHOSTS lookup in the TCP/IP configuration dialog box if you want to use this technique. See "Installing and Configuring TCP/IP for Windows NT Server" later in this chapter for more information.

***HOSTS* File**   The HOSTS file (see also the preceding section) is a text file that lists IP addresses and the corresponding host name. This file is located by default in the \systemroot\ SYSTEM32\DRIVERS\ETC directory. It is designed to resolve TCP/IP host names and FQDNs and is the first mechanism consulted by traditional TCP/IP utilities. It is consulted by NetBIOS-based utilities only after trying the NetBIOS name cache, WINS, b-node broadcasts, and the LMHOSTS file. The HOSTS file is searched sequentially from top to bottom so that frequently used names (such as servers) should generally be listed near the top. The HOSTS file must be located on the local computer.

Domain Name Service (DNS)   Domain Name Service is an IP address resolution method frequently used on UNIX systems. One or more DNS servers are implemented and can then be consulted to resolve names not listed in the local HOSTS (or LMHOSTS) file. Windows NT can be configured to use DNS. Microsoft has included a DNS in release 4.0 of Windows NT Server. Configuring Windows NT to use DNS for name resolution is described in the section "Installing and Configuring TCP/IP for Windows NT Server" later in this chapter.

▶ **See** "Domain Name System Name Resolution," **p. 286**

Dynamic Host Configuration Protocol (DHCP)   DHCP is a protocol that enables IP addresses to be automatically assigned from a pool of available IP addresses centrally stored and managed on one or more servers. In addition, other TCP/IP-related information, such as the subnet mask and default gateway, can also be retrieved. DHCP servers do not share information with other DHCP servers or with DNS servers. The IP address pool managed by a DHCP server must be entirely owned by that server. No other server or individual should be able to assign an address from that pool.

DHCP is defined in RFCs 1533, 1534, 1541, and 1542. It is an extension to, and builds upon, the BOOTP protocol defined in RFC 951, which automatically assigns IP addresses to diskless workstations. Microsoft has designed a server-based service, an administration utility, and client software that implement the DHCP protocol. The installation and configuration of DHCP on Windows NT Server is covered in detail later in this chapter in the section "Implementing Dynamic Host Configuration Protocol (DHCP)."

Windows Internet Name Service (WINS)   WINS is a NetBIOS Name Server (NBNS) implemented as a Windows NT service. Also included with Windows NT Server are an administration utility and client software. It can be used with or without DHCP to register NetBIOS names and resolve them to IP addresses without using b-node broadcasts, which can be problematic in large networks. Name resolution requests are resolved using directed datagrams (network packets) that are routable.

WINS is a dynamic name service that tracks network names as users start and stop client workstations. Multiple WINS servers can be configured to provide redundancy and to improve name resolution performance. Changes to the names database on one WINS server are replicated to other WINS servers set up as Push or Pull partners. The installation and configuration of WINS on Windows NT Server is covered in detail in Chapter 10, "Name Resolution with TCP/IP."

▶ **See** "Implementing Windows Internet Name Service (WINS)," **p. 315**

Now that you have had a brief overview of TCP/IP and some of its elements, you are ready to learn how to install TCP/IP on Windows NT Server.

Installing and Configuring TCP/IP for Windows NT Server

This section teaches you how to install TCP/IP on a Windows NT Server computer. You learn how to install the protocol suite and all the options offered by Microsoft. A variety of client-based utilities for the TCP/IP suite are included in Microsoft's implementation, including connectivity to such utilities as Finger, lpr, rcp, rexec, rsh, Telnet, and tftp.

Both client and server support is provided for FTP (File Transfer Protocol). These utilities enable a Windows NT server or Windows NT workstation to interact with UNIX workstations and other platforms supporting TCP/IP. Notably missing from the connectivity utilities is support for NFS, the Network File System, but this is available from at least three third-party software companies for the Windows NT platform. Microsoft has suggested it may include NFS in a future release of Windows NT Server. A number of diagnostic utilities are also offered including arp, hostname, ipconfig, lpq, nbtstat, netstat, ping, route, and tracert. An SNMP agent, implemented as a Windows NT service, enables a remote network management console, such as Sun Net Manager or HP Open View.

TCP/IP can be installed during the original setup of Windows NT Server, or it can be added at a later time using the Network icon in the Control Panel. In this section, you learn how to add TCP/IP to an existing Windows NT Server installation. Adding it during the initial setup is an almost identical process, so the following steps should still be helpful. You simply follow these instructions when you get to the network portion of Setup.

To install TCP/IP and related services, follow these steps:

1. Choose Settings, Control Panel from the Start menu.

2. In the control panel, double-click the Network icon to open the Network dialog box. Click the Protocols tab (see Figure 9.1). The TCP/IP protocol can be added by selecting the Add button.

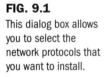

FIG. 9.1

This dialog box allows you to select the network protocols that you want to install.

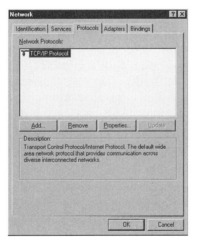

3. A dialog box requesting the full path to the distribution files appears. Enter the location using a drive letter or Universal Naming Convention (UNC) name of a shared network resource (such as a CD-ROM drive), and click Continue. Clearly the UNC name option is only feasible if you have another network transport protocol already installed and operational.

4. Now that you have installed the TCP/IP protocol, you need to properly configure the protocol. Figure 9.2 shows the TCP/IP Properties dialog box. There are five tabs on the dialog.

5. The IP Address tab is used to set the IP address for this workstation (see Figure 9.2). There are two ways to setup an IP address. The first is to obtain the address via DHCP.

FIG. 9.2

This dialog allows you to set the TCP/IP properties for the Windows NT computer.

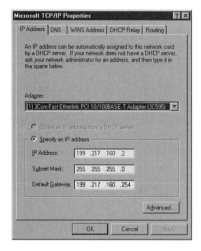

See "Dynamic Host Configuration Protocol (DHCP)" earlier in this chapter for a discussion on DHCP. The other is to statically assign an IP address. If you are using DHCP, simply select the Obtain an IP address from a DHCP server radio button. The DHCP server will provide all of the needed information.

If you are statically assigning the IP address, you will need to obtain a unique dotted decimal IP address from a central authority on your network. This person will also be able to provide the subnet mask. The default router is the main router that is used to forward packets to and from other networks, most likely the Internet.

6. The advance button on the IP Address tab allows the user to configure additional TCP/IP settings for additional adapters. A computer that has more than one network adapter is a multi-homed computer.

CAUTION

If you are unsure what IP address to use, check with the person in your organization who is responsible for managing IP addresses before finishing this process. If you are the person responsible and you are still unsure, review the earlier section "IP Addresses, Host Names, Domain Names, and NetBIOS Names" for guidance, and spend some time planning your IP addressing scheme. It is very important that two computers do not have the same IP address! If you assign two computers the same TCP/IP address, one or both of the computers will not be able to use the network. If this machine was an important server, this server would no longer be available.

N O T E DHCP can be used to configure any of the properties for the TCP/IP protocol. Typically, this includes the IP address, subnet mask, DNS addresses, and WINS addresses. ▮

7. Now press the DNS tab (see Figure 9.3). This tab allows you to enter one or more DNS servers for name resolution. Windows NT has already set your hostname to the machine name that picked for your computer. The domain name should be entered—for instance,

gasullivan.com is a valid domain name. The domain suffix search order allows multiple domain name spaces to be searched.

FIG. 9.3
The DNS tab allows the DNS options for this workstation to be set.

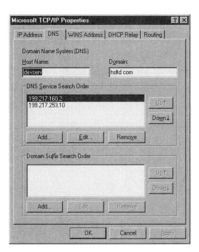

Part

III

Ch

9

8. Click the WINS Address settings tab (see Figure 9.4). If WINS is enabled on your network, you can enter the IP address of a primary and secondary WINS server. If there is a DNS server available on the network, selecting the Enable DNS for Windows resolution check box will have the TCP/IP protocol check the DNS server for name resolution.

FIG. 9.4
The WINS Address tab controls the usage of the Windows Internet Naming Service (WINS).

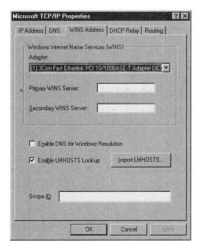

9. The routing tab has one check box; checking Enable IP forwarding enables the static and dynamic, if installed, routing on this computer.

▶ **See** "Routing in Windows NT 4.0," **p. 272**

10. Clicking the OK button will commit the changes and close the dialog box. You will most likely have to reboot the machine so that all of the changes take effect.

In addition to the base protocol, you may want to install some of the TCP/IP specific services. These services include TCP/IP printing, the simple TCP/IP, and the SNMP services (SNMP is the Simple Network Management Protocol that allows the configuration and monitoring of network devices). The TCP/IP printing services allow the user to print to TCP/IP printers. This is most useful when printing to existing UNIX host printers.The simple TCP/IP services installs an FTP server and a Telnet server. The SNMP services allows this computer to become the source of SNMP events or the destination of SNMP messages.

Now that you have learned some of the background information about TCP/IP and how to install and configure it on your computer, you are ready to learn about two additional services that can facilitate the management of IP addresses (DHCP) and NetBIOS name resolution (WINS).

Implementing Dynamic Host Configuration Protocol (DHCP)

In this section, you learn how to configure a DHCP Server. You learn the process of defining a *scope*, configuring client reservations, configuring DHCP clients, testing clients, viewing and managing DHCP client leases, and maintaining your DHCP database. A DHCP scope is a pool of available IP addresses and (optionally) additional addressing information for various shared devices or services. As a DHCP client computer connects to the network, a unique IP address will be assigned and, with the addresses of other shared resources (for example, servers), can be transmitted to the client computer.

The IP address is said to be *leased* to the client computer because it can be returned to the pool of available addresses and used by another client at a later time. You can define global options that will apply to all scopes defined on a DHCP server. You can also define options that apply to only one scope.

You need several pieces of information before you can complete the configuration of DHCP. They are listed here for your convenience. If you are unsure of the answers to some of the questions, read this entire section for additional background on the operation of DHCP and how it is configured. If you are still not clear, remember that you can update the DHCP scope at a later time and force clients to renew their leases, which automatically updates them with new information. You must answer the following questions before configuring DHCP:

■ Will all the computers on your network be DHCP clients? If not, you must be sure to exclude the addresses from the pool of available addresses. In general, servers, routers, and other similar devices should be configured with static IP addresses.

■ What information, in addition to the IP address, do you want to automatically configure? A default gateway? WINS Server? DNS Server?

■ What options can be configured for all clients on the network? What options are shared by all clients on a particular subnet? Are there any options that are unique for specific clients?

■ How many DHCP servers will you need? If your network consists of multiple physical subnets connected by routers, your routers must act as BOOTP Relay Agents as specified in RFC 1542, or you must put a DHCP server on each subnet with DHCP clients. If your router does not support RFC 1542 (as many older routers do not), you may be able to upgrade it to add such support without having to replace the router.

■ What range of addresses, and other information, should be included in the scope defined on each DHCP server? Should any servers have multiple scopes defined? Remember, DHCP servers do not share information with other DHCP servers or DNS servers. Each must have its own set of addresses to offer to the clients it will service. Additional information on defining a scope is provided in the section "Creating a DHCP Scope" later in this chapter.

▶ **See** "The Windows NT 4.0 Multi-Protocol Router (MPR)," **p. 274**

The Advantages of DHCP

DHCP offers several advantages over the manual configuration of TCP/IP addresses, as follows:

■ Users are not required to enter an IP address, subnet mask, or any other addressing information. Therefore, they are much less likely to enter a random address or copy an address from a colleague's computer, reasoning that if it is working, an identical configuration will work on their own computer.

■ The process of manually entering an IP address, subnet mask, and other configuration information is prone to error, even with an educated user population that is cooperating fully with the process. There are too many numbers and settings to expect a large group of users to set them without error. When users change computers or locations, the settings need to be redone.

■ A fair amount of administrative overhead is associated with managing the list of valid IP addresses, even with a DNS. It is also a process that is inherently difficult to divide among several individuals unless they are all knowledgeable about the technology and cooperate fully with one another.

■ DHCP enables users to configure their own computer without having to contact an administrator to get a valid IP address. This eliminates errors, delays, and frustration.

■ When users move their computer to a new location, or travel with a laptop containing a PCMCIA Ethernet adapter or similar device, they will automatically receive a valid address for the new location when they start their computer.

How DHCP Leases IP Addresses to Clients

An overview of the DHCP lease address process may help you to administer the process more effectively. The first step is to configure a DHCP server, as described in the next section. After the server is operational, the basic steps involved in a DHCP client lease are as follows:

1. A client computer starts and initializes an unconfigured version of TCP/IP. Then it broadcasts a request for an IP address. The request contains the computer's hardware address and computer name so that DHCP servers know who sent the request.

2. All DHCP servers that have an available lease that is valid for the client send a response using a broadcast message (because the client does not have an IP address yet). The message includes the client's hardware address, the IP address being offered, the subnet mask, the duration of the lease, and the IP address of the server making the offer. The server must reserve the address in case the offer is accepted.

3. The client accepts the first offer it receives. It broadcasts its acceptance to all DHCP servers with a message including the IP address of the server whose offer was accepted. Other servers release the temporary reservation on their offered addresses.

4. The server with the selected address sends an acknowledgment message with the IP address, subnet mask, and possibly other information defined in the scope as described in the next section. The client receives the acknowledgment and initializes a full version of TCP/IP, and can communicate with other hosts on the LAN or WAN.

Configuring DHCP

A DHCP server is configured using the DHCP Manager utility. Open the DHCP Manager utility by selecting Start, Programs, Administrative Tools, DHCP Manager. The DHCP service is started, stopped, paused, and continued like all services—using the Services icon in the Control Panel or using the Windows NT Server Manager. Make sure that the service, formally named the Microsoft DHCP Server, is started.

The rest of this section describes the procedures you use to define a DHCP scope, set various options, and configure and test DHCP client workstations. You also learn how to reserve certain addresses that are manually assigned (for example, for servers and routers) so that they will be excluded from the pool of available addresses managed by the DHCP service.

▶ **See** "A Flexible Set of Services," **p. 54**

Creating a DHCP Scope   To create a DHCP scope, follow these steps:

1. Start the DHCP Manager.

2. Choose Scope, Create. The Scope Properties dialog box appears. Figure 9.5 depicts a completed scope.

3. Enter the range of IP addresses that will be included in this scope. It is usually a good idea to include the full list of addresses used on this network or subnet and then to explicitly exclude those addresses managed by a DNS or other DHCP server. You may also want to set aside a range of addresses for servers, routers, or other network devices so that you can establish addressing conventions that make it easier to identify shared devices by their IP addresses. For example, within a given scope you might set aside host IDs from .1 to .20 for servers and .250 to .254 for routers and hubs even if they aren't all needed at this time.

4. Enter a Subnet Mask. If you are not subnetting, this will be determined by the *class* of your IP address. For example, **255.255.255.0** would be used for class C addresses suitable for small networks with few (less than 255) hosts. The example configuration shown in Figures 9.4 through 9.10 uses the third octet to subnet class B addresses into 14 subnets.

FIG. 9.5

This dialog box is used to create a scope containing an IP Address pool, excluded ranges, and optional characteristics for the scope.

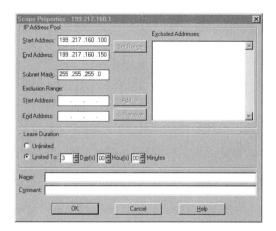

Part

III

Ch

9

5. Enter a Name for the pool and include a descriptive Comment if you want. Set the lease duration based on the volatility of your host population. For example, if you have a very stable network, set a long duration. If you have a small range of addresses that must be shared by an ever-changing group of traveling laptop users, set a short duration.

6. Click OK. A dialog box informs you that the scope has been defined but not activated. You can activate it now or wait and activate it later by highlighting the scope and choosing Scope, Activate.

Another scope is shown in Figure 9.6. This scope would compliment the scope shown in Figure 9.5 on a network with two subnets. A DHCP server would be implemented on each subnet. Each DHCP server can back up the other with a range of addresses from the other scope.

FIG. 9.6

This figure depicts another scope that would compliment the scope shown in Figure 9.5 for a small network involving two subnets.

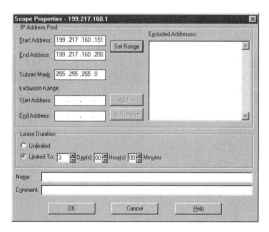

Configuring Global Options To set options that will be provided to all clients from all scopes as they receive an IP address lease, follow these steps:

1. Start the DHCP Manager.

2. Choose DHCP Options, Global. The DHCP Options: Global dialog box appears (see Figure 9.7).

FIG. 9.7

This dialog box is used to configure options that apply to all scopes managed by this DHCP server.

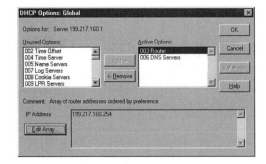

3. Select an option from the list of Unused Options. Click Add to move it to the Active Options list box.

4. Select the option in the Active Options box and click Value. Then click Edit Array. The IP Address Array Editor appears (see Figure 9.8).

FIG. 9.8

This dialog box enables you to specify the addresses of specific optional elements that will be part of this definition. In this case, the addresses listed are for DNS servers defined for all scopes (global).

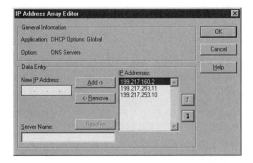

5. Enter the addresses of elements that correspond to the option listed in the General Information box. Click Add.

6. Use the arrow buttons to order the entries from the top down in the order you would like them to be used (not all options will be consulted in this order, depending on the nature of the option used). Click OK to return to the Options: Global dialog box.

7. When you have set all the options that apply globally to all scopes, click OK. Options that are good candidates for global definition are DNS servers and WINS servers because these can be accessed across routers and would therefore be available to multiple subnets.

Configuring Scope Options   To set options that will be provided to clients from a particular scope as they receive an IP address lease, follow these steps:

1. Start the DHCP Manager.

2. Highlight the scope for which you want to set options. Choose DHCP Options, Scope. The DHCP Options: Scope dialog box appears (see Figure 9.9).

FIG. 9.9

This dialog box is used to configure options that apply to only one scope.

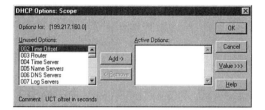

Part

III

Ch

9

3. Select an option from the list of Unused Options. Click Add to move it to the Active Options list box.

4. Select the option in the Active Options box and click Value. Then click Edit Array. The IP Address Array Editor appears.

5. Enter the addresses of elements that correspond to the option listed in the General Information box. Click Add.

6. Use the arrow buttons to order the entries from the top down in the order you would like them to be used. Click OK to return to the Options: Scope dialog box.

7. When you have set all the options that apply to this scope, click OK. An option that is a good candidate for scope-specific definition is the address of the default gateway because many subnets have only one router that is used to connect to the rest of the network.

Configuring Client Reservations   There are occasions when a client computer must always have the same IP address. This can occur based on the needs of a particular application. In addition, if you are using a client workstation as a peer server, and sharing resources with many other clients, it may be useful to reserve its address so that it will not change, much as server addresses are best not to change. To reserve an IP address for a particular client, follow these steps:

1. Start the DHCP Manager.

2. You can view any current reservations by choosing Scope, Active Leases.

3. To enter a new reservation, choose Scope, Add Reservations. The Add Reserved Clients dialog box appears (see Figure 9.10).

FIG. 9.10

The Add Reserved Clients dialog box is used to reserve a particular IP address for a specific computer so that its IP address will never change.

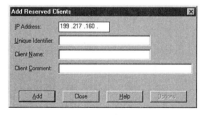

4. The IP Address will already be partially filled in based on the scope you are using. You may want to change part of the address if you are subnetting. Enter the remainder of the host ID to complete the address.

5. In the Unique Identifier box, enter the hardware address of the network adapter in the computer for which you are creating the reservation.

TIP The hardware address for a Windows NT computer can be found by running WINMSD.EXE and clicking the Network button. It can also be discovered on most Windows clients (including Windows NT) by typing **NET CONFIG WKSTA** at a command prompt.

6. Enter a Client Name for this computer. Usually this is the NetBIOS name for the computer, although you can enter anything here without affecting the operation of the lease or the computer in question.

7. Enter a Client Comment, if you want, describing the client computer. Click Add to define the reservation.

Configuring DHCP Clients   You configure clients to use DHCP by clicking the Enable Automatic DHCP Configuration check box in the TCP/IP Configuration dialog box. This is accessed by clicking the Network icon on the Control Panel. Run Network Setup on Windows for Workgroups clients. All other settings can be received from the DHCP server if they are defined in the scope used by this client. Any entries made for other parameters, the default gateway for example, will take precedence over values received from the DHCP server.

Testing DHCP Clients   In this section, you learn how to use the IPCONFIG diagnostic utility to report the status of your current network configuration. You will be able to view the IP address you have leased from a DHCP server and other information passed to your computer from the defined scope. To verify the operation of DHCP, you will view your current address, release it, and then renew a lease. This operation is only for testing or other diagnostic and troubleshooting use. These commands are not required by typical users in the normal course of computer operations.

To test the operation of a DHCP client, follow these steps:

1. Start the client computer and log on to the network. If you cannot even complete this task, you will need to reconfigure your client software. Be sure that you have loaded the correct version of TCP/IP, especially for older Windows for Workgroups clients.

2. Open a command prompt. Type the following command:

   ```
   IPCONFIG /all
   ```

   This displays a full listing of your IP address and all options that were defined globally, for your scope, or for your individual client workstation.

3. If options have been defined for DNS servers, WINS servers, a default gateway, and so on, try using the PING command with their addresses. This will "bounce" a test packet off the other machine and return it to your computer to test basic network connectivity.

For example, using the address of a WINS server defined in the examples used for the figures, you would enter:

```
PING 182.111.200.3
```

You should receive a series of replies with the time it took to make the trip to the remote host and back. Ping other devices configured for your scope or globally on your network.

4. Enter the following command to release your IP address:

```
IPCONFIG /release
```

5. Then re-enter the command:

```
IPCONFIG /all
```

6. You will no longer have an IP address, and cannot communicate with other hosts on the network. Now enter the following:

```
IPCONFIG /renew
```

This renews your lease, probably with the same address (unless another host happened to lease it while it wasn't being used). Check the information you received from the DHCP server using the /all option with IPCONFIG again.

7. This simple series of commands confirms the proper operation of your DHCP client.

Viewing DHCP Client Leases and Reservations   To view the current status of the leases and reservations supplied by a DHCP server, follow these steps:

1. Start the DHCP Manager.

2. Highlight a scope in the left pane of the window and choose Scope, Active Leases. The Active Leases dialog box appears (see Figure 9.11).

FIG. 9.11

This dialog box displays active leases and reservations for a defined scope.

3. You can use the option buttons to sort the listing by name or by IP address. Using the check box, you can show only reservations (without leases). In addition, you can highlight any of the listed leases or reservations and click the Properties button for additional information.

4. You can also use the Reconcile button to validate the listing. This should be done after the DHCP database is restored from a backup copy, or after a system crash.

Maintaining the DHCP Database   At periodic intervals, the DHCP database may need to be compacted using a utility provided for that purpose named JETPACK.EXE. This utility reclaims wasted space in the database left by the process of entries being added and deleted. For large networks, this should be performed approximately once a week. For smaller networks, once a month is appropriate. See "Restoring the DHCP Database" in the Windows NT Server TCP/IP manual for information on restoring a corrupted DHCP database.

To use JETPACK to compact the DHCP database, follow these steps:

1. You must stop the Microsoft DHCP Server service before this operation can be per-formed. Therefore, this operation is best done during off-peak times. Use the Services icon in the Control Panel or the Windows NT Server Manager to stop the service. You can also use the following command:

   ```
   net stop dhcpserver
   ```

2. Open a command prompt and change to the \systemroot\SYSTEM32\DHCP directory. Make a backup copy of the database, just in case it's needed:

   ```
   copy dhcp.mdb dhcp.bak
   ```

3. Use JETPACK to compact the DHCP database creating a new temporary file that will replace the existing database:

   ```
   jetpack dhcp.mdb temp.mdb
   ```

4. Delete the existing database (remember, you have a backup copy):

   ```
   del dhcp.mdb
   ```

5. Rename the compacted temporary database as the in-use database:

   ```
   ren temp.mdb dhcp.mdb
   ```

6. Restart the service:

   ```
   net start dhcpserver
   ```

Using the Point-to-Point Tunneling Protocol (PPTP)

Due to the explosive growth of the Internet, it is now possible to connect to the Internet from most locations in United States with a local telephone call. Access to the Internet is also widely available outside the US although the rate structures and availability vary widely in different parts of the world. Nevertheless, the wide availability of connection to the Internet offers a tantalizing prospect—why not use the public Internet as a means of accessing your organization's private network from other geographic locations? This idea is sometimes re-ferred to as a Virtual Private Network (VPN).

Although the idea sounds promising, the first two concerns that arise are security and reliabil-ity. In order to be useful, information sent over the Internet between the remote client com-puter and a corporate server would need to be encrypted to prevent unauthorized access or eavesdropping. And using the Internet as part of your organization's WAN means that your remote connectivity is only as reliable and available as the Internet itself. Although the reliability track record of the Internet has been pretty good, problems and outages have occurred, and serious concerns have been raised by Bob Metcalfe (inventor of Ethernet) and other industry pioneers.

> **CAUTION**
>
> Encryption for the broadcast of information over the Internet is a quickly changing technology. What was safe one day will be easily compromised on another. Caution should always be taken when sending sensitive data over the Internet.

A group of corporations (Microsoft, 3Com/Primary Access, Ascend Communications, U.S. Robotics, and ECI-Telematics) has formed the PPTP Forum. This forum is working to create a protocol that would enable network traffic to be transmitted between two points on the Internet in a secure manner. The PPTP specification was entered as an Internet draft in June of 1996 and will be proposed as an Internet standard protocol when the forum has completed its work. There are other competing technologies being developed that also offer the opportunity to create VPNs, such as the Secure Wide Area Network initiative (S/WAN).

The PPTP specification enables any type of network traffic (e.g. IPX and AppleTalk) to be encapsulated and transmitted over a TCP/IP network. A complete discussion of the specification is beyond the scope of this book; however, a copy of the specification can be found at the InterNIC's Web site. The current URL for the Internet Drafts index is **http:// www.ietf.cnri.reston.va.us/1id-abstracts.html**.

Internet reliability is a complex issue depending on the cooperation of many organizations. Discussions are underway on how the infrastructure of the Internet could be improved, especially the routers and hubs that connect various physical network segments. The nature of the Internet will make ongoing reliability a somewhat elusive commodity. The Internet is not *owned* by any single organization, and is not (in its entirety) under the direct control of any single entity. As its use continues to grow, there will undoubtedly be points in time when reliability and throughput begin to suffer, then periods of improvement as upgraded equipment and software are implemented. You must make a judgment as to whether the level of throughput and reliability provided are suitable for the application or type of usage you are implementing.

The Remote Access Service (RAS) that is included with Windows NT Server does address the security concerns, and through the use of encryption technology provides a way to deliver network traffic over the Internet that will be highly secure. Although there is no absolute guarantee that a given encryption method is secure, the method being used in the Microsoft implementation of RAS (RSA RC4 with a 40-bit session key) is considered lightly secure. For most organizations, this level of security is adequate for ordinary business communications. Other products offering the capability to use a larger key would be required for sensitive information that must be kept secure for periods of a month or more.

N O T E There is a great deal of information on encryption available on the Web. Use any search engine (e.g., **www.yahoo.com**) to find additional information on this topic, and be sure to check the RSA Data Security, Inc. site for information on their products and technologies. ▓

CAUTION

The level of encryption that is appropriate for your networking needs really depends upon the type of information that is being sent on the network. The more valuable the information is, the more important it is that you spend time and effort securing the data.

PPTP is implemented in a variety of ways. In some cases, special PPTP-compliant hardware is required. A few scenarios that use PPTP are outlined below.

Accessing Your Network Over the Internet

One of the principle uses of PPTP, as already discussed, is to enable remote client computers to use the Internet as a means of gaining access to a private network. There are two different methods for achieving this connection, depending on how the client accesses the Internet. If the client is directly attached to the Internet (e.g. with an Ethernet cable provided by some organization with direct Internet access) the configuration would look something like Figure 9.12.

▶ **See** "Connecting to Your Network Using Remote Access," **p. 374**

FIG. 9.12
A remote client directly attached to the Internet can access your private network in a relatively secure manner using PPTP.

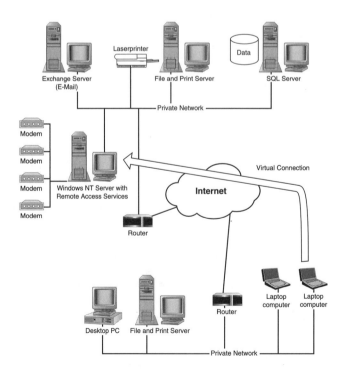

The second method for connecting is for the client to dial into an Internet service provider (ISP). This would look just like Figure 9.12.

Outsourcing Communication Hardware

PPTP offers the possibility of outsourcing your communications infrastructure. Many organizations are using Windows NT Server and RAS to provide mobile- or home-based employees access to their corporate network services. This often turns out to be a system that is harder to manage than it first seems. There are many reasons for this, including the following:

- Modems are hard to maintain. They always seem to fail at the worst hours.
- Modems quickly become obsolete.
- Adequately securing modems and networks can be tough.

Using the PPTP technology, it is possible to use a local ISP. The ISP is maintaining a large communications infrastructure already. Using PPTP, your users dial in to the ISP and access your network. In addition to outsourcing this tricky communications option, utilizing PPTP has these additional advantages:

- Users pay one fee to the ISP. This fee also provides them with Internet access that does not impact the performance of your network.
- If you use a national ISP, such as AT&T WorldNet or the Microsoft Network (MSN), traveling or remote city clients can get access on the same communications infrastructure. They pay only local phone toll charges.

A sample scenario is illustrated in Figure 9.13.

FIG. 9.13
Communication hardware can be outsourced when using the PPTP protocol.

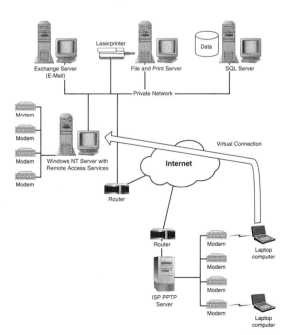

Routing in Windows NT 4.0

The TCP/IP protocol was specifically designed to be routed from one local LAN to another. This allows corporations to form large networks by connecting together many small networks, and forms the basis for the Internet.

This section covers the basics of TCP/IP routing in the Windows NT 4.0 operating system. IP routing is referred to as *static routing* because the routing is based upon a static locally configured routing table. This section also addresses the more advanced concepts in routing, such as how these are addressed in the Multiprotocol Router (MPR) for the Windows NT 4.0 operating system. You will then learn how to properly set up the static and MPR routers.

Static TCP/IP Routing in Windows NT 4.0

All TCP/IP stacks provide the ability to route packets to different addresses. This is one of the primary purposes of the TCP/IP stack. When a packet is leaving the computer, the TCP/IP stack will analyze the packet and decide the appropriate destination to send the packet.

The Internet Protocol (IP) portion of the stack is assigned the responsibility of determining the destination of an outgoing packet. The IP uses the Address Resolution Protocol (ARP) to determine the MAC or physical network address of the destination computer.

Each packet that is sent from a computer goes throught the IP portion of the TCP/IP stack. The IP portion will identify the IP destination of the packet. If the IP address identifies a computer that is on the same subnetwork, the packet is sent directly to the destination computer. Otherwise, the packet needs to be routed through intermediate computers, often called *routers*, to its final destination.

Routing allows for one IP address to become a sink destination for groups of IP addresses. The IP portion of the TCP/IP stack maintains a table of potential destinations for each outgoing packet. Looking at the structure of the routing table will help to understand how the routing performs in Windows NT (see Table 9.1).

Table 9.1 Potential Destinations for Outgoing Packets

Network Address	Netmask	Gateway Address	Interface	Metric
0.0.0.0	0.0.0.0	199.217.177.253	199.217.177.3	1
127.0.0.0	255.0.0.0	127.0.0.1	127.0.0.1	1
199.217.177.0	255.255.255.0	199.117.177.3	199.217.177.3	1
199.217.177.3	255.255.255.255	127.0.0.1	127.0.0.1	1
199.217.177.255	255.255.255.255	199.217.177.254	199.217.177.3	1

Network Address	Netmask	Gateway Address	Interface	Metric
224.0.0.0	224.0.0.0	199.214.177.3	199.217.177.3	1
255.255.255.255	255.255.255.255	199.217.177.3	199.217.177.3	1

Table 9.1 can be acquired for any Windows NT 4.0 system that has the TCP/IP stack installed by typing *route print*. The route command is used to add, delete, and analyze the TCP/IP routing tables.

In Table 9.1, there are the following five columns, with each row in the table a different route:

- **Network Address**—This provides a destination network address. This is the address that is used for matching the outgoing IP address.
- **Netmask**—This is a logical operator set of bits. It is logically read in with the network address and the destination IP address in the packet. The netmask allows TCP/IP to be divided in to logical subnets.
- **Gateway Address**—This is the IP address that the packet will actually be sent to. The gateway address must be an IP address that physically resides on the current subnetwork.
- **Interface**—This is the IP address of the network interface card that is to be used for this route. In machines that have multiple network interface cards installed, this address tells IP which interface card is physically connected to the router.
- **Metric**—The metric column allows multiple gateways to be configured for the same routes. The gateway with the highest metric will be tried first. If this route times out, the next highest metric route will be tried.

The routing table on most Windows NT computers is computed and filled automatically when the sytem is booted up. There are two potential sources for filling in the routing table. The first are the settings for the TCP/IP stack. The second are settings acquired from DHCP.

When a packet is presented to the IP part of the TCP/IP stack, IP will compare the destination address of the packet with each of the network addresses and the netmask parameter. Each bit in the netmask is either a one or zero. If the bit in the netmask is a one, then the destination IP address and network address must match exactly for this route to be chosen for this packet. The IP address that does not have any incorrect bits and has the most ones in the netmask is selected as the best route. If several IP addresses tie in this regard, the route with the lowest metric is selected. If packet does not reach the destination, IP will try an alternative route.

N O T E   Before a packet is sent, the TCP portion of the TCP/IP packet will resolve the hostname to the actual IP address of the destination machine. ■

A short example will explain the determination of how a packet is routed. The first packet is sent to an IP address that is on the sub network 199.217.177.5. Since you are on a class C network and on the computer 199.217.177.3, you do not need to route this packet through an intermediate router. Line 3 of the routing table has a netmask of 255.255.255.0. This means that the first three octets of the destination IP address must match the first three octets of the network address in the routing table. This is exactly the case for this packet. This packet is routed to the NIC card itself. At this point, IP will check to see if it has a MAC address associated with the destination IP address. If there is a MAC address for this destination, the packet is sent to the destination computer. If not, IP will resolve the MAC address for the IP address by using the Address Resolution Protocol (ARP).

A second packet is sent out of this computer; this time, the destination IP address is not on the same physical network. The destination IP address is 207.68.156.73. Each of the lines of the routing table will be analyzed to match this address. It is actually line one that serves as a catch-all IP address. Since the netmask is 0.0.0.0, none of the destination IP address bits must match the network address. So this packet will be sent to the 199.217.177.253 address for routing to its final destination. The 199.217.177.253 address happens to be the IP address that is set up in the TCP/IP configuration screen for the default router address.

Now that we understand how routes are chosen, let's address each of the seven routes shown in this routing table example. The first route is the default gateway route. If no other routes match the destination IP address, this route will be taken. The second route is the loopback address. In TCP/IP packets that are sent to 127.XXX.XXX.XXX, addresses should be echoed back by this same machine. The third line corresponds to the local subnet route. This will result in ARP resolution of the MAC address of the destination machine. The fourth line is the host route for our local machine. Notice that this is pointed to the loopback TCP/IP address and will end in the packet being sent right back to ourselves. The fifth line is a local subnet broadcast address. The packet will be sent to all machines on this subnet. On an Ethernet LAN, this will result in an Ethernet broadcast message. The sixth line is an IP multicast address. IP multicast allows the packet to multicast across special multicast gateways.

Additional static routes may be added to the Windows NT 4.0 TCP/IP routing table so that the NT computer will act like a router. This configuration would occur when you have two subnets and you are using a Windows NT system with two network cards to route packets between the two subnets. For any demanding routing needs, you would want to use the Multi-Protocol Router that is discussed in the following section.

The Windows NT 4.0 Multi-Protocol Router (MPR)

In addition to the static IP routing, many network environments need more full-featured routing capabilities. Windows NT 4.0 has added the Multi-Protocol Router to address these full routing needs. The Multi-Protocol Router adds the following three primary functions to the static IP routing:

- **IP Routing Information Protocol**—The routing information protocol for the Internet protocol.
- **IPX Routing Information Protocol**—The routing information protocol for Novell's IPX networking protocol.

- **BOOTP/DHCP relay agent**—Allows BOOTP/DHCP servers and clients to communicate across a router.

Understanding the Multi-Protocol Router The IP routing that is offered by the Multi-Protocol Router (MPR) improves on the standard static routing by enabling dynamic updates of the routing tables. Dynamic updates of the routing table allows the MPR to learn about how packets can be routed on the network. The Routing Information Protocol (RIP) provides the method for routers to convey their routing information.

In addition to improving upon static IP routing, the MPR adds the routing of IPX packets. IPX is the basis of the SPX/IPX network architecture that the majority of Novell NetWare routers use. The IPX routing in the MPR is also supported by the Routing Information Protocol for IPX. This allows the IPX routing to dynamically update its routing tables.

The ability to relay BOOTP messages is important in an NT environment. When client computers are set up to obtain an IP address from a DHCP server, the client computer does this by using the BOOTP protocol. BOOTP uses an IP broadcast to find a BOOTP server. This IP broadcast is typically limited to the local subnet. In an Ethernet networking environment, the IP broadcast is implemented as a Ethernet broadcast. These broadcast messages are typically not propagated across routers. This means that any client that wants to obtain its TCP/IP settings from a Windows NT DHCP-enabled server will need to be on the same physical network. The MPR allows these protocols to be extended across router boundaries.

▶ **See** "Implementing Dynamic Host Configuration Protocol (DHCP)," **p. 260**

The Routing Information Protocol (RIP) is the most popular method for dynamic router configuration. Dynamic router configuration becomes very important when the number of routers involved in a network increases. The basis of RIP is that a router is set to broadcast the contents of its router table every 30 seconds. The router uses this IP broadcast to advertise its routing table to the rest of the network. When each router on a network receives a broadcast of a router table, the routers increase the hop count for all of the networks in the table update for their own routing table and send the packet on. This continues until the hop count goes over the maximum hops allowed, which is typically 16. As time passes, the routing tables will propagate across the network.

The RIP packets ride on top of TCP/IP or UDP/IP for IP RIP. For IPX-based RIP, the RIP packets ride on top of SPX/IPX. The RIP protocol is the same for both the IP protocol and the IPX protocol.

The MPR system allows routing between any two LAN segments. The current architecture of the Windows NT RAS server and client do not allow you to use the MPR or any other routing system over the RAS links. RAS will provide a remote client a great tool to connect to network resources. It does not provide the ability to setup dial-up routing between two LAN segments. Microsoft is planning to release the capability to establish routing over RAS in a service patch to be released later. RAS can be configured to route packets from the local network to the Internet.

Part III

Ch 9

Implementing the Multi-Protocol Router   To install the components of the MPR, you click the Add button on the Services tab in the Network dialog box. The available services that can be added are the DHCP Relay Agent, RIP for Internet Protocol, or RIP for NWLink for IPX/SPX. Before installing the DHCP Relay Agent or RIP for Internet Protocol, you need to make sure the TCP/IP protocol has been installed. Before installing the RIP for NWLink for IPX/SPX, again you need to make sure that the IPX/SPX protocol has been installed.

To configure the BOOTP/DHCP relay agent, you can go to the DHCP Relay Agent tab in the TCP/IP Properties dialog box. The parameters that you can configure in the DHCP Relay Agent tab include the following:

- **Maximum Hops**—Maximum number of routes that a BOOTP packet can be routed. The BOOTP packet contains a number that tells how many times this packet has been routed. If this number is greater than the Maximum Hops, this packet will not be routed. In general, BOOTP clients are not that many routes from the BOOTP server.

- **Seconds Threshold**—The BOOTP protocol relies on UDP transmission instead of TCP. UDP does not guarantee that a packet is delivered. Therefore, the client and server use a timeout value when waiting for a response. The Seconds Threshold sets the timeout value.

- **DHCP Server Addresses**—This is the address of a DHCP server that will provide this machine's DHCP setup. There is rarely a need to adjust the DHCP settings.

After RIP of IP has been installed, you can enable RIP in the Routing tab of the TCP/IP Setting dialog box. The RIP for IP is configured by using the Registry Editor. The RIP parameters are found under the registry key
`HKEY_LOCAL_MACHINE\SYSTEM\CurrentControlSet\Services\IpRIP\Parameters`. Under this registry key, you will find the following RIP parameters:

- **AcceptDefaultRoutes 0, 1**—If set to the default value of zero default routes, RIP announcements are ignored. Changing this to one has RIP add these routes to the routing table.

- **AcceptHostRoutes 0, 1**—If set to the default value of zero, host route RIP announcements are ignored. Changing this to one has RIP add these routes to the routing table.

- **AnnounceDefaultRoutes 0, 1**—If set to one, default routes are broadcast.

- **AnnounceHostRoutes 0, 1**—If set to one, host routes are broadcast.

- **EnablePoisonedReverse 0, 1**—If set to the default of one, this RIP will broadcast a message when a route received via an earlier RIP message is determined to an invalid route. Allows bad routes to be removed from other routers.

- **Enable Split Horizon 0, 1**—The defualt of one suppresses RIP from broadcasting routes to the same network that the route lies on. If changed to zero, this RIP will broadcast routes that are on the same subnet to routers on that subnet.

- **EnableTriggeredUpdate 0, 1**—The default of one causes the RIP to broadcast immediate change-only messages when changes are made to this router's routing table.

These changes are usually made by a system administrator who is updating the routing table.

- **GarbageTimeout 15–259200 seconds**—Number of seconds a route is kept in the routing table without receiving an RIP announcement containing the route. Eliminates the dead routes on a network.

- **LoggingLevel 0–3**—The level of debug information written to the system log. Zero is no logging and three is detailed logging. The default is level one for logging of errors.

- **MaxTriggeredUpdateFrequency 1–884400**—Number of seconds between triggered updates. RIP waits this many seconds after the last triggered update to send the next triggered update.

- **RouteTimeout 15–259200**—A defualt of 180 seconds, which is the minimum number of seconds that will elapse before a route is marked for garbage collection.

- **SilentRip 0, 1**—If set to one, this RIP is in Silent Mode. In Silent Mode, the RIP will only listen for routing announcements. It will not broadcast any routing information.

- **UpdateFrequency 14, 8844000 seconds**—Number of seconds between routing table broadcasts. The default is 30.

The RIP routing table is the same routing table as the static IP routing tables. Earlier in this chapter, you read that the routing table is managed by the route command line utility.

RIP for IPX/SPX is configured by selecting the Enable RIP routing check box in the Routing tab of the NWLink IPX/SPX Configuration dialog box. The RIP for IPX/SPX has one important configuration setting. In the Routing tab, there is an option to enable routing of NetBIOS broadcast messages, which are Type-20 messages. These messages are used to manage browsing in the Windows NT Sever. Enabling this will allow these packets to cross router boundaries.

> **CAUTION**
>
> NetBIOS broadcast messages can cause a lot of traffic on a network. Routing these packets can cause excessive traffic. If you are not sure, it is best to leave IPX routing turned off.

Routing tables for IPX/SPX are managed using the `ipxroute` command line utility. This utility has many of the same features as the route command for the TCP/IP protocol.

From Here...

In this chapter, you received a tutorial overview of TCP/IP and related technologies that included the reasons they are important and how they operate. You learned how to install, configure, and use TCP/IP and related services. You also learned how to use DHCP and WINS to dynamically assign IP addresses and manage NetBIOS names. For more information on these and related topics, see the following chapters:

Part
III

Ch
9

- For information on setting up WINS or DNS for name resolution on TCP/IP networks, see Chapter 10, "Name Resolution with TCP/IP."
- For information on providing remote access to your network, see Chapter 11, "An Inside Look at Remote Access Service (RAS)."
- For information on gaining access to the Internet and preparing to participate in the Internet community, see Chapter 17, "I-Net Tools and Techniques."
- For information on setting up a server on the Internet, including the World Wide Web, see Chapter 18, "Building a Web with Internet Information Server (IIS)."

Name Resolution with TCP/IP

by Brad Rhodes

This chapter covers the name resolution. Name resolution is important in computer networks because it allows one computer to locate resources that are available on the network. The name resolution issue is complicated by the fact that each of the network architectures addresses name resolution in their own fashion. The name resolution becomes tied to the network architecture.

There is relief on the name resolution issue. Network Operating systems like Windows NT 4.0 are doing a lot more to adopt and integrate the disparate name resolution schemes. This chapter, in particular, discusses how Windows NT provides the ability for using the Domain Name System (DNS) and the Windows Internet Naming System (WINS). ▪

The different forms of TCP/IP host name to address resolution

Learn the different methods that a Windows NT machine uses to resolve the name of a host to the TCP/IP address of a host.

The advantages of the Domain Name Services

Find out the advantages of using a Domain Name System (DNS) server to manage the host name to address tables. Determine if you need to establish a DNS server on your network.

Implementing Domain Name System on Windows NT

Show the user how to set up a Domain Name Server using the DNS server shipped with Windows NT Server. Two detailed examples on how to set up a Domain Name System are provided.

The Windows Internet Naming System (WINS)

Learn how the WINS Server resolves NetBIOS names with dynamically assigned IP addresses.

Name Resolution in the TCP/IP Environment

Computers that are connected over networks using the TCP/IP network protocol address each other using the IP addressing scheme. The IP addressing scheme follows the syntax of four dotted decimal numbers, such as **199.217.160.1**. This address scheme is sometimes called a *dotted octet representation.* This address scheme allows for a clear network topology that relays to computers a lot of the information required for the computers to communicate efficiently.

N O T E The Internet Protocol was specifically designed to enable computers connected to each other through a series of networks to very efficiently determine the destination of a given packet of information. A router can look at the information in the TCP/IP address and quickly determine the best place to send the packet. ■

Name resolution in the TCP/IP network protocol enables network administrators to establish reasonable names for computers on the network. These names are given in an alphanumeric dotted format and are designed so that many people can easily remember or derive the name of the computer. For instance, it is much easier to remember **www.ford.com** than it is to remember the IP address of **198.108.89.236**. Name resolution enables the computer name **www.ford.com** to be resolved to computer IP address of **198.108.89.236**.

In the TCP/IP networking system, there are two common methods of name resolution available. There is a Hosts file for a local and simple method of name to address resolution. The Domain Name System is a distributed method of coordinating the name resolution of connected computers. In addition to the two common methods, there are a couple of less common systems for name resolution in the TCP/IP environment. They include high-end solutions such as X.500, and low-end methods such as a sheet of paper.

Name Resolution and Network Operating Environments

In the past ten years, the Networking Operating System (NOS) has been based upon primarily three network protocols. These protocols are the TCP/IP protocol that began in the UNIX operating system and is the basis for the Internet, Novell IPX/SPX protocol that is the basis of the Novell NetWare operating system, and NetBIOS protocol that was originated at IBM and is the basis of the LAN Manager network operating system.

Although the network operating system can be implemented independent of network protocol, the network protocol ends up heavily influencing how the resources on a network are located. Both Novell and Microsoft currently release their servers with the capability to use multiple protocol stacks. There are several implementations of IPX/SPX and NetBIOS protocols in the UNIX operating system.

How resources are located on a network is the name resolution scheme. A little understanding of how the three network protocols resolve their names will help you understand the complexity, as well as the need, for the DNS system in the TCP/IP protocol.

Novell IPX/SPX Name Resolution   The easiest of the three network architectures is the Novell NetWare IPX/SPX environment. When Novell implemented the IPX/SPX architecture, it knew that its main targeted environment was going to be the small business and that the administration of the system would have to be kept to a minimum. To keep the naming scheme simple, NetWare relied on keeping all of the naming functionality on the server; this is prior to the Novell Directory System (NDS) in NetWare 4.0. If a client wanted to find a resource, it just asked the server. The primary server that enabled the client to access the network was responsible for knowing how to access all of the resources available on the LAN.

This solution works great when there are a large number of clients and few servers. The problem develops when a client wants to begin sharing data with other clients. In this type of network, the server will quickly become a bottleneck just tracking all of the available network resources. In addition, as the network grows, it will be difficult to ensure that the server always knows about all of the resources on the network. With the release of NetWare 4.0 Novell has added the NetWare Directory Service (NDS). The NDS enables the directory of resources and their location to be implemented in distributed database fashion. There are a lot of similarities between the DNS system and the NDS system. The main difference is that the DNS system is primarily used for the location of machines. The NDS system contains information on every aspect of the resources on a network.

NetBIOS Name Resolution   In the design of the NetBIOS network operating protocol, the designers targeted LAN-based workgroups. In the NetBIOS environment, the name of resource and how to connect to it is broadcast over the network. When a client wants to connect to a server resource, the client broadcasts the name of the service that it is looking for. When the server named resource is reached, the server needs to reply to the broadcasting client. The main advantage of this architecture is that it is very simple to implement peer-type servers where all of the clients on the network can easily advertise available resources.

The main disadvantage of this operating environment is the continuous broadcasting of large numbers of packets while clients look for resources on the network. The broadcast packets cannot be routed. The broadcast name requests would quickly use up the available router bandwidth. With the release of Windows NT 3.5, Microsoft introduced the Windows Internet Naming Service that provides a mechanism of letting NetBIOS resources be located from a central resource.

TCP/IP Name Resolution   There are two main forms of name resolution in the TCP/IP networking environment. These are the use of a local hosts text file and the use of the Domain Name System.

These two TCP/IP naming techniques provide different operating benefits and costs. On small networks, the hosts file is easy to understand and is simple to set up and manage. When the network grows, the hosts file becomes unwieldy and the more advanced Domain Name System provides the network administrator an advance naming system. The following two sections provide an overview of the hosts file and DNS naming in a TCP/IP environment.

Hosts File Name Resolution   The precursor to the Internet was a network of research computers called ARPANET. When the administrators began setting up the ARPANET network of computers, they first relied upon a name resolution based on a hosts text file. A sample of a hosts text file relates the format of the information in this file (see Listing 10.1).

Listing 10.1   *HOSTS.TXT*   An Example of the Hosts Text File

```
# Copyright © 1993-1995 Microsoft Corp.
#
# This is a sample HOSTS file used by Microsoft TCP/IP for Windows NT.
#
# This file contains the mappings of IP addresses to host names. Each
# entry should be kept on an individual line. The IP address should
# be placed in the first column followed by the corresponding host name.
# The IP address and the host name should be separated by at least one
# space.
#
# Additionally, comments (such as these) can be inserted on individual
# lines or following the machine name denoted by a '#' symbol.
#
# For example:
#
#      102.54.94.97     rhino.acme.com          # source server
#       38.25.63.10     x.acme.com              # x client host

127.0.0.1       localhost
199.217.160.2        someserv.allnet.net
170.310.133.5        anotherserv.busnet.com
```

N O T E   The hosts file on Windows NT systems with TCP/IP installed and configured is located in the \winnt40\system32\drivers\etc directory. ▪

The records in the hosts file that begin with a pound sign (#) are comments. These records are not processed by the system and are used to make notes so that other administrators can more efficiently read the hosts file. The address records begin with the IP address of a machine in the three dotted decimal notation. The final part of the record is the name of the machine for the given address.

N O T E   It is typical that the names in the hosts file are set up in a hierarchical format. The rightmost part of the name is the top of the hierarchy. ▪

As the number of computers connected to the ARPANET began to grow, it became evident that one central authority would need to keep and maintain a master hosts file for the entire network. The group that ended up with the job was the Stanford Research Institute's Network Information Center SRI-NIC.

A number of issues combine to make this scheme of centrally managing the TCP/IP host names for the entire network increasingly burdensome. The first issue was that someone had to be available to take requests for new network numbers and their associated machine names. Each time someone added a new computer to their network this person would have to make an entry in the master hosts file so that all of the other computers on the network would be able to locate that machine. Additionally, they would need to make the master hosts file available to administrators of all of the machines connected to the network so that they could download the file and update their hosts file. Only after all of this would the new machine on the network be available by name.

As the number of new computers connected to the network per week grew, the pressure to update the master hosts file more often also grew. This growth also meant that the number of computers that had to be manually updated with a new hosts file also grew. The net result was that more and more computers were needing to download a growing master hosts file more often.

One last issue made the hosts file unmanageable when a large number of hosts were connected to the network. The hosts file was typically ordered by the IP address of the machine. The IP address of a machine was resolved by linearly searching through all of the hosts records until a matching host name was found. This linear search would become unreasonably long as the number of hosts gets large. Also, if a host name is added to the hosts file with the same name as that of an existing host, the machine first listed in the hosts file would be the address to get resolved. The second machine listed in the hosts has been replaced by a new machine.

All of the packets that were destined to the second machine now arrive at the first machine. If this second machine was an important mail node, at a university or large company, all of this mail would now be routed to the first machine. This would enable the first machine to impersonate and steal all of the second machine's identity. When a hacker uses this type of a mechanism to look like another machine, either to steal information bound for that machine or to cover his illegal activity, this is known as spoofing.

Domain Name System Resolution The Domain Name System was created to provide a highly scaleable and more manageable solution to the mapping of host names to IP addresses. The DNS system was designed to address many of the problems associated with the Hosts name resolution discussed above.

The DNS system is designed to have the distribution of the naming service spread across large numbers of machines on the network. This way no one machine becomes a single source of failure or bottleneck for the entire network. The DNS system relies upon the concepts of zones, authority, and domains to distribute the name resolution load. The DNS system pushes the responsibility of resolving a name to the DNS server, thereby allowing the client to make one request to the server. The server then issues multiple searches to resolve the address. This enables the resolver client to be very lightweight in its processing, configuration, and memory requirements.

Figure 10.1 provides an overview of the name resolution process for a common name lookup. Here it is seen that the desktop client named **desktop.gasullivan.com** is requesting from the default name server **namesrv.gasullivan.com** the address of **www.microsoft.com**. Figure 10.1 shows that the iterative search for **www.microsoft.com** is conducted by **namesrv.gasullivan.com** on behalf of the client requesting the address. When the IP address is returned to **desktop.gasullivan.com**, it is used exactly the same as if the IP address were gotten from a hosts file.

FIG. 10.1

The desktop client's main DNS server, **namesrv.gasullivan.com**, iterativily searches the DNS name space by contacting other DNS servers.

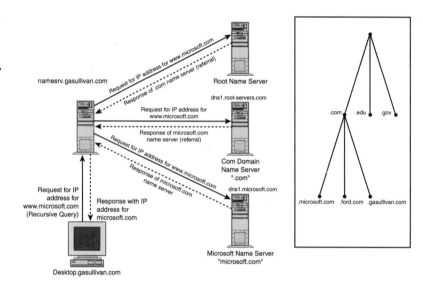

The example shown in Figure 10.1 is not exactly how the name space is searched to resolve the name to an address. If it were the Root domain, name server would be a bottleneck and source of failure for the whole system. In reality, the **namesrv.gasullivan.com** would typically be configured with a set of hints, stored in the "cache" file, that describe where all of the top-level domain name servers are located.

The design of the DNS system was developed by Paul Mockapetris of USC's Information Sciences Institute and was submitted to the Internet Engineering Task Force as RFC's 1034 and 1035 in 1984. A popular implementation of the DNS system was the Berkley Internet Name Domain (BIND) implemented for Berkeley's 4.3BSD version of UNIX by Kevin Dunlap. The source code for BIND was ported to most major versions of UNIX and is the basis for the DNS server in the Windows NT Server system.

The Benefits of Using the Domain Name System Server for Name Resolution

The first section of this chapter introduced the following two primary forms of name resolution in a TCP/IP network:

■ Hosts file name resolution

■ Domain Naming System name resolution

This section helps to determine which network managers will need to consider setting up a full Domain Name System server.

The following are the issues that are important to the consideration of the DNS server:

- Size and complexity of the network
- Connectivity to the Internet
- Typical applications supported by the network

The most important issue in determining the need to establish a DNS server is the size and complexity of the network that is going to be established. The larger and more complex the network is going to be, the more likely the network manager will benefit by establishing a DNS server at the start.

As discussed in the first section of this chapter, the DNS name resolution scheme was designed to relieve the administration headaches that grow from managing the hosts file for name resolution. The more complex a network is, the more the network administrator will benefit from the DNS system's manageability features.

Part
III

Ch
10

The first factor in deciding if you should establish your own DNS is the size and complexity of your network. It is possible to start a network using the hosts file method of resolution and switching over to the DNS server at a later time. Unfortunately, switching a bunch of Windows NT workstations, Windows NT servers, or Windows 95 machines set up from hosts resolution to DNS name resolution involves going to each machine and changing the TCP/IP settings to use DNS. Even on a 25-computer network this becomes a several day task. If it appears that your TCP/IP network will grow to even this modest level, it is likely that you need to consider establishing a DNS server.

The second factor to consider is the connectivity of the network to the Internet. If your network is connected to the Internet via an Internet service provider (ISP), you have the option of getting your DNS services from your ISP. In a typical small network (fewer than ten nodes), the DNS service offered by an ISP will be adequate. Most ISPs offer DNS services for corporate-based connections. The drawback of letting your ISP provide your DNS server is that when it comes time to change any of the addresses on your network, you will have to coordinate these changes with your ISP. This is an error-prone process, and if there are a large number of changes, you will end up spending a lot of time coordinating these changes with the ISP.

The DNS system does not have to only be used on networks that are connected to the Internet. If you are the network manager of a network that will not be connected to the Internet and you want to take advantage of the TCP/IP networking architecture, the DNS system will help manage the naming of the machines on the network. If the network is a large network or a bunch of geographically separated interconnected LANs, the DNS system will be very helpful in managing the network names.

The third factor is the type of applications that are being supported on the network. If you are the network manager of a network that is to provide a large number of Internet-based services to people on the Internet, you will probably want to have a DNS server. The DNS server will enable you to properly configure and name your servers so that people on the Internet will be able to reach the servers. It will come in extremely handy when you decide to move or change the configuration of your Internet servers.

Domain Name System Name Resolution

The most important part of the DNS system is to provide name resolution for a TCP/IP computer. Prior to configuring a DNS server, it is important to develop an understanding of how the DNS system provides name resolution. The following are the two main topics that explain the DNS name resolution process:

- Name space
- The address resolution process

The *name space* is the organization of the DNS system's distributed host name database. The *resolution process* is the way that the name space is searched for the matching host name so that the corresponding IP address can be returned. Finally, the concept of a zone will help you understand how the DNS name space is distributed across a group of DNS servers.

The DNS Name Space

The DNS system client/server architecture highly depends upon distributing the storage of the host name information under its control across large parts of the network. This enables the system to be scaleable, reliable, and manageable. The distributed database enables the DNS to be scaleable as the queries for resolution are distributed to a large number of machines. The millions of queries that are resolved on the Internet each day could never be accomplished on one single machine; they must be distributed to a large number of systems. The distributed database within the DNS provides a more reliable solution by making separate nodes that will duplicate data. The distributed nature provides mechanisms that will copy data from one server to another or refer a query from one server to the next. If any one server is down, the DNS query can typically be resolved by another system.

If an important number of DNS servers are unavailable, only those hosts that are covered by the down DNS servers will be unreachable. The rest of the DNS system remains intact and usable. The distributed database makes the whole system more manageable. The distributed database allows configuration changes in the layout of the data in the DNS system to propagate easily through the system. New servers can be added and old servers can be removed with very little intervention by the network manager.

The distributed database that is the DNS system is laid out like any operating system's file structure. This tree structure is most like the UNIX file system: There is root to the file system, and the subdirectories spawn off of the root (see Figure 10.2).

This tree structure can be traversed up or down the tree to find any one given node. The biggest difference with the DNS system is that the DNS tree resides on more than one machine. The data in Figure 10.2 that contains the information on the **.microsoft.com** domain would reside on a DNS server that is located at the Microsoft facility. The data contained in the

Berkeley domain under the .edu domain resides on a DNS server that is at the Berkeley campus (refer to Figure 10.2).

FIG. 10.2
Here the DNS name space is viewed as the directory or tree structure of an operating system file structure. The files are host names, and the subdirectories are new domain names.

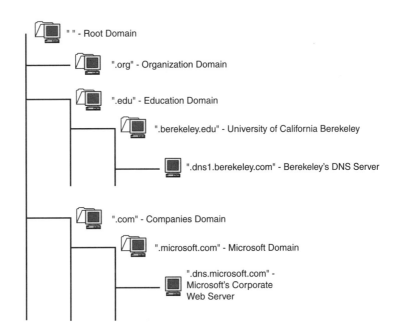

" " - Root Domain

".org" - Organization Domain

".edu" - Education Domain

".berekeley.edu" - University of California Berekeley

".dns1.berekeley.com" - Berekeley's DNS Server

".com" - Companies Domain

".microsoft.com" - Microsoft Domain

".dns.microsoft.com" -
Microsoft's Corporate
Web Server

Part

III

Ch

10

The domain name server *name space* is searched just like the directory tree on a machine is searched. A quick comparison of the directory tree structure search and the search of a file on a file system will help you understand the name space. In the file system search, any one file can be identified by the full path name. In Figure 10.3, the file Wordpad.exe is identified by the full path name c:\Program Files\Accessories\wordpad.exe. In the DNS name space shown in Figure 10.2, the system Web server www at Microsoft is identified by the fully qualified DNS name of **www.microsoft.com**.

The main difference between a DNS name and a file system name is the order of names in the tree. A smaller difference is that the file system uses a slash to separate names and DNS uses a period to separate names. The order of a DNS name is reversed when compared to a file system name space. The file system name space starts with the broad high-level name on the left and goes down the tree to the more specific name as you go to the right. For instance, the full path name of c:\Program Files\Accessories\wordpad.exe starts at the root directory of \.

The Program Files directory is the first level directory underneath the root file system. You traverse the path name until you come to the specific file. The DNS system is organized in the same fashion, except that you start from the right of the fully qualified DNS name. The DNS name **www.microsoft.com** ends with the **.com** high-level domain. This is the first-level domain underneath the root domain name in the DNS name space. You continue to traverse the name space to the left until you reach the actual node.

FIG. 10.3

The file system structure as seen on a Windows NT machine. The subdirectories split off the root and the files are nodes on the subdirectory.

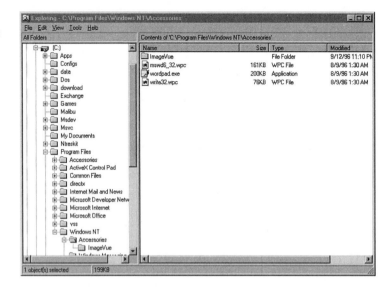

Searching the Name Space for an Address

The main difference between the DNS name database and the file system database is that the DNS name database is distributed across multiple network nodes. This is done through delegation. The DNS system enables the root name server or any other name server to delegate the authority for a given segment of DNS names to another server. This allows the database to be distributed across a large number of nodes but still ensures that any one machine can find and access all of the data.

An example will help to explain how the delegation will take place when a host name is being resolved. Figure 10.4 shows two corporate domains under the **.com** high-level domain: the Microsoft domain and the G. A. Sullivan domain.

In this example, you are on the workstation **desktop.gasullivan.com** and want to access information on the server **www.microsoft.com**. Your workstation is set up to use the DNS server of **name-srv.gasullivan.com** as its default DNS server. To resolve the **www.microsoft.com**, your workstation will ask **name-srv.gasullivan.com** for the IP address of **www.microsoft.com**. The desktop machine **desktop.gasullivan.com** will issue a recursive name resolution query to **name-srv.gasullvan.com**. Remember that **name-srv.gasullivan.com** will resolve the address for the requesting client. This is step 1 in Figure 10.5.

In step 1 in Figure 10.5, **desktop.gasullivan.com** asks **name-srv.gasullivan.com** for IP address of **www.microsoft.com**. This request is a recursive name resolution query. A recursive request tells **name-srv.gasullivan.com** to search the DNS system for the host name **www.microsoft.com**. The DNS server **name-srv.gasullivan.com** should not respond until the host name is located or there is an error locating the host.

FIG. 10.4
A simplified domain tree that shows portions of the G. A. Sullivan domain and the Microsoft domain.

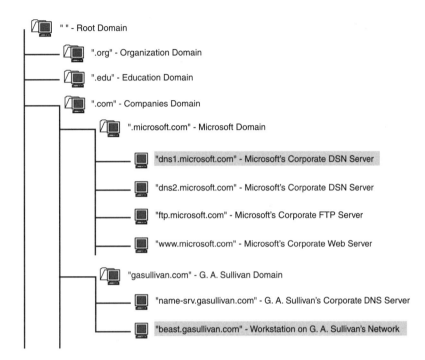

" " - Root Domain

".org" - Organization Domain

".edu" - Education Domain

".com" - Companies Domain

".microsoft.com" - Microsoft Domain

"dns1.microsoft.com" - Microsoft's Corporate DSN Server

"dns2.microsoft.com" - Microsoft's Corporate DSN Server

"ftp.microsoft.com" - Microsoft's Corporate FTP Server

"www.microsoft.com" - Microsoft's Corporate Web Server

"gasullivan.com" - G. A. Sullivan Domain

"name-srv.gasullivan.com" - G. A. Sullivan's Corporate DNS Server

"beast.gasullivan.com" - Workstation on G. A. Sullivan's Network

Part
III

Ch
10

FIG. 10.5
This figure details an example of how the DNS name space is iterativily processed to resolve the destination host.

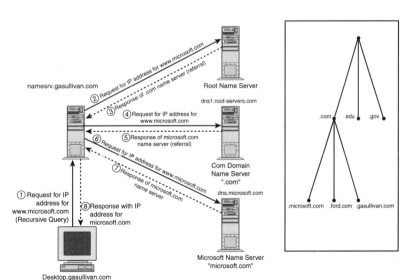

The server **name-srv.gasullivan.com** will recognize that it does not know the address of **www.microsoft.com** and that no servers below **name-srv.gasullivan.com** will know the address of **www.microsoft.com**. In step 2, the request will be forwarded to the next higher level of the domain name space, the root domain. The actual forwarding will be done by the

DNS server **name-srv.gasullivan** for the workstation **desktop.gasullivan.com**. The DNS server **name-srv.gasullivan.com** will send an iterative name resolution query to one of the root name servers for the domain. An iterative query will either return the actual IP address of the host name or will return the IP address of a DNS server that is closer to the host.

The root domain name server will know that it has delegated authority for the **.com** domain to the DNS server **dns1.root-servers.com**. The root name server will tell **name-srv.gasullivan.com** that **dns1.root-server.com** is the authoritative name server for the **.com** domain. This is step 3 in Figure 10.5.

The .com server tells **name-srv.gasullivan.com** that **dns.microsoft.com** is the authoritative name server for the **microsoft.com** domain. This is step 5 in Figure 10.5. Once **name-srv.gasullivan.com** receives this response, it will query **dns.microsoft.com** for the IP address of **www.microsoft.com** (step 6 in Figure 10.5). Because **dns.micorosoft.com** is the DNS server that is authoritative for **www.microsoft.com**, this DNS server will respond to the request with the IP address of **www.microsoft.com**. At this time, **name-srv.gasullivan.com** replies to **desktop.gasullivan.com** with the IP address of **www.microsoft.com.** This is step 8 in Figure 10.5.

This might seem like a lot of activity to resolve the one address. The DNS system provides for caching as a means to reduce the need for so much request response activity. In this example, the DNS server **name-srv.gasullivan.com** will cache several addresses the first time this query is issued. The first piece of information is the host name and IP address of the name server for the **.com** domain. The second piece of information is the IP address and host name for the DNS server that is authoritative for the **microsoft.com** domain, **dns.microsoft.com**. The third piece of information is the actual IP address and host name of the server **www.microsoft.com**. Any further requests for the **www.microsoft.com** server will be answered directly from the cache on **name-srv.gasullivan.com**. If a request is now received at **name-srv.gasullivan.com** for **ftp.microsoft.com** (another server at Microsoft), this request is fulfilled by **name-srv.gasullivan.com** directly asking **dns.microsoft.com**.

This caching scheme is designed to ensure that popular and recently visited sites are found in the cache of the nearest DNS servers. Less frequently accessed sites are flushed from the cache. Each DNS server response in the above example will include a Time to Live (TTL) number. This number is the number of seconds that the domain record should be kept active in a cache. This enables the Authoritative name server—the name server that is responsible for the hosts in that part of the domain—to determine how records pointing to its servers are to be cached. Once the record has been in the DNS server's cache longer than the TTL value, it is flushed and the root name servers are queried again to make sure that most valid data is available.

The Resolver: the DNS Client

The resolver is the portion of the TCP/IP client software that issues a request to a DNS server for a name resolution. The resolver library is automatically called whenever the workstation is configured to DNS for name resolution. There are three types of DNS queries that can be issued to a DNS server: *recursive*, *iterative*, and *reverse*.

NOTE DNS servers will receive queries from DNS clients and other DNS servers. ▓

A *recursive* name resolution query tells the server that it is to either resolve the host name to the IP address of the server or to return an error code. The error code could indicate that the host name does not exist in the domain or that the domain does not exist. Most clients that are not DNS servers will issue a recursive query to their assigned DNS server. This enables the client to issue one request and sit back and wait either for the IP address or an error code to return. This corresponds to step 1 in Figure 10.5.

Iterative queries will return either the IP address of the destination host or the IP address of a DNS server that is closer to the host that is being resolved. This type of query is issued by one DNS server to another DNS server. If the IP address of the destination host is returned, then the DNS server has finished resolving the DNS query and returns the value to the requesting client. If the response to an iterative query is the IP address of another DNS server, this is called referring. The responding DNS is referring the requesting DNS up or down the domain hierarchy tree to a DNS that is closer to the destination host. This type of query is the same as that shown in steps 2–3 and steps 4–5 in Figure 10.5.

This process is very similar to the change directory command in a file system. The DNS server that is resolving the host name will continue up the domain tree until it reaches a point high enough that the destination host is under a lower-level domain. The DNS server will traverse down that branch of the tree until the DNS that is authoritative for the host is reached. This DNS will respond with the IP address of the destination host.

A reverse name request enables the DNS client to request the host name of the host that has a given IP address. The section Reverse Name Resolution explains how the reverse domain name space is constructed. When the client requests the reverse name resolution of an IP address, the reverse name space is searched just like the forward name space. If a client is requesting the host name of the IP address **207.68.156.61**, the DNS servers will search for the host name with a PTR record of **61.156.68.207.in-addr.arpa**. Again, the DNS server handling the request will walk up the domain hierarchy until high enough that the domain is below. It will then walk down the domain hierarchy until the host name for the IP address is exactly matched.

The Internet Name Space

The majority of DNS systems that are set up will be connected to the Internet. The Internet is an extremely large example of the DNS name space. It is a good example of how the distributed DNS database allows a network to be scaled to extremely large sizes. Until recently the Internet was divided into seven top level domains. These top level domains are truly how most people, especially those in the United States, view the Internet. The seven domains are as follows:

- **com**—Commercial sites, such as IBM (**ibm.com**), AT&T (**att.com**), and Microsoft (**microsoft.com**).

Part
III

Ch
10

- **edu**—Educational sites, including schools and universities.
- **gov**—Governmental sites (nonmilitary), such as NASA (**nasa.gov**).
- **mil**—Military organizations in the United States, for example, the U.S. Army (**army.mil**).
- **net**—Networking organizations, including most Internet providers, for example **uu.net**.
- **org**—Noncommercial organizations, usually not-for-profit groups.
- **int**—International organizations.

This original domain hierarchy was dictated by the most powerful organizations that were involved in the Internet during the early formation of the Internet. The majority of these organizations were United States specific organizations. With the explosion of the Internet over the last couple of years, especially in countries outside of the United States, it has become necessary to redesign the domain layout of the Internet. The current domain layout is in accordance with the specification ISO 3166. In ISO 3166, each country gets a domain hierarchy much like the upper-level one shown in the previous list for the United States. So for the Australians there is a domain hierarchy that includes com.au, edu.au, and so on. Not all countries follow this guideline.

Delegation: Zones and Domains

The DNS system has two primary concepts when considering how the name space is divided up. The main and most evident is the concept of Domains. A domain is a division in the name space shown in the name. For instance, the **microsoft.com** domain is a subdomain of the **.com** domain. The division of the name space and placement of the data in this example makes the distinction between a *zone* and a *domain* more clear.

A zone is actually all of the data that is contained under a given DNS server. This is not necessarily all of the data that is associated with the subdomain being managed by the DNS server. For instance, the site **gasullivan.com** is divided into five subdomains and the DNS server **name-srv.gasullivan.com** is the Authoritative DNS server for the **gasullivan.com** domain. The five subdomains of **gasullivan.com** are as follows:

- **training.gasullivan.com**
- **research.gasullivan.com**
- **management.gasullivan.com**
- **systems.gasullivan.com**
- **product.gasullivan.com**

Of the five subdomains of **gasullivan.com**, the research and product subdomains are of a large enough size that they can have their own DNS server (see Figure 10.6). The **srv.gasullivan.com** name server is set up to delegate authority of the research and product domains to **dns1.research.gasullivan.com** and **printsrv.product.gasullivan.com**, respectively.

FIG. 10.6

This expanded **gasullivan.com** domain includes the reverse name domains.

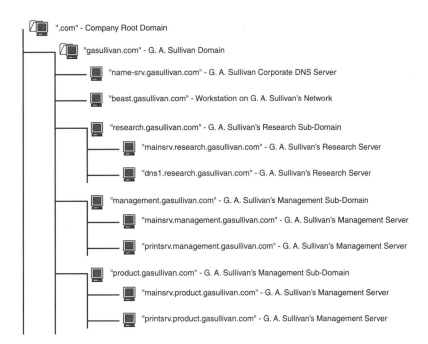

".com" - Company Root Domain

"gasullivan.com" - G. A. Sullivan Domain

"name-srv.gasullivan.com" - G. A. Sullivan Corporate DNS Server

"beast.gasullivan.com" - Workstation on G. A. Sullivan's Network

"research.gasullivan.com" - G. A. Sullivan's Research Sub-Domain

"mainsrv.research.gasullivan.com" - G. A. Sullivan's Research Server

"dns1.research.gasullivan.com" - G. A. Sullivan's Research Server

"management.gasullivan.com" - G. A. Sullivan's Management Sub-Domain

"mainsrv.management.gasullivan.com" - G. A. Sullivan's Management Server

"printsrv.management.gasullivan.com" - G. A. Sullivan's Management Server

"product.gasullivan.com" - G. A. Sullivan's Management Sub-Domain

"mainsrv.product.gasullivan.com" - G. A. Sullivan's Management Server

"printsrv.product.gasullivan.com" - G. A. Sullivan's Management Server

Part

III

Ch

10

The difference between a zone and a domain can now be shown. The domain for **gasullivan.com** includes all of machines that are named ***.gasullivan.com**, ***.training.gasullivan.com**, ***.research.gasullivan.com**, ***.management.gasullivan.com**, ***.systems.gasullivan.com**, and ***.product.gasullivan.com**. The **name-srv** is the authoritative DNS server for this domain. The zone that is attributed to the **name-srv.gasullivan.com** server are those servers that are actually held in the **name-srv.gasullivan.com** databases. Because the research and product subdomains have been delegated to different DNS servers, these servers are no longer in the zone controlled by **name-srv.gasullivan.com**.

A split in the domain is like adding a tree in a directory on a file system. A split in the zone is when the authority for a split in the domain is delegated to another DNS server. It is not possible to have splits in a zone that do not correspond to splits in the name space. For example, all of the machines at the ***.management.gasullivan.com** level must have the same DNS server and all of the machines at the ***.gasullivan.com** level must have the same DNS server. Only when a subdomain is split off of the name space can a new zone be created.

A zone is a single coherent piece of the DNS name space. When one zone is configured to be a backup server for another DNS server, the backup server will request a zone transfer from the primary server. Once the backup has received the zone, it knows that it has the most recent backup of the primary DNS server. Primary domain backup can be used to create a secondary DNS server that mirrors the primary server for reliability and backup purposes. The secondary DNS could also be established to provide faster name resolution for a group of machines that are connected to the primary through a slow or WAN network connection. This way the name resolution packet will not have to flow over the slow network connection.

Reverse Name Resolution

The DNS system provides a method for allowing the resolution of a network nodes host name given the nodes TCP/IP numeric address. This enables a system to log incoming network requests in terms of the host name, not just the TCP/IP address from where the request is coming. Reverse name resolution is very important to the overall architecture of the DNS system.

Several UNIX utilities use the reverse name resolution to verify that the person is coming from a valid machine on the network. For instance, the server part of the FTP connection could double check that you are a valid address on the Internet. The server part of the FTP connection is the ftpd program. The ftpd program could verify that a login request is coming from a valid machine by using the TCP/IP address.

Every packet contains the TCP/IP address of the machine that is making the request. Once ftpd has this TCP/IP address, it can do a reverse name resolution to get the host name of the requesting machine. Now that it has the host name it can do a forward name resolution. This will return the actual TCP/IP address of the requesting machine from the official Internet DNS systems. If this new TCP/IP address does not match the original requested TCP/IP address, this is an indication that the original request did not come from where it stated.

How does reverse name resolution occur in a DNS server? From our discussion to this point, the DNS system is set up to resolve host names to TCP/IP addresses. The DNS server maintains a list that is sorted by the host name. During forward name resolution, the list is searched in the sorted order until the name is found and the TCP/IP address is returned. These sorted searches are much more efficient than a linear search of the host names. Using a small indexing system improves this lookup time even more. Figure 10.7 shows how the names come out in a sorted fashion.

FIG. 10.7

The list of domains is parsed and sorted. The name is broken at the periods and the individual components are reversed. The list is then sorted and built.

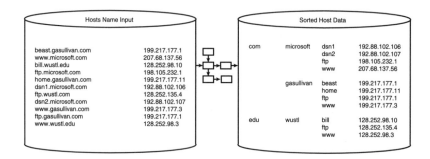

Because the list is already sorted by host name, there are two possibilities for reverse name resolution. The list could be linearly searched on the second element of the list, the TCP/IP address. Or, the list could be duplicated and sorted by TCP/IP address. The linear search would be a problem for two reasons. The first is inefficiency. The second is the spoofing problem that was introduced earlier in the section "Hosts File Name Resolution." Spoofing could occur when a record is added to the DNS host table with a TCP/IP address that is a duplicate of an existing host. Now the reverse name resolution that is relying on the linear search of the

TCP/IP address could return a different host name. Reverse name resolution relies upon keeping a second list that is sorted by TCP/IP address.

It would have been easy to take the initial host name list that is being added to the server and resort the list based upon the TCP/IP address instead of the host name. The DNS system does not do this because the reverse name resolution can solve another very important architectural issue for the DNS system. This is how the domain numbers themselves are assigned and managed. The DNS system uses a second input file and creates a whole new domain space that is tacked on to the root of the main DNS system for tracking the TCP/IP to host name resolution information.

In the name space, the reverse names are stored under a specially created domain. In Figure 10.8, the **arpa** domain is a subdomain split off of the root. There is also the **in-addr** domain that is split off of the **arpa** domain. This special domain constitutes the reverse name space. Under the **in-addr.arpa** domain, the TCP/IP addresses form subdomains.

Part III Ch 10

FIG. 10.8

The current IP address is reversed and it is added to the **in-addr.arpa** domain. This forms the reverse domain name space.

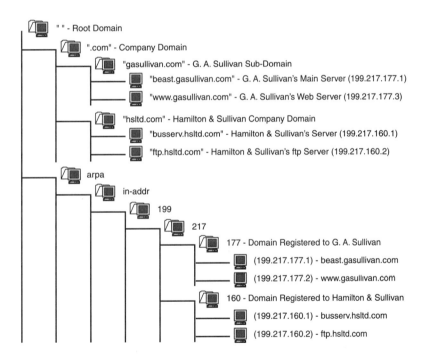

Notice that the address is broken up at the dots and used to form the directory-like structure. The full DNS reverse name resolution domain name of **beast.gasullivan.com (199.217.177.1)** is **1.177.217.199.in-addr.arpa**. The name is pieced together just like the host name. In the host name, the lowest-level node in **beast.gasullivan.com** is **beast**, and this is the first name in the domain name. In other words, the reverse name space names are formed just like the host name part of the name space (see Figure 10.9).

FIG. 10.9
The list of reverse domain names are parsed and sorted like the list of domain names.

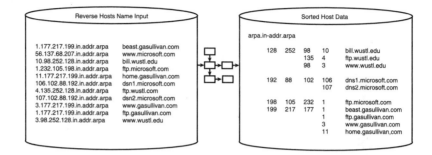

Like the forward name space, the reverse name space is kept in a sorted list in the DNS server. The list is built in exactly the same manner as the forward host name list. This list facilitates the use of indexes to reduce the amount of memory needed to store the list and to greatly reduce the amount of time that it takes to search the list.

The 0.in-addr.arpa and 127.in-addr.arpa Domains

These two special domains under the **in-addr.arpa** reverse name domain solve some minor problems with how DNS replaces the hosts text file for name resolution. Often, TCP/IP applications send requests for the reverse lookup of **0.0.0.0** IP address or the **127.0.0.1** IP address. The **0.0.0.0** IP address is an undefined addresses. It is a waste of network resources to allow resolution of this address to propagate all of the way to the root name server before getting an undefined host or domain error.

The **127.0.0.1** address is the loopback IP address. All TCP/IP systems should route packets sent to this address back to the same machine, loopback. If an application is set up to do reverse name resolution and is getting logon requests from the localhost, then the packet will often contain the IP address of **127.0.0.1**. When the application requests a reverse DNS request on this IP address, if there is not a **127.in-addr.arpa** domain on the server, then this request will again go all the way to the root server before receiving an error or an invalid response.

In order to diminish the impact of requests on these two special IP addresses, every DNS server should define PTR records in the **0.in-addr.arpa** and **127.in-addr.arpa** domains.

> **CAUTION**
>
> It is considered to be in bad taste, or lazy, to set up a DNS server that does not resolve these special domains. If your DNS server does not resolve them and they are not resolved on the client, then these requests are forwarded to the next higher server. This can result in a lot of needless overhead on a busy or large network.

Primary and Secondary DNS Servers

The DNS server system enables a DNS server to be either a primary or a secondary domain name server. A primary domain name server reads its name resolution data directly from files that reside on the server. A secondary server obtains the name resolution data by requesting a zone transfer directly from a primary DNS server. Changes to the machines in a zone must be made to the primary server. The secondary server updates its files from the primary DNS server.

It is highly recommended that any given zone be on two DNS servers, a primary and a secondary. This provides the necessary redundancy that a DNS server requires. If a DNS server is not available for an organization, then anybody trying to get to resources on the network or trying to get out to the Internet will get name resolution errors.

Windows NT Server DNS Specifics

Although the DNS server implemented on the Windows NT Server operating system is guaranteed to inter-operate with the BIND implementation of DNS that many of the UNIX systems are based upon, Microsoft implemented a few additions to the basic DNS server to ensure tight integration with the Microsoft Windows NT Server environment.

Microsoft changed the DNS server code to allow for a tight integration with the WINS naming server. The WINS server and DNS server will now share name spaces. This is primarily done to allow DHCP-registered NetBIOS names that will show up in the WINS server to be resolved by DNS requests.

Microsoft also changed the DNS resolver to enable NetBIOS name resolution and TCP/IP name resolution to interoperate. The DNS resolver is the actual code on a DNS client machine that initiates a name resolution request with a DNS server. Microsoft added a NetBIOS name resolution ahead of the normal DNS name resolution. This allows machines set up for NetBIOS over TCP/IP to use local NetBIOS resolution.

▶ **See** "DNS and WINS Integration," **p. 322**

The Windows NT operating system has roots in the Microsoft LAN Manager server. This server operating system was based heavily upon the NetBIOS networking architecture. The root level of how Windows NT workstation and server operating systems share resources is through a NetBIOS-based protocol. As discussed in "NetBIOS Name Resolution," the NetBIOS architecture relies on broadcasts to resolve names of available servers on the network. This scheme has shown to be very costly on large networks that are interconnected with WANs.

In order to address this problem, Microsoft has implemented the WINS naming database service. The WINS naming service enables the NetBIOS name of a service to be directly mapped to an IP address. Microsoft has since extended the WINS naming service to allow the DNS system in place on many networks to actually provide the name resolution. The WINS server in a DNS server environment will append the NetBIOS name to a configured domain name and pass the resolution request on to the DNS server.

In addition, the DNS server has been enhanced to enable the DNS server to attempt to resolve a host name through a request to the WINS server. The DNS server can be configured with an unlimited number of WINS severs that should be tried for host name resolution requests.

Part

III

Ch

10

When configured in this fashion, the DNS server attempts to resolve the host name from its database files. If it does not find an A record in its local records and the host name is less than 15 characters long, the DNS server will attempt to resolve the name from the WINS servers.

On the Windows NT operating system, the resolver library has been modified over the normal TCP/IP resolver. The Windows NT TCP/IP resolver library is also used to resolve NetBEUI. Microsoft calls the resolver the NetBT networking component. NetBT stands for NetBIOS over TCP/IP. The NetBT component acts a little different than the standard TCP/IP name resolver in that NetBT will look at the name that is being requested. If that name is less than 15 characters long and does not contain any periods, NetBT will attempt a NetBIOS name resolution on the name. If this fails, then NetBT will do a normal TCP/IP name resolution.

The Dynamic Host Control Protocol (DHCP) also presents one challenge to the name resolution. If a client computer on the network is currently configured to use DHCP to obtain the IP address, then the DHCP system enables the network manager to configure a server to dynamically assign IP addresses. There is no provision in the DNS system to allow for dynamic updates of the DNS configuration data. As a result, because the IP address is assigned on-the-fly, it is not possible for someone outside of the current network to establish a connection to a machine that is getting its IP address dynamically. If you are setting up a machine that people on the Internet need to reach, you must to make sure that you assign that machine a static IP address.

DNS Database Records

There are nineteen individual data record types available for the DNS server database. These records follow the basic format of

```
hostname.company.com      IN      A      199.217.160.1
```

Where the first field in the record is the hostname of the machine referenced in the record. The second field is the class type. The class type is almost always IN for the Internet class type. The only other type currently in use is HS for Hesoid used at MIT. The third record is the record type indicator. This is an A record, which is an address record type. The last field in the record is the IP address for the host. Table 10.1 explains all of the individual record types that can be found on the DNS server.

Table 10.1   DNS Record Format

Record Type Indicator	Description
A	Basic address record, which is the most used record in the DNS system. The A record tells how to map a host name to an IP address.
AFSDB	Andrew File System (AFS) cell database server. This enables a client on the AFS system to locate an AFS authenticated name server.

Record Type Indicator	Description
CNAME	Canonical name resource. This enables alias names to be created for the same IP address. For example, if you want to add **ftp.gasullivan.com** to your network and want it to point to an existing machine, such as **devserv.gasullivan.com**, then use a CNAME record of **ftp.gasullivan.com CNAME devserv.gasullivan.com**.
HINFO	The host information record type. This is an optional record that enables the information about the DNS hardware implementation and operating system. RFC 1700 covers the appropriate names to fill in these fields. This record is only rarely used.
ISDN	Same as an A record, but maps a domain name to an ISDN address. This record is experimental and rarely used.
MB	The mailbox resource record. This is an experimental record that is rarely used.
MG	The mail group resource record. This is an experimental record that is rarely used.
MINFO	The mailbox information record. This is an experimental record that is rarely used. Other experimental records that are related to the MINFO are the MB, MG, and MR records.
MR	The mailbox resource record. This is an experimental record that is rarely used.
MX	The mail exchange resource record. This record is at the heart of Internet mail distribution. The SMTP mail transport system relies on the MX record to determine how to find the destination of the SMTP message. Servers that are listed in the MX record need to be running an SMTP messaging server that is properly configured.
NS	Name sever record. It identifies DNS servers for the domain. Every domain must have a NS record in the zone records and in the reverse zone records.
PTR	Reverse name lookup record. This record is used in the **in-addr.arpa** to support reverse name resolution.
RP	Responsible person record. This record is used a lot like the HINFO to provide additional information to those who know to look for it. Multiple records of this type in a domain provide data on those responsible for the domain and how to contact them. Like the HINFO, this is optional and very few people set up this record.

Part
III

Ch
10

continues

Table 10.1   Continued

Record Type Indicator	Description
RT	Route through resource record. This tells an intermediate host how to route data packets to a destination host. The destination host is usually one that is established in an ISDN or X.25 resource record. This record is experimental and rarely used.
SOA	Start of authority record. This tells the DNS systems that this DNS is authoritative for this zone. It contains information on the amount of time that the data from DNS can be cached, and a contact person for this DNS. The rest of the fields in this record affect how secondary backup DNS servers use the data from your DNS server.
TXT	Used to generate general textual information. Could be used to indicate the location of a machine. This record is rarely used.
WINS	A record that points to the IP address of an available WINS server. This is a record that is specific to Microsoft, and cannot be edited in the DNS manager.
WINS_R	This record tells the Microsoft DNS server to use a NetBIOS name request to get the name of a resource.
WKS	The well-known service record database. This record enables certain TCP/IP ports to use a specified protocol. The protocol is almost always UDP or TCP. For example, to set up your SMTP gateway to accept the UDP protocol, you would use **machine.mycompany.com IN WKS 199.217.160.1 SMTP**. At one point, the WKS record was required for SMTP. This has since been dropped: too many sites failed to implement this correctly.
X.25	X.25 resource record. This is very much like the A resource record. It maps a domain name to an X.25 address.

Although this list looks like a long list of selections, there are only four records that really need to be understood. They are the SOA record, the A record, the PTR record and the MX record. If you have these records set up correctly, your DNS should function correctly.

Implementing a DNS Server

The implementation of a DNS server on the Windows NT Server operating system is very similar to the steps that are taken when setting up a DNS server on a UNIX system or any other system. There are a series of implementation level concepts that should be understood prior to implementing a DNS server.

CAUTION

The DNS Manager for Windows NT works much better after you apply the first service patch for Windows NT 4.0. You should apply all of the available patches prior to setting up your DNS server.

There are several ways for the network administrator to get a real boost in establishing a DNS server. The first place to look at getting a head start is from your ISP. If you are the manager of a small network that is currently getting DNS services from your ISP, then your ISP has already established the majority of the information that is needed to configure your DNS server. Most reasonable ISPs will happily provide you with those portions of the configuration files that impact your network.

A second place to get a head start is a utility that creates DNS configuration files from a hosts file. The utility is called h2n, host to name. It is a Perl script that will take an existing hosts file and generate the associated DNS server configuration files. It will not create exactly all of the files in the right format but is a great starting point. The h2n utility can be found in several locations on the Internet using any of the search engines.

A third place that configuration files can be started is from an existing UNIX DNS server. I will discuss how the UNIX DNS server configuration files can be used directly by the Windows NT DNS server. If your network has a DNS server running on UNIX, then consider establishing a backup DNS server on a Windows NT Advanced Server or moving your DNS server from UNIX to Windows NT Advanced Server. In this case, there are two options for setting up the Windows NT DNS server. The first option is to copy the configuration files from UNIX to your Windows NT DNS server directories. The second option is to set up the Windows NT DNS server as a backup DNS server. Once the zone transfer from the primary to the secondary server has occurred, the new Windows NT DNS server will now have all of the configuration files it needs.

Prior to going into the concepts that are important in setting up the DNS server, I should point out one important difference between the DNS server on Windows NT and the DNS server on text-based operating systems, such as UNIX. Windows NT ships with a graphical DNS server administrator tool. This tool greatly simplifies the management of your Windows NT DNS server. By default changes made to the DNS server configuration are stored in the Registry. There is a little known option in the DNS managers options property pages that forces the Windows NT DNS server to read and save the configuration in files instead of the Registry. If you change the setting to use the configuration files, the DNS configuration files from the UNIX system can be copied into the DNS server directory. The DNS server keeps its configuration files in the `\winnt\system32\dns` directory.

When using configuration files instead of the Registry to store DNS configuration information, the DNS manager will behave slightly differently. The subtle differences have to do with the fact that in certain situations the data is not correctly written to the data files. This appears to get better with each Windows NT 4.0 Service Patch. As of Service Patch 2, these differences seem to have diminished to unnoticeable.

Part

III

Ch

10

NOTE Microsoft placed the configuration files for the Windows NT Advance Servers DNS server in the Registry. This configuration information can be found in the Registry key
`\HKEY_LOCAL_MACHINE\SYSTEM\CurrentControlSet\Services\DNS`. ▓

NOTE The configuration data for the DNS server is placed in the Registry for a reason. The Registry in the Windows NT Advanced Server is a database system that is used to store operating system configuration information. The Registry provides a reliable method of storing this configuration information in a centralized place. Windows NT guarantees the integrity of the Registry. Additionally, the Registry is backed up on the recovery diskette. If you change the DNS sever to use files, you will keep the DNS configuration information from getting backed up with the rest of the Registry. ▓

> **CAUTION**
>
> Even when the Microsoft DNS server is configured to boot from the Registry, there are files in the `\systemroot\SYSTEM32\DNS` subdirectory that are essential for your DNS server. This directory should be backed up any time that you make changes to your DNS server.

An Example Setup of the Microsoft DNS Server

This section shows the fundamentals of setting up a DNS server. The network consists of three computers on an external network segment that are outside of the corporate firewall and four computers that reside inside of the firewall. In Figure 10.10, there are two DNS servers set up on the external network and two DNS servers set up on the internal network.

We will step through the setup of the four DNS servers. In this simple network, there is probably not a need to have the internal DNS servers. Name resolution on a small network could be handled by using a hosts file. The external name servers are more important as they tell people on the Internet how to get to your Web and FTP servers.

The External DNS Servers   The first steps in creating the Primary DNS server is to create a new DNS server. First make sure that TCP/IP is properly installed on the Windows NT Server, **www.gasullivan.com**. Also make sure the domain name and workstation name are properly configured.

Creating the New DNS Server   To create a new DNS server, follow these steps:

1. Start the DNS Manager.
2. Right-click the Server list selection item.
3. Select New Server from the pop-menu. This brings up the New Server dialog box.
4. Add the IP address of the new DNS server. This is typically the IP address of the machine where you are running the DNS Manager.

FIG. 10.10

The network configuration for the DNS setup.

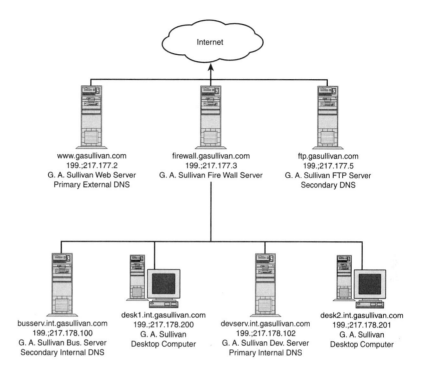

www.gasullivan.com
199.;217.177.2
G. A. Sullivan Web Server
Primary External DNS

firewall.gasullivan.com
199.;217.177.3
G. A. Sullivan Fire Wall Server

ftp.gasullivan.com
199.;217.177.5
G. A. Sullivan FTP Server
Secondary DNS

busserv.int.gasullivan.com
199.;217.178.100
G. A. Sullivan Bus. Server
Secondary Internal DNS

desk1.int.gasullivan.com
199.;217.178.200
G. A. Sullivan
Desktop Computer

devserv.int.gasullivan.com
199.;217.178.102
G. A. Sullivan Dev. Server
Primary Internal DNS

desk2.int.gasullivan.com
199.;217.178.201
G. A. Sullivan
Desktop Computer

5. Click the OK button. This closes the DNS Manager and creates the new zone. Figure 10.11 shows the default zones that are created by the DNS manager when the new server is created.

FIG. 10.11

The DNS Manager has created the default domains.

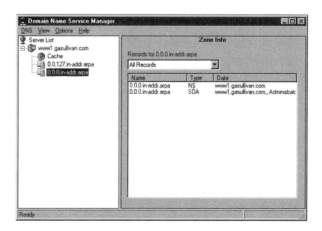

Configuring the 0.0.0.0.in-addr.arpa and the 0.0.0.127.in-addr.arpa Zones On occasion, the DNS Manager does not correctly create the new default zones for our domain. The following steps show how to create these zones and ensure they are properly set up:

N O T E   It is only necessary to create the **0.0.0.0.in-addr.arpa** and **0.0.0.127.in-addr.arpa** zones on DNS if the DNS manager did not create these zones in the previous step. ▨

1. Right-click the server where the new zones are to be created.
2. Choose the Create New Zone option. This brings up the create New Zone Wizard.
3. Enter **0.0.0.0.in-addr.arpa** as the zone name. Select N̲ext to move to the next step in the Create Zone Wizard.
4. Check the Create as a Primary Domain check box. Select F̲inish button to close the New Zone Wizard and create the zone.

Repeat the above steps to create the **0.0.0.127.in-addr.arpa** domain.

Adding the gasullivan.com Domain Records   Now that you have the basic server setup, you can go in and set up the actual zone records. This involves creating two more zone records. The first is the forward zone for the **gasullivan.com** domain. The second zone is the reverse name lookup specified in the **in-addr.arpa** domain, this is the **177.217.199.in-addr.arpa** zone.

N O T E   Creating the reverse domain prior to entering any of the host data will enable you to automatically create PTR records while you are entering the A records for the host. ▨

The first zone to create is the **gasullivan.com** zone. This is done from the DNS Manager with the following steps:

1. Right-click the server where your new zone is to be created.
2. Choose the Create N̲ew Zone option. This brings up the Create New Zone Wizard.
3. Enter **gasullivan.com** as the zone name. Select N̲ext to move to the next step in the Create New Zone Wizard (see Figure 10.12).

FIG. 10.12

The DNS Manager Zone Wizard is used to create a new zone. This is the zone that will hold your domain's specific host data.

4. Check the Create as a Primary Domain check box. Select F̲inish button to close the Create New Zone Wizard and create the zone.

The next step is to create a reverse DNS zone for your domain. The reverse zone for the example is easily calculated from the IP address. The IP address for your domain is **199.217.177**. The DNS reverse domain for this domain is **177.217.199.in-addr.arpa**. Creating this domain is exactly the same as creating the primary domain that we just completed. Figure 10.13 shows the domain with all of the zones completed.

CAUTION

The DNS Manger does not create the PTR record for the DNS server in the reverse name domain. Not having this record will cause your server to be set up incorrectly. There are two ways to create this record. The first is to create the PTR record in the reverse domain directly. (This is done later in this section.) The second is to delete the A record created in the forward name domain, and again add the DNS servers domain name to the forward domain. When adding the DNS servers name to the forward domain the second time, select Create Associated PTR Record in the dialog box.

Part

III

Ch

10

FIG. 10.13

The DNS Manager displays the DNS tree after the new reverse name zone has been created.

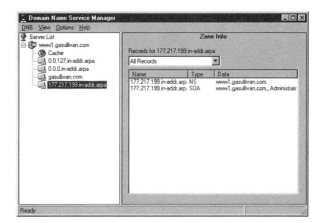

The next step in setting up your DNS servers is to create the backup secondary DNS server for the external network segment. The secondary DNS server is going to reside on **ftp.gasullivan.com.** The steps for this section proceed much like creating the primary DNS server:

1. Start the DNS Manager on the backup DNS server.

2. Right-click the Server List icon and choose New Server from the pop-up menu.

3. Enter the IP address of the new Server. Select Finish to create the new DNS Server.

Next, you will create the **0.0.0.0.in-addr.arpa** and **0.0.0.127.in-addr.arpa** zones in this domain. To do so, repeat the steps you performed in the section "Configuring the 0.0.0.0.in-arpa.addr and the 0.0.0.127.in-addr.arpa Zones."

Again, you need to create two new zones—one for the forward resolution of the **gasullivan.com** domain, the second for the reverse name domain. This time the two domains will be secondary domains:

1. Start the DNS Manager on the backup DNS server.

2. Right-click the Server List icon and choose <u>N</u>ew Zone from the pop-up menu. This brings up the New Zone Wizard.

3. Enter the name of the zone to be created—**gasullivan.com**, in this example. Click the <u>N</u>ext button to go to the the next page on the New Zone Wizard.

4. Select <u>F</u>inish to create the new zone. The DNS Manager displays the new backup server (see Figure 10.14).

FIG. 10.14

The DNS Manager shows the newly created backup DNS server on **www.gasullivan.com**. The X over the domain indicates that the backup has not synched up with the primary DNS.

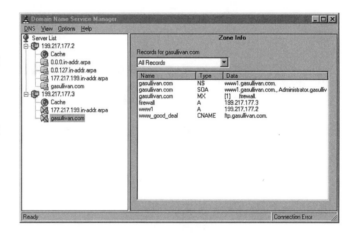

N O T E The DNS Manager is very handy in creating backup domain servers. In the New Zone screen, a hand appears when the Secondary zone option is selected. This hand can be picked up and used to point at the zone that is to be backed up. This will create all of the appropriate zones and attach the backup DNS to the primary DNS server. This is the recommended method of establishing a backup DNS server. ▓

CAUTION

The data will not show up on the backup DNS server until the backup DNS server pulls the data from the primary DNS server. You can force this to happen by stopping and starting the backup DNS server.

Now that you have constructed the two primary zones that construct the forward and reverse domain name spaces for the **gasullivan.com** domain, you can begin to add hosts and other relevant records.

Now you will have to go back to the first DNS server on **www.gasullivan.com**. You need to edit the properties of the **gasullivan.com** zone and the reverse name zone so that they will notify the backup DNS server when changes are made.

Then you will need to add the machines that are on your network so that they appear in your domain. This is done through the DNS manager. You add hosts by right-clicking the zone that is to be added to and selecting the New Host option. This causes the New Host dialog box to appear (see Figure 10.15).

FIG. 10.15

The New Host dialog box is used to add hosts to the domain.

The New Host dialog box contains the host name field and the IP address field. Fill in the host name for your the Firewall server, **firewall.gasullivan.com**, and the IP address **199.217.177.3**. Make sure that you select the Create Associated PTR Record check box so that you do not have to create identical records on the DNS server for the reverse name.

You have now completed the basic requirements for your network to be on the Internet with your own DNS system. Now enhance the external network to provide some additional re-sources by creating a mail system for your inbound e-mail. Your Firewall server provides the capability to accept the e-mail and ensure that it is safely brought into the internal network. Unfortunately, everyone has your main e-mail setup to be sent as **bradr@gasullivan.com**. You need to create an MX record to tell mailers to send e-mail bound for **gasullivan.com** to **firewall.gasullivan.com**. This is done by selecting the New Record option from the zone pop-up menu. The New Record option enables you to create records that are not new host records. Figure 10.16 shows the New Resource Record dialog box for the MX record so that your e-mail will be forwarded to the right machine. (See Chapter 26, "An Inside Look at Exchange Server," for more information.)

Part
III

Ch
10

FIG. 10.16

The New Record dialog box in the DNS Manger enables you to enter the data for the mail exchanger record.

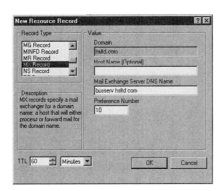

You have one more item to create and that is an alias for the FTP server. You have some extra capacity on your FTP server and can use this capacity to set up a second, smaller Web server. You want the users to get to this new Web sever via the URL **http:// www_good_deal.gasullivan.com**. You do this by creating a CNAME record that points

www_good_deal.gasullivan.com to **ftp.gasullivan.com**. The New Resource Record screen in Figure 10.17 shows how to enter the CNAME record.

FIG. 10.17

The New Resource Record dialog box is used to set up the alias (CNAME) record.

The Internal DNS Servers   Now to create the Internal DNS servers. These servers are necessary to ensure that the firewall is keeping people off of your internal network. Without the internal DNS servers, it would be necessary for your internal workstations to access the DNS servers on the external DNS servers. This opens additional paths for people to enter your network from the outside.

In a sense, creating the internal DNS domain is like creating a subdomain of the **gasullivan.com** domain. The new domain will also result in a new zone that has its data files on the primary DNS server **busserv.int.gasullivan.com**. Begin this by creating a new DNS server on the server **busserv.int.gasullivan.com**. This is done just like the previous example.

First a small aside would be to create a subdomain without creating the new zone. This is a very easy task. This is done by going back to **www.gasullivan.com** and right-clicking the **gasullivan.com** domain. Selecting New Domain will create a subfolder of the **gasullivan.com** domain. The screen below shows the new subdomains that have been created. You can now create machines in the new domains. The domain records are stored in the main zone on **www.gasullivan.com**. The new subdomain is called **int.gasullivan.com** in the DNS Manager. It is the resource records that determine the name of the new subdomain. Figure 10.18 shows the creation of the new subdomain on **www.gasullivan.com**.

Your real objective is to create a new zone. This is a lot more difficult than creating a domain or a sub domain in the same zone. There are five main steps to creating the new zone for the new subdomain:

1. Set up and test the new domain. (This is similar to creating a domain shown in "The External DNS Servers.")
2. Add the backup DNS server for your new domain. (This was also explained in "The External DNS Servers.")
3. Delegate the authority for the new subdomain.
4. Delegate the authority for the reverse subdomain.

FIG. 10.18
The new
int.gasullivan.com
domain has been set
up in the DNS Manager.

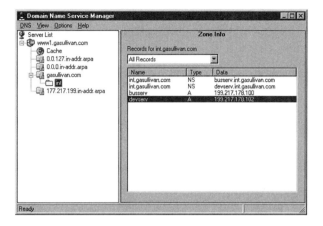

5. Add new host and resource records for hosts on the Internal network.

The first step is to set up and test the new zone on the internal primary DNS server
busserv.int.gasullivan.com. The second part is to add the secondary DNS server on
devserv.int.gasullivan.com and configure it as a back up server. The third step is to delegate
the authority for the new forward name domain from the DNS **www.gasullivan.com** to
busserv.int.gasullivan.com. The fourth step is to delegate the reverse name domain,
178.217.199.in-addr.arpa, for the zone from the DNS server **www.gasullivan.com** to
busserv.gasullivan.com. The fifth part is to add the new host and resource records for the
hosts in the Internal network. The key to creating the new name server it the delegation of the
authority from the upper-level DNS server **www.gasullivan.com** to the lower-level DNS
server.

Figure 10.19 contains the results of creating the new primary internal domain DNS server.

FIG. 10.19
The DNS Manager main
view on the primary
DNS server for the
internal network. All of
the internal domains
and resources have
been created on the
new DNS internal
primary DNS server.

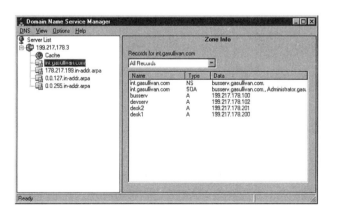

Now to delegate the forward name domain from **www.gasullivan.com** to
busserv.int.gasullivan.com. There are two sets of records that need to be created on

www.gasullivan.com for the delegation to happen. The first set of records let the
int.gasullivan.com DNS servers be seen by higher order DNS servers as the name servers
for the **int.gasullivan.com** domain. These records look like the following:

```
int.gasullivan.com        IN      NS      busserv.int.gasullivan.com
int.gasullivan.com        IN      NS      devserv.int.gasullivan.com
```

Now the problem is that someone looking to get to the name servers do not have the name
servers IP address. This is done by creating two new DNS A records to tell the IP address of
the DNS servers. These records look like the following:

```
busserv.int.gasullivan.com     86400    IN    A    199.217.177.100
devserv.int.gasullivan.com     86400    IN    A    199.217.177.102
```

This gives the forward name resolution delegation to the new name servers.

The reverse name resolution delegation is trickier than the forward domain name resolution.
You must apply to the InterNIC at **www.internic.com** and apply for the new IP address to get
the reverse name resolution domain delegated to you. Another likely source of getting an IP
address that can be delegated to you is to work with your ISP. Many ISPs will submit the paper-
work for you and let you know what the IP address assigned is when the InterNIC registers
you. Once you have the IP address, you simply create the reverse domain name space just like
you did on the first domain. Assume that you got lucky with your InterNIC request and got the
IP address **199.217.178** as your new Class C IP address. There is no reason that you should
expect to get any specific IP address.

After completing the reverse name resolution domain, you will have a domain that looks like
the one shown in Figure 10.20.

FIG. 10.20
The DNS manager after
adding the reverse
domain name space for
the internal network. All
of the internal resources
for the reverse domain
have been added.

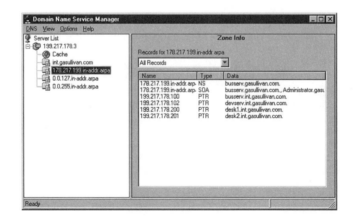

The Cache File

In the DNS system, there are actually two cache files. The first cache file is created by the DNS
manager when it creates a new zone. The second cache file is the DNS server's internal cache
of resolved names.

The cache file that is created by the DNS manager when a new zone is created is actually the root name server hints file. In early incarnations of the DNS server, this file was read into the start of the cache when the DNS server was started. The meaning of the actual cache file changed slightly and it is now necessary to have the root name server hints file also. The root name server hints file is still called a cache file. The root name server hints file enables the DNS system to jump to the top of the domain whenever it is looking for a host that is not in the DNS servers domain hierarchy or its cache. This keeps the DNS server from having to try successive operations to get to the top of the DNS domain hierarchy.

The contents of the `root name hints cache` file should look similar to that in Listing 10.2.

Listing 10.2 *CACHE.TXT* The Default Root Name Hints Cache File

Part
III

Ch
10

```
;
;   Cache file:
;



;
;   Cache file:
;

.                           3631294208  IN    NS    A.ROOT-SERVERS.net.
A.ROOT-SERVERS.net.         1484215808  IN    A     198.41.0.4
.                           3631294208  IN    NS    H.ROOT-SERVERS.net.
H.ROOT-SERVERS.net.         1484215808  IN    A     128.63.2.53
.                           3631294208  IN    NS    B.ROOT-SERVERS.net.
B.ROOT-SERVERS.net.         1484215808  IN    A     128.9.0.107
.                           3631294208  IN    NS    C.ROOT-SERVERS.net.
C.ROOT-SERVERS.net.         1484215808  IN    A     192.33.4.12
.                           3631294208  IN    NS    D.ROOT-SERVERS.net.
D.ROOT-SERVERS.net.         1484215808  IN    A     128.8.10.90
.                           3631294208  IN    NS    E.ROOT-SERVERS.net.
E.ROOT-SERVERS.net.         1484215808  IN    A     192.203.230.10
.                           3631294208  IN    NS    I.ROOT-SERVERS.net.
I.ROOT-SERVERS.net.         1484215808  IN    A     192.36.148.17
.                           3631294208  IN    NS    F.ROOT-SERVERS.net.
F.ROOT-SERVERS.net.         1484215808  IN    A     192.5.5.241
.                           3631294208  IN    NS    G.ROOT-SERVERS.net.
G.ROOT-SERVERS.net.         1484215808  IN    A     192.112.36.4
```

The DNS system maintains an internal cache file where it records not only the host once the name is resolved but all of the DNS servers that it talks to on its way to resolving the host name. The TTL entry in the SOA record tells the DNS server how long to keep the record in the cache.

Substitution and Abbreviations

The setup of the DNS Server shown in the section "The External DNS Server" was done using fully qualified domain names. This is done because it is confusing enough to understand the complexities of the DNS system without adding short, cryptic names that will need to be interpreted before they can be understood. When setting up a DNS server, I always try to use the fully qualified domain name for the machines. This makes the files easier for me to read. The amount of time spent creating the files is small compared to the amount of time spent maintaining the files.

The DNS system has extensive abilities that enable you to abbreviate about any name. If you receive your DNS files from someone else or use the h2n tool, you may end up with all of the names being abbreviated. Therefore it is important to note how the abbreviation occur.

When the DNS server is processing the DNS forward name data, it "knows" that it is processing the data for **gasullivan.com** in the DNS files that were setup. The names of the hosts in the A records in the domain can therefore be abbreviated as the following:

```
www   IN   A     199.217.177.2
```

This will be expanded to:

```
www.gasullivan.com    IN    A     199.217.177.2
```

when it is entered into the DNS database. In this example, **gasullivan.com** is origin for the DNS server during the processing of this record. A second abbreviation is the at sign (@). This is the same as leaving the domain name blank. The origin is substituted for the @. The following record:

```
www.@   IN     A     199.217.177.2
```

is the same as:

```
www.gasullivan.com    IN    A     199.217.177.2
```

There is one last substitution that is worth mentioning. The repeat last name substitution enables you to specify a domain name once and to have multiple records from that domain to the host without repeating the host name. The following section:

```
www.gasullivan.com       IN    A       199.217.177.2
                  IN    CNAME     funnyfarm.gasullivan.com
                  IN    CNAME     crazynames.gasullivan.com
```

is the same as:

```
www.gasullivan.com       IN    A       199.217.177.2
www.gasullivan.com       IN    CNAME     funnyfarm.gasullivan.com
www.gasullivan.com       IN    CNAME     crazynames.gasullivan.com
```

A lot of the existing DNS files use these substitutions extensively.

Tools for Managing the DNS Server

The two primary tools for managing a DNS server on a Windows NT Advanced Server is the DNS manager tool and the `nslookup` command utility. The DNS manager tool enables the network manger to configure the DNS server data. The nslookup tool provides a method of in depth analysis of the DNS server data.

This tool operates a little like the File Explorer in the Windows NT operating system. A domain can be selected and expanded like a directory structure. A node in the domain tree can be configured by double-clicking the node. The main uses of the DNS Manager for creating and maintaining DNS data is described in the previous section.

The `nslookup` command is a query tool that can be used to query the data that is on a DNS server. The nslookup tool has an interactive and command-line mode. It is run in a command window and will be available on any Windows NT machine that has the TCP/IP stack properly installed. Table 10.2 contains the commands that are available in the nslookup tool.

Table 10.2   *nslookup* Commands

Command	Description
exit	Exits the interactive `nslook0up` utility.
finger	Used to Finger a user on a system. The `finger` command is a UNIX utility that enables you to query for information on users connected to the system. For example, `finger bradr@hstld.com` would return information about the user bradr on the host **hsltd.com**. The `finger` command in the nslookup utility will reference the current host when no host is specified. The current host is the last host for which an IP address was resolved.
help	Displays a short list of the commands and their meanings.
ls	Lists information for the DNS domain. This command will list all of the host names and their IP address.
lserver	The `lserver`, `server`, and `root` commands are closely related. The `lserver` command changes the default server to the server specified. The `lserver` command will use the DNS server that was specified as the valid DNS server when nslookup was started. This is the initial DNS server.
root	`Root` is a convenience command. Its use is exactly the same as typing `lserver g.root-server.net`. `g.root-server.net` is the current root server for the Internet.
server	Changes the default server used for DNS queries to the specified host.
set	The `set` command is used in conjunction with the options shown in Table 10.3.
view	Changes how the output of the `ls` command is sorted and listed.

In addition to these commands, there are a number of options that control the behavior of the `nslookup` command. These options, shown in Table 10.3, can be used in the `set` command or passed in on the command line.

Part

III

Ch

10

Table 10.3   *nslookup* Options

Option	Purpose
set all	Lists the available set options on this nslookup system.
cl[ass]=IN	The class is the protocol group. Currently, the only class in wide use is the Internet class. MIT has a domain that uses the Hesiod class.
[no]d2	Turns on and off the highest level of debug information. It basically provides every byte of every packet to and from the server, and provides the most debug information.
[no]debug	Turns on and off the low level of debugging information. It enables more information about each query to be printed.
[no]def[name]	Turns on and off the appending of the machine defined domain name to lookup requests. When requests are a single name, they do not contain the domain; the domain is appended to the name to form the query.
Do[main]= mydomain.com	Changes the default domain. (See the defname option.)
[no] ig[nore]	Turns on and off packet truncation errors.
Po[rt]=53	Changes the default DNS name server port. Useful for debugging. A test DNS system could be established on a unique port and tested by nslookup.
q[uerytype]=A	Changes the query type. By default, DNS is searching for A type records, forward name resolution. If the query is an IP address, then the query type is set to PTR. This option forces the query type.
[no] rec[urse]	Turns on and off recursive queries of DNS severs. nslookup requests recursive lookups by default. This enables you to query a DNS server like another DNS server sends queries.
Ret[ry]=4	Sets the number of retries. After each retry, the time out value is doubled.
[no] sea[rch]	Turns on and off the use of the search list. On is the default. If set to on, the names in the srchlist option and the domain name are appended to the host request until a request is resolved or a list is searched.
Ti[meout]=5	Time out is five seconds. The time out will double with each usage.
Ty[pe]=In	Changes the type of the query. Exactly the same as querytype.
[no] v[c]	Turns on and off the use of a virtual circuit. Default is on. If on, nslookup uses the TCP protocol for name resolution. If off, nslookup uses UDP for name resolution.

Some things that can be accomplished are to lookup the IP address of host. This is typically done by first using the `server` command to change to a DNS and then looking up a hosts name.

The `lserver`, `server`, and `root` commands are used to set the default and initial DNS server. They are primarily used to browse or view the information in DNS servers that are foreign. One common use of the `lserver` and `root` commands is to set your initial server to a server that is correctly resolving names. This is often necessary when you are first setting up your DNS server. When you want to look at some important DNS information, the initial DNS server is used to provide reverse name resolution for the `nslookup` commands. If your server is not correctly configured, then requests that rely on the reverse lookup will not work. Using root or lserver allows this problem to be worked around.

Implementing Windows Internet Name Service (WINS)

WINS is Microsoft's implementation of a NetBIOS Name Server (NBNS). It is implemented as a Windows NT Server service, with an administrative utility program called the WINS Manager and appropriate client software. WINS registers the NetBIOS names used by computers, both clients and servers, as they start. When a Microsoft networking command, such as NET USE, initiates a networking operation using the Windows interface, the subsequent need to resolve a NetBIOS name to complete the command will be handled by WINS. TCP/IP host names can also be resolved by WINS, after the local HOSTS file has been checked, and the DNS (if any) has been consulted.

The Advantages of WINS

The primary advantage of WINS is that it dramatically reduces the amount of broadcast traffic on the network. Because name resolution with WINS is handled by direct communication between WINS servers and clients, broadcast name registration requests and name query requests are therefore minimized. You do not need to configure all clients to use WINS—you can operate a mixed environment. WINS resolves names from clients across routers and can therefore support multiple subnets. If a WINS server is not available, the design of the system still enables clients to use broadcasts so that they are not disabled when the WINS servers are down. WINS servers can replicate the names in their databases to other WINS servers so that a single, dynamic names database is represented and managed across the enterprise network.

How WINS Registers and Resolves NetBIOS Names

To use WINS, you must configure a WINS server and start the service, whose formal name is listed in the Services dialog box simply as Windows Internet Name Service. The steps involved in configuring a WINS server are covered in the next section.

Once you have set up one or more WINS servers and WINS-enabled clients, the process of registering and resolving names involves a number of distinct processes that are carried out in a natural order.

Prior to configuring a WINS server, it is helpful to understand the configuration of the client and how WINS name resolution happens. The steps involved in WINS name registration are as follows:

1. A WINS client is configured with the address of the primary and an optional secondary WINS server. This can be directly configured on the client, or received with an IP address as one of the optional DHCP parameters passed from a DHCP server. As the client starts, it sends its NetBIOS name directly to the WINS server in a name registration request.

2. If the WINS server is available and the name is not already registered to another client, the registration is successful, and a message is returned to the client with a positive registration and the amount of time for which the name is registered, known as the *Time to Live* (*TTL*).

3. If a duplicate name is found, the server sends a name challenge to the currently registered client. If the client responds and affirms that it is using the name, the new registration is denied by sending a message to the requesting client. If the currently registered client does not respond to three queries, the name is released and registered to the new client.

4. If the primary WINS server cannot be found after three attempts by the client using ARP, an attempt will be made to find the secondary WINS server (if the client has been configured for a secondary WINS server). If it also cannot be found with three ARP requests, the client resorts to a standard b-node broadcast to register its name with the local subnet.

A WINS client, by default, will use the h-node (hybrid) implementation of NetBIOS over TCP/IP. The steps involved in WINS name resolution are as follows:

1. When a command is entered or implicitly specified by actions in the Windows interface, a name resolution is required. The NetBIOS name cache is checked first to see if the NetBIOS name mapping to an IP address is available.

2. If the mapping is not in the NetBIOS name cache, a name resolution query is sent directly to the primary WINS server. If no response is returned, the request is sent three times.

3. If the primary WINS server does not respond, the secondary WINS server (if configured) is tried as many as three times. If either the primary or secondary WINS server receives the request, it looks up the name in its database and sends the IP address back to the client, or replies with a `Requested name does not exist` message if it is not listed in the database.

4. If the name cannot be resolved by a WINS server, either because the server is unavailable or because the name is not in the database, a b-node name resolution query is broadcast as many as three times.

5. If the name is still not resolved, the LMHOSTS file (if configured) and the HOSTS file are searched.

6. If the name is not in either LMHOSTS or HOSTS, the DNS (if configured) is consulted.

N O T E An entirely different order is used to resolve host names used in traditional TCP/IP utilities. See "Domain Name System Name Resolution" earlier in this chapter. ■

Configuring WINS

A single WINS server can resolve names for an entire WAN because the requests are sent as directed datagrams and can be routed. A secondary WINS server provides redundancy and fault tolerance. Additional WINS servers can be provided based on the number of client requests received and performance considerations in large network environments. A rough rule of thumb is that a typical WINS server can handle as many as 1,200 name registrations and 700 name queries per minute. A pair of WINS servers should be able to handle as many as 8,000 WINS clients under typical network conditions. If you implement servers with two or more processors, a pair of WINS servers should handle more than 12,000 clients.

WINS servers do not need to be domain controllers as well. They should be configured with a static IP address, subnet mask, default gateway address, and other TCP/IP options. The use of DHCP assigned options is possible, but not recommended.

Entering Basic Configuration Information   To configure the basic operation of your WINS server, follow these steps:

1. Start the WINS Manager.

2. Choose Server, Configuration. The WINS Server Configuration dialog box is displayed (see Figure 10.21).

FIG. 10.21

The WINS Server Configuration dialog box is used to enter or modify the basic values controlling the behavior of the WINS server.

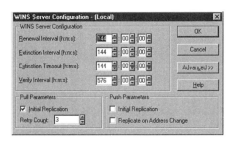

3. The WINS Server Configuration box contains settings for time periods that control the basic behavior of the server: the length of time a name is registered and how often a client must reregister its name. For many installations, the default values are appropriate. Additional information on these settings is available by using the Help button. Click OK after making any adjustments.

4. Choose Options, Preferences. The Preferences dialog box appears (see Figure 10.22).

FIG. 10.22

The Preferences dialog
box enables you to
control the refresh rate
of the Statistics display
in the right pane of the
window and the format
of the address display in
the left pane.

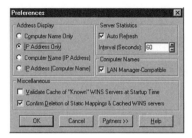

5. The settings you make in the Preferences dialog box control the address display and
   refresh rate of the statistics display. Make any changes you want to configure the display
   to suit your needs. Click OK.

Entering Static Mappings for Non-WINS Clients   If you have non-WINS clients on your
network, you may want to enter static mappings for these computers, especially if they are
involved in resource sharing as is possible with Windows for Workgroups, Windows 95, and
Windows NT Workstation. If another computer attempts to use a shared resource on one of
these devices, the WINS server can still provide name resolution, even though the original
(non-WINS) computer did not register its name. By entering a static mapping, the non-WINS
client appears in the WINS database anyway. To enter a static mapping, follow these steps:

1. Start the WINS Manager.

2. Choose Mappings, Static Mappings. Click the Add Mappings button. The Add Static
   Mappings dialog box appears (see Figure 10.23).

FIG. 10.23

The Add Static
Mappings dialog box
is used to map the
NetBIOS name of a
non-WINS client to an
IP address for inclusion
in the WINS database.

3. Enter the name and IP address you want to register. For normal client workstations,
   click the Unique option button. Click the Close button to return to the Static Mappings
   dialog box. Click Close to close the dialog box.

Configuring WINS Clients   WINS clients are configured by simply entering the address of a
primary WINS server, and optionally a secondary WINS server, into the client's configuration.
This can be done manually, using the Network icon on the Control Panel (run Network Setup
for Windows for Workgroups clients), or you can automatically configure WINS addresses
using DHCP. If you are using DHCP, you can manually configure individual clients, and those
settings will take precedence over the DHCP settings. If you use DHCP to configure WINS
addresses, you must also configure clients using option 046 WINS/NBT Node type or it will

not work. A message box prompts you to do so if you forget. Set this option to 0x8 (h-node, or hybrid).

Viewing WINS Name Mappings   To view the NetBIOS name/IP address mappings currently registered on a WINS server, follow these steps:

1. Start the WINS Manager.

2. Choose Mappings, Show Database. The Show Database dialog box appears (see Figure 10.24).

FIG. 10.24

The Show Database dialog box shows the WINS database and its NetBIOS name to IP address mappings.

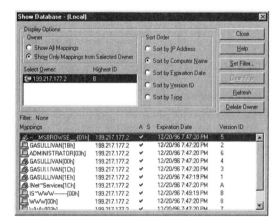

Part
III

Ch
10

3. Click the option button in the Sort Order box that corresponds to the order you prefer. In the Owner combo box, you can select an option button to display all mappings or only those for the server selected in the Select Owner box if you have multiple WINS servers defined. You can also use the Set Filter button to enter name or IP address criteria using the asterisk (*) as a wild card. This displays only matching entries, and can be useful for finding a particular entry in a large list.

Configuring WINS Push/Pull Partners   WINS servers can replicate their mappings database to other WINS servers. When you configure a WINS server to replicate with another server, you can configure the server as a *push partner* with the other server, a *pull partner*, or both. Designating a WINS server as a push partner causes the server to send messages to its partners when its WINS database has received a specified number of changes. When the partners respond, only the *changes* to the database will be replicated to the other servers.

Configuring a server as a pull partner gives you the option to specify a time when requests should be made from its partner. This is the recommended way to provide replication of a WINS database over slow links because you can schedule the transfer for off-peak time periods. For example, two servers on either side of a slow link can each be configured to pull from the other server at different times during the night. A server can be configured to act in both roles with one or more other WINS servers.

To configure a push or pull partner, follow these steps:

1. Start the WINS Manager.

2. Choose Server, Replication Partners. The Replication Partners dialog box appears (see Figure 10.25).

FIG. 10.25

The Replication Partners dialog box is used to configure push and pull replication partners for replication of NetBIOS name/IP address mapping database entries.

3. Click Add. Enter the name of the server you want to replicate to, or from in, the Add WINS Server dialog box. Click OK. The WINS Manager will try to locate the server on the network. If it is found, the name and IP address of the server are added to the WINS Server list. If it cannot be found, you will be asked to enter the IP address of the server in the Validate WINS Server dialog box. Click OK.

4. Highlight the new server or another server in the list, and make a selection in the Replication Options box. The example here will configure both options, but you may want to choose only one. Click the Push Partner check box and then click Configure. The Push Partner Properties dialog box appears (see Figure 10.26).

FIG. 10.26

The Push Partner Properties dialog box is used to configure the replication of changes between the local server and the push partner highlighted in the WINS Server list.

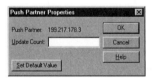

5. Enter the number of changes that can be made to the local database before the changes will be pushed to the replication partner. The smallest number you can enter is 20. Click OK.

6. Click the Pull Partner check box and then click Configure. The Pull Partner Properties dialog box appears (see Figure 10.27).

FIG. 10.27

The Pull Partner
Properties dialog box is
used to configure the
replication of changes
between the local
server and the pull
partner highlighted in
the WINS Servers list.

7. Click OK. Check marks appear in the Push and Pull columns to indicate which relationships have been established.

Maintaining the WINS Database   The JETPACK utility used to compact the DHCP database can be used to compact the WINS database as well. It is recommended that you compact the database if it grows to a size of more than 30M. This maintenance on the WINS database is required for the same reasons you must maintain the DHCP database. See the section "Maintaining the DHCP Database" in Chapter 9 for more information. Also, see "Restoring the WINS Database" in the Windows NT Server Networking Guide for information on restoring a corrupted WINS database. To use JETPACK to compact the WINS database, follow these steps:

1. You must stop the Microsoft WINS Server service before this operation can be performed. Therefore, this operation is best done during off-peak times. Use the Services icon in the Control Panel or the Windows NT Server Manager to stop the service. You can also use the following command:

   ```
   net stop wins
   ```

2. Open a command prompt and change to the *systemroot*\SYSTEM32\WINS directory. Make a backup copy of the database just in case it's needed, as follows:

   ```
   copy wins.mdb wins.bak
   ```

3. Use JETPACK to compact the DHCP database creating a new temporary file that will replace the existing database:

   ```
   jetpack wins.mdb temp.mdb
   ```

4. Delete the existing database (remember, you have a backup copy):

   ```
   del wins.mdb
   ```

5. Rename the compacted temporary database as the in-use database:

   ```
   ren temp.mdb wins.mdb
   ```

6. Restart the service, as follows:

   ```
   net start wins
   ```

Part

III

Ch

10

DNS and WINS Integration

The primary location for the DNS system and the WINS system to integrate is on the DNS server. The Microsoft DNS server that is shipped with Windows NT can be configured to utilize WINS resolution. If the DNS server is configured to use WINS resolution, it will first look try to resolve the host name via the normal DNS name resolution scheme. If the host name is not resolved via the DNS resolution, the DNS server will issue a WINS request. This WINS request is the same as any other client attempting a WINS lookup. If the WINS host name is found, the DNS server will respond to the DNS name query as though the name was found in the DNS servers own data files.

The second location for DNS and WINS integration is on a network client. A Windows NT or Windows 95 network client can be configured for WINS and DNS resolution. This allows the most flexibility in establishing your network. When the client is configured this way, it first looks at the host name that is being resolved. Standard NetBIOS names are always less than 15 characters and do not contain any special characters including the period. If the host name is a standard NetBIOS name, the resolver first attempts a NetBIOS resolution of the host name. This would involve querying the WINS server. If the host is not found this way, the resolver will query the DNS system.

From Here...

In this chapter, you learned how name resolution takes place in the Windows NT system, and about the architecture Domain Name System. You also learned how to setup up TCP/IP domains using the DNS Manager and DNS server. You created a subdomains and learned how to delegate domain authority to the subdomain. You also discovered the tools used to troubleshoot a DNS server.

You also learned about the WINS system and how WINS provides name resolution for the NetBIOS networking architecture

For more information on these and related topics, see the following chapters:

- To explore the setup and management of TCP/IP in Windows NT, see Chapter 9, "Using TCP/IP with Windows NT Server."
- To learn more about the Internet and how Windows NT works with the Internet, see Chapter 17, "I-Net Tools and Techniques."
- For the details associated with how to implement an Internet mail system using the Microsoft Exchange Server, see Chapter 31, "Exchange Server Advanced Topics."

## CHAPTER 11

An Inside Look at Remote Access Service (RAS)

by David O'Leary

Microsoft's Remote Access Service (RAS) provides users with seamless access to their corporate network through a remote dial-up connection. Once connected, users have the same capabilities they would have if directly connected to the network. Because RAS uses the same network protocols for communication as direct office connections, all aspects of standard networking are fully supported. RAS also provides, in conjunction with Windows NT Server, secure network protection via logon validation, access permissions and restrictions, encryption schemes, and callback capabilities.

Some RAS implementations may only include one or two analog modems. Others may have hundreds of modems— mixing analog, ISDN, and ADSL. The uses of RAS are as diverse as the uses of standard networks, but with the added capability of being able to connect to your network from almost anywhere. Through such applications as e-mail, sales force automation, home offices, video-conferencing, and a host of other possible uses, RAS frees employees from the constraints of the office.

Components of a RAS implementation

Learn about the devices involved in a RAS implementation. Understand how they interact, how they communicate, and the responsibilities of each component.

Background information

Learn detailed information about RAS protocols and error detection and correction. Learn about advanced digital data transmission technologies, such as ISDN, ADSL, and cable modems. Easy to understand information is provided on how they work, how they differ, and what applications they best support.

Choosing your hardware

Learn the information you need to know to make important decisions about what modems to choose, how powerful of a machine you will need for your RAS server, what network protocols to support, and the types and numbers of connection devices and associated communication lines you will need.

RAS security

Learn the security features embedded in Microsoft's RAS implementation. Learn how it protects your enterprise. Understand how it was designed to prevent any unauthorized users from gaining access to sensitive information.

As networks become prevalent, the ability of people to dial in and access networks becomes increasingly important. The widespread adoption of client-server technology and other network-centric technologies, such as intranets, has opened up the power of RAS. The work done in *business process re-engineering* has focused on automating processes with network-based applications that, in most cases, can be accessed just as effectively through RAS.

RAS supports all major networking clients, including Windows for Workgroups, Windows 95, Windows NT, UNIX, Mac OS, NetWare, LAN Manager, and OS/2. ■

What's New with RAS in Windows NT 4.0?

With the release of Windows NT 4.0 and Windows 95, Microsoft has made significant changes, additions, and enhancements to the Remote Access Service. The following sections detail these changes.

The Windows 95 Look and Feel

With the incorporation of the Windows 95 look and feel into Windows NT 4.0, significant changes have been made to RAS to make it easier to install, use, and administer. One of the biggest changes is the incorporation of the wizards in the setup/installation process. The RAS Setup Wizard automates many parts of the setup and installation process.

Like in Windows 95, the RAS client application is now called Dial-Up Networking. In addition, the Dial-Up Networking interface, as shown in Figure 11.1, is quite different from Windows 95. It was changed to make it more powerful and to give you more information for troubleshooting problems.

FIG. 11.1
The new Dial-Up Networking interface is easier to use and provides additional features for connecting to remote computers.

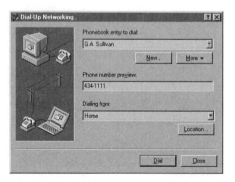

RAS Multilink PPP

The addition of the multilink capability to RAS enables you to increase the bandwidth of a single PPP session by combining two or more physical communication links. This is most commonly used to *bundle* the two B, or *bearer,* channels of an ISDN modem to get a 128 Kbps connection. However, if you have two phone lines and two analog modems (or any combination of lines and modems), you can also use multilink to increase your bandwidth. RAS Multilink is based on the IETF standard RFC 1717, which proposes advances to the PPP protocol with a method for splitting, recombining, and sequencing datagrams across multiple logical data links.

Point-to-Point Tunneling Protocol (PPTP)

PPTP is a protocol created by Microsoft to support multi-protocol *virtual private networks*. Through PPTP, users can use the Internet or any other public network to connect to their corporate networks. This is particularly useful for avoiding long distance charges for users calling from outside of calling areas. PPTP also enables corporations to outsource their remote access needs to Internet service providers or other remote access providers to reduce administrative overhead and costs.

> **N O T E** A virtual private network (VPN) enables users to securely access their private networks through a public network, such as the Internet. To ensure security, VPNs must prevent data from being intercepted and also encrypt the data so that it cannot be read. In addition, VPNs must prevent unauthorized users from gaining access to the private network. ▨

As with any VPN implementation, security is a major concern. The integration of PPTP into RAS enables it to use the same encryption technologies and security mechanisms that RAS uses to ensure that unauthorized users do not gain access to your corporate network or intercept sensitive communication. PPTP is an open industry standard that supports the most common networking protocols (TCP/IP, IPX, and NetBEUI). For more information about PPTP, see Chapter 9, "Using TCP/IP with Windows NT Server."

Part

III

Ch

11

Restartable File Copy

A common problem with transferring large files over analog modems is that a lost connection during this lengthy process forces you to start the process all over again. The Restartable File Copy feature should enable the transfer to continue from where it left off. When RAS detects a disconnect, it remembers the status of your file transmission and, upon reconnecting, attempts to restore the transfer to its previous state.

Auto-Dial and Log-On Dial

If the Windows 95 or Windows NT 4.0 machine is unable to connect to the resource to which it was previously connected through a Dial-Up Networking connection, Dial-Up Networking will automatically be initiated using previously cached information to access the resource. This feature allows for the seamless integration of remote resources. For example, if you use Microsoft Exchange for sending and receiving electronic mail and your Exchange server is located at a remote location, double-clicking the Exchange icon causes Exchange to search for the Exchange server. If the server is not found and was previously accessed through Dial-Up Networking, a dialog box like that shown in Figure 11.2 will ask if you want to use Dial-Up Networking to connect to the remote resource.

FIG. 11.2
The Auto-Dial dialog box pops up when a remote resource cannot be reached.

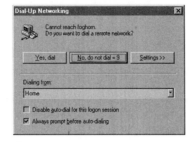

Idle Disconnect

This feature automatically disconnects users who have been inactive for a specified amount of time. This amount of time can be determined by either the Dial-Up Networking client or the server. By disconnecting idle users, this feature can help to free up lines, possibly allowing for the reduction of the total number of supported connections.

Client and Server API Extensions

Microsoft added a number of new APIs to allow for additional RAS monitoring capabilities so that third-party tools, as well as their own applications, can access more detailed information about active RAS connections. For a complete list and detailed descriptions of using the new RAS APIs in Windows NT 4.0, please refer to the Microsoft Developer Network at **http://www.microsoft.com/msdn/**.

The Components of a RAS Implementation

The components of a RAS implementation can vary according to the needs of the enterprise (see Figure 11.3). The two biggest factors in determining the specific components needed are the desired speed and the number of supported users. This section will describe the various components, the role they play, and when they are and are not necessary.

N O T E   Multiport hardware may not be necessary for basic implementations. ▪

FIG. 11.3
A RAS implementation contains many separate components which must all work together to allow remote network connectivity.

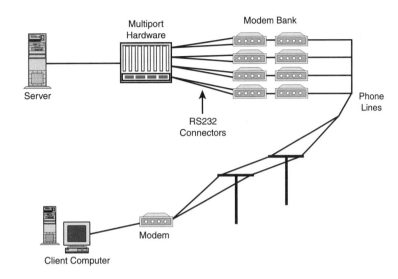

The Server

The RAS server acts as the central communication hub for your remote networking clients. For the purposes of this book, the RAS server is running Windows NT Server 4.0 with RAS installed and running. For users to be able to connect to the LAN, your RAS server must be either the main network server for your corporate LAN or connected to the main domain server for standard network security rights and general networking needs.

Multiport Hardware

If you plan to support only one or two remote access connections to your network, you can probably connect the devices directly to your computer. However, if you plan to support three or more simultaneous connections, you will most likely need to connect your modems to multiport hardware. With multiport hardware, one RAS server can support 256 concurrent connections.

Server Connection Devices

At this time, analog modems are the most common connection device for both clients and servers. However, the maximum transmission rate for this type of device will soon reach its limit, not because of the modems themselves, but because of their transmission medium: the phone system. As the need for faster transmission rates continues to grow, other devices and mediums will increasingly become more dominant.

ISDN has already become a fairly popular technology for increasing bandwidth with transmission rates of up to 128 Kbps. Two other technologies, ADSL and cable modems, which boast even greater transmission rates, should begin to outpace the growth of ISDN within the next year. All of these technologies are discussed in depth in the "Data Lines" and "Communication Lines" sections.

Communication Lines

Most RBR implementations communicate through copper, twisted pair wires—the same as those used in the telephone system. These wires are not the best for data transfer, but because they already connect houses and businesses throughout the world, they have become the most commonly used method (see the following Note).

In general, you will need one dedicated communication line for every device you have. The type of line must match the type of modem. For example, if you plan to support ADSL modems, each modem will need its own ADSL line. The number and types of connections needed depends on the technologies available to your users based on their individual needs. (Information on choosing the types and numbers of connections is in a following section, "Choosing the Type and Number of Communication Lines.")

> **N O T E**   Even though ADSL, ISDN, and analog modems all use the same twisted pair copper wires for communication, the hardware used by the phone company to support these different technologies are very different, and the associated costs passed on to you will vary widely. ■

Client Connection Devices

For now at least, the available client-side devices are the same as the server devices: ADSL, ISDN, and analog and cable modems. However, with the movement toward asymmetric transmissions for which the amount of downstream data is much greater than the amount of upstream data, this may change.

Background Information

The transfer of digital data over analog phone lines is a complicated process because of the large number of variables involved in the communication process. When setting up a LAN, most of the devices involved in the communication are bought, set up, and configured with the sole intention of transferring digital data from one computer to another. However, with remote network access, the data must travel through communication lines and devices that were intended only for the transfer of a voice. Because of this, many things can go wrong.

When something does go wrong, it is not always clear what it was and what can be done to fix it. This section is intended to give you an understanding of all that is involved in modem communication so that you can understand how it works and how to troubleshoot problems more effectively.

Data Lines

The series of copper wires, routing systems, amplifiers, and filters that make up the phone system are by no means the best way to transfer digital data from one computer to another. However, due to the sheer number of twisted pair copper wires running throughout the planet and the existing infrastructure of the modern phone system, this system will continue to be the medium through which the majority of computers will communicate. With the explosion of interest in the Internet and its technologies, modem companies, communication companies, and research laboratories have spent a great deal of time and money in overcoming the inherent weaknesses of digital communication over the existing phone system. As a result, communication is steadily becoming more reliable and much faster.

The early phone network consisted of a pure analog system that connected telephone users directly by wires. This system was very inefficient, was prone to breakdown and noise, and did not lend itself easily to long-distance connections. Beginning in the 1960s, the telephone system gradually began converting its internal connections to a packet-based, digital switching system. Today, nearly all voice switching within the telephone network in the U.S. is digital. Nonetheless, the final connection from the local central office to the customer equipment was, and still largely is, an analog *Plain Old Telephone Service* (*POTS*) line.

Except for cable modems, the technologies I describe all use twisted pair copper wire. Although the wire is the same, the methods used for sending signals over great distances without signal degradation vary widely. This section is intended to give you an overview of the different technologies being used and/or tested. It describes the basics of how they work, their most common applications, and general information about availability.

Analog Phone Lines   Data sent over analog phone lines is routed through the core switching network without alteration; the network treats the data exactly like a voice signal. The core switching network, as shown in Figure 11.4, routes calls from the caller's phone through a series of switches and then to the recipient's phone. The bandwidth limitations of these lines are a result of filters used by the core switching network to reduce line noise in voice transmissions.

FIG. 11.4
Phone calls, along with analog data signals, are routed through a system of switches known as the core switching network to connect the caller to the callee using the shortest possible path.

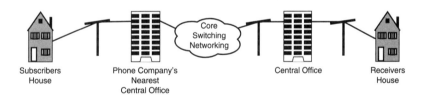

DSL-Based Technologies (ISDN and ADSL)   ISDN (Integrated Services Digital Network) and ADSL (Asymmetric Digital Subscriber Line) are both forms of the DSL (Digital Subscriber Line) technology developed by the Bellcore research arm of the Regional Bell Operating Companies (RBOCs). DSL technologies use the same twisted pair copper wire used for telephone service, but because DSL is a broad-band technology, it cannot be routed through the same series of switches as analog modems. DSL-based modems are fundamentally different than analog modems in that they use digital signaling at the wire level. DSL modems use high-speed computer chips to process the signal and filter out the inherent line noise of copper wires. This enables faster and more reliable connections.

ISDN   ISDN has been around since the late 1970s, but has only recently gained popularity for use in remote access applications. However, due to more advanced DSL forms, such as ADSL, its popularity may be short-lived. ISDN is a switched digital communication product that gives your single phone line the capability to transmit voice and packet data simultaneously over a single twisted pair connection. ISDN transmissions must be routed through special digital switches or over special phone lines known as DS1 (T-1) lines.

There are two basic types of ISDN service: *Basic Rate Interface* (*BRI*) and *Primary Rate Interface* (*PRI*). BRI consists of two 64 Kbps B channels and one 16 Kbps D channel. Using a channel aggregation protocol, such as Multilink-PPP or BONDING, BRI supports an uncompressed data transfer speed of 128 Kbps. PRI is intended for users with greater capacity requirements. Typically, the channel structure is 23 B channels plus one 64 Kbps D channel for a total of 1,536 Kbps. In Europe, PRI consists of 30 B channels plus one 64 Kbps D channel for a total of 1,984 Kbps. BRI is intended for remote access type applications and, as such, it will be the focus of this section.

With BRI, B channels can be used for data transmission only, or in many setups, one channel is used for data and the other channel can be used for voice or data. In other words, you can talk on the phone while simultaneously transmitting data at 64 Kbps or you can transmit and receive data at 128 Kbps.

With ISDN, instead of the phone company sending a ring voltage signal to ring the bell in your phone (in-band signal), it sends a digital packet on the channel. This signal does not disturb established connections, and call setup time is very fast: usually one or two seconds as opposed to 30 to 60 seconds for analog modems. The signaling also indicates who is calling, what type of call it is (data/voice), and what number was dialed. Available ISDN phone equipment is then capable of making intelligent decisions for directing the call.

ADSL   ADSL was designed to maximize downstream transmission rates over single twisted pair wiring. As its name implies, the ADSL transmits an asymmetric data stream with much more data going downstream than upstream (see the following Note). ADSL transmission rates top out at 9 Mbps downstream and 640 Kbps upstream. However, there are many factors involved in ADSL transmission rates. The biggest factor is distance. Unlike analog modems, which transmit data at frequency rates of only up to 3 KHz, ADSL is a broad-band technology that uses a much broader frequency range.

Higher frequencies degrade quickly when transmitted over long distances. As a result, achievable transmission rates for ADSL are largely dependent on the distance between the subscriber's connection and the telephone company's nearest central office. Because of this and because of ADSL's asymmetric nature, ADSL is a technology intended for, and is particularly well suited to, connections to individual homes for such uses as video on demand, home shopping, and Internet browsing.

N O T E   Transmission from a service provider to a subscriber's modem is generally referred to as a *downstream transmission*. An *upstream transmission* is the opposite, going from a subscriber's modem to the service provider. For many Internet-based applications, the data flow is mostly downstream; upstream traffic is largely limited to requests for data. ▪

Cable Lines   Like phone lines, the coaxial cables used for cable TV are also quite plentiful, particularly in the United States. Cable lines enable broad-band transmission, which—if used only for data transmission—supports downstream transmission speeds of up to 36 Mbps. However, most of the bandwidth in today's cable systems is devoted to TV channels. Each TV channel occupies 6 MHz of the spectrum (although some cable companies multiplex several channels into one). In addition, the available bandwidth must be shared between all the homes connected to a particular line. Typical cable systems serve between 500 to 2,500 homes on one line. Further, as is the case with an Ethernet network, too many nodes competing for bandwidth slow network performance. If your neighbors do a lot of downloads, your throughput will suffer unless the cable operator provides additional capacity or extra routers and channels.

The main issue with cable lines being used for digital data transmission is that the current cable infrastructure is set up for one way transmissions, from the provider's transmission site to all connected homes. To become interactive, cable operators must allocate spectrum on the cable for upstream signals and add hardware to receive and retransmit these signals to their servers. Most of today's implementations use low frequencies for upstream transmission because the inherent noise of low frequencies prevents use for television broadcasts.

To use these lower frequencies for upstream transmission, cable operators must filter out this noise somewhere between the *head end* and the cable recipient. Cable operators will also have to modify their cable amplifiers to separate the upstream and downstream signals. In many areas, this will require replacing most amplifiers and running fiber optic cable closer to each home.

Part
III

Ch
11

N O T E   The *head end* is the term for the building from which the cable company broadcasts signals. Head end buildings receive both satellite and traditional broadcast TV signals and then broadcast these channels over the cable lines to each customer.

Finally, cable operators will have to set up a community-wide Internet *point of presence* (*POP*) to serve all the networks associated with a particular head end. This will require the cable companies to plan very carefully and to gain an enormous understanding of TCP/IP networking. They will have to set up routers and servers at the head end and at strategic places around the cable system to manage Internet traffic.

With the many costs and infrastructure changes required for data transmission through cable lines, more focus is being put on the development of DSL technologies for remote access applications.

Connection Devices

Connection devices are the heart and soul of any RAS implementation. They make remote communications possible through whatever medium is chosen. This section discusses the main types of devices.

Analog Modems   Analog modems are by far the most common means of digital communication from remote locations. Advancements in their speed and reliability have enabled users to do much more than before. Through a process called *modulation,* analog modems convert digital data into an audio signal that can be broadcast over the standard telephone system.

Initially, analog modem manufacturers attempted to maximize throughput by maximizing the baud rate (see the following Note). Eventually, it was found that 2,400 signal transitions per second was the upper limit for signal transitions transmitted through the telephone system.

N O T E   *Baud* is the number of discrete conditions or signal elements per second. It signifies the maximum capacity for information carrying of a communication channel in symbols per second. A symbol is a unique state of the communication channel, distinguishable by the receiver from all other possible states. For example, it may be one of two voltage levels on a wire for a direct digital connection, or it might be the phase or frequency of a carrier.

Named after J.M.E. Baudot, the French engineer who constructed the first successful teleprinter, the term *baud* was originally a unit of telegraph signaling speed, set at one Morse code dot per second.

The term *baud* causes much confusion and is usually best avoided when talking about modem communication rates. Use *bits per second (bps)* instead. ■

To surpass this rate, a second technique, called *multiphasing,* is used. Multiphasing sends several 2,400 baud signals at the same time. Each signal is restricted to a specific frequency range so that the signals do not get mixed. This is like several different tunes being whistled simultaneously with each tune being restricted to a certain range of notes. A 28.8 modem sends 14 signals simultaneously at different frequencies. Now, with 33.6 modems, it is believed that we have reached the threshold of the number of signals that can be sent simultaneously because of the limited frequency range available on the telephone system. However, analog modem manufacturers are beginning to explore asymmetric transmissions, like those used in ADSL, to maximize downstream transmission rates. Even so, do not expect modems to get a whole lot faster than the 56 Kbps now reached.

The third method that modem manufacturers use to maximize the throughput of analog modems is compression. Hardware compression works the same way software compression works in such programs as PKZip: It is only effective at compressing data that has not already been compressed. Most large programs, pictures, and sounds have already been compressed and, therefore, do not benefit much from the hardware compression applied to them.

ISDN   ISDN is a fully digital technology that enables computers to communicate by sending digital signals as high-speed pulses at rates of up to 128 Kbps without converting the signal to an analog or audio signal. ISDN devices come in two forms: router and terminal adapters.

An ISDN router connects to your computer or to a networking hub through an Ethernet cable. Your computer will need an Ethernet card to use an ISDN router. In general, ISDN routers are more expensive than a terminal adapter because the router is responsible for deciding when to dial the line, when to hang up, and when to add more speed. It is also responsible for moving Internet packets from the ISDN line to the Ethernet. Routers provide greater speed because they can change speeds without having to call back. A router also provides more flexibility because it is an Ethernet device; therefore, its capabilities can be shared by all computers on the network.

An ISDN terminal adapter connects to your computer's serial port and acts just like an analog modem. Terminal adapters are slightly slower than routers because they are connected to the serial port, which, in most cases, can only handle 115 Kbps. If both B channels are being used for data transmission, this is slightly slower than full capacity. Also, in order to change speeds, the adapter must terminate the connection and reconnect.

ADSL Modems   ADSL is also a fully digital technology. It promises to provide even greater speeds because it is a broad-band technology, meaning it uses much more of the available frequency range for its transmissions.

With ADSL, your modem connects to another ADSL modem at the telephone company's nearest central office. The data is then transmitted over the phone company's backbone using another technology to a third ADSL modem, which then transmits the data to the recipient's ADSL modem (see Figure 11.5).

FIG. 11.5
There are actually four modems involved in an ADSL implementation.

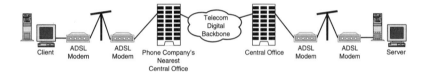

Client   ADSL Modem   ADSL Modem   Phone Company's Nearest Central Office   Telecom Digital Backbone   Central Office   ADSL Modem   ADSL Modem   Server

Part
III

Ch
11

Cable Modems   Like analog modems, cable modems modulate and demodulate the cable signal into a stream of data. Otherwise, the technologies are completely different. Cable modems are much more complicated because they are required to perform many additional functions not required by analog modems. These additional functions can include the following:

- Separating the data signal from the rest of the broadcast stream through the use of a tuner
- Routing and bridging network packets
- Running network-management and diagnostic software
- Encrypting/decrypting data for security and identification purposes

The cable modems in use today have an Ethernet port that connects to the computer (or network) on one side and to the cable connection on the other. An Ethernet adapter needs to be installed in the computer and then connected to the cable's Ethernet port via a standard RJ-45 connector. As far as your computer is concerned, it is hooked directly to the Internet via an Ethernet cable. There are no phone numbers to dial and no limitations on serial-port throughput.

Typically, a cable modem sends and receives data in two slightly different fashions. In the downstream direction, the digital data is modulated and then transmitted in several phases simultaneously with each phase using a 6 MHz allocation, somewhere between 42 MHz and 750 MHz.

Cable modem speeds vary greatly, depending on whether the cable lines are used strictly for transmission and what kind of infrastructure the cable company has for supporting two-way communication. In the downstream direction (from the network to the computer), speeds can be anywhere up to 36 Mbps. Modems this fast are not currently on the market, but should appear sometime in 1997. Few computers will be capable of connecting at such high speeds, so a more realistic number is 3–10 Mbps. In the upstream direction (from computer to network), speeds can be up to 10 Mbps. However, most modem producers will probably select a more optimum speed of between 200 Kbps and 2 Mbps.

In the first few years of cable modem deployment, an asymmetric setup will probably be more common than a symmetric setup. In an asymmetric scheme, the downstream channel has a much higher bandwidth allocation than the upstream channel. This is by design, as current Internet applications tend to be asymmetric in nature.

Cable modems are commonly available, although priced significantly higher than twisted pair modems. Each modem manufacturer currently uses a different data-transmission specification, so cable modems from different vendors are incompatible. Standardization is underway and should be in place soon. However, service for cable modems (that is, cable lines that support data transmission) is only available in a few trial areas. As discussed in a previous section, the cable industry has many changes to make in its communication infrastructure to support this technology. Most experts believe that DSL technologies will be implemented more quickly and cheaply and will become the primary high data rate technology.

Remote Access and Line Protocols

Line protocols establish the method for the transfer of data over a telephone line. Data is packaged by the networking protocol, and then further packaged by the line protocols before being sent over the communication medium (see Figure 11.6). This section covers line protocols supported by Windows 95.

FIG. 11.6

Line protocols are responsible for encapsulating data to transport it through the transmission medium.

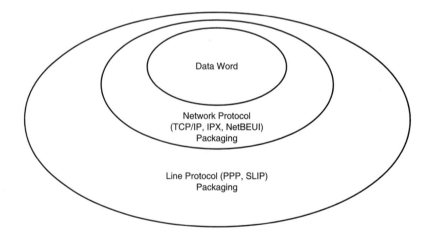

Point-to-Point Protocol   Point-to-Point Protocol (PPP) is a standard encapsulation protocol for the transport of different network protocols across a serial link. It is capable of supporting multiple data protocols on a single connection simultaneously. It also supports link quality testing, header compression, and error detection. Because of its advanced error detection and prevention mechanisms and its built-in extensibility, PPP is quickly becoming the de facto standard for both dial-up accounts and semi-permanent connections.

Serial Line IP   Serial Line IP (SLIP) is a very simple remote-access protocol designed to be easy to implement and to offer connectivity across many different platforms. SLIP is commonly used by Internet service providers (ISPs) to offer Internet connectivity to remote users.

The RAS Line Protocol   Remote access capabilities were first provided by Microsoft in LAN Manager 2.1. For early implementations, Microsoft created its own proprietary line protocol also known as RAS. The RAS line protocol was based on Microsoft's proprietary networking protocol NetBEUI. Because it was based on NetBEUI, the RAS line protocol is only capable of supporting NetBEUI and it does not allow for data compression. Using the RAS Line Protocol, you can connect to Windows for Workgroups 3.11 and Windows NT 3.1 servers running the RAS dial-up server.

Networking and Data Protocols

Part
III

Ch
11

Networking protocols define how data is packaged and prepared for transfer. The actual transfer is then performed by the network adapter, which, in the case of RAS, is the dial-up adapter. This section provides an overview of the networking protocols as they relate to RAS. For more information about networking protocols, see Chapter 4, "Enterprise Planning and Implementation."

TCP/IP   TCP/IP is particularly well-suited to remote access because it was designed by the Internet community specifically for transmitting data on the Internet. Because it was designed to operate in environments where the conditions are not particularly suitable for data transmission, it has strong error detection and correction capabilities. For more information about TCP/IP, see Chapter 9, "Using TCP/IP with Windows NT Server."

NetBEUI   NetBEUI (Netbios Extended User Interface) is a network protocol developed by IBM and Microsoft for use on LANs of 250 nodes or fewer. Microsoft initially used NetBEUI to add networking capabilities to its Windows operating system. NetBEUI is not very well-suited to remote access applications because its error detection and handling capabilities are not as robust as TCP/IP, and it is not routable. However, if your operating systems or line protocols support only NetBEUI, it can be used. For more information about NetBEUI, see Chapter 4, "Enterprise Planning and Implementation."

IPX/SPX   IPX/SPX is the primary network protocol used on NetWare networks. With additions made to it by Novell, it supports routing and works quite well in remote access applications. However, unless Dial-Up Networking clients require IPX/SPX or servers can be accessed only using IPX/SPX, there is no reason to support it. For more information about IPX/SPX, see Chapter 4, "Enterprise Planning and Implementation."

UARTS

A chip known as a *Universal Asynchronous Receiver/Transmitter* (*UART*) is fundamental to serial data communication. In short, this device converts parallel data (e.g., 8-bit bytes) into a serial data stream that can be transmitted over a telephone line. Internal modems are equipped with their own UARTS. External modems, however, utilize the UART incorporated into your PC's COM port. If you are using an external modem, it is important to know what type of UART your COM port is using.

A 16550A type UART is capable of transmitting data at speeds of up to 115,200 bps and are fine for 28.8 modems. If you have an 8250 or 16450 type UART, communication between your computer and modem is limited to 19,200 bps. This can cause the modem's buffer to run empty at times, thus decreasing your effective throughput. If you have an 8250 or 16450 type UART and want to connect a 28,800 bps or higher modem, you may want to consider upgrading your UART. If you have a serial card (or motherboard) with a socketed 8250 or 16450 UART, you can replace the chip with a 16550A. You can also purchase an add-on, high-speed data communication card with 16550A (or equivalent) UART from your local computer store at prices ranging from $20 to $75, depending upon the number of ports and other features.

Error Detection and Handling

Ten to 20 percent of the data sent between modems for RAS is used to ensure that the data sent is exactly the same as the data received and that none got lost along the way. Several mechanisms are used to ensure data integrity. These methods are explained in the following sections.

Cyclic Redundancy Checks (CRC)   Cyclic redundancy checks are used to preserve the integrity of data in storage and transmission applications. CRC can be performed by hardware or software. In the traditional hardware implementation, a single shift register circuit performs the computations and handles data one bit at a time. In software implementation, the data can be handled in terms of bytes or even words.

CRC uses a mathematical polynomial to check the transmission of both bit-oriented and character-oriented sequences. This polynomial interacts through a predetermined algorithm on the data being transmitted to create a remainder that is transmitted in addition to the data. (The remainder comes from dividing the polynomial into the transmitted bit stream.) The polynomial is chosen to be one bit longer than the desired remainder, and the exact bit pattern chosen depends on the type of errors expected.

Framing Errors   All serial communication is set in chunks of data known as *frames*. Frame size is usually determined by the line protocol to maximize throughput with a minimum amount of lost data. To set off the frames, each frame begins with a Start bit and ends with the selected number of Stop bits. The number of bits between the Start and Stop bits is sent across as well. If the Stop bit is not where it is supposed to be due to line interference, a framing error occurs. When a framing error is detected, the frame is resent so that no data is lost.

Hardware Overruns   A hardware overrun occurs when the data in the serial port buffer is not moved in time to another location before new data *overruns* it. This arises when your computer is unable to keep up with the transmitted data, which occurs when you have a very slow computer or when your computer is busy performing processor-intensive activities. Although your computer will generally recover without intervention, large data blocks will need to be re-transmitted, significantly reducing overall system performance. Because one of the variables that causes overruns is system loading, do not be surprised if you find that their frequency varies depending on the programs that are running and how they are being used.

Buffer Overruns   A buffer overrun occurs when the data in the modem's buffer is not sent before new data *overruns* it. This usually signifies a problem with communication between the computer and the modem and can usually be fixed by adjusting your flow control method. Flow control specifies how your modem signals your computer to send additional data or to stop sending data. There are two types of flow control—hardware (RTS/CTS) and software (Xon/Xoff). Hardware flow control tends to give the most reliable connections.

Choosing Your Hardware

The minimum hardware requirements for setting up your Windows NT 4.0 server to support RAS are simply a phone line that can be accessed from an outside number and an analog modem. From this very basic setup, there are many other options. In fact, the number and economy of options increases regularly.

Often, the most difficult part of a RAS implementation is choosing the hardware and getting it all to work together. Resource conflicts, modem incompatibilities, poor documentation, imprecise error messages, incompatible protocols, and line noise all can lead to major headaches for the RAS administrator. That is not to mention the problems associated with relatively new technologies, such as ISDN, ADSL, and cable modems.

Choosing the right hardware and making sure you have installed and configured it properly can save you a lot of time and frustration in the future. This section gives guidelines and pointers for choosing the right numbers and types of hardware to suit your needs.

Choosing Your Connection Devices

You first need to choose the kind of connection devices to use: analog modems or a faster alternative. Consider the following guidelines:

- If users will be using RAS to check e-mail, access the Internet, and/or occasionally access files on your corporate network, a high-speed analog modem (28.8 bps+) should be sufficient for the time being. Prices on 28.8 and 33.3 Kbps modems now are low enough that you really should not consider anything slower, as it can end up costing you more in the long run.

- If your users will be running only text-based, terminal-type programs, and this is all you foresee, consider 14.4 Kbps or faster.

- If your users will be telecommuting or routinely sharing and using files across the network, or will be in need of high-speed access to your company's intranet or the Internet, consider faster alternatives, such as ISDN, ADSL, or cable modems.

TIP   Internal modems are not the most flexible option due to the limitation on the number of expansion slots available in a machine. Also, it is more difficult to monitor and diagnose problems with internal modems.

 TIP   If you need to support several connection devices, then consider using rack-mounted modem pools, which contain up to sixteen devices in a single rack-mounted unit. These banks take up considerably less space than several individual modems, and incompatibility between the modems is less of a concern. In a non-integrated modem bank, cabling is often messy and confusing, and overheating problems can arise.

Deciding the Number of Concurrent Connections to Support

Decide the number of connection devices you need. Because this decision really depends on the needs of your enterprise, this is not addressed here. In making your decision, consider your future needs and options and keep flexibility in mind.

N O T E   Under Windows NT 4.0 Server, RAS is capable of supporting up to 256 concurrent connections. However, to support this many connections, you will need a very powerful machine—at least a dual processor. If you anticipate needing this many connections, it would be wise to split the connections among multiple servers to ease administration, maintenance, and upgrading. ▪

Choosing the Type and Number of Communication Lines

For each connection device, you should have one dedicated line of the same type. For example, if you have eight analog modems, you should have eight dedicated analog phone lines. For both analog and digital phone lines, most phone companies offer a service called a *rollover phone number*, which enables users to dial one phone number, yet access one of many dedicated lines (each assigned to a separate phone number).

N O T E   In order to achieve maximize bandwidth, modems running at 14.4 bps or above must make optimal use of all the frequencies available on an analog phone line. Most phone switches, which companies use to route calls and reduce the number of external lines needed, filter signals to reduce line noise (particularly in higher frequencies). These filters reduce the bandwidth available to modems. This results in slower connection rates and reduced reliability for high speed modems. ▪

Choosing Multiport Hardware

There are two basic types of multiport serial boards: *UART-based* and *intelligent*. UART-based boards simply transfer data between the modems and the computer. Because of limitations in the speed of UARTS and because the processing load falls on the server's CPU, UART-based boards are limited in the number and speed of the modems that they can support.

Intelligent multiport boards have serial port controllers, larger buffers, and they usually contain their own processor-based UART with character recognition and flow control logic. More expensive models also have their own CPU to handle serial I/O and reduce the overall processing load on your server. More powerful boards can support more and faster modems; of course, more powerful boards are more expensive.

N O T E Multiport boards are notorious for having driver-related problems. Therefore, make sure that the hardware you choose is on the Windows NT 4.0 supported hardware list and that there is a current, reliable driver available for it. Whatever you choose, if you need more than one, make sure that they are the same make and model so you don't have to troubleshoot two completely different sets of problems. ▦

In choosing your multiport board, consider the number and speed of modems that you will need to support. Find available boards that support the number of connections you will need. If you need to support more than 16 modems, you will most likely have to purchase two or more boards, which—depending on the board—can either be daisy-chained together or will each require its own expansion slot. The three most important statistics to consider are throughput, CPU usage (or processor load), and price. The main features that affect these statistics are the amount of RAM, the type of UART, and the type and speed of the onboard processor (if present).

Choosing Your Machine

You will need to take all of the preceding information into account when deciding on the system requirements of your RAS server. For most setups, your server will not need to be a dedicated RAS server. The processing load on the RAS server can vary widely depending on the number of connections you plan to support, the speed and type of those connections, and, most importantly, the multiport hardware being used (if it is used).

If you are not using multiport hardware and only have a few connections, the overall load will be very low. With multiport hardware, much of the serial I/O processing should be handled by the multiport hardware; your server will handle most of the networking related load. The documentation that comes with your multiport hardware should have specific information regarding the processing requirements of your server.

Security

Because of the extra level of vulnerability resulting from users being able to access your corporate network without having to physically be in your office, security is a very important part of RAS. The security features offered by RAS, along with the integrated Windows NT Server security, should be enough to keep your private network private if properly implemented and monitored. Microsoft has made security a major issue in both RAS and Windows NT and is using the most advanced and accepted standards in their implementations to ensure the safety of your data.

However, no encryption algorithm is unbreakable. The most advanced hackers have impressive resources at their disposal and will go to great lengths to get what they are looking for. Luckily, advanced hackers tend to focus their efforts on breaking encryption algorithms for the companies that write the encryption algorithms or breaking into sites that have much more interesting data than the average business network contains.

There are many things you can do to ensure the safety of the data contained within your network. This section outlines RAS security mechanisms and how they integrate into the Windows NT Server mechanisms.

Integration with Windows NT Security

The most effective security mechanism that RAS has is its integration with Windows NT. To be able to log in to RAS, you must have an account on the domain on which the RAS server resides and that account must be granted dial-in permission through the Remote Access Admin tool. All security measures that apply to your Windows NT domain also apply to remote access users. Because of this, it is important that you have effective security on your Windows NT domain.

Encryption

Intercepting data from a RAS connection is a very difficult thing. If someone is able to tap into a RAS transmission, encryption prevents him from being able to decipher the captured data. RAS supports several types of data encryption for password authentication and also supports the RSA RC4 encryption algorithm for all data transmission. This section covers the encryption mechanisms used in RAS. For more information about encryption, go to the RSA Data Security World Wide Web page at **www.rsa.com**.

Password Authentication Protocol (PAP)   PAP uses clear text (unencrypted) password authentication for user login. Many third-party remote access applications, such as Trumpet Winsock, can only use PAP for user validation and login. Chapter 12, "Implementing Remote Access Service (RAS)," covers enabling and disabling PAP.

Challenge Handshake Authentication Protocol (CHAP)   CHAP requires a challenge response with encryption on the response. Windows NT RAS server supports the following encryption algorithms in conjunction with CHAP authentication:

- **MS-CHAP**—Microsoft's implementation of the RSA MD4 algorithm. It is the most secure encryption algorithm supported by Windows NT. You can require MS-CHAP authentication by checking Require Microsoft Encrypted Authentication encryption setting for the RAS server, as shown in Figure 11.7. (This is addressed further in the next chapter). Both Windows NT and Windows 95 RAS clients support MS-CHAP for connecting to a Windows NT RAS server.

N O T E   The RSA MD4 is a message-digest algorithm developed by Ron Rivest in 1990. It is meant for digital signature applications where a large message has to be "compressed" in a secure manner before being signed with the private key.

FIG. 11.7

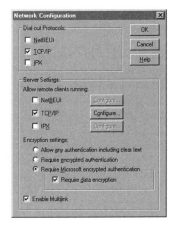

The RAS Network Configuration dialog box enables you to select password encryption settings.

- **SPAP**—A propriety authentication protocol developed by Shiva for use in authenticating encrypted logins from a machine running Shiva's client access software.
- **DES**—Data Encryption Standard. It was developed by IBM and was endorsed by the U.S. government in 1977 as an official standard. Microsoft used DES in early RAS implementations, such as Windows for Workgroups 3.11 RAS and RAS 1.1a.

Part III Ch 11

In addition, Windows 95 and the Windows NT 4.0 RAS *client* support the RSA MD5-CHAP encryption standard, which is used by many third-party PPP servers. The Windows NT RAS *server* does not support RSA MD5 because this method requires a clear-text password for login to the server.

N O T E MD5 was developed by Rivest in 1991. It is basically MD4 with additional safety mechanisms to make it harder to break. Although slightly slower than MD4, it is more secure. ■

RSA RC4 40-Bit Session Key RAS uses the RC4 encryption algorithm for encrypting and decrypting data. RC4 is a variable key-size stream cipher designed by Ron Rivest for RSA Data Security. RC4 is a confidential and propriety algorithm that uses random permutations for encrypting data. It is generally considered secure. It is popular because of its speed, security, and adjustable key size. Adjustable keys are important because keys larger than 40 bits cannot be exported from the U.S. Microsoft's implementation uses a 40-bit key.

Additional Security Features

Because of the serious security concerns presented by a RAS implementation, Microsoft provides additional features that allow you to customize you security setup. These features are described in the following sections.

Callback With callback, after establishing a connection and validating the user, the RAS server hangs up and then calls back to the remote user to reestablish the connection. This can be used as a security mechanism by either forcing a remote user to call from a single number or, if the user is allowed to specify the callback number, by enabling the return phone number to be monitored.

Third-Party Host Security DLLs   For networks in which the basic Windows NT and RAS level of security is not enough, a third-party security DLL can be installed. The security DLL can then authenticate a remote user by reading security information from a database other than the standard Windows NT user account database. For example, the challenge could be a code that the user must provide as input to a cardkey reader. The cardkey reader then displays a response that the remote user types in the terminal window.

Even if the security DLL authenticates the remote user, the RAS server still performs its own authentication. This ensures that RAS security always authenticates a remote user, even if a security DLL is installed that grants access to all users.

Additional Security Techniques

A number of additional steps can be taken to increase the security of remote connections. The measures described in this section should provide most businesses more than adequate protection against unauthorized access to private data.

Restricting Your Remote Access Phone Number   Do not publish your remote access phone number. To be able to break into your domain through RAS, the person must know the phone number to your RAS server. Because of this, one of the most basic steps that you can take to protect your network is to treat the phone number that provides access to your RAS server as an access code. If you are concerned about security, the phone number should probably not be published and should only be given to users as needed.

 Be aware that there are programs that will try all possible phone numbers for an area to detect all numbers on which a modem answers. Once this number is found, the hacker can try to gain access to the network.

Monitoring Access   If you do suspect that an unauthorized person is gaining access to your network, the tools supplied with RAS should help you to monitor RAS access. You can turn on auditing for the RAS function by setting the Enable Audit key to 1 (found in the Registry under HKEY_LOCAL_MACHINE\SYSTEM\CurrentControlSet\Services\RemoteAccess\Parameters). With this enabled, Windows NT records all RAS events into the event log. In addition, all system, application, and security events are also recorded to the Event Log and can be viewed by administrators using the Event Viewer.

Using Firewalls   Where possible, put RAS servers on the *outside* of a firewall. If you are using RAS to enable users to access the Internet, e-mail, or some other public domain, consider protecting private network data behind a firewall. For more information about firewalls, see Chapter 17, "I-Net Tools and Techniques."

Restricting Hours for Remote Users   Specify the hours that remote users are permitted access to your system. Hackers tend to do much of their work or run their automated programs late at night. Restricting the hours during which remote access users can log in provides an extra level of security. Of course, you don't want to be overly restrictive and prevent a user from getting work done, particularly when working late to finish up.

Restricting Dial-In Permissions   Grant dial-in permissions only to those who request permissions. Many domain users do not need remote access capabilities, so it is generally a good security policy to grant dial-in permissions only to those who specifically need permissions.

Enabling Authentication   Set the maximum possible encryption settings. If users will be dialing in from Windows 95 or Windows NT 4.0 machines, choose Require Microsoft Encrypted Authentication and Require Encrypted Data in the RAS Network Configuration dialog box.

From Here...

This chapter is an overview of the devices, technologies, and protocols involved in RAS. With this overview, you should be able to make better decisions while installing and configuring RAS. This chapter also provides an understanding of the various components and how they work so that you can troubleshoot problems as they arise.

As the need for fast, reliable connectivity has increased, modem technology has steadily improved and connectivity options have grown considerably and become much more affordable. As an administrator, it is important to choose reliable options for your RAS server. You should also expect to play a large role in the decisions and setup of your dial-up networking clients. If necessary, consider establishing guidelines or recommendations for dial-up networking clients. If you expect many users to be dialing in from computers they have set up themselves, you should probably write a document or find an existing document to walk them through the setup process.

For more information about the topics addressed in this chapter, see the following chapters:

- For information on networking protocols, see Chapter 9, "Using TCP/IP with Windows NT Server."
- For more detail about RAS, see Chapter 12, " Implementing Remote Access Service (RAS)."
- For insight about RAS hardware and software installation and configuration procedures for both the client and the server, see Chapter 13, "Implementing Dial-Up Networking Clients."
- For information on implementing RAS-related security, see Chapter 25, "Implementing Internet Security."

Implementing Remote Access Service (RAS)

by David O'Leary

This chapter describes the installation and configuration procedures for Microsoft's Remote Access Service (RAS). The Remote Access Service enables authorized users to connect to your corporate network from remote locations, such as their homes, customer sites, and hotel rooms. Once connected, users can copy files, view data, send and receive e-mail, and access all network services as if they were directly connected to your LAN. This chapter provides you with the procedures and detailed information you need to get the Remote Access Service running and to keep it running reliably. For more information about RAS and how it can be used, see Chapter 11, "An Inside Look at Remote Access Service (RAS)."

How to install and configure your hardware for Remote Access Service

Learn procedures for installing RAS-related hardware, including multiport hardware, connection devices, and X.25 smart cards. Learn how to configure your COM ports and modems to maximize throughput.

How to install the Remote Access Service software

Walks through the steps involved in the RAS installation process. Detailed information is presented on all available options to help you customize your RAS installation to the needs of your enterprise.

How to configure Remote Access Service

Gain a detailed understanding of RAS configuration options. Learn how to add devices to your RAS Server and configure them for dialing out, receiving calls, or both.

How to use the Remote Access Admin tool

Learn to use the Remote Access Admin tool to administer and monitor RAS servers throughout your enterprise.

N O T E   This chapter assumes that you will be setting up RAS on a Windows NT 4.0 Server; however, you will find that the setup and administration utilities for Windows NT 4.0 Workstation are identical although limited in the allowed number of concurrent connections. Also, on the server side, the Window NT 3.51 RAS utilities are very similar. ■

RAS can be installed automatically as a part of the initial Windows NT Server installation or after the initial Windows NT Server installation by using the Network applet in the Control Panel. The remaining portion of this chapter assumes that RAS was not installed during installation of Windows NT Server and that you now have a requirement to install it on the server.

N O T E   To be able to add and configure devices and change configuration parameters for networking, you must be logged on as a user with administrative rights to the local machine. ■

The chapter begins by presenting information on installing the hardware required for your RAS server. This section covers hardware for both basic and advanced RAS configurations. Information is presented for the installation and configuration of COM ports, modems, multiport hardware, and X.25 smart cards. You can skip this section if your hardware has already been properly set up and configured and is working properly. ■

Installing the Required Hardware

This section provides general information and guidelines on how to set up and configure RAS-related hardware under Windows NT 4.0. This section assumes that you have already chosen your hardware and that the necessary data lines are already in place. Refer to Chapter 11 for information on choosing hardware. The following devices are discussed:

- Multiport hardware
- Connection devices, such as analog, ISDN, and ADSL modems
- X.25 smart cards

N O T E   Except for modems, most RAS-related devices are considered to be networking adapters. As such, they can be found, installed, and configured from the Adapter tab of the Network applet in the Control Panel. ■

Installing Multiport Hardware

If you plan on connecting more than two modems to your RAS server, you should consider using multiport hardware. Multiport hardware provides additional serial port connections, requires only a single interrupt, and, depending on which multiport device you choose, usually handles much of the processing load involved in supporting multiple modems. For more detailed information on multiport hardware and its uses, refer to Chapter 11. To install your multiport device, follow these steps:

1. Open the Control Panel.

2. Double-click the Network icon to open the Network dialog box.

3. Select the Adapters tab (see Figure 12.1).

FIG. 12.1

The Adapters tab of the Network settings dialog box shows currently used network adapters.

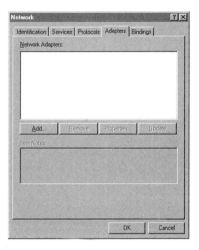

4. In the Adapters tab, click the Add button to bring up the list of available Network Adapters. Windows NT will take a few seconds to build the available network adapter list; then you should see a list like the one displayed in Figure 12.2.

FIG. 12.2

Windows NT displays a list of available network adapters in the Select Network Adapter dialog box.

Part
III

Ch
12

N O T E Although Windows NT supplies many drivers for the most common multiport hardware, you should ensure that you have the latest Windows NT 4.0 driver. Often, the best place to get this is from the hardware manufacturer's World Wide Web page or FTP site. This will be a very important part of your setup. If you get it right the first time, it could save you many future headaches. ▓

5. If you have a driver from the manufacturer, click the Have Disk button. This brings up the Insert Disk dialog box. Type in the path to your driver and hit OK.

6. If you do not have the driver, select your hardware from the list and click OK.

7. Configuration settings are a part of the driver provided for the particular hardware device and therefore vary widely. Consult any information the manufacturer supplies or contact the manufacturer directly for information on configuring its hardware on a Windows NT 4.0 Server.

Installing an X.25 Smart Card

X.25 smart cards, also known as *X.25 pads*, enable you to connect to a X.25 packet-switched network. X.25 pads are often used in implementing a wide area network (WAN) over a public data network (PDN). Because installation and setup procedures vary widely for X.25 adapters, you should refer to your hardware manufacturer's instructions or contact your hardware manufacturer for setup and configuration information under Windows NT 4.0.

In general, you will install the X.25 adapter from the Adapters tab of the Network applet in the Control Panel. Follow the steps given for installing multiport hardware. To ensure reliable communication, make sure you have the latest driver from the manufacturer.

Configuring Your Serial Ports

N O T E   If you are using multiport hardware, refer to the manufacturer's documentation for instructions on configuring its COM ports. ▨

COM ports provide your computer with a way to communicate with external devices, such as modems. However, a COM port can also be used to communicate with an internal device, such as an internal modem. If you plan to attach a modem directly to your machine, whether internally or externally, you will need to use an available COM port and configure it to match your modem's settings. This section gives detailed information on all involved configuration settings and suggests commonly used settings.

COM ports can be configured using the Control Panel of the Windows NT Server (or Workstation). To maximize your chances for successful modem connections the first time, know your modem's communication parameters before starting this procedure.

Follow these steps to configure your COM ports for RAS:

1. Open the Control Panel.
2. Double-click the Ports icon.
3. Click the COM port to be configured, and double-click Settings to display the Settings dialog box, as shown in Figure 12.3. The initial settings displayed will be the Windows NT Server default settings or, if the port had been previously configured, the settings from the previous configuration.

FIG. 12.3

The Settings dialog box displays, and enables editing of, the current settings of the selected COM port. Click Advanced to see the advanced settings for COM1.

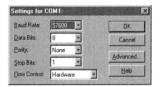

4. Set the baud rate to its highest available speed (see the following Note). This is necessary because if compression is enabled, the effective throughput can far exceed the actual throughput. For a 28.8 modem using the V.34 communication protocol, which defines a hardware compression ratio of four to one, the effective throughput can be as high as 115,200 Bps. (Refer to Chapter 11 for additional details.) The goal is to always keep the modem's buffer filled with information to send out. If the modem's transfer rate is higher than the serial port's, the modem may end up waiting for data to send. Proper flow control settings should keep the buffer from being overfilled.

N O T E   Most modern machines, particularly servers, should have a 16550 or 16550AF UART chip that supports baud rates up to 115 Kbps. However, if you have an older machine with a 16450 UART chip, the maximum baud rate is 19,200 Bps. ▨

5. Select the number of data bits you want to transmit for each character by clicking the Data Bits drop-down list box. The choices are 4, 5, 6, 7, and 8. Eight is recommended.

6. Select the error-checking method by clicking the Parity drop-down list box. Available choices are Even, Odd, None, Mark, and Space. A typical choice is None.

7. Select the number of Stop Bits. This setting controls the number of timing units allowed to pass between each transmitted character. Available choices are 1, 1.5, and 2. One is recommended.

8. Select the Flow Control method by clicking the Flow Control drop-down list box. Flow control defines how the modem communicates with its attached computer. Available choices are Xon/Xoff, Hardware, and None. Hardware flow control tends to be the most reliable method.

9. If you need to change the advanced settings, click Advanced to display the Advanced Settings dialog box, as shown in Figure 12.4. Advanced settings can be used to resolve resource conflicts resulting from multiple resources using the same interrupt or multiple devices assigned to the same address. Normally, the default advanced settings will be sufficient to match the capabilities of your modem. If they are not, consult your modem's documentation or contact the hardware manufacturer to determine the advanced settings to use. When you are satisfied with the advanced settings, click OK.

Part
III

Ch
12

FIG. 12.4

The default settings in the Advanced Setting dialog box are usually sufficient for most remote communication sessions and serial port configuration requirements.

10. Click OK to close the Settings dialog box. Repeat step 3 through step 10 to configure additional serial ports.

11. Click Close to close the Ports dialog box.

When you have completed this procedure, the COM ports should be configured to properly support your modems.

Installing Your Modems

Modems are the backbone of any RAS setup. Ensuring that you have the right modems for the job and that they are properly installed and configured will be key to the success of your RAS implementation. This section is intended to give you the information you need to make the right choices to ensure that you get the maximum reliability and bandwidth from your modems. The following steps take you through the necessary steps to do this:

1. If the modem is an internal modem, you first need to verify that its COM port and IRQ settings match available COM port and IRQ settings on your computer. Refer to your modem's documentation for checking and adjusting these settings on your modem. Available resources under Windows NT can be checked from the Resources tab of the Windows NT Diagnostics applet. Once all settings are properly chosen, turn the computer off and insert the modem into an expansion slot.

   If the modem is an external modem, connect it to a serial port (see the following Note) and turn it on. At least one light should be lit to indicate that the modem has power.

N O T E   If you are connecting an external modem to one of the existing ports on the back of your computer, you should, if possible, use a 25-pin, DB-25 serial port with a 25-pin cable. DB-25 connectors are generally found on most modems and other data communication equipment (DCE) because the serial communication standard, known as RS-232, describes a set of signals that requires a 25-pin cable to carry them.

On the other hand, many modern modem protocols, such as v.34, have embedded the advanced functionality provided by the additional pins within the basic communication protocol and, therefore, require only a nine-pin connection (DB-9). ■

2. Open the Control Panel.

3. Double-click the Modems icon. This displays the Modems Properties dialog box, as shown in Figure 12.5.

FIG. 12.5

The Modems Properties
dialog box enables you
to add and remove
modems and view and
edit each modem's
configuration settings.

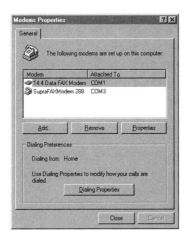

4. Click the <u>A</u>dd button to display the Install New Modem dialog box.

5. If you do not want Windows NT to detect the modem, check the Don't Detect my
   Modem; I Will Select It from a List Box (see the following Note), and then click <u>N</u>ext. If
   you want to choose your modem from the list, skip to step 9.

N O T E Windows NT does a good job of detecting what kind of modem you have and the COM port
to which it is attached. If it is unable to detect your modem, there is most likely a problem
with your modem, its physical setup, or its COM port settings. ■

6. RAS Setup begins searching for your modem by sending signals to available IRQs and
   looking for a response. When it receives a response from an attached device, it will
   continue to query the device to find out what type of device it is. (If you have an external
   modem, you should see the send and receive lights flickering while this happens.) If it
   finds a modem, it will determine its make and model number and the COM port to which
   it is attached. You should see information similar to that shown in Figure 12.6 as RAS
   Setup progresses through the detection process.

Part
III

Ch
12

FIG. 12.6

The detection process
indicates RAS Setup
status as it progresses
through performing
queries of each COM
port.

This could take a couple minutes, particularly if you have several modems attached to multiport hardware. Once all COM ports have been queried and one or more modems found, the RAS Setup Wizard will display a screen like that shown in Figure 12.7.

FIG. 12.7

The RAS Setup Wizard displays information on detected modems.

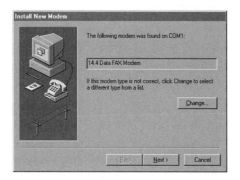

7. The Modem Setup Wizard will display the first device it found. If several modems were found, then clicking Next brings you to the next device. For each device, the Wizard displays the modem name and the attached COM port. If the modem was detected incorrectly, click the Change button and proceed to step 8. If all modems were detected correctly, then skip to step 10.

   If the Wizard was unable to detect your modem or no new modems were found, the Wizard will display an appropriate message and enable you to select the modem from the list of available modems by clicking Next.

8. You should now be looking at the Install New Modem screen of the RAS Setup Wizard. Select the manufacturer and model from the list or, if your modem or manufacturer is not listed and/or you have an updated Windows NT 4.0 driver from the manufacturer, click the Have Disk button and enter the path to the driver, as shown in Figure 12.8. Once the proper modem is selected, click Next.

FIG. 12.8

Setup enables you to use a manufacturer's driver by entering the path to the required files.

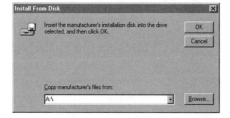

9. Select the COM port that the modem is attached to, and click Next.

10. Windows NT will take a few seconds to install the required files and may require the Windows NT 4.0 Server CD to be placed in your CD-ROM drive. Once this is finished, the Wizard displays a success message and the Next button changes to a Finished button.

11. Click Finish to exit to the Modem Setup Wizard.

Your modem should now be properly installed. Proceed to the next section to configure your modem for your RAS installation.

Configuring Your Modem(s)

Your modem's configurable properties are determined by the driver selected when you installed your modem. Because the Properties dialog box is derived from this driver, the look and configurable settings will vary according to the type, brand, and model of the selected device. Because configurable settings may vary widely, this section will not be able to give you specific instructions as to how to configure your modem. For this reason, you should refer to your hardware manufacturer's documentation for details about your modem's configuration settings. Also, you can refer to Chapter 11, "An Inside Look At Remote Access Service (RAS)," for explanations of applicable settings and protocols, such as flow control, error detection and handling, and compression.

N O T E In many cases, if you found the appropriate drivers for your modems, the default settings should be sufficient. ▧

To open the modem's Properties dialog box, follow these steps:

1. If the Modem Properties dialog box is not already showing, open it by selecting the Modems icon from the Control Panel.
2. Select the modem you want to configure and press the Properties button to bring up the modem's properties.
3. Select the desired settings. (Refer to your hardware manufacturer's documentation and to Chapter 11 for additional information about specific settings.)

At this point, all required hardware should be installed and working properly. It would be wise to test it to verify that it is properly set up and working before installing the RAS software. You can use software supplied with your modem or a program called HyperTerminal which is supplied with both Windows NT and Windows 95. HyperTerminal can be found in the Accessories group of your Start menu. If the Setup Wizard successfully detected your modem, you should not have to worry about testing other than to ensure that your phone cords are properly attached and working.

Installing RAS Software

This section walks you through the steps for installing the RAS software on your server. It presents detailed explanations of the choices offered to help you make an informed decision.

You will need the Windows NT Server CD-ROM for copying RAS files to your machine. Follow these steps to install RAS:

Part

III

Ch

12

1. Open the Control Panel.

2. Double-click the Network icon in the Control Panel to display the Network dialog box.

3. Click the Services tab (see Figure 12.9).

FIG. 12.9

The Services tab enables you to add, remove, and configure network services.

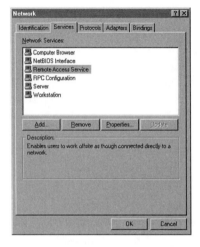

4. Click the <u>A</u>dd button to display a list of available <u>N</u>etwork Services in the Select Network Service dialog box, as shown in Figure 12.10.

FIG. 12.10

The Select Network Service dialog displays a list of available network services.

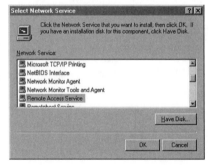

5. Select Remote Access Service from the list, and click OK. This displays the Windows NT Setup dialog box.

6. Enter the path to your Windows NT 4.0 Server CD-ROM and click <u>C</u>ontinue. Windows NT will begin copying the necessary files for RAS to the appropriate directory on your hard drive.

7. When the copy process has been completed, RAS Setup displays the Add RAS Device dialog box, as shown in Figure 12.11. If you installed your modems earlier, they should all be listed in the RAS Capable <u>D</u>evices drop-down list box. If you did not install your modems, click Install <u>M</u>odem and follow the modem installation instructions given in the "Installing Your Modems" section earlier in this chapter.

FIG. 12.11

The Add RAS Device dialog box enables you to add RAS devices by selecting from existing RAS-capable devices.

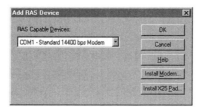

8. Choose one device and click OK. This takes you to the Remote Access Setup dialog box. At this point, the software has been successfully installed and the configuration section begins.

> **CAUTION**
>
> Do not hit the Continue button yet; you still need to configure your modem and network settings. If you leave now, the Setup program will go through binding the service to networking protocols and several other configuration steps and then tell you to reboot the machine before you have even configured RAS to your liking.

Configuring RAS

The Remote Access Setup dialog box enables you to add, remove, and configure RAS devices; and it lets you view and edit RAS network settings. If the Remote Access Setup dialog box, shown in Figure 12.12, is not already displayed, open it by opening the Network icon from the Control Panel, selecting the Services tab, and double-clicking the Remote Access Service entry in the Network Services list.

FIG. 12.12

The Remote Access Setup dialog box displays a list of the current RAS devices. Any devices that you have previously installed should be listed in the Port/ Device/Type box.

Adding, Removing, Cloning, and Configuring RAS Devices

The four buttons displayed at the bottom of the dialog box enable you to configure your ports and communication devices for use with RAS. The following list provides a description of these buttons:

- **Add**—Enables you to add additional devices for use by RAS.

- **Remove**—Enables you to remove an existing device installed for use by RAS.

- **Configure**—Enables you to change the configuration settings for the port. These settings enable you to specify whether the device will be used for receiving calls, dialing out, or both.

- **Clone**—Enables you to copy the modem setup information from one port to another so that the two ports are configured identically. This is a great time-saver when you are installing multiple modems of similar type on different ports.

To add devices, perform the following steps:

1. From the Remote Access Setup dialog box, click the Add button (or you can select an existing device and click the Clone button to copy all of its settings to a device entry).

2. Select an available device from the list. If no more RAS devices are available, you can click the Install Modem button to install additional modems. You can also install an X.25 Pad from this screen by clicking the Install X.25 Pad button.

3. Click OK to add this device and return to the Remote Access Setup dialog box.

N O T E For each device that you add, make sure you click Configure to choose how that device will be used.

The Clone button is particularly useful if you have several modems of the same type connected to multiport hardware. To clone a RAS device, perform the following steps:

1. Install all modems whose settings you want copied.

2. Select a modem from the Remote Access Setup dialog box whose configuration properties you want to be cloned to similar, installed modems. If no devices exist, follow the steps listed above for adding and configuration RAS devices.

3. Press the Clone button. The Setup program will process the list of installed RAS-capable devices that haven't been added yet and add each similar modem to the list of devices with the same configuration as the original selection. If the Setup program could not find any new modems similar to the selection, a message is displayed stating, `There are no more ports of the specified type to clone`.

To configure a RAS device, perform the following steps:

1. Click a modem in the device list box to select it (if it is not already selected), and then click Configure. The Configure Port Usage dialog box, illustrated in Figure 12.13, appears.

2. In the Configure Port Usage box, select whether the device will be used to receive calls, to dial out, or both (though not simultaneously).

 T I P You can use RAS for receiving calls and dialing out simultaneously by using multiple modems. A good method for testing your RAS installation—if you have multiple modems and lines—is to call your RAS server from your RAS server, thereby testing both the dial-out and receiving components.

FIG. 12.13

The Configure Port Usage dialog box enables you to select usage options for a communication device.

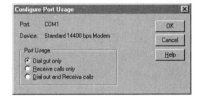

3. Click OK in the Settings dialog box. Then click OK in the Configure Port Usage dialog box to finish your device installation.

Once your ports have been configured to your liking, you need to configure your RAS network settings. The next section explains how to do this.

Network Protocol Configuration for RAS

The Network button on the Remote Access Setup dialog box brings you to the RAS Network Configuration dialog box, (see Figure 12.14). This dialog box allows you to select which networking protocols to use for both the client and the server. Client settings will only be enabled if you have at least one modem configured for dial-out. The server section will not even be seen unless you have at least one modem configured for receiving calls.

FIG. 12.14

The Network Configuration dialog box enables you to configure networking options for RAS. Server settings will only be visible if you have at least one modem configured for dial-out. Client settings will be grayed if no modems are configured for dial-out.

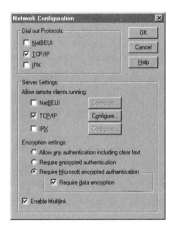

Part

III

Ch

12

For both dialing out and receiving calls, you will need to choose the networking protocols to use. The available options are listed and explained as follows:

■ TCP/IP was designed with distributed networking in mind. It is particularly good at handling the less predictable connections involved with modem communication. It is also the networking protocol of the Internet—for the above reasons. If you want to give remote users Internet connectivity, you will need to use TCP/IP.

■ NetBEUI is Microsoft's networking protocol. It was designed to add networking capabilities to Windows. It is the only networking protocol supported by Windows for

Workgroups. So, if your users will be dialing in from a Windows for Workgroups machine, and you are not using a third-party networking solution, such as Shiva, you will need to use NetBEUI.

■ IPX is predominantly used by NetWare servers. If you have NetWare servers as part of your enterprise network and you want to use RAS to connect to those servers, enable the IPX protocol.

▶ **See** "NetBEUI," **p. 111**

▶ **See** "Internetwork Packet Exchange/Sequenced Package Exchange (IPX/SPX)," **p. 111**

▶ **See** "Transmission Control Protocol/Internet Protocol (TCP/IP)," **p. 112**

Configuring Dial-Out Protocols   In the Dial-Out Protocols combo box at the top of the Network Configuration dialog box, check the appropriate boxes for enabling different dial-out protocols based on your preferences. This section only enables you to choose which protocols to use; setting the parameters of these protocols can be done with the RAS client software supplied with Windows NT or whatever operating system is being used. Client software is covered in Chapter 13, "Implementing Dial-Up Networking Clients."

Configuring RAS Server Network Protocol Settings   The options available under the Server Settings combo box in the Network Configuration dialog box enable you to determine and configure your RAS server's available networking protocols and encryption settings. The choice of protocols depends on your enterprise needs and available protocols being used on your existing network. Do not enable any unnecessary network protocols, as each protocol requires additional network bandwidth and can cause significant performance loss as additional queries must be issued when locating a network resource.

 TIP   The RAS clients can also specify what protocols they want to use for remote connectivity to prevent unnecessary overhead. (Usually, just one is needed.)

Configuration options and procedures for each of the available networking protocols are discussed in the following sections.

NetBEUI   If you want to have users connect to your RAS server—and optionally, the corporate network—using NetBEUI, perform these steps:

1. To allow NetBEUI connections to your RAS server, check the NetBEUI check box in the Server Settings section of the Network Configuration dialog box.

2. Click the Configure button adjacent to the NetBEUI option. The RAS server NetBEUI Configuration dialog box appears (see Figure 12.15).

FIG. 12.15

NetBEUI connectivity options for the RAS server can be configured through the NetBEUI Configuration dialog box.

3. Choose whether to allow full network access or access to the RAS server only for remote NetBEUI clients.

4. Click OK to save your NetBEUI configuration settings.

The Network Configuration dialog box reappears so that you can configure additional protocols.

TCP/IP To configure Transmission Control Protocol/Internet Protocol, perform the following steps:

1. To allow TCP/IP connections, check the TC**P**/IP option.

2. Click the C**o**nfigure button to display the RAS Server TCP/IP Configuration dialog box, as shown in Figure 12.16.

FIG. 12.16
The TCP/IP Configuration dialog box enables you to select TCP/IP settings for connections to your RAS server.

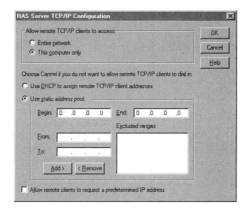

N O T E Each protocol configuration dialog box contains a section for enabling network access options for the selected protocol. ■

3. Choose whether to allow full network access or access to the RAS server only for remote TCP/IP clients.

4. Select the method of assigning IP addresses to dial-in remote clients. One of three alternatives is possible, as follows:

  - **Use D̲HCP to Assign Remote TCP/IP Client Addresses**—DHCP stands for *Dynamic Host Configuration Protocol.* This option enables DHCP assignment of TCP/IP addresses. This enables the RAS server to dynamically obtain TCP/IP addresses from the DHCP server for assignment to remote user PCs connecting to the network using RAS. This method is most useful for minimizing administration overhead.

  - **Use S̲tatic Address Pool**—Assign TCP/IP client addresses from a static pool of available addresses. The static pool sets aside a range of TCP/IP addresses for use by the RAS server for assignment to remote user PCs. Use the B̲egin and E̲nd boxes to specify the static pool address range. You can also use the From and To boxes to exclude certain addresses from the assigned pool. This provides added flexibility for best using available TCP/IP addresses.

- **Allow Remote Clients to Request a Predetermined IP Address**—With this option enabled, users can request a specific IP address. This enables users to always use the same IP address.

5. Click OK to close the RAS Server TCP/IP Configuration dialog box and complete your TCP/IP configuration for RAS.

The Network Configuration dialog box reappears so that you can configure additional protocols.

▶ **See** "Dynamic Host Configuration Protocol (DHCP)," **p. 256**

IPX   The IPX check box enables you to configure the options for enabling IPX/SPX connections using RAS. To configure IPX, follow these steps:

1. Check the IPX check box in the Server Settings area of the Network Configuration dialog box

2. Click the adjacent Configure button to display the RAS Server IPX Configuration dialog box, as shown in Figure 12.17.

FIG. 12.17

RAS allows you to select specific connectivity options for IPX through the IPX Configuration dialog box.

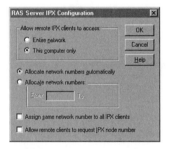

3. Choose whether to allow full network access or access to the RAS server only for remote IPX clients.

4. Select a method for allocating IPX network numbers. One of four alternatives is possible, as follows:

- **Allocate Network Numbers Automatically**—RAS software uses the NetWare Router Information Protocol (RIP) to determine unique network numbers that are available for allocation. The RAS server then allocates that number to the remote client. This method is useful because it requires the least administration overhead for assigning IPX addresses.

- **Allocate Network Numbers**—This is the manual method of allocating the network numbers. This method can be the best choice if you want to have more control over network number assignments for security and monitoring purposes.

To exercise this alternative, simply click the appropriate option button and then enter the first network number in the From box. The RAS server automatically calculates the ending number for you based on the number of available ports.

- **Assign Same Network Number to All IPX Clients**—Enable this check box to assign the same network number to all IPX clients using either the automatic or manual methods.

- **Allow Remote Clients to Request IPX Node Number**—Enable this check box to allow remote clients to request a specific IPX number. This method presents a potential security risk. It enables a remote client to use a previously connected client's node number and potentially impersonate his or her access privileges.

5. Click OK to close the RAS Server IPX Configuration dialog box.

  ▶ **See** "Internetwork Packet Exchange/Sequenced Package Exchange (IPX/SPX)," **p. 111**

User Authentication Settings

This section discusses the encryption techniques used by RAS for authenticating user logon and password information. Encryption settings are one aspect RAS security options used to prevent unauthorized users from gaining access to your server and/or domain. Users can only log on to your RAS server if they are using a RAS-enabled account for the domain. Encryption settings are used to prevent someone from capturing logon and password information by "listening in" to a logon session. To set encryption options, perform the following steps:

1. If you performed the steps in the previous section, you should already have the RAS Network Configuration dialog box open (refer to Figure 12.14). If not, from the Remote Access Setup dialog box, click the Network button. This will display the RAS Network Configuration dialog box.

2. In the Server Settings combo box, select an encryption setting. The possible encryption options are as follows:

   - **Allow Any Authentication Including Clear Text**—Enabling this option button permits remote clients to connect using clear text-based authentication. This method presents a security risk because the logon ID and password are transmitted over an unsecured connection using regular text.

   - **Require Encrypted Authentication**—Enabling this option button permits remote clients to connect using encrypted authentication. This method encrypts the logon ID and password before transmission over the connection line.

N O T E With Require Encrypted Authentication selected, Microsoft supports a variety of encryption algorithms including MS_CHAP, DES, and SPAP. To force the use of MS_CHAP—the most secure password authentication protocol supported by RAS—select Require Microsoft Encrypted Authentication. All of these protocols are described in Chapter 11, "An Inside Look at Remote Access Service (RAS)." ▪

Part

III

Ch

12

- **Require Microsoft Encrypted Authentication**—Enabling this option permits connection using the Microsoft security model. The logon ID and password are authenticated by the Windows NT Server logon service.

3. Enable the Require Data Encryption check box if you require all data (not just the logon ID and password) sent over the remote link to be encrypted. This option is only available when the Require Microsoft Encrypted Authentication option is enabled. Otherwise, it is grayed out and unavailable.

N O T E   As discussed in Chapter 11, RAS uses the RC4 encryption algorithm for encrypting and decrypting data. RC4 is popular because of its speed and proven security. Because RC4 does require some rather involved computations for encryption, it will slow system performance somewhat. If you are not transmitting sensitive information, you can improve performance by leaving this option disabled. ▉

4. Click OK in the Network Configuration dialog box and finish your RAS configuration. The Remote Access Setup dialog box reappears.

The final setting in the Network Configuration dialog box is the Enable Multilink check box. Multilink allows one network session to occur over multiple physical connections. The most common use of multilink is to bundle the two B-channels of an ISDN modem into a single logical connection. Multilink can also be used to bundle any two modems together to increase bandwidth.

▶ **See** "RAS Multilink PPP," **p. 324**

All configuration steps should now be complete. To finish your installation, perform the following steps:

1. Click Continue in the Remote Access Setup dialog box to complete RAS setup and redisplay the Windows NT Setup dialog box containing the path to the installation files.

2. Click Continue in the Windows NT Setup dialog box after verifying that the displayed path to the Windows NT Server installation files is still correct. Setup copies additional files based upon the previously selected protocols and settings for the ports and modems to be used with RAS.

3. When the copy process is complete, the Windows NT Setup dialog box containing the path to the installation files appears again. Click Continue to close the Windows NT Setup dialog box and display the Remote Access Service Setup message box informing you that the Remote Access Service has been installed.

4. When you have finished reading the information in the Remote Access Service Setup message box, click OK to close the box and redisplay the Network Settings dialog box.

5. Click OK to update the network settings, configurations, and bindings.

6. When the network has been updated and reconfigured, the Network Settings Changed message box appears informing you that the network settings have changed and that you must exit and restart Windows NT Server for the new settings to take effect. Either click Restart Now to automatically exit and restart Windows NT Server immediately, or

click Don't Restart Now to close the message box and redisplay the Control Panel window.

7. If you clicked Don't Restart Now, close Control Panel. RAS will start after the next server restart.

The installation and configuration of your RAS server is now complete.

Using the Remote Access Admin Tool

The Remote Access Admin tool included with RAS enables you to set user permissions and monitor active connections on RAS servers throughout your enterprise. If you have multiple RAS servers in your organizations, you can manage all of them from a single Windows NT Server or Windows NT Workstation computer. If you want to configure network settings or add, remove, or configure devices, you will need to refer to the previous section "Configuring RAS."

 TIP If you are familiar with the Remote Access tool provided in Windows NT 3.51, you'll find that except for the new Windows 95 look and feel, the tool is almost exactly the same.

The Remote Access Admin tool can be started from the Administrative Tools group in the Start menu. Figure 12.18 shows the main screen for the Remote Access Admin program.

FIG. 12.18

Remote Access Admin tool can be used to administer all of your RAS servers on the enterprise network.

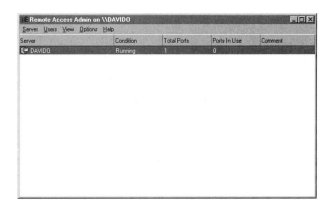

Part

III

Ch

12

The Remote Access Admin tool displays the following information about available RAS servers:

- **Server**—The name of the computer running RAS.
- **Condition**—The status of the RAS service on the server. Options are Running, Stopped, and Paused.
- **Total Ports**—The number of RAS ports configured for use on the machine.
- **Ports In Use**—The ports currently being used by remote users for connection to the server.

■ **Comment**—A descriptive statement about the RAS server machine, such as the machine location.

N O T E   The Remote Access Admin tool is installed by default as part of the RAS server installation process. ▓

The following sections detail some of the administration and monitoring capabilities of the Remote Access Admin tool.

Selecting RAS Servers for Administration

The Remote Access Admin tool enables you to select the RAS server you want to administer by selecting the appropriate PC or domain. You can select a single RAS server to manage, or you can select a complete domain, which would include administering and monitoring all RAS servers within that domain.

N O T E   If you are running RAS on a Windows NT domain controller machine, the default option is to manage RAS servers in the domain. If you are running RAS on a Windows NT Server, the default option is to manage the RAS server on that machine only. ▓

To select a RAS server or domain for administration, perform the following steps:

1. Start Remote Access Admin tool.
2. Choose Server, Select Domain or Server to display a Select Domain dialog box, such as the one illustrated in Figure 12.19.

FIG. 12.19
You can manage all RAS servers in a domain by choosing Server, Select Domain or Server from the menu and then selecting the desired domain.

3. In the Select Domain dialog box, the Select Domain list box shows all the available domains. Select the desired domain from the list or type the name into the Domain text box.
4. Check the Low Speed Connection check box if the connection to the RAS server or domain is going to be over a dial-up link.
5. Click OK to continue, and the RAS servers in that domain will be listed when you return to the main Remote Access Admin window.

After you have selected the RAS server or domain, you can administer it or monitor its operation using the Remote Access Admin tool.

Start, Stop, Pause, or Continue RAS

From a machine with the Remote Access Admin tool, you can start, stop, pause, and continue the RAS on any machine that you proper access rights for.

Starting a RAS   To start RAS, perform the following steps in Remote Access Admin:

1. Choose Server, Start Remote Access Service to display the Start Remote Access Service dialog box (see Figure 12.20).

FIG. 12.20
Start a Remote Access
Service by choosing the
appropriate option from
the Server menu.

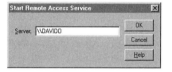

2. Type in the RAS server name by using the \\<computername> notation, and click OK.

3. RAS attempts to start the Remote Access Service on the specified server and displays the updated status on the main Remote Access Admin screen.

Stoping a RAS   To stop RAS, perform the following steps in Remote Access Admin:

1. Select the RAS server on which you want to stop the RAS by selecting it from the list.

2. Choose Server, Stop Remote Access Service to display the Stop Remote Access Service dialog box shown in Figure 12.21.

FIG. 12.21
Stop a Remote Access
Service by choosing the
appropriate option from
the Server menu.

3. Click Yes to stop the service or No to cancel the operation.

Part
III

Ch
12

CAUTION

Stopping or pausing a RAS while users are connected will disconnect those users. If possible, you should use the Remote Access Admin tool to send a message to connected users stating that you will be stopping the RAS and, if appropriate, give them an appropriate amount of time and a phone number where they can contact you if they need you to wait a few additional minutes while they finish a transmission.

4. If you click Yes, RAS attempts to stop the Remote Access Service on the specified server and displays the updated status on the main Remote Access Admin screen. If RAS was unable to stop the service, it will display a message stating the reason.

Pausing a RAS   Pausing allows you to prevent any additional users from connecting to the server, while allowing existing connections to remain. This is useful in cases where you know you will need to shut down the server but do not need to do it immediately and you do not want to force disconnections.

To pause RAS, perform the following steps in Remote Access Admin:

1. Select the RAS server that you want to pause the RAS on by selecting it from the list.

2. Choose Server, Pause Remote Access Service.

3. RAS attempts to pause the Remote Access Service on the specified server and displays the updated status on the main Remote Access Admin screen.

Continuing a RAS   Continuing a paused RAS will allow new users to connect to the RAS server. To continue RAS, perform the following steps in Remote Access Admin:

1. Select the RAS server that you want to continue the RAS on by selecting it from the list.

2. Choose Server, Continue Remote Access Service.

3. RAS attempts to continue the Remote Access Service on the specified server and displays the updated status on the main Remote Access Admin screen.

You can perform the preceding steps on any available RAS server within your enterprise network from a central computer.

Monitoring RAS Ports

The Remote Access Admin tool can be used to monitor the status of your RAS ports periodically to determine their status and user activity. To monitor RAS ports using Remote Access Admin, perform the following steps:

1. Select a RAS server from the list. Choose Server, Communication Ports to display the Communication Ports dialog box, as shown in Figure 12.22. The Communication Ports dialog box lists all the ports configured for RAS usage on the selected server. It also displays any users connected to the port and the time the user started the RAS connection.

2. Select a Port and click Port Status to obtain detailed information about that port. This opens the Port Status dialog box (see Figure 12.23).

3. Click OK to close the Port Status dialog box and return to the Communication Ports dialog box.

4. If any users are connected to the RAS server, you can disconnect them by selecting the appropriate port and clicking Disconnect User.

FIG. 12.22
Monitor the status of your RAS ports using the Remote Access Admin tool.

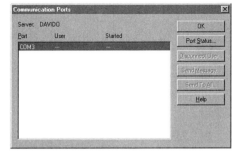

FIG. 12.23
The Port Status dialog box displays detailed information about a configured port and the activity on that port.

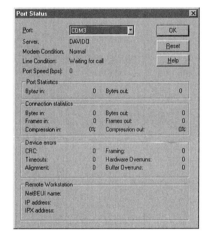

Part

III

Ch

12

CAUTION

You should always warn users before forcing a disconnection. To do this you can use the Admin tool's Send Message button. If possible, give them the time and a method to reply to you before disconnecting them. Forcing a disconnection may cause the user to lose important information or may require them to restart a lengthy download process.

5. You can also send text messages to a selected user or to all connected users by using the Send Message or Send to All buttons.

6. Click OK when you are finished to return to the Remote Access Admin main screen.

Monitoring RAS Connections

RAS enables you to monitor all remote connections by user or by domain. To monitor users connected to your RAS servers, follow these steps:

1. Choose Users, Active Users.

2. The Remote Access Users dialog box appears, as shown in Figure 12.24. All users connected to the RAS servers across the domain are displayed with the server name they are connected to and the time the connection started.

FIG. 12.24
Monitor RAS connections across your domain using the Remote Access Admin tool.

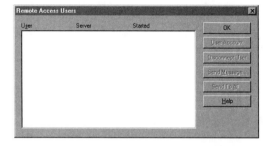

3. You can disconnect a user by selecting the user and clicking Disconnect User (see the previous Caution).

4. You can also send text messages to a selected user or to all connected users by using the Send Message or Send to All buttons.

5. Click OK when you are finished to return to the Remote Access Admin main screen.

Setting User Permissions

The Remote Access Admin tool enables administrators to set up access privileges and dial-in permissions for user accounts in the Windows NT domain. A remote user must have an account on the RAS server or the Windows NT domain to be able to dial-in using RAS.

RAS uses the Windows NT integrated security model to authenticate user logon IDs and passwords. However, you must use the Remote Access Admin tool to set up dial-in permissions for remote users. Use the following procedure to set up dial-in permissions for remote users:

1. Select the server or domain for which you want to set dial-in permissions.

2. Choose Users, Permissions to display the Remote Access Permissions dialog box, as shown in Figure 12.25. This dialog box lists all user accounts available on the server or the domain.

FIG. 12.25
You can grant users dial-in access permission using the Remote Access Permissions dialog box.

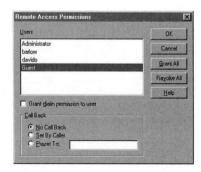

3. You can use the <u>G</u>rant All or Re<u>v</u>oke All buttons to grant or deny dial-in permissions to all user accounts.

N O T E The <u>G</u>rant All and Re<u>v</u>oke All buttons are not available when using a low-speed connection. You must set permissions for one user at a time. ▮

4. You can also set dial-in permissions for an individual account by selecting the account, checking the Grant <u>D</u>ial-in Permission to User box, and clicking OK.

5. The <u>C</u>all Back options determine the method users can use to connect to the RAS server. Using callback, the RAS server accepts a call from a remote user, determines who the user is and from where he is calling, disconnects him, and immediately calls him back to establish a RAS connection.

T I P The callback feature is useful for users who must make long distance calls to connect to the server. Remote users can use the callback option to charge long distance connect charges to a central office number rather than their personal phone numbers. This has the added benefit of consolidating billing records.

Callback is also an effective security measure. Individual user accounts can be configured so as to require the RAS Server to call the user back at a predetermined number before allowing access to the network, making it extremely difficult for an intruder to use the account from another location.

The available options are the following:

- **<u>N</u>o Call Back**—Users dial-in and connect to the RAS server.
- **<u>S</u>et By Caller**—Users provide the server with the callback phone numbers. When this option is enabled, the RAS server prompts the caller for a callback number. This is useful for remote users who travel from place to place and do not have access to a regular number. This can also be an effective security measure as all callback numbers are logged.
- **<u>P</u>reset To**—When this option is enabled, the RAS server initiates a callback to the client at the number indicated in the box. This is a very effective security measure as it only allows users to call from a specified number. However, it can not be used for mobile users or users who need to dial-in from multiple locations.

6. Click OK when you are finished setting permissions to return to the Remote Access Admin main window.

The Remote Access Admin tool is a powerful program for administering and monitoring your enterprise-wide RAS servers. Its single point of management and simplicity of use make it an ideal tool for the job.

Part

III

Ch

12

From Here...

This chapter provides information on the implementation and administration of the server side of Windows NT Remote Access Service. Configuration details are explained, and many of the available configuration options are described to give you a better understanding of some of the more common protocol constraints and settings. The Remote Access Admin tool is also described, and several of the common administrative procedures using this tool are detailed. For more information on these and related issues, see the following chapters:

- To learn about basic concepts concerning network protocols supported by Windows NT and Microsoft BackOffice, see Chapter 4, "Enterprise Planning and Implementation."

- To review basic installation and setup procedures for Windows NT Server, see Chapter 5, "Implementing Windows NT Server."

- To review information on managing and controlling Windows NT Server networks, see Chapter 7, "Administering Windows NT Server."

- To gain a better understanding of the popular TCP/IP transport protocol, see Chapter 9, "Using TCP/IP with Windows NT Server."

## CHAPTER 13

Implementing Dial-Up Networking Clients

by Fred Sebestyen

Starting with the release of Windows for Workgroups (WFWG), and continuing through Windows NT 4.0 today, all of Microsoft's graphical desktop operating systems have the capability to connect to remote networks via modem. The connectivity provided by this software enables people outside of the office to connect to the company network and use network resources just as if they were locally attached. Once a connection is established, the RAS session is virtually transparent to the client computer. ∎

Remote Access Service

Find out how easy it is to configure client computers to connect to your corporate network using Remote Access Service (RAS).

What do you need to use Remote Access Service?

Get an overview of the necessary hardware and connection requirements for a RAS client.

Configuring Dial-Up Networking on Windows clients

You will be guided through detailed instructions for installing client software using each of the Microsoft desktops: Windows for Workgroups, Windows 95, Windows NT 3.51, and Windows NT 4.0.

Configuring clients for Multilink Channel Aggregation

You will be given an overview of what Multilink Channel Aggregation is and how to configure clients for Multilink Channel Aggregation.

Configuring clients to use Point-to-Point Tunneling Protocol

What is Point-to-Point Tunneling Protocol (PPTP)? You will be given an overview of PPTP and guided through the process of setting up and configuring a PPTP client.

Preparing to Use Remote Access Service (RAS)

Many desktop and laptop systems sold today come equipped with a modem. If your system is running Windows for Workgroups, Windows 95, or Windows NT and you have access to a telephone line at your remote location, you probably already have everything you need to use RAS. If you don't currently have a modem, there are many brands and speeds to choose from at a wide range of prices. A faster modem will quickly offset the higher cost in time savings. It is always a good idea to check the Hardware Compatibility List before purchasing a modem to ensure that it will work with your operating system. Methods for using ISDN lines and multiple modems are discussed later in this chapter in the section "Preparing the Client for Multilink PPP."

> **N O T E**   A dial-up connection is only as fast as the slowest modem being used. If your client computer has a 28.8 modem. and the server you are dialing in to only has a 14.4 modem, then your connection will be at most 14.4. ■

Configuring Dial-Up Networking on Windows Clients

RAS has been an integral part of the Microsoft desktop. It supports a wide spectrum of computing desktop software and a wide variety of connectivity hardware. From the most basic hardware—an analog phone line and modem—to the more advanced ISDN lines and terminal adapters (often referred to as *digital modems* or *ISDN modems*), they are all supported with Microsoft's RAS client. Also, as you will see in the "Preparing the Client for Multilink PPP" section using Windows NT 4.0, you can actually use multiple devices to increase the bandwidth on dial-up clients by using *Multilink Channel Aggregation*.

Configuring the Windows for Workgroups Client

With the release of Windows for Workgroups, Microsoft incorporated client software for remote computing into the desktop operating system. Windows for Workgroups also shipped with Mail and Schedule+ included. These applications were designed to work in a network environment and as such, Microsoft provided the means for people who weren't physically in the office to connect to the office network. This section guides you through the process of installing RAS under Windows for Workgroups.

Assuming you have installed Windows for Workgroups with the default settings and did not elect to install networking, you must first install the Remote Access Service in order to use Dial-Up Networking.

Installing Remote Access   The first time that you attempt to use Remote Access, you will be prompted to install the Remote Access Service. The following procedure will guide you through installing the Remote Access Service:

1. Click the Remote Access icon. You will get a dialog box giving you information on Remote Access. This dialog box gives a short introduction as to what Remote Access is and instructs you how to install the service.

2. Press the Install button to begin the installation of Remote Access (see Figure 13.1).

N O T E If you did not have a network card in your computer when you installed Windows for Workgroups, and you installed with the default settings, you do not have Microsoft Networking installed. Microsoft Networking must be installed in order to use Remote Access. ■

FIG. 13.1

The RAS install program will ask you if you want to install Microsoft Windows Network. Click Yes and the Network and Remote Access software will be installed.

Remote Access

The component that you want to install requires Microsoft Windows Network.

Do you want to install Microsoft Workgroup Network now?

[Yes] [No]

3. Click Yes. The Remote Access software and the Microsoft Networking software will begin to copy to your computer.

N O T E When you choose to install Microsoft Networking, you will be prompted to insert the requested WFWG disks in order to install networking and the Remote Access service. In the Remote Access Configuration dialog box, you will be asked what type of modem you have and what port it is connected to. ■

4. Scroll through the list of modems and find the modem that you have connected to your computer. Select the appropriate Modem and COM port and then click OK (see Figure 13.2). Your modem is now installed for Remote Access.

FIG. 13.2

The Remote Access Configuration box is used to tell RAS what kind of modem you have and what port it is connected to.

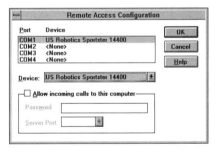

Remote Access Configuration

Port	Device
COM1	US Robotics Sportster 14400
COM2	<None>
COM3	<None>
COM4	<None>

[OK] [Cancel] [Help]

Device: US Robotics Sportster 14400

☐ Allow incoming calls to this computer

Password

Server Port

Part
III

Ch
13

N O T E After your modem is installed on the communications port, you will get a Microsoft Windows Network Names dialog box. This dialog box is used to get information from you to identify your computer for networking. When you are connected to a Microsoft network, everyone connected to the network will be able to see the other computers that are also connected to the network. The name that you enter here will be used for this identification. You will be prompted for the User Name, Workgroup, and Computer Name.

The dialog box defaults the username to the name that you entered when you first installed Windows. The Workgroup should be changed to the domain name of the network that you will be dialing in to, and the computer name should be something that will identify you on the network to other people. ■

5. Make the appropriate entries for User Name, Workgroup, and Computer Name and click OK. The remaining networking software is installed onto your system. When the networking software installation has completed, the system will have to be rebooted.

6. Click the Restart Computer button to reboot your system. After you reboot your computer and startup Windows, you will get a network logon dialog box. This box establishes your identity for the network.

7. Enter your username and password in the dialog box. For consistency, you should use the username and password that you use on your corporate network. The system then asks if you want to create a password-list file for your username. The password-list file is an encrypted list of the passwords you use to connect to shared resources. If your password is not in this file, you will be prompted for a password when you attempt to use a shared resource. If your password is in this file, your connection is re-established without prompting for a password.

8. Select Yes and continue. A Password Confirmation dialog box will appear.

9. Re-enter your password and click OK.

Connecting to Your Network Using Remote Access   Your system should now be configured to use Dial-Up Networking with Windows for Workgroups. To begin using Remote Access, perform the following steps:

1. Click the Remote Access icon in the Network Program Group. The first time that you use Remote Access, it will prompt you that your phonebook is empty (see Figure 13.3). You will be asked if you want to create an entry for the phonebook.

FIG. 13.3

Phonebook entries allow you to make a dial-up connection by picking an entry from a selection list.

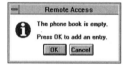

2. Click OK to create an entry for your network. The Add Phonebook Entry dialog box appears. Setting up a phonebook entry is a simple process. It is basically the same as making an entry in a personal phonebook.

3. Enter an Entry Name. This is the name that you would like to use when referring to this entry in the phonebook.

4. Enter the Phone Number of the computer that you will be connecting to.

5. Enter a Description. Provide a meaningful description for your connection, and then click OK.

You are now ready to use Dial-Up Networking to connect with your corporate network. Follow this procedure to start a Remote Access session:

1. In the Remote Access dialog box, highlight the phonebook entry that you would like to use.

2. Click the Dial button. The Authentication screen prompts you for information that is required by the network that you are connecting to. The Authentication screen appears only the first time that you attempt to use the connection (see Figure 13.4).

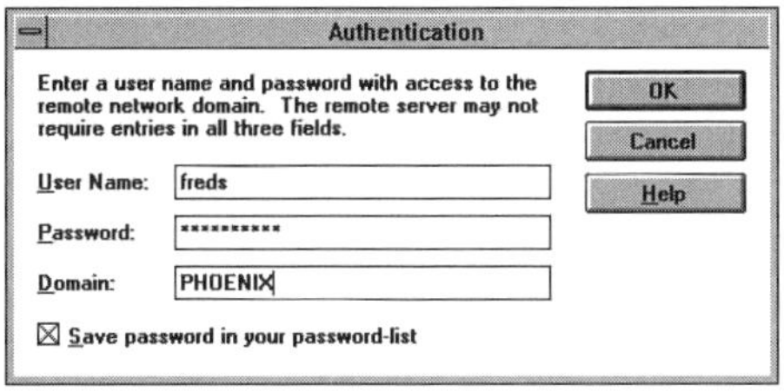

FIG. 13.4
The first time that you use a new phonebook entry, you are prompted by an Authentication dialog box.

3. Enter your User Name and Password for the domain and the Domain Name that you will be connecting to. Make sure that you enter the proper username, password, and domain name because these are going to be used for authentication on the network.

4. When you are finished entering the required information, click OK.

Your system is now set up to use the Remote Access Service. Click dial and connect to your network.

If your network rejects your attempts to connect, check the Network program item in the Control Panel. Select Program Manager, Main, Control Panel. In the Microsoft Windows Network dialog box, click the Startup button. In the Startup Settings dialog box, you must make sure the Log On to Windows NT or LAN Manager Domain check box is selected (see Figure 13.5). Also, make sure that you have the correct Domain Name entered in the dialog box.

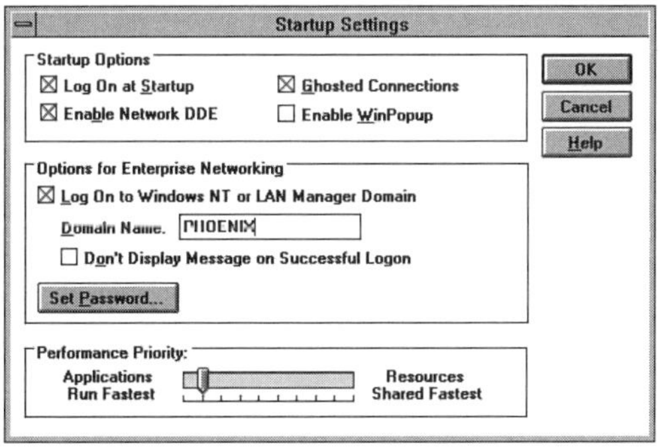

FIG. 13.5
The Startup Settings for Remote Access shows the name of the domain that you are connecting to and your selected startup options.

Part III
Ch
13

CAUTION
The Remote Access Service on Windows for Workgroups only supports the NetBEUI protocol. If your server does not have the NetBEUI protocol installed, you will not be able to connect to your network using Windows for Workgroups.

When you click dial, your modem will access the telephone line and begin dialing your phonebook entry. Depending on the speaker options you have set on your modem, you can hear the phone being dialed, the ring, and then the server's modem pick up and finally the modems negotiating a connection. You will connect to the remote computer and the authentication information that you entered in the Authentication dialog box will be verified by the server (see Figure 13.6). If you entered the correct information, you will be connected and registered on the network.

 If your modem does not respond, there are a couple of things you should check. If you have an external modem, make sure that it is turned on and connected to the appropriate COM port. If you have an internal modem, make sure that the COM port that the modem is using does not conflict with the COM port of your mouse or other serial device. Typically, COM ports 1 and 3 use the same IRQ as do COM ports 2 and 4. You cannot have a device using COM 1 and another device using COM 3 at the same time. The same applies for COM 2 and 4.

FIG. 13.6
After the modems connect, your login information is verified and authenticated on the server.

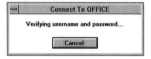

Once you are registered on the network, you can access computers, disk drives, printers, and any other resources on the network just as if you were locally attached. The connection will be limited to the speed of your modem but you will still have full access to your network. Figure 13.7 shows the computers and shared resources on the Phoenix domain.

FIG. 13.7
When you are authenticated on the domain, you can see all of the computers and shared resources on the network.

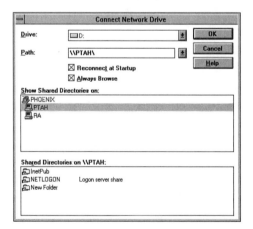

Configuring the Windows 95 Client

With Windows 95 and Dial-Up Networking, Microsoft has made remote computing almost effortless. To connect your mobile or home computer to your office network, all you need is an analog phone line, a supported modem, and the Dial-Up Networking that comes with Windows 95. In this section, you will install the Dial-Up Networking client on Windows 95 for a TCP/IP network.

Dial-Up Networking is not installed by default with Windows 95, but it is almost automatic. To use Dial-Up Networking on your system, you must have a modem that is supported by Windows 95.

This section will guide you through the process of installing your modem on Windows 95 and Dial-Up Networking on your computer.

N O T E Installing a modem consists of two parts: physical installation and software configuration. The physical installation of your modem—connecting it to your computer—is beyond the scope of this book, but should be covered by the documentation included with your modem. The installation described here is the process of telling Windows 95 that there is a modem available and what kind of modem it is. ■

Windows 95 makes installing your modem very easy. Before you begin installing your modem software, you should check to make certain that your modem is ready. If you have an internal modem, make sure that it is properly inserted in your system. If you have an external modem, connect it to your computer's serial port and turn it on.

Installing Your Modem Under Windows 95   Follow these steps in order to begin the installation of your modem:

1. Go to the Start menu and select Start, Settings, Control Panel.
2. Within Control Panel, click the Modem icon. This will start the Install New Modem Wizard (see Figure 13.8). The Install New Modem Wizard will step you through the process of installing your modem.

FIG. 13.8

The Install New Modem Wizard guides you through the installation of your modem.

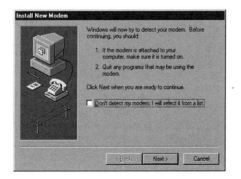

Part
III

Ch
13

N O T E Microsoft has done an excellent job in developing the Modem Detection Wizard for Windows 95. It detects most manufacturer's modems automatically. ▇

3. Leave the Don't Detect My Modem; I Will Select It From a List check box blank and click Next. The Wizard will search your COM ports to determine what type of modem you have and which COM port it is connected to.

4. When the Wizard is finished analyzing your system, you will get a Verify Modem dialog box. It will show you the modem that it detected. If the Wizard finds your modem and selects the right one, click Next.

N O T E If you want to change the modem manually, click Change. You will be presented with a dialog box of manufacturers and models. Look through the list of manufacturers on the left and find the maker of your modem. When you select the manufacturer, the list on the right shows the modem models. Look through the list and select your modem.

If your modem is not in the list, you still have the option of clicking Have Disk. This option enables you to select your modem manually provided that you have a driver disk from the manufacturer. ▇

5. Click OK to continue. Windows will install the proper software for your modem. You will get a message from the Install New Modem dialog box telling you that your modem was set up successfully.

6. Click Finish.

7. You will get a Modem Properties dialog box with the name of your installed modem. At this screen, you can verify that the correct modem was installed. Click OK to continue. The modem is now installed and you are ready to install Dial-Up Networking.

Installing Dial-Up Networking   Dial-Up Networking is not installed by default during the installation of Windows 95. Follow these steps to install Dial-Up Networking.

1. Go to the Control Panel.

 TIP You can install Dial-Up Networking when you initially install Windows 95 by selecting the Communications icon in the Add Windows components dialog box.

2. Click the Add/Remove Programs icon in the Control Panel. You will see the Add/Remove Program Properties dialog box. This is where you can install new applications under Windows 95, as well as add new components, such as Dial-Up Networking.

3. Click the Windows Setup tab. This is where you can install additional components of Windows 95 that do not install by default.

4. Select the Communications check box and click the Details button. Make sure that Dial-Up Networking is selected (see Figure 13.9).

FIG. 13.9

Though it is not installed by default, adding Dial-Up Networking to Windows 95 is a simple procedure.

5. Click OK. This is the only communications component that you will need for the RAS client.

6. Click OK and Windows will prompt you to put in the installation disk.

7. Put the disk in the appropriate drive and click OK. Windows will copy the necessary files from the disk and proceed to install the networking software.

8. When the software installation is complete, Windows prompts you to restart your system. Restart your system after the Add/Remove Program Properties dialog box completes.

Configuring Dial-Up Networking When your system restarts, you will have Dial-Up Networking installed on your computer. Before you begin using Dial-Up Networking, you must check the installed network protocols on your computer. The network protocol that you have installed on your client must be consistent with the network protocol that is supported by the host computer you are connecting to. The Windows 95 client supports a number of networking protocols, including those of other vendors, such as Novell, but we are using Microsoft's TCP/IP in this example. Follow these steps:

1. Click the Network icon within the Control Panel. The Networking program item is where you install and configure the networking components of Windows 95. Make sure the Configuration tab is on top of the Network dialog box. This screen shows the default networking components that are installed (see Figure 13.10). You should see Client for Microsoft Networks, Client for NetWare Networks, Dial-Up Adapter, IPX/SPX-compatible Protocol and NetBEUI installed.

   We are configuring our client for a TCP/IP network and since TCP/IP is not installed by default on Windows 95, we will be installing and using the TCP/IP protocol stack.

2. Click the Add button. You will see a list of network components that you can install.

3. Highlight Protocol and then click Add.

4. Select Microsoft from the Manufacturers list box and TCP/IP from the Network Protocols list box, and then click OK (see Figure 13.11).

Part
III

Ch
13

FIG. 13.10

The Network Configu-
ration dialog box shows
you which network
components you have
installed. It shows your
installed clients,
adapters, protocols,
and services.

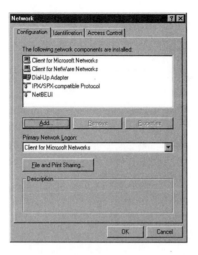

FIG. 13.11

Installing a Network
Protocol is a simple
procedure under
Windows 95.

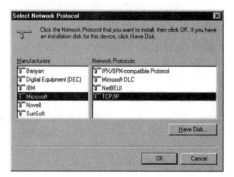

Removing Unnecessary Protocols   After you complete the previous steps and the files have
been copied, the TCP/IP protocol is installed on your system along with the default protocols.
In an effort to keep your system running "lean and mean," you should remove any unnecessary networking components that install themselves by default. In this example, you are connecting to a Microsoft network using TCP/IP, so you will not be using the Client for NetWare
components or any of the other networking protocols.

Follow these steps to remove any unnecessary networking components:

1. To delete the Client for NetWare Networks, click the Client for NetWare Networks and
    click Remove.

2. Select IPX/SPX-compatible Protocol and click Remove.

3. Click NetBEUI Protocol and click Remove.

4. Click OK to continue the installation.

5. Click Yes to continue.

As you can see, Microsoft has made it very convenient to add and remove networking components within Windows 95. Windows installs and configures the networking software and tells you that the system must be restarted before the settings will take effect.

 T I P If your network uses an IPX/SPX-compatible protocol or the NetBEUI protocol, you must use the same protocol for the dial-up client. Your server could be configured with any of these protocols, so check with your system administrator if you need help.

N O T E You should not have any unnecessary networking components or protocols installed on your computer. Always remove any unnecessary components. ■

Making a New Connection   The following steps will guide you through the establishment of a dial-up connection:

1. After your system is rebooted and Windows restarts, you are greeted with a logon dialog box. Enter your Username and Password, and then click OK. This should be consistent with the username that you use to log on to your remote computer.

2. Click My Computer and you should now see a Dial-Up Networking folder. In order to use Dial-Up Networking, you must first create a connection for the computer that you want to dial to. This will be done for every dial-up connection that you have on your Windows 95 client.

3. Click the Dial-Up Networking icon and you will see the Make a New Connection icon.

4. Click the Make New Connection icon to set up a connection to your network. The Make New Connection Wizard makes it easy for you to create dial-up connections (see Figure 13.12). The Wizard will create an icon for each connection you create.

FIG. 13.12
The Make New Connection Wizard steps you through the process of creating a phonebook entry. You will have an icon created for each connection you make.

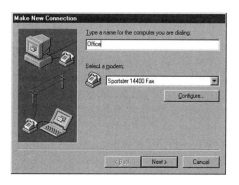

N O T E You will use Make New Connection Wizard for each computer that you make a connection to. The Wizard will create an icon for each of these computers. ■

5. The Make New Connection Wizard steps you through the process of setting up a dial-up connection. First you must enter a name for this connection and click Next.

Part
III

Ch
13

6. You will then be asked to input the phone number you are dialing. Enter the number and click Next.

7. Click Finish and you will have an icon for your new connection.

8. Next you need to change the properties of the new connection. Put your mouse pointer over the new icon and click the right mouse button. This will give you a selection list of options.

9. Click Properties and you will see the properties of the new connection. You must configure the Server Type properties.

10. Click the Server Type button. The Server Types dialog box appears. Make sure that only the protocols that your server supports are checked in the Allowed Network Protocols check boxes (see Figure 13.13).

N O T E   Make sure to de-select any unsupported protocols. ■

FIG. 13.13

Your Server Types selections must match that of the server you are connecting to. Ask your network administrator if you need help configuring your network.

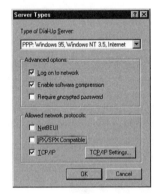

N O T E   Based on your network configuration, you might have to make some changes to the TCP/IP settings. IP addresses for the client computer and the name server are established within the TCP/IP settings. Some networks assign static IP addresses and some networks use DHCP for assigning IP addresses dynamically. Talk to your network administrator for help configuring your TCP/IP settings. Refer to Chapter 9, "Using TCP/IP with Windows NT Server," for TCP/IP configuration. ■

11. Click OK to get to the connection properties.

12. Click OK to continue. You will see the new connection icon you just created and you are ready to connect to the network.

13. Click the icon and you will get a Connect To dialog box.

14. Enter your password and click Connect.

CAUTION

To maximize security, *do not* check the Save Password check box. Selecting the check box would allow anyone who has access to your computer access to your corporate network.

Your modem will pick up the line and dial to your server computer. You can watch the status of your connection as your computer dials, connects, and registers on your network.

The Connected to status box shows when you have a successful connection to your network (see Figure 13.14). It tells you what speed you are connected at and it keeps track of the duration of your connection.

FIG. 13.14

The Connected to status box shows you the status of your connection. It will show you the speed of your connection and monitor the length of time that you are connected to the remote computer.

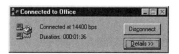

You now have access to all of the computing resources of your network that you would normally have if you were locally attached. Click Network Neighborhood and you will see a list of the other computers on the network (see Figure 13.15).

FIG. 13.15

Once you are authenticated on your remote network, you will see all of the shared resources and other computers on the network.

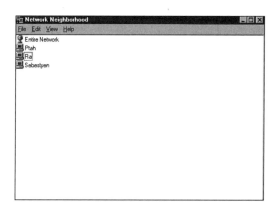

Part

III

Ch

13

Configuring the Windows NT 3.51 Client

RAS is implemented as a service on Windows NT 3.51. You must install this service before you can use Dial-Up Networking. The Remote Access Service is installed on Windows NT 3.51 via the Network configuration program in the Control Panel.

Installing the RAS Software   The following is the procedure to install RAS on Windows NT 3.51:

1. Select the Network icon within the Control Panel. You will see the Network Settings dialog box (see Figure 13.16).

FIG. 13.16

Remote Access runs as a service on NT 3.51. It is installed in the Network Settings dialog box.

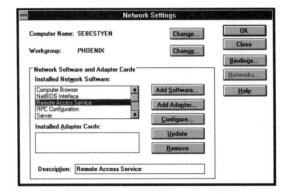

2. Click the Add Software button. The Add Network Software dialog box appears.
3. Scroll down through the list and select Remote Access Service and click Continue.
4. You will be prompted for the installation disk. Put the disk in the appropriate device and click Continue.
5. Windows will install the software necessary to set up Remote Access Service. If you do not have a network card in your computer, you will get a dialog box from NT informing you that automatic restoration of network connections was disabled. For Dial-Up Networking, this is expected and is not a problem; click OK to continue.
6. Remote Access Setup will now configure your modem. You will get a dialog box informing you that it will attempt to detect your modem (see Figure 13.17). Choose OK if you want Windows to do so. Choose Cancel to manually select your modem.

N O T E   It is a good practice to at least give Windows the opportunity to detect your modem. If it's not detected correctly (though it usually is), you can always change it manually. ▦

FIG. 13.17

Remote Access Setup's modem detection dialog box asks if you want it to detect your modem. NT 3.51's modem detection is an easy way to configure a new modem.

7. When NT detects your modem, click OK to close the Detect dialog box.

8. Click OK to close the Port Configuration dialog box. You will now see the Remote Access Setup dialog box.

9. Click the Network button. Make sure that you have the correct protocol selected in the Network Configuration dialog box (see Figure 13.18).

FIG. 13.18

Make sure that you have the proper protocols selected for the network you are connecting to.

10. Click OK to close the Network Configuration dialog box.

11. Click Continue to close the Remote Access Setup dialog box.

12. NT installs and configures the RAS software and brings you back to the Network Settings dialog box. Click OK to continue setting up Remote Access.

13. NT continues configuring your software and then informs you that Windows must be restarted before the new settings will take effect. Make sure that you have all other applications closed, then restart Windows.

Using RAS with Windows NT 3.51 When Windows restarts, you are ready to use Remote Access Service for Dial-Up Networking with Windows NT. When you click the Remote Access Service program group for the first time, you will get a dialog box from Remote Access telling you that the phonebook is empty. You need to click OK to create an entry to connect to your network.

Creating a Phonebook Entry Because RAS has never before been used, there are no phonebook entries set up. Each computer that you want to connect to needs its own phonebook entry. Use the following procedure to set up a phonebook entry:

1. Click OK to create an entry for your network. You will now be in the Add Phone Book Entry dialog box (see Figure 13.19).

Part
III

Ch
13

FIG. 13.19

The Add Phone Book Entry dialog box is where you create an entry for your dial-up connections.

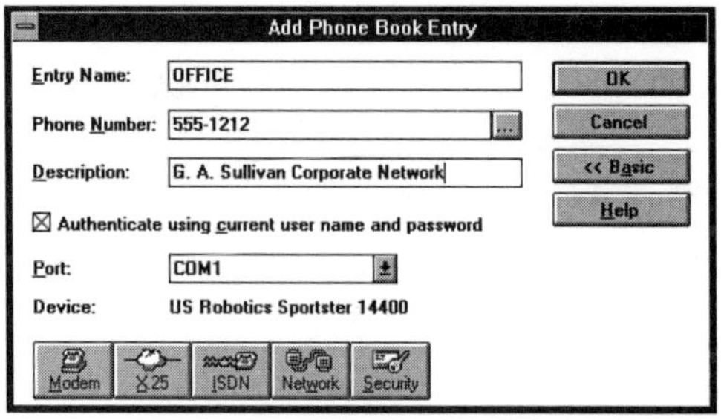

2. Input an Entry Name; this is the company name or server name. Choose any name you like, from 1 to 20 characters with no commas or spaces.

3. Input the Phone Number. This is the phone number of the computer that you are connecting to.

4. Input the Description for your connection. This is for your reference and it is optional.

5. If you set up your remote computer to use the same username and password as that of your corporate network, make sure that the Authenticate Using Current User Name and Password check box is selected.

6. Click the Network button. This is where you will verify that the proper protocol has been installed and configured for your connection.

7. Check your settings, and then click OK. Now you have a phonebook entry to connect to your network.

8. Highlight your network connection in the Remote Access dialog box and click Dial to connect to your network.

N O T E Your computer will dial the remote computer using the phonebook entry that you select. The modems will negotiate a connection and your user ID and password will be authenticated on your network's domain controller. If you have privileges on the domain, you will have access to all of the resources on your network just as if you were accessing through a local network connection. After being authenticated, you can go to the File Manager and make connections to other resources on the network. ∎

9. Select the File Manager icon from the Main program group.

10. Click Disk.

11. Click Connect Network Drive. The Connect Network Drive dialog box appears. You can now see all of the shared resources on your network (see Figure 13.20).

FIG. 13.20

Once you are authenti-
cated on the remote
domain, you can see the
shared resources and
other computers on the
domain.

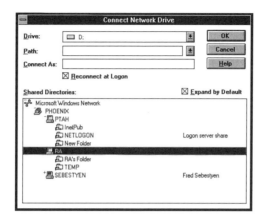

Configuring the Windows NT 4.0 Client

The Remote Access Service used for Dial-Up Networking on Windows NT 4.0 is installed as a service just as it is on NT 3.51. This section will guide you through the installation of RAS under Windows NT 4.0.

Installing the RAS Client Under Windows NT 4.0   Follow these steps to install RAS under Windows NT 4.0:

1. Select Start, Settings, Control Panel from Windows.

2. Click the Network icon and you will be presented with the Network Settings folder.

3. Click the Services tab and you will see a list of the currently installed services.

4. Click the Add button to get to the Select Network Services dialog box.

5. Select Remote Access Services and click OK. Windows will prompt for the installation disk.

6. Insert the installation disk into the requested drive and click Continue.

7. NT will begin to copy the files to your computer. When the installation is complete, you will get a dialog box from RAS indicating that there is no RAS capable device and it asks if you want to invoke the Modem installer (see Figure 13.21). Click Yes to continue.

Part
III

Ch
13

FIG. 13.21

The RAS modem
installer will automati-
cally appear as you
install the Remote
Access Service if there
are no RAS capable
devices installed.

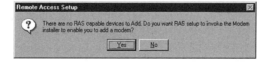

N O T E   You will now get the Windows NT 4.0 version of the Install New Modem dialog box. It
functions the same as the Windows 95 version. If you need help with the Install New
Modem dialog box, refer to the previous section "Installing Your Modem Under Windows 95." ▦

8. When the Install New Modem dialog box is complete, click Finish to install the selected modem. NT will detect and install your modem software for you.

9. When the modem installation is complete, you will be placed back in the Remote Access Setup dialog box within the Add RAS Device dialog box. The modem that you just installed is selected as the RAS Capable Device. Click OK to continue.

10. Click Continue to complete the Remote Access Setup dialog box.

11. Click the Protocol tab; this is where you verify that you are installing the proper network protocol for the server that you are connecting to. Make sure that the network protocol that you have installed is one that is supported by your network.

12. If you need to install a different network protocol, click the Add button and continue with the installation of the new protocol.

13. If your protocol is already installed, click Close to complete the setup. NT installs and configures the RAS software. When the configuration is complete, you are informed that Windows needs to be restarted.

14. Click Yes to restart Windows.

Creating a New Phonebook Entry   After Windows restarts, your modem will be installed and you will also have RAS running on your computer. RAS is disguised as Dial-Up Networking within Windows NT 4.0 to be consistent with the Windows 95 Explorer interface. When your computer restarts, you will have a Dial-Up Networking icon in My Computer. The Dial-Up Networking program is where you set up your connections to remote computers.

Follow these steps to set up a phonebook entry using the New Phonebook Entry Wizard:

1. Click the icon and you will be prompted by the New Phonebook Entry Wizard to make an entry for your network (see Figure 13.22). Type in a name for the entry and click Next.

FIG. 13.22

The New Phonebook Entry Wizard allows you to create an icon for your connection. You can make subsequent connections by clicking the icon.

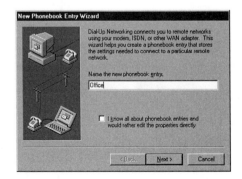

2. Because you are connecting to a Microsoft Windows network, click <u>N</u>ext at the Server dialog box.

3. Enter the phone number and click <u>N</u>ext.

4. Click Finish and your new entry is complete. This is all you have to do to set up your connection. This entry will enable you to connect to your network just by selecting the entry and clicking Dial.

5. Click Dial to connect to your network.

6. The first time that you use your new connection, you will be presented a dialog box requesting your username, password, and domain name of the NT domain that you will be connecting to. Enter your username.

7. Enter your password.

8. Enter the domain name of the NT domain you will be connecting to.

CAUTION

Do not select the Save Password check box. Though this may seem convenient, it also removes a layer of security from your network.

9. Click OK.

10. Your modem will pick up the line and begin to dial the number. When you connect to your network, you will have access to all of the shared devices on your network. Click Network Neighborhood to verify that you have a successful connection. You will see all of the computers that are currently turned on and connected to your network (see Figure 13.23).

FIG. 13.23
Once you are authenticated on the domain, you can see all of the shared resources and computers on the domain.

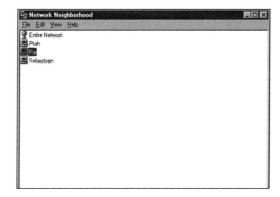

Part
III

Ch
13

Configuring Clients for Multilink Channel Aggregation

Multilink Channel Aggregation, also known as *Multilink PPP*, is a protocol that is being supported by Microsoft in Windows NT 4.0. Multilink PPP enables a computer with Windows NT 4.0 and more than one modem to use those modems at the same time during a single RAS session to achieve maximum bandwidth. Multilink PPP supports the transfer of data across parallel connections simultaneously. This means that if you have two 28.8 modems on your computer and two phone lines, you could connect to your network with both modems at the same time effectively giving you 57.6 Kbps throughput.

▶ **See** "Configuring RAS," **p. 355**

This section will step you through the process of configuring your computer for Multilink PPP. Because RAS installation is not part of Windows NT's default installation, you will first have to make sure that this component is installed and functioning properly on your workstation. Previously in this chapter, you learned how to install modems and RAS. If you need help, refer to the section "Installing the RAS Client Under Windows NT 4.0."

Preparing the Client for Multilink PPP

Assuming your RAS connections are working properly for Dial-Up Networking, there are just a few additional steps that you have to take to enable your client to connect via Multilink PPP.

The first thing that you need to do is install your additional modem or other dial-up adapter. The Multilink PPP supports aggregation of two analog modems, or you can use an analog modem and a digital modem with an ISDN line. Multilink PPP also supports the use of two digital modems with ISDN lines. The only limitation you have is the server you are connecting to must also support the type of hardware connections you are attempting to make.

To install an additional modem for use with RAS, follow this procedure:

1. Select the Control Panel icon in the Main program group.
2. Go to the Network Configuration program.
3. Select the Services tab.
4. Highlight Remote Access Services and click Properties. You will be in the Remote Access Setup dialog box. If your new modem is identical to your existing modem, you can click Clone to copy your existing modem settings and save yourself a couple of steps.
5. If you need to install a new modem, click Modem to install a new modem. Refer to the section "Installing Your Modem Under Windows 95" earlier in this chapter if you need help installing a new modem. Figure 13.24 shows the modems that are installed on the computer.

FIG. 13.24

The Remote Access Setup dialog shows both of your modems that are installed for use with RAS.

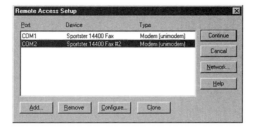

Configuring Your Dial-Up Connection to Use Multiple Lines

Once you have both of your modems installed, you need to set up a modem connection to the remote computer and enable your dial-up connection to use multiple lines. This section will guide you through the process of enabling your connection to use multiple lines.

In order to use any dial-up connection, you must set up a phonebook entry for the connection. Follow this procedure to set up a phonebook entry for your multiple line connection:

1. Select My Computer from the Windows desktop. You will see the Dial-Up Networking program.
2. Click Dial-Up Networking to start the Dial-Up Networking dialog box.
3. Click New to create a new entry for your multilink connection.
4. Enter a name for your connection. Make it something descriptive of the connection. The name can be anything, but you might want to make it something that will remind you that it is a multilink connection (see Figure 13.25).

FIG. 13.25

Creating a new entry for the multilink connection is a little more involved than making a single line connection.

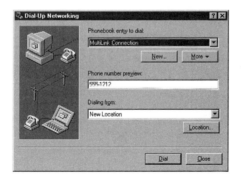

5. Click Next.
6. Because you will be connecting to an NT server, do not select anything on the Server dialog box and click Next.
7. On the Modem or Adapter dialog box you will now see two modems listed. Select one of the modems that are listed and click Next.
8. Enter the phone number of the computer that you will be dialing to and click Next.

9. Click Finish and you will be finished with the first part of configuring your multilink connection.

10. Your multilink connection is now in the selection list of phonebook entries. The setup is complete, but it is only set up for a single line dial-up. It must be configured to use multiple lines in order to use multilink. To configure this entry, select the entry from the phonebook selection list and click More.

11. You will be presented with another selection list of choices. From this selection list, click Edit entry and modem properties.

12. This will bring up the Edit Phonebook Entry dialog box. Click the Basic tab (see Figure 13.26).

FIG. 13.26

You must edit the phonebook entry to support multiple lines.

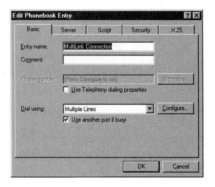

13. At the bottom of the Basic tab there is a drop-down list box for Dial Using, which tells the connection what device it should use to make this connection. The modem that you selected when you initially set up this connection should be listed here. Click this drop-down list box.

14. You will see all of the modems that you have configured on your system. At the bottom of this list box you will also have a selection for Multiple Lines. Make sure that it is selected.

15. Click Configure. When you click to configure multiple lines, you will see both of your modems listed in the Multiple Line Configuration dialog box (see Figure 13.27). The one that you initially set up for this dial-up connection will have its check box selected. To enable a multilink connection, select the check box of the other modem and click Phone Numbers.

16. Enter the number that you will be dialing in the New Phone Number box and click Add.

N O T E Typically, a RAS server is configured having one phone number for dial in. This number will roll over to several available phone lines. The phone number that you enter for your second connection for a multilink session will be the same as the first in most instances. ▪

17. Click OK to close the Phone Numbers dialog box.

18. Click OK to close the Multiple Line Configuration dialog box.

FIG. 13.27

Both lines must be configured for dialing the remote computer.

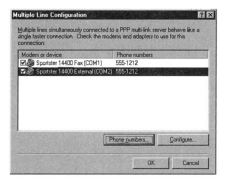

19. Click OK to close the Edit Phonebook Entry dialog box. Your phonebook entry for multilink session is now complete. You can now use this connection to dial-up your server using both of your modems for the connection.

20. To connect to the server computer, click Dial. The modems will pick up the phone lines and dial the numbers. Both modems will dial out and connect to the modems at the server. As the connections are made, you can watch the screen and note the progress of your connections. The dual individual connections are bonded to form a single connection to the server. You are now connected at the combined speed of both of your devices.

 An easy way to tell if you are getting the throughput that you were expecting is to copy a file from the server to your local computer. Select a larger file, and note the size. Copy the same file to your computer twice, once with a single connection and once with the multilink connection, and time how long it takes to copy the files. The multilink session should give you a noticeable improvement in throughput.

 Another way to check on the status of your multilink connection is to use the Dial-Up Networking Monitor in the Control Panel. With this monitor, you can select the modems and watch the status of the throughput on-the-fly.

Configuring a Client to Use Point-to-Point Tunneling Protocol (PPTP)

Just what is PPTP? In this section, we explore PPTP and show you how to set up a PPTP client.

PPTP is a protocol that Microsoft has included in Windows NT 4.0. It enables computers running Windows NT to securely connect to a private network using a modem and an Internet connection. Clearly, this enables corporations to greatly reduce their operating costs for remote clients. This eliminates the need for modem servers with multiple COM ports, banks of modems, and long distance call charges. Even dedicated connections to remote locations can be replaced using PPTP for secure connections via the Internet.

Point-to-Point Tunneling protocol is an offshoot of Point-to-Point Protocol. PPP provides a method for sending network packets over a serial connection, such as a modem link. PPTP expands on this capability by providing the ability to encapsulate one network protocol within another. Using this technique, NetBEUI or IPX packets can be wrapped in TCP/IP packets and sent over a TCP/IP network to a NetBEUI or IPX network. TCP/IP is used to create a "tunnel" through which the NetBEUI or IPX packets travel. Although tunneling provides a secure connection over the Internet, there is a small price in performance, as each packet must be "unwrapped" before it is processed.

The configuration for deployment of a PPTP connection requires three computers—the client computer requiring access to the private network, a computer providing Internet access as an Internet service provider (ISP), and a PPTP server on your private LAN.

In a typical PPTP deployment scenario, you have a client computer that needs access to a private LAN. The PPTP connection is a two-stage process. The client computer first connects to an ISP via the Point-to-Point Protocol (PPP) using Dial-Up Networking. After this connection is complete, the client will establish a second connection using the Point-to-Point Tunneling Protocol to the PPTP server on the target LAN. The PPTP server is connected to both the private LAN and the Internet.

PPTP provides encrypted communications between the client computer and the PPTP server on the LAN. There are typically two levels of security that a PPTP client must pass through before they can connect to the private LAN. First the client must be authenticated on the ISP's network by using a password before being allowed Internet access on that network. Then on the second connection to the PPTP server, the client must be verified and authenticated to the NT domain. The NT Server running PPTP controls all access to the private network.

The PPTP server requires a standard Windows NT logon to have access to the LAN. All PPTP clients must supply a user ID and password. The Windows NT logon over PPTP provides a mechanism that is as secure as logging on to a local computer running Windows NT. The user accounts of remote users must reside in the Windows NT directory service and are administered using the User Manager for Domains.

Once the remote user connects to the private LAN through the PPTP server, they must be authenticated. After a user is authenticated and registered on the network, they have access to all of the network resources just as if they were locally connected to the LAN.

Installing the PPTP Protocol

PPTP is a networking protocol that must be installed onto your system just like TCP/IP, IPX, or any other networking protocol. Follow this procedure to install the PPTP protocol:

1. Select Start, Settings, Control Panel from the Start menu.
2. Click Network.
3. Click the Protocols tab.
4. Click Add. In the Select Network Protocol dialog box that appears, select Point-to-Point Tunneling Protocol and click OK (see Figure 13.28).

FIG. 13.28

Installing the PPTP Protocol is done with the Select Network Protocol dialog box.

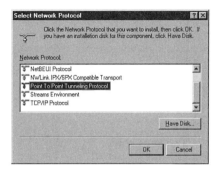

5. The PPTP software will be copied to your computer. During the installation you will get a PPTP Configuration dialog box. There is a selection box for the Number of Virtual Private Networks (see Figure 13.29). This is asking how many different private networks you will be connecting to. In this example, you will only be connecting to one network. Select 1 and click OK.

FIG. 13.29

Select the number of private networks you will be connecting to.

6. You will be prompted by a Setup Message to continue on to the RAS Setup dialog box and configure the PPTP port. Click OK to continue.

7. The Remote Access Setup dialog box appears showing the Virtual Private Network (VPN) device in the RAS capable devices selection box (see Figure 13.30). Click OK to add the VPN device.

FIG. 13.30

The VPN device must be added to the RAS devices.

Part
III

Ch
13

8. The VPN device is added to your list of RAS devices. Click the Continue button to continue. The software is installed and configured.

9. Click Close. Your RAS bindings are configured and you are asked if you want to restart your computer.

10. Click Yes to restart your computer.

When Windows restarts, you will have PPTP installed and you are ready to configure your connections. This section will step you through the process of configuring your computer for PPTP.

Configuring a PPTP Client

To begin the configuration of the Dial-Up Networking connection, you must make sure that you have already installed the network protocols used on the private network on your client computer. Also, you should have configured the Remote Access Service to dial out using those network protocols.

To use a PPTP client, you must create two separate phonebook entries. The first entry is used to create a connection to an Internet service provider. This connection could already be set up on your computer. It would be the entry that you usually use to connect to your ISP. Once the client is connected to the ISP, a second entry is used to connect to the PPTP server on their private network. This section explains how to create these Dial-Up Networking entries.

Editing an Existing Phonebook Entry   The following are the steps to configure an existing entry for a connection to an Internet service provider:

1. Click My Computer.
2. Click Dial-Up Networking.
3. Select the entry and click More.
4. Click Edit entry and modem properties. You will be in the Edit Phonebook Entry dialog box.
5. On the Basic tab, check the Phone Number and Dial Using boxes to make sure you have the correct phone number to your ISP and the appropriate dial-up device selected.
6. Click the Server tab. Check the Dial-up Server Type. Make sure that the PPP: Windows NT, Windows 95 Plus, Internet selection appears. Also check the Network Protocols box to make sure that the TCP/IP check box is selected.
7. Click the TCP/IP Settings button. This is where you must change the TCP/IP settings to conform to your ISP. Each ISP is configured a little differently so check with your ISP to get the correct settings.
8. Click the Script tab. Make sure that None is selected.
9. Click the Security tab. Make sure that the Accept Only Encrypted Authentication option button is selected.
10. Click OK to finish editing your entry.

 T I P   Each ISP's network is configured the way that it wants it configured. Be sure to get the proper settings from your ISP so you can make the connection to its network.

Creating a New Entry to an ISP Using the Phonebook Wizard   Follow these steps to create a new phonebook entry to an Internet service provider:

1. Click My Computer.
2. Click Dial-Up Networking.
3. Click <u>N</u>ew. This will start the New Phonebook Entry Wizard (see Figure 13.31).

FIG. 13.31

You use the New Phonebook Entry Wizard to create an entry for your ISP.

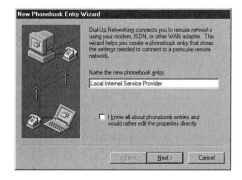

4. Enter a name for this connection and click <u>N</u>ext.
5. Select the <u>I</u> Am Calling the Internet check box and click <u>N</u>ext.
6. Select the dial-up device that you will be using for this connection and click <u>N</u>ext. You should also see your VPN device listed here.

CAUTION

Don't select the VPN device when configuring your ISP connection. It will be configured in the next step.

7. Enter the <u>P</u>hone Number of your ISP and click <u>N</u>ext.
8. Click Finish to complete creating your new connection to your ISP.

N O T E   Although these default settings for a PPP connection will work for connecting to most ISPs, each ISP can configure its network a little differently. Examples are TCP/IP settings for static IP addresses, enabling PPP LCP extensions on the server, and different authentication and encryption policies. Check with your ISP for more information on the required settings. ▓

 You should probably check out your connection to your ISP before proceeding. Open a Web browser and try to hit a couple of Web sites to make sure your connection is working.

With the ISP phonebook entry configured, we must now create a phonebook entry for the PPTP server.

Creating the PPTP Server Phonebook Entry   Follow this procedure to create a phonebook entry for your PPTP server:

1. Click My Computer.
2. Click Dial-Up Networking.
3. Select the ISP entry that you have just created in the previous section and click More.
4. Click Clone entry and modem properties. The Clone Phonebook Entry dialog box appears (see Figure 13.32).

FIG. 13.32

You can clone the ISP phonebook entry to save some time setting up your connection.

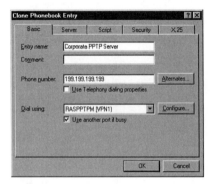

5. Change the Entry Name on the Basic tab to something that will remind you that this entry is for your PPTP connection. This can be anything, such as "Corporate PPTP Server."
6. Enter the IP address of the network interface card in your PPTP server. This IP address should be for the card that is connected to the Internet.
7. In the Dial Using box, select the virtual private network device that was created when you installed the PPTP protocol.
8. Click the Server tab and make sure that PPP: Windows NT, Windows 95 Plus, Internet is selected. Also make sure that your network's protocols are selected in the Network protocols box.

N O T E   For this PPTP connection phonebook entry, you do not have to have TCP/IP selected. Your TCP/IP connection is made to your ISP. You should select the protocol that is supported on your private network. ■

9. Click the Script tab and make sure that the None option button is selected.
10. Click the Security tab, shown in Figure 13.33. Select the Accept Only Microsoft Encrypted Authentication option button and the Require Data Encryption check box. Also, if you configured your client computer to use the same username and password as your private network, select the Use Current Username and Password check box. If you don't check this box, you will be prompted by the PPTP server.

FIG. 13.33

The Security Settings for the PPTP Phonebook Entry should be set to accept only Microsoft encrypted authentication.

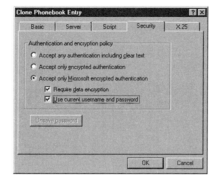

11. Click OK to finish creating your PPTP server phonebook entry.

Connecting to a PPTP Server After you create the two phonebook entries (as described in the previous section), you will be ready to connect to your PPTP server. This section explains how to make that connection:

1. Click My Computer.
2. Click Dial-Up Networking.
3. Click More.
4. Select User Preferences.
5. Select the Appearance tab.
6. Clear the Close On Dial check box and click OK.
7. In the Dial-Up Networking dialog box, select your ISP connection from the Phonebook entry to dial box.
8. Click Dial.
9. After you connect to your ISP successfully, select the entry for your PPTP server and click Dial.

The second connection links through your ISP connection to your PPTP server on your private network. When you connect to your PPTP server through this second connection, all traffic through your modem now travels exclusively to your PPTP server for routing over your private network. You will be able to use your private network as if connected directly via a local connection.

From Here...

This chapter provides detailed instructions for installing and configuring client software for all of the Microsoft GUI desktops. You learned how to install Dial-Up Networking, how to install modems, and how to install and uninstall other networking components. For more information on these and related topics, consult the following chapters:

Part
III

Ch
13

■ If you need more information concerning the TCP/IP protocol and configuring PPTP servers, refer to Chapter 9, "Using TPC/IP with Windows NT Server."

■ For more information on configuring a RAS server, see Chapter 12, "Implementing Remote Access Service (RAS)."

■ See Chapter 15, "Wide Area Network Technologies," for more information on wide area networking as it applies to Dial-Up Networking.

## CHAPTER 14

Windows Integration with NetWare and UNIX

by Brad Rhodes and Bob Thompson

Network managers in the real world seldom have the luxury of working in a homogeneous network operating system (NOS) environment. If your organization runs Windows NT Server as its only NOS, consider yourself lucky. If instead, like many system administrators, you must contend with an installed base of mixed NetWare 3.1x and 4.x servers, a UNIX host here and there, and perhaps a System Network Architecture (SNA) host lurking in the glass house, then read on. ■

Unlock network protocol issues

Investigate the various network protocols that are available on the Windows NT platform, and learn which to use when integrating with other systems.

File system issues

Explore various file system alternatives, and learn how they can help integrate different operating systems.

NetWare integration

Learn how to integrate Windows NT Server into an existing Novell NetWare environment.

Gateway Services for NetWare (GSNW)

Learn how to configure and use GSNW to extend the reach of your NetWare clients.

Directory Services for NetWare

Learn how this tool can ease the job of managing separate directories of users.

UNIX integration

Learn how to integrate with UNIX servers and clients.

Integrating Operating Systems

There are several levels at which two diverse operating environments can integrate. Among them are the following:

- **Network protocols**—The two operating environments can share common sets of networking protocols.

- **Common network applications**—Right above the integration of network protocols is the capability to run small network applications that access both environments.

- **E-mail integration**—E-mail is one of the largest applications, and it is important that UNIX and BackOffice provide great e-mail integration.

- **File and print sharing**—File and print sharing provides the need for the majority of the LANs that have been installed. File and print sharing allow users to store files on a file server and print files on shared printers. This functionality is the driving factor behind the majority of the LANs that have been installed.

- **Common file systems**—Building on the File and Printer sharing is the capability to have one file system that is used on both operating environments. There are currently two competing standards—Microsoft's Common Internet File System and Sun Microsystems' Web Network File System (NFS).

- **Common shared directories**—The integration of directory services enables users to look for resources in one place without regard for operating environment that controls the resources.

- **Common Application Programming Interface**—In addition to sharing and integrating resources, common Applications Programming Interfaces (APIs) between two operating environments enable portability of applications.

- **Remote procedure calls**—RPCs provide a means for one application to call functions that actually run on other servers.

- **Distributed object models**—Distributed object models are designed to facilitate component interoperability in heterogeneous networks.

This chapter explores the capability of Windows NT and BackOffice environments to integrate with Novell NetWare and the UNIX operating system.

Spanning Multiple Network Protocols

Windows NT Server 4.0 uses a protocol-independent networking architecture, which enables it to interoperate with a wide range of NOSs and protocols. With its support for standard network application interfaces, Windows NT Server easily accommodates simultaneous interoperability with Novell NetWare, UNIX, and IBM SNA networks.

NetWare historically has dominated the NOS market, and now holds about two-thirds of both the number of servers installed and the number of workstations using it. Although Windows NT Server is closing the gap quickly, many network managers will find it necessary to support both NOSs on a temporary basis as their organizations make the transition to Windows NT Server. Others will need to provide such support on a more or less permanent basis in organizations that plan for both NOSs to coexist on a long-term basis. Fortunately, Windows NT Server provides excellent tools for both migration and long-term coexistence.

UNIX is a fact of life in most medium and large organizations, and again, Windows NT Server provides many of the tools you need to allow UNIX workstations and hosts to coexist with Windows NT Server. Microsoft has also recognized the continuing importance of mainframe connectivity to the enterprise and has accordingly provided SNA connectivity tools and services with Windows NT Server.

Integration Feuds

Microsoft's chairman, Bill Gates, and Novell's former chairman, Ray Noorda, didn't much like each other or, at least, so it appeared to most observers in the early 1990s. Each seemed determined to make life as difficult as possible for the other, causing much unnecessary suffering among users of Microsoft and Novell NOSs. This disagreement, played out in the trade press over the years, took on the characteristics of an elementary schoolyard spat.

Client-side support promised by Novell for Windows NT was late in arriving and seemed to many to be a conscious action on the part of Novell to cripple acceptance of Windows NT. For its part, Microsoft promoted the use of Gateway Services for Windows NT Server as a means to enable hundreds of clients to access a Novell server running only a five-user NetWare license. Novell broadsides were answered in turn by Microsoft, culminating when Novell threatened suit against Microsoft for bundling Novell client software with Windows, and Microsoft's subsequent withdrawal of that software. To this day, configuring a Windows 3.x client to access a Novell server requires installing client software acquired separately from Novell.

Ray Noorda's departure from Novell and Bob Frankenberg's ascension to the helm appear to have resulted in an uneasy truce in this battle of the Titans, although border skirmishes continue. Microsoft and Novell appear to have realized that neither firm is likely to disappear anytime soon as a key player in the NOS market, and that coexistence better serves both their customers and their own interests. Novell recognizes that Windows NT Server will increasingly appear in previously exclusive Novell shops and, accordingly, is improving NetWare's integration with Windows NT. Plans include porting NetWare Directory Services (NDS) to the Windows NT platform. On its part, Microsoft has implicitly recognized the current dominance of NetWare and now provides excellent tools for coexistence and migration.

Part
III

Ch
14

Windows NT Network and Transport Protocols

Until recently, the fundamental problem with integrating Microsoft, Novell, and UNIX networks has been that each used a different and incompatible transport protocol. Microsoft networks historically have used NetBEUI, Novell networks depended on IPX/SPX, and UNIX networks used TCP/IP. Each network and transport protocol is fast and reliable, and each has advantages and drawbacks, explained as follows:

- NetBEUI requires minimal setup and is easy to administer. Because NetBEUI packets contain no network layer header information, however, they can be bridged only and can't be routed, making NetBEUI usable only for LANs. Microsoft is de-emphasizing NetBEUI for enterprise networking, relegating it to peer networking only.

- IPX/SPX was originally designed for local area networking. Like NetBEUI, IPX/SPX is easy to set up and administer. Unlike NetBEUI, however, IPX/SPX can be routed. Because IPX/SPX was originally designed as a LAN protocol rather than a WAN protocol, it lacks subnetting support, variable packet lengths, and other technical features that make it a less-than-ideal choice as a foundation on which to build an internetwork, at least when considered in isolation. Still, because it combines the ease of use of NetBEUI with much of the flexibility and power of TCP/IP, IPX/SPX can be a good choice as the shared network and transport protocol for a heterogeneous network, particularly one that heavily depends on Novell NetWare servers. Microsoft refers to its IPX/SPX implementation as NWLink.

- TCP/IP was designed from the ground up for internetworking. As the *lingua franca* of the Internet, TCP/IP provides in abundance all the tools needed to build an internetwork. The sole drawback to TCP/IP is that it can be extremely complex to administer, both on the server side and on the client side. If your environment includes UNIX hosts or workstations, or if you want to set up a corporate intranet or connect to the Internet, you must run TCP/IP.

The Novell-centric view is that everyone should speak IPX/SPX. Although Novell has made some half-hearted, expensive, and poorly received attempts to provide native TCP/IP support (for example, NetWare/IP) the Novell world continues to revolve around IPX/SPX. Similarly, in the UNIX universe, you either speak TCP/IP, or no one listens to you. Many networks—particularly those growing from smaller, peer-based environments—depend on NetBEUI, so this protocol, too, needs to be accommodated.

N O T E   Windows NT Server 4.0 installs only NWLink IPX/SPX transport by default, but allows additional transport protocols to run simultaneously. If your network includes NetWare servers, you should leave NWLink installed. If your network includes UNIX hosts, spans multiple sites, or connects to the Internet, you should also load TCP/IP transport when you install Windows NT Server. ■

Fortunately, Microsoft has realized the importance of all three of these protocols to those who need to build heterogeneous networks and has provided support for each of the three protocols in Windows NT Server 4.0. You can run one, any two, or all three of these protocols simultaneously to provide the fundamental network and transport layer support you need to build your network. This broad network and transport layer support provides the foundation for linking heterogeneous networking components.

Integrating Windows NT Server with Novell NetWare

The almost seamless integration of Windows NT Server 4.0 with NetWare is one of the major reasons for the phenomenal growth of Windows NT Server sales. In less than two years, Windows NT Server has grown from an "also ran" product that barely appeared in sales charts to a major competitor of NetWare. Windows NT Server, in contrast to NetWare, provides a superior application server platform. The Microsoft BackOffice suite provides a solid foundation for developing client-server applications, and competing client-server application development tools from other vendors increasingly are being ported to the Windows NT Server environment.

All these applications can be accessed natively by Microsoft clients, as well as by NetWare clients, by using either the Novell NETx network shell or the VLM (Virtual Loadable Module) requester. The IPX/SPX protocol (NWLink) provided with Windows NT Server (see Figure 14.1) enables NetWare clients to communicate with a server application using Novell NetBIOS, Winsock, and Remote Procedure Calls (RPCs).

FIG. 14.1
Connect Windows NT and NetWare servers to a NetWare client with NWLink.

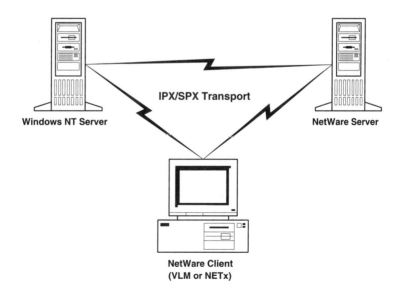

IPX/SPX Transport

Windows NT Server

NetWare Server

**NetWare Client
(VLM or NETx)**

Part

III

Ch

14

Although Windows NT Server's support for diverse network and transport layer protocols has eliminated one problem, still remaining is the issue of what core protocol is used for communication between servers and workstations. Microsoft uses the Server Message Block (SMB) protocol for this purpose, whereas NetWare uses NetWare Core Protocol (NCP). If NetWare clients are to be able to access Windows NT servers, and if Windows NT clients are to be able to access NetWare servers, something must be done to translate between these two fundamental, but incompatible, protocols. Microsoft provides the following two utilities to bridge this gap:

- **Gateway Service for NetWare (GSNW)**—This enables clients running Microsoft client software to access shared files on a NetWare server and to print to NetWare printers. GSNW translates the upper-layer SMB calls to and from NetWare NCP calls. GSNW is included with Windows NT Server 4.0.

- **File and Print Services for NetWare (FPSN)**—This enables Windows NT Server to emulate a NetWare 3.12 server. Novell clients can access shared files and printers in the same way that they would access shared resources on any NetWare 3.12 server. FPSN avoids the translation between SMB and NCP by simply dealing with NetWare clients directly as NCP devices.

With a market share that now stands at about 65 percent and is gradually declining, Novell has little motivation to provide tools to make it easier for Windows NT Server to coexist with, or replace, NetWare. On the other hand, with market share now at about 10 percent and growing explosively, Microsoft Windows NT Server has everything to gain from readily making available such tools to ease coexistence and migration. Fortunately, Microsoft, recognizing its second-place position in the networking business, has taken responsibility for bridging the core protocol gap by providing a set of tools designed to facilitate integration of Windows NT Server with NetWare servers.

Accessing Novell NetWare Servers Using Microsoft Clients

Clients running Microsoft Networking client software can access shared files and printers on a Novell NetWare server in one of the following three ways:

- Use a client operating system, such as Windows NT Workstation or Windows 95, that provides built-in support for both Microsoft Networking and NetWare. As supplied, these clients provide full access to NetWare 3.1x servers. They enable you to access NetWare 4.x servers using *bindery emulation mode,* but don't provide NDS support. You can update your Windows 95 clients to provide full NDS support by installing the Service for NetWare Directory Services, available in Windows 95 Service Pack 1, which you can download from **http://www.microsoft.com/WindowsSupport/**.

- Add a Novell NetWare client protocol stack to a client to provide full access to NetWare services. The Novell NetWare client coexists with the Microsoft Networking client and supports full NDS access on NetWare 4.x servers. You can download the 32-bit client for Windows 95 from **ftp.novell.com/pub/updates/nwos/nc32w952** and for DOS/ Windows 3.1+ from **ftp.novell.com/pub/updates/nwos/cl32dw21**.

- Install Gateway Service for NetWare (GSNW) to enable clients running only Microsoft networking client software to access NetWare server resources via gateway services provided by Windows NT Server.

The method you use for a particular client depends on both the operating system that client is running and the level of NetWare connectivity you need to provide to that client.

Using a Client Operating System with Built-In NetWare Support Windows 95 and the Windows NT 4.0 Workstation and Server versions include the Windows NT Multiple Provider Router (MPR) API, which isn't to be confused with the Multi-Protocol Routing Service. The MPR API provides a consistent application interface to the local file system, remote Windows network servers, and NetWare servers.

▶ **See** "The Windows NT 4.0 Multi-Protocol Router (MPR)," **p. 274**

Any workstation running either of these 32-bit operating systems has access internally to all services needed to use NetWare resources without the need for a separate NetWare-specific protocol stack. NDS isn't supported, although any of these clients can access a NetWare 4.x server running in bindery emulation mode.

Adding a Novell Protocol Stack If your client's operating system doesn't include native NetWare support, or if you require extended access to NetWare 4.1 services, you have no alternative but to install Novell NetWare client software on that client. Novell supplies full-function NetWare client software for numerous workstation operating systems, including DOS, Windows 3.x, Windows 95, Windows NT, OS/2, UNIX, and the Mac OS. The primary drawbacks to installing Novell client software are as follows:

- Additional effort is required to configure each workstation initially.

- Additional ongoing maintenance is required to support a more complex client environment.

- Additional conventional or base memory is needed for the second protocol stack.

N O T E The problems attendant to installing Novell client software are likely to disappear in the long run as Microsoft improves NetWare support in its client operating systems. Both Microsoft and Novell are now shipping 32-bit NetWare clients for Windows 95 that provide NDS support. ■

Part

III

Ch

14

Adding NetWare client support to coexist with an existing Microsoft Networking client is relatively straightforward, but doing so successfully requires that you first understand the fundamentals of how a Novell NetWare client accesses a NetWare server.

Novell clients require an IPX driver to provide network and transport layer services and a shell to provide network redirection. Novell clients can use one of the two following methods for meeting each of these requirements:

- The original Novell client software used a monolithic IPX driver with the NETx shell. The IPX driver, IPX.COM, is generated for each client using the Novell program WSGEN. The resulting IPX.COM file is specific to the individual client because it's hard-coded for the address and IRQ of the NIC, and so forth. The IPX.COM drivers are a nightmare to administer: Each change to a client configuration requires that the IPX.COM for that client be created anew. More important from an interoperability aspect, IPX.COM supports only a single IPX protocol stack.

- The NetWare shell was originally provided in versions specific to the version of DOS being used: NET2.COM was used with MS-DOS 2.x; NET3.COM was used with MS-DOS 3.x; and so on. With the advent of MS-DOS 5.0, Novell shipped a version called NETx, which could be used with any version of DOS. Variants of NETx called EMSNETx and XMSNETx were also provided to take advantage of expanded and extended memory, respectively.

With the advent of NetWare 4.0, Novell altered its client software support. The NETx shell was replaced by the Virtual Loadable Module (VLM) requester. More important from an interoperability standpoint, the IPX.COM was replaced by the Novell Open Datalink Interface (ODI), which breaks down the services formerly provided by IPX.COM into the following layers:

- The link support layer is loaded first by running the program LSL.COM provided by Novell. The link support layer provides a standardized low-level hardware interface, and handles routing of frames to the correct protocol service.

- The Multiple Link Interface Driver (MLID) is loaded next. The MLID is specific to the model of network interface card being used. For example, if you use a 3Com 3C509 Ethernet card, run the MLID 3C5X9.COM. If instead you're using a Novell NE2000 Ethernet card, run NE2000.COM. The MLID provides an interface to the link support layer running below it and to the protocol stacks running above it.

- The protocol support layer is the last ODI layer to be loaded. It provides services for one or more network protocols. For example, IPX services are provided by the program IPXODI.COM, which is often the only protocol support to be found on NetWare clients. However, LSL and the MLID can simultaneously load and service additional protocols, for example, TCPIP.EXE.

Clients that use ODI to provide protocol support can use either the NETx shell or the VLM requesters to provide redirection services. Although the VLM requester provides superior services and reduced memory usage, many NetWare clients continue to use the NETx shell.

In some cases, this is due to incompatibilities between the VLM requester and a few older network applications. In others, it's simply a matter of inertia. Clients that run the IPX.COM are limited to using NETx because the monolithic drivers don't support the VLM requester.

Whether you choose to install NETx NetWare shell or the VLM NetWare requester, ensure that your NICs are using Novell ODI drivers. The older drivers are no longer supported by Novell, are much harder to maintain, and—most importantly—don't let you run other protocols. As mentioned earlier, Windows NT Server is protocol independent. Windows NT Server is bundled with the NWLink protocol, so many NetWare system managers will be happy to learn that they don't have to install a second protocol stack on their clients. Other NetWare administrators may opt to load the Microsoft TCP/IP protocol stack supplied on the Windows NT Server 4.0 CD-ROM, giving their clients simultaneous access to NetWare, Windows NT, UNIX, and the Internet.

Microsoft Networking software uses a methodology similar to, but incompatible with, ODI to communicate with NICs. This method, called the Network Device Interface Specification (NDIS), offers functionality similar to ODI. Fortunately, both Microsoft and Novell provide *shim drivers* (or *shims*) that enable interoperability between ODI and NDIS. Microsoft PC-client software uses the NetWare ODI driver, automatically installing the NDIS-to-ODI shim.

Using Gateway Service for NetWare   The Gateway Service for NetWare is bundled with Windows NT Server 4.0 (see Figure 14.2). Running as a service on Windows NT Server 4.0, GSNW lets one or more Microsoft Networking clients access NetWare resources. Used with Client Service for NetWare and the NWLink protocol, GSNW enables Windows NT Server clients to access shared files on a NetWare server and to print to NetWare printers. Microsoft Networking clients don't need to run the IPX/SPX protocol because the GSNW translates the upper-layer SMB calls to and from NetWare NCP calls.

FIG. 14.2
Microsoft Networking clients access shared resources on a Novell NetWare server with the Gateway Service for NetWare.

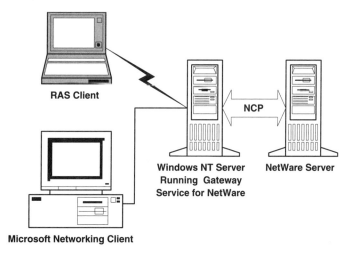

RAS Client

Windows NT Server Running Gateway Service for NetWare

NetWare Server

NCP

Microsoft Networking Client

Part
III

Ch
14

N O T E   An added benefit of using GSNW is that it can be deployed with Remote Access Service to provide remote Microsoft Networking clients access to NetWare file and print services transparently. ▦

▶ **See** "Network Protocol Configuration for RAS," **p. 357**

Before implementing GSNW, the Windows NT Server administrator and the NetWare administrator should consider the following issues:

- **NDS support**—GSNW is intended primarily for use in a NetWare 2.x/3.x environment and doesn't support Novell NDS. Although a GSNW client can access a NetWare 4.x server, it can do so only through bindery emulation mode.

- **Performance**—The GSNW uses a single NetWare connection through which all requests are routed to the NetWare server from GSNW clients. On one hand, this is an advantage because additional NetWare user licenses beyond the single license needed by GSNW don't need to be purchased for each user logging on to a NetWare server from GSNW. The downside of GSNW is that traffic from all GSNW users is routed through a single NetWare connection, so performance can degrade noticeably under a heavy load.

- **Shared rights**—GSNW uses a single connection to the NetWare server, so all GSNW clients use the same NetWare account. This means that all GSNW clients have identical trustee rights and other permissions, which are determined by the settings for that one account. All GSNW users are assigned to the NetWare group NTGATEWAY.

- **Logon scripts**—Microsoft networking clients don't execute NetWare logon scripts.

- **Backup**—The backup software bundled with NetWare doesn't back up GSNW clients.

- **Account management**—Users' access rights for GSNW are managed through the Windows NT account management utilities. NetWare account management utilities are used to manage a single GSNW specific account. All of the NT GSNW user accounts are funneled through this single account.

Configuring a NetWare Server to Use Gateway Service for NetWare   Little needs to be done on the NetWare server to prepare it for use with GSNW, but Supervisor access on the NetWare server is required to use the Novell SYSCON utility to make these changes. To prepare the NetWare server, follow these steps:

1. Log on to the NetWare 3.1x server as supervisor (or supervisor equivalent) and run SYSCON.EXE (see Figure 14.3).

2. Create a new NetWare group with the mandatory name NTGATEWAY (see Figure 14.4). Grant this group the file, directory, and printer rights that you want available to all users of the shared gateway.

FIG. 14.3

Use Novell's
SYSCON.EXE to
prepare the NetWare
3.1x server for the
Gateway Service for
NetWare.

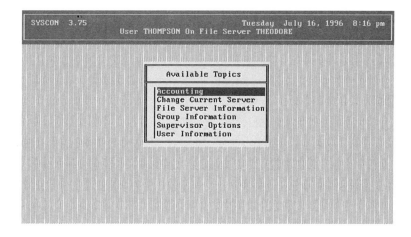

FIG. 14.4

Create the NetWare
group NTGATEWAY and
grant all file, directory,
and printer rights to be
shared.

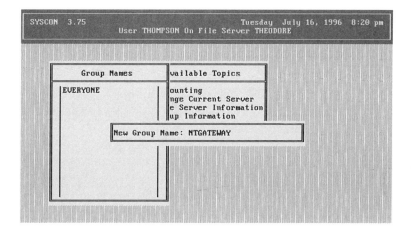

3. Create a new NetWare user with the same name and password as that used to log on to the Windows NT Server running GSNW (see Figure 14.5). This user is granted NetWare Supervisor Equivalent rights. This account is used by the system manager for maintenance and can also be used by the Migration Tool for NetWare, which requires full access to the NetWare server. With this account, logging on to the NetWare server from the computer running Windows NT Server enables you to run NetWare utilities, in addition to using NetWare files and printers.

Part
III

Ch
14

FIG. 14.5
Create a supervisor equivalent user for system maintenance and to run NetWare utilities.

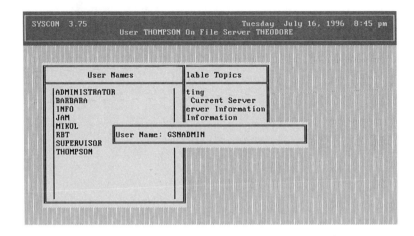

4. Create one or more new NetWare user accounts to be used by GSNW users, and assign each of these accounts to the NTGATEWAY group (see Figure 14.6). Each account inherits the rights granted to the NTGATEWAY group and can also be assigned additional file and directory access rights of its own.

FIG. 14.6
Create NetWare user accounts for shared access to the NetWare server, and assign them to the NTGATEWAY group.

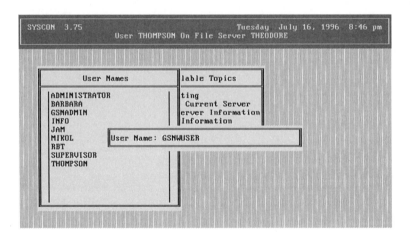

Installing Gateway Service for NetWare   After you make the necessary changes to your NetWare server, the next step is to install the GSNW on your Windows NT Server. Proceed as follows:

1. In Control Panel, double-click the Network tool to display the Network property sheet. Click the Services tab to display installed network services (see Figure 14.7).

FIG. 14.7

You can display installed Network Services in the Network property sheet.

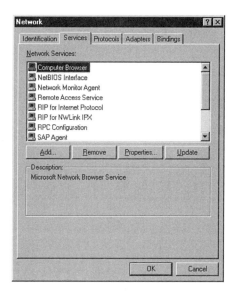

2. Click Add to display the Select Network Service dialog box (see Figure 14.8).

FIG. 14.8

Select Gateway (and Client) Services for NetWare in the Select Network Service dialog box.

3. Select Gateway (and Client) Services for NetWare and click OK to display the Windows NT Setup dialog box (see Figure 14.9).

Part
III

Ch
14

FIG. 14.9

Specify the location of the Gateway Service for NetWare distribution files in the Windows NT Setup dialog box.

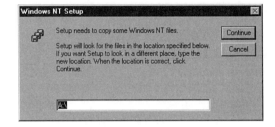

4. In the text box, type the drive and path name where the GSNW distribution files are located, and click Continue to begin copying files. Windows NT Setup displays the progress of the file copying operation.

N O T E At this point, the NWLink IPX/SPX Protocol Configuration dialog box may appear if you have more than one NIC installed in your server or if Windows NT can't automatically configure the protocol. If so, specify which NIC is to be used to link to the NetWare server. Windows NT Server normally detects the correct frame type needed by this NIC to communicate with the NetWare server and installs it as a default, showing the Frame Type as Auto Detected.

If for some reason you need to change the frame type, choose one from the Frame Type list box. Other tunable parameters are stored in the Registry and can be changed by clicking the Advanced button.

There's usually no reason to alter these settings. Make sure that you have a good reason before you attempt to do so. ■

5. After all files are copied, the Network dialog box reappears, with Gateway Service for NetWare now visible as an installed network service (see Figure 14.10).

FIG. 14.10

The Network property sheet displays Gateway Service for NetWare as an installed network service.

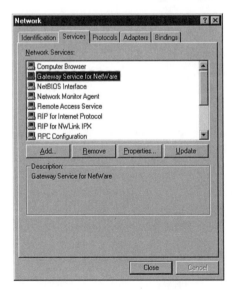

6. Click Close to complete the installation of Gateway Service for NetWare. Windows NT Server then configures and stores the affected bindings.

When the bindings review is complete, the Network Settings Change dialog box appears to notify you that you must restart Windows NT Server before the changes will take effect.

Choosing a Preferred NetWare Server   If more than one NetWare server exists on your network when GSNW is first run, the Select Preferred Server for NetWare dialog box displays to prompt you to choose one of these servers as the default server to which GSNW connects. You can either choose one of the servers as the default preferred server for that logon account, or choose none. Based on your selection, the preferred server is determined as follows:

■ If you specify a server, that server remains your preferred server until you explicitly change it. Because the server that you first attach to performs the logon validation that's then used to determine user access to server resources, specifying a server is normally preferable.

■ If you specify no preferred server, GSNW locates the nearest NetWare server each time you log on. Understand that *nearest* means the NetWare server that responds the fastest at the moment you log on, so if you choose the None option, you can't predict which server you'll connect to.

Enabling the Gateway and Activating Shares   After you create the necessary group and user accounts on the NetWare server and install GSNW, the next step is to enable GSNW. Follow these steps:

1. From Control Panel, double-click the GSNW tool to display the Gateway Service for NetWare dialog box (see Figure 14.11).

FIG. 14.11

Set the preferred server and other options in the Gateway Service for NetWare dialog box

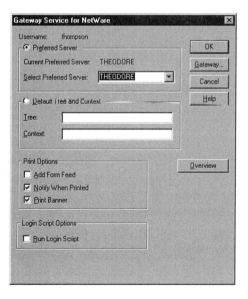

2. Click Gateway to display the Configure Gateway dialog box. Mark the Enable Gateway check box, and fill in the Gateway Account, Password, and Confirm Password text boxes, as shown in Figure 14.12.

FIG. 14.12

Enable the gateway and enter account name and password information in the Configure Gateway dialog box.

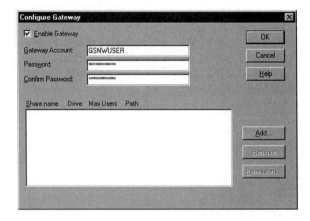

3. Choose Add to display the New Share dialog box (see Figure 14.13). Enter a Share Name by which the resource will be known. Next, enter the Network Path associated with the share. Optionally, enter a Comment to further describe the shared resource. Finally, select a drive letter from the drop-down list to be assigned to the share.

FIG. 14.13

You can enter a share name, specify the associated network path, and designate a drive letter by which the share can be accessed.

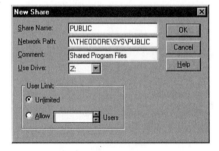

4. The User Limit section enables you to specify the maximum number of users who can access the share concurrently. Select either Unlimited or Allow, and use the arrow keys to specify a maximum allowable number of concurrent users.

5. After you complete all this information, click OK to accept your changes.

6. The Configure Gateway dialog box reappears, with the new share visible (see Figure 14.14). Use the Add button to create additional shares as needed. Use the Remove button to remove unneeded shares.

FIG. 14.14

The completed Configure Gateway dialog box, showing the newly created share.

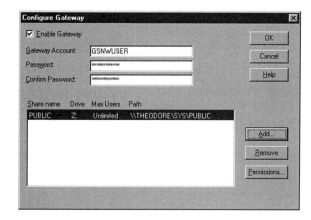

7. To set permissions for the shares you've just created, choose Permissions to display the Access Through Share Permissions dialog box (see Figure 14.15).

FIG. 14.15

Assign permissions for the newly created share in the Access Through Share Permissions dialog box.

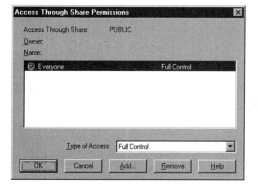

Installing and Configuring a GSNW Print Gateway   Installing a GSNW print gateway enables Microsoft Networking users to print to NetWare printers. After Gateway Service for NetWare is installed and enabled and a print gateway is configured, a NetWare printer appears on the Windows NT Server computer simply as another shared printer. Access to, and control of, shared NetWare printers is determined by setting the properties for the shared printer from within the Printers folder on the Windows NT server. Print jobs sent to the gateway are redirected to the NetWare print queue that the gateway is mapped to.

To install and configure the GSNW print gateway, follow these steps:

1. From the Start menu, choose Settings, Printers to display the Printers folder. Double-click the Add Printer icon to display the Add Printer Wizard (see Figure 14.16).

Part
III

Ch
14

FIG. 14.16

Setting up a shared network printer with the Add Printer Wizard.

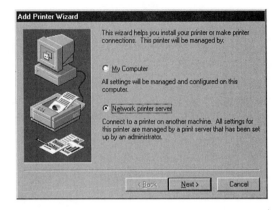

2. Select the Network Printer Server option, and click Next to display the Connect to Printer dialog box (see Figure 14.17).

FIG. 14.17

Displaying available print queues for a Windows NT server.

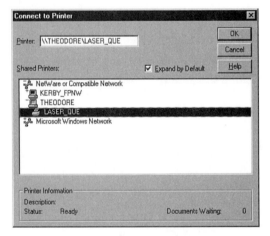

3. In the Shared Printers list, double-click NDS tree names and NetWare 3.1x server names to expand the display and list the shared printers available with each server. When you've located the printer to be shared, select it and click OK.

4. The Add Printer Wizard next prompts you to specify whether you want this printer to be the default printer for Windows applications (see Figure 14.18). Select Yes or No and then click Next.

FIG. 14.18

Specify that the printer won't be the default printer for Windows applications.

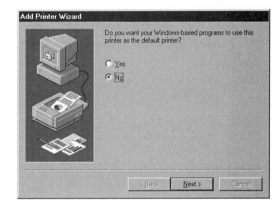

5. The Add Printer Wizard informs you that the printer has been installed successfully (see Figure 14.19). Click Finish to complete the installation and return to the Printers folder. At this point, the shared printer is installed but not yet enabled.

FIG. 14.19

The Add Printer Wizard's final step in adding a print queue for a NetWare printer.

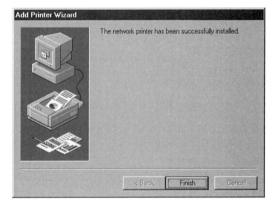

6. To enable the newly created shared printer, right-click its icon to display the context-sensitive menu, and choose Properties to display the print queue property sheet.

7. Select the Shared option button and enter a name for the shared printer (see Figure 14.20).

Part
III

Ch
14

FIG. 14.20
Specify a Share Name for the printer.

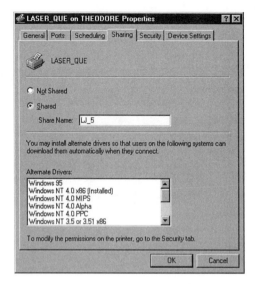

8. Choose OK to accept your changes and return to the Printers folder. Close the Printers folder. The shared printer is now available for use by authorized GSNW users.

Microsoft Networking clients now see the shared NetWare printer as they would any shared printer available on the Windows NT server.

Accessing Microsoft Windows NT Servers Using NetWare Clients

Many LAN administrators are faced with integrating a new Windows NT server into an existing network that includes a large installed base of NetWare clients. You may have scores or hundreds of clients, each already running Novell client software to access the existing NetWare servers. Visiting each workstation to install and configure new network client software is expensive, time-consuming, and disruptive. Fortunately, Microsoft offers a way to avoid this effort and cost by using the existing NetWare client software to access the new Windows NT server.

File and Print Services for NetWare, shown as a diagram in Figure 14.21, is a $100 utility available from Microsoft that runs on Windows NT Server. Running File and Print Services for NetWare causes the Windows NT 4.0 server to appear to Novell clients as a NetWare 3.12 server. Unlike GSNW, the performance of File and Print Services for NetWare is very good and doesn't degrade under heavy load. Microsoft positions File and Print Services for NetWare as a product that not only eases integration of Windows NT into a NetWare environment, but one that also serves as an excellent transition tool.

FIG. 14.21
Emulating a NetWare
3.12 server with the
Windows NT 4.0 File
and Print Services for
NetWare.

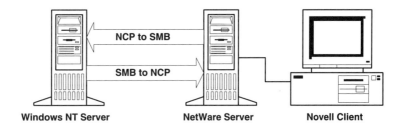

Windows NT Server   **NetWare Server**   **Novell Client**

N O T E It's easy to confuse the purposes of Gateway Service for NetWare versus File and Print
Services for NetWare. They're exactly opposite. Gateway Service for NetWare enables
Microsoft clients to access a Novell NetWare server. File and Print Service for NetWare enables Novell
clients to access a Windows NT server. ■

File and Print Services for NetWare uses as its foundation Windows NT Server's NWLink,
GSNW, and an enhanced version of the bundled Migration Tool for NetWare. With Directory
Service Manager for NetWare an administrator can centrally manage user accounts for both
NetWare and Windows NT servers. See the section "Directory Service Manager for Netware"
later in this chapter.

NetWare clients can access a Windows NT server running File and Print Services for NetWare
by using either the NetWare NETx shell or the VLM requester. Installing File and Print Services for NetWare creates a NetWare volume called :SYSVOL, which has a directory structure
analogous to a NetWare SYS: volume, including the LOGIN, PUBLIC, MAIL, and SYSTEM directories. Clients can continue to use utilities that are compatible with NetWare, including ATTACH,
LOGIN, LOGOUT, SETPASS, MAP, SLIST, CAPTURE, and ENDCAP, to access shared files and printers.

File and Print Services for NetWare also includes an enhanced version of the basic Migration
Tool for NetWare bundled with Windows NT Server. The Migration Tool for NetWare, covered
more fully later in the section "Directory Service Manager for NetWare," translates NetWare
account information to Windows NT Server, re-creating NetWare user and group information,
files and directories, security and permissions, and logon scripts.

CAUTION
Although File and Print Services for NetWare enables workstations running Novell client software to access
the Windows NT server without using Microsoft client software, you must still provide each such client with a
Windows NT Server user access license.

Part
III

Ch
14

Installing File and Print Services for NetWare   To install File and Print Services for NetWare (FPNW), follow these steps:

1. From Control Panel, double-click the Network tool to display the Network property sheet, and then click <u>A</u>dd to display the Select Network Service dialog box.

2. Click Have Disk to display the Insert Disk dialog box. Enter the drive and path where the FPNW distribution files are located, and then click OK to continue.

3. The Select OEM Option dialog box appears (see Figure 14.22). You're installing FPNW, so select File and Print Services for NetWare. Click OK to continue. Windows NT Setup copies the distribution files from the disk.

FIG. 14.22

Installing File and Print Services for NetWare from the distribution diskette.

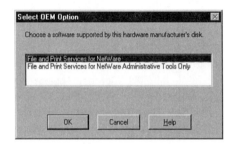

4. After all files are copied, the Install File and Print Services for NetWare dialog box appears (see Figure 14.23). Use this dialog box to specify the location of the NetWare SYS: volume, enter the supervisor account information, and tune server performance. Set the following values:

   • Directory for SYS Volume is completed with the default value of c:\SYSVOL. Accept this location, or specify an alternate drive and directory name. The location you specify must reside on an NTFS partition if you want to set NTFS file access permissions and NTFS directory access permissions to control access to the volume.

   • Server Name is completed with the default value of *SERVER_NAME_FPNW*. Accept this name or specify an alternate server name for users to access this server. The name you specify can't be the Microsoft computer name for the server.

   • Password and Confirm Password requires that you enter and reenter the supervisor account password for the NetWare server.

   • The options in the Tuning section enable you to determine server performance and resource usage, as follows:

      • **Minimize Memory Usage**—Using minimal memory at the expense of slower FPNW performance, this selection is most appropriate for a server that's used primarily for purposes other than sharing files and printers, for example, an application server.

- **Balance Between Memory**—Providing moderately high server performance with moderate memory usage, this choice is most appropriate for a general-purpose server that shares files and printers as well as runs applications.

- **Maximize Performance**—Providing the highest server performance at the expense of increased memory usage, this choice is most appropriate for a server that is dedicated to sharing files and printers.

FIG. 14.23

Specifying volume location, supervisor account information, and performance tuning in the Install File and Print Services for NetWare dialog box.

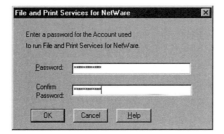

5. After you fill in all required values, click OK to accept your changes. The File and Print Services for NetWare dialog box appears (see Figure 14.24).

FIG. 14.24

Enter the password for the account to be used to run File and Print Services for NetWare.

Part

III

Ch

14

6. Enter and confirm the password to be used to run File and Print Services for NetWare and click OK. Windows NT Setup copies the FPNW distribution files to your server.

7. After all files are copied, the Network property sheet appears, with File and Print Services for NetWare visible as an installed network service (see Figure 14.25).

FIG. 14.25

The Network property sheet, displaying File and Print Services for NetWare as an installed network service.

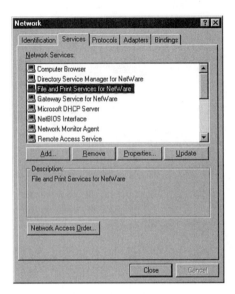

8. Click Close to complete the installation. Windows NT Server begins Bindings Configuration. After configuring the bindings, it stores the bindings and then finally reviews the bindings.

9. After Windows NT Server finishes configuring, reviewing, and storing the bindings, it displays the NWLink IPX/SPX Properties sheet (see Figure 14.26). Enter the Internal Network Number and specify parameters for each NIC. Use the Adapter drop-down list to select each adapter, and specify a frame type. Leave the frame type set at Auto Frame Type Detection unless you're experiencing problems connecting to the NetWare server.

10. Click the Routing tab (see Figure 14.27). If you want your Windows NT server to act as an IPX/SPX router, mark the Enable RIP Routing check box. After you complete the NWLink IPX/SPX Properties sheet, click OK to continue.

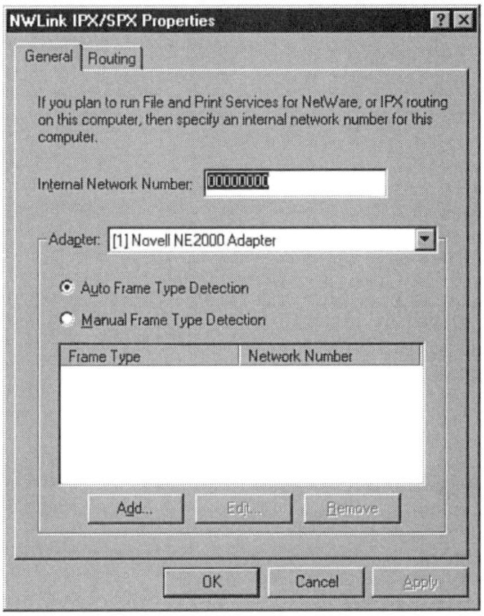

FIG. 14.26

The NWLink IPX/SPX Properties dialog box's General page enables you to specify protocol properties for each adapter.

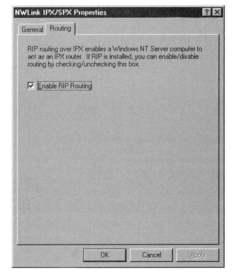

FIG. 14.27

Enable IPX/SPX RIP routing on the Routing page of the NWLink IPX/SPX Properties dialog box.

11. If the internal network number you provided in step 10 is invalid, the NWLink IPX/SPX message box shown in Figure 14.28 appears. When you click OK to return to the NWLink IPX/SPX Properties sheet, Windows NT Server generates a random internal network number for you (see Figure 14.29). Accept this randomly generated number, or enter a correct internal network number of your own. Choose OK to continue.

FIG. 14.28

The NWLink IPX/SPX message box that warns you that the internal network number is invalid.

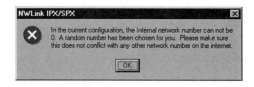

FIG. 14.29

The random internal network number generated by Windows NT Server.

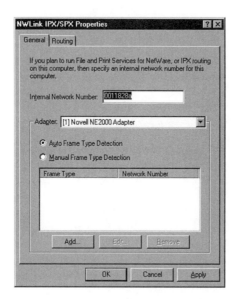

12. Windows NT again configures, stores, and reviews the bindings. The Network Settings Change message box appears to warn you that you must restart Windows NT Server before the changes take effect. After the server restarts, FPNW is available.

Configuring and Managing File and Print Services for NetWare   After you install File and Print Services for NetWare, you must configure it before Novell NetWare resources are available to users. Follow these steps to configure FPNW:

1. From Control Panel, double-click the FPNW tool to display the File and Print Services for NetWare dialog box (see Figure 14.30). The File Server Information section displays various statistics about the associated NetWare file server and the FPNW gateway to that server.

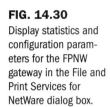

FIG. 14.30

Display statistics and configuration parameters for the FPNW gateway in the File and Print Services for NetWare dialog box.

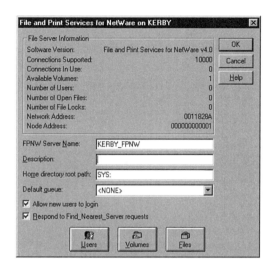

2. The FPNW Server Name text box displays the default name assigned to the FPNW gateway when it was installed. You can assign another name or accept the name as is.

3. Enter a short description of the FPNW gateway in the Description text box, if needed.

4. The Home Directory Root Path text box displays the NetWare volume assigned to this gateway when it was installed. You can assign another volume, or accept the volume displayed.

5. The Default Queue drop-down list is initially set to <NONE>. The list displays all NetWare print queues available on the server. Select one of these queues to specify it as the default print queue for FPNW users.

The Users, Volumes, and Files buttons in the File and Print Services for NetWare dialog box enable you to manage the FPNW gateway, as follows:

1. Click Users to display the Users dialog box (see Figure 14.31). The Connected Users list displays the name, Network Address, Node Address, and Login Time for each user. You can use this list to Disconnect a user, to Disconnect All users, or to Send Message to a user or users. The Resources list displays the Drives and Opens for each resource.

2. After you finish managing users, click Close to return to the File and Print Services for NetWare dialog box.

3. Click Volumes to display the Volumes Usage dialog box (see Figure 14.32). The Volume list displays available volumes. For each volume, Users lists the current number of users accessing that volume; Max Users lists the maximum number of concurrent users allowed; and Path lists the Windows NT Server drive and folder associated with the NetWare volume.

Part
III

Ch
14

FIG. 14.31

Display user statistics and managing users with the Users dialog box.

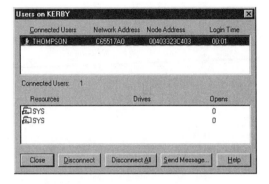

FIG. 14.32

Display volume statistics and managing volumes in the Volumes Usage dialog box.

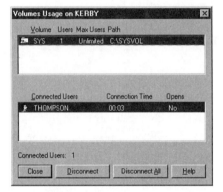

4. The Connected Users list displays the name of each Connected User, Connection Time, and Opens for the volume highlighted in the Volume list. You can disconnect a specific user by highlighting that user and choosing Disconnect, or disconnect all users by choosing Disconnect All. After you finish managing volumes, click Close to return to the File and Print Services for NetWare dialog box.

5. Click Files to display the Files Opened by Users dialog box (see Figure 14.33). The Opened By list displays the name of the user who opened each listed file. For each open file, For displays the permissions associated with that open; Locks displays the number of Locks on that file; and Volume and Path display the location of the file. Click Close File to close a selected file. Click Close All Files to close all files listed. Click Refresh to update the list of displayed files.

6. After you finish managing files, click Close to return to the File and Print Services for NetWare dialog box.

After you finish configuring and managing the FPNW gateway, click OK to accept the changes and close the File and Print Services for NetWare dialog box.

FIG. 14.33
Display file statistics and managing files with the Files Opened by Users dialog box.

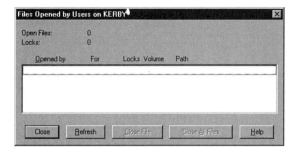

Other Windows NT Server Integration Tools for NetWare

In addition to GSNW and the File and Print Service for NetWare, two other tools are available for Windows NT Server to aid integration with Novell NetWare environments. The Directory Service Manager for NetWare enables you to manage user accounts on Windows NT servers and NetWare servers using a single integrated database. The Multi-Protocol Routing Service enables your Windows NT server to provide software routing to link networks.

Directory Service Manager for NetWare If, in addition to one or more Windows NT servers, your network includes Novell NetWare 2.x/3.x servers or NetWare 4.x servers running bindery emulation, you might consider buying Directory Service Manager for NetWare. Directory Service Manager for NetWare is used initially to export NetWare user account information into Windows NT Directory Services and to subsequently maintain all Windows NT Server and NetWare Server user account information in a common database (see Figure 14.34).

FIG. 14.34
Directory Service Manager for NetWare connects NetWare 2.x/3.x servers to a Windows NT 4.0 domain.

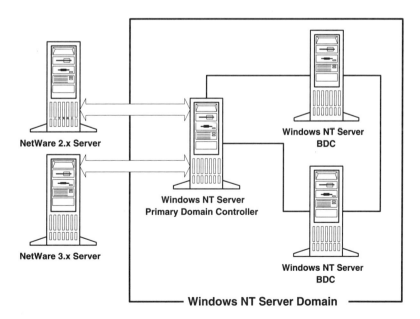

Part
III

Ch
14

During the initial transfer of NetWare user account information, the administrator has the option of creating a map file to re-create the NetWare accounts' passwords, assign a single password to all accounts, or set the password to the username. The *Directory Service Manager for NetWare Administrators Guide* lists the necessary steps involved to import the NetWare servers user account information. The initial setup process is complicated, so Directory Service Manager for NetWare includes a Trial Run option that creates a log file containing the account information that would be migrated to the Windows NT Server.

After you select the user and groups to be propagated to and from the NetWare servers, any changes to those accounts on Windows NT Server are replicated automatically to the NetWare servers. The replication process isn't bidirectional, so all subsequent changes must be made using Directory Service Manager for NetWare. When the initial migration is complete, the Directory Service Manager for NetWare database doesn't reflect any changes made directly to a NetWare server. Once installed, Directory Service Manager for NetWare provides a single network logon (see Figure 14.35).

FIG. 14.35

Creating a single network logon for NetWare clients across two Windows NT domains.

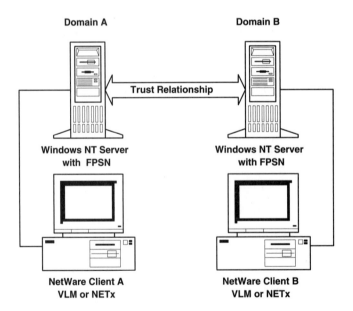

Installing Directory Service Manager for NetWare   To install Directory Service Manager for NetWare, follow these steps:

1. From Control Panel, double-click the Network tool to display the Network property sheet. Click the Services tab.

2. Choose Add to display the Select Network Service dialog box. Windows NT Server 4.0 builds a list of available services and displays them in the Network Service list box.

N O T E If an older version of Directory Service for NetWare is already installed on the computer, it appears in the Network Service list box. Don't select the older version; instead, choose Have Disk to install the current version. ▓

3. Click Have Disk to display the Insert Disk dialog box. In the text box, type the drive and path name where the DSMN distribution files are located, and then choose OK. The Select OEM Option dialog box appears (see Figure 14.36). You're installing the full service, so select Directory Service Manager for NetWare and click OK.

FIG. 14.36

Choose the full Directory Service Manager for NetWare in the Select OEM Option dialog box.

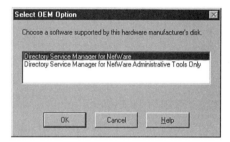

N O T E If you're installing directly from the distribution CD, the DSMN distribution files are located in *d*:\dsmn\nt40*processor*; *d* is the drive letter assigned to your CD-ROM drive, and *processor* is the type of processor installed in your server, such as i386 for Intel computers. ▓

4. After Setup installs the files, the Install Directory Service Manager for NetWare dialog box appears (see Figure 14.37). Enter and confirm a password of your choice for the service account, and click OK.

FIG. 14.37

Enter and confirm the password for the account to be used for DSNW.

5. Windows NT Server returns to the Network property sheet, displaying DSMN as an installed network service (see Figure 14.38).

FIG. 14.38

The Network property sheet displays DSMN as an installed network service.

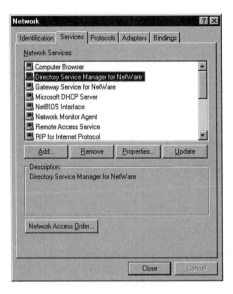

6. Click Close to complete the installation. Windows NT Server configures, stores, and reviews bindings. The Network Settings Change dialog box notifies you that you must restart the server before the changes take effect.

Configuring and Managing Directory Service Manager for NetWare   After you install DSMN, follow these steps to configure and manage it:

> **CAUTION**
>
> This procedure makes changes to the bindery on your NetWare server. Before you begin, be sure to back up the bindery. To do so, log on to the NetWare server as supervisor or supervisor equivalent from a DOS, Windows 3.1x, or Windows 95 client (you can't run the Novell system utilities from Windows NT). Notify all connected NetWare clients to log off. After they do so, run BINDFIX.EXE. Store the resulting three bindery backup files (NET$OBJ.OLD, NET$PROP.OLD, and NET$VAL.OLD) in a safe place before continuing.

1. From the Start menu, choose Programs, Administrative Tools, and Directory Service Manager for NetWare to run the Synchronization Manager. The title bar displays the domain name you're managing. When first run, the Synchronization Manager displays an empty NetWare Server list box, shown in Figure 14.39.

2. From the NetWare Server menu, choose Add Server to Manage to display the Select NetWare Server dialog box (see Figure 14.40). The Select NetWare Server list displays available NetWare servers.

FIG. 14.39

This is the initial status of DSMN's Synchronization Manager. After its first run, the synchronizing manager will display the directories that are synchronized.

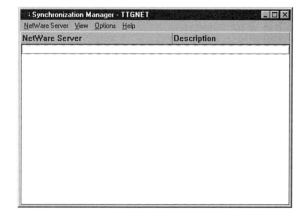

FIG. 14.40

Display available NetWare servers in the Select NetWare Server dialog box.

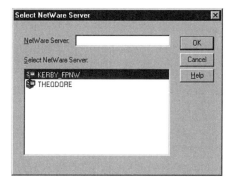

3. Select one of the servers listed and click OK to display the Connect to NetWare Server dialog box (see Figure 14.41). Enter a username and a password. This account must be either the supervisor or another account with supervisor equivalent privileges on the NetWare server.

FIG. 14.41

Specify a username in the Connect to NetWare Server dialog box.

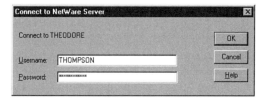

Part
III

Ch
14

4. Click OK to display the Propagate NetWare Accounts to Windows NT Domain dialog box (see Figure 14.42).

FIG. 14.42

The default NetWare users and groups are propagated to Windows NT Server by DSMN synchronization.

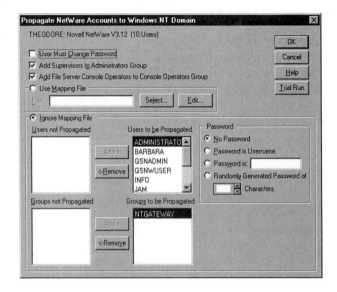

5. By default, all NetWare users are placed in the Users to Be Propagated list box, and all NetWare groups are placed in the Groups to Be Propagated list box. Use the Add and Remove buttons to move users and groups between the list boxes. Also specify the following settings:

   - **User Must Change Password**—If marked, this specifies that a user must immediately change his password when he first logs on.
   - **Add Supervisors to Administrators Group**—If marked, this specifies that Novell supervisor and supervisor equivalent users will be added as members of the Windows NT Administrators group.
   - **Add File Server Console Operators to Console Operators Group**—If marked, this specifies that Novell File Server Console Operators will be added as members of the Windows NT Console Operators group.
   - **Use Mapping File**—If selected, this specifies that individual user propagation parameters are based on the contents of an ASCII mapping file.
   - **The Password section**—This enables you to specify how passwords are assigned on the newly created Windows NT accounts. Select one of the option buttons to determine password assignments, as follows:

No Password—Specifies that the new account won't be assigned a password

Password Is Username—Specifies that the password will be set to the username for each account

Password Is—Enables you to specify a single password that will be used for all newly created accounts

Randomly Generated Password Of—Specifies that each newly created account will have a randomly generated password with the number of characters specified by the Characters spinner box

6. After you complete the Propagate NetWare Accounts to Windows NT Domain dialog box as shown in Figure 14.43, click Trial Run to test your settings. If a problem occurs during the trial run, a message box displays the problem and gives you the opportunity to correct it. Fix any problems reported and rerun the trial run until it completes successfully.

FIG. 14.43

Specify changes to the default settings of the Propagate NetWare Accounts to Windows NT Domain dialog box.

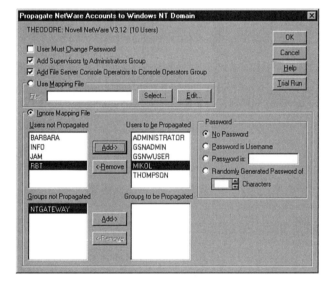

7. When the trial run completes successfully, the Synchronization Manager message box (see Figure 14.44) tells you so. Click Yes to display the trial run log file (see Figure 14.45).

Part
III

Ch
14

FIG. 14.44

The Synchronization Manager's message after a trial run succeeds.

FIG. 14.45

Display the trial-run log file in Notepad.

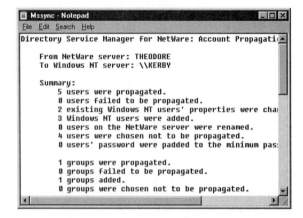

8. Review the log file to make sure that synchronization takes place as expected. When you're satisfied that everything is correct, close the log file to return to the Propagate NetWare Accounts to Windows NT Domain dialog box.

9. Click OK to complete the synchronization. The Synchronization Manager message box (see Figure 14.46) notifies you that you should back up your NetWare bindery before proceeding.

FIG. 14.46

Synchronization Manager's warning to back up your NetWare bindery before proceeding.

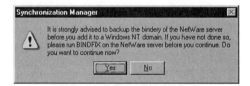

10. When you're satisfied that your NetWare bindery is safe, click Yes to display the Set Propagated Accounts dialog box (see Figure 14.47).

FIG. 14.47
The Set Propagated Accounts dialog box specifies which accounts will be propagated, based on group membership.

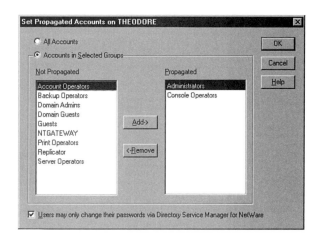

N O T E By default, the Users May Only Change Their Passwords via Directory Service Manager for NetWare check box is marked. If you want users to be able to change their passwords by using standard Novell utilities, unmark this check box. ▪

11. Use the Add and Remove buttons to specify the users to be propagated. After you complete this process, click OK to propagate the accounts and display the Synchronization Manager message box shown in Figure 14.48. Click Yes to remove the users and groups that weren't selected to be propagated from the NetWare server; click No to leave those users and groups on the NetWare server.

FIG. 14.48
Synchronization Manager's message that the selected accounts have been propagated.

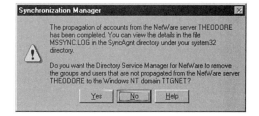

12. The Synchronization Manager appears, with the newly propagated NetWare server visible. Select that server and use the NetWare Server menu to manage the server (see Figure 14.49).

Part
III

Ch
14

FIG. 14.49
Synchronization
Manager displays the
newly propagated
NetWare server,
enabling you to
manage it.

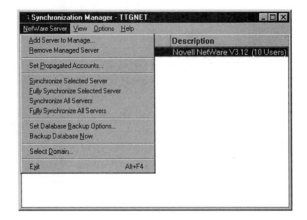

Windows NT Integration with UNIX

This section describes the integration of the Microsoft BackOffice components with the UNIX operating system. Ever since the earlier research releases of UNIX at AT&T, it has been a landmark operating system. The UNIX system has led the way to open computing. The majority of client-server and Internet systems owe a large part of their heritage to the UNIX operating system.

Microsoft has put considerable effort into ensuring that the BackOffice products integrate well with UNIX. This shows Microsoft's commitment to open computing, and ensures that network managers in homogenous operating environments will be able to integrate the BackOffice components into their operations. This section addresses how BackOffice and the UNIX operating system interact at each of these levels.

Network Protocols

Prior to the development of Windows NT, Microsoft developed the Xenix operating system. Xenix was a 16-bit port of the original AT&T UNIX Operating system developed to run on the Intel 80286 processor. In addition, Microsoft joined with IBM to develop the MS-Net or LAN Manager Network Operating System. The LAN Manager operating system provided file and print sharing. The main advantage of the LAN Manager Operating System is that it was installed on top of the main operating systems. The LAN Manager Operating system was primarily supported on OS/2 and UNIX. The LAN Manger was based on the NetBIOS protocol. Sytek Inc., Sunnyvale, California, developed the NetBIOS specification in 1984.

The end result for the Windows NT operating system is broad support of communications architecture. In a heterogeneous network environment, the Windows NT Server provides a large number of connectivity options out of the box. For UNIX, providing LAN manager connectivity is typically an expensive third-party upgrade.

Microsoft has relied heavily on the capability to encapsulate NetBIOS communications traffic into different transport layer protocols. Supported transport layer protocols include TCP/IP, IPX/SPX, and the native Windows NT NetBEUI. Microsoft will increasingly move to network components that do not rely on NetBIOS encapsulation. The Windows NT network components will be engineered to natively speak the differing protocols. See the discussion in the section "Common Internet File System" later in this chapter to see more about how Microsoft is going to sever its ties with the NetBIOS interface.

FTP and Telnet Servers

In order to provide a basic set of connectivity with the UNIX environment, Windows NT ships with the necessary TCP/IP client applications. These client applications include Telnet, FTP, lpr, and SNMP. In addition, the Windows NT resource kit contains very useful UNIX-like servers for these same applications. These server components include a Telnet service, an FTP service, and an lpr service. The lpr service and client applications are common UNIX utilties that allow users on one UNIX machine to print to printers on another UNIX machine.

> **N O T E** In the Windows NT operating system, a server type application is typically run as a service. In the UNIX operating system, a server application is often a *daemon*, which is a background process. ▓

The POSIX operating environment provides many of the commonly used UNIX command-line options. With POSIX and Telnet server service installed, it is possible for a user logged on to a UNIX system to Telnet to a Windows NT server and use many of the same command-line options from the UNIX system. Many server type utilities that have existed on UNIX rely on UNIX commands to get their jobs done. This is why the POSIX system is often important. These UNIX demons could not be ported to Windows NT unless these commands were available.

POSIX for Windows NT is an optional operating system extentsion that is shipped with Windows NT. (POSIX stands for Portable Operating System Interface.) The POSIX standard has been accepted by IEEE and the ISO standards bodies. POSIX specifies a base level of operating system APIs and command-line utilities. This base is very similar to UNIX and includes commands such as ls to list a directory and cd to change a directory. By default, the POSIX subsystem on Windows NT is installed and configured. When a POSIX application is started, the POSIX subsystem is started and application is launched.

For many years, system administrators have remote shelled between UNIX systems to ease administration. The 4.0 version of Windows NT now ships with a rexec client. This enables a NT 4.0 workstation to remote execute a command on a rexec server. The rexec is short for *remote execution*. A command that is proceeded by a rexec will run on a remote host. This has always provided the capability to kick off remote jobs in the UNIX environment. It is now possible to rexec jobs between Windows NT machines and UNIX machines. Windows NT 4.0 does not ship with a service component that provides rexec server capabilities. In order to allow NT 4.0 to be a rexec server, you need to acquire some third-party software. Some providers of these include Seattle Labs, Software Innovations, and Altaman systems.

Part
III

Ch
14

Windows NT 4.0 ships with a shell called sh.exe that is a part of the POSIX subsystem. This command shell supports a limited set of features when compared to a UNIX shell. A large number of UNIX shell scripts could be very useful in the Windows NT environment. In order to use these shell scripts, the Windows NT administrator must install a third-party command shell. Some of the vendors that are offering good third-party shells for Windows NT that are compatible with UNIX shells include Seattle Labs and Altaman systems.

There are three potential sources for FTP servers that are readily available for the Windows NT Server environment. In Windows NT 4.0 Server, the FTP service was integrated as a part of the Internet Information Server (IIS). Normally, the Internet Information Server is installed during the installation of Windows NT 4.0 Server. If you did not install the IIS component, you need to install the IIS at this point.

▶ **See** "File Transfer Protocol," **p. 531**

The FTP server service is an optional component of IIS. To install this component, follow these steps:

1. Open the Control Panel. Double-click the Network applet icon.

2. Click the Services tab and click the Add button.

3. In the Select Network Service dialog box, choose Microsoft Internet Service Manager 2.0 (IIS). Click OK. This brings up the Microsoft Internet Service Manager 2.0 Setup dialog box (see Figure 14.50).

FIG. 14.50

The Microsoft Internet Service Manager Setup dialog box.

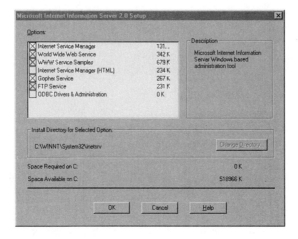

4. In this box, select the IIS components that you want to install. Make sure that the FTP Service is selected. Click OK.

Once the FTP server has been installed, FTP clients can connect to your FTP server. An FTP connection enables users to log on to your server and download files.

▶ **See** "File Transfer Protocol," **p. 531**

FTP servers introduce a point of security contention. The majority of users will want to configure their Windows NT server to allow only anonymous connections and assume that all of the files on the server are available to the outside world. Files that contain sensitive information should not be put in the directories that are available to the FTP server. If you choose to implement your FTP server to allow login accounts, you should be aware that the FTP protocol sends username password combinations over the network in a clear text format. People on the network can potentially snoop the username and password, thereby gaining access to the files on your FTP server.

The Telnet server enables clients on UNIX machines to log on and get a command prompt on your Windows NT server. This enables a remote client to launch batch and shell-script jobs that execute on the Windows NT server. Most major operating systems ship some form of Telnet client either with the operating system or as an add-on tool.

The Telnet server that ships with the Windows NT Server 4.0 Resource is a beta version of the telnet server. The latest release of the inbound Telnet server can be downloaded from **ftp://ntrk.microsoft.com\telnetd**. You will need to pick up this version before installing the Telnet server. To install the Telnet server, perform the following steps:

1. Open the Network Configuration dialog box.
2. Select the Services tab. Click the Add button to open the Add Services dialog box.
3. In the Add Services dialog box, select the Have Disk option.
4. In the Directory File dialog box, enter the path to your Windows NT resource kit Telnet directory. If you have the new beta file from the preceding URL, you should have two options in the Select OEM Option. The first option is the Remote Session Manager. The second option is the Telnetd Service Beta (Inbound Telnet). Choose the Remote Session Manager option.

One last facility that is often found in UNIX networks is the RCP capability. RCP in UNIX stands for remote copy. Remote copy allows one-line copies from a source system to a destination system. RCP is functionally close to FTP but operates a little differently. FTP always requires a user to log on to a server prior to transferring any files. RCP is more automated. RPC sends the username of the current system along with the request to copy the files. The destination system looks at the user ID and sending system's computer name. If the computer name is in a special file, the user identified by the user ID is given permissions as if the person had logged on that server. For this reason, RCP is only possible between systems that have been previously set up.

File and Printer Sharing

The previous section explains how Windows NT and UNIX operating systems are able to install communications protocols that enable them to communicate. This section covers the capability of Windows NT and UNIX machines to share files and printers. The following are two possibilities for sharing files in this fashion:

Part

III

Ch

14

- The Windows NT system can become a client to a UNIX machine that is a file server.
- A UNIX machine can become a client on a Windows NT file server.

The Network File System (NFS)

For Windows NT to become a client on a UNIX server, the Windows NT machine needs a Network File System (NFS) client. The same products that allow an NT workstation to become an NFS client also sell an NT NFS server. When this product is added to an NT system, the NT system will look like an NFS file server to any NFS client.

The Network File System specification was developed by Sun Microsystems Incorporated. The NFS file system heavily depends upon the TCP/IP networking architecture. Like many other file-sharing architectures, NFS integrates into the operating system. When a request is made to open or read a file that is on an NFS-shared mount point, the operating system redirects the file system call to the NFS redirector. A typical NFS network is shown in Figure 14.51.

FIG. 14.51

A typical NFS network.

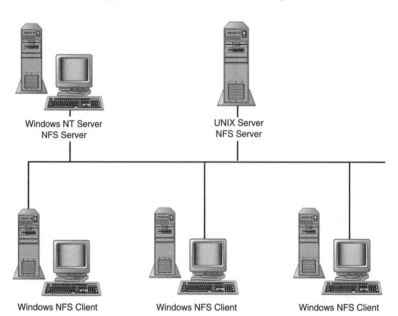

Windows NT Server
NFS Server

UNIX Server
NFS Server

Windows NFS Client

Windows NFS Client

Windows NFS Client

Three RFCs dictate the design and implementation of NFS. RFC 1094 dictates the design of NFS. RFC 1057 defines the RPC specification. RFC 1014 covers the external data representation specification XDR. A good reference for RFCs is found at **http://www.cis.ohio-state. edu/hypertext/information/rfc.html**.

Once the NFS software is installed on Windows NT machine, the Windows NT machine can attach to an NFS share that is available on the network. When users mount the NFS share, they need to log on to the NFS server because Windows NT does not know how to authenticate the user using the Windows NT login on the UNIX server. Typically, having the NFS software display a login window for the user does this.

One provider of NFS server software for Windows NT goes beyond the typical NFS server: The Intergraph Corporation is now shipping the DiskShare and DiskAccess products. The DiskAccess client enables a Windows 95 or Windows NT computer to access NFS mounts on remote machines. The DiskShare product enables the users on Windows NT workstation and server machines to create NFS drive shares. These drive shares are available to any NFS client.

The DiskShare product enables the administrator to create NFS shares directly from the Explorer or My Computer file browsers. It is a multithreaded product that runs kernel mode service. This design provides a scalable-efficient NFS solution for Windows NT.

DiskShare relies on the Windows NT native security to authorize access to resources. It enables the user to create a mapping file that maps an incoming NFS username to a Windows NT username. This mapping can be one NFS username to one Windows NT account name, or multiple NFS usernames to one Windows NT account. The security access to the files in the NFS share are checked using the normal Windows NT file access protocols. NFS relies on UNIX numeric user IDs (UIDs) to determine access to files. The DiskShare product enables the user to map these UIDs to Windows NT user accounts.

In addition, users that are mounting the NFS share from Windows-based clients running Intergraph's DiskAccess client are authenticated using their actual Windows login. See Chapter 4, "Enterprise Planning and Implementation," to understand Windows NT security.

When users are using the DiskAccess product, they are able to view NFS share points like any native Windows NT share point. The DiskAccess product is implemented as multithreaded Ring 0 Virtual Device Driver. This architecture ensures maximum performance when the machine is heavily loaded. When the DiskAccess product is from a Windows NT machine, each user of the machine can configure a login password and username that is sent to the NFS share.

LAN Manager for UNIX

The second alternative to provide file and print sharing between UNIX and Windows NT Server is to install UNIX software that enables the UNIX system to "talk" the Windows NT native networking language. The basic package that facilitates the integration of Microsoft networking into the UNIX operating system is the LAN Manger for UNIX (LMU 2.2). The LAN Manager for UNIX is the result of a partnership between Microsoft and AT&T GIS. In addition to providing LMU for AT&T's version of UNIX, the partnership provides for LMU source code to be sublicensed to other UNIX vendors.

N O T E Due to the three-way split of AT&T, the former AT&T GIS operating unit is changing its name back to NCR. ▧

The success of the LMU partnership has led AT&T and Microsoft to develop Advanced Server for UNIX (AS/U). AS/U is equivalent to Microsoft's Advance Server operating system running on the UNIX platform. The security groups and domain organization are identical between the two products. This allows NT and AS/U servers to serve users on the same domain. From the network clients' perspective, there is no difference between the AS/U and Windows NT Server

Part
III

Ch
14

systems. AS/U ships with native tools for server management that are different from the Windows NT tools. Since the AS/U and Windows NT servers are nearly identical, the administration tools from Windows NT can configure and manage an AS/U server. Likewise, the AS/U tools can configure and operate with Windows NT servers.

There are a large number of possibilities to deploying AS/U and Windows NT in a mixed environment. A small example is provided here to help explain how AS/U and Windows NT Server can integrate. The network diagram is shown in Figure 14.52.

FIG. 14.52
The Advanced Server UNIX platform in a heterogeneous network environment.

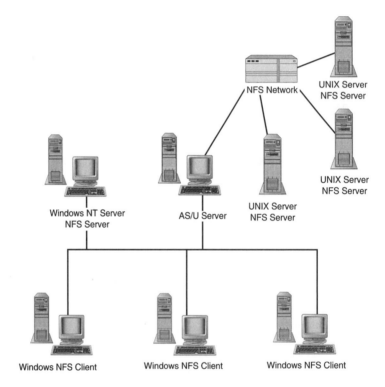

The AS/U diagram in Figure 14.52 shows a network with client workstations running Windows and Windows 95, a Windows NT Server, and several UNIX servers. The UNIX servers have been in place for some time. They share one another's files via the NFS network file system. The UNIX box that is running AS/U allows all of the clients running only Windows Networking to log on to any of the NFS shared drives. In this fashion, the AS/U operating system can provide a gateway from the Microsoft networking protocols to the NFS shared resources.

In Figure 14.52, it is important to note that the AS/U participates in the Windows NT Domain just like any other Windows NT Server. This includes participating in the Windows NT Domain, trust level relationships, and DHCP and WINS integration. The last service that AS/U provides is the capability to abstract the UNIX print spooler. This means that the Windows clients in Figure 14.52 are able to print directly to the AS/U printer share. The AS/U printer share maps the spooled print job to a UNIX print queue, which can reside anywhere on the UNIX network.

AT&T has sublicensed the AS/U source code to DEC for OSF/1 and VMS operating systems, HP for HP/UNIX and SCO for SCO-UNIX, Bull, SNI, and Olivetti operating systems. Unipress is porting the AS/U to Sun's Solaris operating system and IBM's AIX operating system. Almost all of the major UNIX vendors will offer AS/U.

Printer Sharing

Windows NT and Windows NT Advanced Server ships with a printing service that supports UNIX style printing. UNIX systems use a *de facto* standard for managing print jobs. This standard is based on the lpr, short for line printer, and lpd, short for line printer daemon printer client and printer server. The lpr command-line tool was used on UNIX systems to specify the destination and file to print. The lpr tool would then spool the print job to the line printer daemon lpd. The lpd server would manage ensuring that the job was spooled and printed correctly.

The Windows NT lpd is added to the system in the Network Configuration dialog box. You can get to the Network Configuration dialog box by choosing Settings, Control Panel and double-clicking the Network icon. Once you are in the Network Configuration dialog box, click the Add button. This brings up the select network service dialog box. In this dialog box, the lpd service is installed by selecting Microsoft TCP/IP Printing.

Once the printing service has been installed you can send print jobs by setting up a normal printer connected to the lpd spooler. You can also send print jobs directly to the lpd server running on the Windows NT system or a UNIX system. To send a print job from a Windows NT system to an lpd server, use the lpr command-line tool. The lpr command-line tool works identical to the lpr tool in UNIX.

Once the lpd daemon has been set up on the Windows NT system, this system can receive print jobs from UNIX hosts. This enables Windows clients and UNIX clients to share the same printers. The lpq—line printer query—utility allows a user to query the line printer for its status, including number of documents to print.

▶ **See** "Managing Access to Shared Resources," **p. 197**

Once jobs have been sent to the lpd server, you can monitor the status of an lpd server by using the lpq command, which produces a list of all of the jobs currently in the lpd server's printer queue.

In addition to the normal printing of jobs via the lpr and lpd tools, Windows NT has enhanced TCP/IP printing tools. The original tools first shipped with Windows NT covered the base requirements called for in RFC 1179. These enhancements were added to the base solution

Part
III

Ch
14

to address what many UNIX people had come to expect from lpr and lpd tools in the UNIX environment. They include the capability to source jobs from any available port between 512 and 1,023. Windows NT Server 4.0 also has the capability to print multiple data files per control file and to correctly handle host naming when in print-through mode.

Common Shared File Systems

You saw how it was possible for a Windows NT system to adopt the UNIX methods of sharing files and how a UNIX system could adopt a Windows NT method of sharing files. This section describes two new file systems that are being proposed as the standard file system for the Internet.

Why is there a need for a standard file system for the Internet? Currently, the HTTP standard for transmitting data does not provide applications and application developers with a rich set of commands that enable an application to read, write, lock, delete, or share files. The following two standards compete as the common file sharing system for the Internet:

- WebNFS from Sun Microsystems
- Common Internet File System (CIFS) from Microsoft

Neither of these systems is meant to replace the HTTP traffic common with Web browsers. They are more targeted at the older FTP method of transferring files.

WebNFS

The WebNFS specification is a minor upgrade to the NFS specification that has been a popular file-sharing protocol in UNIX systems for a long time. Because NFS is already based on the TCP/IP protocol, the system can be adopted to the Internet without much change.

WebNFS primarily changes the way that an NFS client attaches to a file on an NFS server. The problem with the normal NFS protocol is that it took more than four request response pairs to obtain a mount point and mount the file handle to the mount point. Once the client acquires the mount point, it must issue a lookup command for each component of the directory. For instance, to get the file **nfs://ftp.sun.com/pub/projects/whizbang/src/main.c** would take five lookup transmits. Each lookup transmit would move the client closer to the actual file that is desired.

NFS was designed for the LAN environment in which this type of penalty would not be that big of a problem. When this is translated to the Internet (where the server could be halfway around the world), the multiple requests to traverse the directory would cause a very long delay. The new WebNFS protocol enables the client to jump to the actual file handle with one request.

One additional change to the NFS specification is the inclusion of an URL-based file specifier. An NFS URL looks like **nfs://test.hp.com/pubdir/pcdir/filedir/drivers.txt.** This change enables WebNFS browsers to access NFS files directly.

The advantages of NFS over FTP is that NFS will almost always recover a file transfer that is in progress, whereas FTP is rarely able to recover an interrupted file transfer. NFS is able to handle all of a client's requests over one TCP connection. FTP demands a new request for each new request. This can cause a burden on heavy traffic sites.

The advantages of WebNFS over HTTP are that WebNFS does a better job of managing a client's interaction with the server. It uses fewer resources than equivalent HTTP activity. WebNFS browsers can follow the same links that an HTTP-based browser can. The NFS specification allows multiple simultaneous connections to the server. This enables a WebNFS client to issue five reads for five different files, and the server will begin responding as soon as it can. The data for complex pages can be interleaved. The downside of the WebNFS specification is that CGI scripts cannot be executed.

The main goal of WebNFS is to create an NFS file system that is much more efficient over Internet or WAN type connections. The NFS file system remains geared toward the LAN environment.

Common Internet File System (CIFS)

The Common Internet File System (CIFS) system proposed by Microsoft is a standard Internet file system based on the Server Message Block (SMB) protocol. Microsoft has submitted the CIFS 1.0 specification to the IETF for approval. In 1992, SMB became an X/Open standard. After its approval by X/Open, there were several ports of the SMB to different UNIX systems. One such popular port was the Samba system written for the Linux operating system.

The SMB file sharing system is often referred to as the DOS/Windows File API on the wire. The transmissions are very much like a serialized version of how a DOS/Windows program reads and writes a file. SMB has always had powerful commands. Each of the SMB commands can typically do a lot. This is in contrast to the NetWare protocol, which has taken 30 function calls to do the same that one SMB function call does.

The CIFS is an enhanced version of the SMB file system. The first thing the CIFS does is to remove unneeded components, stripping SMB down to just a file-sharing protocol. This removes printing, login, and file browsing out of the file sharing protocol. The second change was to remove SMB reliance on NetBIOS naming. Under CIFS, the SMB name resolution can use any name resolution, including NetBIOS and DNS. Some carryovers from the SMB to CIFS are the capability to chain requests and advance caching control.

CIFS adds some additional features to SMB to enhance its use as an Internet file-sharing platform. These enhancements include support for Microsoft's DFS file system. The DFS file system enables a network administrator to construct a file share that is the combination of many physical subdirectories. Each of these subdirectories could link to a subdirectory of the root share. Another helpful feature is file or directory change notification. This way, the client could access a share point and ask to be notified when a file appears. CIFS adds client-side cancellation of pending requests, enabling the client to stop a file transfer. CIFS also includes files with 64-bit offsets, Unicode file names, and file streams. CIFS includes fault tolerance improvements and optimizations for slow links.

Part
III

Ch
14

There are some issues facing CIFS being accepted as an Internet standard protocol. These issues mainly are the differences between UNIX and Windows NT. The Windows NT security model uses text-based usernames to identify users. UNIX systems use userIDs to identify users. It is not clear how the text-based CIFS username will be translated to UNIX-based UserIDs. It is even less clear if you are to have a UNIX system using CIFS to connect to another UNIX system. Again, there is no clear way to map the UserID to the username.

The two proposed standards are going to be compared over the next year as they both vie for the number one spot. They both can access files with one command. CIFS actually is a little more efficient in this regard because CIFS can open and lock the file in one request. CIFS is made to enable existing DOS and Windows applications to lock files over the Internet. This could prove to be bad in that a lot of these older applications would lock all of their files. In a large multiuser environment, this could cause problems. The applications written to manage NFS files are primarily targeted at UNIX and are more careful about the locking of files. Table 14.1 gives a list of comparisons for the CIFS and NFS file systems.

Table 14.1   A Comparison of CIFS and NFS

CIFS Architecture	NFS Architecture
Connection oriented	Not connection oriented.
Places burden of managing connection onto the server	Does not support locking to maintain a stateless connection. This will create a problem with PC applications that lock files.
Caching support	Increases complexity of client and server.
Most operations between Client and Server are atomic	Most operations can be repeated whether the previous operation worked or not. Service is stateful.

Remote Procedure Call (RPC) Support

The Remote Procedure Call (RPC) was originally implemented by Sun Microsystems for their version of the UNIX operating system. Sun Microsystems received approval from the Open Network Computing (ONC) as a standard for RPC implementation. This version of RPC is commonly known as the ONC/RPC specification. The Open Software Foundation chose to enhance ONC/RPC to be included as a part of its Distributed Computing Environment (DCE).

RPC enables a procedure on one client to call a function that actually ends up executing on a separate client. This paradigm becomes a very powerful tool for implementing distributed applications. Instead of custom writing the message protocols between the client and server, developers can implement the message passing part of the programs as function calls. In addition, RPC is independent of the network protocol that is used.

The magic of RPC is done by implementing a stub function call that is linked into the RPC program. This stub function call is linked from a library that is generated by running the RPC function calls through an Interface Definition Language (IDL) compiler. The IDL compiler generates a library function that can be called from any language. When the client stub function is called, it marshals all of the arguments to standard format. It packages the arguments to the function call and forwards the call to the server. The server unpackages and unmarshals the arguments. The function runs on the server. Once the server has completed the function, it marshals and packages the return parameters and sends them back to the requesting client.

Marshaling of the arguments refers to the conversion of the arguments to a standard operating system independent format. One of the bigger problems when passing data from one system to another is the variation in the format of the data. Some machines always break word boundaries on 32-bit intervals, while others use 16- or 64-bit intervals. Some machines use *little endian* data representation while others use *big endian*. The *endian* of a processor is the bit ordering within the byte. Marshaling enables the data to be converted and formatted in a standard fashion. This guarantees that the client and the servers can reside on different operating systems with different hardware architectures.

To extend its network computing model in Windows NT, Microsoft has implemented a version of RPC in the Windows NT operating system. The Microsoft RPC version differs somewhat from the DCE/RPC. Primarily the differences are in the RPC directory services. The DCE/RPC directory services are based upon the Cell Directory Services (CDS). Microsoft chose to offer a proprietary RPC Locator with Windows NT server. Microsoft has also included a CDS-compliant directory service. In order to use non-TCP/IP protocols in RPC processing, you will need to use the Microsoft RPC Locator. If you are integrating Microsoft RPC into your existing RPC infrastructure, the CDS directory service ensures that Directory services are available across the enterprise.

RPC directory services provide the client a method of locating services. When a client issues a call to an RPC function, the RPC component uses the RPC Locator to locate a server that is advertising the function that is getting called. RPC then routes the function call to that server.

The Microsoft implementation of RPC supports a wider range of protocols than most RPC offerings. Table 14.2 shows the protocols that are supported and the operating systems that are supported. The key for the table is as follows:

- C stands for Client Support
- N stands for No Support
- S stands for Server

Part
III

Ch
14

Table 14.2   Microsoft RPC Supported Protocols

Protocol	DOS	Win 3.x	Win 95	Win NT	Mac	UNIX
NetBIOS over TCP	C	C	N	C,S	N	N
NetBIOS over IPX	C	C	N	C,S	N	N
NetBIOS over NetBEUI	C	C	C,S	C,S	N	N
TCP/IP	C	C	C,S	C,S	C	C,S
Named Pipe	C	C	C	C,S	N	N
SPX	C	C	C,S	C,S	N	N
DECNet	C	C	N	N	N	N
AppleTalk	N	N	N	N	C	N
Banyan Vines	N	N	N	C,S	N	N
UDP/IP	C	C	N	C,S	N	N
IPX	C	C	N	C,S	N	N
Local Procedure Call	N	N	C,S	C,S	N	N

The Microsoft RPC implementation is a robust distributed computing platform. It is the basis for many of the management tools that are used on Windows NT server. The RPC functionality has become a key technology in the distribution of DCOM type objects.

Directory Services Interoperability

The Network Operating System vendors have really begun to heat up the competition in the delivery of Common Directory Services. These common directory services allow resources on a network to look like they are all organized under one directory tree.

A good example of what this looks like to the end user would be to imagine a directory tree. As the user begins to go up the directory tree, he not only is changing directories on one server, but changing from server to server. As each new server is attached, the user's security is passed to the new server automatically. The user will see a continuous directory tree.

The network managers are another group of people that are driving the use of more common directory services. The benefit of a common directory for network managers is that it is a way to reduce the overwhelming amount of information. Each user ends up with several different usernames on each system and each platform. For instance, a user that uses Windows to logon and use network resources, uses UNIX to process some legacy reports and connects to a SQL database would end up with three separate logins. If all of these products used a single directory source for usernames, then the administrator could configure the user with only one change.

The third group of people to benefit is developers. The process for enabling their applications to manipulate the network resources or usernames requires custom coding for the manipulation of each component. When a directory is in place, the developer can utilize just one set of APIs for the manipulation of users, file sharing, file security, printer sharing, and anything else on the network.

Of course, the real benefit to everyone comes when the directories become cross platform. When directories become cross platform, it will be possible for a user to cross different machines utilizing resources without ever knowing it. At that point, users no longer need to remember that their stock information is on server XYZ.

The drive behind reliable directory services has been led by Banyan, maker of the Banyan Vines Network Operating System, and Novell with the NetWare Directory Services. Microsoft is now offering the OLE/DS. Of these vendors, Novell was beginning to get a large amount of attention in this area. NDS was bolstered by a good client implementation for Windows, Window 95, and Windows NT. The majority of these vendors would like to get a user trapped into using their directory services. This makes it much easier for users to access resources on the vendor's native operating system. See Chapter 8, "Windows NT Server Directory Services," to see the details of Windows NT directory services.

The speed with which the Internet has exploded onto the computing scene has brought to light a common directory service that is now starting to get a lot of attention from all of the main operating system companies: The Lightweight Directory Access Protocol (LDAP) is now being proposed as the best shot at achieving good cross-platform directory services.

The LDAP specification was developed by the University of Michigan and the Internet Engineering Task Force. Currently, LDAP version 2 is the released version of the specifications. LDAP version 3 is currently in the works.

LDAP is a distillation of the Open System Interconnect (OSI) X.500 Directory Service. The X.500 Directory Service has proven to be too much of a burden in all but the largest of organizations. This is especially true for Windows, Mac OS, and DOS clients. LDAP will be used in the following three modes:

- **Organizing Web sites**—Once the currently available Web sites are in a standard directory, it becomes much easier to traverse up and down the tree and mark the location of items. The directory helps organize the seemingly disjointed hyperlinks. Microsoft and Netscape will both support LDAP in their browsers.

- **Accessing sensitive information**—Utilize security to provide users access to sensitive information.

- **Replicating databases**—LDAP was not designed as a replication protocol, but it has all of the necessary components to replicate databases.

Security in the LDAP environment is important because end users will want to control access to information, allowing some people access to the resource and not allowing others. The LDAP 2 specification allows for Kerberos encryption of the password while on the wire. LDAP 3 is looking at implementing the full X.509 security for the directory service.

Part
III
Ch
14

The capability to replicate directory services becomes very important in large organizations or when considering applying LDAP on the Internet. Without replication, the master server of a large network will become a large potential bottleneck. LDAP 3 is offering some forms of replication.

Netscape was an early adopter of the LDAP specification. Netscape is also a company with little or no legacy directory servers to support. As a result, Netscape is the largest proponent of LDAP and the largest user of LDAP.

Microsoft is beginning to release products that have LDAP support in them. Some of these products include the latest version of the Exchange Mail Server and the upcoming version of Internet Explorer. Microsoft has committed to making LDAP a standard offering component of the operating system with the next release of Windows NT. Microsoft is primarily moving forward with its original ODSI and OLE/DS initiatives. The LDAP connector becomes a service provider interface between the native directory and the LDAP directory.

Novell is also adding LDAP support to their NDS directory service. Novell feels that they have a strong directory offering with good OS support and solid multi-master replication. Its approach to LDAP is the least aggressive of the three vendors.

Netscape has rushed out and become a leader in the implementation of LDAP. It is now adding many features that are nonstandard. These features largely address some of the scalability and encryption problems that exist in the deployment of large LDAP networks.

LDAP is quickly becoming one of the more important standards available on Internet.

Common Application Programming Interfaces (APIs)

Again, with Application Programming Interfaces, two approaches can be taken. The first is to port a UNIX application to the Windows NT system. The second is to port a Windows NT system to the UNIX environment.

One advantage that a programmer can make use of is the availability of the OSF/DCE environment on both systems. This means that the communications portion of the application will not need to be ported from one system to the other, but can be used intact on either system.

Porting UNIX Applications to Windows NT

Bringing more of the UNIX API environment to Windows NT will greatly aid in the porting of a UNIX application. There is one application environment that leads in providing this functionality: the NuTCRACKER suite of development tools from DataFocus. Included in the NuTCRACKER SDK are the UNIX environment APIs, a porting guide, and UNIX system libraries. The UNIX system libraries run on top of the Win32 APIs and are tuned to the Windows NT environment. This system includes support for the full UNIX API including fork, exec, pipes, named pipes, message queues, signals, semaphores, and BSD sockets. The tool also includes the MKS Toolkit to aid the UNIX developer. The MKS Toolkit brings vi, cc, and utilities to make the Windows NT development environment more comfortable to the UNIX developer.

The NuTCRACKER X/SDK integrates the X11R5-based X/Server and libraries and the X/Motif libraries to the standard NuTCRACKER SDK. This enables the porting of X Windows applications.

Applications ported to Windows NT from UNIX can maintain a very UNIX-centric look or can take advantage of the newly available Win32 APIs as needed.

A second tool that enables the porting from UNIX to Windows NT is the Portage tool from Cnsynsys Computers Inc. It provides similar functions but it is a full port of UNIX SVR4 and UNIX SVR4.2 system in the Windows NT environment. When fully installed, a command window that is exactly like UNIX runs. The developer works in the text mode or the add-on X environment. The command window functions like the MKS toolkit and the Hamilton C Shell.

Porting Windows NT Applications to UNIX

Microsoft has begun an initiative to support vendors that are porting the MFC and Win32 APIs to the UNIX environment. This initiative is called the Window Interface Source Environment (WISE) in which Microsoft helps these vendors by supplying source code and engineering to help in their implementation of Win32 and MFC on the UNIX. There are two portions of this initiative: the WISE SDK and the WISE Emulator.

Choosing the WISE SDK enables the developer to port the Windows application on the UNIX platform. The resulting application will be targeted at the UNIX system that WISE SDK was engineered for. This produces the most robust and fastest port of the application, but also requires the most time. These tools include support for the latest features of Windows, including OLE, ActiveX, threads, and WinInet APIs. A tool that is considered a leader is the Wind/U toolkit from Bristol Technologies.

The WISE Emulator is more appropriate when the source code for the package is not available. The WISE Emulator will also emulate an x86 processor when it is run on systems that do not have an x86 processor.

In addition to those resources previously mentioned, many other UNIX connectivity utilities are available from third party vendors. Some of these utilities are available as freeware. They include enhanced Telnet and FTP servers, time servers that enable Windows NT systems to receive distributed time updates from UNIX servers, and Finger daemons that enable Windows NT servers to respond to standard Finger requests. Finger requests enable remote users to obtain user information about users on a system. X/Servers enable users of UNIX-based X Windows clients to log on to Windows NT X Windows servers. A good reference starting point for these and other important tools is the Internet Resources for Windows NT Internet Support page at **http://www.microsoft.com/windows/ntserver/tools/isupport.htm**.

Part
III

Ch
14

From Here...

One of Windows NT 4.0 strongest features is its ability to be deployed in a heterogeneous environment. You learned in this chapter that Windows NT 4.0 could be installed in an existing Novell NetWare LAN. You saw that File and Print Services for NetWare allows a Windows NT 4.0 server to look just like a NetWare file and print server. When there is a large network of NetWare clients, this solution allows NT 4.0 to drop into place and appear as just another NetWare resource. Further integration of Windows NT and NetWare allow the two network operating systems to share directory services. Directory services are the key to locating resources on a network. The more integrated the directory services, the more integrated the two operating systems become. The user or the network administrator can move users from NT 4.0 Servers to NetWare servers and back without notice.

In the future, Windows NT, NetWare, and UNIX will continue to increase their ability to integrate. You will see additional work in the area of Lightweight Directory Access Protocol (LDAP) and other directory services integration efforts. For more information on these and related topics, see the following chapters:

- For more information concerning TCP/IP, see Chapter 9, "Using TCP/IP with Windows NT Server."
- See Chapter 16, "The BackOffice I-Net Toolbox," for more information on using BackOffice in an I-net environment.

## CHAPTER 15

Wide Area Network Technologies

by Steve Hays

Businesses and organizations today, in order to share information and facilitate better communication in a global marketplace, are unifying their local area network (LAN) resources to form wide area networks (WANs). WANs enable organizations to take advantage of such innovative ideas as cross-functional project teams, distance learning, collaborative workgroups, telecommuting, videoconferencing, multimedia, and access to corporate data. ■

Building WANs

Take a look at the planning and strategies required for building WANs.

Open System Interconnection

Learn about the Open System Interconnection (OSI) reference model.

Networking services

Discover the communication services used to provide WAN connectivity between an organization's geographically dispersed locations.

Protocols

Look at some of the common protocols for the communication across the WAN.

Understanding WANs

WANs are growing in popularity, responding to corporate needs for communication and reduced communication costs. The geographic expansion of organizations, increasing numbers of telecommuters, and the growth of client-server and intranet applications have increased the demand for WANs. In constructing wide area internetworks to meet this rising demand, network managers continue to struggle with a variety of issues, including evolving services, emerging applications, and remote users.

In addition, the Telecommunications Act of 1996 is bringing many new challenges and opportunities for any organization with locations in the United States. Long distance carriers, cable providers, and local service providers can all now compete to provide local and long distance service. In the long term, customers will benefit from competitive lower rates and a wider selection of services. In the short term, however, there will be great volatility in the availability and pricing of WAN services.

Many of the potential providers are scrambling to define their service offerings and get them to market. Similar trends also exist on a global scale. During these times of rapid change, organizations need to be able to adapt their networks quickly. Therefore, a key characteristic of remote access and internetworking products is the flexibility to combine WAN services or change from one service to another quickly and easily.

The focus of this chapter is the technologies involved in implementing and supporting a WAN. Information provided in this chapter provides an overview of the steps required to create a WAN, the components that make up a WAN, and the technologies used.

Creation and modification of a corporate WAN is done with the consideration of specific business needs in mind. The following are some of the issues to consider when determining the appropriate WAN architecture:

- Demand for connectivity and access to remote resources
- Traffic and performance requirements
- Network and information security
- Reliability, redundancy, and recovery
- Scalability, growth, and evolution
- Central network management
- Costs

These issues are defined in this chapter, which functions as an introduction to WAN technology. Designing, developing, and supporting WANs is a specialized science; expertise can come only through education and experience. WANs and their supporting technologies and services are expanding at an unprecedented rate; however, the capable engineers who can plan implement and manage WANs are in short supply.

Building WANs

Building a WAN is a complex activity. A project of this magnitude requires extensive planning, resources, and commitment from the organization. The nature of the organization along with the goals and objectives sought should determine the scope of the project. The process should be iterative, allowing for contingencies and refinements in the technologies that make up the WAN. For more information on these issues, see Chapter 4, "Enterprise Planning and Implementation."

The entire process can be broken down into the following three distinct phases:

- **Analysis**—The analysis phase is a needs assessment of the organization to create a clear understanding of how the WAN project will achieve the goals of the organization.

- **Design**—In the design phase, the architecture of the WAN is defined in conformance to the business plan. A schedule of project tasks and an order of operation in which these tasks are performed is defined. Responsibilities required to complete the project are assigned to both internal and external resources.

- **Implementation**—The resources, technologies, and equipment come together in the implementation phase to create the WAN. This phase consists of the time and effort involved to physically build the WAN.

  ▶ **See** "Building Your Network," **p. 66**

Again, it is important that this is an iterative process to ensure a long, stable, and secure future for the WAN, and to be sure of its continued value to the organization. As new technologies arrive or the organizational needs change for any number of reasons, there will be a need for continued additions and modifications to the WAN.

To summarize, the design of a WAN consists of the following steps:

1. Identify your requirements.
2. Understand the fundamentals of data communication circuits.
3. Obtain pricing for your area.
4. Evaluate and select the data circuit cost/performance tradeoff that best meets your needs.
5. Understand WAN protocols, and specify organizational standards for them.

By following this straightforward approach, you'll enhance your chance for success.

Open System Interconnection

In order to have program-to-program communication between similar or dissimilar computers, standards must exist. The Open System Interconnection (OSI) reference model is a set of standards that has been developed by the International Standards Organization (ISO). The OSI reference model provides a common ground for manufacturers and service providers to ensure compatibly. Because of the OSI reference model, open systems can be developed with various vendors' equipment and software without the risk of total incompatibility.

OSI Reference Model Layers

The OSI reference model breaks down the communication process into seven layers. Each layer is responsible for providing information and pointers to the next higher layer in the OSI reference model. The application layer makes available network services to software application programs. Each layer describes certain tasks that must be performed by network hardware and software in order for network communication to take place.

Layer 1 through layer 3 support network access, while layer 4 through layer 7 support the communication between the message source and destination. As data is passed through the layers, each layer adds its own information to the packet that defines the configuration the packet is coming from. The data packet is interpreted by the receiver, breaking down each layer and resulting in the reception of the original data. The seven layers are described in the following sections.

Layer 7: Application Layer   This is the layer where applications that facilitate network connectivity reside—for example, FTP, Telnet, and electronic mail—and where network services—including file services, print services, message services, application services, and database services—are provided.

Layer 6: Presentation Layer   This is responsible for translating data into formats that can be readily understood by each computer system. The presentation layer concerns itself with translating differences at the bit level, byte level, or character level, and with file syntax. An example of this might be the translating of data formats between two different computer systems that have different data formats. Computers need to agree on the method of identifying the number of bits that equal a whole character and the file syntax that is used by each. The presentation layer also concerns itself with data compression and encryption.

Layer 5: Session Layer   This provides mechanisms that establish, maintain, synchronize, and manage communication between computer systems. The session layer is responsible for the establishment of connection ID numbers, and relies on the transport layer to provide the information that identifies the correct services. The session layer is responsible for the coordination of acknowledgment numbering and re-transmission procedures. It tracks who initially initiated a conversation.

The session layer is responsible for reestablishing a logical communication session between computers should that session end prematurely. The session layer would either resume the interrupted dialog, or initiate another session to the other computer. The session layer also manages a planned connection release of a communication session.

Layer 4: Transport Layer   This provides reliable end-to-end communication by providing service addressing, flow control, datagram segmentation, and end-to-end error checking. The transport layer ensures that packets arrive in one piece, and makes sure that the data is directed to the appropriate service. The transport layer concerns itself with the *service addressing,* which identifies addresses or ports that point to upper-layer network services.

The transport-level addressing also keeps track of multiple connections or conversations that might occur on a network-attached computer system. The transport layer is also responsible for breaking larger units of data sent down from higher layers into smaller pieces that can be transported across the network. These pieces would then be reassembled at the transport layer of the receiving computer system and passed on to that computer's higher layers.

Layer 3: Network Layer   This is responsible for the internetworking process that needs to occur to reliably send and receive data between networks. It provides logical addressing usually specified in software—not hard coded onto network interface cards—and provides for network routing, flow control, sequencing, and translation. Network-layer flow control monitors network congestion. Network-layer addressing provides addressing that is specific to the logical addressing assigned to a particular network protocol, such as an IP address.

Layer 2: Data-Link Layer   This provides the initial organization of the data bits into a structure called a *data-link frame*. This frame contains the beginning and end of the frame, source, and destination addresses; a method to ensure that the frame does not contain errors that may have occurred in the course of transmission through the transmission media; and an area to provide some basic administrative functions, such as flow control, frame length calculations, and protocol decisions.

The data-link layer is broken into two logical areas, the *Media Access Control* (*MAC*) sublayer and the *Logical Link Control* (*LLC*) sublayer. The MAC sublayer refers to the Media Access Protocol (the way that stations on a network gain access to the media and permission to transmit their data: contention, token passing, polling, and so on), and the physical addressing of stations on the network. This would include the source and destination address sections of the data-link frame.

The LLC sublayer includes portions of the data-link frame responsible for the frame synchronization, flow control, and error checking within the frame. The physical addressing at the data-link layer (used for source and destination addressing in a data-link layer frame) is called a physical address because this address (also called a MAC-layer address) is hard coded into the network interface card in a computer.

This addressing is useful for conveying all the information necessary to direct information to and from computers within a local network. The addressing is usually assigned by the manufacturer of the network interface at the time of manufacture. The first half of the MAC layer address contains hex address information that is unique to each manufacturer; the second half is unique to that individual NIC card.

Layer 1: Physical Layer   This is the foundation of communication between all computer systems. It describes the type of cabling system as the transmission media, the transmission devices that attach to the media, the physical connector specifications, and the electrical or optical signaling characteristics (analog or digital, signal levels, and signal encoding methods). The physical layer also describes the network topology and the distribution of the physical layer transmission media (i.e., in a bus, star, ring, mesh, and so on).

The OSI Reference Model in Action

In the OSI reference model, the left stack represents computer number one, the middle two stacks indicate the routed WAN, and the right stack indicates computer number two (see Figure 15.1). The arrows indicate the path taken by data sent from a program on computer number one to a program on computer number two through the routed WAN.

FIG. 15.1
Communications do not always travel through all of the seven layers of the OSI.

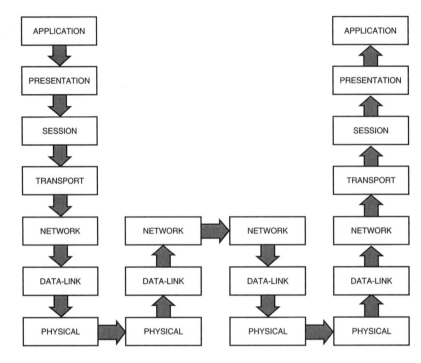

NOTE   Data on the receiving computer traverses the OSI in the opposite order it is sent from the transmitting computer. ▨

Communication between two computer systems begins on one system at the highest layer that communication occurs, goes down through to the physical layer, through the transmission media and network, over to the other computer at the physical layer, and then up through to the highest layer of communication on the other computer. This communication is usually symmetrical. In the case of this type of communication occurring through a routed WAN, the network portion of the diagram can also extend through the physical and data-link layers and to the network layer.

Not all methods of network communication extend to all the layers of the full OSI reference model. For example, communication between programs on differing hosts using TCP/IP might use all layers, while local Windows for Workgroups communication within the same network using the NetBEUI protocol might have communication occurring only at the data-link layer and physical layer levels.

Networking Services

WANs can be as simple as connecting two distant modems over a standard phone line. Most organizations, however, require higher performance than can be achieved through modems. Organizations need to be able to respond to changing communication demands without requiring wholesale revamping of WAN equipment and services. Fortunately, recent network developments have created technologies that offer several choices that meet these needs.

Selecting WAN services is becoming increasingly complex. The number of WAN services to choose from continues to grow, but no single service has emerged as the solution for all situations. Network managers must make constant tradeoffs between cost, performance, and availability. Leased digital circuits, for instance, are widely available but expensive, especially for applications that do not send data continually. Packet services, such as X.25, may be more affordable, but offer lower throughput. Although switched services, such as ISDN, offer higher throughput, they are not yet available in all locations and may be expensive if not used properly.

Price and Availability

To add to the dilemma, there can be great variations in the pricing and availability for a given service from region to region. For example, ISDN service may be available in one exchange, but not in the next. If it is available, the tariffs can vary dramatically from one service provider to the next. In the United States, this variability is only likely to increase in the short term with the deregulation of the telecommunication industry. In the long run, increased competition can result in lower prices and greater flexibility; but it is important for companies to pursue WAN strategies that leverage more than one WAN service to retain flexibility as the market continues to change.

Flexibility is thus important in selecting premise equipment, such as routers. Although it might be advantageous to change or reconfigure WAN services frequently to adapt to changing tariffs and minimize WAN charges, the process of reconfiguring, or even replacing, a piece of equipment to handle a different WAN service can be a barrier. If the process is complex and costly, companies may actually find it easier and less expensive to keep their existing configuration and absorb tariff increases rather than change services. It is only when premise equipment allows flexibility that companies can truly design their wide area networks to best meet both their business needs and budgetary requirements.

Digital Service and Fiber Optics

More than 30 years ago public telephone companies around the world began upgrading their analog services between central offices to digital systems. The phone companies found that digital lines offered more dependable service. Digital services are less sensitive to noise and interference and don't tend to deteriorate with age. Digital systems will either work 100 percent or not at all. Also, digital communication equipment is less expensive than analog. Less circuitry is needed to classify a voltage level as zero or one than to analyze an analog signal for amplitude and frequencies. This enables the phone company to increase capacity for less expense and increase the reliability of its networks.

More recently, developments in fiber optics have once again increased performance and reliability of digital services while cutting the cost of services. Because of the lack of electronic interference, the fiber is more reliable. The data capacity and speed of fiber is orders of magnitude higher than that of copper. For these reasons, fiber is now the media of choice for data transmission. All of the long distance carriers are now equipped with fiber and digital transmitters and receivers.

Many of the Regional Bell Operating Companies (RBOCs) are now upgrading their central office equipment to digital. Also, increase in the use and availability of Integrated Services Digital Networks (ISDN) creates a big push to digital. The ISDN standard, which exists globally, is digital from the ground up.

Although the telephone central office equipment is being replaced by digital equipment, it is still fully compatible with the analog equipment in use today (such as modems, telephones, and fax machines). The following are some popular network services for WANs:

- Regular telephone lines, often called *Plain Ordinary Telephone Service* (*POTS*) lines, enabling the use of up to 33.6 Kbps modems
- Switched 56 digital data circuits at up to 56 Kbps
- ISDN-BRI circuit-switched connections using digital telephone lines at 128 Kbps
- T-1 digital access circuits at 1.544 Mbps
- ISDN-PRI circuit-switched connections using T-1 access circuits
- Dedicated T-1 full-period, point-to-point connection using T-1 access circuits
- Frame-relay, packet-switched connections using T-1 access circuits
- SMDS packet-switched connections using fiber access circuits
- SONET and T-3 digital fiber-based access circuits based around 45 Mbps

Each type of access circuit must have a specific type of *Data Circuit Terminating Equipment,* often also called *Data Communications Equipment* (*DCE*) or *customer premise equipment,* attached to the line in order to be able to transmit data on that circuit.

Service providers usually offer many options as methods of connection through their networks, each with an associated billing agreement. These various options can be summarized as the following three fundamental choices:

- **Full period (dedicated or leased lines)**—Connected all the time and billed at a monthly fixed charge
- **Circuit-switched (dial-up)**—Connected on demand and billed at a monthly fixed charge for the access circuit plus a per-minute usage charge
- **Packet-switched**—Connected all the time and billed at a monthly fixed charge for the access circuit plus a usage charge based on the amount of data transmitted

The following sections describe some of the digital network services and technologies available today. Where high speed analog leaves off is where the digital services start. For the most part, a 33.6 Kbps modem wouldn't support the WAN traffic of businesses today.

Data Service Units and Channel Service Units

Data Service Units (*DSUs*) and *Channel Service Units* (*CSUs*) are required for any data transmission over all-digital links. DSUs and CSUs in the digital environment are the equivalent of the modem in the analog environment. Most manufacturers combine DSUs and CSUs in a single unit because of their complementary relationship. Many of the current analog modems are being built so they can be converted to a DSU and CSU with a simple software upgrade.

The DSU is responsible for the transmission and reception of a signal as well as the buffering of the data and flow control.

The CSU is used to ensure that data terminal equipment (DTE), i.e., computers and network components, do not send signals that could interfere with the telecommunication carrier's network or equipment. The Federal Communication Commission (FCC) requires every digital circuit to be terminated with a CSU.

Virtual Connections

A *permanent virtual circuit* (*PVC*) ensures a connection through a packet network between transmitting and receiving devices. Packet switching uses virtual circuits to make a logical connection to allocate bandwidth on demand between two parties exchanging data. *Logic*, or routing and destination information similar to an address, accompanies each packet through the network. When a device sends a packet onto the network, the logical channel number within the packet verifies that the sending device has a PVC connection to the receiving device. PVCs require no call setup or breakdown processes.

A *switched virtual call* (*SVC*) is similar to a dial-up call because it requires setup and breakdown processes to take place. The calling device sends a packet over the network known as a *call-request packet.* This packet contains a logical channel number as well as the address of the device being called. The network uses this address to route the call-request packet to the remote device, usually a Data Communications Equipment (DCE) device that supports the call on the remote side of the connection. A DCE device establishes, maintains, and terminates sessions on a network.

When the receiving device accepts the call request, it returns a call-accepted packet to the network. The network then sends this packet as a call-connected packet. The channel enters into a data transfer state, establishing an end-to-end virtual circuit.

To conclude the session, one of the devices sends a clear-request packet that is received as a clear-indication packet and then confirmed with a clear-confirm packet. After the call is cleared, the logical channel numbers are made available for another session.

Switched 56

Switched 56 is a digital, time-charged service. As the name implies, the link rate is 56 Kbps with data rates of 150 Kbps to 200 Kbps with compression. Switched 56 is widely available. One good feature of Switched 56 is that it is interoperable with ISDN. That is, a location with Switched 56 service can place calls to and receive calls not only from other locations with Switched 56 service, but also from any locations that have ISDN basic rate service.

As with the office telephone, all you need is the number to call. This enables an organization to use ISDN at all remote sites where it is available and to supplement it with Switched 56 service in other areas, a viable alternative to providing complete interoperability among all remote locations. Switched 56 technology, over the long haul, is expected to be replaced by ISDN equipment.

T-1 and E-1

Availability and economy of T-1 service has increased since it was first offered to the public in 1982. Companies have found that streamlining voice, data, facsimile, and video traffic into a T-1 backbone is more desirable than using the analog networks. T-1s give better control, are easier to troubleshoot and maintain, and are cheaper and faster.

Digital service is based on standard increments of the digital signal (DS). The *DS* refers to the rate and format of the signal, and the *T* designation refers to the equipment providing the signals. DS and T are used interchangeably, for example, DS-1 and T-1, or DS-3 and T-3. DS-0 is 64 Kbps; DS-1 is 24 multiplexed DS-0s plus 8 Kbps for network control overhead, or 1.544 Mbps. With T-1, the 24 channels can individually carry voice or data conversations over the same copper pair required for one analog conversation.

E-1, the European counterpart to the T-1, operates at a rate of 2.048 Mbps. The E-1 is composed of 32 channels at 64 Kbps. Of the 32 channels, 30 are used for voice and data, one for framing, and one for signaling information.

Fractional T-1   In the past, if you didn't need the bandwidth available in a T-1, you had to go to the 56 Kbps line, which didn't provide enough bandwidth in some cases. *Fractional T-1 (FT-1)* provides the option of leasing only the portion of the T-1 that an application requires, as shown in Figure 15.2. For instance, if an application needs only 384 Kbps of bandwidth, a leased FT-1 with DS-0s 0 through 5 would cover the application and provide significant cost savings over a full T-1.

N O T E   T-1 and FT-1 both enable switching of the DS-0s within the network. This provides flexibility and economy in the configuration of multipoint networks. DS-0s can be switched between destinations within the network using a digital access cross-connect switch (DACS) network. ▪

How T-1 and E-1 Work   T-1 and E-1 services can combine voice, data, and video traffic over the same network. Information is encoded using *time division multiplexing (TDM)* for data and *pulse code modulation (PCM)* for voice. PCM digitizes voice when carried over digital circuits between the carriers switches. A TDM divides the combined stream of digital information traveling across a link into equal time slots. On the transmitting end, the TDM takes the data from each channel in sequence and places it into a time slot on the aggregate link known as a *trunk* or *backbone.* On the receiving end, another TDM receives this aggregate stream of data from the trunk and sorts it back into the original channels (see Figure 15.3).

Part

III

Ch

15

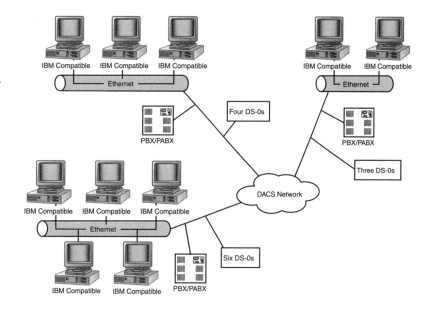

FIG. 15.2
With Fractional T-1 networks, only the DS-0s needed for the application are leased.

FIG. 15.3
A single channel is divided into time slots and each transmitting device is assigned at least one of the time slots for its transmission.

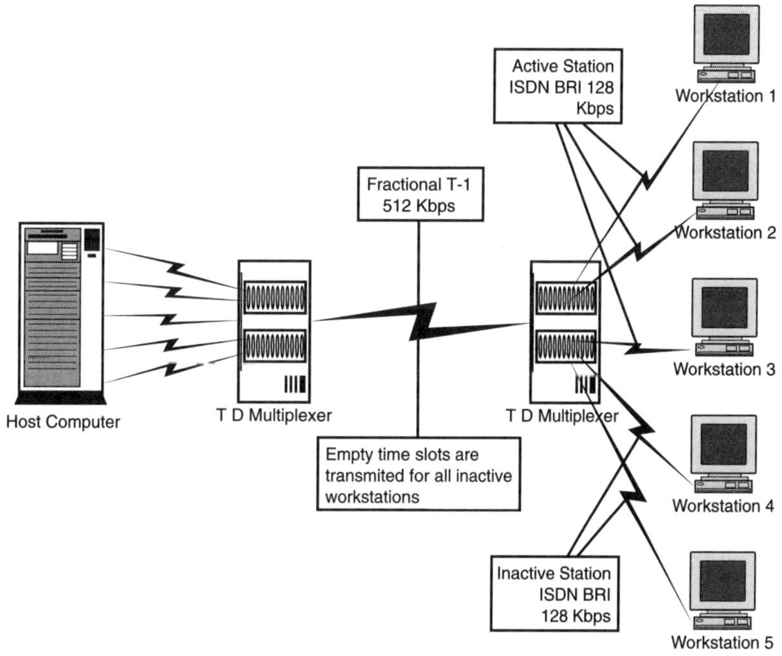

Multiplexers are used to merge a number of digital channels into a single link. For instance, by putting a multiplexer on each end of a T-1, all of the 24 channels of data are sent in aggregate. When the data reaches the destination, the aggregate data is separated into its original channels and distributed. Multiplexers are made up of the following four separate elements:

- **Channel interface units**—These are the ports that provide the physical connection of voice and data equipment to the multiplexer.

- **Buffers**—These are the bulk data storage or memory within the multiplexer. A buffer can store data that can be read and written between the channels and the aggregate TDM link.

- **Time slot interchanger (TSI)**—This combines the information from the channel interface units into an aggregate for transmission over the T-1 or E-1 link.

- **Line interfaces**—These convert the aggregate stream from the TSI to a format that is appropriate for the T-1 and E-1 transmission.

Framing   Framing is the packaging of data so it can be read correctly. T-1 technology was originally based on multiplexing 24 voice channels on two twisted pairs. Each channel carries digitized voice and signaling information in eight-bit bytes, so a frame is formatted consisting of eight bits on 24 channels or 192 bits of data. Added to the framing data is a framing bit in the 193rd position to identify each frame. Each byte is updated 8,000 times per second. This equates to a transmission speed on a T-1 of 192 bits of data, plus one framing bit, times 8,000 seconds for 1.544 Mbps. This description describes what is commonly known as *D4 frame and format*: *frame* is the sequence of 193 bits and *format* is the 24 eight-bit channels or 192 bits.

To understand the term *superframe* (*SF*), consider each of the 24 channels on a T-1 as a time slot. As derived from the previous framing discussion, 8,000 framing bits are traveling across the T-1 per second. That's one framing bit every 125 microseconds. The receiving multiplexer looks for a predetermined sequence of bits every 12 frames. It is these 12 frames that make up the SF. There are 12 frames times 193 bits, or 2,316 bits in an SF.

Within the SF, insignificant bits of data are sacrificed for signaling information necessary for successful completion of the transmission. This process is known as *robbed bit signaling*.

The problem with the D4 frame and format and the robbed bit signaling is that it was designed for voice streams where it wasn't a problem to replace bits in a voice transmission with signaling bits. However, it becomes a significant problem when data bits need to be removed from a data stream. There are fewer, if any, insignificant bits that can be robbed for the signaling process. This is where the *extended superframe* (*ESF*) comes into the picture. ESF increases the size of the SF from 12 to 24 frames, doubling the number of signaling bits available. Also, instead of using 8,000 framing bits, ESF uses only 2,000, leaving 6,000 bits in the 193rd framing bit position for other transmission and error checking functions.

T-1 Fast Packet Technology   *Fast packet technology* extensively improves the way that information is routed on a T-1 backbone. Fast packet improves the level of support that T-1s can provide for your network. The fast packet multiplexers used with T-1s increase the speed and reliability as well as the efficiency and resiliency of the network. Fast packet can be many times more cost effective for data, voice, and video networks than the traditional TDM used in conventional T-1 networks.

NOTE Fast packet technology allocates bandwidth as needed. This requires fewer T-1/E-1 circuits to support applications than a standard circuit switched T-1/E-1 network, which divides bandwidth into fixed channel segments. ■

Remember, a TDM divides the T-1 bandwidth into 24 channels of 64 Kbps feeding voice or data into each of the 24 fixed 64 Kbps channels in the node. In a voice conversation, more than 50 percent of the transmission can be pauses or silence. The classic TDM transfers the silence costing bandwidth, which equates to network performance. Fast packet only allocates bandwidth when necessary. By suppressing silence in voice and idle characters in data, the transmission is many times more efficient.

Fast packet sends data in the same D4 frame that the TDM uses. Instead of allocating one DS-0 per device on the node, fast packet fills the entire packet with data from one channel only with a destination address attached. Fast packet addresses each frame to a single device, so the frame doesn't require any disassembly or reassembly to pass through intermediate nodes.

Integrated Services Digital Network

Integrated Services Digital Network (ISDN) is a digital switched communication service that is accepted throughout the world. ISDN is capable of sending and receiving voice, data, video, and facsimile over point-to-point digital connections. ISDN was designed digitally from the ground up. It represents a standard that is capable of anything from a phone call to WAN connectivity. ISDN is fully compatible with the existing analog services that are available today. ISDN is largely used in telecommuting, videoconferencing, and WAN connectivity.

NOTE Voice, data, video, fax, and more share one digital link in an ISDN network. One D channel carries the signaling and packet data, while multiple B channels are used for digital access. ■

ISDN delivers the following types of services:

- **Bearer services**—Digital telephony, circuit-switched data at 64 Kbps, packet-switched X.25 data, and frame-relay data.
- **Telecommunication services**—E-mail, videoconferencing, voice, and fax.
- **Supplementary services**—Fast dialing, caller ID, call waiting, call forwarding, and three-way calling.

ISDN Basic Rate Interface ISDN *Basic Rate Interface* (*BRI*) service delivers data on one or two 64 Kbps bearer (B) channels for services of either 64 Kbps or 128 Kbps. Its circuit setup and maintenance signaling is taken out of band to a separate 16 Kbps data (D) channel. It is a switched digital service for dedicated, dial-up applications similar to those that use packet-switched technology. This service is provided by the RBOCs on the same twisted pair that is used by the analog telephone network.

With compression, speeds of up to 400 Kbps are possible over a single 2B+D ISDN line. Users can connect to a variable number of other locations for variable periods of time with sustained throughput comparable to fractional T-1.

ISDN BRI is a popular choice for local access. If there is a flat-rate monthly charge between the locations, ISDN BRI makes less sense if you will be making long-distance telephone calls.

ISDN Primary Rate Interface   ISDN *Primary Rate Interface (PRI)* service in North America and Japan delivers service through a standard T-1 (1.544 Mbps) trunk and consists of 23 64 Kbps B channels and one 64 Kbps D channel. In Europe, the service is delivered through an E-1 (2.048 Mbps) and consists of either 30 or 31 B channels and one D channel. PRIs are dedicated trunks that connect to a telephone company's central office. The ISDN PRIs are capable of supporting large numbers of voice and data communication. The B channels are used to transmit the physical data while the D channel is used to distinguish ISDN from other digital alternatives on the analog network and tell the network how to handle the B channel data.

Basically, all current telephone and computing systems can be connected to ISDN through a PRI, including PBXs, LANs, WANs, multiplexers, and videoconferencing equipment.

Broadband ISDN   *Broadband ISDN (B-ISDN)* is the latest ISDN standard that uses fiber optics as a transmission medium. The service supports transmission speeds of greater than 1.55 Mbps and single channel speeds above 64 Kbps. B-ISDN uses ATM as the switching infrastructure.

Asynchronous Transfer Mode

Asynchronous transfer mode (ATM) has grown out of the need for a worldwide standard to enable interoperability of information, regardless of the network or type of information. ATM has been named as the switching and multiplexing technology for Broadband ISDN. There is an unprecedented level of acceptance throughout the industry of both the technology and the standardization process.

In the past, there have been separate methods used for the transmission of information among users on a LAN versus users on the WAN. This situation has added to the complexity of networking, as users' needs for connectivity expand from the LAN to WAN. ATM is a method of communication that can be used as the basis for both LAN and WAN technologies. In time, as ATM develops, the circuits between LANs and WANs will disappear based on this one standard.

In many instances, separate networks are used to carry voice, data, and video, mostly because these traffic types have different characteristics. Data traffic tends to be "bursty:" it doesn't need to communicate for an extended period of time and then sends large quantities of information as fast as possible. Voice and video tend to be more even in the amount of information required, but are very sensitive to the time and order that the information arrives.

ATM does not require separate networks. ATM is the only standards-based technology that has been designed from the beginning to accommodate the simultaneous transmission of data, voice, and video. ATM provides the following key benefits:

- ATM provides a single network for all traffic types: voice, data, and video. ATM enables the integration of networks, improving efficiency and manageability.
- Due to its high speed and the integration of traffic types, ATM enables the creation and expansion of new applications, such as multimedia, to the desktop.
- Because ATM is not based on a specific type of physical transport, it is compatible with currently deployed physical networks. ATM can be transported over twisted pair, coaxial, and fiber optic cables.
- Efforts within the standards organizations and the ATM forum continue to ensure that embedded networks will be able to gain the benefits of ATM incrementally—upgrading portions of the network based on new application requirements and business needs.
- ATM is evolving into a standard technology for local, campus backbone, and public and private wide area services. This uniformity is intended to simplify network management by using the same technology for all levels of the network.
- The information systems and telecommunication industries are focusing and standardizing on ATM, which has been designed from the onset to be scalable and flexible in geographic distance, number of users, and access and trunk bandwidth speeds, ranging from Mbps to Gbps.

ATM Technology   ATM technology is based on powerful, yet flexible concepts. When information needs to be transmitted, the sender negotiates a *requested path* with the network for a connection to the destination. When setting up this connection, the sender specifies the type, speed, and other attributes of the call, which determine the end-to-end quality of service.

Another key concept is that ATM is a switched-based technology. By providing connectivity through a switch instead of a shared bus, the following benefits are provided:

- Dedicated bandwidth per connection
- Higher aggregate bandwidth
- Well-defined connection procedures
- Flexible access speeds

Using ATM, the information to be sent is segmented into a fixed length cell, then transported to and reassembled at the destination. The ATM cell has a fixed length of 53 bytes. The cell is broken into two main sections: the *header* and the *payload*. The 48-byte payload is the portion that carries the actual information: voice, data, or video. The five-byte header is the addressing mechanism.

ATM System Architecture   The ATM layered architecture enables voice, data, and video to be simultaneously transferred over the network (see Figure 15.4). ATM's implementation is supported through its three lower-level layers, as follows:

- The adaptation layer (AAL) assures the appropriate service characteristics and divides all types of data into the 48-byte payload that makes up the ATM cell.
- The ATM layer takes the data to be sent and adds the five-byte header information that assures the cell is sent through the right connection.

■ The physical layer (PHY) defines the electrical characteristics and network interfaces. ATM is not tied to a specific type of physical transport. This layer transports the data on the network.

FIG. 15.4

The AAL inserts data into and extracts data from the 48-byte payload. The ATM attaches and detaches the five-byte header and the payload. The PHY converts cells to the appropriate electrical or optical format.

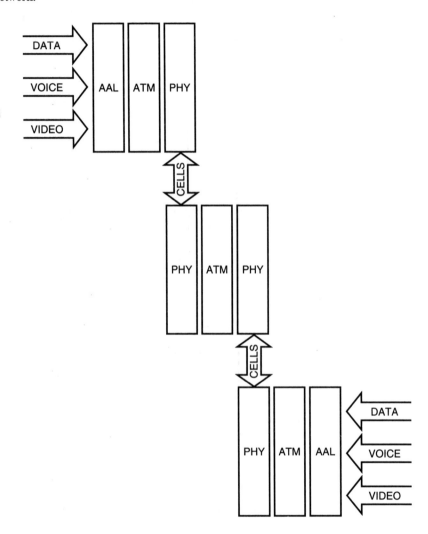

ATM coexists with existing LAN and WAN technologies. ATM specifications are being written to ensure that ATM smoothly integrates numerous existing network technologies at several levels (i.e., B-ISDN, Frame Relay, Ethernet, and TCP/IP).

Frame Relay

Frame relay is viewed as one of the most flexible packet switching technologies for efficiently connecting WANs. Frame relay is tightly linked to fast packet switching technology in that it provides an ideal network access technology for connecting data onto a fast packet switching backbone.

Frame relay provides T-1 level speeds using fast packet switching technology for high performance. Frame relay is a WAN technology based on a packet-oriented communication system. Currently, frame relay service is primarily used for local area network interconnections over public or private networks. Other forms of traffic being passed over frame relay include SNA/SDLC, voice, and video.

Frame relay service has been gaining in popularity over the past few years and most major telecommunication carriers offer user interfaces into the packet-switched network. Typically, bandwidth connections range from 56 Kbps to 1.544 Mbps.

Because frame relay is a packet-oriented network service, the user traffic into the network must first be encapsulated inside a frame-relay frame. This encapsulation is performed by a user-to-network interface (UNI) device called a *Frame Relay Assembler/Disassembler* (*FRAD*). Most LAN-to-LAN bridges and routers available today can be equipped to provide FRAD capabilities.

At the beginning of each frame of user traffic entering into the frame relay network, the FRAD device places header information that contains the frame address. This information is used by the service providers frame relay switching equipment to route the encapsulated traffic to its destination.

Because packets (frames) of user traffic can be routed through various frame relay network paths, including other carrier's frame relay network and switching equipment, frame relay service specifications exist that define this network-to-network interface (NNI).

Frame relay is a WAN technology that caters to "bursty" traffic. The network guarantees the user a *committed information rate* (*CIR*), but permits bursts of data up to the access speed of the connection into the frame relay network. CIR speeds are between 64 Kbps and 1,024 Kbps.

X.25

X.25 is a low speed packet switching technology that is primarily used for interactive, transaction-oriented applications, such as order entry and credit card verification. It is also ideal for sending e-mail and small files across a WAN. For organizations with a multitude of connections, X.25 technology provides bandwidth between 9.6 Kbps to 64 Kbps at a relatively cheap cost. X.25 is useful for character-based terminal emulation and small volume file transfers. Unfortunately, X.25 does not provide enough support for today's businesses. They demand large file transfers, imaging, video links, client-server technology, and much more.

Synchronous Optical Network

The *Synchronous Optical Network* (*SONET*) provides high bandwidth, high reliability, and manageability, and is well-suited for use as a WAN backbone. SONET was introduced in 1984 by Bell Communications and was quickly accepted by the American National Standards Institute (ANSI). SONET rings provide for automatic network backup with 100 percent redundancy so that if there is a point of failure on a fiber ring, service continues on a second ring. SONET rings are currently installed in most major metropolitan areas with larger rings also being installed around multiple major metropolitan areas.

A similar standard, *Synchronous Digital Hierarchy* (*SDH*), is established in Europe. For the next few years, the primary use of SONET will be in large telecommunication carrier backbone networks. SONET requires the use of fiber from end to end. Based on light wave technology, speeds range from 50 Mbps to nearly 2,500 Mbps.

SONET is an international standard, fiber optic transmission concept that is used for broadband transport. SONET offers a variety of optical line rates, all of which are multiples of 51.840 Mbps. SONET provides users with the capability to send signals at multigigabit rates over today's single-mode fiber optic telecommunication links, and contains a rich set of operations, administration, and data management capabilities.

Switched Multimegabit Data Service

Switched Multimegabit Data Service (*SMDS*) is a high-speed, switched data communication service offered by the local telephone companies that is frequently used to connect WANs. SMDS uses the IEEE standard 802.6 Distributed Queue Dual Bus (DQDB) networking technology and is capable of supporting data rates of up to 45 Mbps. Like ATM, SMDS has a 53-byte cell format. Included in the header of an SMDS cell are control, priority, and error-checking information.

With SMDS, organizations have the flexibility they need for distributed computing and bandwidth-intensive applications. At the same time, because SMDS supports both existing and emerging technologies, it provides the scalability that organizations need to support the applications of the future.

Used to interconnect multiple node LANs and WANs through the public telephone network, SMDS eliminates the need for carrier switches to establish a call path between two points of data transmission. Instead, SMDS access devices pass 53-byte cells to a carrier switch. The switch reads addresses and forwards cells one by one over any available path to the desired endpoint. SMDS addresses ensure that the cells arrive in the right order. With no need for a predefined path between devices, data can travel over the least congested routes in an SMDS network providing faster transmission, increased security, and greater flexibility to add or drop network sites.

Because SMDS is connectionless, it is easy for users to build full-mesh networks in which each site is connected to all other sites. SMDS' three-layered architecture contains the following attributes:

- A switching infrastructure comprising SMDS-compatible switches (which may or may not be cell-based)
- A delivery system made up of T-1 and T-3 circuits called *Subscriber Network Interfaces* (*SNIs*)

■ An access control system for users to connect to the switching infrastructure without having to become a part of it

Significant savings are achieved with SMDS because it can deliver the mesh connectivity of dedicated private-line networks with fewer access lines, less terminating equipment, and without the distance-related charges of dedicated networks.

SMDS is the only high-speed, broadband, connectionless data service currently available that offers users a wide range of service features that are generally unavailable on connection-oriented WANs. SMDS offers many features, including the following:

■ High-speed, low-delay connectionless data transport (which sends packets as soon as they are received and requires no call setup)

■ Any-to-any connectivity, sometimes referred to as the *dial tone for data*

■ Multicasting to handle group addressing

■ Addresses like standard telephone numbers

■ Support for key protocols used in local and wide area networking (TCP/IP, Novell, DECNet, AppleTalk, SNA, and OSI)

■ Network scalability

■ SNMP-based network management

■ Call blocking, validation, and screening for the secure interconnection of LANs and distributed client-server applications

SMDS provides users with the cost effectiveness of a public-switched network; the benefits of fully meshed, wide-area interconnection; and the privacy and control of dedicated, private networks. The key benefits subscribers can realize with SMDS include widespread current availability and increased LAN performance. It provides data management features, flexibility, bandwidth on demand, network security and privacy, multiprotocol support, and technology compatibility.

The LAN-like performance features of SMDS make it a natural fit as a backbone network for seamlessly interconnecting Ethernet, Token-Ring, FDDI, and ATM LANs over extended geographic areas. To connect a LAN to an SMDS network requires only a router and an SMDS-compatible DSU/CSU or SMDS host adapter card. Interface guidelines have been developed by the SMDS Interest Group that enable the service to support the networking protocol architectures found in the leading network environments: TCP/IP, Novell's IPX, AppleTalk, DECNet, SNA, and OSI.

Network managers connect to an SMDS carrier switch via an SNI to a T-1 or T-3 circuit. T-1 SNIs are used to access 1.17 Mbps SMDS offerings, while T-3 SNIs are used to tap into 4, 10, 16, 25, or 34 Mbps offerings. A fractional T-3 circuit can be used to access intermediate-speed SMDS offerings.

With the recently announced low-speed SMDS access—56 Kbps, 64 Kbps, and increments of Nx56/64 Kbps—smaller companies and current users of frame-relay technology can take advantage of the SMDS service features. The SMDS Data Exchange Interface (DXI) is used to offer SMDS services at 56 Kbps or 64 Kbps, using the same information formats now employed for on-site connection of SMDS routers to a SMDS DSU/CSU. Because the carrier accepts the data format already produced by the router, a standard DSU/CSU can be used.

SMDS can be used as an alternative to dedicated lines for connecting WANs. The service supports the direct attachment of computing devices for distributed client-server applications such as database access, file transfer, high-resolution imaging, multimedia mail, and workgroup or collaborative computing.

The features of SMDS—such as call screening, verification, and blocking—also enable SMDS service to function as a virtual private network. This means customers can use SMDS as a public-switched alternative to private networks. Subscribers can either deploy SMDS for full mesh connectivity or use SMDS address screening features to limit transmissions within a closed user group.

Because SMDS is able to coexist with dedicated facilities, it enables customers to create hybrid public/private networks. SMDS also allows for the easy expansion of existing networks because new sites can be quickly added to an SMDS net without totally reconfiguring the network. Additions to an SMDS network only require a simple update to a screening database on the SMDS switch.

The separation of the technology-independent SMDS service layer from the technology-dependent access layers enables SMDS to be supported by many different switching technology platforms and different user-to-network interface technologies. The latest SMDS access interface is being defined using public network, multi-service ATM user-to-network interfaces.

WAN Protocols

All communications between devices on a network require that the devices agree on the format of the data. *Protocols* are defined as rules and conventions that govern how devices on a network exchange information. There are a variety of standard protocols to choose from. Each has particular advantages and disadvantages; for example, some are simpler than others, some are more reliable, and some are faster.

The following key functions are required for successful communication across a WAN:

- A method of assigning network addresses to all computers (clients and servers) on the WAN. This is often referred to as a *routed protocol* because the addresses are transmitted along with the information through the network.

- A method of deciding how to route data to a particular address. This is often referred to as a *routing protocol* because it enables you to make routing decisions.

- A method to verify successful information delivery to the far end, often referred to as *end-to-end error checking.*

- Upper-layer protocols: client-server functions, encryption, and information formatting.

N O T E It is important for the sake of compatibility, reliability, and performance that you carefully choose and standardize enterprise-wide networking protocols. ▪

One of the most popular choices to implement WAN protocol functions is the TCP/IP protocol. TCP/IP includes IP for network addressing, OSPF for routing, and TCP for end-to-end error checking. These are widely accepted, open protocols that are published as military standards, but available for anyone to implement. See Chapter 9, "Using TCP/IP with Windows NT Server," for more information.

▶ **See** "Understanding Network Protocols," **p. 110**

Proprietary protocols developed by private companies may or may not be published. Whether this introduces a limitation on adaptability or evolution of your WAN should be considered. Novell's protocol family, referred to as *IPX*, includes their proprietary IPX, RIP, and SPX protocols. These are so widely deployed that they are considered "near open."

In addition, choices must be made for client-server protocols. Popular choices are Windows NT and Novell Core Protocol, among others. E-mail, file transfer, encryption standards, and terminal emulation all fit into the upper layers category. You have many choices for implementing WAN protocols. Ideally, an enterprise will standardize on one set of protocols, thus reducing long-term maintenance and administrative costs.

Some common protocols used in LAN networking do not extend to the OSI network layer. These include DEC LAT, NetBIOS, and NetBEUI. Because they have no provisions for network layer addressing and routing, connecting these protocols between different LANs must be done with MAC layer devices, such as LAN bridges or LAN switches. Protocols that operate at the network layer (such as TCP/IP, IPX/SPX, and DECNet) utilize routers to interconnect networks. Most routers have the capability to route routeable protocols and to bridge non-routeable traffic.

WANs and Windows NT Domains

Windows NT networks with the domain models are perfect for the needs of a WAN. Windows NT provides for a single logon validation point rather than having to log on to multiple servers throughout the WAN. The Microsoft networking model provides for a single security token validation that gives the user credentials that can take the user anywhere the network is connected, reducing the overhead and complexity of logging on to each server individually.

▶ **See** "Understanding BackOffice Security," **p. 112**

From Here...

Today's wide area networks have the capability of transporting data, voice, and images to far-reaching locations throughout an organization's global enterprise. Managing and expanding these crucial wide-area connections requires highly trained professionals who are able to assess, select, and implement the appropriate wide area services and technologies from an ever-increasing array of options.

Network engineers must have the up-to-date knowledge and skills that enable them to implement, configure, and troubleshoot complex wide area networks. They must know how to make maximum use of protocols, circuits, and tools, as well as plan for migration to advanced implementations and build wide area networks that achieve the optimum balance of cost, security, and performance. For more information on these and related issues, see the following chapters:

- To see how Internet naming services work with Windows NT, see Chapter 10, "Name Resolution with TCP/IP."
- For information on the blending of BackOffice with NetWare and UNIX, see Chapter 14, "Windows Integration with NetWare and UNIX."
- For a thorough examination of the I-net capabilities of BackOffice, see Chapter 16, "The BackOffice I-Net Toolbox."
- For a look at implementation on the World Wide Web, see Chapter 18, "Building a Web with Internet Information Server (IIS)."
- For a practical approach to security, see Chapter 46, "Implementing Real-World Security."
- To learn how to support networks, see Chapter 48, "Proactive Network Administration."

Implementing Intranet and
Internet Technologies

## CHAPTER 16

The BackOffice I-Net Toolbox

by Azam A. Mirza

The Microsoft BackOffice suite of products provides a rich collection of built-in functionality for Internet connectivity as part of its core feature set. Windows NT Server has built-in support for the TCP/IP protocol suite and applications. With the release of the Internet Information Server (IIS) as an integrated Windows NT Server product, Microsoft has added support for a World Wide Web server, File Transfer Protocol (FTP) server, and Gopher server to the core set of features provided by the Windows NT Server.

The tight integration of the BackOffice products allows for the use of features previously not available as a single package. Windows NT Server enables the hosting of Web servers and Internet-enabled application servers that can be accessed using the Internet Information Server and its set of client browsing tools. ■

Microsoft Windows NT Server and I-net

Find out about the tools and protocols available within Windows NT Server for Internet connectivity and use.

Internet Information Server features

Learn about the Internet Information Server and its feature set.

Microsoft's Internet strategy and supporting products

Find out how Microsoft envisions the Internet of the future and the products it is developing to meet that vision.

Microsoft Index Server and Proxy Server

Learn about the features supported by Microsoft Index Server and the Proxy Server.

Internet server products from other vendors

Find out about the Internet server product offerings from Netscape Communications Corporation and O'Reilly and Associates, Inc.

Windows NT Server and the Internet

Windows NT Server comes Internet-enabled right out of the box. The TCP/IP protocol suite included with Windows NT Server makes it very easy to get up and running on the Internet. The core TCP/IP protocol suite included with Windows NT Server is as follows:

- **TCP/IP networking services**—This enables computers to communicate with each other using the TCP/IP standard as the communications mechanism. See Chapter 9, "Using TCP/IP with Windows NT Server," for more information.

- **FTP Client**—The FTP (File Transfer Protocol) program is used to transfer files between a user's computer and a remote computer.

- **FTP Server service**—This is a high-level TCP/IP protocol that runs as a Windows NT service enabling users to connect to a Windows NT server using FTP client software for transferring files. The FTP Server facilitates communications between the Windows NT server and the FTP client.

- **Telnet Client**—This is a TCP/IP-based program for connecting to remote computers for the purpose of running command-line programs on the remote machine.

- **Dynamic Host Configuration Protocol (DHCP)**—This enables workstation computers running the TCP/IP protocol to dynamically obtain IP addresses from a Windows NT server. Every computer running TCP/IP must be assigned a unique IP address, and the DHCP protocol facilitates that by centrally managing the assignment of these IP addresses.

- **Windows Internet Naming Service (WINS)**—This enables computers to resolve NetBIOS names to IP addresses. This is somewhat analogous to the function provided by a DNS, which resolves TCP/IP domain names to IP addresses.

- **Remote Access Service (RAS) connectivity using SLIP and PPP**—This enables users to connect to Windows NT Server machines and other Internet host computers using the Serial Line Internet Protocol (SLIP) or the Point-to-Point Protocol (PPP). These protocols enable the use of the TCP/IP protocol when connected to the network with a modem.

In addition, Microsoft BackOffice includes a wide set of server components for implementing a comprehensive Internet solution. Server products are available for a wide variety of functions and needs. The following sections discuss the role and feature sets of these Internet server components.

Internet Information Server

Microsoft Internet Information Server (IIS) is the first in a series of products released by Microsoft as part of the BackOffice suite that enable corporations to take advantage of the enormous potential of the Internet and intranet. IIS is the centerpiece of the Microsoft Internet strategy. It is the glue that brings together the power of the Internet and enables corporations to develop a presence in the Internet community.

T I P Internet Information Server can be downloaded at no charge from the Microsoft Web site at **http://www.microsoft.com**. In addition, IIS is now included on the Windows NT Server 4.0 CD.

IIS provides the basic services necessary to implement a Web site for your corporation. The following are some of the features that IIS supports (which are explained in detail in the following sections):

- Services
- BackOffice Integration
- Server Administration
- Security

▶ **See** "A Guide to Services Provided by the Internet Information Server," **p. 541**

Services

Microsoft Internet Information Server supports three of the most common services on the Internet, which form the basis for creating a functional Web site:

- **World Wide Web (WWW or Web)**—The World Wide Web service is used to publish information on the Internet. WWW is explained in more detail in Chapter 18, "Building a Web with Internet Information Server (IIS)."

- **File Transfer Protocol (FTP)**—FTP is used primarily to transfer files between computers, usually downloading files from remote servers on the Internet. FTP is explained in more detail in Chapter 18.

- **Gopher**—Gopher is a method of providing a catalog of files and directories stored on a Web server for browsing by users. Gopher is explained in more detail in Chapter 18.

BackOffice Integration

The strongest feature of IIS might be its unparalleled integration with the Microsoft BackOffice products. IIS runs as a service installed under Windows NT Server and uses the various built-in NT Server tools and services to its advantage.

N O T E Internet Information Server 2.0 requires Windows NT Server 4.0 operating system. ▓

Security under IIS is provided through integration with the Windows NT Server security model. IIS uses the built-in security to provide user authentication and password validation.

Performance monitoring and optimization tuning services are integrated with Windows NT Server and are provided by the Performance Monitor tool. Web administrators can use the Performance Monitor to analyze disk usage, client connections, server load, and other performance criteria, and handle optimization issues and clear up performance bottlenecks.

▶ **See** "Monitoring Server Performance," **p. 206**

Part **IV**

Ch **16**

IIS uses the NT Server Event Logging service to log events to the application log. Web administrators can consult the event log for errors, warnings, or for keeping track of unauthorized access attempts.

▶ **See** "Viewing Event Logs," **p. 206**

In addition, IIS also leverages the power of other BackOffice products to provide a tight integrated environment for hosting Web sites. IIS includes a connectivity tool for accessing Microsoft SQL Server databases called the Internet Database Connector (IDC). IDC enables IIS servers to connect to ODBC databases and access the stored data.

N O T E   IDC can be used to connect to other databases that have ODBC drivers available, such as Oracle and Microsoft Access. ■

▶ **See** "Using Internet Database Connector and ODBC," **p. 573**
▶ **See** "Dynamic Content with IIS Using dbWeb and IDC," **p. 727**

The Exchange Server Connector enables IIS to connect to the Microsoft enterprise mail system. Users can send and receive mail from the Internet and within their corporate intranets using their Web browsers and an SMTP/POP3 mail client. The tight integration of the BackOffice products is one of the reasons that IIS is a very powerful Web hosting solution for organizations trying to develop an Internet presence.

▶ **See** "Building a Web with Internet Information Server (IIS)," **p. 537**

Administration

IIS provides administration capabilities through the Internet Service Manager. Internet Service Manager is a one-stop solution for managing all IIS services and other Microsoft Internet products, such as the Proxy Server.

▶ **See** "Using the Internet Service Manager," **p. 550**

Internet Service Manager provides a single point of administration for one to many IIS servers. All IIS servers within an organization can be administrated from a single computer running the Internet Service Manager software. IIS even includes an HTML version of the Internet Service Manager, which enables remote administration of IIS servers from sites across the Internet.

▶ **See** "Administering Internet Information Servers Remotely," **p. 555**

Security

As previously mentioned, IIS leverages the power of the Windows NT Server security mechanism. However, IIS provides Web administrators with the flexibility to set up security based on their needs. Web administrators can set up security using one of three security methods, as follows:

■ **Anonymous logon**—This enables logon validation for all user connections. Anonymous logon is used by services, such as FTP and Gopher.

- **Basic authentication**—This is the most basic security scheme; it passes all authentication information using simple text strings. The FTP protocol uses this mechanism for its user logon verification process.

- **Windows NT Challenge/Response**—The authentication method used by Windows NT, Challenge/Response, is the most secure form of user authentication.

In addition, IIS also supports the industry standard Secure Sockets Layer (SSL) security scheme for secure transfer of information between client and server. However, the most important security feature added to IIS has been the introduction of the Proxy Server component. The server provides mechanisms for securing the bidirectional flow of information between an organization and the Internet.

▶ **See** "Proxy Server Features," **p. 686**

IIS also uses the built-in Windows NT Server Point-to-Point Tunneling Protocol (PPTP) to enable organizations to create secure, private intranets across wide-area links using public data networks.

▶ **See** "Using the Point-to-Point Tunneling Protocol (PPTP)," **p. 268**

Microsoft Internet Architecture

Microsoft's Internet architecture is built around the Windows NT Server and the Internet Information Server. Microsoft is releasing a group of Internet server products for the BackOffice family that sits on top of the Windows NT Server and IIS tandem to provide the full set of features required by corporations to implement their Internet strategy initiatives. Figure 16.1 presents an outline of Microsoft's Internet server components strategy designed to make the Internet plan a reality.

The additions to the Microsoft Internet Server components include the following:

- **Membership Server**—This provides security and user authentication services for a corporate World Wide Web site. Membership servers provide links to legacy systems, third-party systems, and other Web sites. Membership Server uses the integrated Windows NT security model for user authentication and password validation.

- **Personalization Server**—This server, designed for providing personalized content on the Web, uses the ActiveX technology to provide corporations with the capability to customize their Web sites based on user preferences. Users can create custom Web pages based on their likes and dislikes and use them as home pages or as their personal Web starting points.

  ▶ **See** "ActiveX," **p. 601**

- **Chat Server**—This server enables corporations to implement Internet Relay Chat (IRC) for carrying out real-time conversation. Users can engage in personal conversations, join a presentation, or attend a conference using the Internet as the connection medium.

- **News Server**—This enables the creation of newsgroups for discussion forums. News Server is based on the UseNet, which uses the NNTP protocol for facilitating discussion groups.

Part
IV

Ch

16

FIG. 16.1
Microsoft Internet
strategy includes a
wide range of server
products for imple-
menting various
Internet functions.

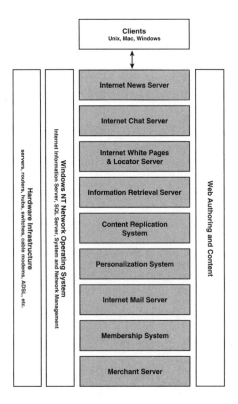

▶ **See** "UseNet: Network Newsgroups," **p. 528**

▪ **Mail Server**—This is an SMTP-based server for enabling e-mail among users.

 ▶ **See** "Electronic Mail," **p. 530**

 ▶ **See** "New Features in Exchange Server 5.0," **p. 886**

▪ **Index Server**—This is a server designed for indexing, cataloging, and searching HTML documents. Users can use the search capabilities of the server to find pertinent information using their Web browsers. Index Server is discussed in more detail in Chapter 21.

▪ **White Pages Server**— This is a directory server that enables users to list themselves, create personal profiles, and search for other users. This server is based on the concept of the White Pages telephone directory, but provides more detailed information storage and retrieval.

▪ **Content Replication Server**—This enables replication of Web site content between multiple servers. Content Replication Server is an invaluable tool for organizations maintaining multiple Web servers in physically disparate locations. With it, Web administrators can create content on a single server and then propagate the changes to all Web servers within an enterprise. Content Replication Server is discussed in more detail in Chapter 21.

■ **Merchant Server**—This provides the tools and security necessary to conduct electronic commerce over the Internet. Merchant Server supports the industry standards for secure credit card processing, handles retail billing operations, and provides order entry and order processing capabilities.

■ **Proxy Server**—This provides a single Internet connecting point for all client machines within an organization, enabling secure Internet connections for corporate users. Proxy Server is discussed in more detail in Chapter 22.

The main concept of this Internet architecture is to enable corporations to build custom Internet solutions. Building on the basic blocks of Windows NT Server and IIS, organizations can pick and choose components that best suit their needs for the kind of Web site they are deploying. To achieve these goals, Microsoft has set guidelines for its products that include the following:

■ **Open standards**—Standards-based architecture provides seamless integration into any corporate environment.

■ **Performance and scalability**—Scalable and optimized components provide the best performance and easy expandability.

■ **Flexibility**—Internet server components are client-side independent. These server products can be used with any client browser or other World Wide Web tools that conform to industry standards and protocols. In addition, all components are extensible through programmatic interfaces, such as ISAPI, MAPI, and ActiveX.

▶ **See** "ActiveX," **p. 601**

▶ **See** "Internet Server API," **p. 527**

▶ **See** "Using ISAPI," **p. 573**

■ **Ease of administration**—All components are manageable through a centralized administration tool based on the Internet Service Manager.

▶ **See** "Using the Internet Service Manager," **p. 550**

Not all of the products of Microsoft's Internet architecture are as yet released. The following sections describe the two components that are currently available and that provide part of the functionality promised by the Microsoft Internet architecture: Microsoft Index Server and Microsoft Proxy Server.

Microsoft Index Server

Microsoft Index Server is the same as the Information Retrieval Server previously described, and enables Web administrators to index and catalog a Web site for search capabilities. Users can search the Web site using keywords, phrases, and sentences for the information they are looking for.

 T I P Microsoft Index Server is available at the Microsoft Web site at **http://www.microsoft.com** on the BackOffice home page.

Index Server provides automatic indexing and cataloging of files, HTML documents, Microsoft Office documents, and other file formats. It provides powerful search mechanisms, so users can query the Web site for data. Index Server supports the following features (which are described in detail in this section):

- Indexing
- Custom queries
- Multiple language support
- Extensibility
- Security

> **See** "Implementing Index Server and Content Replication System," **p. 653**

Indexing   Index Server is an add-on component to the Internet Information Server. It enables Web administrators to index and catalog the entire content of their Web servers. Implemented in conjunction with Windows NT Server and Internet Information Server, Index Server can index and catalog anything from HTML documents to Microsoft Word files, Excel spreadsheets, and PowerPoint presentations.

N O T E   Index Server 1.1 requires Internet Information Server 3.0 running on Windows NT Server 4.0. ■

Users can query indexes or the text within the documents for the information they are looking for. For example, users can look for text strings within a Microsoft Word document. This is a powerful feature that prevents Web administrators from having to convert existing documents to HTML format for indexing and cataloging. They can just publish the actual documents and enable users to find a file or information within a file. Indexing features of the Index Server include the following:

- Multiple language indexing, which enables Index Server to generate index information for sites that support multiple language operation
- Automatic index updates
- Incremental refreshing of indexes, which enables administrators to update index information for files that have changed since the last indexing operation
- Multithreaded indexing to take advantage of multiple processors
- Performance monitoring for best query response time and optimization

Custom Queries   Index Server enables Web administrators to create HTML forms that can be used by users to execute queries against the IIS server. The queries can be customized by selecting various options on the query form to suit the user's needs. The user enters the information into the fields on the screen; then, the Index Server processes the query form through the query engine and finds the information and presents it to the user in the form of HTML documents.

The query forms are special HTML pages that have input controls on them for the user to enter information. The forms are easily created and can be customized to meet the needs of the local Web site content. The form can be created to provide users such options as full site search, restricted search, search through specially formatted documents (e.g., a Microsoft Excel spreadsheet), or search for particular files. Queries can be performed using a variety of criteria, including the following:

- Limited scope searches
- Searches for words and phrases in HTML pages
- Searches for words and phrases within documents, such as Microsoft Word files
- Multiple word searches using Boolean operators, such as AND, OR, and NOT
- Wild-card searches

Multiple Language Support   Index Server has built-in support for seven languages. It is not necessary to run the system in a particular language to be able to use the language support. Web administrators can mix and match different languages in their Web site content, and the Index Server can capably index and catalog the information. Documents created using any of the seven languages can be searched simultaneously. The following languages are supported:

- U.S. English and International English
- Dutch
- German
- French
- Italian
- Spanish
- Swedish

Extensibility   Index Server provides extensibility through a programmatic mechanism called *content filters*. Content filters are a special ActiveX interface that enable programmers to expose the contents of their program files. For example, Index Server uses the exposed content filters to obtain the text contained within a Microsoft Word document. Index Server can thus index and catalog a Microsoft Word file for search and retrieval by users.

Security   Index Server provides a high level of security by leveraging the security features of IIS and Windows NT Server. Index Server implements security at various levels to protect its catalogs and indexed Web pages, and it also provides user authentication facilities before providing search results. The following three security measures ensure a secure and robust search server mechanism:

- **Catalog directory access control**—By default, the catalog directories are created with access permissions only for Web administrators when Index Server is installed. This is done to prevent users from browsing the catalog directories directly using file server shares.

Part
IV

Ch
16

> **CAUTION**
>
> Care should be taken to set the appropriate permissions on catalog directories that are created manually by Web administrators. The catalog directory should allow access privileges for administrators and system accounts only.

■ **Access control for Web pages**—Document access information is stored in catalog files and compared against the logged on user access to make sure the user has appropriate permissions to view the requested page.

 Windows NT auditing mechanism can be used to monitor access control and possible unauthorized access attempts.

■ **Authentication**—This provides user authentication and password validation. A user must be logged on and authenticated before any search query requests can be processed from his account. Authentication is performed using the Windows NT logon validation process.

Microsoft Proxy Server

Microsoft Proxy Server is the latest in a series of BackOffice components being released by Microsoft as part of its Internet architecture. It is a product that enables corporations to provide secure connectivity to the Internet for its corporate users. Proxy Server is a service that runs on the Windows NT server. It supports all Internet protocols, including the following:

■ HTTP

■ FTP

■ Telnet

■ Gopher

■ RealAudio and VDOLive (streaming media)

■ IRC

■ SMTP

■ NNTP

▶ **See** "I-Net Tools and Protocols," **p. 521**

Users utilizing client tools that support any of these protocols can gain access to the Internet through the Proxy Server. In addition, Proxy Server is platform-independent: it can provide Internet access to clients running any operating system and using any tool that employs one of the supported protocols.

Another advantage of Proxy Server is its capability to service TCP/IP requests from non-TCP/IP networks. It provides support for IPX/SPX and NetBIOS protocols. Corporations running IPX/SPX or NetBIOS do not need to convert to the TCP/IP protocol to gain access to the Internet. For example, someone using the Internet Explorer browser on a Novell NetWare network client running IPX/SPX can connect to the Internet through Proxy Server. It will handle passing requests from the client system to the remote server and vice versa. The features supported by Proxy Server include the following:

- Services and protocols
- Integration
- Security

    ▶ **See** "Proxy Server Features," **p. 686**

Services and Protocols   Proxy Server uses the Web Proxy Service and the Windows Sockets Service to monitor Internet requests and connectivity to the Internet. These two services enable Proxy Server to act as a gateway between the corporate network and the Internet and to process requests between the two.

N O T E   Web Proxy Service and Windows Sockets Service enable Proxy Server to act on behalf of a local workstation when connecting to the Internet. The local workstation is kept hidden from the outside world and it seems as though all communication is occurring with only Proxy Server. By isolating corporate machines from the Internet, it becomes very difficult for intruders to obtain the address of a local workstation and gain access to its resources. ▨

Integration   Proxy Server is tightly integrated with Windows NT Server and IIS. The Internet Service Manager, which ships with IIS, is also the administration tool used for managing Proxy servers. In addition, the Performance Monitor tool and the Event Logging service can be used to optimize Proxy Server performance and monitor user activity.

▶ **See** "Monitoring Server Performance," **p. 206**

▶ **See** "Viewing Event Logs," **p. 206**

Security   Proxy Server's main function is to provide secure access to the Internet from corporate networks. First and foremost, Proxy Server leverages the security features built into Windows NT to provide a secure environment and then builds upon them. The security features offered by Proxy Server enable administrators to control access by the following criteria:

- **User**—Access can be controlled at the user level. Users can be granted or denied access to the outside world based on their Windows NT logon names and group permissions.
- **Service**—A certain service can be granted or denied access. For example, a Web administrator might decide to disallow FTP service connections to the Internet to prevent users from downloading virus-infected files. The administrator can disable FTP access through Proxy Server, and all user requests for FTP connections will be denied.
- **Port**—A specific TCP/IP service port can be granted or denied access. For example, direct connections to the Telnet port can be disabled to prevent outsiders from entering the corporate network using Telnet.
- **IP Addresses**—A specific IP address or a range of IP addresses can be granted or denied access.

Part

IV

Ch

16

■ **Domain**—A particular Windows NT domain can be prevented from gaining access to the Internet.

■ **Site**—Access by users to specific sites on the Internet can be denied.

▶ **See** "Administering Proxy Server," **p. 693**

Other Microsoft I-Net Tools

In addition to the server-based Internet tools provided by BackOffice, Microsoft offers a full array of tools for the client-side requirements of the Internet. The Microsoft Internet tools strategy includes tools for WWW browsing, WWW authoring, WWW site maintenance, the extension of Microsoft Office products to support the creation of Web-based applications, and the Visual Basic scripting language for creating Internet-enabled applications. These tools include the following:

■ Internet Explorer

■ Internet Studio

■ Microsoft FrontPage

■ Internet Assistant for Microsoft Word, Excel, and PowerPoint

■ Microsoft Viewer for Microsoft Word, Excel, and PowerPoint

The following is a brief description of each of these tools for enabling client access to the Internet and the WWW.

Internet Explorer   Internet Explorer 3.0 is the latest Microsoft Web browser (see Figure 16.2). Internet Explorer supports the HTML version 3.5 specification. With the VRML add-on, Internet Explorer enables users to explore virtual reality sites. The Internet Explorer feature set includes the following:

■ Full support for multimedia extensions that enable the use of background audio, scrolling marquees, and inline images

■ 32-bit architecture under Windows 95 and Windows NT

■ A consistent interface with the Windows 95 graphical user interface

■ Support for multiple threads for downloading several files simultaneously

■ Support for UseNet news reading

■ Support for displaying tables on a Web page, which enables Web browsers to display information—such as a listing of stock quotes—in a tabular format

■ Support for sizable frames and cascading style sheets

■ Support for the Secure Sockets Layer security scheme for electronic commerce

■ Availability on Windows 95, Windows NT, and the Apple Macintosh

■ Support for VRML

■ Support for Internet news and mail

■ Availability in more than 20 languages

Microsoft WWW site address

FIG. 16.2

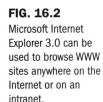

Microsoft Internet Explorer 3.0 can be used to browse WWW sites anywhere on the Internet or on an intranet.

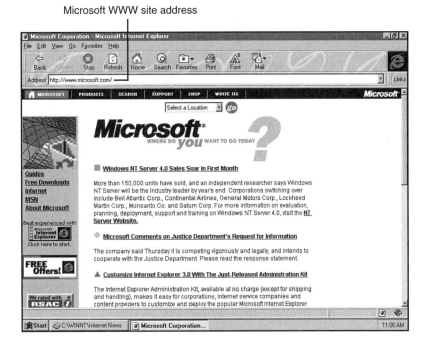

Microsoft FrontPage   Microsoft FrontPage is a component of the suite of Microsoft tools for doing Web-based publishing and creating HTML documents. FrontPage contains a sophisticated set of Web publishing tools that require no programming to create attractive and fully functional HTML-based Web pages. This is in contrast to other HTML development tools that require extensive knowledge of HTML syntax to create Web pages. Figure 16.3 shows the main screen for building Web pages using Microsoft FrontPage.

FrontPage supports a full range of WWW authoring, scripting, and site management tools, and has the following features:

- FrontPage Editor for creating and editing HTML pages
- FrontPage Explorer for graphical management of a Web site
- WebBots (similar to Microsoft Office wizards) for implementing the most common WWW functionality—such as text searches, feedback forms, and threaded discussion forums—without any programming or complex setup
- Wizards to help automate common WWW authoring tasks
- To-do lists for keeping track of the Web site creation and management process

Internet Studio   Internet Studio is Microsoft's high-end Web publishing tool that provides sophisticated Web document authoring and content development capability for commercial and professional WWW developers. Internet Studio offers such features as frame-based layouts, interactive Web pages, and other HTML version 3.0 extensions for creating sophisticated

WWW content. Frames are used in desktop publishing for organizing text around figures and pictures, and in multiple column layouts.

FIG. 16.3

Microsoft FrontPage enables the creation of Web pages using a graphical interface. Menus and toolbars are consistent with other Microsoft products.

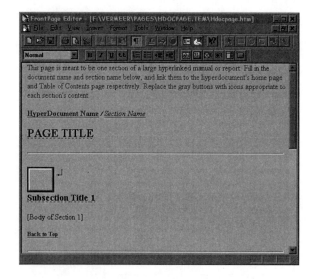

Internet Assistant for Word, Excel, and PowerPoint   The Internet Assistant for Microsoft Word, Excel, and PowerPoint is an add-on product that enables users to create and edit WWW documents directly from within the Microsoft Office applications. With Internet Assistant, users can author documents for the WWW with no HTML or Internet experience.

N O T E   Internet Assistant for Word, Excel, and PowerPoint are incorporated into the respective products as part of the new Microsoft Office 97 suite of applications. The add-on products are avilable for earlier versions of Microsoft Office products. ■

Internet Assistant converts Word documents, Excel spreadsheets, and PowerPoint presentations automatically to HTML, preserving standard formatting elements, such as lists, headings, and bold and italic styles. It also provides a special template for adding hyperlinks, definitions, forms, preformatted text, and other HTML elements. If you want to include HTML elements not directly supported by the Internet Assistant template, you can use the HTML Markup command, which enables you to place native HTML codes in your document.

Internet Assistant is a cost-effective solution for creating Web pages because it is available free of charge from Microsoft. It provides the following features:

- **A familiar authoring and editing environment**—Internet Assistant uses the Microsoft Office environment as its interface and thus provides a familiar set of tools for formatting, spell checking, and so on.

- **Automatic file conversion**—You can create a WWW document from a Word document, Excel spreadsheet, or PowerPoint slide by simply choosing File, Save As from the menu and choosing the HTML file format.
- **HTML version 2.0 support**—Internet Assistant automatically converts text formatting, such as italics, to the appropriate tags in an HTML document.
- **Additional HTML support**—Internet Assistant provides support for additional HTML elements with its HTML Markup command.
- **Hyperlinks**—You can create links between documents on the Internet, on a local network, or on your hard drive.

Microsoft Viewer for Word, Excel, and PowerPoint   Microsoft Viewer for Microsoft Word, Excel, and PowerPoint enables Internet users to view and print Word documents, Excel spreadsheets, and PowerPoint presentations without having the products installed. This makes it possible to have access to Microsoft Office-based documents that are posted on the WWW, in newsgroups, or downloaded from FTP sites.

For example, a user might access the Microsoft Web site and download a product description document that is in Microsoft Word format. If the user does not have Word installed, the user can still view the document using the Microsoft Viewer for Microsoft Word.

If you want to preserve multiple columns, text-wrapping features, embedded objects, and other Word features that HTML does not support, you can publish your document with Microsoft Viewer, which preserves the native format of the document.

Other I-Net Tools

In addition to Microsoft, other vendors are moving fast to develop products for Internet and intranet deployment. This section describes World Wide Web server products from Netscape and O'Reilly.

Netscape Web Server Products

Netscape Communications Corporation develops a wide range of server products for implementing Internet and intranet solutions. Netscape's vision of the ideal Internet architecture is quite similar to Microsoft's, as evidenced by the server products it supports.

Netscape server products are available for a wide range of operating system platforms, including Windows NT, UNIX, IBM AIX, and DEC UNIX. All Netscape products are fully based on open industry standards. The Netscape server family includes the following products:

- **Enterprise Server**—This is Netscape's flagship product for high-performance, high-volume Web sites. This is the server that compares with the Internet Information Server.
- **Mail Server**—This is an SMTP mail server for facilitating electronic mail messaging across the Internet.

- **News Server**—This is an NNTP server for creating public and private discussion groups and for connecting to the Internet UseNet community.

- **Catalog Server**—Netscape's counterpart to the Microsoft Index Server, Catalog Server provides indexing, cataloging, and search capabilities for the Web site.

- **Proxy Server**—This enables corporations to provide secure connectivity to the Internet using filtering and security mechanisms.

- **Directory Server**—This provides user directory information, and is similar to the Microsoft White Pages Server.

- **Certificate Server**—This enables Web administrators to manage their own security key certificates. It provides key issuing, signing, and management using SSL for secure and private communications across the Internet.

- **FastTrack Server**—This is an entry level server for sites that will implement a basic Internet presence. FastTrack Server is easy to install, set up, and administer. It is one of the few commercial servers available that can run on Windows 95.

 TIP Evaluation copies of Netscape's server products can be downloaded from the Netscape Web site at **http://www.netscape.com**.

Netscape markets a collection of its server products under the trade name SuiteSpot, which is an integrated suite of server products that provides a wide range of functionality for developing Internet and intranet solutions. SuiteSpot includes Enterprise Server, Mail Server, News Server, Catalog Server, and Proxy Server. In addition, it includes LiveWirePro and AppFoundry, which are development tools for creating Web content.

O'Reilly's WebSite

O'Reilly and Associates, Inc. (**http://www.oreilly.com**) offers WebSite, a World Wide Web server for the Windows NT and Windows 95 platforms. WebSite is a multithreaded, 32-bit Web server that is known for its ease of use and flexibility. It is probably the server that supports the widest variety of standards: CGI, ActiveX, Java, and Perl scripting. WebSite supports the following features:

- **WebView**—This is a graphical hierarchical tool for managing document links and directory structures. It also provides logging functions, and it includes a wizard for automatically creating Web pages.

- **HotDog**—This is an HTML editor for creating Web documents.

- **Spyglass Mosaic**—It includes the Mosaic Web browser for navigating World Wide Web sites.

- **Security**—It provides support for popular security standards, such as SSL and S-HTTP.

Using Dial-Up Networking

There are several different ways to connect to the Internet using Windows NT and Remote Access Service (RAS). RAS provides connection speeds anywhere from 2,400 bits per second (Bps) to 128 kilobits per second (Kbps), with full support for modems, ISDN, and X.25 connectivity. Using dial-up networking client software, the user can remotely connect to an Internet host (perhaps even a computer running UNIX) that supports SLIP or PPP connections using a modem, for example. Once connected, the user can use graphical tools, such as a Web browser, or the traditional command-line tools, such as FTP and Telnet. For a complete discussion of Windows NT Server RAS capabilities, see Chapter 12, "Implementing Remote Access Service (RAS)."

Another method of using Windows NT and RAS—the one that is most commonly used—is to set up a RAS server on a LAN with a direct connection to the Internet. Mobile and home users can then dial in to the RAS server and connect to the Internet. Some corporate sites set up a RAS server isolated from the rest of the corporate LAN to provide a degree of security. Users can then dial in to two different RAS servers: one for Internet access and one to get to the corporate LAN.

The RAS client and server products provide support for the most popular protocols (NetBEUI, IPX/SPX, and TCP/IP using SLIP or PPP). The breadth of features and the simplicity of configuration and administration make the RAS solution ideal for providing remote connectivity for mobile and home-based corporate users. In addition, RAS has full support for Windows NT security and other dial-up security schemes, such as the Challenge Handshake Authentication Protocol (CHAP) and the Password Authentication Protocol (PAP), for connecting to Internet hosts running a multitude of operating systems.

Part
IV

Ch
16

From Here...

This chapter presented some of the server-based products available as part of Microsoft BackOffice for corporations to use when implementing an Internet or intranet connectivity plan. For more information on some of the topics addressed in this chapter, see the following chapters:

- For information on Internet and intranets, see Chapter 17, "I-Net Tools and Techniques."
- To learn about setting up a Web site, see Chapter 18, "Building a Web with Internet Information Server (IIS)."
- To learn about exploring the Internet using the client Web browsers, see Chapter 19, "Web Browsers."
- For information on creating content for your IIS servers, see Chapter 20, "Using Microsoft FrontPage 97."

- To learn about adding search capabilities to your IIS site, see Chapter 21, "Implementing Index Server and Content Replication Server."
- For delivering active content to the Internet, see Chapter 24, "Using Active Platform to Enhance Your Web Site."
- To ensure proper security measures are taken for your Internet involvement, see Chapter 26, "Implementing Internet Security."

## CHAPTER 17

I-Net Tools and Techniques

by Azam A. Mirza

In Chapter 16, "The BackOffice I-Net Toolbox," you learned about some of the tools and products Microsoft BackOffice provides for developing an effective Internet presence. This chapter focuses on the tools and techniques that make the Internet work. The commercialization of the Internet has caught the corporate world by storm and the possibility of being left behind has created a frenzy among corporations trying to adopt the Internet phenomenon.

The following sections describe some of the Internet tools and techniques, present scenarios for achieving business value from the Internet, and also discuss the increasing role of intrancts in the corporate world. ■

What is the Internet?

Gain an understanding of the Internet by learning about its origin, the current state of Internet technology, and what the future holds for online computing.

Tools and technologies for effectively using the Internet

Explore the tools and services the Internet offers. Some major Internet technologies are discussed in detail, and their importance and value to the user are explained.

How the Internet provides value to the business community

Learn how the Internet has revolutionized the way the world does business today and how corporations are embracing the Internet to enhance their operations and visibility in the global marketplace.

What is an intranet?

Find out how intranets are revolutionizing the corporate network infrastructure and bringing new promise to corporate computing environments.

The I-Net tools and protocols

Learn about the tools and technologies that provide the power, flexibility, and functionality available through the Internet and intranet—collectively referred to as *I-Net*.

What Is the Internet?

In the early 1970s, the United States Defense Advanced Research Projects Agency (DARPA) became interested in the concept of a packet-switched network. DARPA consequently sponsored a research project to design and develop an advanced mechanism for facilitating the flow of information between distributed computers. The Advanced Research Projects Agency (ARPA), as it was known by the time the project got underway, funded the initial creation of the packet-switched network called the ARPANET, which would eventually grow into what is known today as the Internet.

ARPANET initially used the UNIX operating system, the Network Control Protocol (NCP), and a 50 kilobits per second (Kbps) line to connect four computers located at the University of California at Los Angeles, the Stanford Research Institute, the University of California at Santa Barbara, and the University of Utah at Salt Lake City. By the early 1980s, a new protocol for network connectivity and communications—the Transmission Control Protocol/Internet Protocol (TCP/IP)—was proposed and adopted for ARPANET use. As a public domain protocol, TCP/IP was widely accepted by the computing community for connecting to the fledgling ARPANET. By the mid 1980s, ARPANET had grown from the humble beginning of a four-computer network to more than 200 linked networks with thousands of computers.

Recognizing the potential of the ARPANET as a major network for research, education, and communications, the National Science Foundation (NSF) developed the NSFNET in the mid 1980s to provide a high-speed backbone for connecting to the Internet. From the mid 1980s to the early 1990s, the NSFNET backbone was consistently upgraded from a 56 Kbps line to a 1.54 Mbps line to a 25 Mbps line. The NSFNET played a major role in funding the advancement of the Internet as a viable tool for research and development.

Shortly after the NSFNET backbone was put into place, other government agencies in the United States and organizations abroad got into the act with the creation of backbone networks by the National Aeronautics and Space Agency (NSINET), the Department of Energy (ESNET), and numerous European organizations. Over a short period, the Internet grew to become a conglomeration of more than 5,000 networks in more than 60 countries with more than 5 million computers (see Figure 17.1).

With the eventual decommissioning of the original ARPANET and the NSFNET backbone network as it was outgrown, other Internet backbone network providers emerged. Currently, the backbone for the Internet is supplied by a group of national commercial providers, such as AT&T, MCI, and Sprint, as well as several smaller regional providers. Internationally, the backbone is supported by government organizations and private sector corporations.

FIG. 17.1
The Internet now provides connectivity to a large part of the world. (Illustration courtesy of the Internet Society.)

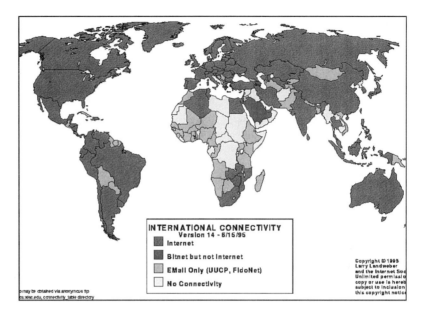

Part

IV

Ch

17

The World's Largest Network

The Internet of the 1990s is a substantial departure from the small network created some 20 years ago for research purposes. With the spread of the Internet's popularity into the business community and private sector, the number of computers connected to the Internet has doubled every year since 1988. It is estimated that by the middle of 1995, more than 20 million users were accessing the Internet and connecting to more than 7 million host computers worldwide.

The initial Internet was nothing more than a collection of connected networks that facilitated the flow of information between computer users. Because the Internet was largely based on computers that ran various versions of the early UNIX operating system, it was mainly a text-based, command-line environment. Also, the slow transmission lines connecting Internet users necessitated the use of techniques that required the least amount of bandwidth for transmission of data. Most early tools and applications used cryptic commands and minimal user interfaces to save transmission overhead. However, as the NSFNET backbone was upgraded to higher speeds and the network became capable of handling higher volumes of information flow, the Internet became a more user-friendly and flexible environment.

Efforts got underway to develop methods of accessing the databases available on the Internet. Early efforts led to the development of tools for searching and retrieving information, such as Archie, Veronica, Jughead, and Gopher. Archie was the first of such tools. It uses a simple method to catalog the information and files available on remote machines and makes the list available to users. Subsequent tools became more and more sophisticated in their approaches, leading to Gopher—which required the use of special Gopher servers for collecting, storing, and displaying information for access by Internet users. Gopher is widely used for providing catalogs of books in libraries and phonebook listings. Veronica and Jughead each provide additional indexing and searching capabilities for use with Gopher servers. Even though all these search and retrieval tools are very sophisticated, they all use text-based user interfaces.

N O T E   The names Archie, Veronica, and Jughead were patterned after the popular comic book characters and are trademarks of Archie Comic Publications, Inc. Veronica and Jughead are both acronyms. Veronica stands for Very Easy Rodent-Oriented Net-wide Index to Computerized Archives, and Jughead stands for Jonzy's Universal Gopher Hierarchy Excavation and Display. Gopher was named after its creators' alma mater: the University of Minnesota Golden Gophers. ▪

Welcome to Cyberspace

With the arrival of the Microsoft Windows graphical user interface in the early 1990s, the continuing popularity of the Apple Macintosh user interface, and the X Windows environment on the UNIX operating system, the graphical user interface became the norm on the desktop rather than the exception. However, the Internet was still largely a text-based environment in a world becoming predominantly graphical. When it became apparent that it was possible to publish information on the Internet for access by the mass population, efforts got underway to develop tools for graphical display of the information.

The key factors responsible for the Internet's exponential growth are the development of the World Wide Web (WWW) (see the section "The World Wide Web" later in this chapter), and a user-friendly way to browse through the information available on it. The development of the Mosaic graphical Internet browsing tool (in 1993) at the University of Illinois National Center for Supercomputing Applications resulted in making the Internet more accessible and much easier to use. Mosaic provided graphical point-and-click navigation of the vast Internet expanse, and enabled people to experience the Internet without having to learn archaic and difficult UNIX utilities and commands.

Naturally, this proliferation of users led to creative approaches to sharing information on the Internet, and as the amount of quality information from an expanding variety of sources increased, the Internet phenomenon became known as the *Information Superhighway* (see the section "I-Net Tools and Protocols" later in this chapter).

Through its first 20 years of existence, the Internet simply facilitated communications between researchers, scientists, and university students. Its primary value was in providing users with the capability to exchange electronic mail (*e-mail*) messages, participate in discussion groups, exchange ideas, and work with each other. The Internet was strictly a nonprofit domain; users resented and shunned anyone who tried to make a dollar from its use. However, in the last three to four years, the Internet has gone through a tremendous transformation. Cyberspace, as it is sometimes referred to, is a place for communicating, advertising, conducting business, and providing information to the masses or the individual.

Networks

The Internet is not a single network, but instead, a combination of thousands of networks spread throughout the world. As mentioned earlier, the initial ARPANET had humble beginnings as a four-node network. As time passed, more and more computers were connected to the initial network. In time, entire networks were connected to the base ARPANET. In the late 1980s, NSFNET came into existence and formed the backbone of a network that connected thousands of Department of Defense agencies, universities, businesses, and research institutions.

Today, the Internet consists of a backbone of networks being maintained by companies, such as AT&T, MCI, and Sprint. This backbone network typically runs at speeds of 45–100 Mbps. It also provides connectivity to the mid-level and regional networks being operated throughout the world.

For example, one of these is the Canadian Network (CA.net), which provides connectivity to most of Canada. These mid-level and regional networks then provide connectivity to local organizations, universities, and Internet service providers (ISPs) who provide or sell Internet connectivity to the commercial and private sectors.

N O T E The multilevel connectivity of the Internet is transparent to the average user and does not in any way affect the capability to explore the Internet. ▨

Protocols

The Internet networks run on a network scheme called TCP/IP: a mechanism that breaks a message into small packets and transmits them over the network. In addition to carrying a piece of the actual message, each packet also carries an identification tag to facilitate the reassembling of the pieces back into the proper order when the message is received. The packets comprising a message are required to reach the proper destination, but they do not have to use the same route or travel through the Internet in a predetermined sequence. When all the packets containing a particular message have arrived at the destination, they are automatically put back together to re-create the original message. This is why the Internet is called a *packet-switched* network. The devices that collect these packets and determine the best transmission routes for them are called *routers*. See Chapter 9, "Using TCP/IP with Windows NT Server," for more information.

Domains and Addresses

Domains provide the Internet with a way to define network groups, computer names, and addresses. All Internet computers are identified by a unique number called the *IP* (*Internet Protocol*) *address*, and even though millions of computers are connected to the Internet (and therefore are in the Internet domain), each IP address must be unique. Thus, an IP address consists of four three-digit numbers, called *octets*, each separated by a dot. The permissible range for an octet is 0 through 255 (for example, **200.215.180.210**).

N O T E Not all addresses are available for general use. Certain ranges in the Class A address space have been reserved for administrative purposes and future usage, thus reducing the total number of available addresses significantly. ▨

N O T E The enormous growth of the Internet has resulted in a shortage of available IP addresses. An inappropriate allocation of addresses in the Class B range has resulted in inefficient address usage. Many organizations have been assigned relatively large Class B addresses when a smaller Class C address range would have sufficed. Efforts are underway to rework the addressing scheme to alleviate the problems.

▶ **See** "A Brief TCP/IP Tutorial," **p. 250**

Dividing the IP address space into classes makes it easier to distribute addresses using the top-down domain-level hierarchy method. Backbone providers are usually assigned Class A addresses, with subsequent lower-level domains assigned Class B, C, or D addresses under that range. For example, Macmillan Computer Publishing USA is assigned a Class C address of **199.177.202.X**, which makes 256 Class D addresses available to Macmillan Computer Publishing to be assigned as it sees fit within its domain. Macmillan's network provider has a Class B address assigned to it, **199.177.X.X**, enabling it to assign more than 65,000 lower domain addresses to its customers. The IP address purposely distributes administration of address assignment to lower levels of the domain hierarchy for autonomy of operations.

N O T E The InterNIC (Internet Network Information Center) is now ultimately responsible for processing all IP address requests and has the final authority for assigning IP addresses to interested parties.

Because it is difficult to remember cryptic numbers, the Internet uses a naming convention called the *Domain Name Service* (*DNS*), which translates IP addresses into names that are easier to remember. For example, the address of the Macmillan Computer Publishing USA Internet server is (currently) **199.177.202.10**. Because it is difficult to remember such a number, the server has been assigned the name **www.mcp.com**. Just like the numeric IP addresses, domain names are also separated by dots for the purpose of creating a name-based domain hierarchy. In terms of domain names, the addresses are read backwards to identify the top-level domain, and so on. With **www.mcp.com**, the top-level domain is the **com** domain. The **mcp** domain is a mid-level domain that is part of the **com** domain, and **www** is one of the names of a computer in the **mcp** domain (it may have other names as well).

Six top-level domains are defined for the United States:

- **gov**—Government organizations
- **mil**—Military organizations
- **edu**—Educational organizations
- **com**—Commercial organizations
- **org**—Nonprofit organizations
- **net**—Network service providers, usually mid-level regional networks

In addition, countries around the world have each been assigned a two-character top level domain name. For example, **uk** is for the United Kingdom, **ca** is for Canada, **au** is for Australia, and **fi** is for Finland. The DNS naming convention allows for 2–4 levels of nested domains—a completely arbitrary selection based on ease of use and simplicity.

N O T E   Recently, the United States has also been assigned a two-character code—namely, **us**—
to identify computers and domains within the United States. However, the previously
mentioned six top-level domains are still predominantly used to identify entities within the United
States—a concession to the country of origin for the Internet. ▇

Dividing computers and networks into domains distributes the administration of the naming
system to lower levels of the hierarchy. Because every computer name on the Internet must be
unique, it is easier to handle the administration by placing the responsibility on the network
administrators to maintain uniqueness within their own domain. For example, the company
G.A. Sullivan can have two computers named "server" and be legal as long as one is in the
gasullivan.com domain (**server.gasullivan.com**), and the other is in the
hamilton.gasullivan.com domain (**server.hamilton.gasullivan.com**). You cannot have both
computers in the **gasullivan.com domain** because their name strings would be identical
(**server.gasullivan.com**). However, because **hamilton** is a subdomain of the **gasullivan.com
domain**, it is possible to have a second computer named "server" within the
hamilton.gasullivan.com subdomain. Therefore, as long as you can append the computer
name to a domain name to make the entire name string unique, you have satisfied the naming
convention.

Part
IV

Ch
17

Business Value of the Internet

The Internet has become a great influence in the business world. Its impact was expected by
some, but has taken the majority of people somewhat by surprise. Business entities of all types
are still struggling to find ways to take advantage of this significant and relatively new resource. The enormous popularity of the Internet has affected the business community in the
following ways:

- ▇ It has motivated companies around the world to rethink how they do business and how
  they reach their target audience. For example, several TV commercials now include the
  Web site addresses of the advertisers.
- ▇ It presents an outstanding opportunity for businesses to reach a mass market audience.
- ▇ It offers opportunities for individuals and organizations to launch businesses using the
  Internet as the vehicle.
- ▇ It is a convenient medium for disseminating enormous amounts of information to a large
  audience. The information is available for users to view at their own leisure and prefer-
  ence.

These concepts are supported by the applications being implemented that utilize the
Internet—and the WWW in particular—for the following business activities:

- ▇ Marketing and advertising
- ▇ Sales
- ▇ Communications

■ Publishing

■ Computer systems support

Marketing and Advertising

The Internet has been recognized by organizations around the world as a new and exciting opportunity for expanding their businesses to reach new and untapped customers. The WWW has leveled the playing field for all organizations big and small by making the medium of communication the same for all. Companies must compete with each other using the same methods and tools and on the strength of their products rather than a glamorous or convincing marketing campaign. This apparently level playing field makes it difficult for organizations to differentiate themselves from each other for attracting customers. However, it also pushes the envelope for coming up with new and exciting ideas for grabbing the attention of the audience.

The most common method of marketing information about a business is to develop a WWW site for introducing products. Many organizations have created WWW sites for introducing customers to their products in the hopes of enticing them to buy the products. Unique and innovative ideas are used by organizations to attract potential customers to their WWW sites. Figure 17.2 shows the Web site maintained by ProSoft for providing WWW users with information about its Internet and intranet training courses.

FIG. 17.2
ProSoft maintains a WWW site for introducing its training courses to potential Internet-based customers.

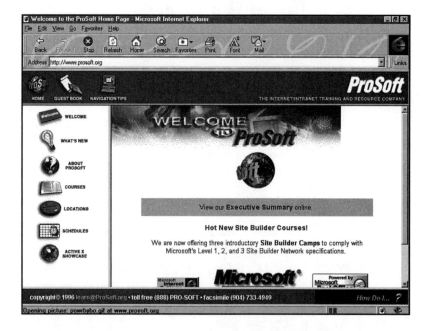

Another, more common method of advertising on the WWW is to buy advertising space on WWW sites commonly visited by Internet users. Organizations providing services to Internet users, such as the Yahoo! WWW search database site, sell advertising space on their WWW sites to finance their operations. Businesses can buy advertising space on other sites that grab users' attention and introduce them to products being offered by organizations around the world. These advertising spots usually also include hyperlinks to the WWW site being maintained by the advertiser, so the users can immediately navigate to that site if they are interested in checking out the products. Figure 17.3 depicts the Yahoo! search database Web site with some advertisements by other businesses.

FIG. 17.3
The Yahoo! WWW search database sells advertising spots on its site.

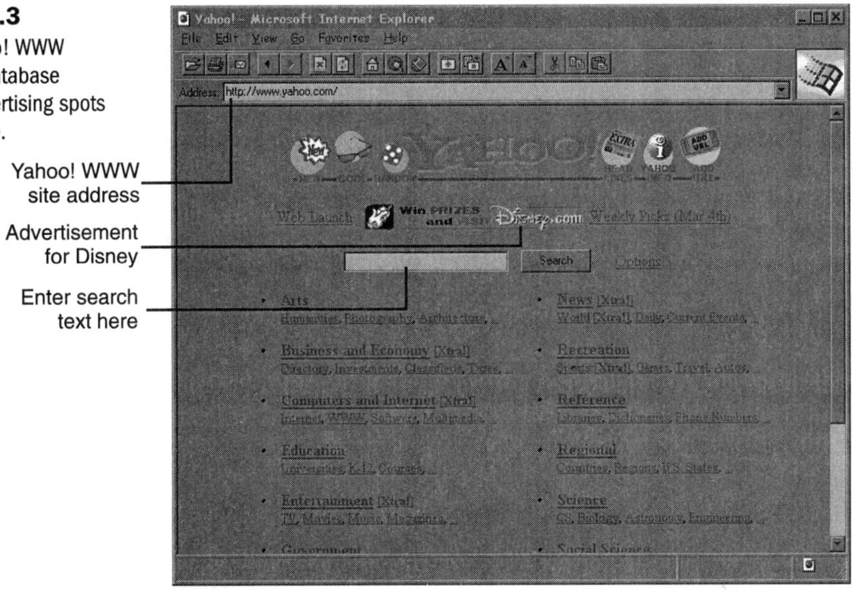

Yahoo! WWW site address

Advertisement for Disney

Enter search text here

Sales

The Internet has always been used for the buying and selling of goods using the electronic medium. In the old days, most activities involving electronic commerce over the Internet were done between individuals. The *Acceptable Use Policy* (*AUP*) for the NSFNET backbone expressly prohibited the use of the Internet for commercial activities and, therefore, prohibited organizations and individuals from selling products over the Internet.

N O T E The Acceptable Use Policy was defined as part of the NSFNET charter and governed all conduct over the Internet. It is a set of guidelines that is still adhered to in some form or another by all Internet users. It defines acceptable and unacceptable behavior for "citizens" of the Internet. ▨

N O T E Before commercial activity was acceptable on the Internet, the only means of buying or selling products over the Internet was through special UseNet newsgroups. These newsgroups were set up to enable users to trade with each other, and are still heavily used. For example, a newsgroup called **misc.forsale.computers.monitors** is for buying and selling computer monitors. The newsgroup **rec.photo.marketplace** is used exclusively to buy and sell photography equipment. ▨

However, after the NSFNET backbone was decommissioned and the Internet became more commercial, changes were brought about to allow commercial activity on the Internet. The World Wide Web became the medium of choice for carrying out electronic commerce. One of the most famous and popular commercial WWW sites is the Internet Shopping Network. The ISN, as it is more commonly called, is one of the first WWW sites developed exclusively to sell products on the Internet. Figure 17.4 displays the home page of the Internet Shopping Network Web site.

FIG. 17.4

The Internet Shopping Network sells a wide variety of computer products to WWW users.

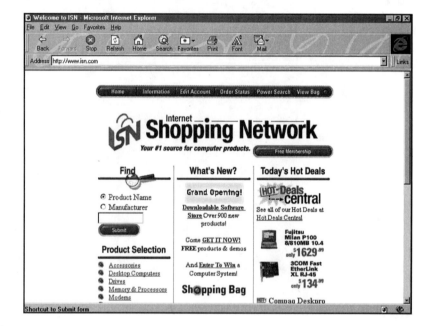

Over the last couple of years, hundreds of WWW sites have sprung up for selling products to the Internet community. They are commonly referred to as *online shopping malls*. The Internet can be used to buy products in any imaginable category from clothes to skiing gear, computers, and boats.

Traditional businesses that have moved the fastest to embrace the Internet have usually been in the apparel retail business and the mail-order catalog business. Such companies as Lands' End, The Nature Company, The Limited, and Damark mail-order catalog have moved quickly to adapt their businesses to embrace the Internet.

The introduction of server products, such as the Microsoft Merchant Server, indicate the importance of electronic commerce on the Internet. These server products make it possible for corporations to engage in full retail sales operations. They support such operations as inventory management, order processing, account management, secure credit card processing, and order entry.

Communication

One of the major advantages of the Internet has been its capability to provide a means of communication among organizations. E-mail and mailing lists provide businesses with a convenient and relatively inexpensive mechanism for communicating with customers and vendors on a one-to-one basis. More and more, business users are using Internet e-mail to keep in touch with each other, exchange ideas and information, and receive customer feedback.

Mailing lists are maintained by organizations around the world to inform their customers of new happenings, product announcements, and other important events. One example of a mailing list is the Microsoft Windows NT Server mailing list available to registered users of Windows NT Server. It informs them of product updates, bug fixes, and upcoming events relating to the Windows NT Server product. For more information, see the sections "Electronic Mail" and "UseNet: Network Newsgroups" later in this chapter.

Part

IV

Ch

17

Publishing

Many organizations have recognized the WWW as a great place to advertise, and they are using the WWW as a means of publishing information about their products and services. The popularity of the WWW as an advertising and marketing tool is evident in the number of sites set up solely for the purpose of advertising products and services. The Internet also presents an enormous opportunity for service providers to develop a presence on the WWW. Virtually overnight, hundreds of businesses specializing in WWW server setup, Web page creation, electronic publishing, and content creation have sprung up around the world. The home page for one such company is shown in Figure 17.5.

FIG. 17.5
WWW content creators, such as Digital Dimensions, Inc., also have their own Web pages.

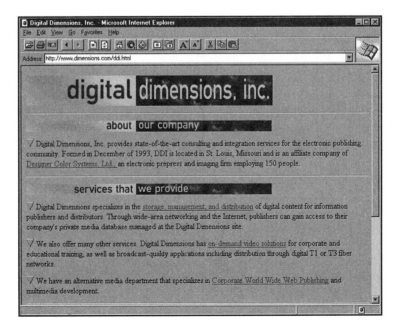

The World Wide Web is also being used as a medium for electronic publishing. Following are examples of popular uses of the Web:

■ Several books have been converted to electronic form and made available on the WWW. The contents of this book are provided in HTML format on the CD-ROM included with this book. (Perhaps you are reading the electronic version with a Web browser right now!)

■ Several newsletters are published by individuals and organizations solely in electronic form and made available on the WWW.

■ The IRS publishes all tax-related materials on the WWW.

■ Web sites are maintained by organizations for providing users with up-to-the-minute news stories and stock market quotes. For example, ESPN maintains a WWW site for up-to-date sports news and information (see Figure 17.6).

FIG. 17.6
The ESPNet SportsZone provides up-to-the-minute sports news, scores, and highlights.

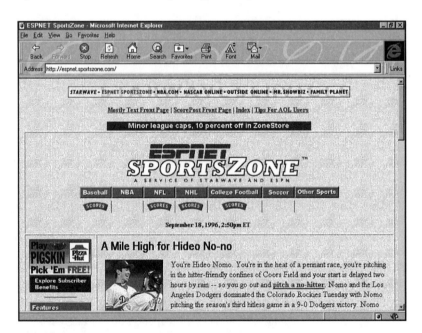

Computer Systems Support

The Internet has also become a vehicle for providing help desk operations to the user community. Corporations worldwide are using the Internet as a means for providing product support and service. For example, General Life Insurance Company uses the Internet to provide its life insurance policy holders with information about their policy status. Figure 17.7 presents a view of the main page at the General Life WWW site.

FIG. 17.7
General Life Insurance Company's WWW site provides an automated mechanism for clients to look up life insurance policy information.

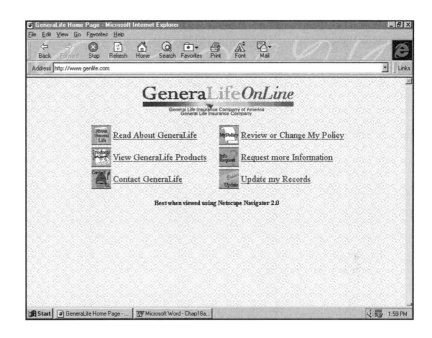

Such companies as Microsoft and IBM have placed their entire help desk knowledge base on the Internet for their customers to use. Product support is fast becoming a very popular and a well-received application for the Internet.

Joining the Internet Community

To join the Internet community and provide other Internet users access to your Internet site, you must have an Internet connection. Internet connections are provided by commercial connection providers called *Internet service providers (ISPs)*. ISPs sell Internet connections based on a variety of pricing and connectivity schemes. When acquiring an Internet connection, consider the following points:

- Choosing an Internet service provider
- Bandwidth requirements
- Special connectivity issues

Each of these topics is discussed in the following sections.

Choosing an Internet Service Provider

Thousands of ISPs around the world provide Internet connectivity. ISPs exist in all flavors and sizes—from such companies as Sprint, MCI, and AT&T to small local and regional organizations. Figure 17.8 illustrates the role an ISP plays in providing your Internet connectivity.

FIG. 17.8

ISPs provide connectivity by selling commercial Internet connections.

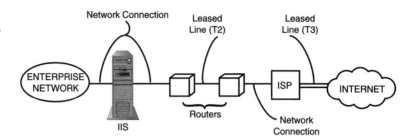

Pricing for Internet connections is based on the kind of connection you desire and its speed. Prices vary widely from one ISP to another. The larger national providers probably will cost more than the smaller, local ISPs. The larger ISPs claim reliability, customer service, and quality as their selling points. Local providers tout the personal attention and easy accessibility of their services. The field is so crowded and so many options are available that Internet connections have become a place for price wars. ISPs are constantly touting their lowered prices and increased bandwidth.

N O T E Select an ISP that provides a good, reliable connection. Unreliable connection is the single biggest complaint against most ISPs. ■

The following are some issues you should consider when selecting an ISP:

■ **Customer base**—How many customers does the ISP have in your region? Who are its customers? Are they organizations that are likely to have needs similar to your own?

■ **History**—How long has the ISP been in business? Will it still be in business next year?

■ **Reputation**—What kind of reputation does the ISP have around town? Are current customers satisfied with its service?

■ **ISP connection to the Internet**—What kind of connection does the ISP have to the Internet? The higher its connection speed, the more traffic it can handle. Most ISPs have speed problems because they do not have sufficient bandwidth available for the number of customers they have. See the next section, "Bandwidth Requirements," for more information.

■ **Customer service**—How big is the customer support staff? What is the ratio of customer support personnel to customers? Does the ISP handle problem calls in a timely manner? Does it have free on-site service? Is the support staff knowledgeable? Does it provide free support for the first 30 days?

■ **Connection speeds**—What kind of connection speeds does the ISP provide? The more choices it has, the more options you have for upgrading in the future to higher speeds.

■ **Cost**—What is the pricing structure? Does it have a flat monthly rate or does it charge by connection time? Does it have any up-front setup charges? Some ISPs charge exorbitant setup charges. Compare costs between ISPs.

Bandwidth Requirements

Internet connections come in a variety of speed choices. For running information publishing sites, anything less than a 56,000 Kbps connection is not enough. Your choice of a connection speed depends on how much traffic you will experience. Start with a suitable speed and upgrade if you experience speed problems as more people find out about your site. Bandwidth options are available in a variety of speeds, as shown in Table 17.1.

> **CAUTION**
>
> I do not recommend modem connections for running a Web server site. The typical modem speeds of 14,400 Kbps to 28,800 Kbps are not fast enough to handle the traffic created by Web servers.

Part
IV

Ch
17

Table 17.1 Bandwidth Options for Sites Running Internet Services

Connection Type	Bandwidth (Kbps)
Leased line	56
Frame relay	56
ISDN	128
Fractional T-1	56–1,540
T-1	1,540
T-3	45,000

Leased line, Frame Relay, and ISDN connections can handle light traffic up to about 25–50 simultaneous connections. Fractional T-1 and T-1 lines can handle anywhere from 100 to 1,000 simultaneous users. Organizations that handle thousands of users at a time have multiple T-1 connections or even a T-3 connection.

 Start with a connection speed that is fast enough to get you up and running, and test your Internet site setup. If in the future you need to upgrade, you can always do so.

Special Connectivity Issues

This section discusses some other connectivity issues that you must tackle before your Internet connectivity is complete. These issues are as follows:

- **IP addresses and DNS registration**—You need IP addresses and DNS name registration for your Internet machines and other computers you are going to connect to the Internet. Most ISPs take care of obtaining IP addresses and registering your DNS domain name for you. To register your organization yourself, you must contact InterNIC (Network Information Center).

N O T E   You can contact InterNIC via e-mail at **http://info@internic.net** or by phone. In the
USA, call 1-800-444-4345. In Canada or elsewhere, call 1-619-455-4600. From overseas,
you may need to use a country code to access the USA when dialing. ■

 T I P   Domain name selection is an important step. Make sure that you select a name appropriate for your
organization because you cannot change your domain name after it is registered. For example,
Macmillan Computer Publishing USA has a registered domain name of **mcp.com**.

■ **Router**—You need a routing device to route traffic from your Web server to the Internet.
Most ISPs provide a router at their end and require you to purchase a router for your
end of the connection. Many router products are available on the market; make your
selection based on your needs, future upgrade needs, and cost.

T I P   Windows NT Server can be set up to provide software routing of your TCP/IP packets. You can
accomplish this task by using static routing tables and the ROUTE.EXE application included with
Windows NT Server. Use of this utility is beyond the scope of this book. Consult Volume 2 of
the Windows NT Resource Kit, *Windows NT Networking Guide*, for more information.

■ **Simple Mail Transfer Protocol (SMTP) mail gateway**—You need to route e-mail
traffic between your Microsoft Exchange Server and the Internet. Your ISP should
provide you with an SMTP routing setup at its end, and you should install an SMTP
gateway at your end to accept traffic from the ISP's e-mail server.

N O T E   Microsoft Exchange Server includes an SMTP gateway called the Internet Mail Connector as
part of the server product. ■

■ **DNS name resolution**—You also need DNS name resolution capabilities to be able to
resolve IP addresses to domain names. DNS software is now available for Windows NT
Server 4.0. You can set up your own DNS server on a Windows NT server machine, or
you can have your ISP provide DNS name resolution for you. Most ISPs provide DNS
services free or for a nominal fee. For more information, see the section "Domains and
Addresses" earlier in this chapter.

User Education and Training

If you are implementing an Internet solution with which users in your enterprise will get access
to the Internet or will be using your intranet IIS machines, then you must spend some time and
resources in educating your users about the Internet, its policies, and how to best utilize it.

You should develop a plan for user training and education. You need to address such user-
related issues as the following:

■ **Internet primer**—Train them about what the Internet is. Users can be directed toward
hundreds of books written on the subject. Small group seminars can be arranged to
introduce users to the Internet.

■ **What the Internet offers**—Teach users to derive value from the Internet. What are some of the resources available?

■ **How to use the Internet**—Show users how to get connected and use the resources available on the Internet. Provide training on using client software, such as Internet Explorer.

■ **Internet etiquette**—Introduce them to Internet policies and practices. Provide users with the Internet "Acceptable Use Policies" document or other guide to *netiquette*. Make sure that users understand what is allowed and what is unacceptable on the Internet. Use a search engine with the keyword netiquette or try **http://www.netwelcome.com**.

N O T E   Your users will be representing your organization to the rest of the Internet world. Make sure that they represent your organization in a positive and acceptable manner. Set up organizational guidelines that define acceptable behavior. ■

■ **Security issues**—Train users on the security issues. Warn them about checking files downloaded from the Internet for viruses. Make them aware of the consequences of carrying out unlawful activities on the Internet, such as copying pirated software.

User training is a time-consuming and costly undertaking. However, it is very important that users are properly educated and represent your organization in a positive manner. The time you invest in training will be repaid many times over.

Defining an Internet Security Plan

One of the most important planning-stage steps is handling the security issues involved with operating Internet sites. When you set up your Internet site, pay special attention to security issues so that you do not provide access to sensitive company information to people from outside your enterprise.

Microsoft BackOffice products provide a flexible security model for making sure that your machines and network are safeguarded against unauthorized intrusion.

The Risks

In addition to the security measures offered by Microsoft BackOffice products, you can take extra steps to ensure that your internal network and information are protected from potential security risks by doing the following:

■ Set up firewalls to prevent unauthorized access to your network.

N O T E   Firewalls, screening routers, and other similar security measures can limit who has access to your network. For example, you can filter user traffic based on IP addresses or security keys. If the remote client trying to connect to your machine is not on the list of allowed clients, it will not be granted access to your network. ■

Part
IV
Ch
17

- Separate your Windows NT Servers running Internet services from the rest of your enterprise network by placing them in their own domain. Then set up a one-way trust relationship to permit only one-way access. Allow users from your enterprise network to access the Internet machines, but do not allow any user accounts from the domain containing the Internet machines (especially Guest) to access your network. Run all Internet services in the security context of a service account from the untrusted domain containing the Internet machines.

- Make sure that your Internet server machines have appropriate file permissions established to prevent unauthorized copying or modifications of files.

- Require password authentication before granting access to sensitive data.

- Require users to change passwords at regular intervals.

- Use the NTFS file system for data storage. NTFS enables very low-level control of file access control.

- Always use encrypted passwords across the Internet.

- Check all files transferred through FTP for viruses.

  ▶ **See** "Security for Your Internet Server," **p. 570**

The Tools

Security has been the number one concern for organizations trying to implement I-net solutions. Because the Internet evolved from an open and distributed environment, security concerns have plagued the network from the very beginning. As compared to the consumer market, the relatively slower acceptance of the Internet in the corporate community can be directly attributed to concerns and issues raised over the secure nature of information transmissions.

The sensitive nature of corporate data makes security of paramount importance in the corporate community. Standards committees have worked very hard to introduce standards for secure communications over the last year or so. The following are some of the tools and technologies developed to implement Internet security:

- Encryption
- Firewalls
- Electronic signatures and IDs

Encryption   Most Web server and browser software products support the *Secure Sockets Layer* (*SSL*) security mechanism for data encryption. SSL encrypts the data being transferred over the network and requires the client to present a valid key before the data can be decrypted. SSL is the most widely implemented security standard for data protection. In addition to encryption, SSL also provides user authentication functionality.

To use encryption technologies, such as SSL, an electronic "certificate" must be obtained from a certifying organization, such as VeriSign. Once installed, the certificates enable Web servers to send encrypted data and request encrypted responses from client browsers.

In addition, the *Secure Electronic Transactions* (*SET*) standard provides a secure method of enabling electronic commerce using WWW technology. SET was mainly designed to handle the exchange of credit card numbers over the Internet.

Firewalls   Firewalls are special software systems that safeguard a network from outside intrusion and from unauthorized access to the outside world from within an organization's network. A firewall is basically a gatekeeper that checks to see if network traffic coming in or going out of a secured environment originates from an authorized user and has appropriate permissions to access the destination resource.

> **N O T E**   An infamous firewall software product called SATAN created a considerable amount of publicity due to the reverse nature of the product. SATAN could be used to find loopholes in an organization's network infrastructure. ■

T I P   Proxy servers, such as Microsoft Access Server, are products that perform firewall functions to keep intruders from coming in or going out of a secure network. See Chapter 22, "Implementing Microsoft Proxy Server," for more information.

Electronic Signatures and IDs   Electronic signatures are a recent development that take the concept of security to the lowest and most personal level by assigning electronic identification to individual users of the Internet or intranet. With systems enabled for the use of electronic signatures, every operation performed by the user requires a valid electronic signature and the signature is then authenticated using a central database set up by the signature issuing organization to determine if the signature is valid.

Electronic signatures are a valuable addition to environments in which very sensitive information is being accessed, such as credit card processing systems. Users can use their credit cards to purchase products and then verify their purchase for approval by providing a matching electronic signature. They can also be used in e-mail systems to ensure that a message is indeed from the person who signed the message, and even that the contents of the message have not been altered. As a greater variety of human interaction is performed in networked environments, the capability to positively identify an individual becomes vital.

What Is an Intranet?

As the world races to connect to the Internet, an unexpected phenomenon is taking place. Corporations trying to figure out profitable and beneficial uses for this emerging global network have found a way to enhance the power and usefulness of their own internal networks as well. The intranet model, a younger and more contained sibling of the Internet, has emerged. An intranet is a scaled down version of the Internet—not in functionality or features, but in size and scope.

Your Own Private Internet

Intranets are internal, corporate-wide networks based on technology used for the Internet. Whereas the Internet provides corporate networks with connectivity to the global network of networks, intranets enable corporations to build internal, self-contained networks that have important advantages over existing network technologies. The intranet process model and its network connectivity architecture hold several major advantages over traditional networking architectures.

Not only is an intranet an excellent solution on its own, it can also be a great stepping stone to enterprise connectivity to the global Internet. Corporations hesitant about embracing the Internet can move at a slower pace and implement an internal intranet before making the leap to the global network. Since the technologies and tools used are identical, the move to Internet connectivity is only a matter of scaling an intranet to the bigger Internet. Figure 17.9 shows the corporate intranet Web site for G. A. Sullivan.

FIG. 17.9

G. A. Sullivan's internal Web site is used to disseminate corporate information to employees.

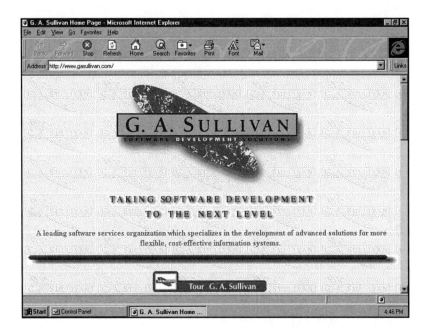

The Power of Internet Technologies

Leveraging the technologies used throughout the global Internet framework and scaling them down to the enterprise level provide intranets with immense advantages. The Internet networking concept has served millions of interconnected networks very well over a long period of time. Utilizing the same tools and techniques to enhance the networking capabilities of an enterprise is a logical solution. Some of the advantages of an intranet are as follows:

- Cost-effective networking
- A new process model
- Platform independence

Cost Effective Networking   Companies are realizing the cost effectiveness of the intranet network architecture. It is relatively inexpensive to set up an intranet. The technologies at the core of an intranet are open, standards-based, and widely implemented. The server software for setting up a World Wide Web (WWW) server, often referred to as a *Web server*, is usually inexpensive and is available from a multitude of vendors, such as Microsoft and Netscape. The client workstations on an intranet use inexpensive and easy-to-use Web browser software for connecting to the Web server. However, setup, installation, and operation of an effective corporate intranet are not trivial tasks and require a lot of time and effort on the part of the developers.

The networking infrastructure needed for setting up a basic intranet is already in place in most corporations. Note, however, that a rapidly growing intranet may eventually place extensive demands on an existing infrastructure in terms of hardware and networking resources.

A New Process Model   Intranets implement a hybrid architecture that brings together the best features of the client/server process model with those of the host-based process model. The intranet architecture is geared toward ease of deployment, centralized control of information, and simple administration of resources. In the intranet process model, the server is responsible for providing information and requested data to the intended users. In addition, the server holds the key to the graphical user interface presented to the user through the client browser software.

Client workstations (typically desktop PCs) use Web browser software to display information sent by the server. The server controls the layout and content of the information. This makes management and administration of information very reliable because it is centralized. However, the client is not just a dumb terminal. It does perform operations, such as information caching and local storage of information downloaded by the user. In other words, the intranet architecture is a process model that takes the best from the client/server world and combines it with the best attributes of the traditional host-based architecture employed by mainframes and minicomputers.

Platform Independence   An important advantage of intranets is their capability to bring together heterogeneous systems into a common interoperable network. The corporate world has spent millions of dollars and many years trying to connect disparate and incompatible systems into a seamless and interoperable network. The results have not been completely satisfactory. As the intranet architecture was developed from the ground up to be able to connect different systems together, it lends itself well to the corporate culture in most organizations where different systems, such as PCs, Macs, and UNIX-based workstations, must coexist.

Part
IV

Ch
17

Business Value of an Intranet

Intranets present enterprises with a unique and exciting opportunity to bring together technologies that were difficult to implement before. As mentioned previously, the cost effectiveness and platform independence of the intranet model bring true heterogeneous networking to the enterprise for the first time. As more and more enterprises understand the power of the Internet networking model, they are racing to embrace the technology. Corporations around the world are implementing intranet networks within their enterprise to avail themselves of these advantages.

It is important to note that intranets can be stand-alone networks or can be connected to the Internet at the same time. This provides your enterprise users with connectivity to the internal network and outside world using the same networking technologies and tools. Users do not have to use and adopt different methods and processes when moving between an intranet and the outside world. For example, currently most enterprises implement multiple e-mail systems to provide connectivity to the internal network and to the outside world. For each outside entity they must connect to, a corporation must embrace a system that is compatible with the other side. With Internet technology, all communications can occur over a single e-mail system.

Intranets provide added value to an enterprise in the following areas:

- Communications
- Publishing
- Workgroup applications

Internal Communications

The following communication tools facilitate information exchange among users of a corporate intranet:

- **E-mail**—A messaging system for exchanging information between users within an intranet or across the global Internet.
- **Bulletin Boards**—A "Post-it Notes™" system for disseminating information to a group of users on a corporate intranet.
- **Discussion Groups**—A forum for exchanging ideas and engaging in discussions on various topics.
- **Chat Rooms**—A place where users can interactively "talk" to each other using tools specifically designed for use across an intranet.
- **Remote Access**—Enables remote connection to the corporate intranet through dial-up networking.

Most popular among communication tools are e-mail messaging systems and discussion group reading and posting programs. In addition, tools are becoming available for using the multimedia hardware on client workstations (speakers and microphone) to provide digital phone facilities over the Internet. Users can speak to each other using their computers rather than a traditional telephone. There are also tools for providing live feeds of television and radio broadcasts.

Live video and audio products provide support for streaming media. It is possible to transfer feeds from satellite transmissions directly to intranet networks and make them available to users. Users can watch live seminars from their desktops using their browsers, watch news broadcasts, or gain access to broadcasts of educational classes, for example. Such browsers as Navigator and Internet Explorer have add-on products available that make it possible to see and hear live video and audio broadcasts. Various vendors provide tools for this purpose; the ShockWave add-on product is the most widely used.

These tools can be effectively used within a corporate environment to provide users with intranet-based digital phone capabilities, the ability to bring corporate seminars and presentations to user desktops, and the capability to provide videoconferencing facilities for users in different geographic locations.

Intranet Publishing

Intranets provide a means for corporations to use electronic publishing for disseminating information to their users. A Web site can be established that is used as the clearing house for information that needs to be transmitted to users. Users can connect to the Web site using their Web browsers and navigate through the Web pages to reach the information they are looking for. The common electronically published material on intranets includes the following:

- **Phone Directories**—Users can access corporate phone directories using their Web browsers, and look up the phone numbers of associates within the company.
- **Employee Handbook**—Employee handbooks can be made available to corporate users in electronic form.
- **Product Catalogs**—Corporate product catalogs can be electronically published for quick and easy reference.
- **Reference Manuals**—Reference manuals can be placed online for employees to use when needed.

Since the users are most often going to use a Web browser, it provides a single point of entry for a wide variety of tasks.

Workgroup Applications

Workgroup applications provide users with productivity tools for better working together. The most popular workgroup application of the past decade has been the Lotus Notes system. In a major endorsement of intranets and intranet technologies, IBM has recently announced plans to migrate the Notes environment to the World Wide Web platform. Other vendors such as Netscape and Microsoft have also launched initiatives to address the growing need for intranet productivity tools.

Netscape's upcoming Communicator product is a combination of browser, e-mail, groupware, discussion, and collaboration software for facilitating group activities and enhancing team productivity.

Microsoft is building team collaboration and group connectivity features into its server and client product lines to facilitate better information retrieval and sharing among groups of users.

The Architecture of a Sample Intranet

In a typical intranet, client workstations utilize a networked environment to connect to servers that facilitate requests for information and data. At its most basic level, an intranet requires a single Web server, a network infrastructure based on the TCP/IP networking protocol, and client workstations located within the same physical location. At the other end of the spectrum, an intranet can consist of hundreds of Web servers and thousands of client workstations located all around the world, connected through a complex array of networking components.

Whatever the scope, careful planning must go into setting up the infrastructure for a corporate intranet. In most large organizations, several servers will be needed to host the various components of an intranet. However, in smaller organizations, even a single server can be used to set up a basic intranet. Figure 17.10 presents a sample design for intranets that can satisfy the needs of many organizations.

FIG. 17.10

An intranet can comprise a collection of servers providing services to a heterogeneous and dispersed client base.

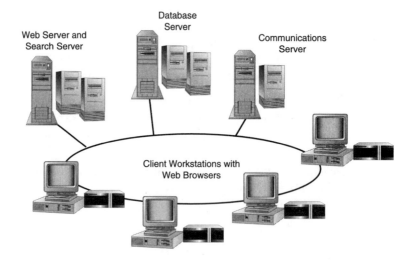

Note that separate machines for various server functions are shown for clarity and ease of understanding. The different server software packages shown in Figure 17.10 (Web server, database server, and so on) can be run on a single server. The choice of the number of Web servers and the selection of separate machines to perform the various operations will depend on the following:

■ The amount of information being processed

■ The number of clients being supported concurrently

■ The speed and performance capabilities of the different server machines

It is always a good idea to start small with a basic intranet setup and build upon that foundation. Intranet server software packages are available for all popular server platforms, such as Windows NT, OS/2, Macintosh, NetWare, and various flavors of the UNIX operating system.

So far, UNIX has been the overwhelming server operating system of choice for setting up Internet and intranet Web servers. This is due to the fact that the Internet was originally designed on UNIX-based machines. The perceived notion is that UNIX is better suited for the high-performance requirements of the Internet.

However, Windows NT has taken major strides in the last year as a viable Web server platform alternative, and is gaining popularity among corporations deciding to implement I-net technology. Ultimately, the selection of a server operating system to use depends more on corporate guidelines and the availability of in-house technical expertise than on what other organizations might be using. Each of the previously mentioned server operating systems is a worthy candidate for potential Web server implementation. It is unnecessary to set up a UNIX-based Web server in an organization where another server operating system is the standard.

Client workstations can be based on any operating system that has Web browser software available. Typical client workstations are a combination of PC, Macintosh, and UNIX systems. Finding a Web browser software package is usually not a problem for these operating systems because such companies as Netscape and Microsoft provide browser support for a wide range of client platforms.

Part
IV
Ch
17

If the corporate intranet is going to expand beyond the local area network (LAN) and encompass an organization's wide area network (WAN), then consideration must also be given toward maximizing throughput across slower WAN links.

Several strategies are available to handle an intranet spanning a WAN. Some corporations may opt to have individual divisions, groups, or subsidiaries install, operate, and manage their own intranets, creating a web of smaller intranets. Under such circumstances, cooperation and coordination between the various intranet administrators becomes an important consideration. A centrally created and managed intranet to service the entire organization is another possibility. This simplifies management, but may increase user training needs due to the IS support staff being centrally located.

It should become obvious from these considerations that installing, operating, and maintaining a corporate intranet is not a trivial task. Careful planning and design must go into implementing a sound intranet solution. However, with proper planning, an intranet can deliver measurable ease of use, interoperability of dissimilar platforms, centralized administration, and levels of productivity, performance, and functionality as yet unattained by other networking technologies.

I-Net Tools and Protocols

The WWW and the graphical Web browsers are probably the single most important reason for the widespread popularity of the Internet in the last few years. Web browsers, such as Netscape Navigator and Microsoft Internet Explorer, provide a graphical user interface that makes the information available on the Internet easier to find and more fun to investigate. By enabling users to gain access to the Internet in a point-and-click manner, a whole new class of users was introduced to the online world of computing. The Internet was quickly transformed from the network of networks to the Information Superhighway.

However, the Information Superhighway consists of much more than the pretty sites that encompass the World Wide Web. It is truly a global information store for the following:

- Doing research
- Communicating across geographic and cultural boundaries
- Engaging in commerce
- Providing huge amounts of informational and retrieval services

These capabilities are available through the many services on the Internet, such as the following:

- The World Wide Web
- Web Browsers
- UseNet: Network Newsgroups
- Electronic Mail
- Telnet
- File Transfer Protocol (FTP)
- Gopher

Each of these services is described in the following sections.

The World Wide Web

The World Wide Web consists of computers connected to the Internet throughout the world that provide graphical access to information stored on those computers. A WWW server may be set up for the purpose of information publishing, education, or to enable electronic commerce. The characteristic that makes the WWW unique is its capability to provide multimedia features, such as pictures, bitmaps, animation, video, and sound. Figure 17.11 shows a corporate informational WWW site set up by G. A. Sullivan.

N O T E The term *WWW site* refers to a computer running WWW server software enabling Internet users to connect to it using WWW browsing software.

The following languages and interfaces are used by Web servers and browsers to facilitate communications between them:

- Hypertext Transport Protocol (HTTP)
- Hypertext Markup Language (HTML)
- Uniform Resource Locator (URL)
- Virtual Reality Modeling Language (VRML)
- Common Gateway Interface (CGI)
- Internet Server API (ISAPI)

- Secure Sockets Layer (SSL)
- Common Internet File System (CIFS)

Each of these is described in the following sections.

FIG. 17.11
Organizations such as G. A. Sullivan use the WWW as a means of providing corporate information and news to their clients and prospective customers.

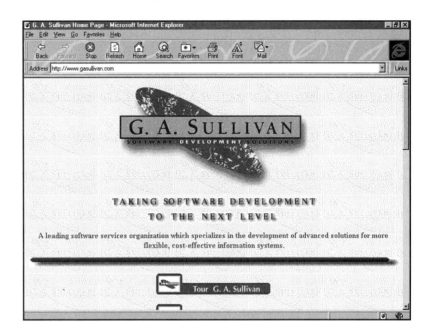

Hypertext Transport Protocol   Hypertext Transport Protocol (HTTP) defines a uniform method for connecting to Web servers using hypertext links. A user can click a link embedded within a Web document, and the system uses the appropriate protocol to connect to the system servicing that link. HTTP also defines mechanisms for retrieving documents from Web servers.

Such Web browsers as Internet Explorer and Navigator use the HTTP protocol to connect to Web sites. An URL address (defined in the section "Uniform Resource Locator" later in this section) is actually an HTTP addressing mechanism that provides the necessary information for making the HTTP link.

Hypertext Markup Language   The Hypertext Markup Language (HTML) is the scripting language used to define WWW server information content. HTML is a plain-text ASCII scripting language that uses embedded control codes like the word processors of old to achieve the formatting of text as well as graphics, images, audio, and video. The information is then stored as files on a WWW server. When a Web browser accesses the file, it is first interpreted by the browser, the control codes are decoded, and the formatted information is presented to the user in a graphical format referred to as a *Web page*.

The WWW and HTML were both developed at CERN (French acronym for European Laboratory for Particle Physics) in 1990. HTML 1.0 was the version used by initial Web browsers, such as Mosaic. The current standard being used is HTML3, which incorporates tables, figures, and other advanced features into WWW document creation. Figure 17.12 presents an HTML document for a Web site home page, and Figure 17.13 shows the page as it looks when viewed using Internet Explorer.

N O T E   CERN is a high-energy physics research center in Switzerland. Much cutting-edge computer science research is conducted at CERN. ▪

N O T E   Mosaic is the graphical Web browser developed by the National Center for Supercomputing Applications at the University of Illinois at Urbana-Champaign. ▪

FIG. 17.12
HTML source documents are used to create WWW home pages.

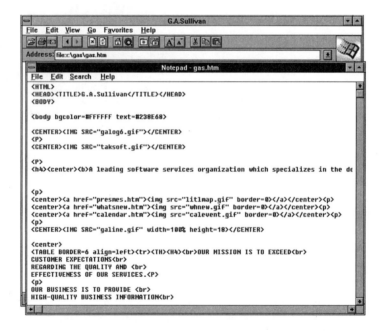

The *HT* in HTML stands for *Hypertext*—an important concept in WWW browsing. Hypertext, or *hyperlink*, refers to links defined within normal textual documents that enable a user to jump to another part of a document. The Windows help system is an example of a document-based system that uses hypertext links. By clicking highlighted or underlined words, users can navigate easily throughout the help system—even between different help files.

The WWW takes the same concept to the next level by enabling hypertext links between Web pages and even WWW sites. By clicking hypertext links defined on a Web page, users cannot only navigate within the same WWW site and view different pages, but can even jump to links pointing to sites on other WWW servers in remote locations. This powerful feature enables navigation of the Internet in a manner never possible before the advent of the WWW.

FIG. 17.13

Microsoft Internet Explorer is the browser software that allows users to view information on the WWW.

Part
IV

Ch

17

The HTML standard is platform-independent because it does not incorporate any codes that specify platform-unique parameters. For example, the codes might specify what size font to use, but not the type of font. That is left up to the browser to determine based upon the platform on which it is running and the fonts available on that machine.

Uniform Resource Locator   The WWW uses a standard called the *Uniform Resource Locator (URL)* for identifying services and machines available across the Internet. The URL is used for identifying the kind of service being used to access a resource, such as FTP, WWW, Gopher, and so on.

An URL uniquely identifies a machine, service, or product over the Internet. An URL has three parts:

- **Scheme**—Identifies the kind of server making the service available, such as FTP, WWW, or Gopher.
- **Address**—Identifies the address of the resource, such as **www.microsoft.com**.
- **Path**—Identifies the full path to the resource being used, such as **/home/images/ image1.gif**.

For example, the URL for accessing the Microsoft FTP server for downloading a file called README.TXT is **ftp://ftp.microsoft.com/readme.txt**. This means that the service being used is FTP (the scheme), the server address is **ftp.microsoft.com** (the address), and the file to download is **readme.txt** (the path). To further explain the URL format, every URL scheme is followed by a colon (:), which is followed by two slashes to indicate that an address follows.

Simply put, URLs are a way for identifying resources on the Internet in a consistent manner.

Virtual Reality Modeling Language The Virtual Reality Modeling Language (VRML) is a scripting language for displaying 3-D objects on the WWW. The VRML addition to the WWW enables the display of interactive 3-D worlds (for example, a virtual computer-generated model of a university campus) that can be traversed by the users accessing them. The capabilities and opportunities afforded by VRML are only limited by the imagination of the Web page author and available bandwidth. VRML promises to provide the capability to visit virtual worlds on the WWW, walk through them, and experience the multimedia power of the WWW. Microsoft maintains a sample Web page to demonstrate the capabilities of the VRML technology, as shown in Figure 17.14. If you would like to view such a site, use a search engine (such as **http://www.yahoo.com** or **http://www.webcrawler.com**) and execute a search on VRML.

▶ **See** "Significance of Bandwidth," **p. 72**

FIG. 17.14
Microsoft Internet
Explorer can be used to
view VRML 3-D objects.

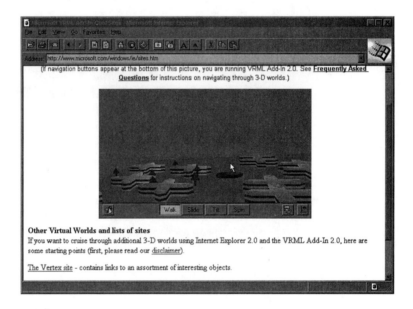

Common Gateway Interface The Common Gateway Interface (CGI) is a standard for extending the functionality of the WWW by enabling WWW servers to execute programs. Current implementations of WWW servers enable users to retrieve static HTML Web pages that can be viewed using a Web browser. CGI extends this idea by enabling users to execute programs in real time through a Web browser to obtain dynamic information from the WWW server. For example, a WWW site may provide up-to-the-minute stock quotes by executing a program that retrieves the stock prices from a database.

N O T E The WWW server at **www.prosoft.com** uses the method just described to provide users schedules of training classes for various locations around the country. It executes a program to retrieve quotes from an online database. ■

The CGI interface basically serves as a gateway between the WWW server and an external executable program. It receives requests from users, passes them along to an external program, and then displays the results to the user through a dynamically created Web page.

The most common usage of the CGI standard is for querying information from a database server. Users enter queries into a Web page, the WWW server accepts the data, sends it to the application or processing engine that will process the data, accepts the results back from the processing engine, and displays the results to the user.

The CGI mechanism is fully platform independent and can transfer data from any browser that supports CGI to any WWW server that also supports CGI. Because a CGI program is basically an executable file, there are no constraints on what kind of program can be executed through a CGI script. A CGI program can be written in any language that can create executable programs, such as C/C++, FORTRAN, Pascal, Visual Basic, or PowerBuilder. CGI programs can also be written using operating system scripts, such as Perl, UNIX script, or MS-DOS batch files.

▶ **See** "Using CGI," **p. 572**

Part
IV
Ch
17

Internet Server API

Internet Server API (ISAPI) refers to a set of programming APIs introduced by Microsoft for writing applications for the Microsoft Internet Information Server. ISAPI provides the same functionality as CGI, but in a little different manner.

ISAPI applications are dynamic-link libraries (DLL) rather than executables or scripts. Thus, when an ISAPI DLL is installed on the IIS server, it is loaded the same time the server is started. This provides exceptional speed and power to ISAPI applications as compared to CGI scripts that must be loaded each time they are accessed. However, this also takes away some of the flexibility that CGI provides in terms of application development options and capability to upgrade installed applications on-the-fly. To upgrade an ISAPI application would require bringing down the IIS server.

ISAPI has garnered a lot of attention due to its remarkable speed advantages and is an excellent solution for building Web-based applications. ISAPI applications can be developed in any development tool that enables the creation of 32-bit Windows NT DLLs. Examples of such tools include Visual C++, Visual Basic 4.0, Delphi, and PowerBuilder.

▶ **See** "Using ISAPI," **p. 573**

Common Internet File System

Common Internet File System (*CIFS*) is a protocol that enables remote sharing and opening of files across the Internet. Rather than downloading files before they can be opened or read, CIFS provides users with direct read/write access to the files. CIFS does away with the need for local storage of remote files before users can open the file.

CIFS is an enhanced version of the native file sharing system used by such operating systems as Windows 95, Windows NT, and OS/2, and is based on the *Server Message Block* (*SMB*) protocol. CIFS can run over TCP/IP links and is specifically optimized for slower dial-up connections. CIFS supports the Domain Name System (DNS) for name resolution across the Internet.

▶ **See** "Name Resolution in the TCP/IP Environment," **p. 280**

UseNet: Network Newsgroups

UseNet is a distributed discussion system that consists of a set of discussion groups called *newsgroups*. Newsgroups are organized in a hierarchy based on subjects, such as recreation, sports, news, information, and religion. Each hierarchy includes anywhere from a few groups to thousands of groups and can be subdivided into minor hierarchies. They are organized similarly to the structure of a hard disk with its directories and subdirectories.

UseNet uses the TCP/IP-based Internet backbone as its transport mechanism. The standard used by UseNet news (or netnews) for propagation of UseNet traffic is called the *Network News Transport Protocol* (*NNTP*). NNTP is a higher-level protocol that runs on top of the TCP/IP protocol to facilitate communications between various servers running the UseNet server software.

N O T E   In the early days of the Internet, another service, *UUCP*, was predominantly used for propagation of UseNet news. UUCP stands for *UNIX-to-UNIX Copy*. The service is still used, but has been mostly replaced by the faster and more flexible NNTP protocol. ▨

N O T E   The recreation hierarchy, designated by the *rec* keyword, is subdivided into lower-level hierarchies, such as **rec.arts**, **rec.games**, **rec.pets**, **rec.sports**, **rec.travel**, and so on. The **rec.pets** newsgroup, for example, can be further divided into lower-level hierarchies, such as **rec.pets.dogs**, **rec.pets.cats**, and so on. ▨

The newsgroups enable users with the appropriate news-reading software to view articles posted to these groups, post their own articles, and reply to articles posted by other users.

After an article is posted into a UseNet newsgroup, the article is broadcast using the NNTP service to other computers connected to the Internet and running the NNTP service. UseNet groups are different from mailing lists because they require central storage of articles at an NNTP server computer for viewing by all members of the network connected to that computer.

At last count, there were more than 19,000 UseNet newsgroups for topics ranging from distributed computer systems to daily soap operas. A multitude of UseNet news-reading software programs are available on the Internet as shareware programs and also as commercial packages. Some Web browsers, such as Microsoft Internet Explorer and Netscape Navigator, have news-reading capabilities built in. Figure 17.15 shows the user interface of a shareware product called Free Agent used for reading newsgroups. The same company also offers a more complete version of the program called Agent version 1.0.

FIG. 17.15

Free Agent is a shareware UseNet news-reading program with powerful features such as news threading, offline reading, filtering, and so on.

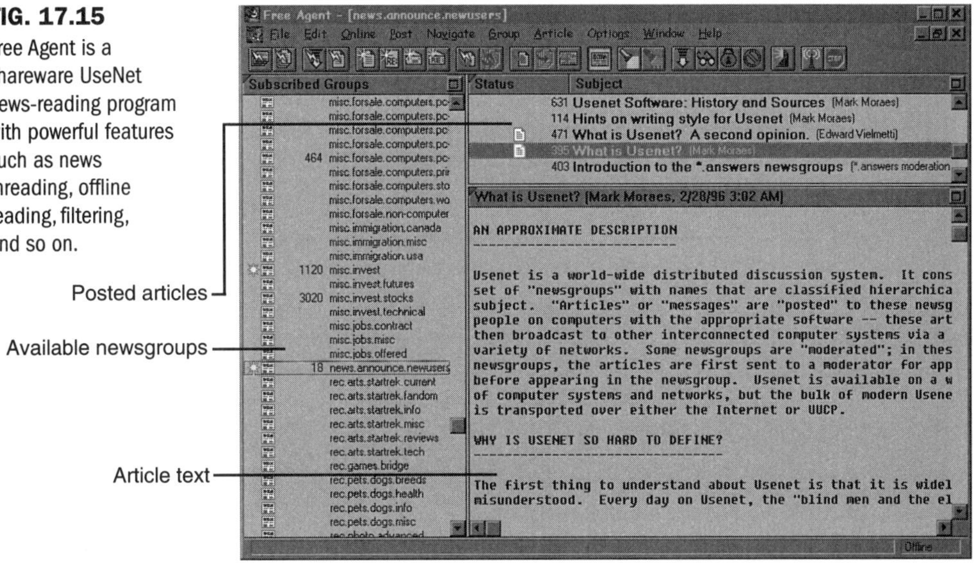

Posted articles

Available newsgroups

Article text

The latest news-reading programs, such as Free Agent, provide the following sophisticated features:

- **Message threading**—This enables users to follow a particular discussion topic by reading all posted articles about the subject; for example, a group of articles on the discussion of dog house training in the **rec.pets.dogs** newsgroup.

- **Kill files**—This is used for ignoring articles the user may not want to read; for example, directing the newsreader to ignore all articles that include the word *Pitbull* in article headers in the **rec.pets.dogs** newsgroup.

- **Filtering**—This enables users to selectively read only the articles they are interested in and ignore the rest; for example, filtering all articles in **rec.pets.dogs** newsgroup except for those that contain the keywords *Alaskan* and *Malamute* in the article headers.

- **Rot-13**—This is an encryption technique for making articles unreadable. The main purpose of this technique is to post articles that might be offensive to certain users. By encrypting the articles and including a warning about its contents, users can be made aware of the sensitive nature of the subject matter. Most newsreaders include the rot-13 encryption/decryption technique.

- **Post/reply/e-mail**—This enables users to post articles to newsgroups, reply to posted articles, or send private e-mail to the author of a particular article.

- **Binary file viewer**—This enables automatic viewing of posted binary image files. Some posted articles might have binary files attached to them, such as a bitmap image. Sophisticated newsreaders enable users to view these images on-the-fly without having to download them and use an external viewing program.

Part

IV

Ch

17

Electronic Mail

Electronic mail, or *e-mail,* is the most prevalent service on the Internet. E-mail enables Internet users to send messages to each other using a service called the *Simple Mail Transfer Protocol (SMTP).* Just like NNTP is used to transfer UseNet news, SMTP is used to transfer e-mail messages. SMTP also runs as a higher-level service on top of the TCP/IP protocol.

E-mail provides a fast and cost-effective method of communication that is remarkably useful. E-mail messages can travel across the world in a matter of minutes to reach their destinations. Even though the WWW has been instrumental in bringing the Internet to the masses and transforming it into the Information Superhighway, the speed, effectiveness, and simplicity of the e-mail concept have made it the most widely used service over the Internet.

N O T E   The Internet community affectionately refers to the normal postal mail as *snail mail* due to its comparative slowness. ■

Numerous commercial and shareware software packages are available for receiving and sending e-mail messages using the SMTP service. Popular proprietary e-mail programs, such as Microsoft Mail, Microsoft Exchange, and Lotus cc:Mail have special interfaces for receiving and sending SMTP-based e-mail. Microsoft Exchange Server is a part of BackOffice and is covered in Chapters 28 through 33.

An offshoot of individual, user-to-user e-mail connectivity is the invention of mailing lists. As the name suggests, mailing lists are similar in concept to the mass mailings you receive through the postal service. However, on the Internet, you must subscribe to a mailing list. Users just send a simple message to the mailing list administrator asking to be included in the list and shortly thereafter will start receiving messages originating from the list as normal e-mail messages.

Telnet

Telnet is a service that enables users to log on to remote computers (that is, other computers on the Internet) and remotely execute programs on those computers. It is a mainstay of the old Internet days when users could log on to remote computers and run applications and programs on those computers. Today, Telnet is used mainly for remote administration of computer systems and for accessing Internet hosts to run command-line applications, such as Ping and Finger. Figure 17.16 presents a sample Telnet session for connecting to a remote computer system.

N O T E   Ping and Finger are two utility programs with origins in the UNIX operating system. Ping enables users to send an echo signal to another machine using the TCP/IP protocol. It is used to test the network connection. Finger enables users to find out how many users are connected to a machine and who they are. It also reports more detailed information about a particular user, if desired. ■

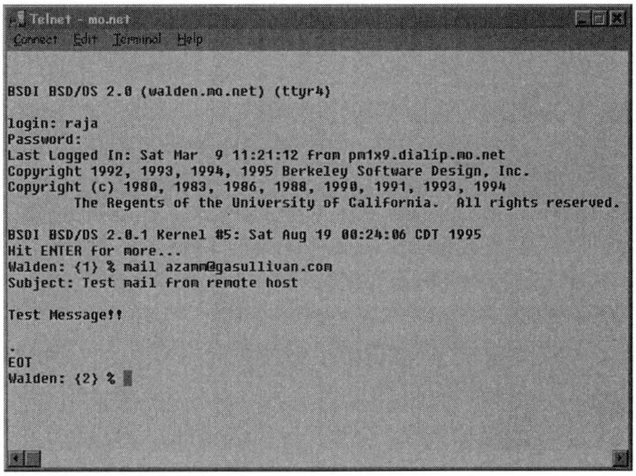

FIG. 17.16

Telnet can be used to connect to remote Internet hosts and execute programs on the remote machine.

Telnet is inherently a command-line application interface that uses the popular VT-100 terminal emulation for displaying information to the user. When users log on to a remote machine using Telnet, they are presented with a command-line prompt. Users can execute any command-line programs using Telnet.

The TCP/IP protocol suite bundled with Windows NT includes a Telnet client as part of the TCP/IP utility programs.

N O T E The Windows NT Resource Kit includes a Telnet server for accessing a Windows NT Workstation or Windows NT Server machine. The Telnet server enables users to log in to a machine using a Telnet client, such as the one included with Windows NT. ■

File Transfer Protocol

File Transfer Protocol (FTP) is one of the earliest and most commonly used services provided by the Internet. It is a simple file transfer utility that enables a user to transfer files between his computer and a remote computer running the FTP server service.

N O T E FTP servers enable users to log on to a machine using FTP clients. All TCP/IP-based services require special server programs to facilitate access by client programs. Under Windows NT, most server programs, such as WWW Server, FTP Server, SQL Server, and Telnet Server run as operating system services. ■

The TCP/IP protocol suite included with Windows NT includes an FTP client and an FTP server as part of the TCP/IP utility programs.

The FTP system is platform-independent and facilitates file transfers between disparate systems, such as a UNIX workstation and a DOS PC. The FTP protocol allows for the transfer of both plain-text ASCII files and binary files. Figure 17.17 presents a sample FTP session with the **ftp.microsoft.com** server site.

Part

IV

Ch

17

FIG. 17.17

Use FTP to transfer files between a local computer and a host computer (both on the Internet), such as Microsoft's FTP server.

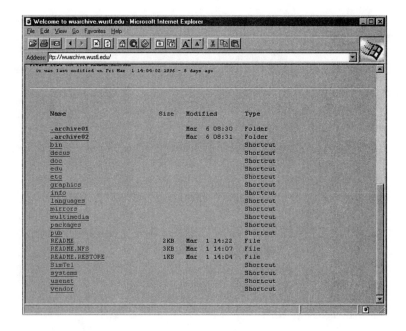

FTP uses a command-line interface that requires users to know and understand FTP keywords for transferring files. Many graphical FTP programs also are available that facilitate point-and-click use of FTP services. The FTP standard defines a basic set of commands that must be supported by all implementations of the FTP service.

Because FTP uses clear text for transfer of information between client and server, it is not a very secure service. FTP should not be used for transferring sensitive files or information. For example, when connecting to a host computer, users are required to enter a logon ID and password. The logon ID and password are passed from the client to the server using clear text, and as such, there is a potential for the information being intercepted and viewed by a third party.

A powerful feature of the FTP service is its capability for *anonymous logon*. An anonymous logon is similar in concept to the guest account on Windows NT machines. It enables users to log on to a machine and have viewing and reading rights on predetermined directories and files on the system. Users can download files using anonymous FTP from any FTP server that allows anonymous logon. Anonymous FTP makes the FTP service more secure than normal by limiting the capabilities of the client.

▶ **See** "A Flexible Set of Services," **p. 54**

▶ **See** "Managing Access to Shared Resources," **p. 197**

Gopher

Gopher was developed for retrieving information from an online database, such as the IRS catalog of tax forms. As with all high-level TCP/IP services, Gopher also uses the client-server process model to facilitate the transfer of information between a user running the Gopher client and a Gopher server. Figure 17.18 shows a sample session with a Gopher server.

FIG. 17.18
Use a Gopher client to connect to a Gopher server.

Gopher server address ⎯

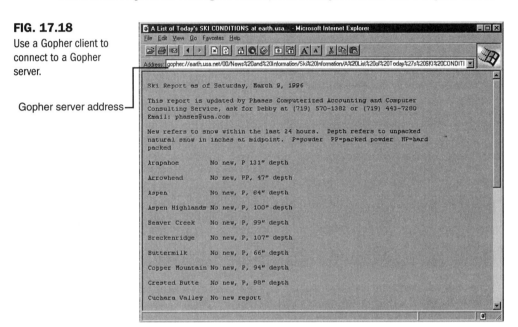

Gopher is similar in concept to the FTP service; however, it only enables retrieval of information and has no provision for uploading information to the server. Nonetheless, Gopher does provide the following significant advantages over FTP:

- It has a user-friendly interface for information retrieval and display, as opposed to the command-line interface of FTP.

- It provides access to more information and resources, such as program files, online phone book databases, online catalogs, UseNet news, and plain text files. FTP, on the other hand, is primarily used for downloading such files as shareware programs, text documents. and other file-based information.

- It provides a simple menu system for accessing the information. Even if used with a terminal-based textual interface, Gopher displays menus, lists, and other text formatting features to graphically display information and is a vast improvement over the cryptic command-line structure of the FTP service.

- It enables jumping between information stored on different servers. It uses a mechanism similar to hyperlinks to connect distributed Gopher servers together and for linking information between them. Users can start from a particular Gopher server and navigate to other Gopher servers across the Internet. In contrast, FTP only enables connection to a single server at a time and users cannot navigate between servers. Users must log off and log on to switch between FTP servers.

Part
IV

Ch
17

Additional Services

Other services are on the Internet in addition to those already mentioned. Although they are perhaps less important, they still are useful, and you may find a reason to use some of them. The Internet is still growing, and new services are created and offered from time to time. The following is a brief list of a few additional services:

- **Mailing lists**—These are informational mailings to which users can subscribe. Mailing lists usually are created for specific discussion topics, special interest groups, or specific products (for example, a mailing list for the Canon EOS Cameras). Mailing lists are sent to all subscribers through the e-mail system.

- **Wide Area Information Servers (WAIS)**—This enables users to access vast amounts of information for browsing and retrieval. It is designed to search indexed material using keywords or phrases. The WAIS (pronounced *waze*) concept is one of the few Internet technologies to have come out of the commercial sector rather than the research and education community. WAIS was originally developed to publish information for easy access by corporate employees. For example, the entire phone directory for a large multinational corporation can be put on a Wide Area Information Server for easy access by company employees using the Internet. The major difference between WAIS and WWW is the protocol used.

- **Internet Chat or Internet Relay Chat (IRC)**—This is a mechanism for engaging in interactive communications with a group of users. IRC enables users to engage in conversation in real time. However, the mode of communication is text-only.

- **Shareware and freeware**—Software and tools are available all across the Internet for users. Most of these programs are written by other users and made available to the Internet community free of charge or for a nominal fee. The main purpose of software sharing is to provide benefit to fellow Internet users.

This is only a partial list of what the Internet offers, and as time goes by and technology advances, you are sure to see other applications added.

What the Future Holds

What does the future hold for the Internet? The Internet backbone transmission rates have progressed from an initial 50 Kbps to more than 100 Mbps. Plans are currently underway to upgrade the backbone to achieve transmission rates of 1 Gbps (gigabit per second) in the very near future. Significant increases in Internet transmission rates are necessary to accommodate the rapidly growing Internet population.

On the client access side, the advances have been even more dramatic. The Internet has evolved from a network of supercomputers accessible via 300 bps lines to a network of networks accessible from millions of locations at speeds of up to 45 Mbps. Today, the lowest acceptable access speed for the average user connecting to the Internet is 28.8 Kbps, and 64–128 Kbps ISDN lines are quickly increasing in popularity.

In the near future you can only expect these access speeds to increase by an order of magnitude. Cable modems with transmission rate claims of 5–10 Mbps are already on the horizon. Advances in *ATM* (Asynchronous Transfer Mode—a new standard for network connectivity) technology promise to put 25–100 Mbps network connections on corporate desktops, and eventually this technology will trickle down to the individual user. Because ATM technology is scalable, transmission rates will only go up from here. Additionally, satellite connections will provide increased access speeds for the Internet community.

Advances on the software side will be as interesting. The current push is to develop standards for securing financial transactions on the Internet. When the standards are in place, you can expect to see a multitude of software applications ranging from secure online shopping to online banking and online trading of financial instruments. Electronic commerce—a means for doing financial transactions, such as credit card purchases, stock purchases, and automatic fund transfers from bank accounts—will become a common occurrence as users conduct their day-to-day business using the Internet.

Part
IV

Ch
17

Such tools as the InternetPhone, which enables users to carry on a real-time, audio-based conversation with others using the Internet, have already broken new ground toward a new class of multimedia applications for the Internet. With the increase in available access speeds, you can expect to conduct extensive audio- and video-based interactive sessions on the Internet. The Internet will become a place where people can interactively communicate with one another.

If the Internet maintains its current rate of growth—and there is every indication that it will—most of the world's population could have Internet access by the end of the century.

Internet users will also have a host of professional and personal productivity applications and tools available for them on the Information Superhighway. The Internet is sure to provide the following:

- The capability to conduct electronic commerce for credit card purchases, stock purchases, fund transfers, wires, and other financial transactions.
- Multimedia, 3-D interactive information stores where users can browse through information using text, audio, and video. For example, users can visit an online version of the Microsoft corporate campus and get a tour of the facilities.
- Real-time audio for online communications using such tools as the InternetPhone.
- Interactive video enables users to watch highlights of events as they happen. Examples include watching news, sports highlights, and information services.
- Virtual tours enable users to walk through online representations of information stores, such as libraries.

The possibilities on the Information Superhighway are limitless. During the rest of this decade, you will witness the development of technologies and applications well beyond the dreams of the original Internet creators when they conceived the idea some 20 years ago.

From Here...

This chapter presents the Internet and intranet as viable technologies for businesses to provide connectivity within their organizations and to the global network. For more information on the topics discussed in this chapter, see the following chapters:

- For information on other Internet components available for Microsoft BackOffice, see Chapter 16, "The BackOffice I-Net Toolbox."

- For information on Internet Information Server implementation, see Chapter 18, "Building a Web with Internet Information Server (IIS)."

- To learn about exploring the Internet using the client Web browsers, see Chapter 19, "Web Browsers."

- For information on creating content for your IIS servers, see Chapter 20, "Using Microsoft FrontPage 97."

- To learn about setting up a secure Internet connection by using the Microsoft Proxy Server, see Chapter 22, "Implementing Microsoft Proxy Server."

- To ensure that proper security measures are taken for your Internet involvement, see Chapter 25, "Implementing Internet Security."

- To explore how the Internet can be used in business, see Chapter 49, "Building BackOffice Applications."

Building a Web with Internet Information Server (IIS)

by Azam A. Mirza

In Chapter 16, "The BackOffice I-Net Toolbox," you learned about the various server-based products that Microsoft BackOffice provides for implementing a comprehensive Web solution. The Internet Information Server (IIS) is the glue that brings together the power of all these components. In this chapter, you learn how to set up IIS on your enterprise network to provide Internet and intranet services for your users.

Detailed information is provided to help you set up IIS for your enterprise, configure services on your IIS, and learn to use the Internet Service Manager for managing your enterprise IISs. You also learn about IIS security features and how to set up a secure IIS infrastructure. Finally, you learn how to create content for your IIS services and publish information for use by your enterprise users and the Internet community. ∎

Resource requirements for implementing the Internet Information Server

Learn about the hardware, software, and human resource needs for setting up and running an IIS-based Web site.

Services provided by Internet Information Server

Learn about the services provided by the Internet Information Server and the features they support.

How to set up Internet Information Server

Learn how to set up and install the Internet Information Server. Issues relating to TCP/IP configuration are discussed.

Internet Information Server security

Learn about setting up security for the Internet Information Server and how the security features of Windows NT Server can be used to secure your Internet connectivity infrastructure.

Creating content for Internet Information Server services

See how to create and publish content for your Internet Information Server services for internal enterprise use and the Internet community.

Resource Requirements

An important consideration in developing an Internet presence is the resources your organization is willing to invest in developing the infrastructure for running an effective IIS site. Running an IIS site requires the following types of resources (which are described in the following sections):

- Hardware
- Software
- Human resources

Hardware

The amount of traffic your IIS machine will handle determines the kind of hardware platform you need. A checklist of hardware items that you need for an IIS site includes the following:

- **Computer System**—A machine that will run your IIS site
- **Router**—A device used for routing TCP/IP traffic over the Internet
- **Internet Connection**—A connection to the Internet, such as an ISDN line or a T1 leased line

The choices available in terms of the computing platform are numerous. The first choice to make is the kind of processor your IIS machine should use. IIS is available for the following processor systems:

- Intel
- MIPS
- Alpha
- PowerPC

Any one of the preceding systems would be a good choice for running your IIS site because IIS is equally supported on these platforms. Multiprocessor systems are also an option when considering a system for an IIS site because of their higher processing power. You can monitor the processor utilization of your IIS machine using the Performance Monitor tool included with Windows NT.

You should get as much memory as possible in your system for better performance. If you are going to be running a site that will handle many users and numerous simultaneous connections, you should start with at least 64M of RAM. If your server has additional services running on it (for example, SQL Server, Exchange Server, and so on), you should add at least an additional 16M for IIS. You can monitor the memory usage of your IIS machine using the Performance Monitor tool provided with Windows NT to see if your server would benefit from the addition of more memory.

▶ **See** "Using the Performance Monitor," **p. 1664**

Another important consideration is the available hard disk space. World Wide Web files can take up a lot of disk space. If your site is going to use multimedia features, such as sound, images, and video clips, you will need a large amount of space to store multimedia files—perhaps several gigabytes. Make sure that your machine has enough hard disk space and can be expanded easily in the future. You can monitor the hard disk usage and performance of your IIS machine using the Performance Monitor tool provided with Windows NT.

 TIP Get a hard disk subsystem that is as fast as possible. The most time-consuming aspect of running IIS services is the hard disk access while loading Web pages or transferring files using FTP (if there isn't one). A hard disk subsystem based on the SCSI standard is usually the fastest option with the most flexibility for future storage expandability. A Fast/Wide SCSI system can provide throughput of 10-20 Mbps with the option of installing up to 15 SCSI drives in a single daisy chain.

Deciding whether you should buy a new machine for running IIS or use an existing system depends on your needs and the funds available for setting up your IIS machine.

Software

The IIS software itself is a part of the BackOffice suite of applications. However, you will need other software to set up a complete IIS site. IIS provides all pieces for setting up WWW, FTP, and Gopher sites. Nonetheless, to create content for these sites, you need to acquire additional software packages. Content creation for your WWW service requires using such software packages as Microsoft Internet Studio, Microsoft FrontPage, or Internet Assistant for Microsoft Word. Other WWW content creation packages also are available.

In addition to the software already mentioned, you may need additional applications if you want to create a server that attracts attention, generates excitement by taking full advantage of multimedia data types, and uses the latest techniques. If this is your goal, you should investigate applications for the following processes:

- Creating, capturing, and digitizing images
- Creating sound files
- Capturing video
- Compressing files

A multitude of choices is available in each of the preceding software categories; make your decisions based on available features, cost, and your own preference.

Human Resources

Operating an IIS site requires your organization to devote some human resources. You need a person or group of people to manage your various servers and services. Many options are available for deciding how you can allocate human resources to manage your Internet connectivity. The following guidelines help you estimate the number of people needed to operate your IIS site. Figure 18.1 shows how human expertise is utilized in putting together an IIS site.

Part

IV

Ch

18

FIG. 18.1

Expertise in various aspects of Internet and network administration is needed to operate an IIS site.

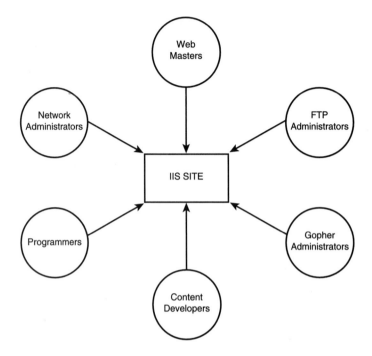

It is not necessary to assign a different person to each of the jobs. For example, one person might be the Webmaster, FTP administrator, and Gopher administrator for your entire enterprise, or you might need separate people to do each of those jobs. The choice depends on how much activity is handled by your IIS site. The following is a list of the tasks that need to be performed to operate an IIS site:

- **Network administrator**—You need a network administrator for setting up and managing the machine and the Internet connection. The network administrator needs to be proficient in TCP/IP networking and related issues, such as router setup and configuration.

- **Webmaster**—This is the person in charge of operating your WWW site. The Webmaster has ultimate responsibility for the content of your site, its policies, usage control, and all other related issues.

- **FTP administrator**—The FTP administrator is responsible for operating the FTP service.

- **Gopher administrator**—The Gopher administrator is responsible for operating the Gopher service.

- **WWW content developer**—The WWW content developer is responsible for the creation of content for your WWW site using HTML development tools.

- **Programmer**—This is the person responsible for creating applications using the Common Gateway Interface (CGI), Internet Server API (ISAPI), and so on.

If you are operating a site where the content stays static most of the time, you might be able to administer the entire suite of IIS services using one person. If you operate a site with a lot of published content that changes regularly, however, you might need more than one person to manage all your services. The choice depends on how much work there is to do.

▶ **See** "Hypertext Markup Language," **p. 523**

▶ **See** "Common Gateway Interface," **p. 526**

▶ **See** "ISAPI," **p. 1636**

A Guide to Services Provided by the Internet Information Server

An important part of planning your IIS configuration is the type of services you will be offering. IIS provides control over the services you can install, set up, and run as part of your Internet implementation plan. The type of services you offer depend on what your intent is in using IIS. If you want to run a server exclusively providing WWW services (without FTP and Gopher) to your enterprise or the Internet, then you can install just the WWW service. Many organizations are using IIS to implement WWW services only. The Web is a powerful and flexible system that provides a great deal of impact. However, WWW is probably the most complex and time-consuming of the three services to set up, run, and maintain.

> N O T E   The complexity in running a WWW site stems from its enormous flexibility and breadth
>   of features. Creating attractive and useful content for Web sites demands much time
> and effort. ▨

If your intent is to provide file transfer capability for your users, then you can implement the FTP service. It provides a fast and simple way of transferring files between remote machines. The FTP service included with IIS is very easy to set up and maintain. Setting up FTP, however, does require that you pay special attention to security concerns to safeguard your system against intruders.

FTP is also the only one of the three services that enables client machines to transfer files to your IIS machine. If you want to provide users with the capability to upload files to your system, then you must use the FTP service included with IIS.

The Gopher service is similar to FTP but provides enhancements, such as menu structures, hyperlinks, and richer content formatting capability. Gopher services are easy to set up under IIS. Gopher servers are most suited to publishing textual, static information that does not require the overhead involved in implementing HTML Web pages. The most widely used implementations of Gopher servers are for library catalogs, phone directories, and other text-based information stores. If you would like to build a fast and easy catalog system, then Gopher is the service of choice. For more information, see "Creating the Content for IIS Services" later in this chapter.

IIS provides an integrated set of services for managing all your Internet connectivity needs. The combination of popular Internet services with a centrally managed environment makes IIS an ideal choice for your intranet or Internet servers.

The Internet Information Server (IIS) was designed from the ground up to be an integrated part of the Microsoft Windows NT Server platform. IIS runs as a set of integrated Windows NT Server services leveraging the built-in features of Windows NT Server (that is, Service Manager, Performance Monitor, and the Windows NT Server security features).

IIS offers a high-speed, secure, and robust means of publishing information on the Internet. The Internet security options, such as the Secure Sockets Layer (SSL), Secure Transaction Technology (STT), and the Cryptography Application Programming Interface (CAPI), also provide a method of conducting safe and secure transactions on the Internet. They provide for the building and deployment of Internet-enabled applications that use the latest in encryption and security technologies. (For information on security issues, see the section "Security for Your Internet Server" later in this chapter.)

The following sections describe the three services provided by Internet Information Server.

▶ **See** "A Flexible Set of Services," **p. 54**

World Wide Web

The WWW service delivered within IIS provides a powerful mechanism for publishing information to a large user base. Furthermore, the functionality available in the WWW service provided by IIS is not limited to just creating static HTML pages.

The World Wide Web service in IIS enables users to immediately publish existing files, WWW documents, and other information for access by the Internet community or for local LAN access by the corporate network. The WWW service includes the following features:

- Performance optimization under the Windows NT Server architecture.

- The Windows NT Server Directory Services, which require user IDs and passwords for protected WWW documents.

- Integration with the Windows NT security model, which provides a very secure WWW server.

- Virtual directories, which is an alias to the physical directory on the server. Virtual directories provide a simpler and direct path to subdirectories that might have long and complex physical paths on the hard disk. They also provide a simple security measure by hiding the actual directory structure from the users.

- Built-in SSL security, which provides secure financial and commercial transactions across the Internet.

- Virtual server capability, which enables the hosting of multiple Web sites on one Windows NT Server computer, thus making management and administration simpler.

- Graphical administration of all aspects through the Internet Service Manager.

Figure 18.2 depicts the IIS administration screen of the Internet Service Manager. The WWW service within IIS supports the capability to do the following:

■ Execute programs on the server

■ Manage and organize your published information in directory trees

■ Provide users access to your server directory structure using virtual servers and virtual directories

FIG. 18.2

The IIS administration utility, called the Internet Service Manager, provides a graphical interface for the administration of services.

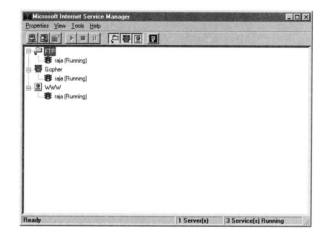

Each of these features of the WWW service is discussed in the following sections.

▶ **See** "Hypertext Markup Language," **p. 523**

Server Applications An important aspect of any well-designed WWW site is its capability to enable users to execute remote programs on the server using hypertext links. In addition, users can also trigger application execution by filling out an HTML form and submitting it for processing by the server. The WWW service within IIS fully supports the concept of running server-based applications by providing support for the standard called the Common Gateway Interface (CGI).

> **CAUTION**
>
> The capability to execute programs on your WWW server does increase the security risk involved by providing unauthorized users a chance to break into your system using the application. Extra care should be taken to prevent users from gaining read/write access to your program executables and script files.

IIS also supports a new Application Programming Interface (API) for writing Internet-enabled applications called the Internet Server Application Programming Interface (ISAPI). Both the CGI and the ISAPI methods enable you to write applications that can do almost anything. You can use any language, such as C/C++ and Visual Basic, to write applications that can be run using the CGI or ISAPI interface.

Using the CGI method, you can execute operating system batch language scripts (for example, BAT or CMD files) to execute programs for your WWW service. The ISAPI method differs from CGI in one important aspect: ISAPI programs are compiled as dynamic-link libraries (DLLs) that are loaded by the WWW server at server startup. This provides ISAPI applications with a performance edge over CGI-based scripts or applications. However, ISAPI DLLs are loaded as part of the inital IIS startup and increase startup times. In addition, ISAPI DLLs are loaded in the same memory space as IIS, and a misbehaving DLL can cause the IIS service to hang.

▶ **See** "Common Gateway Interface," **p.526**

Managing Directories   The WWW service enables you to organize the information you want to publish in directories in a manageable manner. By distributing information across multiple directories, you can divide information into logical collections. The WWW service can then be configured to enable users access to these directories, all their subdirectories, and the files stored in them.

N O T E   Whenever you install a new WWW server, IIS automatically creates a root directory for your server. The root directory, \InetPub\wwwroot by default, is given the alias Home. It is the starting point for all Web browsers to view the information published by your WWW server. ■

In addition to using the Home directory for publishing information, you can also use the concept of *virtual directories*, which enable you to distribute information across directories that are not subdirectories of the Home directory. They can also be used to place information on a different drive or a network drive. A discussion on creating virtual directories for WWW publishing is presented in the section titled "Directories" later in this chapter.

N O T E   All virtual directories used by your WWW service must reside within the same Windows NT domain. ■

Even though virtual directories might exist anywhere within your Windows NT domain, they are presented to the user as a single directory tree existing as subdirectories of the Home directory. The Home directory is the root of all directories being used by your WWW service. This makes it simple to present the information to the user in a manner that can be easily navigated.

Virtual Servers   *Virtual servers* enable you to create more than one WWW server on the same machine. By default, every machine has a single domain name and IP address (for example, **www.mcp.com** or **199.177.202.10**). Virtual servers enable you to attach additional IP addresses and domain names to a server to make it appear that you are using multiple servers to service user information needs.

You might want to create WWW servers for different departments within your enterprise, for example, marketing and systems. You do not need to set up a different machine for each department's WWW server. You can use a single machine by creating virtual servers on that machine called marketing.mcp.com and systems.mcp.com.

By segmenting the same machine into multiple virtual servers, you can divide the information you publish into logical collections and use the same machine to hold the information content. Users wanting to connect to the marketing information will go directly to the marketing WWW site, and users wanting to connect to systems information will go directly to the systems WWW site.

See "Using Property Sheets to Configure Your Internet Information Server" later in this chapter for more information.

FTP Service

The FTP service built into IIS provides some powerful features for allowing FTP access to your site. The FTP server supports anonymous logon for providing access to the Internet community for file uploads and downloads for an IIS site. The virtual directories and virtual browsing functions of IIS enable administrators to provide fast, efficient access to the directories and files available on the network. The integrated security built into IIS enables the administrators to restrict access based on user IDs and passwords to files and directories.

The FTP service enables users to employ such tools as Internet Explorer to connect to your FTP server. You can also use other FTP client software, such as the Windows NT FTP client, to connect to the FTP server.

The WWW service has replaced or enhanced most of the functionality available through FTP. However, the WWW service cannot be used to copy files from the client to the server. FTP is the only service that provides this functionality.

Part

IV

Ch

18

> **CAUTION**
>
> Extreme care should be exercised when permitting users to copy files to your server. Make sure that you check all files for viruses. It is a good idea to limit incoming files to a single directory to facilitate the process of checking them.

FTP provides an easy, simple, and maintainable system for publishing a large number of files. FTP enables transfers of files no matter what format they are in. You can use FTP to transfer text, image, or executable files. Figure 18.3 shows the Internet Service Manager screen for the FTP service. (For more information, see "FTP" later in this chapter.)

Gopher Service

The Gopher service in IIS enables you to publish information from large file archives. The IIS Gopher service supports all features of the Gopher standard. In addition, the Gopher service in IIS supports the Gopher+ selector strings, which enable clients to obtain additional information from the server, such as the Gopher server administrator name. You can use tag files on your Gopher server to enable links to other Gopher servers across the enterprise or the Internet.

FIG. 18.3
Internet Service
Manager is the tool
used for administering
IIS services, such as the
FTP service.

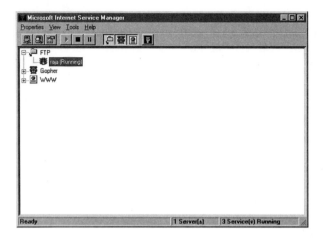

The Gopher service enables corporations to provide a graphical point-and-click interface for its users to access information stored in online databases. Figure 18.4 shows the Internet Service Manager screen for the Gopher service.

FIG. 18.4
Internet Service
Manager is the central
administration tool for
all IIS services, such as
the Gopher service.

The Gopher server in IIS can be used to set up corporate catalogs of employee information accessible only by the corporation's employees. It can be used to publish a catalog of company products for browsing by customers over the Internet. It can also be used as an online reference system for product user manuals. For more information, see "Gopher" later in this chapter.

Setting Up Your Internet Information Server

In this section, you learn how to set up IIS. IIS enables you to set up services for running a WWW site, an FTP site, and a Gopher site. Before you can install IIS, you need to complete the following tasks:

■ Set up and configure a computer with Windows NT Server 4.0 with Service Pack 1a installed.

N O T E During the installation of Windows NT Server 4.0, you will get the option of installing IIS. You can install IIS at that point or use the Setup program later to install IIS. The two procedures are identical, and this chapter outlines the procedure for installing IIS on a preconfigured Windows NT Server 4.0 machine. ■

N O T E Internet Information Server can only be installed on machines running Windows NT Server 4.0 with Service Pack 1a installed. ■

■ Make sure that you have the logon ID and password for an administrator account with full permissions on the new IIS server computer.

■ Disable or remove any previous versions of IIS, especially beta versions.

■ Make sure that TCP/IP is installed on your computer. (See Chapter 9, "Using TCP/IP with Windows NT Server," for more information.)

■ If you have any other WWW, FTP, or Gopher services running on your computer, you must disable them. For example, the FTP service included with Windows NT Server must be disabled.

■ Using the Control Panel Network applet, make sure that an Internet domain name is defined for your machine under the DNS configuration option.

Part

IV

Ch

18

CAUTION

The Internet domain name should be the domain name provided by InterNIC if you have requested a registered domain name and IP addresses. If you are just creating an intranet server and you are not connected to the Internet, you can safely create your own domain name after checking with other network administrators to be sure that one isn't already in use. It should be a unique name and should not match any existing Windows NT domain names.

■ Plan your directory structure for your WWW, FTP, and Gopher publishing files.

Make sure that you have performed the preceding tasks before starting IIS installation.

To install IIS, follow these steps:

1. Choose Start Menu, <u>R</u>un.

2. In the Run dialog box, enter **<path>:\inetstp.exe** for the command line where **<path>** refers to the location of the setup file, for example, d:\i386\inetsrv\inetstp.EXE.

3. Click OK.

You can also open a command prompt and enter *<path>*:**\inetstp.exe** at the command line.

N O T E During setup, you can click the Help button at any time to get help on installing IIS. ▨

After you have started the Setup program for IIS, perform the following steps:

1. Read the Welcome screen shown in Figure 18.5.

FIG. 18.5

The Internet Information
Server 2.0 Setup
Welcome screen
provides information
about running the Setup
program.

2. Click OK. A dialog box appears offering installation options (see Figure 18.6).

FIG. 18.6

This dialog box offers
the opportunity to select
specific services to
install or to select all of
them, as shown here.

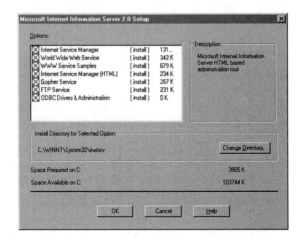

3. Check all options that you want to install. By default, all available options are installed automatically except for the HTML version of the Internet Service Manager. The HTML version of Internet Service Manager allows administrators to remotely manage IIS servers across the Internet.

4. By default, IIS is installed in the `<%winntroot%\system32\>inetsrv` directory. Click the Change Directory button if you want to change the installation directory for IIS. The Change Directory dialog box appears.

5. Type in the IIS installation directory path or select it from the directory list box and click OK. Click Cancel to return without changing the installation directory.

6. If the installation directory you specified does not exist, you will be prompted by the system prior to its creation. Click Yes to create the directory and continue with the installation.

7. When the installation directory is created, the Publishing Directories dialog box appears, as shown in Figure 18.7.

FIG. 18.7

The Publishing Directories dialog box enables you to specify the root directory for the published content that will be offered by each of the three services.

Part

IV

Ch

18

8. Publishing directory locations for WWW, FTP, and Gopher services are displayed. By default, all publishing directories are installed in a directory called InetPub under the root directory for the system drive. You can accept the default location, click the appropriate Browse button to select new locations for each service, or type in the directory locations manually. Click OK when finished.

 You might want to specify a different drive and location for your publishing directories to separate them from your IIS installation location. This is a particularly good idea if you will allow users to upload files to your server using FTP, or if you plan to run server-based applications from your Web pages. By separating the publishing directories from your IIS services, you can help avoid accidentally assigning improper permissions that could lead to corrupted system files. It is simply easier to manage your server with all published data on a separate drive.

9. If the publishing directories you specified do not exist, the Setup program asks if you want to create them. Click Yes.

10. IIS Setup now completes installation of all components by copying files to the installation directories. The IIS Setup Progress dialog box appears to confirm that the Setup program is still active and display its current progress.

CAUTION

The DNS domain name must be specified for the machine on which you are installing IIS. If a domain name is not specified, IIS Setup displays a warning message to inform you to do so.

---

11. If you selected the ODBC drivers option from the Installation Options dialog box, Setup displays the ODBC Driver installation dialog box. Select the drivers you want to install and click OK.

12. After the setup is completed, the setup success dialog box appears.

13. Click OK to end the installation process.

Setup automatically starts all services you installed by default and creates a Start Menu group for IIS called Microsoft Internet Server. To make sure that everything has been installed properly, you should verify that all IIS services have been started and check the event log for possible errors. You can check the status of IIS services using the Services applet in the Control Panel. Check the event log using the Windows NT Event Viewer. IIS events appear in the Applications log.

N O T E As part of the IIS installation process, a sample WWW tour of IIS features is set up automatically. Make sure that you navigate through the sample pages to get an idea of what a WWW, FTP, and Gopher site setup looks like. ■

Now that you have successfully installed IIS, you can configure your IIS services by using the Internet Service Manager. The next section discusses the Internet Service Manager in detail.

Using the Internet Service Manager

The Internet Service Manager is the graphical tool used for administering all IIS servers in an organization. Internet Service Manager enables the configuration and monitoring of all IIS services from a central location. By default, the icon for the Internet Service Manager is placed in the Microsoft Internet Server Start Menu Group during setup.

 The Internet Service Manager is automatically installed on your IIS server during installation, but it can also be on machines other than the server. This enables remote administration of IIS servers from any Windows NT workstation or another Windows NT server.

The Internet Service Manager can be run from any computer running Windows NT Workstation or Windows NT Server that is connected to the same network as the IIS server. It can also be run from a computer connected to your enterprise network from the Internet. Internet Service Manager uses the Windows NT security protocol for user authentication and enables secure connections to IIS over the Internet and from remote administration computers (see Figure 18.8).

FIG. 18.8
The Internet Service Manager main window shows a single server (named RAJA), which is running all three services available with IIS.

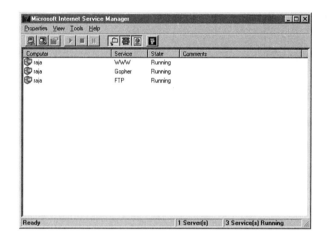

Internet Service Manager can be used to perform the following administration tasks on IIS servers:

- Find all Internet Information Servers connected to a network.
- Connect to individual Internet Information Servers.
- View Internet Information Server data as a report, by service, or by server.
- Start, stop, or pause Internet Information Servers.
- Use *property sheets:* tabbed dialog boxes that enable you to configure the services on Internet Information Servers.

Each of these tasks is explained in detail in the following sections.

Finding Internet Information Servers

Internet Service Manager can find all servers running IIS on your network. It uses one of two methods to find servers running IIS: Windows Internet Name Service (WINS) and TCP/IP broadcasts.

If WINS is used on your network, Internet Service Manager automatically finds any servers running IIS services. This is accomplished because servers running IIS services automatically register with WINS servers. Therefore, when an Internet Service Manager attempts to find servers running IIS services on its startup, WINS returns the addresses of registered servers.

Part
IV

Ch
18

However, if WINS is not being used on your network, then the Internet Service Manager uses TCP/IP broadcasts to find servers running IIS services.

> **CAUTION**
> Internet Information Server cannot find servers running IIS services across routers by using TCP/IP broadcasts. To find servers running across routers, you must use WINS.

You can query for servers running IIS on your network by choosing Properties, Find All Servers. The Finding All Servers dialog box is displayed while the system searches for IIS servers (see Figure 18.9).

▶ **See** "Windows Internet Name Service (WINS)," **p. 256**

FIG. 18.9
The Properties, Find All Servers menu option enables you to discover servers running IIS services on your network.

Connecting to Internet Information Servers

After you have used the Internet Service Manager to find the servers running IIS services on your network, you can connect to those servers for administrative purposes. To perform administrative tasks, you must be logged on with an account belonging to the Administrators group on IIS. To connect to a server running IIS services, perform the following steps:

1. Choose Properties, Connect to Server.
2. In the server name dialog box, type in the name of the server that you want to connect to.

Alternatively, perform these steps:

1. Choose Properties, Find All Servers.
2. When the list of found servers is displayed, double-click the server name that you want to connect to.

After you have connected to a server, it will be added to your Internet Service Manager window. The stoplight icons representing the various services will indicate the status (started, stopped, or paused) of the services running on the server, and you will be able to open the properties sheets for the server to configure its services.

Viewing Internet Information Servers

Internet Service Manager's simple and elegant graphical user interface provides a lot of flexibility for administrators. You can choose to view the information being displayed by Internet Service Manager in three different styles:

- Reports view
- Servers view
- Services view

To switch between different views, choose the appropriate viewing option from the View menu. Each of these views is discussed in the following sections.

Reports View Reports view is the default view used by the Internet Service Manager. It lists all the servers running IIS services in alphabetical order. One line is used for each installed service. The Reports view is the only view that enables you to sort information alphabetically. You can sort by server name, service type, service state, and comments. To sort, click the column headings in the Reports view. Figure 18.10 shows the Internet Service Manager running in Reports view.

 T I P You can use sorting to quickly find out the state of services running on your network. For example, by clicking the state column and sorting the listed servers by server state, you can determine which services are stopped or paused on your network.

FIG. 18.10
When viewing servers running IIS services using the Reports view, you can sort the displayed information by clicking a column heading.

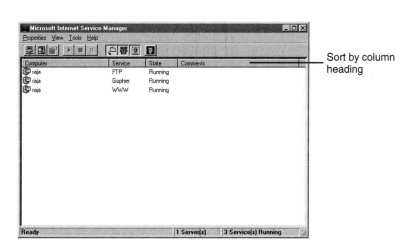

Sort by column heading

The Reports view is most useful when you only have one or two servers running IIS services. If many servers on your network are running IIS services, it is easier to view information using one of the other two views.

Servers View   The Servers view lists servers running IIS services on the network by computer name. You can double-click the plus sign next to a server name to display the IIS services running on that server. Figure 18.11 shows the Internet Service Manager running in Servers view.

FIG. 18.11

The Internet Service
Manager window is
viewing a server running
all IIS services using the
Servers view.

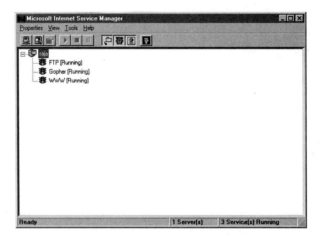

Servers view is most useful when you are trying to determine the status of services on a particular computer running IIS services.

Services View   Services view displays the information by service type for computers running IIS services on your network (see Figure 18.12). You can double-click the plus sign next to the service name to display the servers running that service.

FIG. 18.12

The Services view in
the Internet Service
Manager provides an
easy way to determine
which servers are
running a particular
service.

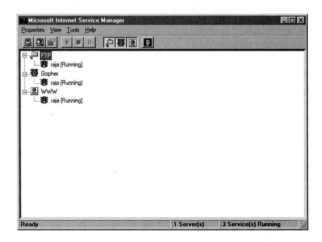

Services view is most useful for enterprises running multiple servers in distributed sites. It makes it easy to determine which servers are running a particular IIS service.

 T I P You can apply filters in any view by choosing the service filter commands from the <u>V</u>iew menu. For example, to view only WWW services, you can deselect the FTP and Gopher options in the <u>V</u>iew menu. Choose <u>A</u>ll to clear the filter and view all services.

Administering Internet Information Servers Remotely

You can install the Internet Service Manager on any computer running the Windows NT Workstation and Windows NT Server operating systems and administer any server running IIS services from a central administrative computer.

You can install Internet Service Manager over the network by creating a share to the \Admin$ directory on the Internet Information Server installation CD-ROM and connecting to it from the remote computer. You can then run the Setup program for the Internet Information Server remotely from the newly created share and install the Internet Service Manager component only on the remote machine.

Internet Service Manager can be used to administer servers running IIS services from the Internet also. IIS Setup includes a component for an HTML-based Internet Service Manager for use across the Internet. The HTML Internet Service Manager is a collection of HTML pages designed specifically for administering IIS servers. The HTML Internet Service Manager uses Microsoft Internet Explorer to administer IIS servers remotely. Figure 18.13 shows the startup screen for the HTML Internet Service Manager.

Part
IV

Ch
18

FIG. 18.13

The HTML-based Internet Service Manager component is actually a set of HTML files that can be accessed using Microsoft Internet Explorer to administer IIS services.

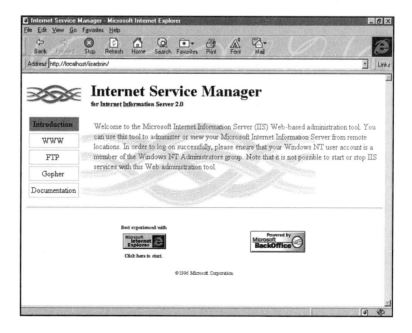

The HTML files for using Microsoft Internet Explorer as the HTML Internet Service Manager are installed in the `<%winroot%\system32\InetSrv\iisadmin>` directory. To connect to an IIS server for administration purposes, all you need is the URL address to the `iisadmin` directory (**http://localhost/iisadmin/** in Figure 18.13.) However, to gain access, you must be logged on to the local machine using a logon ID and password that belongs to the Administrators group on the IIS server machine.

N O T E   A Start Menu icon is also created for the HTML Internet Service Manager under the Microsoft Internet Server group once the component is installed. ■

N O T E   You cannot use the HTML Internet Service Manager to start, stop, or pause IIS services on the machine you are administering. ■

Once connected, the options available for administration of IIS services are identical to the ones available through the regular Internet Service Manager. Figure 18.14 presents the Service Properties screen for the WWW service using the HTML Internet Information Server.

FIG. 18.14

You can access the WWW Service Properties dialog box using the HTML Internet Service Manager.

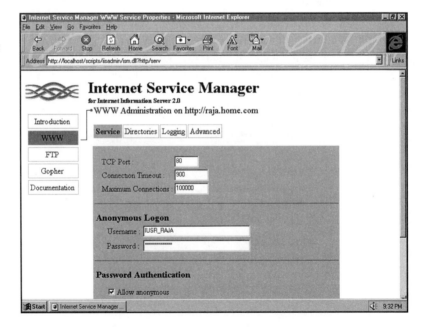

The options available are identical to the WWW Service properties dialog box accessible through the regular Internet Service Manager. The properties dialog boxes for FTP and Gopher are also identical to their regular counterparts. Please refer to the section "Using Property Sheets to Configure Your Internet Information Server" later in this chapter for information on setting WWW, FTP, and Gopher service properties.

CAUTION

If you are going to use Internet Service Manager across the Internet, make sure that you are using a Windows NT Logon ID and password and the Windows NT Challenge/Response authentication protocol for user validation. Do not use the clear text method for sending passwords across the Internet.

Starting, Stopping, and Pausing Services

You can use the Internet Service Manager to change the state of IIS services running on your network with a simple procedure. Services can be in one of three states:

- Running (started)
- Paused
- Stopped

To change the state of an IIS service running on a computer, follow these steps:

1. Select the service you want to start, stop, or pause in the Internet Service Manager.
2. Choose Properties, then select Start Service, Stop Service, or Pause Service.

You can also use the appropriate toolbar button to start, stop, or pause a service.

The graphical view of the Internet Service Manager makes it easy to determine which services are started, stopped, or paused. For example, by using the sort option in Reports view, you can sort services by service state to get a quick snapshot of which services are running.

Using Property Sheets to Configure Your Internet Information Server

Internet Service Manager enables the configuration and management of IIS services by using property sheets. Property sheets are tabbed dialog boxes for configuring all options for a particular service. You can use property sheets to configure all three IIS services: WWW, FTP, and Gopher. The property sheet for each of these services is described in detail in the following sections.

WWW   To configure the WWW service running on a server, double-click the WWW service name or computer name in any of the views to bring up the WWW Service Properties dialog box (see Figure 18.15).

The Service Properties dialog box displays tabs for each category that can be configured. The WWW property sheets can be used to configure the following categories (which are described in detail in the following sections):

- Service
- Directories
- Logging
- Advanced

Part

IV

Ch

18

FIG. 18.15
The WWW service is being configured in the Internet Service Manager.

Property sheets

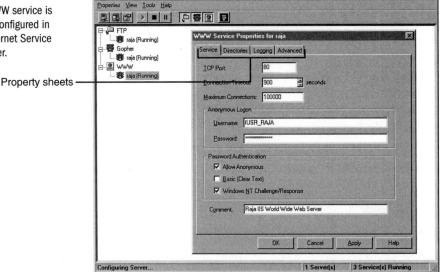

Service The WWW Service tab is used to set various connection options for your WWW server (see Figure 18.16). To set Service options, click the Service tab on the WWW Service Properties dialog box and perform the following steps:

1. In the TCP Port box, specify the TCP/IP connection port that the service will use for enabling connections to IIS. The default is port 80 for the WWW service. For most environments, the default should be satisfactory.

2. In the Connection Timeout box, specify the number of seconds before a user is disconnected from your IIS machine. The default value is 900 seconds (15 minutes). You can increase or decrease this value based on your preference. Idle users will be disconnected after the specified time period to free up server resources.

3. The Maximum Connections box is used to limit the number of users that can simultaneously connect to the WWW service. The default value is 100,000 connections. The setting for this field depends on your network bandwidth, the available resources, and the speed of your server running IIS.

4. The Anonymous Logon options enable you to specify the username and password that will be used by the WWW service to facilitate anonymous connections to your server. By default, IIS creates and uses the account IUSR_*computername* to facilitate anonymous logons. Most Internet sites allow anonymous logons for user connections.

You can control the access allowed to the IUSR_*computername* anonymous account by changing its permission using the User Manager or by specifying another account on your network as the anonymous logon account.

5. The Password Authentication options enable you to specify the method used for authenticated logons. If your server does not allow anonymous logons or the client software requests user validation, the authentication schemes specified will be used. Three authentication options are available:

- **Allow Anonymous**—If checked, the WWW service uses the anonymous logon ID and password set up in the preceding step for authenticating all user connections.

- **Basic**—If checked, Basic authentication uses clear text to verify user connections. If used in conjunction with the SSL security scheme, it enables the use of encrypted logon IDs and passwords. All browsers support the basic authentication mechanism.

> **CAUTION**
>
> Transmitting clear text passwords over the Internet can compromise your network security. It is possible to capture passwords over the network using protocol analyzers.

- **Windows NT Challenge/Response**—If checked, this uses the Windows NT Challenge/Response authentication method. This is the most secure form of user authentication. Internet Explorer 2.0 or higher supports this authentication method.

6. The Comment box is used to specify the comment displayed by the Internet Service Manager in the Reports view.

7. Click OK to continue, or click Apply to immediately enforce the changes.

Part
IV

Ch
18

FIG. 18.16
WWW Service and its properties can be configured using the Service tab on the WWW Service Properties dialog box.

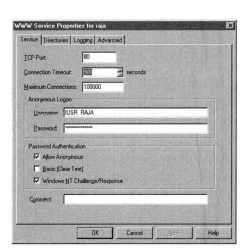

Directories   The WWW Directories tab, as shown in Figure 18.17, is used to set up directories used by the server and set their properties.

FIG. 18.17

IIS's default directories are listed on the Directories tab.

The Directory list box lists the current directories set up for the WWW service. It displays the following information:

- **Directory**—The path to the directory being used
- **Alias**—The path name for users to get to the physical directory location
- **Address**—The IP address of the virtual server if the directory resides on a virtual server
- **Error**—System errors with the directory mapping, such as inability to read directory contents

IIS by default creates three directory mappings for your WWW service:

- **Home**—The home directory points to the root directory set up by IIS for your WWW service. It has an alias of <Home>. There can be only one home directory for every IIS machine.
- **Scripts**—The scripts directory has an alias of /Scripts.
- **IISAdmin**—This is the directory for administering the IIS server using the HTML Internet Service Manager. The directory has an alias of /iisadmin.

If checked, the Enable Default Document option enables you to specify the default document that will be loaded if a user does not specify a file name when connecting to your WWW service. By convention, if there is a default.html file in the directory being accessed, that file is loaded as the initial document when a user first accesses that directory. However, you can specify another file as the initial document to load, such as home.html.

T I P You can specify a default document in every directory to be displayed if the user does not specify a file when connecting to that directory.

If checked, the Directory Browsing Allowed option enables you to provide access to the directories and files stored under your root WWW directory. When this occurs, the user is presented with a hypertext listing of your directory structure similar to the Windows File Manager format.

N O T E Virtual directories are not displayed even if directory browsing is enabled. To view a virtual directory, users must know the URL address or use a hyperlink to get to them. ■

▶ **See** "Uniform Resource Locator," **p. 525**

You can use the Add, Remove, and Edit Properties buttons to specify the directory structure for your WWW service. To add a directory, follow these steps:

1. Click Add on the Directories tab. The Directory Properties dialog box appears (see Figure 18.18).

FIG. 18.18

Add new directories to your WWW service using the Directory Properties dialog box.

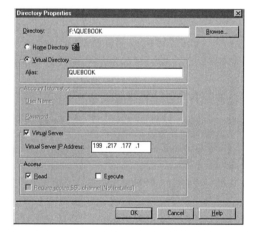

2. Specify a new directory name in the Directory box or use the Browse button to select a directory.

CAUTION

If you specify a directory name, you need to create that directory manually. Internet Service Manager does not automatically create the directory for you. If the directory does not exist, the Directory list box displays an error message.

3. Select the Home Directory option button or the Virtual Directory option button. If you select Virtual Directory, specify the alias to use for the directory.

4. If the directory you specified is a network share name (for example, \\servername\ path), you can use the Account Information options to specify a username and password to use to connect to the network share. The Account Information options are only available for directories specified using the network share name method.

5. If the directory you are adding points to a virtual server, check the Virtual Server option and specify a Virtual Server IP Address. You must use a valid IP address. Virtual servers and virtual directories make it appear that more than one WWW server is available to users using the same machine.

N O T E The default directories created by IIS do not have IP addresses assigned to them. You must do so manually. To create virtual servers, you must assign IP addresses to the home directory and all virtual directories on an IIS machine for each virtual server you will create. ▪

T I P To bind additional IP addresses to your network card, use the Network applet in the Control Panel. Your computer will then be a *multihomed* host in TCP/IP terminology.

▶ **See** "Installing and Configuring TCP/IP for Windows NT Server," **p. 256**

6. The Access check boxes enable you to specify user access permission for the directory. Click the Read check box to provide users read access to a directory.

7. Click the Execute check box if this is a directory for storing executable programs. The option is enabled by default for the Scripts directory created by IIS, which stores program executables.

CAUTION

For security reasons, you should never provide users with read access to directories containing executable programs and scripts because this may enable them to copy your program files.

8. The Require Secure SSL channel option enables you to use SSL security for accessing the contents of this directory.

9. Click OK to return to the Directories tab.

If you want to remove a directory, simply select the directory in the Directory Properties dialog box and click Remove. To edit properties for a directory, select the directory in the Directory Properties dialog box and click Edit Properties. The Directory Properties dialog box appears. Make the appropriate changes and click OK to return to the Directories tab.

Logging The WWW Logging tab is used to specify logging options used by your WWW service (see Figure 18.19). Logging can be used to store information about those who accessed your WWW service and the information they accessed. Logging information can be stored in log files, or you can use an ODBC-compatible database, such as Microsoft SQL Server, to store logging information.

FIG. 18.19

WWW service Logging options can be used to record user activity on IIS machines.

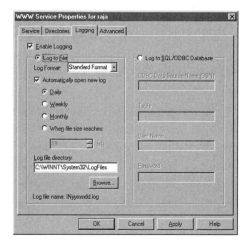

T I P You can use a single log file or a single Microsoft SQL Server database to store logging information from multiple IIS machines if you want to consolidate the information in one location.

To configure Logging options, click the Logging tab on the WWW Service Properties dialog box and follow these steps:

1. Click the Enable Logging check box to start logging for the WWW service.

2. Choose the Log to File or Log to SQL/ODBC Database option button.

3. If you choose the Log to File option, you have the following options:

   • **Automatically Open New Log**—This creates a new log based on the options available. Specify a new log file logging interval by selecting Daily, Weekly, Monthly, or When File Size Reaches.

   • **When File Size Reaches**—This specifies the file size in megabytes when a new file is to be created.

   • **Log File Directory**—This specifies the directory name and path where all log files will be stored. Alternatively, you can use the Browse button to specify a directory.

   • **Log File Name**—This displays the naming convention that will be used to store the log files. The *yymmdd* will be replaced with the two-digit year, month, and day numbers to create unique names for log files.

N O T E   If you do not use the Automatically Open New Log File option, the same log file will be
used indefinitely. You must select an existing directory or manually create a new directory
for log files using the File Manager or the MKDIR command. ▨

4. If you chose the Log to SQL/ODBC Database option, you must configure the following
   options:

   - **ODBC Data Source Name (DSN)**—Specifies the name that will be used to
     connect to the database for logging

   - **Table**—Specifies the name of the table that will store the logging information

   - **Username**—Specifies the username that will be used to connect to the database

   - **Password**—Specifies the password that will be used to connect to the database

N O T E   You must use the ODBC Applet in the Control Panel to create the specified system ODBC
data source. ▨

5. Click OK to continue, or click Apply to immediately implement the changes.

> **CAUTION**
>
> Logging to an ODBC data source is slower than logging to a file. For sites with heavy traffic, you should
> consider logging to a file for performance reasons or adding processing power to the server to support the
> additional load. For example, you can add a processor and higher performance disk subsystem.

Advanced   The WWW Advanced tab is used to specify access limits and to control the network traffic on your IIS machine (see Figure 18.20). You can choose a default access option
that either grants access to all users or denies access to all users. Then you can specify
individual computers or groups that are the exceptions to the default.

FIG. 18.20

The WWW service
Advanced tab can be
used to specify access
control properties and
network usage limits.

For example, if you want to use an IIS server as an intranet server for your organization only, you would deny access by default and add the IP addresses of your computers as exceptions to be granted access. If many computers are on your network, you can specify one or more groups of computers by using a domain name or IP address and subnet mask corresponding to the groups. Your server must be configured to use DNS in order to employ this option. See Chapter 9, "Using TCP/IP with Windows NT Server," for more information.

In this section, the option of granting access by default and entering exceptions that will be denied access is described.

To configure Advanced options, click the Advanced tab on the WWW Service Properties dialog box and follow these steps:

1. Select the Granted Access option for access control on your IIS machine. By default, all computers are granted access to your IIS machine.

2. To exclude computers from having access to your IIS machine, specify those computers with the Add button. The Deny Access On dialog box appears (see Figure 18.21).

FIG. 18.21

The Deny Access On dialog box is used to deny access to selected computers when a default policy that grants access to everyone has been chosen.

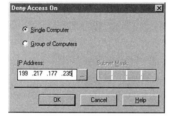

3. In the Deny Access On dialog box, specify the computer or the group of computers that will be excluded using the IP addresses for those computers. For a group of computers, you must also specify a subnet mask used by the group.

4. Click OK to return to the Advanced tab.

5. The specified computer or group of computers will show up in the excluded list. You can specify more computers to exclude or remove computers from the list by selecting them and clicking Remove. Use the Edit button to change the Deny Access On properties for a computer from the list.

6. Click the Limit Network Use by all Internet Services on This Computer option button to place a limit on network bandwidth usage by your IIS machine. This controls the amount of outbound information the IIS services on this server can send to clients on the network. The Maximum Network Use box enables you to enter a limit. The default is 4,096 Kbps. Enter a value suited to your network usage needs.

7. When finished, click OK to continue or click Apply to immediately enforce the changes.

FTP   To configure the FTP service running on a server, double-click the FTP service name or computer name in any of the views to bring up the FTP Service Properties dialog box, which displays tabs for each category that can be configured. The categories are as follows:

- Service
- Messages
- Directories
- Logging
- Advanced

The Directories, Logging, and Advanced tabs are identical to those used for the WWW service. Refer to the earlier section, "WWW," for more information on setting these options. The Service and Messages tabs, which are different for the FTP service, are outlined in the following sections.

Service   The Service tab on the FTP Service Properties dialog box is used to set various connection options for your FTP server (see Figure 18.22). To set Service options, click the Service tab on the FTP Service property sheets dialog box and follow these steps:

1. In the TCP Port box, specify the TCP/IP connection port that the service will use for enabling connections to the IIS server. The default is port 21 for the FTP service. For most environments, the default should be satisfactory.

2. In the Connection Timeout box, specify the number of seconds before a user is disconnected from your IIS machine. The default value is 900 seconds (15 minutes). You can increase or decrease this value based on your preference. Idle users will be disconnected after the specified time period to free up server resources.

3. The Maximum Connections box is used to limit the number of users that can simultaneously connect to the FTP service. The default value is 1,000 connections. The setting for this field depends on your network bandwidth, the available resources, and the speed of your server running IIS.

4. The Allow Anonymous Connections options enable you to specify the username and password that will be used by the FTP service to facilitate anonymous connections to your server. By default, IIS creates and uses the account IUSR_*computername* to facilitate anonymous logons.

N O T E   Most FTP users use *anonymous* as their usernames and their e-mail addresses as passwords to log on to FTP servers. In such instances, the IUSR_*computername* account is used for validating permissions for files and directories. ▪

T I P   You can control the access given to the IUSR_*computername* anonymous account by changing its permissions using the File Manager. Alternatively, you can specify another account on your network as the anonymous logon account.

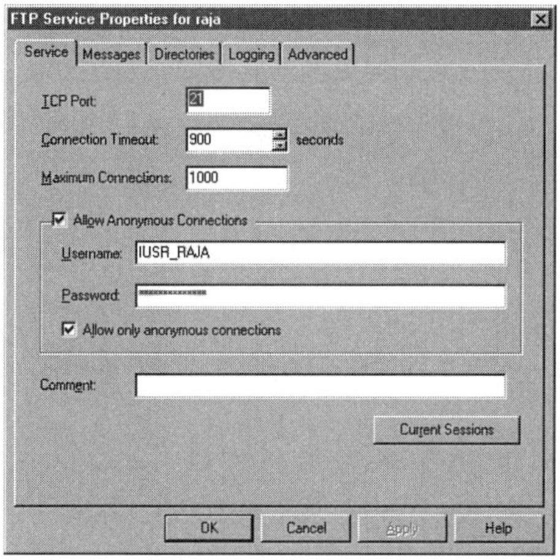

FIG. 18.22

FTP Service connection options are set using the Service tab on the FTP Service Properties dialog box.

5. The Allow Only Anonymous Connections check box disables logon permissions for all users except anonymous logons. This is used to prevent users with administrative privileges from gaining access to additional resources beyond those for which the anonymous FTP account has been granted permissions. This can be a useful method for ensuring that only selected resources are available through the FTP service.

CAUTION

The FTP protocol uses clear text for transmitting passwords (which are not encrypted prior to transmission) and is not a secure method of communication. It is possible to capture information, including passwords, transmitted over the network using protocol analyzers. This is why FTP is mostly used to transfer files and information of a non-sensitive nature.

6. The Comment box is used to specify the comment displayed by the Internet Service Manager in the Reports view.

7. Click the Current Session button to display users currently connected to your FTP server.

8. On the FTP User Sessions screen, you can view the users currently connected to your FTP Server. You can disconnect users by selecting them from the list and clicking the Disconnect button. You can disconnect all connected users by clicking the Disconnect All button. They will be immediately disconnected, and any transfers in progress will be aborted.

9. Click Close to return to the Service tab.

10. Click OK to continue, or click Apply to immediately enforce the changes.

Messages   The FTP Messages tab is used to display messages to clients connected to your FTP server (see Figure 18.23). You can display a welcome message when they initially connect, perhaps to explain the services offered. You can also display an exit message when they disconnect and a maximum connections message to notify users that the FTP service is already supporting the maximum number of users for which the server is configured.

FIG. 18.23

The Messages tab allows system administrators to set up greeting messages for users connecting to the FTP service.

To set Messages options, click the Messages tab on the FTP service property sheets dialog box and perform the following steps:

1. In the Welcome Message text box, enter the text to be displayed to clients when they first connect to your FTP server.

2. In the Exit Message text box, enter the text to be displayed when connected clients log off your FTP server.

3. In the Maximum Connections Message text box, enter text to be displayed when the maximum number of allowed client connections has been reached.

Gopher   To configure the Gopher service running on a server, double-click the Gopher service name or computer name in any of the views to bring up the Gopher Service Properties dialog box. You can then configure the following categories:

- Service
- Directories
- Logging
- Advanced

The Directories, Logging, and Advanced tabs are identical to those used for the WWW service. Refer to the earlier section, "WWW," for more information on setting these options. The Service tab, which is different for the Gopher service, is outlined in this section.

The Gopher Service tab is used to set various connection options for your Gopher server (see Figure 18.24). To set Service options, click the Service tab on the Gopher service property sheets dialog box and follow these steps:

1. In the TCP Port box, specify the TCP/IP connection port that the service will use for enabling connections to the IIS server. The default is port 70 for the Gopher service. For most environments, the default should be satisfactory.

2. In the Connection Timeout box, specify the number of seconds before a user is disconnected from your IIS machine. The default value is 900 seconds (15 minutes). You can increase or decrease this value based on your preference. Idle users will be disconnected after the specified time period to free up server resources.

3. The Maximum Connections box is used to limit the number of users that can simultaneously connect to the Gopher service. The default value is 1,000 connections. The setting for this field depends on your network bandwidth, the available resources, and the speed of your server running IIS.

4. The Service Administrator Name and Email information is used by the Gopher server to supply clients with information about who to contact in case of problems.

CAUTION

Make sure that the Service Administrator account name and e-mail address you specify is valid. Otherwise, mail sent by users will be bounced back to them.

5. The Anonymous Logon option enables you to specify the username and password that will be used by the Gopher service to facilitate anonymous connections to your server. By default, IIS creates and uses the account IUSR_*computername* to facilitate anonymous logons.

6. The Comment box is used to specify the comment displayed by the Internet Service Manager in the Reports view.

7. Click OK to continue, or click Apply to immediately enforce the changes.

Part
IV

Ch
18

FIG. 18.24

Gopher service connection options can be set using the Service tab on the Gopher Service Properties dialog box.

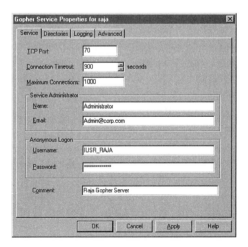

Security for Your Internet Server

Installing and operating an IIS server involves paying special attention to the security issues involved. If you are running a server being accessed by thousands of users from around the world, security of your server content and other computers on your enterprise network becomes an important issue. IIS was developed with security as one of the most important design goals. Microsoft fulfills the security needs of administrators by integrating security for IIS with the security model built into Windows NT.

Windows NT provides powerful security features for user authentication, access control, and auditing. IIS leverages these capabilities of the Windows NT operating system to provide security for its Internet-based services.

Windows NT uses a security model that handles security for all services using a single logon authentication mechanism. By creating user accounts and setting access permissions for those accounts, administrators can control what resources and services are available to users. You can minimize the chance of security problems for IIS machines by adopting the following standards:

- **User Accounts**—User accounts enable you to control who is allowed access to your resources. By restricting IIS access to valid user accounts, you can minimize the chances of security problems.

- **IUSR_*Computername* Account**—The IUSR_*computername* account is created expressly for the purpose of enabling anonymous connections to your IIS services. IUSR_*computername* accounts only have the capability to access resources managed by the IIS server and thus cannot gain access to network resources, such as network shares. By using the IUSR_*computername* account for all your Internet client connections, you can manage all user permission and security issues more easily.

N O T E   The IUSR_*computername* is created as part of the IIS installation process. ■

- **File System Security**—Make sure that you secure all your content files by setting the appropriate permissions on your WWW, FTP, and Gopher files. Use the NTFS file system to store your files. Using NTFS, you can set permissions to determine what users and groups have permissions to access files and directories. Make sure that the appropriate access rights are granted to the IUSR_*computername* account for accessing the WWW, FTP, and Gopher files.

- **Access Control**—If necessary, use the Internet Service Manager property sheets Advanced tab for WWW, FTP, and Gopher services to configure which computers or groups of computers have access to your IIS services. If you are going to be operating an intranet, it is a good idea to only grant access to computers that are a part of your enterprise.

■ **Auditing**—Use the auditing features of Windows NT in conjunction with the NTFS file system to keep records of file access and user activity. You can regularly examine the audit logs to check for unauthorized access.

  ▶ **See** "Setting Up Auditing," **p. 149**

  ▶ **See** "Setting Permissions on Shared Resources," **p. 200**

In addition, the Internet Service Manager includes a tool for creating Secure Sockets Layer (SSL) security keys for your IIS server. Figure 18.25 shows this tool—the Key Manager—that is used for creating and installing SSL keys on your IIS server.

FIG. 18.25

Key Manager can be used to create, set up, and manage security keys for SSL-based secure transactions on your IIS server.

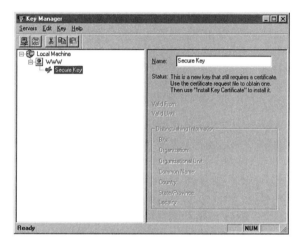

Part

IV

Ch

18

N O T E To complete installation of a newly created key, you must obtain a key certificate from a certificate issuing organization, such as VeriSign. ■

  ▶ **See** "Implementing Internet Security," **p. 759**

Creating the Content for IIS Services

The most difficult and time-consuming task in your efforts to set up IIS services is to create content for your services. After you have configured your IIS machine, set configuration parameters using Internet Service Manager property sheets, created directory structures, and handled security issues, you will need to create the data files that constitute the content displayed to users accessing your IIS services.

The three services provided by IIS each require you to follow content creation guidelines that enable them to service user requests for information quickly and efficiently. The following sections discuss content creation and publishing issues for the three IIS services: WWW, FTP, and Gopher.

WWW Publishing

WWW content creation and information publishing requires you to create special files called *HTML documents.* HTML files are simple ASCII text files that can be created using any text editor, such as Notepad. However, using a text editor and writing HTML files requires you to know the scripting syntax used by the language. Most content creators use special tools designed expressly for the creation of HTML documents (for example, Microsoft Internet Studio and Microsoft FrontPage).

▶ **See** "Hypertext Markup Language," **p. 523**

 When creating your WWW service content files, make sure that your files do not take a long time to load. HTML files that include a lot of large images may take a long time to load over client connections with slow modems.

HTML files are a combination of text, links to other files, links to images, links to sound files, and so on. You must create the image files, sound files, and other file types that will be employed by your WWW service using tools that enable the creation of such files. For example, you can create sound files using the Sound Recorder utility included with Windows NT. After you have created the content files for your WWW service, you can copy the files to the appropriate directories for access by clients using browsers, such as Internet Explorer.

> **CAUTION**
>
> Make sure that you set appropriate permissions on your content files. Provide only read permissions for HTML files and Execute permissions for executable programs and scripts. You should set permissions through both the Internet Service Manager and the NTFS file system security.

In addition to the creation of HTML documents for Web browsing, you can also allow users to remotely execute applications on your WWW server to accomplish tasks. For example, a WWW server providing phone book directory assistance might require you to enter a search name on an HTML page and then click an execute button on the page to query an online phone database for the information. Such dynamic tasks are accomplished by creating executable programs that can receive data from Web pages, parse the information, and return the results back to the user.

IIS uses two methods for creating dynamic WWW content (which are discussed in the following sections):

- Common Gateway Interface (CGI)
- Internet Server API (ISAPI)

Using CGI   To create CGI applications, you can use any programming language that enables you to create Windows executable programs. You can also use a scripting language, such as Perl for Windows NT, to create executable scripts.

After you have created your application, you can make it available to your users by simply placing it in the /Scripts directory. The /Scripts directory is a directory created by the IIS installation program for holding executable programs and scripts. By default, the /Scripts directory has only execute permissions to prevent users from copying or replacing your directory contents.

TIP Use the File Manager to set appropriate permissions on all your /Scripts directory files.

After your application is created and appropriately set up in the /Scripts directory, clients can run your application in one of two ways.

If your application requires no data input, you can create a hypertext link on a page to execute your application. For example, a hypertext link to run an application that displays a quote of the day would look something like "Click Here to Get the Quote of the Day." Users can click this hyperlink on a Web page and get their quote of the day.

If your application requires data from the users to execute, you can create an HTML form that prompts them for input. For example, you might want users to register before accessing your WWW site. To do so, you can create a simple page that requires each user to enter a name and e-mail address. After entering the information, the user clicks a Submit button to start an application that stores the information in a server-based database file.

▶ **See** "Common Gateway Interface," **p. 525**

Using ISAPI   The ISAPI method uses the exact same concepts as CGI but is different in one very important respect: ISAPI applications are created using the Microsoft BackOffice Software Developers Kit and are Windows NT DLLs. As such, ISAPI applications are loaded as server runtime DLLs at server startup. Only one instance of an ISAPI application is needed to service requests from multiple clients. By contrast, every request for a CGI application starts a new instance of the application.

▶ **See** "ISAPI," **p. 1636**

Because ISAPI applications are loaded at server startup, they provide a significant performance boost over CGI applications that are loaded when a client request comes through. However, loading all ISAPI DLLs at server startup results in a longer startup time. And as mentioned previously, ISAPI DLLs are loaded in the same memory space as the IIS server and a misbehaving ISAPI DLL can hang the entire IIS subsystem.

IIS includes a powerful feature for creating database-enabled WWW content called the Internet Database Connector. The Internet Database Connector, in conjunction with ODBC, enables you to create Web pages to publish information contained in back-end databases, such as Microsoft SQL Server. The following section discusses the Internet Database Connector feature of IIS.

Using Internet Database Connector and ODBC   Using the Internet Database Connector interface and ODBC, you can create Web pages that enable you to retrieve and display information from databases, such as Microsoft SQL Server. The Internet Database Connector is an

Part
IV

Ch
18

ISAPI application called HTTPODBC.DLL. This application is nothing more than an interface that uses ODBBµLo communicate with the databar' The Internet Database Connector can be used to do the following:

- Retrieve rows from a database and display them to users using Web pages
- Insert, update, and delete rows from a database based on user input from a Web page
- Perform other database commands supported by your database, such as executing stored procedures on Microsoft SQL Server

FTP Publishing

Creating the content for your FTP service is a straightforward and simple procedure. After you have decided what files need to be made accessible to users, you can copy those files to the appropriate FTP directories.

> **CAUTION**
>
> Make sure that you set appropriate permissions on your content files. Most FTP directories should only have read permissions. Provide a directory for user uploads with write permissions. You should set permissions through both the Internet Service Manager and the NTFS file system security using File Manager.

FTP directory structure is usually created to logically group files by function or topic. For example, you can have an FTP server that provides users access to software patches and online user guides. You can create a directory structure in which all software patches are stored under a directory called *patches* and user guides are stored under a directory called *guides*. This reduces directory clutter and provides users with an easy way to get to the files they are looking for.

Gopher Publishing

Creating content for your Gopher server is similar to FTP. You can place Gopher files in the appropriate directories for browsing by users.

> **CAUTION**
>
> Make sure that you set appropriate permissions on your content files. Gopher directories should only have read permissions. You should set permissions through the NTFS file system security using File Manager.

Gopher enables you to create links to other Gopher servers using a technique called *tag files*. Tag files are special ASCII files stored in the Gopher directory, and they define links to other Gopher resources across the network and the Internet. Microsoft provides a utility called gdsset for creating tag files. Tag files are stored as hidden files. You can edit tag files using any text editor.

To get more information on creating tag files and the syntax for the gdsset utility, type **gdsset** at the Windows NT command line.

From Here...

This chapter presents the features of Internet Information Server, as well as instructions on setting up and installing IIS, securing your IIS installation, and creating content for your IIS services. For more information on these and related issues, see the following chapters:

- For information on other Internet components available for Microsoft BackOffice, see Chapter 16, "The BackOffice I-Net Toolbox."
- To learn about using various Web browsers to connect to World Wide Web sites, see Chapter 19, " Web Browsers."
- For information on creating content for your IIS servers, see Chapter 20, "Using Microsoft FrontPage 97."
- To learn about using the Microsoft Search Server to add advanced cataloging and search capabilities to your IIS site, see Chapter 21, "Implementing Index Server and the Content Replication System."
- To learn about controlling access and implementing access security for your Internet connection, see Chapter 22, "Implementing Microsoft Proxy Server."
- To explore how the Internet can be used in business, see Chapter 47, "Building BackOffice Applications."

Part
IV

Ch
18

## CHAPTER 19

Web Browsers

by Robert S. Black

Although Web browsers are not explicitly a part of Microsoft BackOffice, they are an important component of the computing landscape. Web browsers enable users to view information easily. Users of BackOffice probably have the need to integrate the use of their Web browsers.

Explanations of both Microsoft Internet Explorer and Netscape Navigator are included in this chapter. Even though Navigator is not a Microsoft product, its widespread use warrants discussing it. You will learn many of the features of these two browsers, including how to use them to access the World Wide Web on the Internet or to access an intranet within your own organization. ◼

How to use Microsoft Internet Explorer and Netscape Navigator

Learn the many features of both Internet Explorer and Netscape Navigator, such as browsing, changing the display, quickly accessing sites, reading and posting to newsgroups, and sending e-mail.

Web page components and how to use them

Look here to find out how to use HTML, Java, ActiveX, VRML, scripting languages, and other add-ons and utilities.

Web browsers for the Internet and intranets

Stay current with the latest features of Web browsers, and learn some of their many uses.

Understanding Web Browsers

Both Microsoft Internet Explorer and Netscape Navigator are available from a variety of sources. In addition to conventional retail sales, both can be downloaded from their makers' Web pages. Both are often packaged with other software. Internet Explorer is free for everyone, while Netscape makes Navigator free for students, but charges a nominal fee for everyone else. This chapter deals with Internet Explorer 3.0 and Navigator 3.0.

Navigator and Internet Explorer can both be run on a variety of platforms. Microsoft offers version 3.01 of Internet Explorer for Windows 95, Windows NT 4.0, Windows NT MIPS, Windows NT for PowerPC, Windows NT for DEC Alpha, and Windows 3.1. It also has version 2.1 for Macintosh, which is not discussed in this chapter.

Netscape offers Navigator version 3 for the following platforms: Windows 3.1, Windows 95, Windows NT, UNIX: AIX, UNIX: BSD/386, UNIX: HP-UX, UNIX: IRIX, UNIX: Linux, UNIX: OSF/1, UNIX: SunOs 4.1.3, UNIX SPARC Solaris 2.3, and UNIX SPARC Solaris 2.4.

Additionally, there are many other Web browsers available for users of various software platforms. For example, IBM produces Web Explorer specifically for users of the OS/2 operating system.

The end of this chapter focuses on components and features of Web pages, such as Java, ActiveX, scripting languages, VRML, Active Server Pages, and Magic Cookies.

Please note that this chapter is extremely time-sensitive. At the time of publication, this chapter was as up-to-date as possible, but new developments occur daily in Web browsers, their add-ons, and the development tools used. This chapter provides a good overview of the material. To keep up to date with developments, browse a variety of sites on the Web such as **http://home.netscape.com/**, **http://www.microsoft.com/**, and **http://www.javasoft.com/**. Additionally, explore the Web for relevant topics by using your favorite search engine. For more background information on the Internet, intranets, and their utility, see Chapter 17, "I-Net Tools and Techniques."

What Are Web Browsers?

Initially, Web browsers enabled users to view only World Wide Web pages. Now, Web browsers are a means of accessing most features of the Internet, such as e-mail, FTP, and newsservices via Web pages. A Web page is a document written in Hypertext Markup Language (HTML). Most browsers can read this format and display a combination of graphics, text, and sound to the viewer. Users can navigate the Web by single-clicking hyperlinks, which the browser uses to move users from page to page.

In addition to World Wide Web viewing, browsers can view any document that is in the above mentioned HTML format. This is why intranet use is becoming so popular. Intranets enable an organization to pass information via the same mechanism as the World Wide Web, while letting only authorized users see the text.

The function of Web browsers continues to expand. It is conceivable that Web browsers will soon provide users with full Internet access, including total e-mail services.

Addresses

How does the Web browser know where to look for a desired document? The browser uses an address, also called a *Universal Resource Indicator* (*URI*), to determine which document to access. The URI—commonly, but often erroneously, referred to as a *Universal Resource Locator* (*URL*)—uniquely indicates the location of a document. An address is made up of the following four components:

- **Protocol**—The protocol informs the browser what type of information it is to display. For example, **http** indicates a Web page, **news** represents a newsgroup, and **file** means the file is on, or is mapped to, a local drive.
- **Domain**—The domain indicates the location of the server with the information. The domain can be represented as a domain name, such as **www.gasullivan.com**, or the IP address of the server, such as **111.111.111.111**.
- **Path**—The path is the directory in which the file is listed.
- **File name**—The file name is the name of the HTML file; typically, this has a **.htm** or **.html** extension. The file name is often not displayed for the default page for a particular path. Often, this is a file named **index.htm** at a particular site.

N O T E Because virtually everyone refers to Internet addresses as URLs, this book follows that convention.

It is important to understanding the naming convention for sites so that you know the source of the information that you are reading or downloading. This discussion is expanded in the section "Security" presented later in this chapter.

Part
IV

Ch
19

Hypertext Markup Language (HTML)

Hypertext Markup Language (HTML) is a collection of standardized codes placed in text documents. Web browsers read the documents and translate the codes into font, spacing, and placement decisions that appear on the browser display screen.

An HTML page tells the browser how to present a document to a viewer. The page can also contain other information, such as scripting or tags, to create more powerful Web pages.

Microsoft Internet Explorer

Internet Explorer, Microsoft's Web browser, has many capabilities. It can view Web pages, navigate the World Wide Web, start a Telnet client, play audio, display VRML, send e-mail, view newsgroups, and carry out many other functions. Internet Explorer also has NetMeeting, a program that enables voice communication over the Internet and allows users to see and work on the same whiteboard and share common applications.

Users can download the latest version of Internet Explorer at **http://www.microsoft.com/ie/download**.

Navigating with Explorer

To access a specific Web site, type the name of the URL in the Address drop-down box at the top of Explorer, as shown in Figure 19.1, and press Enter. For example, type **http://www.gasullivan.com**. You navigate using the following features:

- **Hyperlinks**—To move to another site specified on the page, click the name once. Typically, the name will be in a different color from the rest of the text and underlined. This text is called a *hyperlink*. The hyperlink has another URL associated with it, so the Web browser visits the specified site.

- **Back button**—To move back to the site you were viewing, click the Back button. Each click of the Back button moves you to the page that was accessed immediately before the one displayed.

- **Forward button**—You can move using the Forward button only if the Back button was used to get you to the current screen. It is always grayed out when disabled.

 The Go menu option displays a list of Web sites recently traversed. A check next to the Web site name indicates the current Web page. Forward will move you down the list while Back will move you up it.

- **Home button**—The Home button moves you to the default page that Microsoft Internet Explorer loaded.

- **Search button**—This moves you to the default search page. A *search page* is a Web page whose function is to locate information on the Web. You can change which page is displayed by following the procedure explained in the following section "Changing Default Pages."

Changing Default Pages   To change the default home page, perform the following steps:

1. Choose View, Options. The Options dialog box appears.
2. Click the Navigation tab (see Figure 19.2).
3. Select Start Page from the Page combo box by clicking the arrow and selecting it from the list.
4. Type the URL of the home site in the address box, for example, **http://www.gasullivan.com**.

Similarly, you can change the search page by following the same procedure, by selecting Search Page in step 3 instead of the Start Page.

FIG. 19.1

Typing the URL in the Address box brings up the desired page.

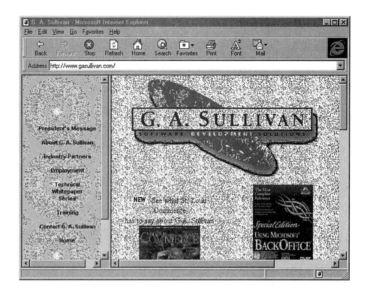

FIG. 19.2

Setting the Start Page to **http:// www.gasullivan.com** will cause this page to appear every subsequent time Internet Explorer is started.

Part
IV

Ch
19

Changing Fonts   To change the size of the words displayed on the screen, click the Font button on the toolbar. This increases the size of the font until it has reached the maximum size and then sets the size to the smallest possible font.

To change the actual font displayed, perform the following steps:

1. Choose View, Options. The Options dialog box appears.

2. Choose the General tab, and then click the Font Settings button at the bottom right of the tab.

3. Select the font from the Proportional Font or Fixed-Width Font drop-down list box.

4. Click OK when you have chosen the font you desire.

N O T E   Some Web pages have default fonts that Internet Explorer will not override.   ■

Using Favorites   *Favorites* are markers that save a reference to a particular Web page. To save
the current page for quick reference, perform the following steps:

1. Click the Favorites button.
2. Choose Add to Favorites.
3. Type the name you want to call the page in the Name text box.
4. Click OK.
5. Verify that the site was added by clicking Favorites and noticing the new item in the list.

To delete an item from the Favorites menu, perform the following steps:

1. Click the Favorites button.
2. Choose Organize Favorites.
3. Select the link that you want to delete.
4. Press the Delete button. Your operating system may prompt you to make sure that you
   really want to delete the link. Confirm your decision.

Printing

The Print button prints the page being viewed by the browser. The entire page, including
graphics and text, will be printed—not just the area that is viewed.

Refreshing

Refresh requests the Web page from the server again. You might press the Refresh button
because the Web page has been updated since last loaded, the site is cached on the local hard
drive and did not read from the network, the connection to the site was broken, or because of a
display problem.

Finding Information in a Document

If a Web page has a large amount of text, it may be difficult to find a certain piece of information that you are looking for. Internet Explorer can search for a particular word or phrase on
the current Web page. To find a particular word or phrase, perform the following steps:

1. If the page has multiple frames, click the desired frame to search.
2. Choose Edit, Find (or press Ctrl+F). The Find dialog box appears (see Figure 19.3).
3. At the Find prompt, type the word or words you want to search for.
4. Check the boxes to indicate whether you want to Start From Top of Page and whether
   Internet Explorer should Match Case of the words you typed.
5. Click the Find Next button. Internet Explorer highlights the word or words if they
   match, but returns a message box if nothing was found.

FIG. 19.3
You can search the current page for specific text.

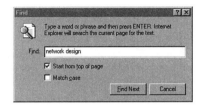

N O T E Internet Explorer only searches text, so if the word you are looking for is in a graphic or a control, Internet Explorer will not find it. ▪

Copying Features from Other Web Pages

Internet Explorer enables you to look at the HTML script that generates the displayed Web page on the browser. You can use this function to copy features from other Web pages.

To view a Web page's HTML script, choose View, Source. This opens Notepad with a script of the HTML. To view the HTML script, you could also right-click and select View Source. Finding the script for the desired feature may be difficult. Matching text between the Web page and source script may help to narrow the specific lines that you are searching for.

If the Web page is using frames, you will not see the source for any of the material inside the frames. To view the material inside the frames, perform the following steps:

1. Right-click the frame whose source you desire to see.
2. Select View Source.
3. Follow the preceding find procedure.

Internet Mail

There are many programs available to use e-mail. Microsoft, however, has incorporated a mail program as a part of Internet Explorer.

Setting Up Internet Mail When selecting the Read Mail option from Internet Explorer for the first time, the user has the option to set up mail via a Setup Wizard. Before beginning, make sure you get your SMTP and POP3 mail servers and POP3 account name. To set up Internet Mail, perform the following steps:

1. Select Mail from the toolbar, and click Read mail.
2. The first time, a Setup Wizard appears. Read the instructions and follow the next prompts.
3. Type your name and e-mail address in the appropriate text boxes. Click Next.
4. Type the name of your mail servers and logon name similar to that shown in Figure 19.4. Click Next.

FIG. 19.4
Input the name of the
mail servers to properly
configure Internet Mail
to send and receive
e-mail.

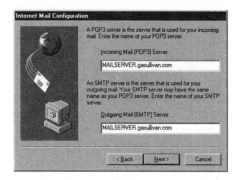

5. Type your logon name for your e-mail account. If you enter your password, then anyone who uses Internet Mail on your computer will have access to your e-mail account.

6. Select the name of the connection from the drop-down list box. Follow the rest of the instructions from the Wizard, and you will be set up to send and receive e-mail.

Using Internet Mail   To read a message, click the description of it in the top window. To compose a message, click the New Message button, type the e-mail address of the recipient in the To text box, and type your message in the text field that appears. If you want to reply to a message, select the message and click the Reply to Author button on the toolbar.

No messages will be sent or received until you click the Send and Receive button. This button will get all messages from the mail server and send out all of the messages that you have composed.

Internet News

A component of the Internet also supported by Internet Explorer is the *newsgroup*—a collection of messages associated by topic. Users have the capability to respond to others' messages by posting to the newsgroup or e-mailing the sender. Users can also generate new posts to a newsgroup.

There are newsgroups for a large variety of subjects. You'll encounter newsgroups about products, events, hobbies, and many other interests.

Setting Up Newsgroups for Internet News   When selecting the newsgroups option from Internet Explorer for the first time, the user has the option to set up the newsreader with a Setup Wizard. You need to subscribe to a newsserver. Ask your company, organization, or Internet service provider for information regarding your newsserver. You will need the newsserver's name to set Internet News. To set up newsgroups with Internet Explorer, perform the following steps:

1. Click the Mail button at the top toolbar, or choose Go.

2. Select Read News.

3. The first time that you do this, a Setup Wizard will appear. Follow the instructions. When the Wizard prompts you for your name and e-mail address, type in a name that you want

other subscribers to the newsgroups to see you as. Some people use their e-mail addresses, their names, or made-up names. You can change your name later.

It is important that you put your correct e-mail address, or you will not be able to send or receive mail via the newsreader. Again, you can change your e-mail address in the program. Subsequently, Internet News will launch without the Setup Wizard.

4. Click Next. Internet News prompts you for the name of your newsserver. Type the name. The first entry will be your default news service. That only matters if you have more than one provider.

5. After clicking Next, indicate the manner that you want to connect to your newsserver. If you connect via modem, you will need to select the name of your connection from the list box.

6. Click Next and then Finish; you have completed the setup.

If you choose to bypass any portion of the setup, you can change the settings in the program. Select News, Options, and the Server tab. On this tab you can edit your name, e-mail address, and newsserver. To change your name or e-mail address, type the change in the appropriate blank. To delete a newsservice, click the service and click remove.

To add a newsservice, perform the following steps:

1. Click News, Options. The Options dialog box appears.

2. Click the Sever tab (see Figure 19.5).

FIG. 19.5
Configure the e-mail address and name that will appear to other users of a newsgroup.

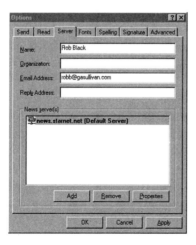

3. Click the Add button.

4. Type the name of the newsserver in the News Server Name text box. If you want the newsserver as your default server, click the Set as Default button at the bottom of the screen.

Subscribing and Unsubscribing to a Newsgroup Subscribers to a newsgroup are able to compose, read, and reply to messages for that particular newsgroup. To subscribe to a newsgroup, perform the following steps:

1. Choose News, Newsgroups, or type Ctrl+W. You can also click the Newsgroups button on the toolbar at the top of the page. The Newsgroups window appears, as shown in Figure 19.6.

FIG. 19.6

Subscribe to a newsgroup by clicking the name of the unsubscribed newsgroup and pressing the Subscribe button.

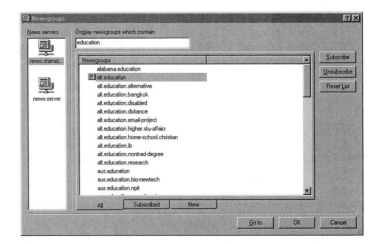

2. Many newsgroups will appear in the list. Type some text in the Display Newsgroups Which Contain text box. This text will shorten the list to only newsgroups that contain the text in the name. For example, if you were looking for a newsgroup about football, then you might type **football**. All of the sites that are available from your newsservice provider will appear.

T I P When typing text to find a listing of sites, it may be helpful to type a period before and/or after the name that you type. For example, if you are looking for a newsgroup on ants and type the word **ants**, Internet News will return a listing that contains **consultants** and **giants**. On the other hand, typing **.ants**, **ants.**, or **.ants.** might be more helpful in returning the desired results.

3. Click the desired newsgroup name.
4. Click the Subscribe button on the right of the screen. Now you are subscribed to the newsgroup.

To unsubscribe from a newsgroup, select the desired newsgroup from the Newsgroups window, and choose Unsubscribe.

How to Read and Respond to Posts Once you have subscribed to a newsgroup, you are ready to read and reply to messages. To read a message, select the desired newsgroup from the Newsgroups window, and click Go To. The Internet News window appears with the newsgroup open (see Figure 19.7). Now, simply go to the message of interest.

FIG. 19.7
Clicking an item in the upper window causes the message to appear in the lower window.

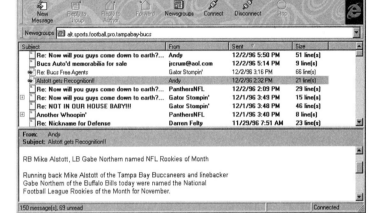

To post a message, perform the following steps:

1. Click the New Message button on the toolbar at the top of the page.

2. Type your message in the blank space on the bottom of the window.

3. To post your message to the newsgroup, click the leftmost button on the toolbar (the pin with a piece of paper).

Replying to a message is different than posting a message in that the message will be associated with the original message for others to view. Replying lets one follow the conversation thread more easily. To reply to a message, perform the following steps:

1. Click the message that you want to reply to.

2. Press the Reply to Group button on the toolbar.

3. Type a message, and click the Post Message button. The message will be posted with Re: inserted before the subject of the original message.

Additionally, when viewed in Internet News, the message can be displayed by clicking the plus sign to the left of the message. The reply message is listed below and indented in relation to the original message.

If you want to send e-mail to the author you can do this by clicking the Reply to Author button, typing a message, and sending it. You must have configured Internet Mail to use this feature, as it sends mail via Internet Mail to the author.

Using NetMeeting

NetMeeting is Microsoft Internet Explorer's real-time voice Internet phone software. NetMeeting enables users to talk to each other in real time using their Internet connection with no additional charge other than their normal Internet connection charges. NetMeeting also provides whiteboard, chat, resource sharing, and multiconference.

Part
IV

Ch
19

> **T I P** Microsoft gives you the opportunity to download NetMeeting when you download Internet Explorer. You
> can download NetMeeting from **http://www.microsoft.com/ie/download**.

Setting Up NetMeeting   Before you begin the setup of NetMeeting, you should have a microphone and soundcard installed. If you already have these items, follow these steps to implement NetMeeting:

1. Download NetMeeting from Microsoft at **http://www.microsoft.com/msdownload/
   netmeeting.htm** by following the instructions that Microsoft provides.

2. Once the NetMeeting Setup program has been downloaded, run it by clicking its icon.

3. Follow the prompts given by the setup program. Agree to install the software.

4. Read and agree to the licensing agreement. NetMeeting will unpack and set up the files
   in the appropriate directory.

5. Restart your system so NetMeeting's settings will take effect.

6. Run NetMeeting by clicking its icon. The first time, NetMeeting's Setup Wizard will run.

7. Click Next after reading the information on the first screen. (Continue clicking Next
   throughout the setup process to progress to the following screen.)

8. Enter your first name, last name, and e-mail address (see Figure 19.8). You can also
   enter your city, state, and comments. Other users in a conference will be able to see this
   information.

FIG. 19.8

Microsoft stores your
e-mail address along
with the rest of this
information on a server
so that you can
communicate with other
users without directly
exchanging IP
addresses.

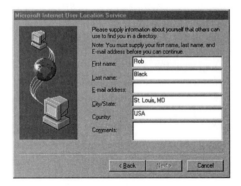

9. Choose the server on which you want to leave your information so that others can
   contact you (see Figure 19.9). Microsoft has a variety of servers including
   **uls.microsoft.com, uls1.microsoft.com, uls2.microsoft.com, uls3.microsoft.com,
   uls4.microsoft.com,** and **uls5.microsoft.com**. It is possible that others have servers
   that provide user location services. Your Internet service provider may have such a
   service. Selecting **uls.microsoft.com** makes you easier to locate for others. If you
   choose to have your name posted on the server, when you log on to NetMeeting, anyone
   else using it will be able to see your e-mail address, first name, last name, and any other
   information that you provided in step 8.

FIG. 19.9

Choose a server for your contact information, and decide whether to make your information public.

10. Configure the sound and voice for NetMeeting. NetMeeting will check to see if your sound card is enabled for full or half duplex audio. If both users of a NetMeeting session have full duplex audio, then they can speak simultaneously; otherwise, they need to speak one at a time.

11. Select the speed of your connection.

12. Tune your microphone. If you do not have a microphone, you can often plug headphones into your input and speak into them.

13. Finish the wizard, and you are ready to begin NetMeeting. All of the options set with the Setup Wizard can be changed by choosing Tools, Options in the NetMeeting client.

Joining a Session   While your computer is running the NetMeeting client, a message box and ringing noise will occur. You can choose to accept or decline the invitation to the session. If you accept, NetMeeting will set up the conference. While connected, there are several functions available for communicating.

Using Chat   Sometimes it is more efficient to use the chat screen than voice transmission. The chat screen enables users to send text in place of audio. One would use Chat to make information more clear or so simultaneous discussions can take place when both users do not have full duplex audio. Also, three or more users cannot transmit voice, so chat would be necessary to enable "talking."

To use chat, simply click the Chat button on the tool bar at the top of NetMeeting. The chat screen will pop up for all the users in the conference. Type what you want to say in the bottom window and press return or click the button on the right to send it.

Using Whiteboard   Whiteboard is a multi-point function of NetMeeting that enables users to manipulate the same graphics at the same time. With whiteboard, users can illustrate points with graphics to a group of people.

To use whiteboard, click the whiteboard button on the toolbar at the top of NetMeeting. The whiteboard will pop up for all users to draw on. Graphics can be captured from other windows by clicking the Select Area button on the toolbar on the left of the screen. This button is depicted by a window with a dotted line around it.

Part

IV

Ch

19

Transferring Files   To send a file to a member of a conference, click the Send File button on the toolbar at the top. Choose a file to send and the recipient.

To receive a file, a window will appear while in a conference prompting you to accept or decline the file being transmitted, as shown in Figure 19.10.

FIG. 19.10
Transferring files from one computer to another is easy using NetMeeting.

Hosting a Session   To begin a session, click the Call icon on the toolbar on the top. Select a name from the list in the specified user location server, input the IP address of the desired person, or choose the person's name from a call list or type in the name for a given server. If the user accepts, then NetMeeting will set up the call as depicted in Figure 19.11. If the user declines or the operation times out, you can make another call.

FIG. 19.11
Hosting a session with NetMeeting allows the user to decide who is allowed in a conference.

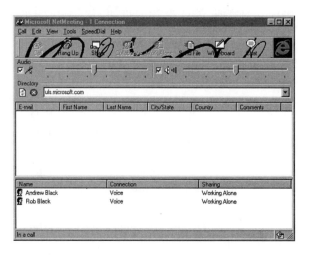

Internet Explorer 3.0 has many features to enable users to use Internet resources more effectively. Its browser lets you explore the World Wide Web, its mail program allows you to send and receive mail, and its news program enables you to join and participate in newsgroups. Netscape Navigator has similar functionality to allow you to use Internet resources. The choice between these two leading Web browsers (or even another alternative) can be a difficult one, especially since they are regularly updated and "leapfrog" each other with new functionality. The features of Netscape Navigator are outlined in the following section.

Netscape Navigator

Like Internet Explorer, Netscape Navigator has a variety of features. Navigator can view Web pages, navigate the World Wide Web, start a Telnet client, play audio, display VRML, send e-mail, view newsgroups, and carry out many other functions. Netscape Navigator also has CoolTalk: a software like Microsoft's NetMeeting that enables voice communication over the Internet, and enables users to share common applications and see and work on the same whiteboard.

 Users can download the latest version of Netscape Navigator at **http://home.netscape.com/ comprod/mirror/client_download.html**.

Navigating with Navigator

To access a specific Web site, type the URL in the Location drop-down box at the top of Navigator, as shown in Figure 19.12, and press enter. For example, type **wysiwyg://2/http:// www.prosoft.org/**. You navigate using the following features:

- **Hyperlinks**—To move to another site specified on the page, click the name. Typically, the name will be in a different color from the rest of the text and underlined. This text is called a *hyperlink*. The hyperlink has another URL associated with it, so the Web browser visits the specified site.

- **Back button**—To move back to the site you were viewing, click the Back button. You could also right-click the Web page and select Back from the drop-down menu. Each click of the Back button moves you to the page that was accessed immediately before the one displayed.

- **Forward button**—You can move using the Forward button only if the Back button was used to get you to the current screen. It is always grayed out when disabled.

 The Go menu option displays a list of Web sites recently traversed. A check next to the Web site name indicates the current Web page. Forward will move you up the list while Back will move you down it.

- **Home button**—The Home button moves you to the default page that Netscape Navigator loaded.

- **Net Search**—Clicking Net Search below the Location box moves you to Netscape's default search page at **http://home.netscape.com**.

Part
IV

Ch
19

FIG. 19.12

Typing the URL in the Address box brings up the desired page.

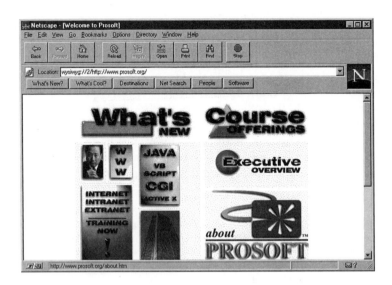

Changing the Default Home Page

To make Netscape load a specific Web page as the default start page, perform the following steps:

1. Choose Options, General Preferences. The Preferences dialog box appears.

2. Click the Appearance tab.

3. In the frame in the middle of the page titled Startup, make sure that the Netscape Browser check box is checked and the Browser Starts With option Home Page Location is selected (see Figure 19.13).

FIG. 19.13

The Appearance tab enables the user to specify which page Netscape is to load and to change some appearance functions.

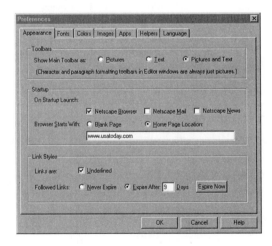

4. Type the address of the site in the text box. For example, if you type **www.usatoday.com**, then your browser will load the USA Today Web site.

Changing Fonts

To change the font displayed from the default font, perform the following steps:

1. Choose Options, General Preferences. The Preferences dialog box appears.
2. Click the Fonts tab.
3. Click the Choose Font button for the font that you want to change. The Choose Base Font pop-up screen appears.
4. Change to the desired font.

N O T E   Some Web pages have default fonts that Navigator will not override. ▨

Using Bookmarks

Bookmarks are used to save the location of frequently referenced sites for quick reference. To save the current page, perform the following steps:

1. Choose Bookmarks.
2. Choose Add Bookmark. The current page will now appear on the bookmark list.

You can see the bookmark by clicking the Bookmark toolbar button. The item appears at the bottom of the list.

To delete an item from Bookmarks, perform the following steps:

1. Choose Bookmarks, Go to Bookmarks.
2. Select a bookmark and press the Delete button. You could also select a bookmark and choose Edit, Delete.

To get the bookmark back, follow the preceding Add procedure.

To order the bookmarks on the list, perform the following steps:

1. Choose Bookmarks, Go to Bookmarks.
2. Click a bookmark icon, and drag it to where you want it to appear in the list.

Printing

The Print button prints the page being viewed by the browser. The entire page, including graphics and text, will be printed—not just the area that is viewed.

Part
IV

Ch
19

Reloading

Reload refreshes the current displayed site. There are several reasons for reloading a page: It is possible that the site has been updated since last loaded, the site is cached on the local hard drive and did not read from the network, the connection was lost, or another picture problem.

Finding Information in a Document

If a Web page has a large amount of text, it may be difficult to find a certain piece of information that you are looking for. Netscape Navigator can search for a particular word or phrase on the current Web page.

To find a particular word or phrase on the current Web page, perform the following steps:

1. If the page has multiple frames, click a frame to search.
2. Press the Find button.
3. At the prompt, type the word or words that you want to search for.
4. Check the boxes to indicate whether you want to search upward or downward. Also, click the Match case check box if you want Navigator to match the case of the text that you typed.
5. Click the Find Next button.

Netscape highlights the word or words if it finds a match; otherwise, it returns a message box informing you that nothing was found.

N O T E   Netscape Navigator only searches text, so if the word you are looking for is in a graphic or a control, Netscape Navigator will not find it. ■

Copying Features from Other Web Pages

Navigator enables you to look at the HTML script that generates the displayed Web page on the browser. You can use this function to copy features from other Web pages. To view a Web page's HTML script, perform the following steps:

1. Choose View.
2. Choose a document source, which opens a window with a script of the HTML.

If the Web page is using frames and you want to view the source of a particular frame, then perform the following procedure:

1. Click the frame in question.
2. Choose View.
3. Click the frame source option. The HTML of the active frame will appear in a window.

Internet Mail

There are many programs available to use e-mail. Netscape, however, has incorporated a mail program as a part of Netscape Navigator.

Setting Up Netscape Mail   Before starting the Netscape Mail program, you should configure the settings from Netscape Navigator. You will need information about your SMTP server, POP3 server, and logon name from your network administrator or Internet service provider. To set up Netscape Mail, do the following.

1. Choose Options, Mail and News Preferences. The Preferences dialog box appears.
2. Click the Servers tab and type the name of the appropriate servers and your POP3 user name (see Figure 19.14).

FIG. 19.14
Configure Netscape
Mail to send and
receive e-mail.

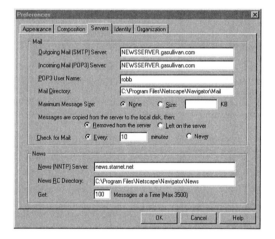

3. Type the name of the mail directory that you will use on your local hard drive.
4. Select whether you will leave the mail on the server or remove it.
5. Choose the interval that Netscape Mail checks for mail.

Using Netscape Mail   To start Netscape Mail, choose Window, Netscape Mail. The Netscape Mail client will start. Clicking the envelope icon at the bottom-ight corner of Navigator's browser window will also start up Netscape Mail. The following functions are available:

- ■ **Getting mail**—Click the Get Mail button to receive mail. If you set Netscape Mail to get your mail at a given interval, you only need to click the Get Mail button when you want Netscape Mail to check for new mail.

- ■ **Reading mail**—To read mail, click a description of the mail item (see Figure 19.15). The text will appear on the screen. To reply to this message, click the Re:Mail button and type your message.

FIG. 19.15

Netscape Mail main screen is used to read and organize e-mail.

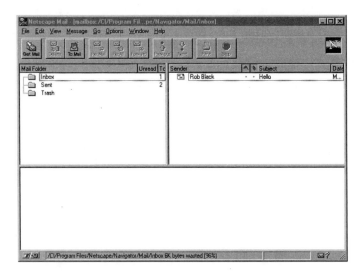

■ **Sending mail**—To send a new message, click the To:Mail button. Type your message and then click the Send button on the top right.

Netscape News

In order to read, compose, and respond to messages, the news server must be configured correctly. To configure the news server, perform the following steps:

1. From Navigator's main page, choose Window, Netscape News. This launches the Netscape News client.

2. Choose Options, Mail and News Preferences.

 You can also set up Netscape News from the Navigator Options menu.

3. Type the name of your news server in the News (NNTP) Server text box toward the bottom of the display. Get the name of your newsserver from your system administrator or Internet service provider. For example, the name of your newsserver might be **news.starnet.net**.

4. Type the name of the directory in which you want Netscape to store news files on your hard drive or leave the name listed as a default.

5. Select Options, Preferences and click the Identity tab. Type in the name you want for other users of the newsgroup to see you as in the Your Name text box. Type in your e-mail address in the Your e-mail text box. You can run the news client without this step, but you will not be able to post new messages or reply to existing ones.

6. Type the number of messages that you want for Netscape News to retrieve at one time. The News client is configured and you can launch it.

To add a new newsgroup, Choose File, Add Newsgroup. A window will appear, prompting you for the name of the new newsgroup. Enter it in the Type in a Newsgroup to Add to the List text box.

If you don't know the name of the desired newsgroup, you can find it by selecting one of four options from the Options menu: Show All Newsgroups, Show Subscribed Newsgroups, Show Active Newsgroups, and Show New Newsgroups (which shows all of the newsgroups that have been added since the last time you checked).

N O T E The first time you sign on, there are no new newsgroups. To obtain a list of the available newsgroups, you must select Show All Newsgroups. Since the list of all possible newsgroups is extremely large, the first time you select this option you may have to wait for a long time while the data is being transferred to your computer.

Show Active Newsgroups shows all of the newsgroups that you are subscribed to that have messages that you have not already read. Show Subscribed Newsgroups shows all of the newsgroups that you are subscribed to. ▨

To subscribe to a newsgroup, right-click the name of the unsubscribed newsgroup and select the Subscribe option. To unsubscribe to a newsgroup, right-click the name of a subscribed newsgroup and select the Unsubscribe option.

To read a message in a newsgroup, click the name of the newsgroup you want to view and then click the name of the message in the list box on the right side of the display. The text of the message will appear in the bottom portion of the window.

To reply to a message, you must have set up your user name and e-mail address. After selecting a message, click the Re: Mail, Re: News, or Re: Both button. Re: Mail will send the original author an e-mail of your response. Re: News will post a new message to the newsgroup with your response. Re: Both will send the original author an e-mail *and* post the same message to the newsgroup. This message will appear below and indented in relation to the original message that was posted. Clicking the plus sign to the left of a message shows all of the responses to that message.

To post a new message, click the To: News button and type a message in the text box that appears. To send the message, press the Send button at the top left of the toolbar. Similarly, you can use the To: Mail button to send e-mail without starting up a mail client.

Part

IV

Ch

19

CoolTalk

CoolTalk is Netscape's real-time voice Internet phone software, which enables users to talk to each other in real time using their Internet connection with no additional charge over and above their normal connect charges. CoolTalk also provides whiteboard, chat, and resource sharing.

Setting Up CoolTalk   When installing Netscape Navigator, a message box will appear to see if you want to install CoolTalk. Click Yes, and the Navigator Setup will install CoolTalk.

Once you start up CoolTalk, choose Options and select the Conference tab. Type the host name of your computer. If your computer has a DNS name, then you can use that as the name for the computer. If your computer does not have a DNS name, then you will have to use the IP address of your computer. If your computer does not have a dedicated connection (a dial up connection from home, for example), then you will have to change your IP address each time you start CoolTalk.

Joining a Session   When you are logged in to CoolTalk, a message box will appear if someone is asking you to join a session. You can either <u>A</u>ccept or <u>R</u>eject.

After joining a session, you may speak into your microphone to send an audio transmission or use one of CoolTalk's many features.

FIG. 19.16

Press Accept to join a session or Reject if you do not want to join.

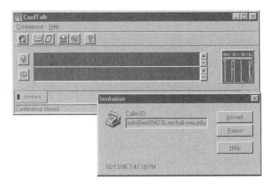

Using Chat   In addition to having the capability to communicate with voice, you can also use a chat window to type messages. You may want to do this because of poor sound quality, or to send a message as the other person is talking.

To chat, click the Chat Tool icon (a picture of a typewriter) on the toolbar. The Chat Tool will launch. You can type and edit a message in the bottom window. To send the message, type Ctrl+Enter or press the microphone icon on the top left of the toolbar at the top. The ongoing conversation is kept in the upper Log File window.

Using Whiteboard   Whiteboard enables users to manipulate the same graphics at the same time. With whiteboard, users can illustrate points with graphics to a group of people.

To use whiteboard, click the Paint button on the toolbar at the top of CoolTalk. The whiteboard will launch and enable both users to draw. Graphics can be captured from other windows, regions of the screen, or the entire desktop by choosing Capture and then the appropriate command. When selecting a window, CoolTalk will minimize, enabling you to click the window that it should capture. When selecting a region, CoolTalk again closes to enable the user to click the desired region of the screen. In both cases CoolTalk will re-size and enable the user to indicate where the selected graphics should appear.

Hosting a Session   Click the Start Conference button (which contains a picture of two people) on the toolbar. Enter the Domain Name Server (DNS) or the IP address of the desired person. CoolTalk will make a request to the specified computer. If the user does not have the CoolTalk Watch Dog or CoolTalk running, then the session will be refused. (The CoolTalk Watch Dog is a program that monitors for incoming messages, but the user does not have to have CoolTalk running.) The other user has the same option as you to accept or decline. If the user chooses to accept, then you will be notified, and CoolTalk will negotiate the connection. You will be able to use the whiteboard, chat, or voice functions of CoolTalk.

Plug-Ins

Plug-ins are programs that provide Netscape Navigator with additional functionality. These programs are often written by outside vendors who want to add a specific capability to Navigator such as enabling it to display VRML or use ActiveX Controls.

To see which plug-ins are installed, choose Help, About Plug-ins. Netscape presents information about both the plug-ins installed on the system and company that makes them.

Using ActiveX with ScriptActive Plug-In   Unlike Microsoft Internet Explorer, Netscape does not support ActiveX Controls. It does, however, support plug-ins. NCompass Labs make ScriptActive, an ActiveX plug-in that enables users to use ActiveX Controls and read Web pages with VBScript.

Installing ScriptActive   To install ScriptActive, perform the following steps:

1. Download ScriptActive from **http://www.ncompasslabs.com** following the site's download instructions.
2. Once the file has been downloaded, click the file's icon on the desktop to install NCompass ScriptActive.
3. You will be asked if you want to continue. Click the Yes button, and ScriptActive will unpack the necessary files.
4. Read and accept the license agreement. You have 30 days to evaluate the software before you have to pay. Students and members of nonprofit, charitable organizations are not required to pay.

Using ScriptActive   Once installed, SciptActive enables Netscape Navigator to read HTML files formatted for certain ActiveX Controls automatically. If an ActiveX page does not appear correctly, you will need to run the NCompass HTML conversion utility. The page may not appear correctly, depending on how the tags are embedded in the HTML.

To convert an HTML page with ActiveX Controls to one that Netscape Navigator can read, do the following:

1. Copy the Web page you want to convert to your hard drive.
2. Run NCompass HTML Conversion Utility. The Conversion Tool dialog box appears (see Figure 19.17).

Part

IV

Ch

19

FIG. 19.17

You can alter a Web page so that the ActiveX Control can be viewed with Netscape Navigator using the ScriptActive Conversion Program.

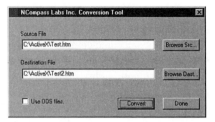

3. Type the name of the file on your hard drive in the Source File field you want Navigator to read. You cannot use the World Wide Web address; you must use the file that is on your hard drive.

4. Type the path and name of where you would like the file to be outputted in the Destination File field.

5. Press the Convert button. If the path and destination were specified correctly, the conversion utility will report a successful conversion.

6. Read the new Web page with Netscape Navigator. The ActiveX Control will now be displayed.

> **CAUTION**
>
> These converted HTML pages will not work correctly with Internet Explorer or with Netscape Navigator without the plug-in.

Web Page Components

Thus far, this chapter has explained how to use the Internet Explorer and Netscape Navigator Web browsers. To administer or design a Web site, it is important to understand some of the inner workings of Web pages. This section explains some of the different aspects of a Web page and also provides a starting point for Web page designers and a reference for all who are interested in Web pages.

Web Design Tools

Many Web design tools are available on the market today. Each has features assigned for a specific task. Some are designed for programmers, while others are for Web page designers with little or no programming experience. Most of these tools allow for easier writing of HTML, but some do not allow for every feature of HTML to be included. Often there is an easy option for inserting Java applets or ActiveX Controls, which are discussed in the following two sections of this chapter. It is important to define your needs before searching for the right product for your situation. Some Web design tools include Netscape Navigator Gold and Adobe PageMill. For information on one of Microsoft's tools, consult Chapter 20, "Using Microsoft FrontPage 97."

Java

Java applets are compiled Java programs that can run on Web browsers. Applets enable user interaction and animated graphics on a Web page. The same applet can run on a PC, a Macintosh, or a UNIX system.

Java is an object-oriented programming language that runs on multiple platforms. It is similar to C++; however, it has a different method of garbage collection, is more stringent about being object-oriented, and does not have pointers. Sun Microsystems developed Java to run independently of the platform it is on.

An applet runs on a virtual machine, which is a platform-specific program used to run Java. Java can be viewed with several browsers, including Internet Explorer, Netscape Navigator, and Sun's HotJava browser. Although the Java language itself is not limited, the browsers that run Java prevent it from executing unsecured actions on your computer, such as reading and writing to your disk. In a worst case scenario, a Java applet could waste your system resources, such as CPU cycles or network bandwidth. The above method to prevent damage to data is sometimes called a sandbox design which is further presented in the "Preventing Damage to Your Data" section later in this chapter.

There are a variety of software products that can be used to write Java applets. Sun's Java Developer Kit (JDK), Symantec's Café, Microsoft's Visual J++, Borland's JBuilder, and Type Solutions' Studio J++ are some of the Java compilers currently available.

ActiveX

ActiveX is a product of Microsoft's *object linking and embedding* (*OLE*) technology. ActiveX has the capability to be embedded in HTML, as well as for the traditional uses for OLE technology, replacing OCX components.

Part
IV

Ch
19

There are many different uses for ActiveX technology. It provides a unified model for behavior for both the Web and personal computers. ActiveX Controls are the interactive controls (e.g., buttons or menubars) that users can incorporate into HTML pages. Active scripting is the scripting used in HTML pages to control the actions of ActiveX Controls. Additionally, Microsoft uses ActiveX as a virtual machine to run and integrate Java applets in Internet Explorer. For more information on ActiveX, see Chapter 23, "Using Active Platform to Enhance Your Web Site."

To incorporate ActiveX Controls into your Web pages, include a tag to an existing ActiveX Control in your HTML document, and make the control available for those who want to view your Web page. Just including an ActiveX Control in your Web page will probably not give you the desired effect for your page. To make the control do many operations will probably require that you write code in JavaScript or VBScript.

Currently, ActiveX can only be used on Internet Explorer and on a PC. Unlike Java, ActiveX does not have the limitation to prevent it from becoming a security hazard. More on security is discussed in the "Security" section later in this chapter.

Scripting Languages

Although HTML enables Web page developers to change the layout and format of Web pages, it does not support user interaction except with hyperlinks. User interaction can be implemented via a variety of methods such as ActiveX, Java, and scripting languages. A *scripting language* is text that can be written inside an HTML document.

Probably the most important feature of a scripting language is the capability to do processing on the client computer instead of the server. For example, if a user is prompted to type in registration information for purchasing a product and leaves a required field blank, without scripting, the information would be sent to the server. The server would recognize the information as incorrect and send back an appropriate response. This process wastes time and resources. It wastes the resources of the server and the bandwidth of the transmission line.

With scripting, certain responses can be immediate and the server and connection do not have to be used. A script could make sure that the information is in the correct format so that the server would only have to validate certain types of data (such as logon name and password). More than just saving time, scripting also is useful in integrating Java applets and ActiveX Controls, enabling these components to be used more effectively.

There are several differences between scripting and Java applets and ActiveX Controls. Scripts are an interpreted language listed in a text file, while ActiveX Controls are compiled programs with tags in the HTML script. Java applets can be compiled programs or intepreted bytecode, which is harder to read than a script but entirely possible. This means that users can see what is occurring in the code of scripts, so validating passwords with scripting is not recommended and should be done on the server.

Also, in many cases, scripting is an easier and quicker way to implement certain functions than using Java applets or ActiveX Controls. Additionally, access to where scripting languages can write is different than applets and ActiveX Controls. ActiveX Controls can read and write to the entire area that the user can access. Java applets do not have the capability to write to your hard drive at all. Scripting languages can write to your hard drive in a limited fashion. Both Internet Explorer and Netscape Navigator enable writing to a single file. (See the section "Magic Cookies" later in this chapter.)

> **CAUTION**
>
> Your browser determines where scripting languages can write. If you have a browser from an unreliable source, it could read or write to your local domain. Also, unreliable plug-ins could give scripting languages the same capability. To prevent against these potential risks, make certain that your software provider is reputable.

The following sections describe two of the prevalent scripting languages for Web pages.

JavaScript   JavaScript, created by Netscape with contributions from Sun, resembles Java code stylistically with some exceptions. Because JavaScript is interpreted, it does not do strong type casting. It is object based, and variables do not have to be explicitly declared. JavaScript is support by Netscape Navigator and Sun HotJava, while Internet Explorer supports JScript, Microsoft's version of JavaScript. Using JavaScript is free and information on the syntax and how to use it are available with links from the Netscape home page at **http:// home.netscape.com**.

VBScript   VBScript, like the name implies, is a subset of the Visual Basic (VB) programming language. VBScript includes variants as the only data type, has no capability to read or write to files except on the server and Cookie files, and there are cosmetic differences. For information on the syntax and specifics, see **http://www.microsoft.com/vbscript**.

VBScript is only implemented in Internet Explorer. Microsoft has just released Microsoft Script Debugger which is currently the only development environment for both VBScript and JavaScript.

Choosing a Scripting Language   Deciding which script to use and whether to use Java applets or ActiveX Controls (or both) depends on your particular situation. Currently, Java applets and JavaScript provides for the best, most universal solution. JavaScript can run on Internet Explorer, Netscape Navigator, and Sun HotJava, while VBScript can only be used with Internet Explorer. Java can run on many operating systems, such as Windows, Macintosh, and UNIX. ActiveX technology can currently run on only the Windows operating systems.

If your needs are for a corporate intranet, you can choose the best option to meet the needs of your existing system. For example, if your company has many Visual Basic programmers and runs Windows exclusively, then VBScript and ActiveX Controls might be the best solution.

Magic Cookies

Magic Cookies, or Cookies, are data packets that are sent to your browser from a World Wide Web Server and stored in a file. There are two chief uses for Cookies.

Web sites sometimes use Cookie information to store information about you from visit to visit. This data—such as how many times you have visited a particular Web site or information that stores your preferences so that a particular Web page is customized to suit your needs—typically stores the state of information for a particular Web page and is stored locally on your machine. The Web site can access your Cookie file and use the information from your previous visits.

Another use is to maintain information about the state of your computer for scripting. Information can be stored on your machine instead of the server to make the process move faster. For example, a Web site that uses multiple pages for registration can use Cookies to store important information so that the newly loaded page does not have to query information back from the server.

You can instruct both Internet Explorer and Netscape Navigator to produce a warning message when your Cookie file is going to be used.

> **CAUTION**
>
> Do not edit your `cookies.txt` file manually. Afterward, you could have problems when viewing Web sites that use this information.

To enable a Cookie warning for Internet Explorer, perform the following steps:

1. Choose View, Options.
2. On the Advanced tab, click the Warn before Accepting Cookies check box. (When cookies are sent, you will be notified.)

To enable a Cookie warning for Netscape Navigator, perform the following steps:

1. Choose Options, Network Preference.
2. On the Protocol tab, click the Accepting a Cookie check box.

N O T E   Cookie files for different Web browsers are stored separately. Therefore, information saved when visiting a Web site with Internet Explorer, for example, cannot be accessed when viewing the same site through Netscape Navigator. ▪

Security

Making sure that transactions across the Internet are secure is an important issue if the Internet is going to become a more effective means of communication. For secure transactions to occur, information needs to be able to be passed securely and identities on both ends of the transaction need to be verified. The integrity of the data needs to be certified as well.

There are additional security concerns for the users of Web browsers. Users need to be able to trust that the data sent to them will not have a detrimental effect on their computers. There are dangers that threaten both Internet and intranet users, such as levels of access to sites. Finally, there are security concerns that are similar to Internet problems, but ultimately unique to intranet users. Chapter 25, "Implementing Internet Security," provides a broader overview of the Internet security.

Secure Internet Transactions   There are many requirements for assuring secure Internet transactions. First, both parties' identities must be verified. Both Internet Explorer and Netscape Navigator support identity verification with *site certificate support* and *client-side certificates*. These digital certificates ensure that the entity on the other end of the transaction is the person or organization it claims to be. With this identity verification, sites can support unique pages for each user because each person has a distinct identifier.

The second element of secure transactions is the protection of data so that others cannot view it. This security can be achieved with data encryption. Encryption is a mechanism that converts data so that only the holder of the key can decrypt it. The encryption process uses a mathematical procedure that, without the key, would take years to solve with the most powerful computers in the world. (The length of time actually depends on how many bytes is used in the encryption.)

Standards for encryption are still in a state of flux. Both Internet Explorer and Netscape Navigator support some form of data encryption. Microsoft is developing CryptoAPI, which enables programmers to use encryption in programs without having to write the program that does the encryption. Also, CryptoAPI will have a common interface to make interaction between processes easier.

▶ **See** "An Introduction to Cryptography," **p. 762**

▶ **See** "The Microsoft Security Framework," **p. 769**

Preventing Damage to Your Data The three main concerns for data security on a client machine are scripting languages, Java applets, and ActiveX Controls. These programs running on a Web browser could perform malicious actions if preventive measures are not taken. A program might read or overwrite data that it should not have access to. There are several mechanisms to prevent malicious actions by programs running on a Web browser.

N O T E HTML does not have access to other files on your computer.

One strategy that is currently implemented for both Java and scripting languages on both Internet Explorer and Netscape Navigator is to *sandbox* the problem. *Sandboxing* means to prevent certain actions, such as reading and writing to disk, from taking place except on the server from which the data originates. Sandboxing prevents the most dangerous malicious actions, but reduces the power of the application considerably.

The Java programming language allows for reading and writing to disk, but Web browsers' virtual Java machines do not let the applet read or write except to the server of origin. Therefore, no compromise of data can occur. There are a few exceptions to this rule. The following data can be read from a client machine:

- The version of Java that is running on the client
- The name and version of the operating system
- The character delimiter used to separate files and paths
- The end of line character

It would be difficult to use this data in a malicious manner. The only way for Java applets to create problems is by using up client resources, such as wasting CPU cycles and bandwidth across the network. These problems could be easily rectified by stopping the applet, and no permanent damage to the client machine would occur.

Browsers use a similar strategy for scripting languages. Scripting languages are restricted to where they can read and write. Unlike Java, scripting languages can write to Cookies. It is possible that a scripting language could corrupt a Cookie file, but the possible damage is minimal.

Intranet Security   Verification of controls in an intranet environment is different from that of the Internet. On the Internet, a company's reputation stands behind the product. The company can make certain that its product has not been tampered with by instituting the proper internal controls. Customers can verify that they are receiving data directly from the company and no one has altered it. No such guarantee occurs with an internally developed ActiveX Control or Java applet. Without the proper internal controls, a rouge programmer could cripple a company by corrupting or stealing data.

Active Server Pages

Active Server Pages enables a Web site to custom make Web pages for their users. The advantage of Active Server Pages is that the page is generated on the server side so that the user browsing cannot see the underlying functions that make the Web page work. Remember that the source of a Web page can be viewed.

Active Server Pages is ideal for a Web site that wants to restrict its data displayed, depending on a user's access level or preferences. A user on the client browser enters a logon name and password. The server validates the user and determines the appropriate information to be displayed on the page. The information shown may be totally different from that of another user, although the URL is identical for both. For more information about Active Server Pages, see Chapter 23, "Using Active Platform to Enhance Your Web Site."

VRML

Virtual Reality Modeling Language (VRML) is a standard for the animation of geometric shapes. It enables the viewing and manipulation of three dimensional objects via Web pages with a special VRML browser. Users can change the perspective of the animation. For example, a user could walk through a three-dimensional building. The user could also manipulate the position of the objects in the animation.

Viewing VRML   VRML is an interpreted, not compiled, language, so it must be viewed by special Web browsers. There are a variety of VRML browsers, including some plug-ins to Navigator and Internet Explorer. Navigator 3.0 comes with the Live3D plug-in, while Internet Explorer is packaged with VRML 1.0 ActiveX Control. These browsers and plug-ins can be found by searching for VRML with the Web search engine of your choice.

Unlike certain other items that can be viewed with a browser, there is no security danger. The only data that is downloaded is the script that generates the VRML and the graphics. The VRML browser does the actual compilation that determines how the picture will be rendered and how the user can move through the rendered world.

Creating VRML   As mentioned above, VRML is an interpreted language, which means that you can write VRML with an ASCII text editor, but it would be a time-consuming process due to the complexity of the VRML. This problem will be exacerbated in the near future with all of the new features of VRML.

The solution to this problem is a software package that can help users generate VRML sites. There are a number of such packages, which vary greatly in price and quality. Use your favorite Web search engine to find the latest VRML design packages.

Utility and Practicality of VRML   Currently, VRML is not as practical as other means of presenting graphics to Web users. There is not yet sufficient bandwidth for VRML to load quickly enough to make it an efficient means to display moving pictures.

One might wonder how VRML could be used for purposes other than games. There are a wide variety of potential applications. Two examples are selling real estate and producing assembly instructions. Currently, real estate brokers use the World Wide Web to sell property more effectively. When VRML can be displayed more quickly, real estate brokers will be able to display entire houses in VRML, so customers can move throughout the house rather than just seeing an outside picture of the house. Products that require assembly could be explained easily with a VRML demonstration of putting the product together. Users could change their perspective and see how all the pieces fit together.

History and Other Browsers

Considering its wide acceptance in businesses and homes, it is remarkable that the World Wide Web has only been in existence since 1991. The Web was first conceived in 1989 when Tim Berners-Lee proposed a system to exchange information in various formats that could be viewed on different platforms for the exchange of data between high-energy physicists from around the globe. The World Wide Web's growth in scope and users can be traced to its ease of use and the broad, valuable source of information that it provides.

Although this chapter chiefly deals with Internet Explorer and Netscape Navigator, there are many browsers available on the market today. Many have a special niche, such as a VRML browser or a browser for a particular operating system. The following are some of the more notable browsers available:

- **HotJava**—Sun produces the HotJava browser. It is in direct competition with Internet Explorer and Netscape Navigator, but does not yet have the functionality of either. For more information, go to **http://www.javasoft.com/products/HotJava/**.

- **Notes Web Navigator**—Lotus makes Notes Web Navigator, a browser that is integrated with the Lotus Notes product. The Lotus Web site is **http://www.lotus.com/comms**.

- **PointCast**—PointCast is a new company that integrates its Web browser into a screen saver. PointCast extracts information from around the Web based on the request you make and places it on your screen as a screen saver. See **http://www.pointcast.com** for more information.

- **PowerBrowser**—Oracle makes PowerBrowser, which integrates a server program with your Web browser so you can list Web pages on the Internet. Oracle's site is **http://www.oracle.com**.

■ **Mosaic**—One of the first Web browsers, NCSA Mosaic is still available from **http:// www.ncsa.uiuc.edu/SDG/Software/Mosaic/**.

The Future of Web Browsers

Both Microsoft and Netscape are moving browser technology to the desktop. Internet Explorer 4.0 will be tightly integrated with the user's on-screen computer desktop so that information from all sources—the World Wide Web, an intranet, or users' hard drives—can be accessed and managed with the Web browser. It can then become the primary information retrieval application, and be used instead of My Computer or Explorer to access local files and documents.

Netscape Communicator will be a package of integrated components for many forms of communication and information access. Communicator will have a common editing environment for e-mail, Web, and newsgroup documents. A single address book will be able to be used for e-mail and Netscape's real-time collaboration software. Communicator will also include a calendar and scheduling program, in addition to the Navigator Web browser. This version of Navigator will support ActiveX technology.

Microsoft has additional plans for Internet Explorer 4.0. It plans to have an integrated Web view of all information, not just Web pages. Internet Explorer 4.0 will have enhanced multimedia capabilities, including DirectX and Dynamic HTML. DirectX is a common set of API calls that enables software to make the same calls independent of the device it is calling. DirectX will enable 3-D, direct draw, and picture updates to be faster.

Dynamic HTML enables users to edit the HTML in a Web page that they are viewing. It also can be used to quickly animate graphics. For example, by changing the position of an object on a page, it will move across the page. Dynamic HTML allows the HTML page to be altered at a regular interval so that the object moves across the page. Digital Wallet, which will enable secure commercial transactions over the Internet (e.g., credit card transactions), will be part of Internet Explorer 4.0.

There will also be a large number of vendors supporting ActiveX technology. Microsoft has announced that Visual Basic 5 (VB5), a graphical user interface programming language, will have control creation abilities, enabling the user to make ActiveX Controls with VB5.

Web browsers will move from computers to other appliances. Already, there are televisions that have Web browsing capabilities. Eventually it is possible that cars or microwaves could have Internet connections. Users could find directions or e-mail a repair service indicating they have a problem with a product.

The world of Web browsing is still in its infancy. With increasing communication speeds and less costly software and hardware, the power of the Web will only increase.

From Here...

This chapter has explained how to use both Netscape Navigator and Internet Explorer. You have learned how to browse and use e-mail and newsgroups with both packages. This chapter also explains some of the major components that constitute Web pages. To use these components more effectively and to understand more about the Internet and intranets, consult the following chapters:

- For information on the Internet and intranets, see Chapter 16, "The BackOffice I-Net Toolbox."

- If you are interested in Web page development, check out Microsoft's development software, Microsoft FrontPage 97, in Chapter 20, "Using Microsoft FrontPage 97."

- For additional information on Active Server Pages and the Active Platform in general, see Chapter 23, "Using Active Platform to Enhance Your Web Site."

- For more in-depth information on Internet security, see Chapter 25, "Implementing Internet Security."

Part
IV
Ch
19

## CHAPTER 20

Using Microsoft FrontPage 97

by Allen Carson

FrontPage 97 is essentially a suite of programs that provides the Web site Administrator and authors all the tools necessary to create and manage Web sites for private or commercial purposes. FrontPage 97 consists of the following four main components:

- FrontPage 97 Explorer
- FrontPage 97 Editor
- FrontPage 97 Server
- FrontPage 97 server extensions

Components and resource requirements

Learn what the basic FrontPage 97 components are and what minimum hardware and software configurations are needed to use them.

Install FrontPage 97 and creating an initial Web site

Find out how simple it is to install FrontPage 97 and how to use the Corporate Presence Wizard to create a small to medium sized Web site.

Explore and customize your new Web site

Find out how you can use the FrontPage Explorer to examine the various links, directory structures, and file details that make up your Web site. Learn how to use the FrontPage Editor and the To Do List to customize your Web site to fit your specific needs.

Administer and maintain your Web site

See how the various features and utilities included with FrontPage 97 can be used to administer the daily activities of your Web site and to maintain your site to accommodate your changing business environment.

FrontPage 97 Explorer

The FrontPage 97 Explorer is the tool you use to create, configure, and manage your Web site. It has a graphical interface with two main views to help you navigate your Web site. The Folder view displays an overview of your Web site file structure, and the Hyperlink view gives you the layout of your pages with the links so you can easily visualize how users will browse them. The following are some of the FrontPage 97 Explorer features:

- Wizards and templates, to create entire Web sites or to help create many commonly seen types of Web pages
- Automatic adjustment of links when pages are moved or renamed
- The capability for many different users to modify the same Web site from different locations
- A To Do List, which helps manage the tasks necessary for creating and managing a Web site
- Moving and hosting Web sites or pages to servers that may be running on different platforms
- Maintenance and repair of the external links on a Web site

FrontPage 97 Editor

The FrontPage 97 Editor is the tool used to create and modify the pages of your Web site. It is a graphical editor with an interface like a word processor. You do not have to possess an understanding of Hypertext Markup Language (HTML) to use the FrontPage 97 Editor, but if you do have such knowledge, you can use the FrontPage 97 Editor to insert and edit raw HTML data. The editor displays the page you are editing in the same format as an HTML browser. The following are some of the features of the FrontPage Editor:

- What-you-see-is-what-you-get (WYSIWYG) editing of HTML forms, including framesets, images, forms, WebBot components, and hyperlinks
- Drag-and-drop editing of most file types
- WebBot components, which automate many of the more common Web page functions
- Support for client-side and server-side image maps
- Automatic conversion of Rich Text Format (RTF) and text (TXT) files to HTML
- Automatic conversion of many image file types to Graphics Interchange Format (GIF) or Joint Photographic Experts Group (JPEG or JPG)
- Easy image manipulation and placement
- Multilevel undo for all Web page editing operations

FrontPage 97 Server

The Personal Web Server included with FrontPage 97 could be used as a server for your Web sites, but that is not its real purpose. It is provided mostly as a means to test your Web pages in an environment as close as possible to a fully functional Web server. The FrontPage 97 Explorer and Editor make use of the Personal Web Server to access and save your Web sites and pages.

FrontPage 97 Server Extensions

The FrontPage 97 server extensions are provided for a variety of commercial Web servers so the WebBots and automation capabilities of FrontPage 97 can be used on servers other than the one included in FrontPage 97. The servers supported with FrontPage 97 server extensions include the following:

- **NCSA**—Extensions are available for versions 1.5a and 1.5.2, but not for version 1.5.1.
- **CERN**—Version 3.0.
- **Apache**—Extensions are available for versions 1.0.5 and 1.1.1.
- **Netscape**—Currently, extensions are available for Netscape Commerce Server 1.12, Netscape Communications Server 1.12, Netscape Enterprise 2.0, and Netscape FastTrack 2.0.
- **O'Reilly and Associates WebSite**
- **Microsoft's Internet Information Server**—Extensions are available for Versions 2.0 and higher.

For a complete list of servers supported through the server extensions, see the Microsoft site at **http://www.microsoft.com/frontpage/softlib/current.htm**. It is advisable to check this location often as the list of supported servers rapidly changes.

Getting Started with FrontPage 97

The easiest way to get started with FrontPage 97 is to use one of the wizards or templates to create a base Web site and then customize it to suit your purposes. First, however, review the resources and installation procedure required for FrontPage 97 described in this section.

Resource Requirements

In order for FrontPage 97 to properly operate and provide reasonable performance, a minimum hardware and software configuration is required. Fortunately, the list of required minimum components is very small and is limited to random access memory (RAM), hard disk space, operating system versions, and communications protocols. Recommended configurations that exceed the minimum configurations are also indicated where appropriate. The minimum (and recommended) configurations are as follows:

- 8M RAM (16M recommended) if using FrontPage 97 with Windows 95

- 16M RAM (24M recommended) if using FrontPage 97 with Windows NT
- 12M free disk space (includes Personal Web Server and the server extensions)
- Microsoft Windows 95 or Windows NT (version 3.51 or higher)
- Winsock compliant version 1.1 (32-bit) Transfer Control Protocol/Internet Protocol (TCP/IP) stack

N O T E   Although only 12M of disk space is required for FrontPage 97 and the Personal Web Server, you will need much more additional disk space for the content of the Web sites that you will create. ■

▶ **See** "System Requirements," **p. 127**

Installing FrontPage

To install FrontPage, run the installation utility program SETUP.EXE. This will start the InstallShield Wizard to guide you through the setup process. FrontPage 97 will first ask you to specify a destination directory. The default is FrontPage on the disk where Windows is installed. You can accept this default or specify another location. FrontPage 97 then asks you for a directory in which to store the Web Server files and the Web site content you will create. The default directory is FrontPage 97 Webs. You will then be asked to select either the Standard installation or Custom installation.

The Standard installation installs the client software along with the Personal Web Server and any necessary server extensions. The installation software detects when you are running a Web server other than the Personal Web Server and attempts to install extensions for that server. If a server is detected, it will be listed along with the extensions available for it.

You will then be asked to specify a folder or group for the FrontPage 97 icons. The default is Microsoft FrontPage 97. At this point, FrontPage 97 will display a screen summarizing the installation parameters that you have selected along with a confirmation button. Once you click the Next button, the installation proceeds automatically.

The Custom installation enables you to install the following software:

- **Client software**—This is the FrontPage 97 Explorer and Editor.
- **Personal Web server**—FrontPage must use a Web server to function. If you already have a Web server on your system, FrontPage 97 will probably be able to work with it. If this is the case, you will need to install the correct server extensions to enable FrontPage 97 to function correctly.
- **Server extensions**—The FrontPage 97 installation program will detect what server extensions are needed if possible and install them. If you want to have this done automatically, it is important to have the server installed and running before installing FrontPage 97.

▶ **See** "Internet Information Server," **p. 480**

The difference between Standard and Custom installation is that Custom will allow you to choose the components that you want to install. It is recommended for advanced users only.

Using the Corporate Presence Wizard

The Corporate Presence Wizard will create a sample Web site for a small or medium sized company. It will ask the user several questions to help customize the Web site. To use the FrontPage 97 Wizard to create the corporate Web site, perform the following steps:

1. When you start the FrontPage 97 Explorer, it presents the Getting Started with Microsoft FrontPage dialog box, as shown in Figure 20.1. You can open an existing Web or create a new Web by Importing, using a wizard, or creating a blank FrontPage Web. Alternatively, if FrontPage 97 is already open, close any open Webs, and choose File, New, FrontPage 97 Web.

FIG. 20.1

The Getting Started with Microsoft FrontPage dialog is shown by default when the FrontPage 97 Explorer is started. You may disable it by de-selecting the Show Getting Started Dialog checkbox. It may be re-enabled later through the General tab on the Options dialog.

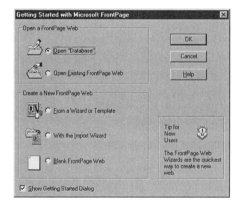

2. You will be given a list of Wizards from which to choose. For this example, choose the Corporate Presence Wizard.

3. You will be asked to provide a server in which to place the created Web site. If you do not have authoring permission on any servers, you can elect to place the Web site in a disk folder. There is an option for specifying the Secure Sockets Layer (SSL). See more about this in the section "Security Issues" later in this chapter. You must also provide a name for the Web site that you are creating.

4. FrontPage 97 will ask you to specify a name and password for creating this Web site.

5. After an introduction screen, you are asked to specify which main pages you would like included on your Web site. The selections that you may choose from are Home (required), What's New, Products/Services, Table of Contents, Feedback Form, and Search Form. For this example, select all possible pages.

6. FrontPage 97 then asks what topics you want for the home page. The Selections that you may choose from are Introduction, Mission Statement, Company Profile, and Contact Information. Again, select all options.

7. You are then asked for the What's New page topics. The allowed options are Web Changes, Press Releases, and Articles and Reviews. Select them all.

8. FrontPage 97 then enables you to specify the number of products and services your company provides. Use the default, three products and three services, for this example.

Part

IV

Ch

20

9. You can then select options for each products or services page. The options for products are Product Image, Pricing Information, and Information Request Form. The options for services are Capabilities List, Reference Accounts, and Information Request Form. For this example, select all options.

10. FrontPage 97 then asks what information you would like for your form page to ask. Available choices are Full Name, Job Title, Company Affiliation, Mailing Address, Telephone Number, Fax Number, and E-mail Address. Select all items.

11. You then need to specify how you want the information to be stored: tab-delimited or Web-page format. For this example, choose the tab-delimited format.

12. FrontPage 97 then enables you to specify the options for the table of contents page. Available options are Keep Page List Up-To-Date Automatically, Show Pages Not Linked Into the Web, and Use Bullets for Top-Level Pages. Select Keep Page List Up-to-Date Automatically and Use Bullets for Top-Level Pages.

13. You then specify what items you would like to appear at the top and bottom of each page. Options for the top of the page are Your Company's Logo, Page Title, and Links to Your Main Web Pages. Options for the bottom of the page are Links to Your Main Web Pages, E-mail Address of Your Webmaster, Copyright Notice, and Date Page was Last Modified. For this example, check all options.

14. FrontPage 97 then enables you to choose a style for your Web site. Style options are Plain, Conservative, Flashy, and Cool. Use Flashy for this example.

15. You can then select the color scheme for your Web site. For this example, use the default options.

16. FrontPage 97 then enables you to include the "Under Construction" sign on your pages. Do not include it for this example.

17. FrontPage 97 then needs your company-specific information. Use the defaults for this example.

18. You are asked whether or not to show the To Do List. For this example, show the To Do List.

19. Click the Finish button. FrontPage 97 creates the pages for the Corporate Presence Web site.

Now that you have created the corporate Web site, it will be used as a basis for the examples in this chapter. Continue on to the next section for a quick overview of how to use the FrontPage 97 Editor.

Using the FrontPage 97 Explorer

Now that the Web site has been created, you can use the FrontPage 97 Explorer to navigate through your Web site and organize its files and links. The Explorer is also used to maintain the permissions and properties of your Web site. (Permissions and properties are maintained through the Web Settings, Permissions, and Options dialog boxes. These dialogs will be covered in the section "Other FrontPage Management Tools.") FrontPage 97 Explorer has two main views on a Web site: the Hyperlink view and the Folder view.

The Hyperlink View   To show the Hyperlink view, click the Hyperlink view button on the toolbar, or select View, Hyperlink from the menu. The Hyperlink button on the toolbar is indicated in Figure 20.2. This view shows the relationships of the links in the Web site. As depicted in Figure 20.2, the Tree pane (left side) shows the Web site in a tree structure. By clicking the plus sign next to a page, the page is expanded to show all of the links on that page. Once a page is opened, it can be closed again by clicking the minus sign next to it. The various icons used for each page are descriptive of the type of page or link with which they are associated.

FIG. 20.2

The FrontPage 97 Hyperlink view shows the relationships of the links in the Web site. The Tree pane on the left can be expanded or collapsed by clicking the plus and minus signs next to the icons.

Hyperlink view button

Show FrontPage 97 Editor button

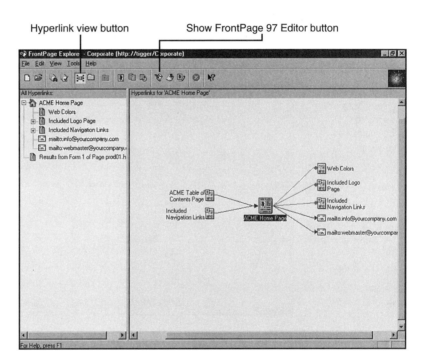

TROUBLESHOOTING

Where is the root of my Web site? I can't find it. For the Outline view to identify the root of your Web site, the URL of the page must be `index.htm`. If you import this Web site from a UNIX server, the root of the Web site will likely be `index.html`, and FrontPage 97 will not correctly identify it. To rename the file, switch to the folder view, right-click the file, and select Rename from the pop-up menu, or select Edit, Rename from the menu.

Part
IV

Ch
20

The Link pane (right side) shows the selected page in the center of the display, along with the links to and from that page. Links displayed in blue indicate the linked page is visible, while links displayed in gray indicate the page is hidden. For a complete discussion of hidden pages and their advantages, see the "Taking Advantage of Hidden Directories" section later in this chapter. You can use the toolbar buttons to chose whether or not to display links to images, multiple links, or links within the page. When you select a page on Tree pane, it is centered in the Link pane.

The Folder View   The Folder view displays the directory structure of the files in your Web site (see Figure 20.3). This view allows you to easily find a specific file and view its location within your Web site. The Folder view supports the moving of files by drag-and-drop, and will automatically update the links between files helping to prevent broken links.

FIG. 20.3

The FrontPage 97 Folder view utilizes the Directory pane and the Summary pane to display the organization of the files in your Web site and provide detailed information about each one.

Directory pane ———

Summary pane ———

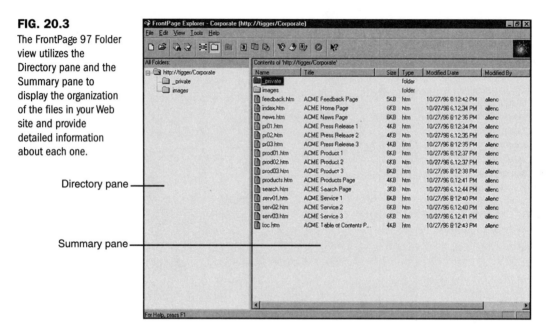

The Directory pane displays the directory structure of the Web site. The Summary pane lists the files in the selected directory, along with several columns of information about that file. The columns that can be displayed in the Summary pane are the following:

- **Name**—The file name that the item is stored under
- **Title**—The title of the page that was set in the editor
- **Size**—The size of the file
- **Type**—The type of file, commonly .HTM, .HTML, .GIF, or .JPG.
- **Modified Date**—The last time and date the file was modified
- **Modified By**—The user who last modified the file
- **Page Uniform Resource Locator (URL)**—The URL of the file (normally, the same as the file name)
- **Comments**—The comments as entered in the Properties dialog box

To open a folder, you can either single-click the folder in the Directory pane, or double-click the folder in the Summary pane. A document can be opened by right-clicking it and selecting Open or Open With in the pop-up menu.

The To Do List FrontPage 97's To Do List provides the Webmaster with a tool to organize the task necessary to set up and maintain a Web site. When the Corporate Presence Wizard created this Web site, one of the things that it did was to create a To Do List to help inform you of the tasks necessary to customize your Web site. To open the To Do List, choose Tools, Show To Do List. This displays the FrontPage To Do List dialog box that displays all of the entries in the list (see Figure 20.4). The To Do List is one of the features of FrontPage 97 that will allow you to keep track of project tasks that can be assigned to different persons. Some of the wizards and FrontPage 97 Editor commands will make additions to the To Do List.

FIG. 20.4

The FrontPage To Do List dialog box displays information about each task entry in the To Do List. Any changes made to the sort order and column sizes are lost when the dialog is closed.

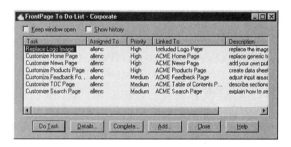

The FrontPage To Do List dialog box displays the following information on each task:

- **Task**—The task to be done.
- **Assigned To**—Who the task is assigned to.
- **Priority**—Priority of the task (high, medium, or low).
- **Completed**—Shows the status of the task, but will not display unless the Show History option is selected.
- **Linked To**—The page with which the task is associated.
- **Description**—A description of the task.

It is possible to sort any of the columns by clicking the column heading. The FrontPage To Do List dialog box enables you to take the following actions:

- **Do Task**—Opens the FrontPage 97 Editor with the page associated with the task.
- **Details**—Shows the details associated with the task.
- **Complete**—Marks the task as done.
- **Add**—Adds a new task to the list. This opens the Add To Do Task dialog box. With this dialog box, you can add a new task to the list, specifying a person to assign it to, a priority, and a description of the task.

The following are the two option check boxes on the FrontPage To Do List dialog box:

■ **Keep Window Open**—Keeps the window open while you are performing a task.

■ **Show History**—Toggles the display of the Completed Column and shows tasks that are marked as completed.

Figure 20.4 shows the To Do List after the Corporate Presence Wizard has finished. Note that the Wizard has made entries into the list, showing some of the tasks necessary to customize the Web site it created into a site that is customized for your company. Each task may be reassigned to another person by clicking the Details button and entering another user's name. The Details dialog box may also be used to change the priority or change the description of the task. By keeping the To Do List up to date, you should be able to quickly view the status of any of the Web sites under your control. For an example of using the To Do List to complete a task, see the section "Using the FrontPage 97 Editor."

Spelling Checker   FrontPage 97 implements a cross-file spelling checker. The spelling checker may be invoked on a single page by selecting Tools, Spelling in the FrontPage 97 Editor; or it may be run on the entire Web site by pressing the Spell Check button on the toolbar or by choosing Tools, Spelling in the FrontPage 97 Explorer. When you invoke the spelling checker, the Spelling dialog box is displayed. This dialog allows you to add pages with spelling errors on the To Do List.

Verify Links   One of the most difficult chores facing Webmasters is that of verifying all of the external links from a Web site. To help accomplish this, FrontPage 97 includes the Verify Links tool. To start this tool, choose Tools, Verify Links. This displays the Verify Links dialog box, which contains all the external links from the Web site as well as the following information about each of these external links:

■ **Status**—The status of the link, which is initially a yellow dot followed by a question mark (meaning unverified)

■ **URL**—The actual address of the link

■ **Linked From**—The title of the page followed by the URL in parentheses that contains the link

When you start the verify task, which—depending on the size of the Web site and the speed of your connection—may take several minutes, the Verify button changes to a Stop button, and FrontPage 97 attempts to verify each link. As the links are verified, the status is marked. Correct links are marked with a green dot followed by the word *OK*, and broken links are marked by a red dot followed by the word *Broken*. At the bottom of the dialog box, a percent complete indication is given. After verification is complete, a summary of broken links is given.

The Verify Links dialog box enables you to take any of the following three actions to correct any identified problems:

■ **Edit the link**—Clicking the Edit Link button displays a dialog box showing the incorrect link and all of the pages on which it occurs. You are enabled to edit the link with the option of changing all of the occurrences of that link. After the link has been changed, its status is changed to a gray dot followed by the word *Edited*.

■ **Edit the page**—Clicking the Edit Page opens the page in the FrontPage 97 Editor.

■ **Add a task to the To Do List**—Clicking the Add <u>T</u>ask adds a task entry to the To Do List and marks the status of the link with a gray dot followed by the words *To Do*.

After the links have been edited, the list should be verified again.

Recalculate Links   The Recalculate Links command updates the display for the current Web site in which you are working. This enables you to view changes that have been made by other authors. It also updates the text indices that are used by the search bots. Depending on the size of the Web site, this may take several minutes.

Using the FrontPage 97 Editor

To illustrate some of the basic ways the FrontPage 97 Editor can be used, you will use the items added by the Wizard in the To Do List to customize the Corporate Presence example. Display the To Do List by clicking the Show To Do List button. To replace the logo image, perform the following steps:

1. Right-click the image, and select Image Properties from the pop-up menu.
2. You will be enabled to enter a path to the new image or browse for a new image.
3. Clicking Browse brings up the Image dialog box. This dialog box enables you to select images from the current Web site, a file path, or the FrontPage 97 clip art library. The library has images in several categories.
4. Once you have made the changes, click the Save button to save them in the Web server.
5. FrontPage 97 will ask you if you want to mark the task on the To Do List as done. Since the task has been completed, you should select <u>Y</u>es to mark it completed.
6. If the Show History box is checked, the completed item will be displayed with the completion date in the Completed column.

To customize the home page and remove that item from the To Do List, perform the following steps:

1. Highlight the Customize Home Page task, and click the Do Task button. This item indicates that there is some generic text that was added by the Corporate Presence Wizard which needs to be replaced by something more descriptive of your Web site.
2. FrontPage 97 will open the home page in the FrontPage 97 Editor. The To Do List has a link to the page that needs to be changed. Note that it is not necessary for you to look for the page; FrontPage 97 will open it automatically for you.
3. The Corporate Presence Wizard put comment text in each area describing what kind of text should be there (see Figure 20.5). You should delete the comment text and replace it with the text you want. When the cursor is moved over the comment text, the WebBot icon is displayed. Right-clicking while the WebBot icon is present will display the WebBot pop-up menu.

FIG. 20.5

A generic Web page is displayed by the FrontPage 97 Editor in which the Corporate Presence Wizard has inserted generic comment text. This needs to be replaced by company-specific text as the page is customized.

WedBot icon ─┘

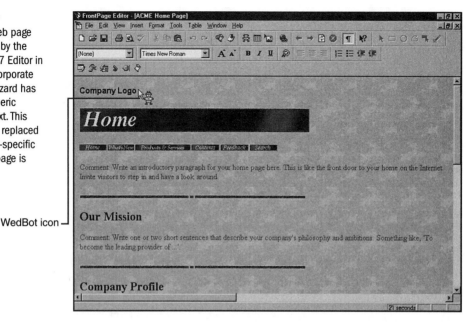

4. You should continue through the To Do List, and complete all the items specified by the Wizard.

These two items in the To Do List were used to illustrate the way that the different components of FrontPage 97 work together to help you administer changes and maintain your Web site. The other items in the list are handled in a similar manner and are left as an exercise for the reader.

Inside FrontPage 97

This section describes some of the internal workings of FrontPage 97. Some of the areas that will be covered include the function of the Root Web, how the Smart HTML engine works, the way the directories are laid out, and how to make use of the Wizards that are included with FrontPage 97. This section will also cover server issues such as what the server extensions are, and some security topics. Also covered are file management and version control tools, along with more advanced topics including templates, WebBots, scripts, and database connectivity.

Although it is not always necessary to understand how FrontPage 97 works to use it, familiarity with these mechanisms will explain some of the behaviors of FrontPage 97. This can be especially important if you intend to use WebBots on servers that do not have server extensions installed.

The Root Web

The root Web is the FrontPage 97 Web site that is always provided by the server. To access this Web site, supply the name of the server without any Web name specified. You can modify this Web site, but you must be aware that if you update the server, it may be overwritten. All FrontPage 97 Web sites are considered children of the root Web site and may inherit permissions from it. If you have no need to provide different security schemes, you should set the desired security on the root Web site and have all Web sites inherit that setup.

The types of permissions that may be set are the users and computers that have Administer, Author, and Browse permissions. If all your Web sites can have the same security scheme, then it would be easier for you to manage the security by setting it in one place and having all Web sites inherit their security from it. Otherwise, you will need to set each Web site's security individually.

SHTML Engine

The Smart HTML (SHTML) engine is the component of FrontPage 97 that makes the WebBots work. On Windows NT 3.51 and Windows NT 4.0, the SmartHTML engine resides in the `_vti_bin` directory of each Web site.

WebBots are one of the more powerful features of FrontPage 97. They are active components that work in conjunction with the server to add interactive content to your Web pages. Normally such interactive content would require scripting on the Web page, an executable that would run on the server, and connectivity software (such as a Common Gateway Interface (CGI) program) to connect the two. WebBots allow authors to create rich interactive content without the need for sophisticated programming techniques.

When the editor saves a page to the server, the server extensions scan the incoming page to determine if there are any WebBot items on the page. If there are, the server parses the page and saves a copy with the SmartHTML components replaced by the HTML generated by the WebBot.

If you look at the raw HTML in a page that contains WebBots, you will notice the `<!--VERMEER` tags. These denote the WebBot component parameters.

FrontPage 97 allows for two versions of WebBots: *static* and *dynamic*. Static WebBots do not change when the page is fetched by a browser. A dynamic WebBot is one that must change each time the page is fetched. An access counter is a good example. Allowing for two types of components does not force the server to parse each WebBot every time the page is browsed; thus, there are significant processing time savings.

The dynamic WebBot components are primarily used for database updates and queries.

The Directory Structure

When you install FrontPage 97, you set the directory for it to install under. During the install process, it creates several directories under the install directory for its own purposes.

The \FRONTPAGE97 directory structure is as follows:

- **\BIN**—This directory stores the executables for the FrontPage 97 client.
- **\BOTCACHE**—This is a working area for the WebBots.
- **\ISAPI**—This directory contains DLLs for the Internet Server Application Program Interface (ISAPI).
  - ▶ **See** "Internet Sever API," **p. 527**
- **\PAGES**—This directory stores the page-based wizards and templates.
- **\WEBS**—This directory stores the Web-based wizards and templates.
- **\DATA**—This directory stores the FrontPage 97 tutorial.
- **\CLIPART**—This directory stores the various lines and bullets used when building a Web site with a wizard.
- **_VTI_BIN**—This directory stores a copy of the three executables (SHTML, AUTHOR, and ADMIN) for each Web site.
- **\IMAGES**—This directory contains the graphic undercon.gif used in a new Web site built from scratch.
- **\SAMPLES**—This directory is initially empty.
- **\SERVSUPP**—This directory contains miscellaneous DLLs and configuration files.
- **\TEMP**—This is a temporary directory for FrontPage 97.

The \FRONTPAGE WEBS directory structure is as follows:

- **\SERVER**—This directory contains the personal Web server executables.
- **\CONTENT**—This directory contains a subdirectory for each Web site that you create.

Taking Advantage of Hidden Directories

Hidden directories are those directories in the FrontPage 97 Content hierarchy that begin with an underscore (_). These directories are normally used for common header files and color definition pages. These pages are invisible to the search WebBots in the sense that they are not included in the search lists or in generated tables of content. These directories are also used by the Discussion Web Wizard. If you desire the discussion content to be searched by WebBots, it will be necessary to rename the directories or to set the option on the Advanced tab in the Web Settings dialog box. This also will enable users to directly browse these files.

FrontPage 97 Wizards

FrontPage 97 includes several Web Wizards to automate the construction of many of the more common types of Web sites. Although these Web sites are probably not exactly what you will want to create, in all likelihood, one of the Wizards will provide the basis for the type of Web site that you want. It will then be a relatively easy task to use the FrontPage 97 Editor to customize the Web site to your needs. The Wizards are as follows:

- **Normal Web Wizard**—The Normal Web Wizard creates a Web site with a single blank page.
- **Corporate Presence Wizard**—The Corporate Presence Wizard creates a framework for a small company Web site.
- **Customer Support Web Wizard**—The Customer Support Web Wizard creates a Web site to provide customer support services intended especially for software companies.
- **Discussion Web Wizard**—The Discussion Web Wizard creates a discussion Web site.
- **Empty Web Wizard**—The Empty Web Wizard creates an empty Web site. This Wizard is most useful for creating an empty space that can be used to import a Web site from another server.
- **Import Web Wizard**—The Import Web Wizard takes you through the steps necessary to import an existing Web site into FrontPage 97 from the local disk or an attached disk.
- **Learning FrontPage Wizard**—The Learning FrontPage Wizard is a tutorial to use in getting started with FrontPage 97.
- **Personal Web Wizard**—The Personal Web Wizard creates a simple personal Web site.
- **Project Web Wizard**—The Project Web Wizard creates a Web site to manage a project containing the members, status, schedule, archive, and discussion areas.

FrontPage 97 Server Extensions

FrontPage 97 server extensions consist of executables that run on the same computer as the server. The server extensions are necessary to support the WebBots, and the security and access permissions implemented by the FrontPage 97 Explorer. If you are not the administrator of your network, you will probably need to contact the administrator to inquire about installing the appropriate server extensions. The Microsoft Web site lists several Internet service providers (ISPs) who already support the FrontPage 97 server extensions, along with information on how to become a registered FrontPage WPP (Web Presence Provider) at **http://microsoft.saltmine.com/frontpage/wpp/list/**.

The server extensions provide three main functions, as follows:

- The functionality required to support the FrontPage 97 environment, including storing documents, maintaining the To Do List, and determining the relationships among the files that make up the Web site.
- The Application Program Interfaces (APIs) that are necessary for such functions as permissions, image maps, and configuration.
- The functionality required by the interactive WebBots (such as search bots and discussion group bots).

Server extensions generally communicate with the server through some type of Common Gateway Interface (CGI). UNIX servers generally run the extensions in a forked process, which will not share the same address space, while Windows-based servers will run the extensions in the context of a dynamic link library (DLL), which will be in the server's

Part
IV

Ch
20

address space. For permission and configuration information, the server extensions must initiate the communication protocol.

▶ **See** "Using CGI," **p. 572**

Due to these and other differences in the way servers are implemented, FrontPage 97 must be tailored to support each server's needs. The differences are isolated in the drivers within the server extensions. This allows 80 to 90 percent of the server extensions program to remain identical between servers. Because of this, a single edition of the server extensions will often contain drivers for more than one vendor's server on that platform.

Security Issues

FrontPage 97 also includes a new security model that provides greater control for the FrontPage administrator. Privileges can now be assigned to either groups or to users remotely through HTTP, and FrontPage administrators no longer have to be NT administrators to assign or change privileges.

As an extra security measure, FrontPage 97 supports the Secure Sockets Layer (SSL) protocol, which allows you to remotely author and administer your Web site in a secure environment. It also allows you to create hyperlinks to secure Web pages.

▶ **See** "Defining an Internet Security Plan," **p. 513**

FrontPage 97 provides for Web site security in the following three main areas:

■ **Access Control**—FrontPage 97 uses permissions to control access in the User, Author, and Administrator domains. These permissions are added and modified through the Permissions dialog box which is displayed by selecting Tools, Permissions from the menu. For more information on setting permissions, see the section "Other FrontPage Management Tools." Users must be granted the necessary permissions before they can browse the Web site. Authors must be granted the correct permissions before they can make changes to individual files. Administrators must possess the required permissions before they can grant permissions to others. Additionally, access control is built directly into the server itself; control is not passed through to the system. Usernames (login IDs), passwords, and Internet Protocol (IP) addresses are also utilized to help control access.

▶ **See** "Understanding Information Networks," **p. 28**

■ **Proxies**—Often, to support the security requirements of Web sites, it is necessary to use FrontPage 97 to copy a Web site to a server that is outside the firewall. FrontPage 97 will handle this on either side of the firewall. It enables you to specify a proxy server and list the servers that should be accessed directly without going through the firewall. FrontPage 97 enables the user to specify a username and password combination to use for authentication at the proxy. Once the FrontPage 97 client has the needed security information, the user need not be aware that a proxy is in use. Proxies are set up through the Options dialog box, which is opened by selecting Tools, Options from the menu.

▶ **See** "Microsoft Proxy Server," **p. 488**

■ **Encryption**—FrontPage 97 now supports secure sockets. Secure Socket Layer (SSL) is a low-level protocol that provides secure communications between the server and the browser. SSL uses authentication and encryption technology developed by RSA Data Security, Inc. In general, SSL (U.S. government approved) uses a 40-bit key size for the RC4 stream encryption algorithm. For domestic purposes, the full encryption algorithm could be implemented, thus providing for a 128-bit key size. The encryption established between the browser and a server remains valid over multiple connections.

▶ **See** "An Introduction to Cryptography," **p. 762**

Although FrontPage 97 uses these features to provide a means to secure your Web site, Web administrators need to be aware of the following security issues:

■ **Web Bot Security Issues**—Although WebBots automate many of the more mundane tasks of managing a Web site, they do open up possible security risks. The Save Results WebBot used by most forms enables the user to save the results to a file specified by the file path. If the server is run as the root, and the CGI scripts run as root, then authors can set a form so the results can be written to any file on the server's file system. It may not be possible to overcome these security issues on some servers. The network administrator needs to be aware of these problems when deciding whether or not to allow interactive WebBots to be used.

■ **Securing using the Windows NT File System (NTFS)**—When FrontPage 97 is running on NTFS, it is possible to use the security inherent in NTFS to implement page-level security. This can be accomplished by setting the permissions on the individual directories within the Web site file structure. Setting security this way enables making use of the protections implemented by Windows NT. This is a powerful argument for using NTFS on a server system.

▶ **See** "Configuring Hard Disk Space," **p. 159**

■ **Securing using the File Allocation Table (FAT) File System**—Unlike NTFS, there is no file-level security under the FAT file system. The only way to implement page-level security on FAT-based Web sites is to create different Web sites for each area where different permissions are needed. It is then possible to set different access permissions on each Web site using the Permissions dialog box. Note that this is only possible if the Web sites do not inherit permissions from the root Web site. Since Web sites can have links between themselves, these child Web sites can be linked together to form a larger Web site.

Part
IV
Ch
20

Using FrontPage 97 Explorer to Manage Your Web Site

The FrontPage 97 Explorer is the tool used to manage the structure and configuration of your Web site. It is used to create and maintain the permissions, links, passwords, and other security options. The Explorer is not used to edit the pages, but it is tightly coupled to the editor, and supports drag-and-drop to and from it. This section will also illustrate how to use the FrontPage 97 Explorer to manage the files that make up your Web site. It will allow you to easily import, export, delete, and rename files.

Managing Files   Using FrontPage 97 Explorer, you can import files into your Web site. Once the files are in your Web site, there are tools to rename, delete, and maintain the properties on those files. The files can also be maintained in different folders for organizational purposes.

Importing Files   To import files into a Web site, first open the Web site into which you want to import the files, and choose File, Import. This opens the Import File to Web dialog box (see Figure 20.6).

FIG. 20.6

The Import File to FrontPage Web dialog box displays files and addresses on the import list and provides for import list maintenance (adding files, editing URL addresses, and removing files).

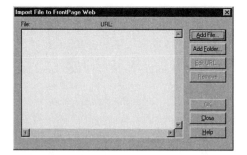

This dialog box displays any files currently on the import list. There are also buttons that enable you to perform the following tasks:

- Add files to the import list
- Edit the URL of a file on the import list
- Remove files from the import list
- Close the import list

When you click the Import Now icon on the FrontPage Explorer dialog box, the files selected from the import list will be imported into the current Web site.

Exporting Files   You can export any files from the currently open Web site. To do this, highlight the desired file in the FrontPage Explorer dialog box, and choose File, Export Selected. FrontPage 97 will display the File Open/Save dialog box to enable you to specify the directory and name to use to export the selected file. You can export any file that is in the currently open Web site.

Deleting Web Sites   If you want to delete the Web site in which you are currently working, choose File, Delete Web. The Delete Web command is only enabled if you have a Web site open. FrontPage 97 will display a confirmation dialog box. Once you delete a Web site, there is no way to recover it.

Renaming Files   To rename a file, highlight the file, and choose Edit, Rename. You can also right-click the file, and choose Rename from the pop-up menu.

Deleting Files   To delete a file, highlight the file, and choose Edit, Delete. You can also delete a file by right-clicking it, and choosing Delete from the pop-up menu.

Displaying Properties   To display the Properties dialog box for a file, highlight the file and choose Edit, Properties. The General tab of the Properties dialog box will display the file name, title, type, size, and location. The Summary tab of the dialog box displays the created and modified file data and enables you to view and edit the comments.

Moving or Copying Files   To move or copy files, use a combination of the Cut, Copy, and Paste commands. To move a file, cut it from one location, use the Folder view to go to a different location, and then paste the file in its new location. To replicate a file in a different location, copy it, move to the desired location, and then paste it. The following list explains the commands:

- **Cut**—To cut a file from a location, select the file, and choose Edit, Cut. This will remove the file from its current location and place it on the Clipboard.

- **Copy**—To copy a file, select the file, and choose Edit, Copy. This will place a copy of the file on the Clipboard while leaving the original in place.

- **Paste**—To past a file from the Clipboard, use the Explorer to open the desired directory, and choose Edit, Paste. This will insert the contents of the Clipboard into the current directory.

Other FrontPage Management Tools   FrontPage 97 provides the administrator with a set of extremely powerful tools to change the configuration and options for the Web site. This section describes these tools and how to use them effectively to maintain the Web site.

The Permissions dialog box enables you to set the permissions on the Web site based on the user's name or the user's Internet Protocol (IP) address (see Figure 20.7). To open the Permissions dialog box, choose Tools, Permissions.

FIG. 20.7
The Permissions dialog box is used to set permissions on the Web site. To add new permissions and continue to work in this dialog, click Apply.

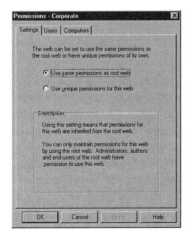

Part
IV

Ch
20

Permissions may be created and modified based on a user's ID or a computer IP address. This will allow the administrator to enable or disable specific users or specific computers. The tabs in the Permissions dialog box are as follows:

■ **Settings**—This tab displays and modifies the permission settings for this Web site. If you choose the option to use unique permissions for this Web site, the other tabs will allow Administer, Author, and Browse permissions by user name and IP address. If the option is chosen to inherit permissions from the root Web site, these options will be disabled.

■ **Users**—This tab enables Administer, Author, and Browse permissions to be set by user-name. To add a user, click the A̲dd button. You will be prompted for the user's name and password, along with the permissions that you want to assign. To delete a permission, highlight the desired user, and click the R̲emove key. This tab also enables you to give Browse permission to everyone.

> **CAUTION**
> The Delete key will not ask for a confirmation, so exercise caution when deleting a permission.

■ **Computers**—This tab enables Administer, Author, and Browse permissions to be set by IP address. Its behavior is similar to the User tab.

The password enables access to the entire Web site. To change the password for the current user, choose T̲ools, C̲hange Password. This opens the Change Password dialog box as depicted in Figure 20.8. You are required to enter the current password, along with the new password and a confirmation.

FIG. 20.8

The Change Password dialog box is used to change the current user password. No change can be made until the old password has been entered correctly for the identified username.

The FrontPage Web Settings dialog box enables you to edit Web site parameters and specify the type of image maps the Web site supports. It also provides a means to select the validation language for the form fields. To change the settings for the current Web site, choose T̲ools, W̲eb Settings. This opens the FrontPage Web Settings dialog box as illustrated in Figure 20.9.

FIG. 20.9

The FrontPage Web Settings dialog box enables you to edit Web site parameters and specify the type of image maps the Web site supports.

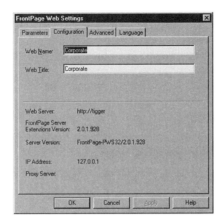

This dialog box has four tabs, which are as follows:

- **Parameters**—This tab enables you to add, edit, or delete defined parameters to use in your Web site in conjunction with the Substitution WebBot. To edit these parameters, select the desired parameter, and click Modify. Clicking Add or Modify opens the Parameter Modification dialog box. To delete a Parameter, select the desired parameter, and click the Remove button.

> **CAUTION**
>
> The Remove dialog box will not ask for a confirmation, so use caution while in this dialog box.

- **Configuration**—The Configuration tab displays the Web server, extension version, server version, IP address, and proxy server. It also enables you to view and edit the Web site name and Web site title.
- **Advanced**—The Advanced tab enables you to edit several Web site parameters, including image maps, validation scripts, options, and recalculate status, as follows:
  - The Image Maps area of this tab is used to set the type of image map (client-side or specified server) you want to use for the current Web site.
  - Validation Scripts are used to specify the language used to validate the form fields.
  - Options configures the FrontPage 97 Explorer to show the documents in hidden directories.
  - The Recalculate Status area shows the status of text indexes and WebBot date components.
- **Language**—The Language tab enables you to view and edit the Default Web Site Language and the Default HTML Encoding. The Default Web Site Language setting will decide the language used to send error messages from the Web server to the Web browser. If your Web pages are in a different language, you should change this so that the error messages will match the language of your content. The Default HTML

Part

IV

Ch

20

Encoding setting will select the character set to be used for any new pages that will be created. You may change the encoding options on individual pages by selecting the desired encoding from the General tab of the Page Properties dialog box.

The Options dialog box enables you to set the general options for FrontPage 97. It also provides a method to set up associations with any editors you would like to use for the various types of documents on your Web site. To open the Options dialog box, choose Tools, Options (see Figure 20.10).

FIG. 20.10

The Options dialog box enables you to set the general options for FrontPage 97 and provides a method to set up associations with any editors you want to use on your Web site. Note that when you set an option, it is set for all FrontPage 97 Web sites.

This dialog box has three tabs, which are explained as follows:

- **General**—This tab enables you to select general options for FrontPage 97. There is an option to display—or not to display—the opening dialog box, an option to warn when WebBot components (scheduled image and scheduled include) are out of date, and an option to warn when text search indices are out of date.

- **Proxies**—This tab enables Hypertext Transport Protocol (HTTP) proxies to be set up.

- **Configure Editors**—This tab enables the editors for various types of files to be configured. To configure an editor, click Add to display the Add dialog box. In this dialog box, you specify the extension of the file, the editor name, and the command line for the editor. The Modify button enables you to change an editor, and the Remove button removes an editor from the list. When the editors are configured, they will appear in the pop-up menu under Open With, which is displayed when the user right-clicks a document.

Version Control   FrontPage 97 works in conjunction with Microsoft Visual SourceSafe providing a reliable way to manage the process of Web page development by one or more persons. When Version 5.0 of SourceSafe is properly configured, the Check In and Check Out commands appear. Use the Check In command to commit the changes that have been made in a document to the Source Safe library. Use the Check Out command to reserve a document from Source Safe so that the user is able to safely make changes to it.

For more information, see the white paper titled "Microsoft Visual SourceSafe and FrontPage 97" on the Microsoft FrontPage 97 World Wide Web site at **http://www.microsoft.com/ssafe/techinfo/frontpage.htm**.

Advanced Topics with FrontPage 97 Editor

The FrontPage 97 Editor is a very powerful and extensive HTML editing tool. This section does not cover all of the commands available in the editor. To do so would require an entire book. This section covers the more advanced features of FrontPage 97 that set it apart from other HTML editors.

Using FrontPage 97 Templates   FrontPage 97 has templates that will assist you in creating several basic types of pages. There are several templates that lay out simple examples of the type of page that you want to create. The following are the *simple templates:*

- **Normal**—Creates a normal (blank) page that is not based on a template
- **Bibliography**—Creates a page that references printed or electronic documents
- **Confirmation Form**—Inserts controls for a sample confirmation form
- **Directory of Press Releases**—Creates a directory of press releases sorted by date
- **Employee Directory**—Creates an alphabetized listing of employees with a table of contents
- **Employment Opportunities**—Creates a list of available jobs with a form to ask for more information
- **Feedback Form**—Lays out controls for a sample feedback form
- **Frequently Asked Questions (FAQ)**—Creates a page that answers common questions about a topic
- **Glossary of Terms**—Creates a page defining related terms
- **Guestbook**—Lays out controls for an example of a guestbook or sign-in page
- **Hotlist**—Lays out an example hotlist or links page
- **Hyperdocument**—Creates a hierarchical document divided into sections
- **Lecture Abstracts**—Creates a page describing a lecture to be used with the Seminar Schedule Template
- **Meeting Agenda**—Creates an agenda for an upcoming meeting
- **Office Directory**—Creates a listing of the locations of your company's offices
- **Press Release**—Creates a press release for use with the Press Release Directory Template
- **Product Description**—Creates a page describing a product with features, benefits, and specifications
- **Product or Event Registration**—Lays out controls for a sample registration page
- **Search Page**—Creates a page to search for keywords across all of the documents in your Web site

- **Seminar Schedule**—Creates the main page describing a seminar event (for use with the Lecture Abstract Template)
- **Software Data Sheet**—Creates a data sheet describing a software product
- **Survey Form**—Creates a survey form to collect information from browsers and stores it on your server
- **Table of Contents**—Creates a table of contents for your Web site
- **User Registration**—Creates a page for users to register for your Web site
- **What's New**—Creates a page describing new additions to your site, sorted by date

The following are *interactive templates:*

- **Form Page Wizard**—Takes you through the steps needed to lay out the controls for a basic form page
- **Frames Wizard**—Assists you in creating a frameset, which is a page containing several independent windows that each refer to a separate URL

 TIP If you are going to lay out your frameset from a grid, it will be easier if you create each frame's URL prior to starting the Frames Wizard.

To start the Frames Wizard, select File, New, and select the Frames Wizard from the list of templates. The Frames Wizard takes you through the following steps:

1. The first dialog allows you to choose from a template or design to make a custom frame page.
2. If you decide to use the existing templates, you will be allowed to choose from one of the following: Banner With Nested Table of Contents, Main Document Plus Footnotes, Navigation Bars with Internal Table of Contents, Nested Three-Level Hierarchy, Simple Table of Contents, or Top-Down Three-Level Hierarchy.
3. If you choose to lay out your own frameset, the Wizard will allow you to specify the number of rows and columns and their sizes.
4. After your framset is layed out, you need to specify the URL for each frame. The Wizard will present a representation of your grid, and you will need to select each frame and enter a name and URL for it. You may also specify the margin widths, scrolling options, and whether or not the frames are sizable.
5. Enter an alternate URL for browsers that do not support frames.
6. Set a title and URL for the frameset.
7. If you used a template, the Wizard will create the files needed for each frame in your frameset.

Custom Templates　　To create a custom template from a page that you have created, open the page in the FrontPage 97 Editor, and choose File, Save As. Once you have saved the new template, it appears in the menu of templates along with the standard ones that come with FrontPage.

Working with Images   One of the most important aspects of the World Wide Web is its capability to make use of graphics as a means of communications. Because of this, no Web page management or editing tool would be complete without extensive image manipulation capabilities. To this end, FrontPage 97 has a complete interface that allows you to insert and edit images and their properties while viewing them in the same way that they will be viewed on your pages. The FrontPage 97 Editor also provides an intuitive method of setting up image maps.

Inserting Images   To insert an image into a Web page, place the cursor at the desired location, and choose Insert, Image. A dialog box will display all of the images in the current Web site. You also have two buttons: From URL and From File. The From URL button enables you to load an image from the URL that you specify. This image will not be saved in the local Web site. The From File button enables you to browse the local computer and select an image. When you choose this option, FrontPage 97 will ask if you would like to save the image in the current Web site. FrontPage knows how to interpret the following image formats:

- Graphics Interchange Format (.GIF)
- Joint Photographic Expert Group (.JPG, .JIF)
- Windows Bitmap (.BMP)
- Tagged Image File Format (.TIF)
- Microsoft Paint (.MSP)
- Windows Metafiles (.WMF)
- SUN Raster (.RAS)
- WordPerfect Graphics (.WPG)
- PC Paintbrush (.PCX)
- Encapsulated Postscript (.EPS)
- Targa (.TGA)
- Macintosh Paint (.MAC)
- Kodak PhotoCD (.PCD)

Images are only stored in GIF or JPG format within FrontPage. If you import an image file that is less than 256 colors, it is converted and stored in the GIF format. If it has more than 256 colors, it is converted and stored in JPG format.

Image Properties   After you insert an image, right-click it and select Properties from the pop-up menu, or choose Edit, Properties. You will see the Image Properties dialog box displayed, as shown in Figure 20.11.

Part

IV

Ch

20

FIG. 20.11

The Image Properties dialog box has three tabs for manipulating and controlling property settings for the image files.

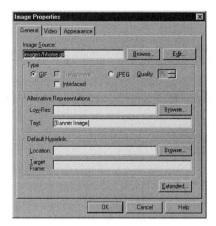

You can select the way you would like the image to be saved—in GIF or JPG—explained as follows:

- **GIF**—This enables you to select the Transparent and Interlaced options. The Transparent option enables you to specify a transparent color that allows the background to show through. Only one color can be selected as transparent. This option is available only for GIF images. The Interlaced option causes images to be painted coarsely at first, and then clearly. This is useful on large images.

- **JPG**—This enables you to specify the Quality option, which allows you to make the image smaller and, therefore, make the transfer quicker.

The following are other image properties that you can set by using the Image Properties dialog box tabs:

- **Layout**—Enables you to specify the image alignment, spacing, and border thickness

- **Alternative Representations**—Enables you to specify an alternative text representation or a lower resolution image representation

 In Microsoft Internet Explorer 3.0, alternative text is shown as ToolTip style windows when the mouse pointer is over an image.

- **Default link**—Enables you to specify a link for the image

Image Maps   To associate an image with multiple links, perform the following steps:

1. Select the image.

2. Using the Image toolbar, define the hotspot areas. You can create rectangular, circular, or polygonal hotspot areas. After the area has been defined, the Create Hyperlink dialog box will open, allowing you to specify the hyperlink properties (see Figure 20.12).

Draw A Circular Hotspot button ——— Select A Transparent Pixel button—

Draw A Rectangular Hotspot button   Highlight the Hotspots button ￢

Select A Hotspot button   Draw A Polygonal Hotspot button

FIG. 20.12

The Image toolbar has buttons on it to select a hotspot, draw a rectangular hotspot, draw a circular hotspot, draw a polygonal hotspot, highlight the hotspots, and select a transparent pixel.

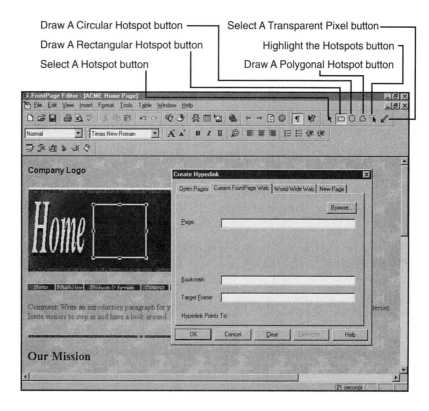

3. To associate the hotspot areas with a link, select the area and click the Link button on the toolbar, choose Edit, Hyperlink, or right-click the hotspot and select Image Hotspot Properties from the pop-up menu.

To help you lay out the hotspot areas, you can click the Highlight Link button on the Hotspot toolbar. This will blank out the original picture and display only the highlight areas.

It is possible to have a link associated with an entire image, as well as having hotspot links. With this type of setup, the hotspot images take precedence over the full image link. If you click an image on an area other than a hotspot, it will go to the full image link.

These hotspots can be client-side or server-side. FrontPage 97 supports either mode. The hotspots are set up the same regardless of how the image maps are generated. The type of image map is set with the FrontPage 97 Explorer in the Web Settings dialog box under the Advanced tab. An image can have a single link or multiple links associated with it.

Single Link   To associate an image with a single link, select the image, and click the Link button on the toolbar, or choose Edit, Hyperlink. This creates a single link associated with the entire image.

Insert from a Text or RTF File   To insert text from a file, place the cursor in the desired position, and choose Insert, File. It is possible to insert text files (.TXT), HTML files (.HTM, .HTML), or Rich Text Format files (.RTF).

Part

IV

Ch

20

N O T E   Inserting text from a file is not the same as using the Annotation WebBot. Inserting from a file will modify the text only when the page is edited. If the file changes, this inserted text will not change automatically. To set up a file for insertion at server time, see the section "Annotation Bot." ■

You will then be given the options for formatting the inserted text, as follows:

■ **One Formatted Paragraph**—Converts the text to a single paragraph with line breaks

■ **Formatted Paragraphs**—Converts each paragraph to formatted text

■ **Normal Paragraphs**—Converts each paragraph to normal text

■ **Normal Paragraphs with Line Breaks**—Converts each paragraph to normal text, preserving the line endings

Using FrontPage Bots   FrontPage 97 WebBots are dynamic objects that are executed when a Web page is saved or browsed. Most WebBot components generate HTML that is sent to the browser. This enables the user to automatically update HTML without resorting to CGI scripts. Some WebBot components work when the page is served to the browser, and other WebBots handle user interaction. If a WebBot runs when the document is served, it will be able to function when the Web site is hosted on another server (if it is published to the server using the FrontPage 97 Publishing Wizard).

When you are editing a page that has WebBots on it, the bots will appear as normal text until you move the cursor over one. At this time, the cursor will change to the WebBot cursor. While the WebBot cursor is displayed, you can get the properties of that WebBot by right-clicking and selecting WebBot Component Properties from the pop-up menu (refer to Figure 20.5).

Annotation Bot   The Annotation Bot is a way of putting text on a page that is seen in the FrontPage 97 Editor but is not displayed when a user views the page with a browser. Annotation text appears purple and in the same font and size as the current style. To insert an Annotation Bot, perform the following steps:

1. Place the cursor at the desired position and choose Insert, WebBot Component.

2. Select Annotation Bot from the list of bots.

3. Enter the annotation text in the text box.

Confirmation Bot   The Confirmation Bot enables you to echo information that the user has entered. To insert a Confirmation Bot, perform the following steps:

1. Place the cursor at the desired position, and choose Insert, WebBot Component.

2. Select Confirmation Bot from the list of bots.

3. Enter the field name to be echoed.

HTML Markup Bot   The HTML Markup Bot provides a way to enter HTML that FrontPage 97 does not support. When FrontPage 97 is serving a page to a browser or the FrontPage 97 Editor, it checks the HTML for correctness. If it encounters any HTML that it doesn't understand, the HTML is stripped from the page. If you use another editor (such as Notepad) to enter unsupported HTML, it will not appear on the page. A way around this is to use the HTML Markup Bot. To add an HTML Markup Bot, perform the following steps:

1. Place the cursor at the desired position, and choose Insert, WebBot Component.
2. Select HTML Markup Bot from the list of bots.
3. Enter the desired HTML in the text box.

> **CAUTION**
>
> Due to the nature of the HTML Markup Bot, the HTML will not be checked for correctness. Therefore, it is up to you to verify the code.

HTML Markup Bots are marked as <?> on a yellow background in the editor.

Include Bot   The Include Bot is a way to insert a file into a page. This is useful if you need to insert some text several places in your Web site. If the text changes, you then need to edit it in only one place.

 Before you begin to insert an included file, create the file for the text and import it into your Web site. This is necessary because you will need to specify the URL when you insert the WebBot. You can specify the URL before you create it, but you risk broken links.

To insert an Include Bot, perform the following steps:

1. Place the cursor at the desired position, and choose Insert, WebBot Component.
2. Select Include Bot from the list.
3. Specify the URL of the file to be included.

The URL of the file will be displayed in the FrontPage 97 Editor.

Scheduled Image Bot   The Scheduled Image Bot is a way to display an image for a specified time period. If the time/date is outside the specified period, the browser will show an alternate image or nothing at all, and the editor will show the alternate image or *[Expired Scheduled Image]* if no alternate image is specified. To insert a Scheduled Image Bot, perform the following steps:

 Because you are inserting an URL, it would be helpful to create the image before you insert the Bot. You can enter the URL before you create it, but you risk creating a broken link.

1. Place the cursor at the desired position, and choose Insert, WebBot Component.
2. Select Scheduled Image Bot from the list of bots.
3. Browse to select the image to include.
4. Specify the begin and end date.
5. If you want, you can specify an alternate image to display if the date is outside the date range.

The object on the page is really a WebBot and not an image. Due to this, you cannot specify properties of the image—just properties of the Bot. This also means that you cannot set hotspots in the image.

 T I P   If you need to specify image parameters or set image hotspots, you can use the Scheduled Include Bot to include a page that has the image you want to include.

Scheduled Include Bot   The Scheduled Include Bot is used the same way as the Scheduled Image Bot, but it offers you more formatting options than the Scheduled Image Bot. To insert a Scheduled Image Bot, perform the same steps as with the Scheduled Image Bot, selecting the Scheduled Include Bot instead.

Search Bot   The Search Bot enables you to insert a search form into a Web page. To insert a Search Bot, perform the following steps:

1. Place the cursor at the desired position, and choose Insert, WebBot Component.
2. Select Search Bot from the list of bots.
3. Set the Search For text. This is the text that appears by the input field for the search text.
4. Set the width of the search field.
5. Enter the label for the Search button.
6. Enter the label for the Reset button.
7. You can specify the pages to search by entering a word list to search. If you have a discussion group, you can enter the discussion group directory. *All* searches all pages not in a hidden directory. If you want to exclude some pages from a search, you can place them in a hidden directory.
8. You can also specify other information to display: the closeness of the match, the file date, and the file size.

Substitution Bot   The Substitution Bot enables you to include any variables that have been defined for the Web site. To include a Substitution Bot, perform the following steps:

1. Place the cursor at the desired position, and choose Insert, WebBot Component.
2. Select Table of Contents Bot from the list of bots.
3. Select the variable that you want to substitute from the list.

Table of Contents Bot   The Table of Contents Bot creates a table of contents for your Web site that is be automatically re-created. To insert a Table of Contents Bot, perform the following steps:

1. Place the cursor at the desired position, and choose Insert, WebBot Component.
2. Select Table of Contents Bot from the list of bots.
3. Specify the starting point for the table of contents. A good starting point is your home page (index.htm).
4. Specify the heading size for the table of contents.

5. Check Show Each Page Only Once to suppress multiple listings for each page. If you do not check this, there will be an entry each time a page is referenced.

6. Check Show Pages With No Incoming Links to show all pages, including those that have no links to them.

7. Check Recompute Table of Contents When Any Other Page Is Edited to generate the table of contents when any page in the Web site is edited. This may be time-consuming, so if you don't check this option, you must save the page again with the Table of Contents Bot on it to generate the table of contents again.

Timestamp Bot   The Timestamp Bot is a way to insert the last time a page was edited or automatically updated. To insert a Timestamp Bot, perform the following steps:

1. Place the cursor at the desired position, and choose Insert, WebBot Component.

2. Select Timestamp Bot from the list of bots.

3. You can select the last edited date or last automatically updated date, and specify the time format.

Using Forms   Forms are a way to collect organized data from the browsers of your Web pages. With FrontPage 97 forms, it is possible to collect the data in text, HTML, or formatted text. A form can be set up several ways in FrontPage, as follows:

- Use the Form Page Wizard from the File, New command in the FrontPage 97 Editor.

- Use the Feedback Form Template from the File, New command in the FrontPage 97 Editor.

- Construct your own form using the Insert, Form Field command to insert form components on a page that already exists.

  ▶ **See** "The Interactive, Dynamic Web Site," **p. 728**

If the form is going to be a complicated one, it is probably easier to have the Form Page Wizard create the form for you, and then fill out the rest of the page. To use the Form Page Wizard, perform the following steps:

1. Choose File, New in the FrontPage 97 Editor.

2. Select Form Page Wizard from the list.

3. Provide an URL and a page title for the form page that you want to create.

4. FrontPage then enables you to select a series of components to place on the page that is to be created. These components range from nearly complete forms (Contact, Account, Product, Ordering, and Personal Information) to simple form elements (Boolean, Date, Time, Range, Number, String, and Paragraph).

5. For the more complex sections, it is possible to select from a number of options you want to include in that section.

6. When there are a number of sections entered in the list, you can reorder the list, or remove any undesired elements.

7. After all the desired sections have been selected, you can specify how the sections are presented, whether or not a table of contents is generated for this page, and how the fields will be aligned.

8. It is then necessary to specify the method for handling the file, and the name of the result file, if necessary. The results may be saved to a Web page, a text file, or with a custom CGI script.

9. After the page has been created, you can customize the page by adding text or other items you want on the page.

> **CAUTION**
>
> FrontPage's Form Wizard defaults the Results file to the TEMP directory under the main FrontPage 97 directory. For the form to function correctly, it is necessary to move it to a directory in the current Web site. The hidden directory _private is generally a good choice.

Database Connectivity   FrontPage 97 now includes a Database Connectivity Wizard to help the user set up pages that will run database queries and insert the results set into HTML pages. The following components are needed for database connectivity:

- **Open Database Connectivity (ODBC) compliant database**—Any database that is ODBC compliant can be set up to be used with FrontPage 97.

- **Internet Database Connection (.IDC or IDC) file**—This file contains the information specifying how to connect to the database, the Structured Query Language (SQL) statement to execute, and the HTML Extension file.

- **HTML Extension File (.HTX or HTX)**—This file describes how to format the results of the query. It is a standard HTML file with IDC parameters added.

The first step in connecting a database is to configure the database as a system (Data Source Name, or DSN). This will set up the database as a system-wide datasource. To do this, run the ODBC Administrator and click the System DSN button. This will open the System DSN dialog box. This dialog box enables the user to set up a datasource with a driver that is already installed, or add or delete a driver. Once the database has been set up, an HTML extensions file will be needed. To create an HTX file, perform the following steps:

1. Open the FrontPage 97 Editor, and choose File, New.

2. Select Database Results from the list of file types. This creates a blank HTX file.

3. To add fields in the HTX file, choose Edit, Database, and select the desired field.

4. From this menu, database column values or IDC fields can be inserted into the results file.

The Internet Database Connector Wizard shown in Figure 20.13 is the tool to use to create the IDC file. To run the Wizard, choose File, New in the FrontPage 97 Editor, or click the Database Connectivity button on the toolbar.

FIG. 20.13

The Internet Database Connector Wizard shows the ODBC datasource as NorthWind and `Scripts/ database.HTX` as the template for the results of the query.

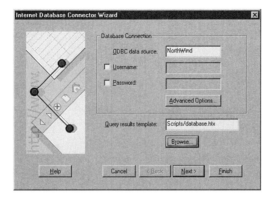

The Internet Database Connector Wizard will walk the user through the following steps:

1. Specify the ODBC datasource. This is the name that was set up as the System DSN. The example uses the Northwind database included with Microsoft Access.

2. A Username and Password can also be set if needed.

3. Set the Query Results Template. This is the name of the HTX file created previously. The Browse button enables you to browse the current Web site for a document.

4. Click Next to display the SQL options. This specifies the SQL statements to run (see Figure 20.14). To specify more than one SQL statement, click the combo box to create another query. If more than one query is specified, the results of each query are displayed in separate detail sections of the HTX file.

FIG. 20.14

The Internet Database Connector Wizard displays one query: `Select * from Employees`. Employees is a table in the datasource set up earlier.

Part

IV

Ch

20

5. This dialog box also enables the user to enter Parameters. To add a parameter to the query, click the Insert Parameter button, and the dialog box enables a Form Field name to be entered.

6. Click the Next button to open the dialog box to specify any default parameters (see Figure 20.15). If the query is run because the user submitted a form, the default parameters are combined with any form parameters. If the query is run because the user followed a link to the IDC file, the default parameters are the only ones used.

FIG. 20.15

The Internet Database Connector Wizard parameter dialog shows that no default parameters have been entered. Form parameters may be set with the Form Properties dialog box.

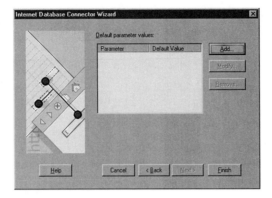

7. Clicking Finish opens the Save dialog box to enable you to specify where you want to save the IDC file.

N O T E The IDC file should be saved in a directory where the permissions are set so that scripts are allowed to run. ■

Once the IDC file has been created, it can be used as a link from another Web page, or it can be set up as a form handler. To set it as a form handler, create the form and then right-click to bring up the Form Properties dialog box, as follows:

1. From the Form Properties section, select Internet Database Connector from the combo box.

2. Click the Settings button to display the Settings For Database Connector dialog box.

3. This dialog box enables you to specify the IDC file to use as the form handler. Clicking the Edit button opens the Internet Database Connector Wizard to edit the IDC file.

Inserting Java Applets FrontPage 97 now provides support for Java applets. In the previous version of FrontPage, it was necessary to insert Java applets using the Unsupported HTML Bot. To add a Java applet, first import the class file (xxx.class) into the current Web site. Then from the FrontPage 97 Editor, choose Insert, Other Component, Java Applet. This opens the Java Applet Properties dialog box, which enables you to specify the following:

- **Applet source**—The name of the class file.
- **Base URL**—The URL for the location of the class file.
- **Alternative text for browsers that do not support Java**—This message is displayed when a browser that does not support Java attempts to display the page.
- **Applet parameters**—This section specifies the names and values for the Java applet.
- **Applet size**—Controls the size of the applet on the page.
- **Layout**—Specifies the alignment of the applet in relation to text on the page.
- **Extended attributes section**—Enables other attribute/value pairs to be added to the APPLET HTML tag.

When a Java applet is present on the page, it is denoted by a Java applet graphic that appears as a blue capital *J* at a 45 degree angle. The applet properties can easily be edited by right-clicking the graphic and selecting Java Applet Properties from the pop-up menu.

Inserting Netscape Plug-Ins   Netscape plug-ins are files that extend Netscape Navigator to enable it to handle non-Netscape file types. ActiveX files are a good example. To insert a Netscape add-on, choose Insert, Other Components, Plug-In. This opens the Plug-In Properties dialog box. This dialog box enables you to specify the location of the plug-in by browsing the local disk or the Web site. The dialog box also enables you to edit the size and alignment characteristics for the add-on.

▶ **See** "Plug-Ins," **p. 599**

Inserting ActiveX Components   With the introduction of ActiveX components, Microsoft has expanded the capabilities of Web pages. ActiveX Controls are essentially smaller versions of Object Linking and Embedding (OLE) controls. By themselves, they are not all that powerful, but with the combination of ActiveX Controls and VBScripts, the Web page becomes a (somewhat independent) platform for programming. To insert an ActiveX control, choose Insert, Other Components, ActiveX Control. This opens the ActiveX Control Properties dialog box, as depicted in Figure 20.16.

▶ **See** "ActiveX Technologies," **p. 711**

FIG. 20.16

As the title implies, the ActiveX Control Properties dialog box enables you to specify the control parameters and layout settings for the selected ActiveX Control.

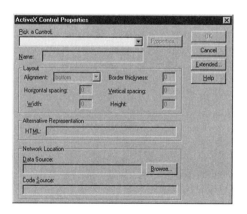

The dialog box enables you to edit the following properties:

- ■ **Pick a Control**—This drop-down list box will display the controls currently installed on your system. If you know the class ID, you can install a control that is not present on your system.

- ■ **Properties**—If the ActiveX Control is loaded on your system, and it supports editing properties, press this button and the Tabular Properties Editor will open and enable you to specify the properties for the control. If the control is not loaded on your system, or if it does not support editing, the Object Parameters dialog box will open. To use this dialog box, you must know the name of each property.

- **Name**—This is the name you will use to refer to the control in the scripts that you write for this page.

- **Layout**—This area will enable you to specify the size and alignment for the control.

- **Alternative Representation**—This enables you to specify the URL of an alternative representation for browsers that do not support ActiveX.

- **Data Source**—This enables you to specify the URL for a file that contains runtime parameters (if necessary) for the control.

- **Code Source**—This enables you to specify the URL to use for downloading the control if the control is not on the browsing computer.

- **Extended**—The Extended button enables you to specify parameters that are not directly supported.

Once the control is inserted, it appears under the name you specified along with all of its properties in the Actions window in the Script Wizard.

Inserting Scripts   Scripts are a way of adding interactive content to your Web page. Scripts are generally written in either JavaScript or VBScript. JavaScript is a very simplified form of Java that can be inserted into the HTML of the Web page. JavaScript scripts are supported by Netscape Navigator and Internet Explorer. VBScript is a simplified version of Visual Basic that is also included as part of the Web page HTML. VBScripts are supported by Internet Explorer and by Netscape Navigator with an add-on.

FrontPage 97 supports *inline scripts*, or *event scripts*. Inline scripts are run when the page loads. Event scripts are run when triggered by actions on a form or ActiveX components. This section is not intended to serve as a lesson in script writing. There are excellent tutorials available for JavaScript at **http://java.sun.com**, and for VBScript at **http://www.microsoft.com**. I strongly encourage you to review these (if necessary) before continuing.

▶ **See** "Scripting Languages," **p. 602**

You can insert scripts into your page by either adding them with the HTML Bot or by using the Script dialog box. This dialog box generally makes it easier to add scripts to a page, but it does not recommend mixing different types of scripts on the same Web page (see Figure 20.17). To add a script to a page, choose Insert, Script, or click the Script dialog box icon on the toolbar. The Script dialog box appears.

You can add the script in the Script window of the Script dialog box. Selecting VBScript causes the Script Wizard to create VBScript and insert it into the page. Selecting JavaScript causes JavaScript to be inserted. The Other option is for future expansion. The Run Script on Server check box is currently not implemented. If you insert the script without using the Script Wizard, it is not necessary to select the Language option.

N O T E   Microsoft does not recommend using scripts of differing types on the same page in FrontPage 97. Doing so will create unpredictable results. ▪

FIG. 20.17
The Script dialog box
allows you to specify
either VBScript or
JavaScript. The Other
selection is for future
expansion.

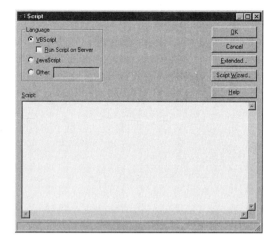

When a script is added to the page, a script icon is displayed. The script icon is a Green *J* on a
yellow background for JavaScript scripts, or a Visual Basic code icon for a VBScript. Alternatively, you can use the Script Wizard to insert a script.

N O T E   An icon cannot be displayed if the inserted script is associated with a form field or an
ActiveX Control that already exists. ▪

To run the Script Wizard, select the language option you want, and click the Script Wizard
button in the Script dialog box. The Script Wizard dialog box depicted in Figure 20.18 will be
displayed.

FIG. 20.18
The Script Wizard is
shown inserting a
VBScript into the ACME
Home Page. Form
elements or controls
would show in the
Events window and the
Wizard would allow you
to link them with
actions from the Action
window.

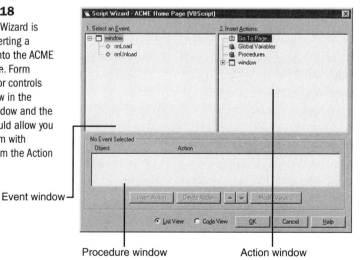

Event window ⏤

Procedure window   Action window

The Script Wizard display is divided into the following three sections:

- **Event window**—The Event window shows the events associated with this Web page in a tree structure. There are events for the window, along with events that are associated with any form elements or ActiveX components. To expand a branch, click the plus icon. To collapse a branch, click the minus icon. To remove an event handler from a specific event, right-click the event, and select Delete Event Handler from the pop-up menu.

- **Action window**—The Action window displays defined procedures and variables for this page. To add a new procedure or variable, right-click anywhere in the window, and select the desired action from the pop-up menu.

- **Procedure window**—The Procedure window provides two views: the List view and the Code view. The List view displays a list of the actions associated with the selected event, along with buttons that enable you to add or delete events. If the action involves a variable, the Modify Value button enables you to change the variable that is used. The Code view displays the code generated by the actions and enables you to type code directly into the window.

The Script Wizard user interface is the same regardless of whether you are using VBScript or JavaScript. The only difference is in the type of code generated.

Inserting Background Sounds   An inserted background sound will be played when the page is opened with a browser. To insert a background sound, perform the following steps:

N O T E   Although Windows NT supports file names with spaces in them (which is common among sound files), if you specify a file name with spaces for a background sound, it will not work. You must rename the file to remove the spaces. ■

1. From the FrontPage 97 Editor, choose Insert, Background Sound. This displays the Background Sound dialog box.

2. The Current Web tab enables you to insert sound files that are already in the current Web site, while the Other Location tab enables you to browse the local drive or specify an URL for the sound file.

3. Select the desired sound file.

4. If the file was specified to be in a location other than the current Web site when the page is saved, FrontPage 97 will ask whether the file is to be saved in the local Web site. If you click Yes, the file will be imported.

5. The number of times the sound should be repeated can be specified by selecting Page, Properties, and editing the sound area on the General tab.

CAUTION

Background sounds inserted with this tool are not supported in Netscape Navigator.

Inserting Videos   FrontPage 97 supports video (`Microsoft.avi`) files being inserted into Web pages. To insert a video file, choose Insert, Video. This opens the Image Properties dialog box. Use the Video tab of this dialog box to specify the source of the video, the repetition, and the start event of the video. The Appearance tab of the dialog box can be used to specify the size and alignment of the video in the same manner as a normal image file.

N O T E   Netscape Navigator does not support videos without a plug-in. A video appears as a graphic that cannot be retrieved when viewed with a Netscape Navigator.

▶ **See** "Plug-Ins," **p. 599**

Inserting Marquees   A marquee is a line of text that scrolls across the page in the browser. To insert a marquee line, select Insert, Marquee from the FrontPage 97 Editor. This opens the Marquee Properties dialog box. The dialog box enables you to specify the following:

- **The text of the marquee**—If you highlighted text on the page when you selected the Marquee command, it will use that text.
- **Movement direction**—This specifies the direction the text will move.
- **Movement speed**—This is the speed at which the text moves.
- **Behavior**—This is the behavior of the movement, as follows:
  - **Scroll** is similar to a stock ticker.
  - **Slide** starts the text from the starting direction to the opposite side of the page. The text remains on the screen at all times.
  - **Alternate** causes the text to alternate from side to side from the starting direction. The text remains on the screen at all times.
- **Alignment**—This specifies how the marquee is aligned with ordinary text.
- **Size**—This specifies the size of the marquee text.
- **Repetitions**—This is the behavior of the scrolling, as follows:
  - **Continuously** causes the text to move as long as the page is displayed.
  - **Times** causes the selected behavior to occur the chosen number of times.
- **Background color**—This specifies the background color of the marquee region.

CAUTION

Marquees are runtime bots, and therefore will not function properly on Web servers that do not have the FrontPage 97 extension installed.

Marquees are not supported on all browsers. On a browser that does not support marquees, the text of the marquee will be displayed left justified.

Part

IV

Ch

20

Using the FrontPage 97 Publishing Wizard

The FrontPage 97 Publishing Wizard is a free tool you can download from the Microsoft Web site that enables you to upload a Web site to another server. Its address is **http:// www.microsoft.com/frontpage/freestuff/fs_fp_pbwiz.htm**.

The Publishing Wizard exports the entire Web site, or just the files that you specify through the SHTML engine, so that the WebBots you have used will work with the server to which you are uploading. If you want the runtime bots to work, it is necessary for the hosting system to have the FrontPage 97 extensions installed. The Publishing Wizard will warn you of any WebBots requiring runtime support from the hosting server.

N O T E   On UNIX servers, the case of the file name is significant, while under Microsoft Windows NT, it is not. If you have used upper- and lowercase in your FrontPage 97 file names, then the links must reflect this, or broken links will result when you upload to a UNIX server. ■

From Here...

In this chapter, you learned how to install and use FrontPage 97 to develop and manage your Web site. This includes using FrontPage 97 wizards to create the basic outline of your site, and FrontPage 97 Editor to customize the site to fit your needs. In addition, you have learned how to liven up your pages with active content using VBScript, JavaScript, images, and access to your databases. This chapter is not intended to be a complete reference for FrontPage 97, as an entire book could have (and has) been devoted to the subject. The following chapters in this book provide more information on using Internet technologies:

- For more information on how to set up and manage intranet and Internet tools to work in conjunction with FrontPage 97, see Chapter 16, "The BackOffice I-Net Toolbox."

- For information on how to set up and use Microsoft's Internet Information Server, see Chapter 18, "Building a Web with Internet Information Server (IIS)."

- For information on the different Web browsers and how to design for the most popular types, see Chapter 19, "Web Browsers."

Advanced I-Net Development

Implementing Index Server and the Content Replication System

by Don Benage

This chapter introduces you to two relatively new members of the Microsoft BackOffice family. Index Server works hand in hand with Internet Information Server (IIS) by building indexes of the content that is published by IIS. Queries, both simple and advanced, can then be created by simply filling out a form using your Web browser. The contents of the form are processed by IIS and a search is made for matching content. The results are sorted, formatted, and returned to the user.

The Content Replication System (CRS) provides an important capability: copying Web content from one server to another. There are many reasons why this is necessary in a typical corporate intranet or professional Web site. These reasons are outlined, and the features provided by CRS are explored. In addition, this chapter provides the key planning concepts and network architecture of CRS. The procedures for testing, monitoring, and maintaining CRS are also provided. ■

Index Server overview

Discover the features of Index Server and the manner in which it works with Internet Information Server (IIS).

Creating a query

Learn the procedures for creating queries—both simple and advanced.

Index Server architecture and administration

Although this product is largely self-maintaining, there are a few things you should know about configuring Index Server and how it operates.

Content Replication System (CRS) overview

Review a description of the Content Replication System and its operational characteristics.

CRS network architecture

Explore the proper way to deploy CRS in a small corporate intranet or the international Internet environment.

CRS maintenance

After installing and testing CRS, learn how to monitor and maintain it during daily operations.

An Index Server Overview

Index Server provides content indexing for both IIS and Peer Web Services (PWS), the Web server component provided by Windows NT Workstation. After it has been installed and configured, it will automatically maintain up-to-date indexes of the content that is stored on a Web server. Index Server is largely self maintaining. There are no complicated maintenance procedures, and the product is designed to run unattended 24 hours a day, seven days a week. As new content is added to the Web server, it automatically updates its indexes in an incremental fashion by incorporating any new entries required without having to re-index all content on the Web server.

Index Server will not only index Hypertext Markup Language (HTML) Web pages, but also documents created with Microsoft Office products. It is capable of "seeing" the contents of the following types of documents:

- Microsoft Word
- Microsoft Excel
- Microsoft PowerPoint
- HTML
- Plain (ASCII) text

In addition, it will index binary files based on their ActiveX properties but, of course, it cannot scan the contents of such files. Other document types can be indexed by creating custom document *filters*, but they are not supported by the standard filters included with the product.

The resulting index that is created is based not only on keywords in the text, but also on the Microsoft Office properties (summary and custom) or ActiveX properties of the file or document. All Microsoft Office document formats include a number of standard properties, such as Title, Subject, Author, Category, and Keywords. In general, the properties of a Microsoft Office document can be viewed by selecting File, Properties. In addition to the standard properties for a document, custom properties can be added by users.

Several sample query forms are provided that can be used to search for content that contains a particular keyword or phrase (see Figure 21.1). This sample query shows only the most rudimentary form of searching that is available. Custom query forms can be created that make it easy for users to formulate complex queries. These queries can perform searches using document properties, including custom properties that are tailored to specific applications if desired.

FIG. 21.1
Sample query forms can be used without modification to search for documents or Web pages on your indexed servers.

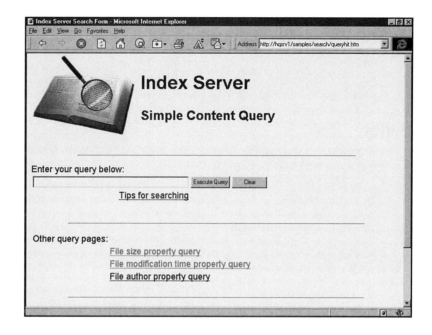

Index Server Architecture

Index Server is designed to run virtually maintenance free. Unless you need to create filters for custom document types, you may never need to worry about the underlying processes that make this product work. However, at some time something may go wrong that requires troubleshooting and an understanding of the way indexes are created and queries are resolved can be useful. In addition, you may simply be curious about how content and property-based indexing is accomplished. An overview is presented here with additional details provided in the following sections. Some details are suppressed for clarity. See the product documentation for full details on all processes.

The process begins when a document is added to an indexed directory on a server. A *scanning* process recognizes that a new file has been added and invokes another process called CiDaemon. The document is analyzed and then *filtered* using an appropriate filter dynamic link library (DLL) and a word-breaker DLL. (Index Server handles multiple languages, and uses different language-dependent rules to determine what to index.) The filtering process identifies keywords and properties that are extracted out of the document and added to the random-access memory (RAM) resident *word lists*. These word lists are subsequently incorporated into *shadow indexes*, which are eventually incorporated into the *master index*.

At some time, a user will open a query form and submit a query to the Index Server engine. The query is processed using information from the query form and a special type of file called an *Internet data query file* (which carries an .IDQ extension). The query is processed, and the returned results are formatted as a Hypertext Markup Language (HTML) page with the aid of

Part
V

Ch
21

another type of file called an HTML extension file (.HTX file). The results are presented to the user's Web browser for display.

By creating custom query forms or custom .IDQ and .HTX files, the query process and the format of the results can be tailored to suit particular needs. The default forms and files are suitable for general purpose indexing and reporting.

Queries

Anyone who has spent time "surfing" the World Wide Web has probably had an opportunity to use one of the *search engines*. These professionally run sites provide sophisticated searching capabilities based on the same type of indexing that is possible with Index Server. Search engines, such as Yahoo!, Lycos, WebCrawler, and AltaVista, provide content indexes at thousands of Web sites on the Internet. Often, after a Web site is found with one of these large search engines, you still need to find a particular page or document of interest.

Web sites that have a local search engine capability make it much easier to find exactly the subject matter you are after. You can use Index Server to provide such a search capability for both public Web sites and intranet sites that you manage. As the amount of subject matter that you include in your site grows, this capability will quickly become a necessity rather than a nice extra feature.

If you have used a public search engine or have other database experience, you already have a good idea what queries are all about. Information is entered into a form specifying what you are interested in finding. This form is then submitted to the Index Server engine for processing. The queries must be expressed in a *query language* that has many powerful features. Index Server's query language supports the following capabilities:

- *Boolean operators* (AND, OR, and NOT) can be used. For example, robot AND human finds documents with *both* words; robot OR human finds documents with *either* word.

- The *proximity operator* (NEAR) can be used to specify that two search items must appear in the same area of the document. For example, fiscal NEAR responsibility should find documents that address *fiscal responsibility*, even if the explicit phrase does not appear in the document.

- Queries are case-insensitive (for example, uppercase and lowercase letters are treated the same). For example, *Robot*, *ROBOT*, and *robot* are all treated the same in a query.

- The *wild card* (*) can be used to match a variable number of arbitrary characters at the end of a word. For example, pre* matches *prehistoric, prefix, preparation, prevention*, and all other words beginning with *pre*. (This is an example of a query that probably needs to be refined to be useful.)

- An additional wild card operator (**) will find words based on the same *stem* word. For example, write** will match *write, wrote, written*, and *writing*. Note that while most of these words would match writ* (using the standard wild card), *wrote* would not. This operator is very useful for matching words that change form as tense changes (*fall* versus *fell*, for example) and other similar situations that confound matching with the standard wild card.

- Punctuation (for example, period, comma, and semicolon) is ignored.

- Certain words are designated as *noise words* (for example, and, the, it), and are completely ignored. The list of noise words (which is in `<systemroot>\system32\noise.enu` for
the English language by default) can be edited if desired. Noise words, also called *stop words*, are never indexed and, therefore, will never result in a hit if included in a query.

- You can use noise words as part of a phrase by enclosing the phrase in quotation marks. The word *and* is both a noise word and a Boolean operator. If you want to search for the phrase *salt and pepper*, you should enclose the phrase in quotation marks (`"salt and pepper"`). Without the quotation marks, `salt and pepper` will match documents that have both words in them, but do not necessarily contain the phrase. Because noise words are not indexed, they can never be found unless they are part of a phrase.

- *Free-text queries* are supported. These are queries that ask a question in English (or some other language). To enter a free-text query, you must precede the query with the `$contents` operator. For example, the query `$contents how do birds fly?` will attempt to find documents that mention birds and flying.

- Queries based on properties take the form `@property operator value`. For example, to find all documents smaller than 4096 bytes, you would enter `@size < 4096`. See the product documentation for a list of supported property names.

This list provides the basics of forming queries that Index Server can resolve. It is possible to create custom forms that simplify the process of formulating queries for a particular subject matter area. This is especially desirable if the user community at your organization is unfamiliar with query processing. However, many sites will not need to customize the query process at all.

The mechanics of actually resolving the query involve the use of some special files. The original query is combined with information in an Internet data query (.IDQ) file. This file specifies how the query is to be processed. There are two possible sections in an .IDQ file: the *names section* and the *query section*. The names section is optional and is used only to define nonstandard column names that can be referred to in the query. This section is not needed for standard query processing. The query section is used to specify parameters that are used when the query is processed.

Parameters in the .IDQ file are specified in a *variable=value* format. A variety of parameters are available to control the behavior of query processing. For example, the location of your *catalog* that contains all indexes created by Index Server is specified in a variable called `CiCatalog`. Another variable, `CiMaxRecordsInResultSet`, controls how much information can be returned as results. The variable `CiColumns` controls the columns that are returned in the results page, and should match the columns referenced in the .HTX file that is used to format the results.

Part
V

Ch
21

HTML extension files (with a .HTX extension) are used to format the results. These files are created using HTML with conditional statements based on the variables defined and created in the .IDQ file that was used for the query being handled. Depending on your interest in customizing the query process, it can be enlightening to review the sample files provided to see how they are designed. The most basic query is handled with the following files, assuming you have accepted all defaults during installation:

- `c:\InetPub\wwwroot\samples\Search\query.htm`—This is the basic query form that is presented as a sample for you to test the use of Index Server. By default, it is not linked into any home page on your Web server. You must add a link to this page or connect to it by entering the URL directly into your browser (**http://<*servername*>/samples/ search/query.htm**) if you want to use it.

- `c:\InetPub\scripts\samples\Search\query.idq`—This is the Internet data query file that corresponds to the basic query form. You can read the comments provided, which describe the variables used and make suggestions for configuration changes that a Webmaster might make.

- `c:\InetPub\wwwroot\samples\Search\query.htx`—This is the HTML extension file for the results that are returned by queries created with the two preceding files. This can also be customized to change the way the information is presented.

Now that you have been introduced to the query process, the action that occurs behind the scenes to index the content on your Web servers is described. The next few sections track the various actions that occur when new content is added to an indexed directory on your Web server, culminating in a set of entries in the master index.

Scanning

Indexing starts with a scanning process. By default, all *virtual roots* defined on your IIS server will be indexed. You can add additional virtual roots and include them in the indexing process as needed. You can also exclude virtual roots from indexing if you desire. These virtual roots can be directories on the Web server machine itself, or shared directories on other servers.

Windows NT supports automatic change notification and will initiate the scanning process when new files are added to the server. Other file servers (for example, Windows 95 and Novell NetWare) do not support this feature, and must wait for a periodic, scheduled scan to occur.
A Registry entry (`ForcedNetPathScanInterval`), which can be configured by the administrator, controls the frequency of these scans.

There are two types of scans that are performed by Index Server: *incremental scan* and *full scan*. The first time a directory is scanned, a full scan of all contents is performed. Thereafter, only an incremental scan is necessary to accommodate the changes that have occurred. Occasionally, an additional full scan could be necessary. For example, after a server suffers a catastrophic failure, a full scan is needed. No administrator intervention is normally needed, even for this type of recovery operation. Index Server has been designed to recover from failures automatically unless an unusual circumstance should occur and go undetected (for example, Registry corruption). A full scan or an incremental scan can be forced at any time by the administrator.

Filtering

Once a directory has been scanned, a three-step filtering process takes place, described as follows:

1. A filter DLL examines the document and extracts the text and properties that are accessible. For many binary files (that don't have a corresponding custom filter), only properties would be able to be extracted.
2. A second DLL, known as a word-breaker DLL, parses the text and any textual properties into words.
3. The resulting list of words is compared with the list of noise words, which are removed and discarded. The remaining words will be processed and included in the index.

Filtering occurs under the direction of the CiDaemon process, which is spawned by the Index Server engine (see the following Note). It must analyze the list of documents that have been scanned and sent for indexing to determine which is the appropriate filter DLL and which is the appropriate word-breaker DLL. As previously mentioned, different filter DLLs and word-breaker DLLs are required to handle documents of different types and in different languages.

N O T E *Daemon* is another name for a background process that runs without requiring user intervention. The term is most commonly used in UNIX environments. In a Windows NT environment, the term *service* has roughly the same meaning and is used much more frequently.

In addition to generating words to be merged, the filtering process also generates a *characterization*. This is a short summary of the item being indexed that can aid the user in deciding if this is a document or file that is of interest. The Registry key `GenerateCharacterization` is set to `1` (by default). If this entry is set to `0`, characterizations will not be generated.

Index Server is designed to be operational 24 hours a day, seven days a week. Therefore, it does most of its work in the background and attempts to work only when the server is idle. It also closes any documents that it is processing as quickly as possible if they are requested by another user or application. Filtering of that document will automatically be retried later.

CAUTION

If directories on shared network drives (on another server) are being indexed, the files that are opened by Index Server will *not* be quickly released when another user or process requests them. This feature (quickly releasing files needed elsewhere) is not available when indexing shared network drives. Therefore, the filtering process may temporarily hold a file lock on a document while it is being filtered. Use discretion when deciding which directories should be indexed.

To avoid interfering with other more urgent processes on a server, the CiDaemon process runs in the idle priority class by default. In other words, it filters documents only when there is no other work of a higher priority to perform. If you intend to use Index Server on a fairly busy computer, this could result in lengthy delays before documents are filtered and a subsequent backlog will occur. To increase the priority of the CiDaemon process—understanding that this may impact the throughput of other work on this server—you can set the `ThreadPriorityFilter` Registry key to `THREAD_PRIORITY_NORMAL` and the `ThreadClassFilter` to `NORMAL_PRIORITY_CLASS`.

Part
V

Ch
21

CAUTION

Changing any of the Registry entries as described in this chapter, especially the priority level, should be approached with extreme care. Improperly editing the Registry can result in corruption of information and the need to reinstall the operating system and restore the most recent backup. This operation should be attempted only by experienced administrators, and only after a current backup is made and the RDISK utility is run to create an updated repair disk.

When the filtering process is complete, the resulting word lists are merged as described in the next section.

Merging and Index Creation

Indexes are used in many different computer applications. There are many different types of indexes for different purposes. The indexes created by Index Server are designed for the purpose of rapidly resolving the search queries used when trying to locate documents or other content on Web servers. The words and properties that have been extracted during the filtering process by CiDaemon are merged into a permanent index that is stored on disk.

Because Index Server must operate in an environment in which many other activities are being performed (potentially) on the same machine concurrently with its operations—including the need to resolve queries based on the current content and indexes that already exist—a multi-step process is used that culminates in a single, up-to-date index. Depending on the load placed on the server and the amount of new information that is being added, there are intermediate stages that result in a more complex state than a single index.

As already described, the filtering process results in *word lists*. These can be thought of as mini-indexes for a small collection of documents. They are stored in RAM as they await further processing. If a power loss occurs, these word lists are lost, but Index Server is designed to recover automatically from such an event. Because they exist in RAM, the creation of a word list is very fast.

Word lists are merged to form *shadow indexes*. These are stored on disk and will, therefore, survive a power loss. More than one shadow index can exist in the *catalog,* which is the directory containing all indexes for an Index Server. The process of merging word lists (and occasionally other shadow indexes) to form a shadow index is called a *shadow merge*. During the shadow merge process, additional compression is performed on the information stored in word lists to further optimize storage and retrieval.

A *master merge* is eventually performed to create the *master index*. During this process, all shadow indexes and the current master index are merged to create a new master index. At any given moment, there is only one master index. If the server has had an opportunity to "get caught up," then there will not be any shadow indexes or word lists—just the master index. In other words, if there is sufficient processing power and no new documents are added for a period of time, the natural progression of things will result in a single master index and no other index structures. As new documents are added, the process starts again. Index Server is capable of operating properly in any intermediate state, but is most efficient when working with just the (complete) master index.

The total number of indexes on a very busy server can grow as high as 255. If the server is so busy that even more shadow indexes would be required, the server will fail and some reconfiguration will be required to provide faster disk subsystems, additional CPU power, or other additional resources so that it can accommodate the load required. A master merge on a very active machine can be a complex and lengthy process. The automatic recovery capability of Index Server includes even this complex operation. System failure in the midst of a master merge operation is fully and automatically recoverable.

Installing and Using Index Server

Now that you know how Index Server operates, it is time to learn how to install and use this powerful tool. The following procedure assumes that you have already installed Windows NT Server and IIS. In addition, you should be logged on with administrative rights to the machine, which is set up as an Index Server. If you want to index the contents of other file servers or Web servers, you should define additional *virtual directories* on the IIS WWW service using the Internet Service Manager. You can add additional virtual directories at a later time if you prefer. For more information about defining virtual directories, see Chapter 18, "Building a Web with Internet Information Server (IIS)."

To install Index Server, follow these steps:

1. Insert the appropriate CD or connect to a shared network directory containing the Index Server distribution file.

2. Launch the executable distribution file (`is11enu.exe` for the English language version).

3. A Welcome dialog box is displayed. Click the Continue button.

4. Another dialog box is displayed (see Figure 21.2). This dialog box requests the location (the full physical path) of the IIS scripts directory so that it can install Index Server sample scripts. By default the directory is `c:\InetPub\scripts`. A virtual directory can also be used. Either accept the default, or override it with your preferred location. Click the Continue button.

FIG. 21.2
This dialog box is used to specify the location of IIS scripts.

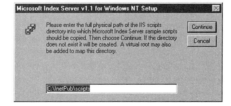

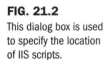

Part

V

Ch

21

5. Another similar dialog box is presented. Enter the location of the IIS virtual root. By default, this is `c:\InetPub\wwwroot`. Again, either accept the default, or override it with your preferred location. Click the Continue button.

6. A final dialog box requests the location to store the Index Server catalog (the collection of indexes including the master index). By default, this is `c:\ISIndex`. Choose a location for the catalog to be stored, or accept the default. Click the Continue button.

7. A file copying progress bar is displayed. When all the files have been copied, you are informed that the process is complete, and the URL for the sample search page (also called a query form) is provided. By default, this is **http://<*servername*>/Samples/Search/queryhit.htm**. Index server has been successfully installed.

Once you have installed Index Server, you naturally will be eager to test its functionality. If you already have an operational Web server with an interesting collection of content, all you need to do is wait. Index Server's operations are automatic, and the scanning, filtering, merging, and index creation process occurs without further intervention. Depending on the amount of content and the load placed on the server, you should allow anywhere from ten minutes to several hours for the indexing process to produce useful results.

You can start by reviewing the online Index Server Guide. This is accessible by choosing Start, Program, Microsoft Index Server, Index Server Online Documentation (see Figure 21.3). Alternatively you can connect to this Web page by manually entering the URL (**http://<*servername*>/srchadm/help/default.htm** by default).

FIG. 21.3
Index Server includes online documentation in HTML format.

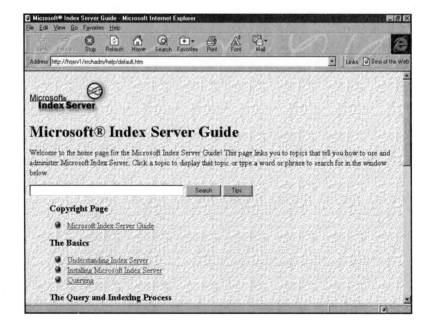

Once an appropriate period of time has elapsed, you are ready to try a search. Choose Start, Program, Microsoft Index Server, Index Server Sample Query Form (see Figure 21.4). This Web page is the sample query form that is discussed in the introduction to this chapter. It enables you to test the search capabilities of Index Server.

FIG. 21.4

The sample query form provided with Index Server is a working search page that can be used without modification or customized to meet specific needs.

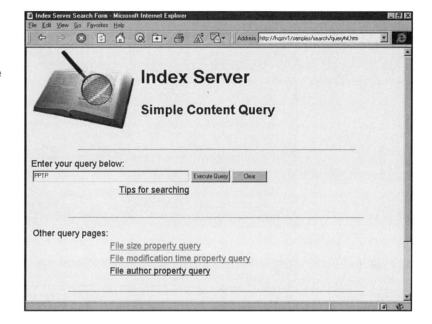

To test your Index Server, follow these steps:

1. Open the sample query form as described in the preceding paragraph.

2. Enter a keyword or phrase that you believe will result in a successful query result. Click the Execute Query button.

3. The results of your query are returned and displayed in your browser (see Figure 21.5). In addition to listing the documents or pages that matched, a *characterization*, or short summary of the document, is automatically generated.

4. Depending on the type of documents returned in your result set, the manner in which your browser is configured and the software installed on your computer, you may be able to click a hyperlink in the results and directly open a matching document. In Figure 21.6, a Microsoft Word document has been opened in the browser window.

5. Choose Go, Back, or click the Back toolbar button. This takes you back to the query results page. At the bottom of this page, you can click the New Query hyperlink to return to the query form (or, in this example, you could just click the Back button one more time).

6. You can continue refining your search by entering new queries until you find the document you want. Simply close your browser when you are done.

Part
V

Ch
21

FIG. 21.5

The results of a query are formatted in HTML and returned to your browser for display.

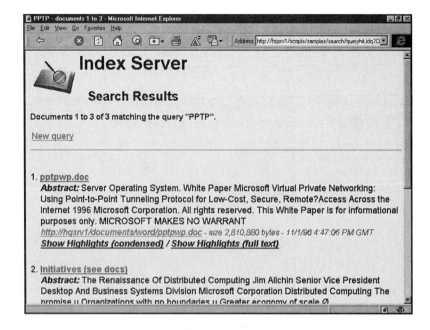

FIG. 21.6

If properly configured, the Microsoft Internet Explorer (version 3.01 for Windows NT shown here) can host documents within its window, such as this Microsoft Word document.

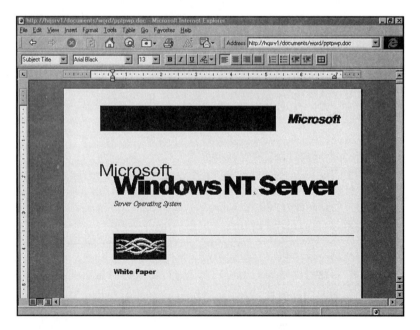

You are now familiar with the main procedures for using Index Server. By design, it is easy to use and manage. With the growth of most Web sites, indexing is becoming a critical feature that is needed to help people find the information they need. Index Server fills this important role with a minimum of work on your part. The next section discusses another member of the BackOffice family called the Content Replication System.

The Content Replication System

The rapid growth of the Internet, and particularly the World Wide Web, took most people by surprise. In a very short time, the Web has grown from an interesting novelty to a useful tool for communicating with the world. This is not to discount the important role it has played for years in the academic and defense communities. In these environments, which have large populations of highly trained individuals, the Internet has long been a widely used and powerful tool. But it wasn't until the invention of the graphical Web browser and the concurrent improvements in network and computer hardware that it gained wide appeal to "ordinary" people.

Thanks to a growing audience, the Internet has now become an excellent platform for organizations to communicate with potential constituents, customers, and other businesses (to the lament of some early Internet users). With this growth has come a rapid maturation in the process and tools used to build and manage Web sites and the content that drives them.

A natural metamorphosis has taken place in many organizations as the sophistication of their Web sites has evolved. Starting with a single interested experimenter, these efforts now may involve one or more Webmasters coordinating the work of graphic artists, musical and sound clip editors, animation specialists, and other special purpose content experts. What is more, all of this content must be organized, and (even worse) constantly updated. In order to cope with these challenges, Webmasters have begun to use some traditional tools for new purposes and to foster the development of an entirely new set of special purpose tools.

Source control systems, used in the past to coordinate the orderly interaction of a group of programmers working together on a body of computer code, have been pressed into duty to manage Web content. These systems not only enable users to "check out" and "check in" files, but also track revisions and even restore an older version if the latest becomes corrupted. Microsoft's SourceSafe is an example of this genre, and a white paper is available on the Microsoft Web site (**http://www.microsoft.com/ssafe**) describing the use of this product for Web content management.

A new entry in the Web management repertoire is the Microsoft Content Replication System (CRS). This product is designed to move Web content from one computer to another. There are a variety of scenarios in which the product can be used, and a number of methods that are supported. This section does the following:

- Introduces the product in more detail by outlining some scenarios in which the product would be useful.
- Describes how to set up CRS.
- Walks you through a sample replication.

Although the product could be used to replicate arbitrary information, it is specifically engineered to be used in a Web server environment. For example, one option enables you to specify the content to be replicated by providing a Uniform Resource Locator (URL)—basically, a Web address.

Content Replication Scenarios

In this section, a variety of scenarios involving the need for content replication are explored. In addition, the role that CRS can play is outlined in order to familiarize you with the type of work this product can perform. Because this is a relatively new product category that is much less familiar than others (e.g., word processing), it is important to spend a little time understanding how it is used before actually deploying it in a production environment.

If you have a modest Web site with under 50 pages managed by a single author, these scenarios will not reflect your environment. When your site grows to hundreds or thousands of pages with dozens of authors, some content management tools are necessary.

A simple example is presented first. Only two computers are involved in this scenario, although it could be a component in a much larger architecture. Figure 21.7 represents a Web content developer's desktop computer linked to a Web server. The content developer may be using a variety of tools to create Web pages and test them on a Peer Web Server, such as that provided by Windows NT Workstation. The tools used to create the pages is unimportant in terms of CRS.

FIG. 21.7

In this simple content replication scenario, Web content is pulled from a desktop computer to a server.

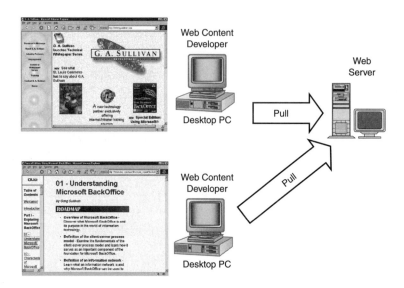

On the same network is a Web server: a Windows NT Server running IIS. The same server is also running CRS. This server would typically be a more powerful machine than the Web developer's desktop computer, and may be locked in a wiring closet for security reasons. Because of its greater power and security, it is a suitable platform for sharing information with a large number of concurrent users and, therefore, an appropriate target to place the Web content that has been developed.

At regular intervals—perhaps every night or once a week—content is *pulled* (copied) from the developer's computer to the Web server. The only action required by the developer is to make sure he has placed *finished* Web pages at the designated link location specified in the replication. This could even be a simple "under construction" page, but it should never be content that yields errors. A partially finished page or series of pages that are actively being developed should be kept in a different location during construction. The developer can point his own browser at this temporary location for viewing and testing links, then copy to the pickup location when he is satisfied with the results.

All activities performed by CRS are managed as *projects*. Even a very complex architecture involving many servers and other computers in locations around the world can be broken down into a collection of projects. In this first scenario, all that is needed is a simple pull replication project. To create the project, the URL of the Peer Web Server being used by the content developer is provided and the destination to which the content should be copied. This location should be an active URL on the Web server that will act as the final destination of this content.

One of the key advantages of using CRS, even in this very simple scenario, is the capability to automate the administrative task of moving the content to the active Web server. The Web developer is presumably involved in this activity regularly—perhaps even full time—but it is a nuisance to require intervention by an administrator in order to move the content to the server. However, it may be unacceptable to provide administrative access to the server to a group of Web developers. By automating the process, the content is moved to the right place, simply and securely, at a regularly designated interval.

The next scenario builds on the first, and demonstrates a situation in which CRS plays a more valuable role. In this example, shown in Figure 21.8, the content on a single Web server is replicated to three additional servers. Depending on the network architecture and links between the servers, it may be possible to copy the information *simultaneously* to the three servers at once. This is a feature of CRS that can be useful if the links between the servers are deemed reliable.

If the links between servers are subject to regular outages, a *frame* copy can be used. With this feature, content is broken down into frames and sent with error correcting protocols that can detect if a frame has become garbled during transmission. In addition, replication projects that are interrupted can be restarted at the point of disruption; they do not need to restart at the beginning as required when using standard file transfer protocols. This can be a critical feature if you are replicating very large files or a large collection of small files over the Internet or private WAN.

Part

V

Ch

21

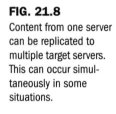

FIG. 21.8

Content from one server can be replicated to multiple target servers. This can occur simultaneously in some situations.

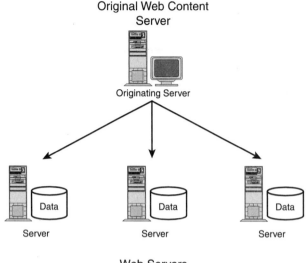

Original Web Content Server

Originating Server

Data Server

Data Server

Data Server

Web Servers

Figure 21.9 shows this scenario developed even further. The content is replicated from a single originating server to a *staging server*. From here, it is replicated over the Internet in a series of discrete projects to three other Web servers in different locations. This distribution is done for the purpose of providing content at a location near its intended audience. Although in theory any Internet user can reach any public server, reliability and throughput will be enhanced by local availability if you intend to serve a large population of users.

At each of these locations, the content is further replicated to multiple local servers for the purpose of providing scalability and redundancy. If a single server fails, the site as a whole is still available due to the availability of one or more backup servers. In addition, the load can be distributed among the servers to provide improved responsiveness during peak access times.

The final scenario is an example involving a very large corporate Web site. In Figure 21.10, each department is responsible for creating Web content describing its products or services. A central group of Webmasters creates the primary home page (www.companyname.com) and manages the overall infrastructure of servers and replication projects.

Each department can be assigned a primary URL that corresponds to a virtual root on the corporate Web server. This location is referenced by a link from the main home page. It is also the target of a content replication project that moves content from a departmental staging server to the primary Web servers at regular intervals. The department's own Web content developers can build whatever structure they want within their own pages and can refer to other well-defined URLs in other departmental pages. If references are made to another department's content other than the virtual root, care must be taken to ensure that the URLs don't change without notification.

FIG. 21.9
A relatively sophisti-
cated replication
scenario involving
multiple locations with
multiple servers at each
is shown here. A staging
server is used as a
distribution point.

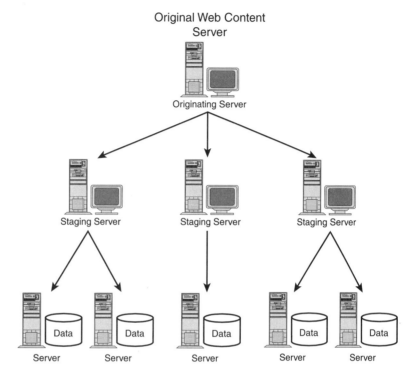

Original Web Content
Server

Originating Server

Staging Server   Staging Server   Staging Server

Data   Data   Data   Data   Data

Server   Server   Server   Server   Server

Web Servers

The primary administrative chore then becomes the maintenance of CRS projects. CRS lends itself to automatic monitoring through its support of Performance Monitor counters. Alerts can be created in Performance Monitor to notify the appropriate administrators by launching a batch file or application. You could use this mechanism to send an e-mail message or trigger a beeper.

There are additional features for automatic server and process monitoring built into SQL Server and Exchange Server that can be used to monitor the services that implement CRS, create entries in the Windows NT event log, and restart services or even reboot servers auto-matically. For more information about automating network administration tasks, see Chapter 50, "Proactive Network Administration."

▶ **See** "Monitoring Your Site," **p. 1027**

Setting Up the Content Replication System

In this section, you learn how to install CRS on a server. If you intend to use the command-line interface exclusively, then any Windows NT server with sufficiently powerful components (processor, disk drive subsystem, and network interface) will suffice. CRS can be run on either Windows NT Server or Windows NT Workstation. Clearly, if the CRS system is also intended to act as a Web server (as opposed to just a staging server for information that is being moved), it must be running IIS.

Part
V

Ch
21

FIG. 21.10

The maintenance of a large corporate Web site can be automated by using CRS.

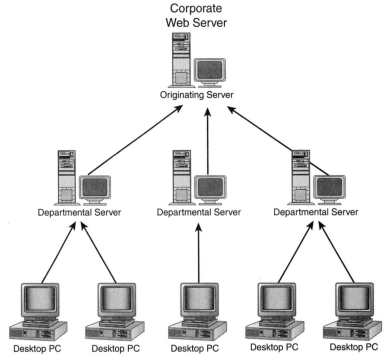

Corporate
Web Server

Originating Server

Departmental Server   Departmental Server   Departmental Server

Desktop PC   Desktop PC   Desktop PC   Desktop PC   Desktop PC

Original Web Content
Developers

Most people will want to take advantage of the CRS Web Administration tool, even if they occasionally use the command-line interface for auxiliary tasks or to confirm the status of a project. This tool is somewhat different from other BackOffice administration tools. It is Web browser-based, which a growing number of BackOffice products are adding, but this is still fairly new. Also, it uses a different style of buttons and controls than you may be used to if you manage other BackOffice products. You may also find it necessary to use the Refresh button to update the display more often with this tool than most others in the BackOffice administration suite, primarily because of its Web-based design. It is, however, relatively easy to learn and use.

NOTE In order to use the Web Administration tool, you must install CRS on a Windows NT 4.0 system that has been configured to use the NTFS file system. In order to ensure security, the CRS Web Administration tool is not supported on disk drives configured with FAT partitions. ■

As with all BackOffice products, administrative tasks can be initiated from client computers connected to the server over the network. In order to run the CRS Web Administration tool on a client computer, you must be running either Microsoft Internet Explorer 3.01 (or later) or Netscape Navigator 3.0 (or later).

In order to administer CRS, you must be able to access the Web Administration tool through IIS. This is subject to IIS security restrictions as described in Chapter 18, "Building a Web With Internet Information Server (IIS)." In addition, you must be an administrator for the Windows NT system that runs CRS. You should also create a *service account* to run CRS services using the User Manager for Domains utility. For more information about Windows NT security, see Chapter 7, "Administering Windows NT Server."

▶ **See** "Creating a Service Account," **p. 195**

To install CRS, follow these steps:

1. Insert the distribution media (usually a CD) into a drive on your Windows NT computer. Find the Setup program and launch it. You will see the dialog box shown in Figure 21.11. Click the OK button.

FIG. 21.11

The InstallShield Self-extracting EXE dialog box begins the installation of CRS.

2. After another intermediate dialog box that requires no response (but simply updates you on the preparation process), you are presented with the Welcome dialog box for the Setup program (see Figure 21.12). Click the Next button.

FIG. 21.12

This is the Welcome dialog box for the Content Replication System.

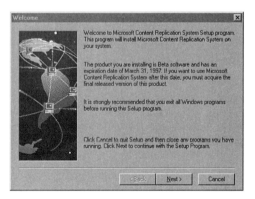

3. A license agreement dialog box is presented next. Carefully read the license and click Yes to accept the license agreement. The next dialog box displays the names of any services that must be stopped in order to complete the installation (see Figure 21.13). Click Yes to stop the services and continue installing CRS.

Part
V

Ch
21

FIG. 21.13

This dialog box lists the Web-related services that must be stopped before the installation process can continue.

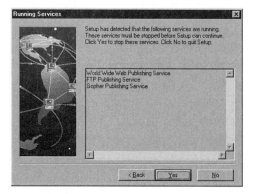

4. A series of messages informing you about services being stopped follows; then, a Registration dialog box is displayed. Enter your Name, and your Company (if appropriate). Click the Next button.

5. You are now prompted to select the directory in which you want CRS installed. Select the directory you want to use, or accept the default (which is automatically created), and click the Next button.

6. The Web Administration and Document Directory dialog box asks you for the virtual root on your Web server that will contain the Web Administration tool and online documentation (see Figure 21.14). Click the Next button.

FIG. 21.14

The Web Administration and Document Directory dialog box is used to select the location for the Web Administration tool and the product documentation.

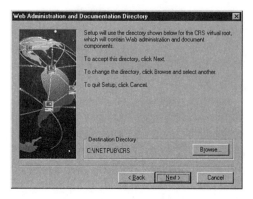

7. You must now choose the setup type, either Typical or Custom. If you select Typical, the Setup program will install standard components without further input. If you select Custom, the dialog box shown in Figure 21.15 is displayed.

FIG. 21.15
The Select Components dialog box is used to customize your CRS installation.

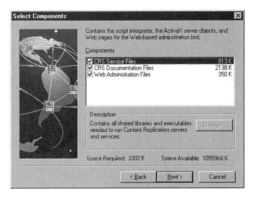

8. You can select those elements of the system you would like to install, and ensure that adequate disk space is available. When you are satisfied with your selections, click the Next button. The CRS Service Account dialog box is displayed (see Figure 21.16).

FIG. 21.16
Use the CRS Service Account dialog box to select the service account that will be used by CRS.

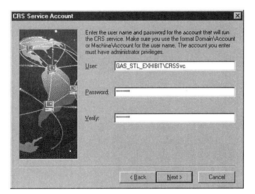

9. The service account establishes the security context that the CRS service will have during its execution. Select the account you created earlier (or task switch to User Manager for Domains and quickly create the account). Click the Next button to continue.

10. The Schedule Service Account dialog box is presented. This is typically the same account used for the CRS service. Select an appropriate account and click the Next button to continue.

11. Select the folder to contain the CRS shortcut icons to start the Web Administration tool and review online documentation. Either choose a folder or accept the default.

12. A confirmation dialog box gives you an opportunity to review all your choices. Click Next to begin the actual installation. When setup is complete, a final dialog box offers you an opportunity to view the CRS Start Page. Click the Finish button to complete setup and view the Start Page (see Figure 21.17).

Part
V
Ch
21

FIG. 21.17
The CRS Start Page provides an introduction to CRS and links you to the Web Administration tool.

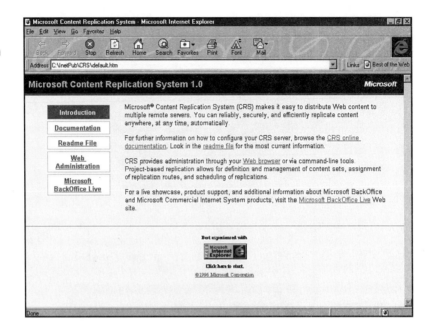

You are now ready to use CRS to move Web content on your network. This is described in the next section.

Using CRS to Move Web Content

There are two interfaces that can be used to control CRS. The first is a Web browser-based interface that uses JScript applications to create and monitor the status of projects. The second is a comprehensive command-line interface. Both of these interfaces are described in this section.

Remember that *all replication events are managed as projects* —no matter how complicated an architecture you want to create. These projects operate on pairs of servers, either pulling or pushing information from one server to the other. Even large replication architectures spanning global networks are based on this simple concept. In the next two sections you will learn how to create both push and pull projects, the basic ingredients for all replication scenarios.

It is a good idea to experiment with CRS in a lab environment before deploying it on your production servers. This is generally true of all BackOffice products, but can be especially important with a product like CRS that is capable of moving very large amounts of information, and consequently having a big impact on network bandwidth and server performance. When it comes time to implement CRS on your production environment, you should have a good idea what will happen, based on the tests you have performed. You want to know how long a typical operation will take, the best time of day to perform that operation, and the impact a replication project will have on active Web users.

Pull Projects   A *pull project* is designed to connect to a source URL (a Web address) and copy the content it finds there to a specified target directory on the server that is running the pull project. The server "pulls" the content from the source, hence the name.

You can either request that all content at the source be pulled, or only a specified number of levels be copied. If you specify a limit of two levels, for example, the initial page (typically `default.htm` or `index.htm`, depending on how the server is configured) will be copied, and the links on that page will be followed. The content of the linked pages will be copied, and the links contained in them will be followed and copied. This is what is meant by two levels deep.

To create a pull project using the Web Administration tool, follow these steps:

1. Launch the Web Administration tool. This can be done by using the icon from Start, Programs, or directly by entering the URL into your browser (**http://servername/crs/ admin/crs.pgi** by default). This opens the CRS Web Administration tool's initial page (see Figure 21.18).

FIG. 21.18

This figure depicts the first page of the Web Administration tool for CRS, a browser-based administration utility that lets you manage Servers, Projects, Routes, or configuration Settings.

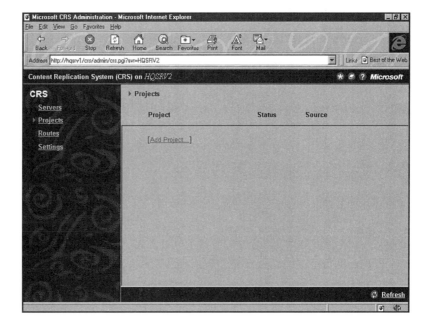

2. Click the Add Project link.
3. An Add Project dialog box is displayed (see Figure 21.19). Enter a Name for the project, and select the type (Pull replication in this example). Click the OK button.

FIG. 21.19

The Add Project dialog box enables you to create a project and select the type of replication that you want to use.

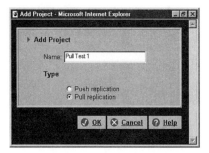

4. The Project Source/Target page is displayed (see Figure 21.20). Enter the Source URL from which content will be pulled, then enter the number of levels the replication should pull (the depth of links that it should follow). Click the All button to pull the entire Web site from that virtual root.

FIG. 21.20

The Source/Target page is used to specify the source and destination for your project.

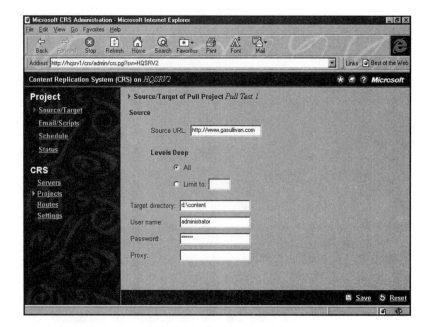

5. Enter the Target directory. This is the fully qualified path name on the local server (the server that is running this CRS project). You can optionally enter a user name, password, and proxy server name if required to access the source server. Click Save, and then click the Projects link to return to the main Projects page. Click the Schedule link. This presents the Schedule page.

6. Select the Replicate Automatically button, or click Add Schedule to add a specific scheduled date and time (see Figure 21.21).

FIG. 21.21
The Add Schedule dialog enables you to specify when the replication occurs. Select the days of the week, and the time of day.

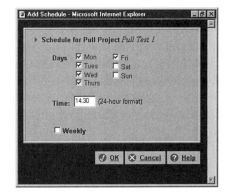

7. Select the schedule for this project and click the OK button to return to the Schedule page and continue.

8. Click the Email/Scripts link. This will present the Email/Scripts page (see Figure 21.22). E-mail notification can automatically be sent on success or failure of a replication event, or every time the event executes. You can also run a script before any content is received on the server, or after it is all received. This script may be used for notification, for routine maintenance chores, or other application specific purposes. Click Save, and then click the Projects link again.

FIG. 21.22
The Email/Scripts page is used primarily for notification purposes

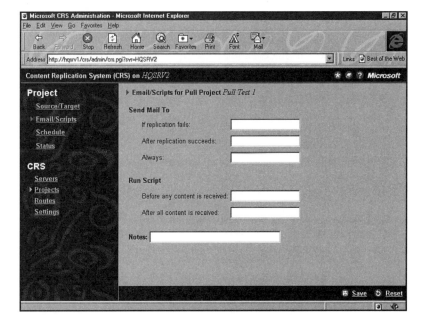

9. You should now see your project added to the list on the Projects page (see Figure 21.23). It should have a status of Idle. Click the Idle link.

FIG. 21.23

The Projects page will list all active projects, and show their current status. You can remove a project by clicking the waste can icon to the left of the project's name.

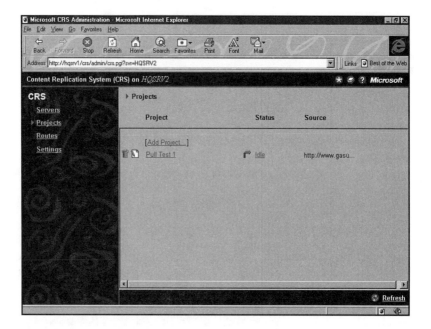

10. A Project Status dialog box will be displayed (see Figure 21.24). This dialog can be used to start a project immediately, regardless of the scheduled times that may have already been set for this project. Click Start if you want to test your new project. The State displayed on the dialog box will be updated from Idle to Running to reflect the new status of the system.

11. Click OK when you are done with this project. You can enter additional projects to monitor, or exit the CRS Administration tool by choosing File, Close from the menu.

Push Projects A *push project operates* in a reverse manner from a pull project. It is initiated on the source server, and "pushes" content to one or more destination servers. In addition, a push project must be defined on both the source and destination servers, although only the source server is configured for a target (destination).

To create a push project using the Web Administration tool, follow these steps:

1. Launch the Web Administration tool. This can be done by using the icon from Start, Programs, or directly by entering the URL into your browser (**http://servername/crs/ admin/crs.pgi**, by default). This opens the CRS Web Administration tool's initial page (refer to Figure 21.18).

2. Click the Add Project link. An Add Project dialog box is displayed.

3. Enter a Name for the project, and select the type (Push replication, in this example). Click the OK button.

FIG. 21.24

In addition to starting a project, the Project Status dialog box can also be used to stop an executing project, or to rollback (undo) the effects of an earlier replication.

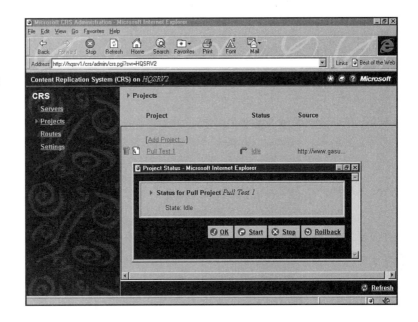

4. The Project Source/Target page is displayed (see Figure 21.25). Enter the Project Directory from which content will be pushed, and then select an option button to indicate which subdirectories (if any) should be copied with the main project directory. Click the Add Target link.

FIG. 21.25

The Source/Target page for a push project is used to specify the project directory to be replicated, whether or not to include sub-directories, and to add Targets (destinations) for the push event.

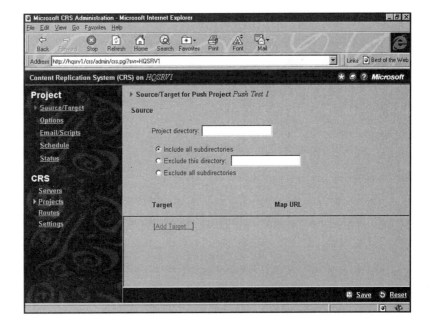

Part
V
Ch
21

5. The Add Target dialog is displayed (see Figure 21.26). Enter the name of the Target machine (for example, HQSRV2). You can also specify that a *route* (a predefined chain of linked servers) should be used as the target, although this is beyond the scope of this book. Click OK and then Save. You can now click the Projects link to return to the main Projects page.

FIG. 21.26

The Add Target dialog box is used to specify the target of this replication event. Only one machine can be specified in a target, but multiple targets may be defined for the same project.

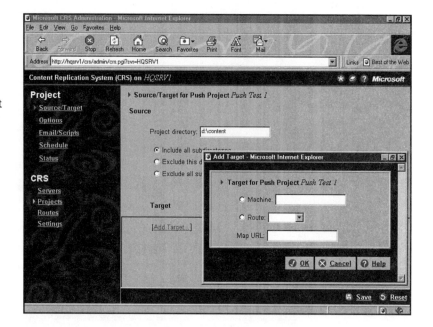

6. You should now see your project added to the list on the Projects page. It should have a status of Idle.

7. In order to complete the configuration of the push replication project, you must repeat steps 2 and 3 on the target server. Click the Servers link and enter the name of the destination server in the Select Server dialog box. You will be connected to the destination server, and any currently defined projects will be displayed.

8. Click the Add Project link. An Add Project dialog box is displayed.

9. Enter the same project name that you used on the originating server, and a project directory that will receive the replicated content—but you need not specify a target server since this server is the final destination.

10. Click Save and return to the Projects page to verify that the new project is visible.

11. You have now completed the configuration of the push project. In order to start the project, you should once again connect to the originating server, go to the Projects page, and click the Idle link to open a Project Status dialog. Then click the Start button to start the project.

12. Click OK when you are done with this project. You can enter additional projects to monitor, or exit the CRS Administration tool by choosing <u>F</u>ile, <u>C</u>lose from the menu.

This brief introduction to the Content Replication System should give you a solid basis on which to build additional knowledge and experience with this new member of the Microsoft BackOffice family. This product is only in its first release, and it will undoubtedly continue to be enhanced with additional features and capabilities. With the growing use of the Web, and the challenges inherent in managing the large volume of content necessary for a great Web site, the importance of this type of tool will multiply.

From Here...

This chapter presented the features available in two Microsoft BackOffice family components: Index Server and the Content Replication System. It provided detailed information on installing, configuring, and using these components to help manage your Web site. For more information about the topics addressed in this chapter, see the following chapters:

- For information on other Internet components available for Microsoft BackOffice, see Chapter 16, "The BackOffice I-Net Toolbox."
- For information on using the Internet and building internal intranets to serve the needs of your organization, see Chapter 17, "I-Net Tools and Techniques."
- For information on Internet Information Server, see Chapter 18, "Building a Web with Internet Information Server (IIS)."
- To learn about client applications that let you access the Internet's World Wide Web, see Chapter 19, "Web Browsers."
- For information on creating content for your IIS servers, see Chapter 20, "Using Microsoft FrontPage 97."
- To learn about Proxy Server to improve I-net access performance and enhance the security of your IIS site, see Chapter 22, "Implementing Microsoft Proxy Server."
- To explore how the Internet can be used in business, see Chapter 47, "Building BackOffice Applications."

## CHAPTER 22

Implementing Microsoft Proxy Server

by Azam A. Mirza

In other chapters in Part V, "Advanced I-Net Develop-ment," you learn about the I-net and the various server based components that come together to provide I-net connectivity. This chapter discusses in detail the Microsoft Proxy Server component of the BackOffice family of prod-ucts. Proxy Server is a higher level server component that sits on top of the Internet Information Server (IIS) to provide a particular piece of the I-net connectivity puzzle.

The main purpose of Proxy Server is to act as an access control gateway for providing clients connectivity to the Internet. Proxy Server enables secure, two-way communi-cations between clients on a local network and the Internet by passing requests between the local network and the Internet. The Proxy Server services client re-quests and server responses but masks the identities of the client and server from each other. In, addition, Proxy Server uses access control lists to limit outgoing access by clients and access from the Internet by unauthorized users.

Resource requirements for implementing the Proxy Server

Learn about the hardware, software, and other requirement needs for setting up and running a Proxy Server.

How to implement Internet access control using Proxy Server

Learn about the components that come together to provide Internet access control using the Proxy Server.

How to set up Proxy Server

Learn how to set up and install the Proxy Server.

Administering Proxy Server services

Learn about administering the Proxy Server using the Internet Service Manager. Configuration of Proxy Server services is discussed in detail. Use the Proxy Server Auto Dial feature to establish dynamic Internet connectivity.

How to secure Proxy Server

Learn about securing your Proxy Server installation from unautho-rized access and tampering by setting security policies and appro-priate server permissions.

> **N O T E**   To the Proxy Server, a client is a computer, software, or service that makes a request for
> information from a server machine on a network. A server is a computer, software, or
> service that responds to the request. ■

The following sections detail the resource requirements for setting up and installing the Proxy Server, its features, and administration. Special attention is paid to issues relating to security when providing enterprise-wide Internet connectivity. ■

Resource Requirements

Careful planning in implementing an effective solution is very important to the success of an organization's Internet connectivity. The setup of a Proxy Server requires special attention to the requirements for hardware and software.

Proxy Server not only requires special hardware considerations, it also requires certain software components for proper installation and operation. Each of these requirements is discussed in detail in the following sections.

Hardware

The hardware requirements in terms of running a Proxy Server machine are identical to the requirements for Windows NT Server 4.0 an Internet Information Server.

▶ **See** "Choosing Your Hardware," **p. 337**
▶ **See** "Resource Requirements," **p. 538**

However, in addition to the machine running Proxy Server, there are other hardware components that play an important role in setting up an effective Proxy Server implementation.

One of the most important considerations is the storage subsystem. The Proxy Server caches frequently accessed Web sites and documents on its local hard disks. The use of a fast and high throughput subsystem can substantially increase system performance and server response time.

In addition, get as much memory as possible in your Proxy Server machine. A typical installation with 64M of RAM is not unreasonable. The memory requirements will be greatly influenced by the number of users being supported and the number of simultaneous connections being handled.

 The use of the NTFS file system for the hard disk subsystem is a good idea due to its high throughput, fault tolerance, and security features.

 It is a good idea to spread the Proxy Server storage requirements across multiple physical disks to improve system performance.

▶ **See** "Configuring Hard Disk Space," **p. 159**

The speed of the Internet connection is also very important. The choices most commonly available currently include the following:

- ■ **Analog modem**—A minimum speed of 28.8 Kbps modems should be used. The analog modem connections are not very fast and cannot handle high load requirements. This modem should only be used when the number of simultaneous users will be very low. Analog modems are the most cost-effective means of providing Internet connectivity.

- ■ **ISDN**—With typical speeds of 64–128 Kbps, these connections provide good connectivity for low to medium sized load situations. ISDN is fast becoming an affordable means of providing connectivity to the Internet.

- ■ **T1 or higher**—T1 lines provide connectivity speeds of 1.54 Mbps. Higher capacity lines are also available, such as T3 and ATM. The cost for such high speed connectivity is considerably higher. However, for situations that require high throughput and must support a lot of simultaneous connections, these lines are a very good choice.

Software

The Proxy Server is a component of the Microsoft BackOffice suite of server components. However, since Proxy Server is a higher level component, it requires certain BackOffice components for its operation.

The following software components are required for successful installation of Proxy Server:

- ■ Microsoft Windows NT Server version 4.0
- ■ Microsoft TCP/IP services for Windows NT Server
- ■ Microsoft Internet Information Server version 2.0

> **CAUTION**
>
> You must upgrade the Windows NT Server installation by installing the Windows NT Server 4.0 Service Pack 1 maintenance update to your Proxy Server machine. The Service Pack is included on your Proxy Server CD.

Make sure the appropriate drivers are installed for the network cards, modems, or ISDN adapters being used.

 The machine running the Proxy Server can be a Primary Domain Controller, Backup Domain Controller, or a stand-alone server. However, it is recommended that you configure the Proxy Server machine as a stand-alone server to improve performance and security.

▶ **See** "Understanding the Server's Role," **p. 109**

Proxy Server Features

Microsoft Proxy Server provides a rich and powerful combination of functionality and ease of use for establishing corporate-wide secure Internet connectivity. It acts as a gateway between the local network and the external Internet. It leverages the Microsoft BackOffice suite of server products to provide advanced security, high performance, reliability, and ease of use features. Some of the features supported by Proxy Server include:

- **Multi-Protocol support**—In addition to TCP/IP, Proxy Server also supports the IPX/SPX protocols on the local network. This enables Proxy Server to service Internet requests from non-TCP/IP clients. Organizations can continue to use IPX/SPX for their internal networks and get the benefits of Internet connectivity through the use of Proxy Server.

- **Security**—Proxy Server enables a single point of Internet connectivity from the internal network. It takes away the need to connect individual clients to the Internet by acting as a gateway between the local network and the Internet.

- **Ease of use**—Proxy Server keeps up with the traditional attributes of Microsoft BackOffice products by being easy to install, administer, and support. It is administered through the standard Internet Service Manager administration utility.

- **Standards compliant**—Proxy Server complies with standards for proxy services and supports most commonly used protocols, such as HTTP, HTTP-S, SSL, FTP, Telnet, and SMTP. In addition, Proxy Server also supports Windows Sockets version 1.1 applications.

- **Performance**—It leverages the power, scalability, and extensibility of the Windows NT Server environment to provide exceptional performance and reliability.

- **Access control lists**—Proxy Server uses access control lists to manage access by user, service, port, IP address, and domain. It can filter both incoming traffic and outgoing traffic.

Proxy Server provides its functionality through two Windows NT services that run on a server machine: *Web Proxy service* and *WinSock Proxy service*. The following sections detail some of the features supported by these services.

Web Proxy Service

The Web Proxy service provides some of the basic functionality needed to implement the Proxy Server. It is a standards-based service that supports the common Internet protocols, such as HTTP, FTP, and Gopher.

N O T E The Web Proxy service is CERN-proxy compatible, which is the standard used by most popular proxy implementations. ▪

Some of the features supported by Web Proxy include the following:

- Popular Internet protocols, such as HTTP, FTP, and Gopher.
- Standards compliant.
- Uses the TCP/IP networking protocol for communications.
- Provides support for secure logon validation and password encryption.
- Provides powerful caching support for Web objects.
- Provides logging capabilities through the use of log files or by logging to a database.
- Administered through the Internet Service Manager.
- Provides powerful access control capabilities by filtering access based on user, domain, IP address, group, or port number. Filtering can be applied on both incoming and outgoing traffic.

WinSock Proxy Service

The WinSock Proxy service provides services for Windows applications that comply with the Windows Sockets version 1.1. Some of the features supported by the WinSock Proxy service include the following:

- Support for IPX/SPX in addition to TCP/IP on the local network.
- Support for Windows NT Challenge/Response authentication mechanism for logon and password validation.
- Access control based on user, group, protocol, or port. Controls both inbound and outbound traffic.
- Enables site filtering based on domain name and IP address. Users cannot access Internet sites they do not have permissions for.
- IP address masking. Hides internal network addresses from the Internet community to provide an extra layer of security and protection from unauthorized access.
- Administered through the Internet Service Manager.
- Powerful logging capabilities to a file or ODBC database.

Having learned about the features of the Proxy Server, the following sections discuss its installation, setup, and administration functions.

Setting Up Your Proxy Server

In this section, you learn about installation and setup of a Proxy Server machine. Proxy Server installs the Web Proxy and WinSock Proxy services to control Internet access and network security. Before you can install Proxy Server, you need to complete the following steps:

1. Set up a computer with Windows NT Server version 4.0 or higher. Make sure the TCP/IP services are installed during Windows NT Server installation.

2. Install the Windows NT Server 4.0 Service Pack 1.

N O T E   Service Pack 1 is included on the Proxy Server CD. ▪

3. Install Internet Information Server version 3.0.

 T I P   IIS can be installed during the installation of Windows NT Server 4.0 or at a later time by using the IIS Setup program. During the installation process, you will get the option of installing IIS. You can install IIS at that point or use the Setup program later to install IIS. The two procedures are identical, and this chapter outlines the procedure for installing IIS on a pre-configured Windows NT Server 4.0 machine.

▶ **See** "Setting Up Your Internet Information Server," **p. 547**

4. Make sure you have an administrator logon ID and password that you can use to install Proxy Server.

Make sure these steps are completed before you attempt to install the Proxy Server software.

Installing Proxy Server

To install the Proxy Server, follow these steps:

1. From the Start menu, choose Run.

2. In the Run dialog box, type **<*path*>:\setup.exe** for the command line, where **<*path*>** refers to the CD-ROM location where the Proxy Server CD is located. For example, d:\setup.exe.

3. Click OK.

N O T E   During setup, you can click the Help button at any time to get help with installing the Proxy Server. ▪

N O T E   You can also open a command prompt and enter **<*path*>:\setup.exe** at the command line. ▪

After you have started the Setup program for Proxy Server, perform the following steps:

1. Read the Welcome Screen shown in Figure 22.1.

2. Click Continue. The Proxy Server Setup dialog box appears (see Figure 22.2).

FIG. 22.1

The Proxy Server Setup Welcome screen provides information about running the Setup program.

FIG. 22.2

The Proxy Server Setup dialog box enables you to change the default installation directory for Proxy Server.

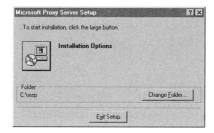

3. If needed, change the folder where Proxy Server will be installed by clicking the Change Folder button; otherwise press the Installation Options button.

4. The Installation Options dialog box appears, as shown in Figure 22.3.

FIG. 22.3

The Proxy Server Installation Options dialog box enables you to select the various services that will be installed during Proxy Server installation.

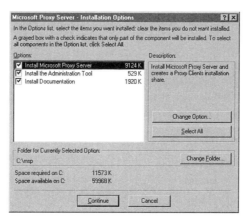

5. By default, all options are selected. Make the appropriate selections for your needs and click Continue. (For a first-time installation, you should install the Proxy Server and the Administration tool. Documentation files can be installed at a later time if so desired.)

6. The Proxy Server Cache Drives dialog box appears (see Figure 22.4). Assign appropriate disk space for caching by selecting a drive, entering a value for Maximum Size (MB), and clicking Set. When done, click OK.

FIG. 22.4

Cache drives are used by Proxy Server to store frequently accessed data files.

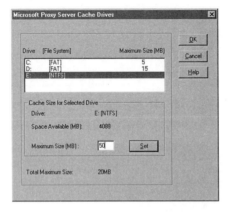

N O T E   You must assign at least one drive and 5M of disk space for caching. The minimum recommended caching space for Proxy Server is 100M plus 0.5M for each client being serviced by the Proxy Server. ▪

   It is a good idea to use NTFS drives for caching. They provide better performance and security.

CAUTION

Do not use removable media or CD-ROM drives as caching drives.

7. The Local Address Table Configuration dialog box appears, as shown in Figure 22.5. Define IP addresses being used by your internal network here. You can define multiple ranges from the pool of your IP addresses. However, each range must be a contiguous block of IP addresses. Click OK.

8. You can also create an LAT by using the Construct Table button. When pressed, the Construct Local Address Table dialog box appears (see Figure 22.6). This dialog box enables you to include some pre-defined private internal network IP ranges as part of your LAT. It also enables you to obtain IP address ranges from your network adapter cards and from internal routing tables.

FIG. 22.5

Local Address Tables (LATs) enable you to define the IP address ranges that constitute your internal network.

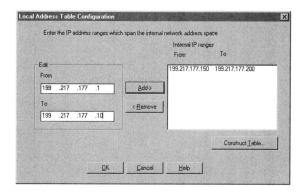

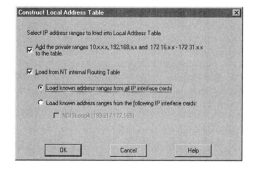

FIG. 22.6

The Construct Local Address Table dialog box enables you to include some pre-defined IP ranges as part of your internal network.

 TIP It is a good idea to use the Construct Local Address Table dialog box to include the pre-defined ranges, and then add any other internal network ranges to the list.

9. When finished, click OK to return to the Local Address Table Configuration dialog box.

10. If you need to add any other IP address to the LAT table, use the From and To boxes and the Add button to add the ranges to the LAT table list.

11. When finished, click OK. The Client Installation/Configuration dialog box appears, as shown in Figure 22.7.

12. Use the WinSock Proxy Client combo box to set up the options for installing WinSock clients from this server. Choose the method clients will use to connect to the Proxy Server. Clients can connect to the server by using its name or IP address.

CAUTION

If using a DNS name, make sure the name displayed in the text box is correct, and ensure that the DNS server has an appropriate entry for the Proxy Server name.

FIG. 22.7

The Client Installation/ Configuration dialog box enables you to set up the options for installation of WinSock and Web Proxy clients.

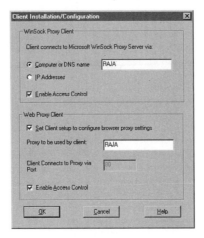

The <u>E</u>nable Access Control check box enables Proxy Server security and ensures that only clients with appropriate permissions can use the WinSock Proxy service. If disabled, all clients will have access to the WinSock Proxy service.

13. Use the Web Proxy Client combo box to set up the options for installing Web Proxy clients from this server. If you click the <u>S</u>et Client Setup to Configure Browser Proxy Settings check box, the client Setup program will automatically configure the Web browser software to use the appropriate Proxy Server. Make sure the correct Proxy Server name is listed in the text box.

N O T E   The Set Client Setup to Configure Browser Proxy Settings feature works only with Netscape Navigator and Microsoft Internet Explorer Web browsers. ■

N O T E   You cannot configure the Connect Clients to Proxy via Port setting here. The setting is preset for Internet Information Server. You must use the Internet Service Manager to change this value. The configuration of this option is covered later in this chapter. ■

The <u>E</u>nable Access Control check box enables Proxy Server security and ensures that only clients with appropriate permissions can use the WinSock Proxy service. If disabled, all clients will have access to the WinSock Proxy service.

14. When finished, click <u>O</u>K. The Setup program will install the necessary files and complete the Proxy Server setup.

   To uninstall Proxy Server, select the Uninstall option from the Proxy Server Program group.

At this point, Proxy Server installation is complete. You can use the Proxy Server program group to start the Internet Service Manager and administer Proxy Server services.

Administering Proxy Server

A powerful combination of tools and services are provided in the BackOffice suite for administering the Proxy Server. The central administrative tool for Proxy Server is the Internet Service Manager provided with Internet Information Server. The Proxy Server Setup program modifies the Internet Service Manager so it can also manage the Web Proxy and the WinSock Proxy services. In addition, tools included with Windows NT Server, such as the Performance Monitor and User Manager, can be used to administer various facets of the Proxy Server.

The following sections discuss Proxy Server administration in detail.

Using the Internet Service Manager

The Internet Service Manager is the focal point for most Proxy Server administration tasks. In particular, the Internet Service Manager is used to administer the two services provided by the Proxy Server: Web Proxy service and WinSock Proxy service.

To administer Proxy Server services through Internet Service Manager, follow these steps:

1. From the Start menu, select Programs, Microsoft Proxy Server, Internet Service Manager.

2. The Internet Service Manager is displayed, as shown in Figure 22.8. All services running on the currently selected server are listed.

FIG. 22.8

The Internet Service Manager can be used to administer Proxy Server services.

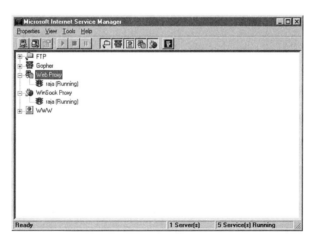

3. If managing a different server, connect to that server by choosing Properties, Connect.

N O T E   Internet Service Manager can be used to administer local, as well as remote, Proxy Servers. ■

4. You can also list all servers running Internet services on the network by choosing Properties, Find All Servers.

5. Once connected to the desired server, you can administer the particular Proxy Server service by double-clicking the computer name next to the service.

The Internet Service Manager uses property sheets to configure and manage services running on the server. Property sheets are tabbed dialog boxes for configuring all options for a particular service.

The following sections describe in detail the configuration options for the two Proxy Server Services: administering Web Proxy service and WinSock Proxy service.

Administering Web Proxy Service   To configure the Web Proxy service, from the Internet Service Manager screen, double-click the computer name next to the Web Proxy service. The Web Proxy Service Properties dialog box appears with the Service tab selected (see Figure 22.9).

FIG. 22.9

The Service tab enables you to configure basic service options for the Proxy Server.

The Web Proxy Service Properties dialog box displays tabs for each category that can be configured. You can use property sheets to configure the following Web Proxy service categories:

- Services
- Permissions
- Caching
- Logging
- Filters

Each of these categories is discussed in detail in the following sections.

Services   The Service tab sets basic options for the Web Proxy service (refer to Figure 22.9). To set these options, click the Service tab and follow these steps:

1. The Product ID number and the Comment text box are used by the system to identify the Proxy Server. Enter a comment that can be used to identify the Web Proxy service.

Part
V

Ch
22

2. The Enable Internet Publishing check box determines if the Proxy Server will allow outside Internet users to gain access to Web servers on the local network. By default, this box is unchecked.

> **CAUTION**
>
> Be careful about enabling the Enable Internet Publishing check box. Make sure you understand the security risks and take appropriate measures to counteract unauthorized access to your Web sites and corporate network.

▶ **See** "Windows NT Security Overview," **p. 226**

▶ **See** "Defining an Internet Security Plan," **p. 513**

3. Pressing the Current Sessions button displays the Web Proxy Service User Sessions dialog box, as shown in Figure 22.10. This allows administrators to view the user connections currently using the Proxy Server service.

FIG. 22.10

The Web Proxy Service User Sessions dialog box can be used to dynamically monitor user activity across the Proxy Server.

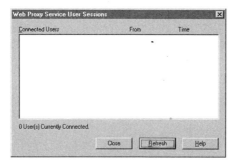

4. The Edit Local Address Table (LAT) button on the Service tab enables administrators to make changes to the LAT table as discussed earlier.

5. Once finished, click Apply to commit changes or click OK to close the Properties dialog box and continue.

Permissions   The Permissions tab is used to configure access control permissions for the Web Proxy service (see Figure 22.11).

The Permissions tab can be used to control access for the following Internet services:

- **FTP Read**—If granted permission, a client can use the FTP protocol to download files from the Internet using his Web browser.

- **Gopher**—Clients can access Gopher file servers through their Web browsers, if granted access control.

- **WWW**—WWW browsing is enabled by allowing clients access to the WWW service. This access control handles both HTTP and HTTP-S protocols.

- **Secure**—Enables SSL (Secure Sockets Layer) access for clients. Clients can browse sites that implement SSL security features.

FIG. 22.11

The Permissions tab allows administrators to control client access to the Web Proxy service.

Permissions are granted on a per-service basis. You will need to setup access lists for each service individually by selecting the appropriate service in the Protocol drop-down list box. To grant users and groups permissions to the various Internet protocols, use the Add button. This brings up the Add Users and Groups dialog box, as shown in Figure 22.12.

FIG. 22.12

The Add Users and Groups dialog box is used to grant Internet access permissions.

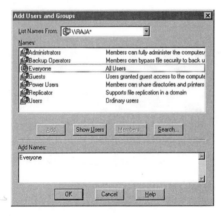

Once finished, click the Apply or OK button to commit changes.

Caching   The Caching tab is used to configure caching information for the Web Proxy service (see Figure 22.13).

Once enabled, caching stores the most frequently accessed locations and documents on the local storage subsystem. The main purpose of caching is to optimize system performance.

FIG. 22.13

The Caching parameters are critical for optimal Web Proxy service performance.

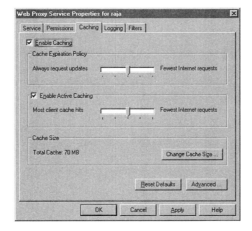

To set caching options, follow these steps:

1. Set appropriate values for the Cache Expiration Policy and Enable Active Caching options.

N O T E It is best to experiment with these values and monitor the results to determine what is the best setting for your network needs. ■

2. The Change Cache Size button enables administrators to expand or contract the size of the allocated cache disk space. Typical cache sizes are about 2–4M for each concurrent user connected through the proxy server.

3. The Reset Defaults button restores the original caching values.

4. The Advanced button displays the Advanced Cache Policy dialog box, as shown in Figure 22.14. This dialog box can be used to set a maximum size limit for cached objects and to reuse expired objects from cache when the Web site is unavailable.

FIG. 22.14

Advanced caching options allow fine-tuning of caching performance.

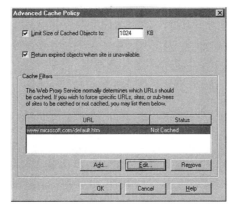

5. The Cache Filters combo box options enable administrators to specify sites that should be especially cached or not. Pressing the Add button brings up the Cache Filter Properties dialog box, which allows you to add specific URL locations for the cache filters (see Figure 22.15).

FIG. 22.15

By caching frequently visited site URLs, performance can be greatly improved.

6. Once finished, click the Apply or OK button on the Caching tab to commit changes.

   ▶ **See** "Performance Monitor," **p. 190**

Logging   The Logging tab is used to configure event logging options for the Web Proxy service (see Figure 22.16).

FIG. 22.16

The Logging tab can be used to set up elaborate reporting for trouble-shooting purposes.

Logging information can be stored in log files; or you can use an ODBC-compatible database, such as Microsoft SQL Server, to store logging information.

 You can use a single log file or a single ODBC database to store logging information from multiple servers.

To configure logging information, click the Logging tab and follow these steps:

1. Click the Enable Logging check box to start logging for the Web Proxy service.
2. Choose the Regular Logging or Verbose Logging option. The Verbose option provides more detailed textual descriptions of log entries whereas the Regular option provides logging codes.
3. Choose the Log to File or Log to SQL/ODBC Database option button.
4. If you choose the Log to File option, you have the following choices:

-   **Automatically Open New Log**—Create a new log based on the options available. Specify a new log file logging interval by selecting Daily, Weekly, Monthly, or When File Size Reaches.
-   **When File Size Reaches**—Specify the file size when a new file should be created in megabytes.
-   **Log File Directory**—Specify the directory name and path where all log files will be stored or use the Browse button to specify a directory.
-   **Log File Name**—Display the naming convention that will be used to store the log files. The *yymmdd* will be replaced with the two-digit year, month, and day numbers to come up with unique names for log files.

N O T E   If you do not use the Automatically Open New Log File option, the same log file will be used indefinitely. You must select an existing directory or manually create a new directory for log files using the File Manager or the MKDIR command. █

5. If you chose the Log to SQL/ODBC Database option, you must configure the following options:

-   **ODBC Data Source Name (DSN)**—Specifies the name that will be used to connect to the database for logging.
-   **Table**—Specifies the name of table that will store the logging information.
-   **User Name**—Specifies the username that will be used to connect to the database.
-   **Password**—Specifies the password that will be used to connect to the database.

N O T E   You must use the ODBC applet in the Control Panel to create the specified system ODBC data source. █

6. Click OK to continue, or click Apply to immediately implement the changes.

CAUTION

Logging to an ODBC data source is slower than logging to a file. Sites with heavy traffic should consider logging to a file for performance reasons or adding processing power to the server to support the additional load, such as adding a processor and higher performance disk subsystem.

Filters The Web Proxy Service Properties Filters tab is used to specify access limits and to control the network traffic on your Proxy Server (see Figure 22.17). You can choose a default access option that either will grant access to all users or deny access to all users. Then you can specify individual computers or groups that are the exceptions to the default.

FIG. 22.17

The Web Proxy service Filters tab can be used to specify access control properties and network usage limits.

In this section, the option of granting access by default and entering exceptions that will be denied access is described.

To configure Filters options, click the Filters tab on the Web Proxy Service Properties dialog box and follow these steps:

1. Select the Enable Filtering option for access control.

2. To exclude computers from having access, you can specify computers that will be granted access using the Add button. This displays the Grant Access To dialog box (see Figure 22. 18).

FIG. 22.18

The Grant Access To dialog box is used to grant access to selected computers when a default policy that denies access to everyone has been chosen.

3. In the Grant Access To dialog box, specify the computer or the group of computers that will be granted access using the IP addresses for those computers. For a group of computers, you must also specify a subnet mask used by the group of computers. You can also specify a Domain name.

4. Click OK to return to the Filters tab.

5. The specified computer or group of computers will show up in the included list. You can specify more computers to exclude, or remove computers from the list by selecting them and clicking Remove. Use the Edit button to change the Grant Access To properties for a computer on the list.

6. When finished, click OK to continue, or click Apply to immediately enforce the changes.

Administering WinSock Proxy Service   To configure the WinSock Proxy service running on a Proxy Server, double-click the computer name running the service to bring up the WinSock Proxy Service Properties dialog box. This dialog box displays tabs for each category that can be configured. The categories are as follows:

- Services
- Protocols
- Permissions
- Logging
- Filters

The Service, Logging, and Filters tabs are identical to those used for the Web Proxy service. Refer to the previous section for the Web Proxy service for more information on setting these options. (The Protocols tab, which is different for the WinSock Proxy service, is discussed in this section.)

The WinSock Protocols tab is used to define or reconfigure existing Internet protocols that clients can use to access resources on the Internet (see Figure 22.19).

FIG. 22.19

The Protocols tab defines parameters for the various Web access technologies.

The Proxy Server comes equipped with a large number of protocol definitions, such as RealAudio, VDOLive, SMTP, POP3, and NNTP. By defining protocols for the common Internet protocols, access can be granted or denied to clients using the Permissions tab. To add a protocol definition from the Protocols tab, follow these steps:

1. Choose the protocol in the Protocol Definitions drop-down list box and click the Add button. The Protocol Definition dialog box is displayed (see Figure 22.20).

FIG. 22.20
The Protocol Definition dialog box can be used to add support for additional Internet protocols.

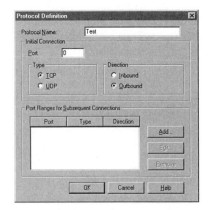

2. Provide a Protocol Name in the text box.

CAUTION

The protocol name and port number must be unique for each new protocol.

---

3. In the Initial Connection box, provide a Port number.

 Most common protocol port numbers are defined in the PROTOCOL file located in the <systemroot\system32\drivers\etc> directory. You can print that file to have a list of protocol and port numbers handy.

4. Select the protocol type.

5. In the Direction box, specify if the protocol will be used for inbound or outbound traffic initially.

6. Use the Port Ranges for Subsequent Connections combo box to specify additional port ranges for protocols that facilitate both inbound and outbound traffic. The FTP protocol and the Telnet service are examples of two-way traffic protocols.

7. Click OK to save the new protocol definition.

Proxy Server Auto Dial Configuration

The Proxy Server Auto Dial feature is provided for scenarios when your organization's Internet connection is not permanent. A permanent, or dedicated, connection maintains constant connectivity to the Internet. A non-dedicated connection establishes itself as needed. Usually, non-dedicated connections are terminated when there has been no traffic for a certain period of time and re-established when Internet traffic is generated.

The Proxy Server Auto Dial feature provides dynamic connection of non-dedicated Internet connections. When a client machine generates an Internet request, the Proxy Server recognizes it, re-establishes the Internet connection, and services the client request.

To configure Auto Dial, follow these steps:

1. From the Start menu, choose Programs, Microsoft Proxy Server, Auto Dial Configuration. This displays the Microsoft Proxy Auto Dial dialog box (see Figure 22.21).

FIG. 22.21
The Dialing Hours tab can be used to set valid times for Dial on Demand connectivity.

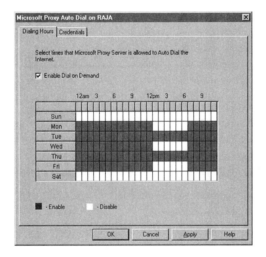

2. Click the Dialing Hours tab.

3. Select the Enable Dial on Demand check box.

4. Select time slots when Proxy Server can dynamically establish a connection to the Internet. If time slots are setup, users can only connect to the Internet during those times. All requests during invalid times are denied by the Proxy Server.

5. Select the Credentials tab (see Figure 22.22). It is used to provide logon authentication information for establishing Auto Dial connections.

6. Select the appropriate entry from the RAS phonebook entries list.

7. Provide a User Name and Password that can be used to connect to the Internet.

8. Optionally, provide a Domain name if required for connectivity.

9. Click Apply or OK to commit changes. Auto Dial configuration is complete.

FIG. 22.22

The Credentials tab is used to provide logon authentication information for establishing an Auto Dial Internet connection.

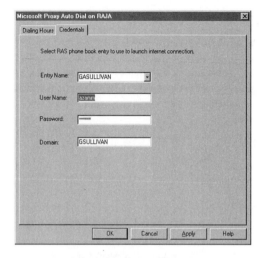

Monitoring Proxy Server Performance

There are a multitude of ways to monitor Proxy Server performance. Proxy Server uses the Windows NT built-in monitoring tool called Performance Monitor to provide administrators with a means to gauge system performance and diagnose problems.

In addition to the Performance Monitor, the Windows NT logging system records events for Proxy Server. The built-in Proxy Server logging mechanism can also be used to gain insight into the server operation and performance.

Proxy Server also provides SNMP-based monitoring capabilities. If you are using SNMP-based monitoring tools, Proxy Server provides MIB files that can be used to enable SNMP monitoring.

However, Performance Monitor provides the most well-integrated and easy to use means of monitoring system performance for Proxy Server. When Proxy Server is first installed, three Performance Monitor objects are created to monitor Proxy Server activity. These include the following:

- **Web Proxy Server Cache**—Monitors the performance of the Web Proxy service caching mechanism
- **Web Proxy Server Service**—Used to monitor the Web Proxy service performance
- **WinSock Proxy Server Service**—Used to monitor the WinSock Proxy service performance

To monitor Proxy Server performance, follow these steps:

1. From the Start menu, choose Programs, Microsoft Proxy Server, Monitor Microsoft Proxy Server Performance. The Performance Monitor screen appears (see Figure 22.23).

FIG. 22.23

Performance Monitor can be used to monitor Proxy Server activity and diagnose performance bottlenecks.

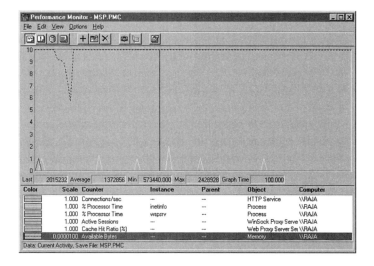

2. To view additional counters, choose File, New Chart.

3. Choose Edit, Add to Chart. The Add to Chart dialog box appears.

4. In the Add to Chart dialog box, select an object to monitor, such as the WinSock Proxy Server service.

5. Select a counter from the counters list.

6. Click Add, and then click Done.

▶ **See** "Performance Monitor," **p. 190**

Implementing Server Security

Installing and operating a Proxy Server involves paying special attention to the security issues involved. If you are running a server being accessed by thousands of users internally, security of your server and other computers on your enterprise network becomes an important issue. Microsoft accomplishes the security needs of administrators by integrating security for Proxy Server with the security model built into Windows NT Server.

Windows NT provides powerful security features for user authentication, access control, and auditing. Proxy Server leverages these capabilities of the Windows NT operating system to provide security for its Internet-based services.

Windows NT uses a security model that handles security for all services using a single logon authentication mechanism. By creating user accounts and setting access permissions for those accounts, administrators can control what resources and services are available to users.

You can minimize the chance of security problems by adopting these standards:

■ **User Accounts**—User accounts enable you to control who is allowed access to resources. By restricting access to valid user accounts, you can minimize the chances of security problems.

■ **IUSR_*Computername* account**—The IUSR_*computername* account is created expressly for the purpose of allowing anonymous connections to IIS services. IUSR_*computername* accounts only have the capability to access resources managed by the IIS server and thus cannot gain access to network resources, such as network shares. By using the IUSR_*computername* account for all your Internet client connections, you can manage all user permission and security issues more easily.

■ **File system security**—Make sure that you secure all your content files by setting the appropriate permissions on your server files. Use the NTFS file system to store your files. Using NTFS, you can set permissions to determine what users and groups have permissions to access files and directories.

■ **Access control**—If necessary, use the Internet Service Manager's Filters tab for Proxy Server services to configure which computers or groups of computers have access to the Internet and which outside domains or users have access to your internal network. If you are going to be operating an intranet, it is a good idea to only grant access to computers that are a part of your enterprise.

■ **Auditing**—Use the auditing features of Windows NT in conjunction with the NTFS file system to keep records of file access and user activity. You can regularly check the audit logs to guard against unauthorized access.

▶ **See** "Understanding BackOffice Security," **p. 112**

▶ **See** "Setting Permissions on Shared Resources," **p. 200**

From Here...

This chapter presented the features available in Microsoft Proxy Server, how to set up and install Proxy Server, how to administer your Proxy Server, and how to secure your installation. For more information on these and related topics, see the following chapters:

■ For information on other Internet components available for Microsoft BackOffice, see Chapter 16, "The BackOffice I-Net Toolbox."

■ For information on Internet Information Server, see Chapter 18, "Building a Web with Internet Information Server (IIS)."

■ To learn about exploring the Internet using the client Web browsers, see Chapter 19, "Web Browsers."

- For information on creating content for your IIS servers, see Chapter 20, "Using Microsoft FrontPage 97."

- To learn about adding search capabilities to your IIS site, see Chapter 21, "Implementing Index Server and the Content Replication System."

- To ensure that proper security measures are taken for your Internet involvement, see Chapter 46, "Implementing Real-World Security."

- To explore how the Internet can be used in business, see Chapter 47, "Building BackOffice Applications."

Part
V

Ch
22

## CHAPTER 23

Using Active Platform to Enhance Your Web Site

by Azam A. Mirza

As part of its strategy to deliver components that enable Microsoft BackOffice as the backbone of Internet technologies, Microsoft has added a high-level component to Internet Information Server (IIS) that delivers cross-platform support, open standards, and a tightly integrated set of tools for delivering dynamic Web content to users.

The Active Platform is an open architecture based on industry standards for creating Web sites and Web-enabled applications for the Internet and intranets. Active Platform provides a means for Web developers to create Web content that can be used across hardware platforms and operating systems.

Features provided by the Active Platform

Learn how the Active Platform technologies come together to provide the means for developing dynamic, interactive, and resourceful Web sites. The three Active Platform technologies—ActiveX, Active Desktop, and Active Server Pages—are introduced.

Installing Active Server Pages

Learn about installing Active Server Pages and enabling your Web site to handle ActiveX technologies.

Creating content for your Web site using Active Server Pages technologies

Learn how you can integrate the power of Active Platform in your Web site to enhance its functionality and features. Learn about the ActiveX scripting mechanisms, ActiveX components, and Active Server Pages objects for accessing server features.

> **N O T E** Microsoft's Web site, **www.microsoft.com**, contains extensive information about Active
> Platform and other Internet technologies. It is a good idea to periodically visit the site for
> the latest information about Microsoft tools and products. ▨

Active Platform Features

The Active Platform leverages such technologies as HTML, scripting mechanisms (such as
CGI and Perl), Microsoft Component Object Model (COM), Java support, and the underlying
operating system services to deliver dynamic, interactive, and customizable content to client
desktops on the Internet and intranets.

> **N O T E** Java is an Internet object-oriented development language, loosely based on C++, that was
> developed by Sun Microsystems, Inc. ▨

> **N O T E** Component Object Model (COM) is the core Microsoft technology for building reusable,
> object-oriented components for use in developing applications and server objects. COM is
> the underlying methodology that controls all Microsoft strategic initiatives. ▨

▶ **See** "Hypertext Markup Language," **p. 523**

▶ **See** "Using CGI," **p. 572**

By providing a high-level platform that sits on top of Internet Information Server (IIS) and the
operating system, Microsoft has created a platform that frees the Web developer from worry-
ing about underlying details and operating system idiosyncrasies. Developers can build Web
sites that conform to the Active Platform specs and not worry about the hardware platform and
operating system that the site will run on. (See Chapter 16, "The BackOffice I-Net Toolbox,"
for more information.)

Active Platform not only brings uniformity to the server side for Web-enabled applications, it
also encompasses the client side with the same open architecture to deliver a cohesive means
of displaying content residing on Active Platform servers.

There are three main parts to the Active Platform that make it possible to create, deploy, and
use powerful Web-enabled applications for the Internet and intranets. These include the following:

- ▨ ActiveX technologies
- ▨ Active Desktop
- ▨ Active Server Pages

Figure 23.1 shows the relationship between the various Active Platform components.
The following sections describe these technologies in more detail.

FIG. 23.1
Active Platform technologies form the basis of the Microsoft Internet initiative.

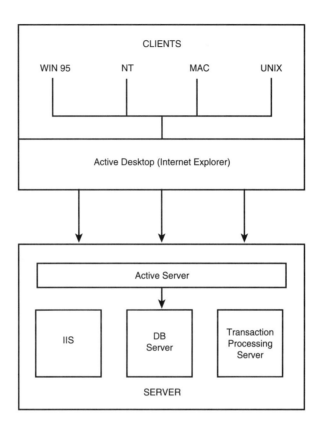

ActiveX Technologies

ActiveX technologies refers to the tools and standards that work as the glue to bring dynamic, interactive content to your Web site. *ActiveX technologies* are a set of software standards, components, and tools that work on different operating systems and heterogeneous networks to enable the Active Platform. The following are some of the technologies included in the ActivcX standard:

- **Dynamic HTML**—An extension to HTML technology that enables Web developers to create dynamic, on-the-fly Web pages. Dynamic HTML pages are created in response to the completion of an ActiveX application and display the results to the user. For example, an ActiveX database access object might query a relational database, obtain the resultset, create a dynamic HTML page to display the resultset, and send the dynamic HTML page to the client browser for display to the user.

N O T E For more information about Dynamic HTML, refer to the Microsoft Web site at **www.microsoft.com**.

- **Language independent scripting support**—Full support for scripting mechanisms, such as CGI and Perl. ActiveX supports open scripting standards that provide scripting support in various languages and on all supported platforms. Scripting can be executed on both the client browser and the Web server components through the use of an ActiveX scripting engine.

N O T E ActiveX supports two very powerful scripting mechanisms through its ActiveX scripting engine: VBScript and JScript. With these two scripting mechanisms, no special procedure is required to process the code. ▓

N O T E Internet Information Server 3.0 supports compilation-free execution of server-side scripts. ▓

- **System services**—ActiveX provides access to operating system services through its component architecture model. Active Platform can access operating system services on supported platforms, such as Windows, Macintosh, and the various flavors of UNIX.
- **Development tools**—Support for ActiveX is incorporated into all Microsoft development tools for creating ActiveX components. These include Microsoft Visual C++, Microsoft Visual Basic, and Microsoft Visual J++. ActiveX components can be written in any language that supports the creation of such components.

N O T E Microsoft Visual Basic 5.0, Control Creation Edition is the first commercial tool available for creating ActiveX Controls for incorporation into Web sites. ▓

- **Java support**—ActiveX technologies provide full support and interoperability for the Java technology and Java applets.

N O T E Active Server Pages, discussed later in this chapter, include the Java Virtual Machine for running Java applets and JScript. ▓

- **Visual InterDev**—A Web application development tool for creating active content Web sites. Visual InterDev is the next generation of Web-development tools that use visual metaphors to make Web development easier. It fully supports ActiveX technologies for creating both client-side and server-side components.

N O T E Visual InterDev is the Web-development tool that provides a single development environment for all Microsoft development tools—such as Visual C++, Visual J++, and Visual Basic—for creating ActiveX-enabled applications. ▓

- **ActiveX Data Objects (ADO)**—ActiveX provides a new mechanism for accessing databases using ODBC (Open DataBase Connectivity). ADO is similar to the DAO (Data Access Objects) and RDO (Remote Data Objects), and provides developers with a means to access the data stored in corporate relational databases. Developers can create HTML pages with scripts that take advantage of ADO constructs to access databases or create Active Controls that are data-aware.

T I P Microsoft Visual Basic 5.0, Control Creation Edition can be used to create data-aware ADO controls.

These ActiveX technologies and tools encompass the entire Active Platform on both the client side and the server side. Some are implemented as stand-alone tools for enhancing the Active Platform environment, while others implement specific functions on the client side and the server side.

Active Desktop

The Active Desktop is the client component of the Active Platform environment. The Active Desktop enables the creation of applications that run on the client systems under a multitude of operating systems and hardware platforms.

The Active Desktop provides developers with a means of writing applications to a common interface to ensure the capability to run on multiple operating systems and hardware platforms. Active Desktop includes support for language-independent scripting, dynamic HTML, system services, and ActiveX component technology. The Active Desktop provides the following advantages over proprietary solutions:

- A single delivery mechanism for providing user interface objects
- Support for language-independent, client-side scripting capabilities
- Support for the dynamic HTML technology
- Support for client-side ActiveX components and Controls created with such tools as the Microsoft Visual Basic 5.0, Control Creation Edition
- Support for Java applets through the Java Virtual Machine, the Java runtime compiler, and the Java JIT (Just-In-Time) compiler

The Active Desktop is fully integrated with the Microsoft Windows 95 and Windows NT operating systems. It provides full support and access to the extensive set of APIs available for the Windows operating system environment.

The main delivery mechanism for the Active Desktop is Microsoft Internet Explorer Web browser. Figure 23.2 presents an example of a Web site using ActiveX components and being accessed through the Microsoft Internet Explorer Active Desktop.

ActiveX Controls used as part of the Active Desktop environment provide a powerful way of adding functionality to your Web site.

Active Server Pages

Internet Information Server 3.0 includes components for enabling your Web site for Active Platform. The component that provides server-side ActiveX functionality is called the Active Server Pages (ASP).

FIG. 23.2

The Microsoft Network Web site provides a highly ActiveX-enabled Web experience.

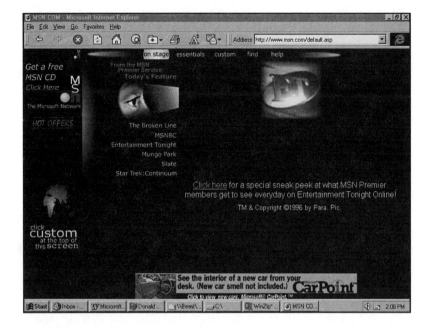

N O T E Active Server Pages denotes the product that has previously been referred to as the ActiveX Server and code named Denali. ■

The Active Server Pages is a high-level component that takes advantage of the scalable, high-performance capabilities of Windows NT Server to provide developers with a rich environment for creating server-side Web applications. Active Server Pages includes full support for Windows NT Server system services, database access, transaction processing, and message queuing.

The following sections provide information about installing Active Server Pages, and using and creating Active Server Pages components and applications.

Installing Active Server Pages

Active Server Pages are provided as an add-on component to Internet Information Server. To install Active Server Pages, you must have the following software components already in place:

■ Windows NT Server version 4.0 with the Windows NT Server version 4.0 Service Pack 1 installed

■ Support for TCP/IP installed as part of the Windows NT Server setup

■ Internet Information Server version 2.0 or higher

N O T E Active Server Pages can be downloaded from the Microsoft WWW site at **www.microsoft.com**. ■

To install Active Server Pages, perform the following steps:

1. From the Start menu, click Run.

2. In the Run dialog box, type **<path>:\asp.exe**, where *<path>* refers to the location where asp.exe resides. This will run the Active Server Pages Setup Wizard to install the software.

3. Read the license agreement displayed, and click I Agree to continue. The welcome screen will be displayed, as shown in Figure 23.3.

FIG. 23.3
The Setup Wizard for Active Server Pages walks you through the installation steps.

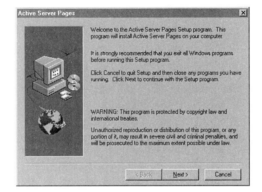

4. Click Next to continue.

5. If there are any IIS services running, the Setup Wizard will ask you to stop these services (see Figure 23.4). Click Yes to stop running IIS services.

FIG. 23.4
IIS services must be stopped before Active Server Pages can be installed.

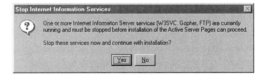

6. The Select Options dialog box appears, as shown in Figure 23.5. By default, all options are checked. Available options include the following:

   - **Active Server Pages Core**—This option is selected by default and cannot be unchecked. It installs the core components needed to provide support for the Active Server Pages.

   - **ODBC 3.0 + Access Driver**—This option installs support for ODBC 3.0 and the driver for accessing Microsoft Access databases using ODBC.

   - **Documentation and Samples**—This option installs the online documentation and the examples used to illustrate Active Server Pages technology.

   - **Java VM**—Installs support for the Java virtual machine for running Java applets.

FIG. 23.5

The Select Options dialog box enables you to install additional Active Platform components, such as ODBC support and the Java Virtual Machine.

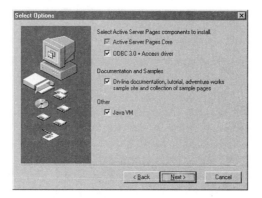

Select the components you want to install and click Next. The Setup Wizard will prompt you for a location for the documentation and samples files (see Figure 23.6).

FIG. 23.6

Samples and documentation files can be installed on a different drive and directory from the server components.

7. Click Next to accept the default or click Browse to change the location. The samples and documentation files will be installed in the specified directory.

8. The Setup Wizard will install the files necessary for Active Server Pages. Once setup is complete, the Wizard displays a dialog box showing the components that were installed, as shown in Figure 23.7.

9. Click OK to complete the setup of Active Server Pages.

 As part of the installation process, additional entries are added to the Microsoft Internet Server program group. The Active Server Pages RoadMap entry is particularly useful. It provides a set of HTML documents that includes samples for Active Server implementation and online documentation.

Once Active Server Pages is installed, you are ready to develop content for your Web site that can take advantage of the Active Server Pages functionality. The following sections describe how you can use ActiveX technology to bring a new level of sophistication and performance to your Web site.

FIG. 23.7
A summary of installation results is displayed for your review.

Creating Active Content for Your Web Site

Active Platform and Active Server Pages in particular provide the means for creating truly interactive and multimedia content for your Web site that take advantage of the latest technology in Internet and intranet development. With ActiveX-enabled content, you can create Web sites that provide a truly information-intensive experience for the users. This section discusses some of the tools and techniques you can use to bring the next level of sophistication to your Web presence.

There are several methods Web developers can use to create ActiveX content for their Web sites. ActiveX content created for Active Server Pages can also be referred to as *server-side ActiveX applications*.

Server-side applications do all processing on the server and free the client system from handling information that it might not be familiar with. All HTML pages displayed on the client browsers are created by the server and sent to the client for display to the user. However, server-side applications do place a high premium on the performance capabilities of the server. A site with a lot of server-side applications can slow down tremendously during high traffic times if the server is not powerful enough to handle it. The following are some of the methods and tools provided for handling server-side ActiveX development:

- Active Server Pages scripting
- Active Server Pages objects
- Active Server Pages components

Active Server Pages Scripting

Microsoft Active Server Pages provides a mechanism for handling scripting functions on Internet Information Server. Through the use of ActiveX scripting, Web developers can create dynamic, interactive Web-based applications that take advantage of the high-performance capabilities of the server machine. Figure 23.8 presents a model of the Active Server Pages scripting mechanisms.

FIG. 23.8

Active Server Pages can host a variety of scripting engines for processing scripting languages.

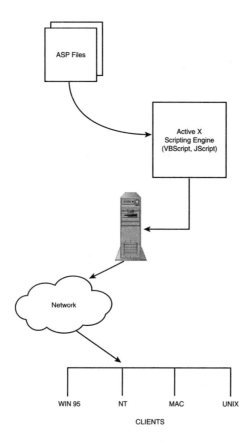

With server-side ActiveX scripting, developers can write applications that generate dynamic HTML pages based on the requirements and then make the pages available to the client browsers as needed. The client browsers need not support scripting and ActiveX technology. Because the HTML pages are created by the server, they can easily be displayed by any client browser.

▶ **See** "Hypertext Markup Language," **p. 523**

Active Server Pages scripts are ASCII text files that are similar to HTML files, but include special directives to identify the scripting commands. An Active Server Pages script file has an extension of .ASP, which identifies it to the server as a script file rather than a simple HTML file.

N O T E Active Server Pages scripts can contain any combination of text, HTML tags, and script commands. ■

 You can convert any HTML file to an Active Server Pages script file by renaming it with an .ASP extension. The Active Server Pages will then treat the file as a script file rather than a simple HTML file.

However, to really use the power, functionality, and flexibility of Active Server scripts, you must extend your HTML file with scripting commands. The default scripting language used by Active Server Pages is the Microsoft Visual Basic Scripting Edition, also referred to as VBScript. However, scripts can be written in any language, such as Perl, REXX, and JScript.

Active Server Pages includes a scripting engine for VBScript that enables it to handle VBScript commands. Because a scripting engine is a Component Object Model (COM) object, other scripting engines can be written that enable Active Server Pages to handle scripts in a particular scripting language.

Since Active Server Pages is just a host for the scripting engine object, multiple scripting engines can be installed on a single server for handling scripts written in various languages. With Active Server Pages, developers can easily switch between different scripting languages within the same script file using special tags. The sample script in Listing 23.1 shows how you can switch between VBScript and JScript code.

Listing 23.1 Using Tags to Switch Between Scripting Languages

```
<HTML>
<SCRIPT LANGUAGE=JScript RUNAT=Server>
<JScript code here>
<SCRIPT LANGUAGE=VBScript RUNAT=Server>
<VBScript code here>
</HTML>
```

As noted, scripting engines extend the functionality of HTML pages by adding additional tags and scripting commands that can be interpreted by the Active Server Pages scripting engine.

N O T E For a complete scripting language syntax reference, refer to the VBScript or JScript language reference included with the Active Server Pages documentation. ▨

Active Server Pages Objects

Active Server Pages includes support for COM objects that enable developers to extend its functionality. The VBScript scripting engine previously mentioned is actually a COM object that is hosted by the Active Server Pages. In addition, Active Server Pages provides functionality for some common objects to carry out certain common tasks. These include the following:

- `Application` object
- `Request` object
- `Response` object
- `Server` object
- `Session` object

Each of these objects provides certain common functionality through a set of events, methods, and properties that is available to all scripts and ActiveX components running in the Active

Server Pages object space. To use objects, you must first create an instance of that object through object instantiation. However, since the previously listed objects are a part of Active Server Pages, they do not require object instantiation and are available for use at all times. These objects are discussed in more detail in the following sections.

N O T E   The following sections provide a description of the objects, properties, and methods available to utilize Active Server Pages functionality. For specific programming examples on how to use these objects, please refer to the online product documentation and tutorials. ▨

The *Application* Object   The Application object is used to share information among all users of a particular ActiveX script application or ActiveX component application. It provides support for the following methods:

- **Lock**—The Lock method prevents other clients from modifying Application object properties.
- **Unlock**—The Unlock method enables other clients to modify Application object properties.

N O T E   An Active Server Pages script application refers to all .ASP scripts stored in a particular virtual directory. ▨

▶ **See** "Managing Directories," **p. 544**

▶ **See** "Virtual Servers," **p. 544**

N O T E   For specific examples on how to utilize the Application object, refer to the Application object online reference. ▨

The *Request* Object   The Request object retrieves user responses through client browsers for processing by the Active Server Pages. Some of the tasks that can be performed through the Request object include getting information about the client browser type, getting information submitted through HTML forms, and getting information stored in server variables or passed through cookies. The Request object provides the following collections:

- **ClientCertificate**—The values of fields stored in the client certificate that is sent in the HTTP request.
- **Cookies**—The values of cookies sent in the HTTP request.
- **Form**—The values of form elements in the HTTP request body.
- **QueryString**—The values of variables in the HTTP query string.
- **ServerVariables**—The values of predetermined environment variables.

N O T E   A *cookie* is an identification token passed from the client to the server that identifies the path to a particular Web resource, such as an URL, a login name, a property value, and so on. ▨

N O T E For specific examples on how to use the Request object, refer to the Request object online reference. ■

The *Response* Object A Response object is primarily used to send information back to the client. Typical uses of the response command include sending text and other stream output back to the client or redirecting clients to another URL document on the Web. Response object also supports a buffering mechanism for storing information until processing is complete before a response is sent back to the user. The Response object includes support for the following collections, properties, and methods:

Part
V
Ch
23

- **Cookies**—The Cookies collection provides access to the values stored for cookies.
- **Buffer**—This property sets whether the page output should be buffered or not.
- **ContentType**—This property specifies the HTTP content type for the Response object.
- **Expires**—This property specifies the length of time when a page cached on the browser is discarded.
- **ExpiresAbsolute**—This property specifies the date and time when a page cached on the browser is discarded.
- **Status**—This property provides the value of the status line returned by the server.
- **AddHeader**—Sets the HTML header name to the specified value.
- **AppendToLog**—Adds a string to the end of the Web server log entry.
- **BinaryWrite**—Writes the given information to the current HTTP output without any character-set conversion.
- **Clear**—Erases any buffered HTML output.
- **End**—Stops processing the .ASP file and returns the current result.
- **Flush**—Sends buffered output immediately to the client.
- **Redirect**—Sends a redirect message to the browser, causing it to attempt to connect to a different URL.
- **Write**—Writes a variable to the current HTTP output as a string.

    ▶ **See** "Uniform Resource Locator," **p. 525**

N O T E For specific examples on how to use the Response object, refer to the Response object online reference. ■

The *Server* Object The Server object provides access to methods and properties of the Web server. The methods and properties include the following:

- **ScriptTimeout**—A property used for setting script execution timeout value
- **CreateObject**—A method for creating instances of Active Server Pages objects
- **HTMLEncode**—Applies HTML encoding to the supplied string
- **MapPath**—Maps a virtual server directory path to a physical path
- **URLEncode**—Applies URL encoding codes to a supplied string

N O T E For specific examples on how to use the `Server` object, refer to the `Server` object online reference. ▣

The *Session* Object   A `Session` object is used to store information about a particular client session. `Session` objects are valid for an entire client session. Any time a client requests an HTML page from the Active Server Pages, a `Session` object is automatically created and is discarded when the client session is terminated. `Session` objects include support for the following methods and properties:

- ▣ **Abandon**—The `Abandon` method destroys a `Session` object and releases its resources.
- ▣ **SessionID** —The `SessionID` property returns the session identification for the current user.
- ▣ **Timeout**—The timeout period for the session state for this application in minutes.

N O T E For specific examples on how to use the `Session` object, refer to the `Session` object online documentation. ▣

Active Server Pages Components

Also included with the Active Server Pages is a set of ActiveX components for performing certain frequently accessed operations. Active Server Pages components are actually automation servers and are designed to run on your Web server as part of a Web application. These are server-side components—not user-interface components—that run as a process to extend the functionality of your Web server scripts.

Server components are typically invoked from .ASP script files. However, Active Server Pages components can be invoked from a variety of sources, including ISAPI applications, CGI scripts, executable files, or other Active Server Pages components. Some of the components prepackaged with the Active Server Pages include the following:

- ▣ Advertisement Rotator component
- ▣ Browser Capabilities component
- ▣ Data Access Object component
- ▣ Content Linking component
- ▣ TextStream component

These five components perform certain very specific tasks as part of a Web server environment. They are discussed in more detail in the following sections.

▶ **See** "Using ISAPI," **p. 573**

▶ **See** "Using CGI," **p. 572**

N O T E The following sections provide a description of the components provided by Microsoft as part of Active Server Pages. For specific programming examples on how to use these components, refer to the online product documentation and tutorials. ■

Advertisement Rotator Component The Advertisement Rotator component makes it easy to display advertisements for sponsors and partner Web sites. With an Advertisement Rotator component, you can display advertisements for other companies and provide links to their Web sites.

Part
V
Ch
23

The Advertisement Rotator component automatically rotates advertisements displayed on a page based on a predetermined schedule. Each time a client accesses a page, a new advertisement is displayed as part of the page.

N O T E The information about when to display a new advertisement and which advertisement to display is stored in a special file called the Rotator Schedule File. ■

The Advertisement Rotator component also records the number of times users see a company's advertisement and also records the number of times users click a particular advertisement to jump to an advertiser's Web site. Each jump to an advertiser's Web site is recorded in the Internet Information Server activity logs.

▶ **See** "Logging," **p. 562**

Browser Capabilities Component The Browser Capabilities component provides the Active Server Pages with information about the capabilities of the client browser. When a browser first makes a connection with a Web server, it sends a *user agent* HTTP header to the server. The header contains a string that identifies the browser and its version number.

▶ **See** "Hypertext Transport Protocol," **p. 523**

This information is compared to the information stored in a file called the BROWSCAP.INI file. If the header information matches the information in the file, the rest of the information is retrieved from the file. However, if the header information does not match any of the entries in the BROWSCAP.INI file, the default browser properties are used instead.

T I P The BROWSCAP.INI file includes browser information for the most common browsers. Information about other browsers can be added to the file by editing its contents and adding those entries.

Data Access Object Component The Data Access Object component uses the ActiveX Data Objects (ADO) to provide access to data stored in a relational database. ADO uses the ODBC mechanism to access the database. The ADO interface is similar to the Database Access Objects (DAO) used by such tools as Visual C++ and Visual Basic. It offers ease of use, high speed, and low memory overhead as benefits.

The main advantage of ADO over DAO is the capability to create data access objects independently. You do not need to go through an object hierarchy to gain access to resources. Each object can be created individually and used by the application. This results in significantly fewer programming steps, lower memory requirements, and higher performance. ADO provides the following enhancements over DAO for building Web-enabled, data-aware applications:

- Independent object creation
- Batch updating
- Stored-procedure support with parameters
- Support for cursors, including server-side cursors
- Support for returning a set number of rows in a resultset
- Multiple recordsets

N O T E   For examples of using the Data Access Object component and the ActiveX Data Objects, refer to the samples included with Active Server Pages. ▦

Content Linking Component   The Content Linking component manages a list of URLs so that you can refer to the pages through bookmarks. The Content Linking component can be used to create a table of contents for your Web pages, and previous and next navigational links to Web pages.

The Content Linking component is most useful when you are building Web pages that require navigation through a group of related information pages. For example, discussion forum messages can be threaded using the Content Linking component.

N O T E   For more information on using the Content Linking component, refer to the online component reference documentation. ▦

TextStream Component   The TextStream component is used to provide input and output capabilities for your Web server applications. Applications can read and write to text files stored on the server. The TextStream component uses the VBScript FileSystem object to achieve its functionality. The `FileSystem` object provides access to the server computer's file system.

N O T E   For more information about the `FileSystem` object, refer to the online VBScript language reference. ▦

From Here...

This chapter presents the features available in Microsoft Active Platform initiative and specifically the server-side components included as part of the Microsoft BackOffice suite. For more information on these and related subjects, see the following chapters:

- For information on other Internet components available for Microsoft BackOffice, see Chapter 16, "The BackOffice I-Net Toolbox."
- To learn about accessing the World Wide Web using client-side browser software, see Chapter 19, "Web Browsers."

■ For information on creating content for your IIS servers, see Chapter 20, "Using Microsoft FrontPage 97."

■ To learn about adding search capabilities to your IIS site, see Chapter 21, "Implementing Index Server and the Content Replication System."

■ To learn about providing Internet connectivity to your enterprise, see Chapter 22, "Implementing Microsoft Proxy Server."

■ To ensure proper security measures are taken for your Internet involvement, see Chapter 46, "Implementing Real-World Security."

■ To explore how the Internet can be used in business, see Chapter 47, "Building BackOffice Applications."

Part
V

Ch
23

## CHAPTER 24

Dynamic Content with IIS Using dbWeb and IDC

by Jeff Thurston

There is little doubt that the Internet will continue to grow in terms of the number of users, the number of sites, the volume of content, and accessibility. Bandwidth problems that once precluded the use of large volumes of information and dazzling graphics are rapidly disappearing. This is resulting in World Wide Web (WWW) site publishers becoming increasingly creative, thereby raising expectations of what a useful site should be. Users are no longer content to view sites with static content, and unless current information is presented, chances are they will never make a second visit.

Similarly, the intranet continues to become more prevalent. Companies of all sizes are using intranets to increase accessibility to key corporate data. Policy manuals, company telephone listings, product information, benefits information, and special-events calendars are just some of the myriad uses for this growing technology.

Most important of all, new levels of functionality are enabling WWW site publishers to reach a growing audience. Unlike traditional media—such as television, newspapers, magazines, and billboards—the Internet and intranets are

Discover two predominant dynamic information publishing tools

Two publishing tools are available to ease the process of publishing dynamic information on your Web pages. Explore the tools, their requirements, and the steps required to install and configure these tools on your system.

A closer look at the Internet Database Connector and dbWeb

Take a closer look at the major features and benefits of each of these tools. Discover their similarities as well as their differences. Learn how to transform your static Web pages into dynamic and exciting representations of the data important to your viewers.

Deciding which information publishing tools to use

Depending on your needs and the complexity with which you intend to publish information from your database, one tool may prove to be more useful than the other. Discover the strengths of each of these tools as well as some tips used to determine which tool will most completely meet your needs.

providing a way for publishers to collect as well as distribute information. At a minimum, WWW site publishers can collect information showing interests based upon the number of times a particular page is viewed. At the other end of the spectrum, such information as name, location, income, interests, and various other demographic data can be retrieved and stored for later use.

Regardless of its use, it is becoming increasingly necessary to include dynamic and interactive content in any successful WWW site. This need will only grow as Internet technologies penetrate homes and businesses around the globe. ■

The Interactive, Dynamic Web Site

Most WWW publishers will agree that the need for interactive and dynamic content is a critical component of any good site. Until recently however, the creation and maintenance of sites containing these components required considerable effort on the part of developers. Solutions that did exist usually exhibited poor response times, poor quality, or both.

The tools landscape is rapidly changing, however. New tools are appearing on the market nearly each day, and the race to be the number one tool provider is yielding tools of exceptional value and functionality.

As a leader in Internet technology, Microsoft has released two tools that provide developers with the ability to quickly create interactive and dynamic Web sites. These tools are the Internet Database Connector (IDC) and dbWeb. This chapter provides a brief overview of both tools.

What Is Interactive Content?

It has not been so long ago that most WWW sites consisted primarily of text documents that included embedded links to other text documents or simple graphics. Users were able to navigate these sites by selecting link indicators, thereby activating a link and causing the target document to subsequently be displayed. Although some might argue that this is interactive, it does not begin to compare with the level of interaction that is possible today.

For the most part, the WWW is not based upon the concept of a session. Users move from document to document with little regard to where they've been and, more importantly, leave little or no trace of who they are. A request for a document usually consists of a connection as an anonymous user, a download of one or more documents, and finally a disconnection from a server.

With current technology, however, it is possible to simulate a session to provide a personalized version of a single document or an entire Web site. Such sites as the Microsoft Network (**http://www.msn.com**) and the Wall Street Journal Interactive Edition (**http://www.wsj.com**) enable users to maintain a personalized home page. Each time a user visits one's home page, content is presented based upon information the user has provided during a registration process. For example, if the user indicated an interest in baseball, relevant information about baseball would be presented each time the page is accessed.

Although the content may be valuable to the user making the request, the registration process also provides the WWW publisher with an opportunity to collect useful information about the user. Such information as name, age, income, and interests can be collected and stored in a database. Later, that information can be used to provide valuable information about the types of people who visit the WWW site.

What Is Dynamic Content?

Maintenance represents a major portion of the efforts required by a WWW site. Some companies have armies of Hypertext Markup Language (HTML) developers, graphic artists, content authors, hardware engineers, network engineers, and so on. Others, however, may rely on a single person for all new development and maintenance. Regardless of the situation, it is important to use every tool available to provide the most value with the least drain on resources and budget.

Dynamic content is generated as it is requested, usually based upon specific criteria provided by the user. In contrast, static content is created and stored; the same content is presented to the user each time it is requested. Therefore, the use of dynamic content can significantly increase the volume of information available to your users without significant effort required of the WWW team.

Part
V

Ch
24

As an example, consider the company wanting to publish product information on its WWW site. A catalog metaphor, complete with company logo in the upper-left corner is decided upon. The initial creation of these pages is rather simple: Key in the text and a few headings, include the graphic, add some footer information, such as the copyright notice, and save.

Several months later, the company decides to update its logo. Maybe the new logo now sports a drop shadow and is nearly the same size; maybe it is a different shape entirely. Regardless, each HTML document must now be updated with the new logo, possibly requiring reformatting to maintain a balanced, professional appearance.

Using dynamic content tools such as Internet Database Connector (IDC) or dbWeb, document templates can be used to present such data in a consistent manner. The template would likely include the graphic, basic formatting attributes such as background graphic or watermark graphic, and the copyright information. This template would then be used by dbWeb or IDC to generate HTML documents dynamically as users made specific requests. More importantly, when changes to such items as logos become necessary, only the templates need updating.

It does not take long to understand the power provided by these tools. Even if your site has only a handful of similar pages, it may be advantageous to use either IDC or dbWeb to generate dynamic content.

Choosing the Right Tool for Your Situation

The two tools provided by Microsoft—Internet Database Connector (IDC) and dbWeb—ease both the creation and maintenance of interactive and dynamic WWW sites. Both of these tools are based upon Microsoft's Internet Server Application Programming Interface, more commonly referred to as ISAPI. The primary difference is that the IDC tool provides a facility with which the developer is able to create and use custom SQL and formatting via HTML-based templates. These templates contain tags recognizedby IDC to generate the actual HTML document sent to the user.

In contrast, the dbWeb tool uses *wizard* technology and a full-featured graphical user interface (GUI) to enable the developer to quickly create dynamic content by selecting options and providing key values. The option settings and key values are stored in a central Microsoft Access (MDB) database.

The tradeoffs these tools represent are no different than the vast majority of development tools. IDC requires more effort but provides more flexibility. On the other hand, dbWeb is simpler to use but offers limited functionality with which to create content. Although it can be argued that dbWeb enables content to be created quickly, a basic understanding of HTML and SQL yields results with IDC just as quickly in most cases.

For most users, the deciding factor may be the skills required by the tool. A good understanding of both SQL and HTML are required in order to effectively use IDC. SQL statements must be built and inserted into IDC query files. Resultsets are then presented based upon IDC tags embedded into a standard HTML document.

No such knowledge is required to use dbWeb. Queries are built using list boxes and combo boxes. Similarly, output options are set using user-friendly dialog boxes. Only when more complex queries or output are required does the developer need an understanding of HTML keywords or special formatting.

Major Features of dbWeb and Internet Database Connector   As shown in Table 24.1, these two tools have much in common. They both use ODBC for database connectivity and both are built upon ISAPI. Their differences, however, are significant. IDC is merely a filter that replaces tags embedded within an HTML document with data values; whereas dbWeb is a full-featured, self-contained application. While dbWeb is capable of both creating and serving dynamic content, IDC is capable only of serving it. Creation of the files required by IDC to generate dynamic content demands the use of a tool such as Microsoft FrontPage, or at the very least a text editor. The tool you use will depend upon the complexity with which you intend to present your content, and the skills you possess in HTML and SQL.

Table 24.1   Comparison of Features

Feature	IDC	dbWeb
Template creation	Requires other tools	Schema Wizard/Schema Editor
Template storage	.IDC files	`dbWeb.mdb`
HTML extensions	Yes	Yes
Extension files	.HTX	(DBX files) .HTM
ISAPI extension	Yes	Yes

Feature	IDC	dbWeb
Database connectivity	ODBC	ODBC
Requires knowledge of HTML	Yes	No (but recommended)
Requires knowledge of SQL	Yes	No (but recommended)
Supported by Microsoft	Yes	No
Source	Included with IIS 2.0	**http://www.microsoft.com**

Benefits of Using dbWeb   The benefits of using dbWeb are many. The most compelling reason for most, however, is the ease with which dynamic content can be published using this tool. Because the process is nearly entirely facilitated by a GUI (the dbWeb Administrator), most users are able to build dynamic content with a minimal amount of effort. Additionally, fairly complex WWW sites can be assembled with little or no knowledge of SQL or HTML. Other benefits include the following:

- **Ease of use**—The dbWeb Administrator makes the creation of dbWeb *schemas* fast and easy. With the assistance of the Schema Wizard, a simple schema can be created in minutes. With a minimal effort, basic schemas can be extended to provide multiple-table joins, automatic links, and customized page headers and footers.

- **Extendibility**—Through the use of .DBX files, basic schemas can be easily enhanced to include such features as banded reporting, HTML tables, graphics (such as company logos and watermarks), and additional links. Since .DBX files are simply HTML documents with additional tags recognized by dbWeb, nearly any feature of HTML can be implemented using .DBX files.

- **Powerful query features**—The capability for users to search for information is extremely powerful. The Query By Example (QBE) functionality provided by dbWeb provides this functionality. Through the Schema Editor, the developer needs only to specify the columns to be queried and set the appropriate properties. dbWeb will then build the required HTML documents dynamically that enable users to input the target values for the selected columns and submit the query to the database.

- **Powerful maintenance features**—With very little effort, forms to facilitate the insertion, update, and deletion of data can be easily added to any dbWeb solution. Based upon the columns selected in the Schema Editor, dbWeb is able to dynamically build the appropriate HTML documents that enable users to maintain the underlying database.

- **Connectivity to diverse data sources**—Although this benefit can be attributed almost entirely to the features of ODBC, the fact that dbWeb uses ODBC is a major benefit. Because of this, dbWeb can connect to nearly any popular data source, including Microsoft SQL Server, Microsoft Access, Oracle, Paradox, Microsoft Visual FoxPro, dBASE, and any other data source for which there are 32-bit ODBC 2.50 drivers available.

Benefits of Using the Internet Database Connector Although dbWeb provides a quick and easy way to publish dynamic content, it has limitations. Because the Internet Database Connector is implemented as a mechanism that simply issues SQL statements and allows for the custom formatting of the resultset, there are few limitations associated with IDC. Other benefits include the following:

- **More control**—Just as with dbWeb, HTML documents can be built that enable users to supply query parameters. Although it would take considerably more effort to build elaborate QBE forms such as those created by dbWeb, doing so is quite possible. Because total control is with the developer, even more elaborate QBE forms are possible.

- **Supported by FrontPage**—The creation of the IDC query files (.IDC) and IDC format files (.HTX) is supported directly by FrontPage via wizards. This greatly reduces the amount of time required to assemble an IDC solution.

- **Connectivity to diverse data sources**—Although not unique to the IDC, the use of ODBC is certainly a significant benefit. This feature enables IDC to connect to nearly any popular data source for which there are 32-bit ODBC 2.50 drivers available.

dbWeb

Microsoft dbWeb is a utility that enables developers to quickly and easily create dynamic content for their Internet or intranet sites. Through the GUI application called dbWeb Administrator, developers are able to specify the columns that make up Query By Example (QBE) forms, result forms, maintenance forms, and links between them.

Installing dbWeb on Your System

To install dbWeb, you must first obtain the dbWeb Setup files. Version 1.1a is available from the CD-ROM included with this book. To check for the availability of a newer version, consult the Microsoft dbWeb home page as described in a following section "Where to Find dbWeb."

Requirements for Installing dbWeb Microsoft dbWeb can be installed on nearly any PC capable of running the I386 version of Windows NT, including PCs with a 486, Pentium, Pentium Pro (or higher), or a compatible processor. At this time, Alpha, MIPS, PowerPC, and foreign versions of Windows NT are not supported. Specific requirements include the following:

- U.S. Versions of Windows NT 3.51 with Service Pack No.4 or No. 5 or Windows NT 4.0 (Server or Workstation). dbWeb will not install on Windows 95.

- Microsoft Internet Information Server 1.0 or later, or Microsoft Peer Web Services included with Windows NT Workstation 4.0.

- Approximately 10M of hard disk space.

- Microsoft ODBC 2.50 or greater. ODBC Desktop Driver Pack 3.0 is available from the CD-ROM included with this book.

- A Web browser, such as Microsoft Internet Explorer 2.0 or later is recommended. Internet Explorer 3.0 is also available on the CD-ROM included with this book.

N O T E dbWeb may stop running unexpectedly if ODBC has not been upgraded to 2.50 or greater or if Service Pack No. 4 or greater has not been installed when running with Windows NT. Both of these updates are available on the Microsoft Internet site. ■

T I P It may be necessary to reboot your machine after upgrading ODBC to ensure that the latest DLL images are loaded into memory.

N O T E Service packs for Windows NT Server can be obtained from the Microsoft Windows NT Server Technical Support page on Microsoft's WWW site. The URL is **http://www.microsoft.com/ntserversupport**.

Service packs for Windows NT Workstation can be obtained from the Microsoft Windows NT Workstation Technical Support page, which is also on Microsoft's WWW site. The URL is **http://www.microsoft.com/ntwkssupport**.

Windows NT Workstation and Windows NT Server use the same service pack. In addition to the WWW pages mentioned, the service pack can be downloaded from Microsoft's FTP server at **ftp://ftp.microsoft.com/bussys/winnt/winnt-public/fixes/usa/NT351/**. At the time of this writing, the current service pack is No. 5, which is located in the `ussp5/i386/` directory. ■

Part

V

Ch

24

Before installing dbWeb, Microsoft Internet Information Server or Microsoft Peer Web Services must also be installed. The dbWeb Setup application will stop the IIS service if it is running, but will restart it when the installation is complete.

Tips for Configuring a Development Workstation

Development using dbWeb or Internet Database Connector can be done on a machine configured with Windows NT Workstation 4.0. It is not necessary to have Windows NT Server 3.51 or 4.0, nor is it necessary to have Internet Information Server installed. The Peer Web services that ships with Windows NT Workstation 4.0 is compatible with both dbWeb and Internet Database Connector.

If SQL Server is the target database, it is also possible to use Microsoft SQL Server, Developer Edition. Although SQL Server requires Windows NT Server, SQL Server, Developer Edition will operate on Windows NT Workstation.

Finally, although it is not necessary to have the development machine connected to a LAN, it is necessary to have networking services installed and running. If a network interface card (NIC) is not installed in the development machine, install the MS Loopback Adapter instead. This enables Microsoft networking to operate as if the machine is connected to a LAN.

Where to Find dbWeb The dbWeb files can be downloaded from the Microsoft Web site. They are packaged in two forms: a 7.45M self-extracting .EXE file named dbweb11a.exe or six self-extracting files named `disk1.exe` through `disk6.exe`. The latter option provides for downloading to floppies. Other sources of useful information include the following:

- **The dbWeb home page**—Visit the dbWeb home page located at **http://www.microsoft.com/intdev/dbweb** for additional information, such as a brief description of dbWeb, a dbWeb FAQ, and updates. This page has links to all of the files mentioned, as well as alternate links to Microsoft's FTP server (**ftp://ftp.microsoft.com/developr/msdn/dbweb/**).

- **The dbWeb tutorial**—It might also be beneficial to download the dbWeb tutorial from the dbWeb home page. This 50-page document can be viewed online as an HTML document, or a 277K Microsoft Word document that can be downloaded instead. The tutorial explains much of what is needed to successfully develop a dbWeb solution.

  Included are three different tutorial scenarios, including one that discusses the Schema Wizard, another that takes a more in-depth look at the schemas (including linking schemas to provide a drilldown metaphor), and a third that demonstrates the usage of extended multi-record and single-record schemas.

- **Peer support**—Microsoft dbWeb is provided free of charge and is unsupported by Microsoft. Peer support is available from the Microsoft newsgroups, however. The dbWeb newsgroup is available on the Microsoft News Server **msnews.microsoft.com**. The group URL is **news:microsoft.public.inetserver.dbweb**.

N O T E   As of the time of this writing, the current version of dbWeb is 1.1a. Check the dbWeb home page located at **http://www.microsoft.com/intdev/dbweb/** for a description of what is included in this new version, or the availability of newer versions. ▓

The files required to install dbWeb can also be found on the CD included with this book, as well as on the Windows NT Resource Kit.

Installing dbWeb   Installation of dbWeb is facilitated by a Setup Wizard. The first and second screens simply presents a welcome message as well as the usual copyright warnings and license agreement. The third screen, shown in Figure 24.1, asks for the destination directory to be provided. Most users will accept the default.

FIG. 24.1

The dbWeb Setup Wizard asks for the destination directory to be specified prior to installation.

The Setup Wizard will next allow the installer to specify which components are installed as shown in Figure 24.2. While most users will want to install all components, it may not always be necessary.

FIG. 24.2
The dbWeb Setup Wizard allows some or all of the provided components to be installed as needed.

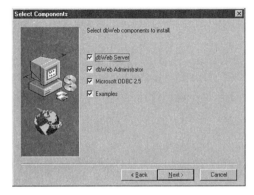

Finally, the dbWeb Setup Wizard will next attempt to determine the default HTML and scripts directory for the IIS installation as shown in Figure 24.3. Most users will accept the defaults provided; however, different directories may be provided as indicated.

FIG. 24.3
The dbWeb Setup Wizard allows the default HTML and scripts directories to be overridden; however, for most users this is not recommended.

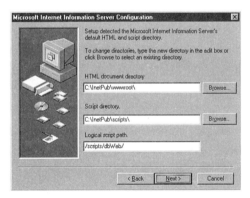

If IIS service is running, the dbWeb Setup Wizard will ask to stop the service before continuing. Once the service is stopped, setup will copy the necessary files as required. The dbWeb service is then registered and the default ODBC Data Source Name (DSN) is created. Finally, setup asks to restart the machine to ensure all of the proper images are loaded into memory.

Once the installation routine has been successfully completed and the machine has been restarted, ensure that ODBC version 2.50 or greater is installed. The dbWeb icon should then be available on the Start menu for use.

Configuring dbWeb   Using the dbWeb Administrator Preferences Editor, many of the default values used when creating new schemas can be changed. Prior to creating a schema, these items should be configured for your installation. To invoke the Administrator Preferences Editor, start the dbWeb Administrator and choose Edit, Preferences.

The Administrator Preferences Editor is implemented using a tabbed dialog box, which includes two tabs. The Schema Defaults tab provides for the configuration of the default values used in the creation of a new dbWeb schema. The General tab, shown in Figure 24.4, includes the following items:

- **Default Schema Database**—Change this item to cause the dbWeb Administrator to open a different dbWeb Repository Database by default. Note that once the dbWeb Administrator is started, any database can be opened using the Open option on the File menu.

- **dbWeb Server Name**—The dbWeb Administrator can be used on a machine other than the one on which the dbWeb Service is running. Enter the name of that machine here, or simply enter \\. if the service is running on the local machine.

FIG. 24.4

The General tab of the dbWeb Administrator Preferences Editor is used to change the default values used in the creation of new dbWeb schemas.

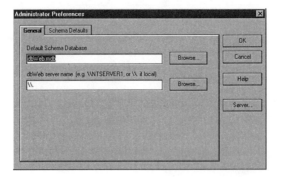

The Schema Defaults tab is where the default values for the Schema Editor are maintained (see Figure 24.5). Setting these defaults affects the default values that are provided upon creation of a new schema. The available items include the following:

- **Page Help URL**—An HTML document generated by dbWeb includes various links, depending on the form, that enable the user to obtain help for the entire page or form. This is the default URL for the page-level help document. Note, however, that each schema can have a separate page help URL.

- **Column Help URL**—Similar to the Page Help URL option is the capability to obtain help on an individual column. Enter the URL for an HTML document from which the user can obtain help on columns in general. The URL of a more specific help document can be specified for each individual column in the column properties editor.

- **Mail Comments To**—Nearly all of the documents generated by dbWeb include a link that, when selected, invokes the user's e-mail editor and inserts the provided mailing address in the Send to field. This is a convenient way to enable users to notify those responsible for the Web site of problems or other feedback.

- **Max Rows for New Schema**—So that the user is not bombarded with resultsets that might otherwise be thousands of rows in length, a maximum row count can be specified for each schema. This feature enables the developer to limit the number of rows returned to the user to a reasonable value.

- **Column Length**—When a column is added to a form or result page, the length of the column can be specified in the column properties editor. Use this field to set the default value for this property. In many cases, however, the length of columns is individually set.

FIG. 24.5

The Schema Defaults tab of the dbWeb Administrator Preferences Editor is where defaults for the Schema Editor are maintained.

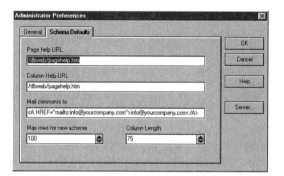

Additional preference settings can be specified using the Server Preferences Editor. To invoke this editor, click the Server button on the Administrator Preferences Editor. As with many of dbWeb's editors, the Server Preferences Editor is implemented using a tabbed dialog box. The first of these tabs is the Paths tab, which includes the following settings (see Figure 24.6):

- **Path to Client Stub**—When dbWeb schemas are requested from within HTML documents, the dbWeb Client Stub is called upon to handle the routing of the request. The dbWeb Client Stub is the ISAPI extension responsible for communicating with the dbWeb Service. This path should be relative to the Web server root. This value should be modified only if the dbWeb Client Stub cannot be found at the location specified by default.

- **Client Stub Name**—The actual name of the dbWeb Client Stub can be specified using this field. The content of this field is seldom modified; however, previous versions of dbWeb implemented the Client Stub as an .EXE file, and with future updates to the dbWeb tool, it may be necessary to modify this value as part of the update process. It might also be used to replace the default dbWeb Client Stub with one of your own.

- **Path to HTML Dir**—This field contains the path to the default location of the HTML documents used by dbWeb. Although most HTML documents are generated dynamically to a cache directory, static documents such as Page Help, Column Help, and About are searched for in this location.

- **About Filename**—This field contains the name of the HTML document that contains version information about dbWeb.

FIG. 24.6

The Paths tab of the dbWeb Server Preferences Editor is used to specify default paths for major dbWeb components.

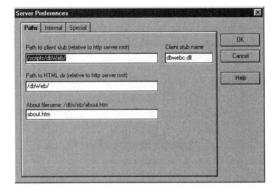

The second tab of the Server Preferences Editor is named Internal and is shown in Figure 24.7. The options of this tab include the following:

- **Beep On Error**—When checked, a beep is sounded on the viewer's machine when an error occurs.

- **Maximum Concurrent Users**—Use this field to set the maximum number of users allowed to access your schema at one time. The default setting is 5 and is typically sufficient.

- **IP Log**—By selecting this option, a log is kept with information on each request dbWeb processes. The log, named DBWIP.LOG, includes such information as the requester's IP address and the schema and method requested.

- **Log Path**—The log is kept at the path specified in this field, which is a path relative to the Web server root. Because the log is typically kept in the dbWeb application directory, a fully qualified path name is typically provided as the default.

- **Data Source Name**—Just as dbWeb enables users to access databases supported by ODBC, the dbWeb Service itself uses ODBC to connect to the dbWeb Repository Database. Specify the ODBC Data Source Name (DSN) defined for the database that will contain dbWeb schemas. Note that this data source may point to any valid DSN based upon an ODBC 2.50 32-bit driver. The default DSN is named dbwebschema.

- **User ID**—If the dbWeb Repository Database, discussed in more detail in the next section, has been configured with security, specify the User ID required to connect to the database in this field. By default, this field is blank. The security options for an Access database can be set with the Microsoft Access application. Refer to the Microsoft Access documentation for specifics.

- **Password**—A password is typically specified along with a User ID if security has been invoked on the dbWeb Repository Database. Specify that password in this field.

FIG. 24.7
The Internal tab of
the dbWeb Server
Preferences Editor is
used to set options
pertaining to the
operational mainte-
nance of the dbWeb
solution.

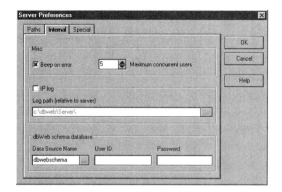

The final tab of the Server Preferences Editor is the Special tab, which is shown in Figure 24.8.
The options of this tab include the following:

- **HTML Header Type**—The HTML Header type can be selected as Full or Custom.
  Select Custom to enable the Custom Access Header and Custom Secure Header to be
  specified.

- **Custom Access Header**—Special HTML can be specified in this field, which is then
  displayed in the event the logon information provided by the user is invalid.

- **Custom Secure Header**—Special HTML can be specified in this field to request logon
  information from the user.

FIG. 24.8
The Special tab of
the dbWeb Server
Preferences Editor is
used to set options
which determine the
type of HTML generated
by dbWeb.

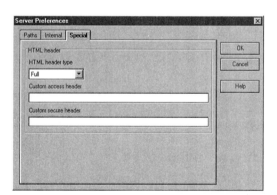

Under normal circumstances, the options in the dbWeb Server Preferences Editor should
remain set to their default values. These options are provided for advanced developers and
should only be altered during development or to fine-tune a busy dbWeb solution.

The Components of dbWeb

The dbWeb tool has several components—both physical and conceptual—that all work together to provide a rather comprehensive solution. The physical components, such as software and database files, are as follows:

- **The dbWeb Service**—The dbWeb Service is installed by Setup. It is a 32-bit, multithreaded Windows NT service that is capable of handling requests from multiple clients simultaneously. By default, the image of the service is located in the dbWeb\Server directory and is named dbwebsrv.exe.

  The dbWeb Service is no different from any other Windows NT service in that it can be started and stopped using the Services applet in the Control Panel. Unlike IIS or SQL Server, this is the only way to start or stop the service manually. Also, as with other services, the startup mode can be set to Automatic, Manual, or Disabled.

- **The dbWeb ISAPI Client Stub**—The dbWeb Client is an ISAPI extension, which by default is installed in the scripts\dbweb directory of the IIS directory (\inetsvr by default). The dbWeb Client is responsible for routing requests to the dbWeb Service as well as routing formatted query results back to IIS.

- **The dbWeb Administrator**—A dbWeb solution is created primarily with the dbWeb Administrator application. This application provides for the maintenance of schemas, which are based upon registered ODBC data sources. It also allows for the registration of these ODBC data sources, a step that must precede the creation of schemas.

- **The dbWeb Schema**—Although maybe not the traditional definition of schema, dbWeb uses the term to define the structure of a set of one or more views of the data in a database. Using a schema, dbWeb Service is able to dynamically create an HTML document to be sent back to the requesting user. Schemas are stored in the dbWeb repository database.

- **The dbWeb Repository Database**—The dbWeb service maintains its DSN registrations and schemas in a Microsoft Access 2.0 database. By default, this database is installed in the dbWeb\Admin directory.

 It may be desirable to upsize the dbWeb repository database from Microsoft Access to Microsoft SQL Server. Doing so can result in better performance. For further information on upsizing your dbWeb repository database, see the dbWeb FAQ at **http://www.microsoft.com/intdev/dbweb/dbwfaq.htm**. The procedure is described in the "Technical Tips and Tricks" section.

CAUTION

Do not attempt to convert the dbWeb Repository Database from Microsoft Access 2.0 format to a newer format. Doing so renders the database unreadable by the dbWeb Administrator.

The conceptual components are the *soft* components of a dbWeb solution. These components include the following:

- **Data Source Registrations**—Before queries can be issued, ODBC Data Source Names must be registered in the dbWeb database. These registrations include the ODBC DSN, a default database, a user ID and password, and other parameters that control the ODBC connection.

- **Schemas**—In order for queries to be issued and resultsets returned, such information as format and the query itself must first be defined. The dbWeb schema is just that: a definition of the query and the multiple ways in which its results are displayed.

- **QBE Forms**—In many cases, it is desirable to allow the user to provide parameters for queries. QBE forms provide this functionality by presenting a form that allows for comparison operators to be selected and target values to be specified.

- **Tabular Forms**—Resultsets are displayed in one of two forms, one of which is the tabular form. In this layout, column names span the top of the form, and multiple rows from the resultset are displayed under each of these names. The result is a form that is similar to a table.

- **Freeform Forms**—The other type of presentation for a resultset is the freeform form. In this layout, a single row of the resultset is displayed and the column names are located along the left side of the form.

- **Insert, Update, and Delete Forms**—These forms enable data to be inserted into the database or existing data to be updated or deleted. The presentation is similar to the freeform form; however, submission of the form triggers an action query of the appropriate type to be issued.

- **Automatic Links**—It is usually desirable to present a parent/child relationship as a drilldown. This is done in dbWeb as an *automatic link*. When these links are selected, another schema containing child data is presented. Links are defined through the Properties Editor by supplying an URL in the Automatic Link URL property.

- **DBX Tags**—HTML tags that handle resultsets from the database are not available. Therefore, it becomes necessary to provide HTML extensions that can be read by dbWeb to generate dynamic HTML documents. These documents, containing only valid HTML tags, are then sent on to the user by Internet Information Server.

- **dbWeb Methods**—Schemas are selected by embedding dbWeb methods in HTML documents. These extended URLs usually include a schema name followed by a question mark (?) and a method name. For a complete listing of dbWeb methods, see the dbWeb online help.

Part
V

Ch
24

The Role of ODBC

It is important to note that the use of ODBC enables databases of virtually any type to be accessed by either the IDC or dbWeb. The only requirement is an ODBC driver for the version of ODBC being used.

Related Microsoft Knowledge Base Articles

Microsoft Knowledge Base article Q155255 documents a problem that causes IIS to stop responding. This article refers to article Q151186, which discusses an update to JET.

The problem described in these articles may also cause Microsoft Access queries to run slowly on Windows NT 4.0. This may be relevant if an Access database is being used as the data source for your Web page. Article Q143163 describes this problem and also recommends the update.

This update is recommended especially when using IDC and dbWeb together. The update can be downloaded from **ftp.microsoft.com** and is named MSJTWNG.EXE.

ODBC 2.50 is distributed with dbWeb 1.1 and should be installed on the machine that is to run dbWeb. The dbWeb's Setup application installs an ODBC setup image in the dbWeb\Odbc32 directory. Run setup.exe from that directory to install ODBC 2.50.

ODBC 2.50 provides support for System Data Source Names (DSN), which are required for using ODBC with Microsoft Internet Information Server (IIS). System DSNs enable Windows NT services to access ODBC without the need of a user account. Both IIS and dbWeb are implemented as Windows NT services and therefore require this capability.

N O T E   Be sure to create all ODBC data sources as System DSNs. Both IDC and dbWeb can use only System DSNs. ▓

Use the ODBC Administrator to define DSNs for use with dbWeb. The utility can be invoked in many ways, as follows:

- Select the ODBC applet from the Control Panel
- From the Windows NT Start menu, usually labeled as ODBC Administrator 32
- Select ODBC Manager from the Utilities menu in dbWeb Administrator
- Press the Manage button on the Data Source Registration Editor in dbWeb Administrator

Administering Your dbWeb Installation

The dbWeb Administrator utility provides the vast majority of the functionality required to administer a dbWeb solution. It is sometimes necessary, however, to use other tools and utilities to provide setup for, or to extend the basic capabilities of, dbWeb. The following sections describe some of the procedures you will use to set up and maintain your dbWeb solution.

Registering an ODBC Data Source   To register a DSN for the first time, ensure that the Data Sources and Schemas node is selected in the main tree view of the dbWeb Administrator. This is the root node and therefore should be the topmost node. Notice that as this node is selected, the first of the three buttons on the toolbar changes to read New Datasource. Press this button to invoke the Data Source Registration Editor, as shown in Figure 24.9.

FIG. 24.9

The dbWeb Data Source Registration Editor is used to register data sources for use in the dbWeb Administrator.

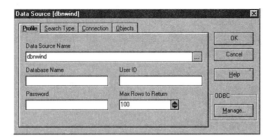

To modify an existing DSN registration, select the appropriate node. The text in the second button in the toolbar should change to Modify Datasource if it is not already labeled as such. Press this button to invoke the Data Source Registration Editor. Removal of a DSN registration is as simple as selecting it from the main tree view and pressing the Delete Datasource button.

The first step to creating a dbWeb solution is to register the ODBC data source upon which your schemas will be based. This is done using the dbWeb Administrator. If a shortcut to the dbWeb Administrator application has not yet been installed on your Start menu, locate the application executable, `dbwebadm.exe`, in the `dbWeb/Admin` directory using a directory browsing utility, such as Windows NT Explorer.

For convenience, a button has been placed on the Data Source Registration Editor dialog box labeled Manage. Click this button to invoke the ODBC Administrator to create additional DSNs as needed.

The Data Source Registration Editor is implemented using a tabbed, dialog box control. The following tabs are available while creating or editing a DSN registration:

CAUTION

Care should be taken when deleting a DSN registration because all related schemas are automatically deleted. Although a confirmation dialog box is presented upon the request to delete a DSN registration, there is no indication that the related schemas will also be deleted.

- **The Profile tab**—Upon the launching of the Data Source Registration Editor, the Profile tab is displayed by default, enabling the DSN and related information to be specified. The name of the DSN as specified in the ODBC Administrator is entered in the Data Source Name edit box. The ellipses (…) button to the right of the edit box causes a list to be presented from which a DSN can be selected.

 TIP The data source list window is small by default, but you can use your mouse to increase its size to see the entire name for all of your DSNs.

The Database Name field allows for the database name to be specified. Because the database name is usually specified during the creation of the DSN, it is not always necessary to specify it here. The database name must be specified in either one place or the other, however.

 T I P When creating the SQL Server accounts used for dbWeb access, specify the default database. Doing so ensures that if a database name is not specified in either the ODBC DSN or in the dbWeb Data Source Registration, the default database is automatically connected to.

The User ID and Password fields allow for connection credentials to be specified as defined by the database administrator. Note that if the DSN is defined to use a Trusted Connection to the SQL Server, these fields are ignored and can therefore be left blank.

- **The Search Type tab**—The setting selected in the Search Type tab depends on the database being connected to. Most larger database servers, such as SQL Server and Oracle, are case-sensitive, whereas most smaller database engines, such as the JET engine used by Microsoft Access, are not.

  If you are connecting to SQL Server, Oracle, or some other database server that is case-sensitive, select the Always Perform Case Insensitive Searches option. If you are using JET, FoxPro, Paradox, or any other database engine that is case-insensitive, select the Use Default Searching as Defined by Your Datasource option.

- **The Connection tab**—The Connection tab enables the duration of the ODBC connection to be configured. The options include the Disconnect from Datasource after Using It Each Time option and the Disconnect after x Minutes option. How this option is set depends greatly on the types of connections users will need and the performance of those connections.

  The default is to disconnect after three minutes, which is adequate in most cases. To tune the performance, it may be necessary to increase the connection time out value to reduce the overhead of multiple reconnects to the database.

- **The Objects tab**—The Objects tab merely provides a way to view the objects in the selected data source. Viewable objects include tables, views, and procedures. This tab provides an excellent way to test your connection without the need for repeatedly opening and closing the Data Source Registration Editor.

Creating a Schema   Once the data source is registered, one or more schemas can be defined for that data source. To add a schema, a data source node or a peer schema node must be selected from the tree control in the dbWeb Administrator. Upon doing so, the first of the three buttons in the toolbar changes to read New Schema. Pressing this button causes a dialog box to appear enabling a schema to be created using either the Schema Wizard or the Schema Editor.

The Schema Wizard   The Schema Wizard is useful for getting a quick start at creating the most simple queries. Because multiple tables cannot be joined by the Schema Wizard, most schemas require the use of the Schema Editor.

Not unlike many of the wizards used in other popular products, the Schema Wizard consists of a series of dialog boxes that prompt for pertinent information in an intuitive manner. The user is guided through the process of creating a schema, step by step. Until all required information is provided on a given page, the user is prevented from moving to the next step.

Navigation is also similar to many other wizards. Along the bottom are buttons that enable the user to move forward (the Next button) and backward (the Previous button). Also provided is a Cancel button, enabling the user to leave the wizard without saving changes, and a Finish button, which becomes available when all of the required information has been provided on all the pages of the wizard.

The dbWeb Schema Wizard consists of five dialog boxes asking for the minimum information required to create a schema. These are as follows:

Part
V
Ch
24

- **Choose a Table**—This page requires the primary table to be selected, upon which a drilldown can be defined. The table chosen here should be the parent table for which there is at least one child.

- **Choose the Data Columns to Query**—This page enables data columns to be selected that are to be included in the Query By Example form for the given schema. A dbWeb QBE form enables the user to provide criteria with which a query is to be executed. An example of a QBE form is shown in Figure 24.10.

FIG. 24.10
A dbWeb Query By Example form allows the user to provide criteria upon which a query is based.

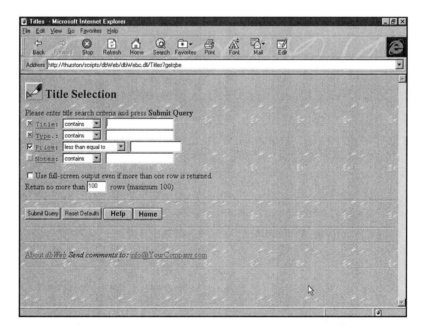

■ **Choose Tabular Form Data Columns**—This page is similar to the QBE page in that it allows for the desired data columns to be selected. The dbWeb Tabular form provides for the presentation of a resultset, such as that resulting from a QBE query. An example of a Tabular form is shown in Figure 24.11.

FIG. 24.11
A dbWeb Tabular form displays a multiple row resultset in table form.

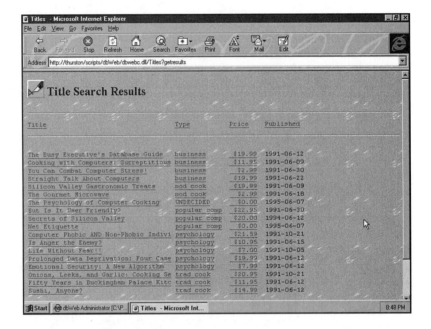

■ **Specify a Drilldown Automatic Link**—This page enables the user to select the column used to select a row or rows from a related table. This column is typically a foreign key into another table. When the user clicks the drilldown, the value of this column is used as a parameter for the next query.

■ **Enter Schema Name**—The final page of the wizard provides for the schema to be named. Unless changed on the Schemas tab of the Schema Editor, this name will appear in the caption bar of the client browser, and therefore a meaningful name should be used. To move directly into the Schema Editor after completion, check the Modify the New Schema When Finished option prior to pressing the Finish button.

The Schema Editor The Schema Editor provides a facility for the creation and management of dbWeb schemas. The Schema Editor is implemented using a tabbed dialog box and allows for the maintenance of all aspects of a dbWeb schema. A brief description of each tab follows.

To invoke the Schema Editor to create a new schema, first select either a data source node or a peer schema node from within the target data source. Doing so causes the text on the first button to change to New Schema. Press this button to invoke a blank Schema Editor.

Editing an existing schema is similar. First select the schema to be edited, then press the Modify schema button. Note that the text for this button changes as a schema is selected in the tree control.

 TIP To maximize performance, dbWeb caches much of the schema information. It is therefore sometimes necessary to stop and restart the dbWeb service in order for changes to take effect.

There are two types of schemas: those based on tables or views and those based on procedures. See the discussion on the Database Object Type grouping of the Schema tab for details on selecting between a table/view-based schema and a procedure-based schema. The following describes the tabs that are available when creating a schema based on tables or views:

Part
V
Ch
24

■ **The Schema tab**—Provides the capability to change basic schema information. The information that can be changed includes the following:

- The Schema Name is that which appears in the tree control of the main dbWeb Administrator window. This name is also used to call the schema from within HTML documents.

- The Browser Title Bar field contains the title that is displayed in the client's browser to be specified. These titles should be very brief but descriptive because it is the text saved in the Favorites menu of Internet Explorer.

- The Mail Comments to field enables an HTML mail link to be specified, which then can be used by the viewer to send mail to a particular user. This field must contain valid syntax for an HTML link, including the `<A HREF="...">` and the `</A>` tags.

- The Page Help URL field allows for a path to an HTML document or any other valid URL to be specified as a help page. The link is presented as a 3-D Help button on the displayed page. This value is provided by default as the value specified in the dbWeb Administrator Preferences.

- The Default Max Rows field allows for a maximum number of rows to be set. This becomes a necessary feature when large databases are used. Such databases could potentially return thousands of rows for a given query, resulting in unwieldy or unusable resultsets to be displayed.

- The Allow Actions On Data grouping enables actions to be carried out on the data by the viewing user. The actions include Insert, Update, and Delete. If any one of these three options is selected, the Ins/Upd/Del tab becomes enabled. Note that if the Database Object Type is set to be a procedure, this grouping along with the SQL grouping are disabled as these options are not valid with that object type.

- The SQL grouping has a single option, which is labeled as Select Distinct Records Only. When this option is set, duplicate rows of data are suppressed. Depending on the structure of the underlying database, this option may or may not have an effect on the resultset generated by the schema.

- The Database Object Type grouping allows for the selection of either Table(s) or View(s) or Procedures. Changing this option changes the mode of the Schema Editor entirely; some of the tabs change and some of the options become unavailable.

CAUTION

If the Database Object Type is changed after any information is entered, this information is discarded, and the Schema Editor is reinitialized as if a brand new schema were being created.

- **The Table tab**—Used to specify which tables are included in the schema. To add a table to the schema, select a table name from the list box on the left and use the <u>A</u>dd button to move it to the list box on the right. Optionally, the A<u>d</u>d All button will move all of the available tables to the list box on the right.

  If more than one table is selected, each table *must* be joined to at least one other table resulting in all tables being joined either directly or indirectly. This is done using the Join tab.

- **The Join tab**—Used to define how multiple tables are joined together to result in a single resultset being returned. Just as with a SQL statement, each table used must be joined to the other tables either directly or indirectly.

  To create a *join*, press the <u>N</u>ew Input button. Doing so invokes the Join Editor, enabling a single column in the left list box to be joined to a single column in the right list box using the operator selected from the drop-down combo box in the middle. Define all joins for all tables by repeating this process.

 If an Access database is being used, it is not possible to create outer-left and outer-right joins using the standard *= and =* operators. The suggested workaround is to create a QueryDef in the Access database and use its resultset in your dbWeb schema as you would any other table.

Also on the Join Tab is a Constraints list box. To add a constraint, press the <u>N</u>ew Constraint button, which invokes the Constraint Editor. To add a constraint, select the column from the list on the top, a comparison operator from the drop-down combo box in the middle, and finally a value in the text box at the bottom. As noted on the screen, numeric values should not be enclosed in quote marks; textual values on the other hand, should be enclosed in quotes.

- **The QBE tab**—Used to specify which tables are available in the Query By Example form. Through this form, the viewer is able to specify target values for one or more of these columns and subsequently submit a query based on these values. QBE forms are called from HTML documents using the GetQbe or GetXQbe dbWeb methods.

 For a list of all available dbWeb methods, click the <u>H</u>elp button on any of the editors, which invokes dbWeb Help. Once in Help, click the <u>C</u>ontents button and select the Developer's Reference link. A link to the dbWeb Methods page is available there.

■ **The Properties Editor**—Invoked by pressing a button labeled Properties, which is found on the QBE tab, the Tabular tab, the Freeform tab, and the Ins/Upd/Del tab (see Figure 24.12). This editor is used to change the attributes of the schema, the selected form, or a selected column. Consult the dbWeb Help file for more information on the meaning and valid values for these properties.

 T I P The Properties Editor and the Computed Column Expression Builder can be invoked from a context-sensitive, tear-off menu, which is presented in response to a right-click of the mouse.

FIG. 24.12
The Properties Editor is where the attributes of a schema are modified.

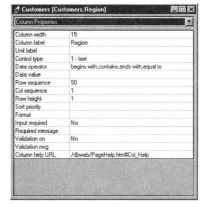

Part
V

Ch
24

■ **The Computed Column Expression Builder**—Invoked by pressing a button labeled Computed Column (see Figure 24.13). This button is found on the QBE tab, the Tabular tab, and the Freeform tab. The editor provides a space for an expression to be built and includes a tree control from which `table.column` combinations can be inserted. The data type of the expression can be specified using a drop-down combo box.

FIG. 24.13
The Computed Column Expression Builder dialog box provides the ability to create computed columns.

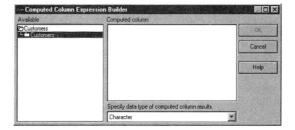

■ **The Tabular tab**—Used to specify which columns are included on the Tabular form for this schema. These forms present multiple rows in a simple tabular fashion where column names are listed across the top and data is listed in rows. Tabular forms are called from HTML documents using the `GetXTabular` and possibly the `GetResults` or `GetXResults` dbWeb methods.

■ **The Freeform tab**—Used to specify which columns are included in the Freeform form for this schema. These forms are used to display a single record at a time where the column names are down the left instead of across the top. Freeform forms are called from HTML documents using the `GetXFreeform` and possibly the `GetResults` or `GetXResults` dbWeb methods.

■ **The Ins/Upd/Del tab**—Used to specify which columns are available on the Ins/Upd/Del form. This same form is used to insert, update, or delete rows in the underlying database. Note that only one table per schema can be modified using this functionality. These functions are called from HTML documents using the `Insert`, `Update`, and `Delete` dbWeb methods.

■ **The DBX tab**—Used to attach .DBX files to the schema. Two different .DBX files are possible, depending on whether the resultset is a single-record resultset or a multi-record resultset. Press the Browse button to select an existing .DBX file or use the Editor button to create a new one using the integrated DBX Editor.

N O T E A single-record resultset is one that contains only one row from the underlying database, whereas a multirecord resultset contains two or more. ■

Linking Your Schemas Together It is often desirable to call one schema from another in response to the viewer's selection of an automatic link. In most cases, this will be a mechanism that represents a parent/child relationship in the database itself. An example might be a schema that lists active clients and a link to another schema that lists the active projects for the selected client. It may also be a link to a different view of the same data. These links are created with the Automatic Link Editor, which is shown in Figure 24.14.

FIG. 24.14

The Automatic Link Editor is used to define the links between different views of the same schema or different schemas altogether.

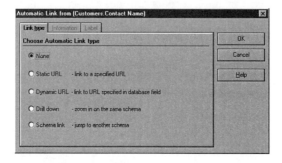

To invoke the Automatic Link Editor, the column that is to be the source of the link must first be selected. This can be done from either the Tabular tab or the Freeform tab. Doing so causes the Properties button to become available; pressing this button causes the Properties Editor to be displayed. As the Automatic Link URL property is selected, a small button labeled with ellipsis points (...) becomes available that, when pushed, causes the Automatic Link Editor to be displayed. Several types of links are supported by dbWeb, as follows:

■ **None**—Selecting this option causes the Automatic Link URL property to be cleared when the Automatic Link Editor is closed. When this option is selected, the Information and Label tabs become grayed, indicating their unavailability.

■ **Static URL**—If a static URL is to be linked to regardless of the row selected, select this option. Once selected, finish defining the link by selecting the Information tab.

Enter the URL in the URL edit field, including the required HTML tag. As an option, dbWeb can automatically wrap the URL in an HTML `<A HREF=>` tag. Select the Jump To option if this is the case. Similarly, the URL can be wrapped in an HTML `<A HREF="mailto:">` tag by selecting the Mail To option.

Finally, the actual data retrieved from the database can be effectively hidden by supplying text in the Label tab. This text appears instead of the actual data. If the data is to be used as the link label, ensure that this field is left blank.

■ **Dynamic URL**—When a different URL is to be linked to depending on the row, select this option. To use this option, the current column must contain an URL. Notice that when this option is selected, the column name is provided automatically on the Information tab.

Just as with the Static URL, the URL can be wrapped by dbWeb depending on the option selected. If the entire HTML tag is included in the column data, the Plain Text option is used. Otherwise, one of the other options should be selected.

■ **Drilldown**—A drilldown link is most useful for linking two forms together based upon a single-part primary key. It is typically used when only a subset of a row's columns will fit in a tabular form. Using a drilldown link, the entire record can be displayed using the Freeform form in the same schema.

Another use, however, is to narrow the scope of a query that returns a large number of rows. For example, the Publishers schema, based upon the `dbpubs` DSN in the dbWeb samples demonstrates links that enable the user to click a city, state, or country. By doing so, a resultset containing the publishers for a given city, state, or country is returned.

The link is defined on the Information tab. Press the New Criteria button to invoke the Criteria Editor, from which a column and comparison operator can be selected. The criteria typically consists of a single-part primary key and the equality comparison operator.

TIP

If your criteria require a multipart primary key to be defined, consider using a schema link to link to a different schema. The schema link allows for multiple criteria to be defined on different columns in both the source and target schemas.

■ **Schema link**—The schema link is undoubtedly the most powerful of the automatic links. Using this option, an entirely different schema, and therefore an entirely different query or table, can be selected.

This kind of link is typically used to drill down on a foreign key from the parent to the child table. For example, if a tabular form was used to display all of the clients for a software consulting form, the user could double-click the client's name, and through a schema link a query of that client's projects could then be displayed.

To configure the link, first select the target schema by clicking the small button with the ellipsis points (…) on it. Clicking the <u>N</u>ew Criteria button then enables the link or links to be defined. This is typically a single- or multipart foreign key.

DBX Files and Tags   To enhance both the input and output of dbWeb, consider using .DBX files. These files allow for the output of a dbWeb schema to be formatted in nearly any way possible with HTML. More importantly, however, is the capability of dbWeb to format your results using report banding features common to most report building tools. Report banding enables a section of your HTML document to be repeated for each row in a resultset.

N O T E   The creation and maintenance of .DBX files require an understanding of HTML. ■

.DBX files are simply HTML files with tags recognized by dbWeb embedded in them. For example, the \TBON and \TBOFF tags identify the start and end of a repeating section, respectively. Other tags identify columns from the resultset. Because .DBX files can be used for QBE forms as well as Insert/Update/Delete forms, extensions to HTML INPUT tags can also be used.

To use a different .DBX file for single-record or multi-record resultsets, define a new schema. This is just one of a handful of reasons why it is often necessary to have different input schemas and resultset schemas.

Create .DBX files for your schemas using a simple text editor, such as Notepad, or with the DBX Editor supplied with dbWeb Administrator. The DBX Editor is available by pressing the Editor button on the DBX tab of the Schema Editor.

Use your favorite HTML editor, such as Microsoft FrontPage or Internet Assistant for Word, to generate the HTML for your basic document. Once the majority of the HTML has been generated, use Notepad or the DBX Editor to add the .DBX tags.

All DBX tags must adhere to a format that is recognized by dbWeb. That format is as follows:

\TOBJ\T{*Table Name*}**\TCOL\T**{*Column Name*}**\T**

Substitute the actual names of the table and column as indicated when editing your .DBX files. HTML formatting tags can be placed before and after the tags.

N O T E   For an overview of the available HTML tags, consult the Microsoft Site Builder Workshop site. The URL is **http://www.microsoft.com/workshop/author/newhtml/default.htm**. ■

The banding tags also must adhere to a specific format. A repeating section must start with a BON tag and end with a BOFF tag. The format for the BON tag is:

`\TBON\TMATCH\T{Table Name}\T{Column Name}\T`

Again, substitute the actual names of the table and column as indicated when editing your .DBX files. The tag for the BOFF tag is as follows:

`\TBOFF\t`

Calling dbWeb Schemas from HTML Documents   Once you have created your schemas using the dbWeb Administrator, you need to embed references to them in your HTML documents. This is typically done by referring to the dbWeb Client Stub followed by the schema name. This is then followed by the query operator, a question mark, and the desired dbWeb method.

The following example is a portion of the dbWeb test page, which is installed with dbWeb to test the installation. The name of the file is DBWTEST.HTM. By default, it is installed in the dbWeb folder located in the wwwroot directory:

```
...
<I><A NAME="Microsoft"><H4>Microsoft Internet Information Server Test</H4></A></I>
<UL>
<B>Pubs Examples</B><BR>
<LI><A HREF="/scripts/dbWeb/dbWebc.dll/Titles?getqbe">Titles</A>
<LI><A HREF="/scripts/dbWeb/dbWebc.dll/Authors?getqbe">Authors</A>
<LI><A HREF="/scripts/dbWeb/dbWebc.dll/Stores?getqbe">Stores</A>
<LI><A HREF="/scripts/dbWeb/dbWebc.dll/Publishers?getqbe">Publishers</A>
<LI><A HREF="/scripts/dbWeb/dbWebc.dll/Author_Titles?getqbe">Author_Titles</A>
<LI><A HREF="/scripts/dbWeb/dbWebc.dll/Store_Sales?getqbe">Store_Sales</A>
</UL>
...
```

As shown by the previous code, the Titles schema is called through a reference to the dbWeb Client stub. The stub is located in the /scripts/dbWeb directory, the path of which is relative to the wwwroot. The getqbe method is called when the user selects the link shown as Titles on the user's browser screen.

Viewing the Visitor and Error Logs   As indicated by the IP Log option in the Server Preferences Editor, dbWeb is able to keep a log of the activities it is requested to perform. The visitor log is written as text files to paths specified using the preferences editor. By default, the log is located at C:\Dbweb\Service\DbwIP.log. The columns in the log are thread ID, date, time, IP address, dbWeb method, and any method parameters.

dbWeb reports its errors using the Windows NT Event Log. To view the errors, select the Application log in the Windows NT Event Viewer, and look for entries that contain dbWeb in the source column. Note that all requests, even those that result in an error, are also logged to the visitor log as well.

The Internet Database Connector

The Internet Database Connector (IDC) is an ISAPI extension installed as a standard component of the Microsoft Internet Information Server. Through this extension, access to ODBC data sources is provided.

IDC uses two types of files to define the way information is requested and the results of the request are formatted. These files are Internet Database Connector files (.IDC) and HTML Extension files (.HTX). The connector files provide a query and a few connection parameters. The resultset is then formatted using the extension files, based upon tags placed within them.

Unlike dbWeb, IDC is not an application capable of creating and maintaining dynamic content templates. It is merely the filter component which is capable of parsing HTML documents with embedded IDC tags and responding to them accordingly. By providing queries in connector files and sophisticated HTML in the format files, much can be done to produce dazzling dynamic content.

N O T E   Development using the IDC requires a thorough knowledge of both SQL and HTML. A basic
understanding of ODBC is also recommended. ▓

The IDC is installed when IIS is installed, so unlike dbWeb, there is nothing more to install. The only additional requirement is that ODBC 2.50 must be installed on the machine.

> **CAUTION**
>
> The ODBC driver for Microsoft Access 2.0 is not compatible with Internet Information Server or the Internet Database Connector. It is therefore necessary to use the ODBC 2.50 driver.

IDC is implemented as a .DLL named `Httpodbc.dll`, which is installed in the IIS directory by default. This ISAPI extension is mapped in the registry to handle files with the .IDC extension.

Based upon field values and option settings in these files, queries are issued to the ODBC data source. The resultset is then formatted based upon special tags in the HTML extension file specified in the .IDC file. The resulting HTML document is then routed back to the client browser by IIS.

Internet Database Connector Files

Internet Database Connector files have the extension .IDC and contain the SQL statement of a query. Also included are a handful of required option fields that specify the ODBC DSN and the output format file. The IDC files can also include one or more of the optional fields used to further customize the way the query is issued. The following fields are required in every IDC file:

- ▓ **Datasource**—The name of a System ODBC data source name must be specified to enable IDC to connect to the data source. Use the ODBC Administrator to create system ODBC DSNs.

■ **Template**—The resultset of an IDC query is formatted and set to the user's browser based upon formatting tags embedded in HTML extension files. These files have an .HTX extension. .HTX files are simply HTML documents with special tags recognized by IDC.

■ **SQL Statement**—The SQL of the query to be issued. Unless advanced options are specified, the dialect of this SQL statement must be ODBC compliant.

The query statement specified in the IDC file can be any valid SQL statement. This includes `INSERT`, `DELETE`, and `UPDATE` queries. While not a common query construct, SQL Data Definition Language (DDL) can also be used in the IDC files to create tables, indices, constraints, stored procedures, triggers, or even drop the same objects. The SQL that can be used is dependent upon the ODBC driver and the underlying database server.

The following snippet of code shows the contents of `viewbook.idc`, an IDC sample file included with IIS. Note that the `Datasource` is an ODBC DSN named `Web SQL`. Two optional fields, `Username` and `Expires`, are included in this example. They indicate that `sa` is the username to be used to gain access to the database and that the resultset is held in cache for two seconds before being considered expired. Expired resultsets are requeried when their results are next requested:

Part

V

Ch

24

```
Datasource: Web SQL
Username: sa
Expires: 2
Template: viewbook.htx
SQLStatement:
+SELECT FirstName, LastName
+FROM Guests
```

A SQL statement can be of nearly any length, depending on its complexity. Regardless, it is advisable to break up your SQL statement into multiple lines for readability. To do so, ensure that a plus sign (+) is used at the beginning of each new line.

There are many other fields that can be included in the IDC files. For a comprehensive discussion of these fields, consult the online documentation included with IIS. The IDC is discussed in Chapter 7, "Administering Windows NT Server."

Using Query Parameters

In many instances, it is desirable to let the user specify criteria for a search. This can be done using standard HTML constructs, as shown in the following code snippet taken from Chapter 8 of the IIS documentation, "Publishing Information and Applications." Note that all of this code is standard HTML; nothing specific to IDC has been used with the exception of the action being defined to call the .IDC file:

```
<FORM METHOD="POST" ACTION="/scripts/samples/sample2.idc"><P>
Enter YTD sales amount: <INPUT NAME="sales" VALUE="5000" ><P>
<INPUT TYPE="SUBMIT" VALUE="Run Query">
</FORM>
```

In this example, the user is asked to provide a value for YTD sales. The default is 5,000, which can be overridden by the user. When the user clicks the Run Query button, the form's SUBMIT method is called, which is defined to call SAMPLE2.IDC. The code from SAMPLE2.IDC, which is again borrowed from the IIS documentation, is as follows:

```
Datasource: Web SQL
Username: sa
Template: sample.htx
SQLStatement:
+SELECT au_lname, ytd_sales
+ from pubs.dbo.titleview
+ where ytd_sales > %sales%
```

Note that the SQL statement includes %sales% in the where clause. This is the value supplied by the user. For example, if the user had supplied 2,000 instead of the default 5,000, %sales% would be replaced by 2,000 before being submitted to the ODBC driver for processing. The resultset would then include only those rows where the value in the ytd_sales column is greater than 2,000.

Just as the user is asked to provide a value using a standard text edit control, standard HTML Select Multiple list boxes can also be used to specify input. Just as %sales% variable was referenced in the .IDC file in the previous example, so can a variable defined as a Select Multiple list box. IDC conveniently replaces the variable name with the actual values.

> **CAUTION**
>
> Pay close attention to the condition described in the "Using Select Multiple List Boxes in HTML Forms" section of Chapter 8 in the IIS online documentation. This discussion describes the significance of the placement of single quote marks around the variable name defined by the HTML SELECT MULTIPLE tag.

HTX Files

HTML Extension files are very similar to dbWeb's .DBX files in purpose. These files contain special formatting tags embedded in a standard HTML document. These tags determine how the resultset of a query is formatted. These tags are enclosed with special delimiters, <%tag%> or <!--%tag-->. The tags available for use in .HTX files include the following:

- <%begindetail%> and <%enddetail%> delimit a section where rows returned from the data source appear.

- <%if%>, <%else%>, and <%endif%> control the inclusion of a block or blocks of HTML code that is returned to the client browser depending on a condition being met. Two IDC built-in variables can be used within the if tag. They are CurrentRecord and MaxRecords.

In addition to these tags, any column can be included by enclosing the name of the column in the standard HTX delimiters. For example, to include the column CustomerName in the HTML document, use <%CustomerName%> in your .HTX file.

Also available in the .HTX files are all of the HTTP variables defined and populated by IIS. A comprehensive list of these variables and their contents are described in Chapter 8 of the IIS online documentation.

Microsoft FrontPage Integration

The .IDC files required by IDC can be easily created using the FrontPage Editor's Internet Database Connector Wizard as shown in Figure 24.15. This Wizard quickly collects the information necessary to generate an .IDC file automatically. FrontPage will also use the Wizard for subsequent edits of the .IDC file. To invoke the Database Connector Wizard, select File, New, and then select Database Connector Wizard from the list of available templates.

FIG. 24.15

The FrontPage Editor's Database Connector Wizard collects the information necessary to generate an IDC file automatically.

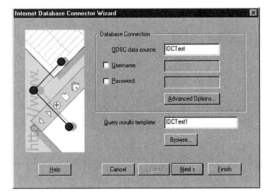

Result templates (.HTX files) can be just as easily created with FrontPage's Database Results template. Selecting this template yeilds a blank editor window in which any HTML document can be created. The primary difference however is the Database submenu located on the Edit menu. This menu provides for the insertion of IDC tags into the HTML document. Refer to the FrontPage documentation for specifics on these items.

From Here...

This chapter is an overview of two tools used to create and maintain dynamic content with Microsoft Internet Information Server. By comparing and discussing many of the major features of each tool, it should be possible to determine which tool is best for the needs of most developers.

In addition to learning about the topics discussed here, it will likely be necessary to consult other chapters in this book to ensure that the solution provided with these tools is complete, secure, and error-free. For additional information on these topics, consult the following chapters:

- For more details on starting, stopping, and configuring Windows NT services such as IIS, dbWeb, and SQL Server, see Chapter 7, "Administering Windows NT Server."
- For a discussion of Internet Information Server, see Chapter 16, "The BackOffice I-Net Toolbox," or Chapter 18, "Building a Web with Internet Information Server (IIS)."

Part

V

Ch

24

## CHAPTER 25

Implementing Internet Security

by David L. Williams

The overwhelming global acceptance of the Internet is providing unprecedented levels of connectivity to computer users around the world. While the potential benefits of this newfound communications infrastructure are immeasurable, many of the possible pitfalls are still unknown. One thing on which most experts would agree, however, is that there has never been a greater need for computer security technologies than there is today. In fact, as more and more people begin to use the Internet for electronic commerce, the need for reliable network security will continue to grow.

This chapter explores the many security issues related to the Internet and explains some basic security concepts and the technologies behind them. It then explains how these technologies fit into the new Microsoft Internet Security Framework and how this framework will help to secure the data of most Internet users. ■

Overview of cryptography

Gain a basic understanding of the technologies forming the foundations of the secure Internet communications protocols.

Microsoft's Internet Security Framework

Learn about the components that make up the Internet Security Framework defined by Microsoft and understand what roles these pieces play in the overall system.

Applying the security protocols

Learn how to apply the technologies described to create a secure environment with Internet Information Server and Internet Explorer.

Internet Security Concerns

The recent explosion in the number of individuals with access to the Internet and its proto-cols—either through high-speed T1 connections at the office or modem dial-up connections at home—has caught the attention of corporate America. They see this new global, high-speed communications medium as a way to maintain closer contact with partners, suppliers, and customers. Some of the benefits include the following:

- Real-time information sharing with partners and suppliers
- More responsive and less expensive customer support facilities
- New sales and advertising channels
- Improved communications and information sharing within an organization

Because of these benefits, many companies have eagerly connected their private networks to the Internet, used the Internet to connect once isolated local area networks (LANs), or begun running Internet protocols on their internal LANs to exploit the information-sharing tools of the World Wide Web. Yet there are a number of security concerns associated with transmitting information—especially sensitive information—across the Internet. These concerns include the privacy, integrity, and authentication of data transmitted across the network.

Privacy

Perhaps the most widely held concern, when it comes to Internet security, is the privacy of transmitted data. The problem is one of transmitting information across a public network with-out that information being seen by an unknown, possibly hostile, third party. The privacy re-quirement varies greatly depending on the parties involved and the purpose of the information exchange. For instance, most individuals rarely worry about whether their e-mail is seen by someone for whom it is not intended; it is probably not terribly interesting.

However, internal corporate memos transmitted from headquarters to a branch office might make for more interesting reading. Corporations tend to jealously guard that information they deem sensitive to their business operations, as this knowledge—if made available to a competi-tor—could easily equate to lost revenues or market share. In fact, there are a number of highly skilled, unscrupulous individuals around who intentionally intercept such information in order to make it available to those competitors willing to pay for it. Any security mechanism for Internet communication must adequately address this issue.

Integrity

In addition to privacy, it is essential to have confidence in the integrity of transmitted informa-tion. Because of the way the Internet is constructed, any information transmitted from one point to another is often stored temporarily on any number of machines along the way (see Figure 25.1). At any of these intermediate destinations, it is possible to compromise the integ-rity of the transmitted data through either accidental or intentional actions.

FIG. 25.1
Data transmitted across the Internet typically resides on various machines while in transit.

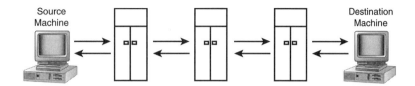

In other words, an individual with malicious intent could alter the content of the transmitted data at any point along the path after it leaves the source machine and before it arrives at the final destination. One possible reason for doing this is to mislead the recipient in order to gain some advantage. A recipient who did not know the data had been altered would assign it whatever confidence the source warrants.

Another situation might involve a file, possibly a program, that has been placed in an area for download. This file could be altered from its original form either before or after being placed on the server. In the case of a data file, it is possible to change or delete data values in order to mislead the recipient. For a program file, it is possible to attach a virus so that when the program is run, the virus infects the destination machine. It is, therefore, extremely important in the open world of the Internet to have a reliable means of detecting data and files that have been altered.

Authentication

As if privacy and integrity were not enough to deal with, the issue of authentication is one that must be answered before any real commerce can be conducted on the open Internet. *Authentication* is the act of verifying that a connected client or server is indeed the client or server it claims to be. It is also used to confirm that a file or set of data did, in fact, originate from a known, trusted source.

It is currently possible on the Internet for a machine to intercept a message or a request sent to a specific IP address, and pretend that it is the intended machine (see Figure 25.2). For instance, a machine may masquerade as a server with which a client is attempting to communicate. In this way, a dialogue may begin between the client and the false server. The client may be misled into giving out information to the server, assuming that it is the machine for which the data was intended. This is a technique known as *masquerading*, or *spoofing*, and can work in the opposite direction as well, with the machine masquerading as a valid client and communicating with a valid server.

FIG. 25.2
A machine masquerading as one party in a communication session can appear authentic to an unsuspecting first party.

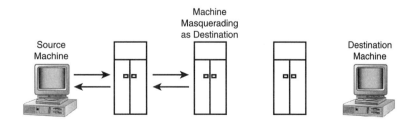

Part
V

Ch
25

When it comes to electronic commerce and online credit card transactions, it is vital that the user is confident the server to which he or she transmits private information (such as an account number) is indeed the machine the user believes it to be. Without this confidence, the grand vision of full-blown electronic commerce on the Internet cannot become reality. Authenticating the commercial site to the satisfaction of the user is the key to raising this confidence.

An Introduction to Cryptography

Given the concerns regarding the safe and private transmission of information across the Internet, it may seem that the best course of action is not to use the Internet at all, except possibly to access the latest sports scores on ESPN. However, all of these concerns can be addressed using techniques developed in the field of cryptography.

Cryptography is the science of translating messages into a form that is safe for transmission such that, if intercepted, they are extremely difficult to restore to the original data. Cryptography dates back to the ancient Egyptians and has been used throughout history for securely transporting military and diplomatic secrets. The recent application of high-speed computers to the field of cryptography has yielded more versatile and secure cryptographic systems.

Today's systems employ a technique known as *encryption* in which complex algorithms are used to transform the digital representation of the information from one mathematical space to another. To perform the encryption, the user utilizes a special algorithm and a unique numeric value called a *key*. To retrieve the encrypted information, the user must know the corresponding algorithm to decrypt the data and another key, which is in some way related to the key used during the encryption process.

Private-Key Encryption

Until recently, most computer encryption was performed using some type of *symmetric algorithm*. This is an algorithm in which a single key is used for both encryption and decryption along with some specified mathematical function (see Figure 25.3). Using this approach, data is encrypted by passing it and the key through the mathematical function to produce data that is completely unintelligible.

To decrypt the data, the encrypted data and the same key are passed through the inverse of the function. The complexity of the function and the length of the key (how large the number is) determine how difficult it will be to break the encryption without having the key. The major advantage of a symmetric cryptographic system is speed.

Probably the most widely known symmetric cryptographic algorithm is the Data Encryption Standard (DES) algorithm. DES is a very good encryption algorithm that typically uses a 56-bit key. (The key, represented in binary form, could use up to 56 bits.) There are a few limitations to remember, however, when using private-key encryption.

First, because DES and other forms of private-key encryption use a single, private key to perform both the encryption and decryption, any two parties sharing encrypted information must know the private key used for encrypting that information. Therefore, it makes sense to generate the keys as needed and exchange them just prior to transmitting the encrypted data. Since anyone with knowledge of the private key can decode and read the encrypted data, this exchange of keys requires a secure channel. However, a secure channel cannot be established until the exchange of keys is completed. Because of this paradox, the keys must be stored somewhere on each local machine prior to transmitting the data. This means that, when the size of the network grows, the number of keys to be maintained grows exponentially, soon becoming unmanageable (see Figure 25.4).

FIG. 25.3
In private-key encryption, a single key is used to perform both encryption and decryption of message data.

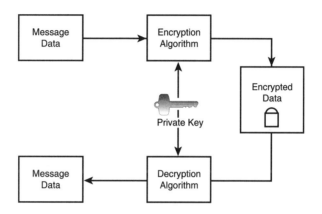

FIG. 25.4
As more and more computers on a network require secure communications using private-key encryption, the number of keys to be maintained grows exponentially. This not only poses a problem in terms of maintaining keys, it also compromises the confidentiality of these keys.

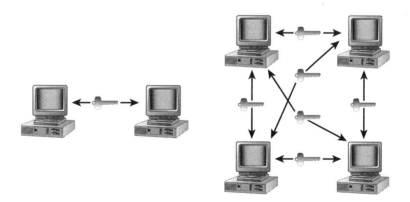

Second, because the keys must be known prior to the exchange of information, two parties have knowledge of any private key. This implies a trusted relationship between the two parties. If either party violates this trust, intentionally or otherwise, the privacy mechanism breaks down.

Public-Key Encryption

Many of the limitations of private-key encryption were overcome by the advent of public-key encryption. This method for encryption was first put into practice in 1977 by Ronald Rivest, Adi Shamir, and Len Adleman when they created the RSA encryption algorithm. This system consists of two keys: one private and one public. The private key, as the name suggests, is always kept secret. The public key can be made known to anyone without jeopardizing the security of the system.

Public-key encryption works on the basis of a one-way, trap-door function. In a one-way function, the computation in the forward direction is relatively simple, but the calculation in the reverse direction is extremely difficult. A trap-door function is a one-way function in which the reverse direction is easily calculated if a specific piece of information is known. That piece of information for a public-key encryption algorithm is the private key. The public key can be calculated from knowledge of the private key, but the opposite is inherently more difficult. That is why it is safe to make the public key available to anyone.

To perform public-key encryption, the data to be encrypted is passed as one input to the encryption function, with one key from the public/private key pair as the other input. To decrypt, the encrypted data is passed through the decryption function along with the other key from the pair (see Figure 25.5). Public-key encryption works the same way in both directions. In other words, data encrypted using the public key can be decrypted using the private key, and data encrypted using the private key can be decrypted using the public key.

FIG. 25.5

In contrast with private-key encryption, two keys are required to complete an information transfer using public-key encryption.

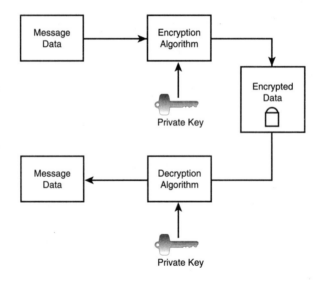

One drawback to public-key encryption is speed. Because two keys are known instead of just one (as is the case for private-key encryption), the public-key algorithms require a longer key in order to obtain the same level of security. This generally translates into more computational time required to process the algorithm.

The RSA system makes it practical to implement encryption on a large network. Public keys can be kept in a public area or distributed by a server and obtained by users as needed. Someone who wants to send an encoded message simply looks in a directory (much like a telephone book) to find the public key of the recipient, and uses that key to perform the encryption. Once the message is encoded, only the private key of the intended recipient will successfully decode the message. If the message is intercepted along the way, the individual intercepting it sees only a garbled mess and has very little hope of breaking the code without utilizing a tremendous amount of computing power. In addition, this approach presupposes no prior relationship between the parties in question, and no trust is implied or required to keep the key private.

Network Credentials

It is now apparent that data encryption is a possible solution to the problem of maintaining privacy while transmitting information across the Internet. Two more concerns still remain regarding the safe and confident utilization of an unsecured network: integrity and authentication. As it turns out, one way to address both of these problems is to employ a mechanism known as a *digital signature*.

Digital Signatures

A digital signature is just what its name implies. It is a digital code that can be attached to an electronic document and is analogous to a handwritten signature in that it uniquely identifies the individual creating it. The idea behind it is actually quite simple, and makes use of the public-key encryption technology previously described. The basic premise revolves around the one-way, trap-door functions. Specifically, any data encoded with a particular private key can only be decoded using the corresponding public key. Conversely, any data that can be decoded with a certain public key could only have been encoded with the corresponding private key. Because only a single entity knows the private key, successful decoding of data with a particular public key therefore uniquely identifies the owner of the related private key.

Part

V

Ch

25

In practice, the raw data is generally not directly encoded. It is first passed through something called a *hashing algorithm*. This hashing algorithm generates a *cryptographic digest*, which is a unique, short-hand representation of the original data. This digest is much easier to work with than the raw data and generally requires much less processing power to encode and decode. Since encryption, especially public-key encryption, is an expensive process in terms of central processing unit (CPU) cycles, and the hashing algorithms are generally much less complex, there can be a significant reduction in processing requirements. Also, this difference in processing requirements becomes even greater as stronger encryption is used.

To create a digital signature, the information to be transmitted is passed through a hashing algorithm to create a cryptographic digest. The digest is then encrypted with the author's private key, and transmitted along with the original text to the recipient. The recipient then decrypts the transmitted digest with the author's public key. In addition, he also creates a new digest by employing the same hashing function on the message body. If the newly created digest matches the decrypted digest, then the decrypted digest could only have been created using the author's private key. Since the key is private, only the author would have access to it, and the source of the document is confirmed. Also, since the two digests match, the document could not have been altered after the author signed it, and the integrity of the document is established (see Figure 25.6).

FIG. 25.6
Digital signatures can
be used to verify both
the authenticity and
integrity of a document.

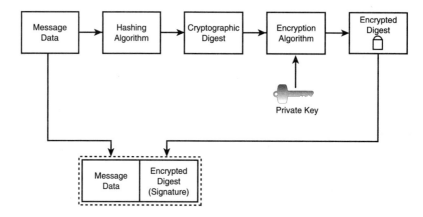

In practice, the sender generally transmits his public key along with the message so that the recipient is not required to look it up. The problem with this approach is that if someone forged the message and then sent his public key to verify the message, the only thing verified is the integrity of the message—not the author. In order to authenticate the author, another mechanism known as a digital ID, or certificate, is employed.

Certificates

A *certificate* is a set of digital data containing an individual's public key and identity information that has been signed by a well-known, trusted third party. This trusted party, known as a *certification authority (CA)*, can be a part of the internal corporate information systems (IS) department, or a commercial supplier of certificate services. This approach enables the transmission of the sender's public key in the form of a certificate along with the signed document. The recipient verifies the certificate with a well-known public key, which is either stored locally on each machine or in a central location. After the recipient validates the certificate, the signature is validated by using the public key contained in the certificate. This process, once completed, authenticates the author of the information and verifies the integrity of the data.

One advantage to this approach is the difficulty required to masquerade as someone else. Because the key used to begin the authentication process is well-known and will only decode information encrypted with the private key of the trusted third party, it is virtually impossible for any unauthorized individual to masquerade as the trusted party. This promotes the element of trust in the system because anyone wanting to sign a message must be known by the trusted party. In addition, the trusted party provides an extra check by specifying the public key for the signing party. Another advantage is that the machine receiving the information need not be physically connected to the trusted authority. The only thing required at the receiving machine is knowledge of the public key of the trusted authority.

The most widely accepted certificate format is the X.509 standard defined by the Consultative Committee in International Telegraphy and Telephony (CCITT). Figure 25.7 shows an illustration of the X.509 format.

FIG. 25.7
The X.509 certificate provides a standard mechanism for validating a user's public key.

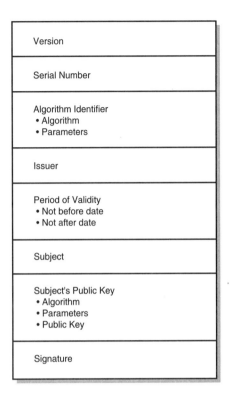

Version
Serial Number
Algorithm Identifier • Algorithm • Parameters
Issuer
Period of Validity • Not before date • Not after date
Subject
Subject's Public Key • Algorithm • Parameters • Public Key
Signature

Part
V

Ch
25

Certificate Hierarchies

Microsoft Corporation has been working closely with VeriSign, Inc., one of the leading certification authorities, to define technologies for use in authentication and validation. They have a vision that goes beyond the idea of a single, trusted party providing authentication services. Clearly, a single authority could not handle the workload involved with maintaining verification information on every user of the Internet. Therefore, Microsoft and VeriSign envision a hierarchical approach to the verification process (see Figure 25.8). It makes sense for small groups—such as departments, corporations, and government agencies—to maintain records on their own users and validate them appropriately.

However, communicating between those groups requires a higher-level authority to perform the necessary validation. A hierarchy would exist in which local authorities would be validated by high-level authorities. Those, in turn, would be validated by still higher-level authorities. Ultimately, a single, topmost authority would maintain records on the other authorities. In this way, no matter how wide an area the transmission covers, the recipient simply traverses up the hierarchy until he reaches a level that provides the required measure of trust. In addition, it seems likely that multiple, parallel hierarchies would exist in order to provide different types of authentication.

FIG. 25.8

The certificate hierarchy could be utilized for authentication when parties associated with different local entities want to exchange secure information. Instead of direct authentication of the parties, the low-level authorities authenticate the parties and high-level authorities verify the low-level authorities.

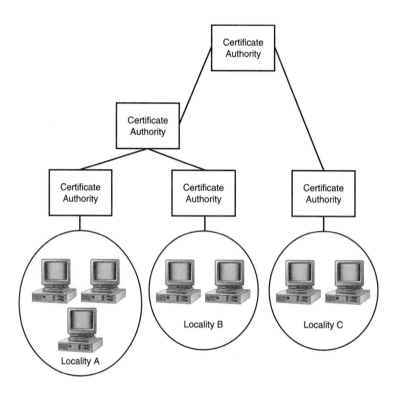

Code Signing

Among the current predictions about what the future of the Internet will bring, many people talk about the potential for full electronic software distribution. Currently, software vendors develop their software, create disks and manuals, place them into boxes, stamp a logo on the box, shrinkwrap the whole package, and ship countless numbers of the packages to various resellers around the world. The consumer then travels to the local computer store, purchases the software, takes it home, and installs it. The expectation for the future—much to the dismay of the software resellers—is for the user to simply download an electronic copy of the software and manuals directly from a server on the Internet. In all likelihood, the software would also install itself, making this method of distribution much easier for the consumer.

Until recently, this scenario would be unthinkable due to the risk of viruses, software piracy, and the lack of a secure means of transferring payment to the vendor. However, the public-key encryption, digital signature, and digital certificate technologies come together in a powerful technique referred to as *code signing*. In this process, the software vender obtains a certificate from a certification authority. The vender then signs the software along with a copy of the certificate using his private key. This way, the entire package is secure and verified by the CA. To use Microsoft's analogy, encryption with the private key equates to shrinkwrapping the package, and the digital certificate equates to a notary seal. The one item not addressed in this scenario is the electronic payment method. This is discussed in the "Secure Electronic Transactions (SET)" section later in this chapter.

The Microsoft Security Framework

Given that brief overview of the technologies involved, it is now time to discuss Microsoft's plan to use their Internet Security Framework to support secure computing over the Internet. This framework is a comprehensive set of technologies—both public-key and password-based—that cover the entire range of secure Internet computing requirements. According to Microsoft, this framework is meant to enable the user to do the following:

- Exchange information securely across public networks
- Control access from the Internet to private, corporate networks
- Engage in electronic commerce

In this framework, Microsoft supports many of the current standards for secure communications on the Internet, as well as supplementing and enhancing a few of them. Its goal is to facilitate a migration to secure network computing without requiring existing security systems to be discarded. In addition, many of the network security features, such as digital certificates, integrate into the existing security model for Windows NT so that network administrators can use the tools with which they are already familiar. This also serves to further blur the distinction between the Internet and the intranet.

Part

V

Ch

25

Authenticode

The Internet Security Framework includes a set of utilities, dubbed Authenticode, that enable the user to digitally sign files and then verify that the files were signed correctly. These utilities are part of the ActiveX Software Development Kit (SDK) and are freely available from Microsoft. The utilities included are the following:

- MakeCert
- Cert2SPC
- SignCode
- PeSigMgr
- ChkTrust

N O T E In order to use the Authenticode utilities, the CryptoAPI must already be installed and running. To check this, go to a command prompt and type **api ***. This command will generate a series of success messages. If no messages are generated, the CryptoAPI is either not installed or not running.

Microsoft recommends the following steps for using these utilities to sign a file:

1. Run MakeCert to generate a public/private key pair, associate the keys with a specified publisher's name, and create an X.509 certificate signed by a root key. If no root key is

specified, it generates one for you. (A *root key* is the public key of a certification authority.)

2. Run Cert2SPC to create a software publishing certificate (SPC), which wraps the X.509 certificate into a signed data object.

CAUTION

The software publishing certificate generated by Cert2SPC is for test purposes only and is not for use in signing files or software intended for publication. To obtain a valid SPC, contact a certification authority.

---

3. Run SignCode to create a digest of the file and sign the digest using the private key generated in Step 1 and the SPC generated in Step 2.

Once the file is signed, it is a good idea to verify both the signature and the integrity of the file, as in the following process:

1. Run PeSigMgr to confirm that the valid SPC was correctly embedded into the file.

2. Run ChkTrust to create a new digest of the information stored within the file and compare it to the encrypted digest that is stored within the signed data object in the file.

Qualifications for Software Publishing Certificates

In order for the system to work as promised, it is vital for the public to maintain confidence in the assurances offered by the software publishing certificates. Toward this end, Microsoft has put forth some suggested criteria to be applied consistently to each SPC applicant. This would ensure that certain standards are met by the applicants, regardless of the authority supplying the certificate.

In their criteria, Microsoft differentiates between commercial and individual software publishers. The qualifications for these two types of publishers differ somewhat.

Individual Qualifications   To obtain an individual SPC, the user must meet the following qualifications:

- The applicant must provide positive identification, including name and address. These identification credentials will be validated prior to issuance of a certificate.

- The applicant must sign a pledge to refrain from publishing software that he knows, or should have known, contains viruses or other malicious code.

Commercial Qualifications   In order to obtain a commercial SPC, the applicant must meet the qualifications specified for the individual publisher plus the two following additional requirements:

- The applicant must achieve a predetermined level of financial standing as indicated by an approved financial rating service.

■ The applicant must agree to generate and store his private key using a dedicated hardware solution.

Wallet

The *wallet* resides on the user's computer or hardware device, such as a hard card, and provides a mechanism for secure storage of private information, such as digital IDs, certificates, electronic receipts, credit card numbers, and private keys. The wallet is a service accessible through a standard programming interface and available based on an access control policy. Some information, such as private keys, will be made available for use programmatically, but will not be directly accessible. The user can transport the wallet from one device to another by means of the *Personal Information Exchange* protocol.

Personal Information Exchange

Personal Information Exchange (PFX) is a set of platform-independent protocols that enable the user to transport personal, secure, sensitive information across some unsecured medium. It enables users to maintain a single set of personal ID information and import or export it anytime the user requires a physical relocation. For example, if a user is working at the office and must go home to complete the work, that individual can use PFX to transport the information to a home computer. This is true even if the two computers are based on different platforms.

Part
V

Ch
25

N O T E To transfer personal information between different platforms, PFX must be implemented on both platforms. ■

PFX defines different modes of operation, depending on the circumstances of the transfer and the security required. It describes the following two secure protocols for multi-platform exchanges:

■ Direct exchange is for direct transfer of personal information.

■ Key generation is for the implicit transfer of keys. This operates by regenerating them at the destination.

For the purposes of discussion in this chapter, emphasis is given to the *Direct Exchange* protocol. This protocol defines a *primary data unit* (*PDU*) referred to as a safe. A *safe* is a secure "container" for holding private data during transport, and can be imported or exported on any compliant platform. The safe is segmented into four "compartments" to handle the following different types of data:

■ Private keys

■ Certificates and certificate revocation lists

■ Miscellaneous secrets (account numbers, credit card numbers, and so on)

■ Extensions

The PFX protocol also defines something referred to as *baggage,* which can hold private key information that has already been protected with an encryption algorithm. The purpose of carrying the baggage outside the safe is to avoid *superencryption,* in which certain pieces of data are encrypted multiple times. The entire safe and baggage, along with a version tag, are included in an integrity-mode wrapper to preserve the integrity of the data. This wrapper cannot keep anyone from tampering with the data, but it will enable detection of such tampering.

To exercise the direct exchange of information, the user must decide between two types of privacy modes and two types of integrity modes, based on the kind of transfer to be made. All four modes are as follows:

- Public-key privacy mode
- Password privacy mode
- Public-key integrity mode
- Password integrity mode

As discussed earlier, the privacy modes exist to ensure the secrecy of the data being transferred, and the integrity modes allow for detection of any damage or alteration of the data. The public-key privacy mode performs standard public-key encryption using a single-purpose public key for the destination platform. This privacy mode is the most secure and provides results suitable for transporting the data across a public communication channel. The public-key integrity mode uses a private key from the source platform to create a trusted digital signature (signed by a CA) to protect the integrity of the package.

N O T E   The keys used for the PFX protocol are platform-specific and are dedicated for use with PFX. They are not associated with any user.

The password privacy mode is interesting in that it does not actually use a specified password to protect the data. Instead, it uses a combination of the username and password to generate a reproducible private key used for symmetric encryption (private-key encryption) of the data. The key is then regenerated at the destination utilizing the same process, and that key is used to decrypt the data. The strength of this mode is determined by the length of the password (which should be long and difficult to guess), but it is not suitable for enabling public transport of the data.

The password integrity mode works in much the same way. A unique, integrity key is generated based on the password supplied. Then, a *message authentication code (MAC)* is created as a unique function of the data and integrity key. The MAC is then regenerated on the destination platform using the same password and transmitted data. The newly generated MAC is then compared to the transmitted MAC, verifying integrity.

In general, it is much better to use the public-key modes when possible. However, using these modes requires advance knowledge of the destination platform as well as the keys for that platform. If access to the keys exists, use the public-key privacy mode. It allows for public transport of the data. If not, password mode can be used, but this requires physical protection of the data during transit. An example of this would be a floppy disc stored in a safe. The integrity modes are not as critical because each will protect the data from tampering. However, it is always better to provide the extra security of public-key encryption whenever possible.

Certificate Server

As discussed in the "Network Credentials" section, certificates afford the capability of authenticating a user's digital signature by providing the digital equivalent to a notary seal supplied by a trusted party. Use of these certificates makes it easy to authenticate the parties involved in network connections and authors of electronic documents. Microsoft's certificate server enables control to be exercised over certificate management. Its primary functions are as follows:

- Manage existing certificates
- Issue new certificates upon request
- Revoke certificates and keep track of those that have been revoked

The use of the certificate server enables organizations to take control of authentication on a group, department, or enterprise level. In addition, the organization maintains total control over the policies and procedures in effect regarding the issuance of certificates. Also, the server is policy independent and has no predefined criteria for determining certificate recipients. This ensures that the organization has flexibility in adapting its procedures over time. Moreover, it enables the certificates to be mapped to Windows NT permission groups, providing powerful use of current security settings as well as familiar tools.

Thanks to its use of the CryptoAPI, the certificate server is isolated from the encryption keys themselves. This provides added security as well as enabling the use of any key management system according to individual needs. It also maintains transport independence, which means that requests for certificates can be received from the following variety of sources:

- HTTP forms
- E-mail
- Microsoft Exchange address book

Finally, the certificate server maintains adherence to standards, such as the X.509 certificate format. As such, it works with non-Microsoft clients, such as Netscape's Navigator Web browser. It also supports alternate certificate formats, allowing for use with third-party security systems as well as future changes in the certificate specifications.

Secure Channel Services

No security framework would be complete without a specification for private communications between two points. Microsoft, therefore, defines secure channel services, which are responsible for establishing and maintaining a secure point-to-point connection with the following properties:

- The connection is private.
- The connection is reliable.
- The connection is authenticated.

A private connection means simply that no unauthorized party can view the information passed between the two points. Actually, it is possible for a third party to "eavesdrop" on the communications due to the structure of the Internet. However, anything seen would be unintelligible because of the encryption performed on the data prior to transmission. Therefore, the data passed from application to application along the connection is kept private.

A reliable connection is one in which errors are detected if they exist. This is accomplished using a digital signature on a hash made from the text of the data, then transmitting this signed hash along with the data. On the receiving end, if the signed hash—which cannot be successfully modified—matches what the hash of the data should look like, the integrity of the data is demonstrated with confidence. Should an error be detected, it may be possible to correct the error through retransmission. If not, the secure connection is terminated.

An authenticated connection is one in which at least the server is proven to be authentic. Optionally, the server may request the client to authenticate itself as well. The authentication is performed by means of a digital certificate signed by a trusted third party. Authenticating the connection makes it virtually impossible for anyone to masquerade as the server and attempt to get the client to reveal its secrets.

To achieve this secure connection, Secure Channel Services defines three protocols with which it will operate. These are Secure Sockets Layer (SSL) 2.0, SSL 3.0, and Private Communications Technology (PCT) 1.0. In addition, Transport Layer Security (TLS) will be supported upon its release. The underlying mechanisms for all of these protocols is quite similar. The basic process involves the following actions:

- The client initiates a connection to the server with a client hello message and a list of possible cryptographic protocols to use for the session.
- The host responds, passing the client a certificate for authentication, a public key for encoding the response, a connection ID, and its choices for protocols to use during the session.
- The client authenticates the host, creates a random master key from which will be derived (on both sides) the symmetric keys for encrypting data for the link (one key used for data traveling from client to server, the other for data traveling from server to client), encrypts the master key with the server's public key, and transmits the encrypted master key and the connection ID to the server.
- The server derives the symmetric session keys from the master key, optionally sends a challenge to the client, and sends an encrypted session ID to the client.
- If the client was challenged, it now responds to the server with its certificate of authenticity.
- From this point on, all communications across the link are encrypted using symmetric (private-key) encryption and each record is accompanied by a message authentication code (MAC), which is derived from a function of the original data, and a private key, providing an integrity check for the record.

The goal of the Secure Channel Services is to provide a secure socket connection without incurring a major performance penalty. It provides quick reconnect times in addition to encryption and message authentication. It uses public-key encryption for the handshake and key exchange phase, then switches to private-key encryption for all remaining communications.

All data flowing across the secured channel is broken into records of a manageable size. A MAC is added to the record to ensure integrity. The record and MAC are encrypted using a symmetric encryption algorithm and transmitted across the channel. On the receiving end, the packet is decrypted using the same symmetric key. The MAC is then compared with one newly generated from the received data. If the integrity is confirmed, the record is then forwarded to the receiving application.

To enable all of the protocols to interact, a universal client hello format was devised. This allows great flexibility in terms of connecting clients running one protocol with servers running another, and provides for backward compatibility. For instance, it enables an SSL 3.0 client to connect with an SSL 2.0 server, or a PCT 1.0 client to connect with an SSL 2.0 (or 3.0) server.

Secure Sockets Layer (SSL)   SSL 2.0 operates almost exactly as in the process described in the previous section. It is the first of the protocols supported by Secure Channel Services, was defined by Netscape Communications, and appeared originally in late 1994. SSL has gained significant popularity with the support of many of the large publishers of World Wide Web server and client software. However, there are a few weaknesses to version 2.0. Critics complain that it requires too many handshake rounds to establish a connection. It also contains a possible security hole during the client authentication phase.

To address some of these problems, Netscape revised SSL with a new 3.0 version. Among the most important improvements provided in this new version is the reduction in the number of rounds required in the initial handshake phase. This reduces the overhead significantly with regards to establishing a new connection. SSL is also backwards compatible with 2.0.

Private Communications Technology (PCT)   PCT was developed by Microsoft in late 1995. It is based heavily on the SSL protocols and uses essentially the same record format. Its key improvements revolve around speed. It requires fewer messages and shorter message structures than SSL 2.0. The exchange of messages during the handshake phase has been shortened so much that establishing an initial connection without authenticating the client requires only one message in each direction, and no connection requires more than two messages in each direction.

The primary differences between SSL and PCT are as follows:

- The message structures and message rounds required during handshake are shorter and simpler in PCT.
- PCT provides more choices in the selection of cryptographic algorithms.
- PCT uses different keys for message authentication and encryption.
- PCT fixes the security hole in the SSL 2.0 client authentication.

Transport Layer Security (TLS)   Moving toward a unified, open standard, Microsoft has offered a discussion draft called *Secure Transport Layer Protocol (STLP)*. It has become known as TLS, and it attempts to combine the SSL 3.0 and PCT protocols. It starts essentially with SSL 3.0 and adds features from PCT. The goal is to provide a single protocol that is simpler, more robust, and more scaleable than either SSL or PCT.

CryptoAPI

To make it easier for developers to take advantage of the technologies discussed in this chapter, Microsoft has produced the CryptoAPI. This application programming interface (API) provides services to enable developers to readily add cryptographic, as well as certificate, management functions to their 32-bit applications without requiring them to have in-depth knowledge of the underlying implementations or algorithms. It also protects the sensitive private key information from direct access by the applications utilizing the cryptographic functions.

Currently there are two versions of this API. Version 1.0 provides all of the basic encryption and decryption functionality in addition to key management facilities. Version 2.0 implements all of the version 1.0 functionality and adds functionality for using and managing certificates. Version 2.0 provides calls broken into the following four functional areas:

- **Certificate encode/decode**—This manages the encoding and decoding of certificates.
- **Certificate store**—This provides a means to store, retrieve, enumerate, verify, and use certificates.
- **Base cryptography**—This provides extremely low-level cryptographic functions and provides a means for communicating with cryptographic service providers (CSPs).
- **Simplified cryptography**—This provides high-level cryptographic functions that wrap some of the functions contained in the base cryptography group. This is the easiest approach to CryptoAPI programming.

Cryptographic Service Provider

The CryptoAPI functions abstract out a security layer and insulate the developer from the details of that layer. They also take a "black box" approach, enabling the functionality of the security layer to be implemented as separate modules called *cryptographic service providers (CSPs)*. Each CSP provides its own implementation of the CryptoAPI. The underlying algorithms and key sizes may differ as well as the methods of implementation. For example, the CSP bundled with the system is called the Microsoft RSA Base Provider. This CSP implements the CryptoAPI using RSA encryption algorithms and key lengths suitable for export out of the United States. Another CSP may implement strong encryption (long keys) not eligible for export. Still another may require use of a smart card for verification of the user. Multiple CSPs can reside on a system simultaneously. The application, prior to exercising any of the cryptographic functions, first acquires a handle to the desired CSP.

To install a CSP, first obtain a copy of the CSP on whatever distribution media is supplied by the vendor. Then execute the setup procedure provided with the distribution. This procedure should copy all necessary files to their appropriate places and perform any registry modifications required.

Security Support Provider Interface (SSPI)

The *security support provider interface* is a layer residing between an application and the CryptoAPI. It provides applications with a very high-level interface to security functions and enables any application using SSPI to connect to any security modules using SSPI. These security modules provide applications with an authenticated connection. They are usually implemented using the CryptoAPI and provide a level of abstraction and extensibility to the system.

Secure Electronic Transactions (SET)

In order to fund many of the ventures now appearing on the Internet, it is clear that some type of secure electronic transfer of funds will need to be possible. In addition, it will need to be such an easy process that the average consumer with a computer at home will feel just as comfortable purchasing an item from the Internet Shopping Network as from the Cable Shopping Network. One might feel that all of the encryption and authentication technology just discussed would be fine for making online purchases with credit cards. In fact, that may be a fair assumption. However, there are a couple of limitations associated with making electronic transactions using only those technologies:

- Although it is possible to authenticate a client computer, it may not be possible to determine that the person using the credit card is the person who owns the credit card. Although this is also a problem when taking credit card numbers over the phone, it becomes even more of a risk with the Internet due to the increased potential for abuse.

- There really is no need for the merchant to know all of the information concerning a credit card—only whether the account has enough funds and how to get paid from the bank issuing the credit card.

To answer this need, dozens of corporations have been working on protocols for implementing an electronic payment system. One protocol has begun to emerge from a combination of two previous front runners. *Secure electronic transactions (SET)* is a protocol defined jointly by VISA and MasterCard, with the help of a partnership of companies, including GTE, IBM, Microsoft, Netscape, SAIC, Terisa, and VeriSign. With the support of these industry giants, it is not difficult to see why SET has become the leading contender for an electronic transaction standard.

SET is an open specification which provides for the protection of payment card purchases on any type of network. The primary goals of SET include the following:

- Ensuring the privacy and confidentiality of the information involved in an electronic transaction

- Guaranteeing the integrity of the transaction

- Authenticating both the card holder and merchant

The steps involved in making an online purchase using SET are demonstrated by the following sample session:

1. The customer, using Internet Explorer (or Netscape Navigator), browses the site of an online merchant.

2. When the customer decides to make a purchase, an encrypted SET charge slip is transmitted to the merchant along with a credit draft for the specified purchase amount.

3. The merchant contacts a processing bank to obtain approval for the transfer. The charge slip (still encrypted) and a copy of the draft are sent to the bank (the charge slip never having been seen by the merchant).

4. The bank contacts VISA to authorize and settle the transfer.

5. VISA approves the transfer for the processing bank and notifies the issuing bank of the transfer.

6. The processing bank notifies the merchant that the transfer was approved.

7. The merchant sends an electronic receipt to the customer. The receipt is electronically signed by the merchant using the merchant's private key and is legally binding.

8. At the end of the month, the issuing bank sends the customer a credit card statement containing (among other things) the purchase from the merchant.

9. The customer (presumably) pays the issuing bank (maybe electronically).

Although this may seem like a long and complicated process, it is not that different from the process taking place today. However, in the scenario above, no credit card was ever physically handed to a merchant and no credit card number was given over the phone.

Securing Internet Information Server

Whether you are using Internet Information Server (IIS) in an Internet or intranet environment, you are opening your server to access by a number of users. In most cases, these individuals will be unknown to you. Therefore, it is absolutely essential to take every possible precaution in securing the server against unauthorized access. In order to accomplish this, it is necessary to understand the security process implemented by IIS to restrict server access.

IIS Security Process

The security process implemented by IIS involves traversing a set of security layers, each of which must be successfully passed in order to move to the next layer and eventually to the requested resource. There are essentially four such security layers standing between a user making a request for a resource through IIS and the requested resource, as follows:

1. IIS first checks the Internet Protocol (IP) address of the user against a list of allowed IP addresses. If the IP address is rejected, the security check fails.

2. IIS validates the username and password against the valid Windows NT user accounts. Even users accessing the IIS services by anonymous access have a user account set up specifically for the anonymous user.

3. Any resource requested from IIS must reside in a directory (or directory tree) that has been identified to IIS. A request for any resource residing outside one of these predefined (virtual) directories will be denied. Also, IIS enables the setting of permissions on the directories defined. These are permissions imposed by IIS and are in addition to any NTFS permissions found.

4. Any user requesting a resource must have appropriate NTFS permissions for that user. For instance, if a file is requested by a user, that user's Windows NT account must have read access to the file, or the request is denied.

Given this list of security layers, it seems prudent to address each layer and apply the most rigid requirements possible, according to the type of access you want to allow. This way, unnecessary security holes can be eliminated and the risks of unauthorized access to your server minimized.

Filtering IP Addresses   The first line of defense for IIS is to filter out IP addresses for any unauthorized clients. This may or may not be feasible for your particular case, as it depends a great deal on whether IIS is being used for an Internet or intranet server. If this is an Internet server, it seems likely that anyone is welcome and no filtering will be used unless you want to single out individual addresses from which users may be harassing your server. However, an intranet is a much more limited system, and IP filtering may be a good fit. In fact, subnet masks provide a good means to block out (or allow) large groups of IP addresses.

To set up IP filtering, you have two basic choices. You can either grant access to everyone except those specifically listed as blocked, or deny access to everyone except those specifically listed as granted. The following are the steps for blocking an IP address:

1. Start the Internet Service Manager.

2. Click the Advanced tab.

3. Click the Granted Access option button. This specifies that all users will be granted access unless explicitly listed in the denied access list.

4. Click the Add button.

5. If you want to enter a single address to block, click the Single Computer option button. In the IP Address box, type the IP address to be blocked. If you would rather use a name, click the button next to the IP Address box, and type the name of the computer to be blocked (e.g., **www.gasullivan.com**).

6. If you want to block a range of addresses, click Group of Computers. In the IP Address box, enter the first IP address in the range. In the Subnet Mask box, type the subnet corresponding to the group to be blocked.

7. Click the OK button.

8. In the Advanced tab, click the OK button.

The following is the process for granting access to an IP address:

1. Start the Internet Service Manager.

2. Click the Advanced tab.

3. Click the Denied Access option button. This specifies that all users will be denied access unless explicitly listed in the granted access list.

4. Click the Add button.

5. If you want to enter a single address to allow access to, click the Single Computer option button. In the IP Address box, type the IP address to be granted access. If you would rather use a name, click the button next to the IP Address box, and type the name of the computer to be granted access (e.g., **www.gasullivan.com**).

6. If you want to grant access to a range of addresses, click Group of Computers. In the IP Address box, enter the first IP address in the range. In the Subnet Mask box, type the subnet corresponding to the group to be granted access.

7. Click the OK button.

8. In the Advanced tab, click the OK button.

Windows NT User Accounts   Anyone who has browsed the World Wide Web probably knows that the vast majority of sites do not require a username and password. They use an anonymous account that works for anyone accessing the site. That will probably also be the case for you if you are running a general Internet site. However, an intranet site could operate either way depending upon the type of information being shared. For sharing general information, such as memos or postings, it may be preferable to allow anonymous access. However, for something like a departmental server or a Web application that has a small, known user base, it may be wise to create Windows NT user accounts for each user and to challenge users with username and password authentication before allowing access.

There are a couple of points to consider before making this decision. First, since the gopher service is always an anonymous protocol, the discussion here centers on File Transfer Protocol (FTP) and Hypertext Transfer Protocol (HTTP) access. With FTP, it is generally safer to allow anonymous access rather than authenticated. That may sound backwards, but the reason is simple. FTP does not encode password information prior to transmission. Therefore, anyone watching the network with a protocol analyzer would be able to intercept the username and password information in plain text. In other words, by requiring authentication, you are actually putting the account at risk. Therefore, it is better to limit what is available via FTP and to allow anonymous access to that information.

> **CAUTION**
>
> FTP is one the most difficult of all the Internet protocols to secure. For this reason, it is strongly recommended that you consider carefully your requirements for running the FTP server.

Second, IIS supports both HTTP basic authentication and the Windows NT Challenge/ Response protocol for client authentication. Both of these authentication methods enable the client to send username and password information to the server. However, in basic authentication, both the username and password are transmitted in plain text. This creates the same risk of interception as in FTP authentication. Clients implementing the Windows NT Challenge/ Response authentication protocol, however, transmit an encrypted username and password. This eliminates the risk of interception and provides much greater security. To date, however, Internet Explorer version 2.0 and higher are the only browsers supporting this protocol.

N O T E   The plain text authentication information is not a problem if secure channel services are utilized. In this case, all data traveling across the link is encrypted, regardless of the protocol being used. ▪

IIS Directory Access   No directory can be accessed through IIS until a virtual directory is created for it. The virtual directory is a directory name that is mapped to a physical directory on either a local or remote disk. A Uniform Resource Locator (URL) referencing the virtual directory is remapped by IIS to the physical directory to access a requested resource. Therefore, be sure to create virtual directories only when absolutely necessary.

Further, when creating virtual directories with IIS, it is possible to set any of three permission types (depending on the type of service) for the virtual directory and all subdirectories: read, write, and execute. It is important not to overlook these permission settings, as they are separate from any permissions maintained by NTFS and provide another level of security. The general rules for setting these directory permissions are as follows:

- **Read**—This permits clients to read or download documents, and should be granted for any directory containing information to be published. This would include HTML files, Microsoft Word documents, Adobe Acrobat documents, text files, and graphics files.

- **Write**—This permits clients to upload information to the server, and should be used cautiously. Always ensure that these directories are at the bottom of the directory tree, and thus contain no subdirectories. Also, any data uploaded to these locations should be treated with extreme caution. This permission setting is only available for the FTP service.

- **Execute**—This permits a client request to invoke executables, such as CGI scripts or ISAPI extensions. This is also something that should be approached with caution. CGI applications and ISAPI extensions are heavily utilized and provide much of the database connectivity now in place. However, it is essential that execute permissions are tightly controlled and limited in scope. This permission setting is only available for the WWW service.

Part

V

Ch

25

CAUTION

In general, it is bad practice to enable both read and write privileges on any given directory. Therefore, it is a good idea to segment a site to keep all relevant documents together and all related executables together, but separate from one another. Also, it is wise to install the publishing services on a completely separate disk partition from the one containing the Windows NT operating system. This provides a fairly good barrier between the server and the operating system files.

To set or modify access permissions for a virtual directory, perform the following steps:

1. Open Internet Service Manager.
2. Double-click the WWW service.
3. Click the Directories tab.
4. Select the folder for which you want to set permissions.
5. Click the Edit Properties button.
6. Select the appropriate check box.
7. Click OK, and then click OK again.

NTFS File Permissions   The last line of defense lies in NTFS's capability to restrict user access on a file-by-file basis. Ensure that all user and group privileges are appropriately restricted. Follow the guidelines outlined in the previous section, "IIS Directory Access," to determine which permissions to set for files in the IIS publishing directory trees. Also, do not allow the anonymous user account any access to files outside these trees.

Security Policies   The most important thing to remember about security is that any secure system is only as good as its weakest link. More often than not, that weak link is in the enforcement of the security policy. One example of this is a mainframe system which requires user ID/password authentication to log on. If it is possible to call a help desk and get a password changed for a specified user ID without presenting any form of identification, the policy has been circumvented.

It is often difficult to decide what the security policies should be for an organization. There are always tradeoffs in security versus usability, and the policies depend upon the individual needs of the organization involved. However, once the policies are put into place, it is important to follow them consistently, or unexpected security holes may appear.

Implementing Secure Channel Services

When it comes to an Internet application involving electronic commerce or an intranet application enabling access to sensitive information, enabling secure channel services on the server seems prudent. This enables all data flowing between the client and server (both directions) to be encrypted for privacy and integrity. Secure channel services can be enabled on a directory basis so that it is enforced only for data requiring secure transport. This way, a single server can host multiple applications: some secure, some not, and some requiring secure channel services for only portions of their available data.

> **CAUTION**
>
> Use of secure channel services does impose a performance penalty. For this reason, it is a good idea to determine which parts of the site really contain sensitive information and which do not. Then, only implement secure channel services on those portions required.

N O T E   To enable secure channel services on the entire Web site, just enable these services on the root IIS directory. Otherwise, enable services on each directory as desired. ■

To enable secure channel services on IIS, the following steps must be performed:

1. Generate a key pair and a request file.
2. Obtain a certificate.
3. Install the certificate on IIS.
4. Activate secure channel services on the desired directories.

Generating Keys   In order to generate keys for use in obtaining certificates, IIS comes with a utility called the Key Manager. This utility can be accessed by either clicking the Key Manager icon in the Internet Information Server program group, or launching the Microsoft Internet Service Manager and selecting Tools, Key Manager. Once Key Manager is open, perform the following procedure:

1. Choose Key, Create New Key.
2. Fill in all information in the Create New Key and Certificate Request dialog boxes.

CAUTION

Commas should not be used in the fields for the Certificate Request dialog box. They indicate an end-of-field marker, and will cause Key Manager to generate an improper certificate request without warning the user.

3. Click the OK button.
4. Another dialog box appears prompting you to re-enter the password. This is just to ensure that the password was not typed incorrectly. Enter the password again and click the OK button.

Upon completion of the form, the Key Manager will generate a file containing the key pair just created, and a second file containing a certificate request. Also, the name of the new key appears in the Key Manager window. You are now ready to obtain a valid certificate.

CAUTION

Do not use the key generated by Key Manager on the Internet until a valid certificate is obtained from a certification authority. This can be either an internal authority or a commercial authority, such as VeriSign.

Obtaining and Installing Certificates   Once you have a certificate request file, you can obtain a valid certificate. The procedure for this may vary from one CA to another, and will depend on the type of certificate requested as well as the type of CA. Eventually, you will receive a valid certificate from the CA. It is now time to install this certificate on IIS. To install the certificate, perform the following steps:

1. Start Key Manager by either clicking the Key Manager icon in the Internet Information Server program group or launching the Microsoft Internet Service Manager and selecting Tools, Key Manager.
2. Select the key pair that corresponds to the certificate request file used to obtain the certificate.
3. Select Key, Install Key Certificate.
4. Select the certificate file containing the certificate supplied by the CA, and click Open.
5. When prompted, type the same password that you used when you created the key pair.
6. Select Servers, Commit Changes Now.
7. Click OK to commit the changes.

Enabling Secure Sockets Layer   In order to use the newly installed certificate, it is necessary to enable Secure Sockets Layer on at least one virtual directory for IIS. This can be done for the root directory to secure the entire site or on a directory-by-directory basis, but any subdirectories of secure directories are also secure. Simply perform the following procedure:

1. Start the Internet Service Manager.
2. Double-click the WWW service to open the Service Properties dialog box.
3. Click the Directories tab.
4. Select the folder for which SSL security is desired, then click Edit Properties.
5. Select the Require secure SSL channel option, and then click OK.

N O T E   Once a directory is set to require SSL, an URL referencing a document from the secure directory must use **HTTPS** rather than **HTTP**, indicating the secure connection. ▧

Security and Internet Explorer

Internet Explorer 3.0 provides facilities for implementing most of the security mechanisms described in this chapter. These features provide the capability to complete the client side of the security framework when implementing an intranet application as well as providing client authentication in a public Internet environment. In addition, it affords protection against false server sites or malicious applications through authentication of the server and validation of the application's author.

Certificates

Internet Explorer manages certificates that enable authentication to a server, identifying you uniquely as you connect to the server. It also enables you to specify both trusted publishers and certification authorities. If you access a site from which you begin to download active content, Internet Explorer presents you with a notification of the publisher's certificate if one exists. You can then proceed to download the content or block it. Also, you can specify that all future software published by the same vendor or any publisher with credentials from the same certification authority be considered safe, and that no such future notification is needed (see Figure 25.9).

FIG. 25.9

Microsoft's Internet Explorer 3.0 displays the certificate accompanying downloaded software and prompts the user for the appropriate action.

Once a publisher or certification authority has been added to the list of trusted publishers, it is possible to view and delete them from the list by performing the following steps:

1. Select View, Options.
2. Select the Security tab.
3. Press the Publishers button to view all trusted publishers and certification authorities.
4. View or remove any software publisher or CA from the list.
5. Press the OK button.

In addition to software publishing, there is a similar mechanism for the recognition of trusted servers. More specifically, it is possible to indicate that any server possessing a certificate from a trusted CA should be trusted. To view and/or delete a CA from this list, perform the following steps:

1. Select View, Options.
2. Select the Security tab.
3. Press the Sites button to view all trusted certification authorities.
4. View or remove any CA from the list.
5. Press the OK button.

Part

V

Ch

25

Finally, it is possible to view personal certificates as well. These personal certificates are used for client authentication to a server and uniquely identify the user. They are used to certify anything from e-mail addresses to credit cards and bank accounts. The procedure for obtaining and installing a certificate varies from one CA to another. Generally, a request is made containing all personal information pertaining to the type of certificate desired. After verifying all of the information, the CA delivers the digital ID using an appropriate means. The certificate is then installed into Internet Explorer, usually in some automated process.

To view any installed personal certificate, perform the following steps:

1. Select View, Options.
2. Select the Security tab.
3. Press the Personal button.
4. Select the certificate from the list, and press the View Certificate button.
5. Press the OK button.

Active Content

In addition to utilizing certificates for authentication, Internet Explorer also provides protection from active content, such as ActiveX Controls and Java applets. This protection integrates quite closely with the digital certificates because much of the protection offered involves trusting applications whose source is trusted.

Both Java applets and ActiveX Controls are appearing on wide numbers of sites across the Internet. It is important to understand exactly what risks are involved with running these executables downloaded from the Internet.

Java applications do not actually exist as executable code, but rather as a set of operations to be performed by the Java Virtual Machine. Alternatively, a *just-in-time* (*JIT*) compiler will compile the Java byte codes into local machine code, which then gets executed directly on the processor. The important point to remember is that in both cases, there is a layer between the downloaded program and the processor. This layer isolates the machine from the Java program and provides protection for the computer. Because of this, Java programs are tightly restricted in their capability to access the local computer's hardware and are, therefore, generally safer to run.

In contrast, ActiveX components are compiled executable modules that run directly on the local hardware and can access nearly anything they want—constrained only by the specific operating system safeguards. For instance, it has been demonstrated that an ActiveX component could shut down a Windows 95 computer without the permission of the user. Fortunately, this demonstration did nothing malicious and warned the user prior to performing the shutdown; but it was a grave reminder of the type of havoc that could be wreaked if malicious intent existed.

It is valid to point out that software downloaded from a trusted source probably will not contain malicious code, especially since the integrity is also checked—disallowing any tampering.

However, errant code is not detected and could accidentally produce similar results. This is really no different than with any software purchased and loaded in a traditional manner. Therefore, the same judgment should be applied when deciding which ActiveX components are to be allowed to run.

To access the settings for allowing and disallowing content based on ActiveX and Java, perform the following steps:

1. Choose View, Options.
2. Select the Security tab.
3. Press the Personal button.
4. In the Active Content frame, select the desired security settings, as follows:
   - Select Allow Downloading of Active Content to enable pages with active content to be downloaded.
   - Select Enable ActiveX Controls and Plug-ins to enable controls to be downloaded and run.
   - Select Run ActiveX Scripts to enable JavaScript and Visual Basic Script programs (which run on the browser) to execute. Disabling this setting will cause many buttons and other controls in downloaded documents to lose functionality.
   - Select Enable Java Programs to enable Java applets to download and execute.
5. Press the Safety Level button.
6. Select the security level desired. The recommended settings are generally a good idea.
7. Press the OK button to exit the Safety Level dialog box.
8. Press the OK button to exit the Options dialog, and the Apply button to apply the changes without closing.

Secure Communications

Obviously, secure communications would be somewhat useless if only the server supported it. Therefore, Microsoft included support for secure communications in Internet Explorer 3.0. In fact, Internet Explorer 3.0 supports SSL 2.0 and 3.0, as well as PCT. These protocols run fairly seamlessly and require very little input from the user. In fact, it is sometimes difficult to tell if a secure page is being accessed, except for the **https** in the URL and the extra lock icon appearing at the bottom right of the Internet Explorer's main frame. The user does have some control, however, over the types of protocols run and what warnings are to be seen. To modify these values, perform the following steps:

1. Select View, Options.
2. Select the Advanced tab.
3. In the Warnings frame, select any warnings you want to receive.
4. To select security protocols allowed, press the Cryptography Settings button.
5. Select any protocol to be allowed.

Part

V

Ch

25

6. Press the OK button to close the Cryptography Protocols dialog box.

7. Press the OK button to exit the Options dialog, and the Apply button to apply the changes without closing.

Web Ratings

Anyone who has surfed the Internet, even for a short time, will probably admit to being just a little overwhelmed by the sheer enormity of it. It is not at all difficult to become lost—following link after link with little hope of ever retracing the exact path you took to get to a destination. The recent proliferation of search engines has made it much easier to find information relating to a given topic without relying on luck. It is now possible to perform a search on a subject by simply keying in a word or group of words and being presented with anywhere from zero to ten million documents pertaining in some way to those words. It is up to the individual user to decide what is relevant and what is not.

In addition to all of the research papers published by universities, information offered by various organizations, and personal items posted by individuals, the Web has become home to a growing number of sites offering mature subject matter. It is up to the individual to determine what is offensive. There has been a recent outcry against the ease with which anyone, no matter what age, can access this material via the Internet. Attempts have been made on various regional and national levels to restrict what may be published, but to no avail. Many people simply do not realize that censorship by a single country could not work unless that country was also willing to restrict connections to any country with contrary policies.

The Internet is truly a global entity. How then can individuals restrict small children from gaining access to these sites or filter what they themselves see? The answer lies in ratings. By rating Web sites, it becomes possible for the user to filter those sites based on individual criteria for the ratings. In this way, access can be restricted, or *filtered,* based on preset criteria, saving precious time from manually sifting through the list of sites returned from your query.

Platform for Internet Content Selection (PICS)

One standard put forth by the World Wide Web Consortium has caught on very quickly. The PICS specification has gained the acceptance of many larger Internet software vendors. PICS defines an infrastructure for associating labels with content. It consists of the following two basic components:

- Rating systems, which define the criteria for rating the content.
- Rating labels, which describe the actual rating information.

PICS does not actually define any rating system, but allows for definitions to be made. In fact, any group or individual can create a rating system to meet specific needs. Once a rating system is defined and a page is rated using the appropriate labels, a browser using the rating system will filter the page according to the user's criteria. If the criteria are met, the browser displays the page; otherwise, it only displays a message indicating why the page could not be viewed.

When talking about rating systems, most people automatically think about sexual or violent content. However, it would be just as appropriate to devise a system based on something else entirely, such as the amount and type of technical content in a publication. In this way, users on a corporate intranet could filter out documents based on their technical level in any given area.

N O T E   It is theoretically possible to incorporate multiple ratings into a single document. This means documents on an intranet could be organized into different categories, with each document containing a rating one or more categories. The documents could then be filtered by the user based on multiple criteria. ■

Recreational Software Advisory Council (RSACi)

One of the most popular of the early rating systems defined for the Internet is from the Recreational Software Advisory Council, called RSACi. This system ships with Internet Explorer 3.0 and is likely to be popular with parents of small children. It is an easy to understand, head-on approach to rating. It essentially defines four categories of ratings—shown in Table 25.1—each of which is then divided into levels that define the rating.

Table 25.1   Categories in the RSACi Internet Rating System

Level	Description
Violence	
1	Creatures killed; creatures injured; damage to realistic objects; fighting—no injuries
2	Humans killed; humans injured; rewards injuring non-threatening creatures
3	Blood and gore; rewards injuring non-threatening humans; rewards killing non-threatening creatures; accidental injury with blood and gore
4	Wanton and gratuitous violence; rape
Language	
1	Mild expletives
2	Expletives; non-sexual anatomical references
3	Strong, vulgar language; obscene gestures
4	Crude or explicit sexual references
Nudity	
1	Revealing attire
2	Partial nudity
3	Frontal nudity; non-sexual frontal nudity
4	Provocative frontal nudity

Part
V

Ch
25

continues

Table 25.1 Continued

Level	Description
Sex	
1	Passionate kissing
2	Clothed sexual touching
3	Non-explicit sexual activity; sexual touching
4	Sex crimes; explicit sexual activity

To utilize the RSACi system, the user sets the desired level for each category. Any document with a rating in any category exceeding the allowable level for that category will not be permitted. The publisher must fill out a questionnaire and submit it along with a processing fee to RSACi. The application can be for a single document, a branch or directory of a Web site, or an entire site. RSACi then responds with a rating that is incorporated into the HTML documents to be published.

Incorporating Ratings into HTML Documents

Incorporating ratings into an HTML document is a relatively straightforward process. It is probable that the HTML authoring tools will eventually aid in this task, but for now it is accomplished with the aid of a standard text editor, such as Notepad. First, obtain a rating for your document based on the rating system you want to incorporate. In the case of RSACi, submit a questionnaire, and you will receive a set of rating labels. A sample rating tag looks something like this:

```
<META http-equiv="PICS-Label" content='(PICS-1.0
"http://www.rsac.org/ratingsv01.html" l gen true comment "RSACi North America
Server" by "RSAC " for "http://www.gasullivan.com" on "1996.09.27T08:15-0500"
exp "1997.09.27T08:15-0500" r (n 0 s 0 v 0 l 1))'>
```

This tag uses the RSACi rating system to rate a fictional document on G. A. Sullivan's Web site. The rating is valid between the dates of 9/27/96 and 9/27/97. The actual rating values are shown last and are simply indicated by a set of label/value pairs. For instance, *n 0* corresponds to a rating of no nudity. In fact, this tag indicates no nudity, sex, or violence. However, the language rating of 1 indicates that mild expletives are used.

Once you have the ratings, open the HTML document in a text editor, and insert the tag into the header section of the document. When it is pasted in, save the document and exit. Listing 25.1 is an example of the resulting document.

Listing 25.1 Simple HTML Document Containing RSACi Rating

```
<HTML>
<HEAD>
<META http-equiv="PICS-Label" content='(PICS-1.0
"http://www.rsac.org/ratingsv01.html" l gen true comment "RSACi North America
```

```
Server" by "RSAC " for "http://www.gasullivan.com" on "1996.09.27T08:15-0500"
exp "1997.09.27T08:15-0500" r (n 0 s 0 v 0 l 1))'>
</HEAD>
<BODY>
This is a page containing MILD EXPLETIVES !
</BODY>
</HTML>
```

Controlling Access to Documents with Internet Explorer

With all of the information about rating systems on the Internet, it would be nice to be able to use that information to restrict access to certain types of material for children, students, and possibly employees. Internet Explorer 3.0 provides a simple means to accomplish this by incorporating a control center called Content Advisor (see Figure 25.10).

FIG. 25.10
Internet Explorer's Content Advisor enables an administrator to restrict access to content based on document ratings.

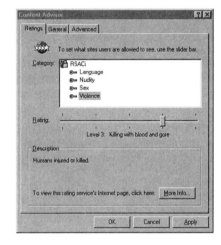

Part
V

Ch
25

To access Content Advisor, follow these steps:

1. Select View, Options. This brings up the Options dialog box.
2. Click the Security tab.

There are two buttons associated with Content Advisor. One enables or disables the use of any rating settings, and the other launches Content Advisor to enable modification of the settings. First time selection of either button brings up a dialog box prompting you to enter a new supervisor password to be used when changing settings. Subsequent selection will require you to enter the supervisor password to proceed. Without this password, no one can to enable, disable, or modify any of the settings.

> **CAUTION**
> Make sure you remember the supervisor password. If you forget it, you will have to reinstall Internet Explorer to change or override any settings made with Content Advisor. If you write this password down, make sure it is not available to those who are restricted.

To enable or disable the Content Advisor settings, select the leftmost button in the Content Advisor section of the Security tab. This button will be labeled either Enable Ratings or Disable Ratings, depending on the current state of the system. Once the button is pressed, Internet Explorer prompts for the supervisor password. If it is entered correctly, Internet Explorer displays a dialog box indicating the success of the action.

To modify the actual rating settings, click the button labeled Settings. Again, you are prompted for the supervisor password. Just enter it and press OK. The Content Advisor dialog box appears containing three tabs: Ratings, General, and Advanced. The Ratings tab enables you to set specific values for a selected rating system and category. To change settings, go to the Category list and click the category you want to change. A slider control appears below the category list. Just slide the control left or right until you achieve the desired Rating level as described just below the slider. When you are satisfied with the settings of all categories, press the Apply button to save the changes (or OK to save and leave the Content Advisor). If you feel that you accidentally changed some settings, pressing Cancel will discard changes and exit.

The General tab enables you to change the supervisor password and set two options. The first option—Users Can See Sites Which Have No Rating—means just that. If this option is selected, any page containing no rating information is allowed to be viewed. Currently, there are a large percentage of sites with no rating information. If those were all blocked, it might be too limiting to the user, depending on the circumstances involved. The second option, Supervisor Can Type a Password to Allow Users to View Restricted Content, provides an override mechanism. If this option is set when a restricted page is encountered, Internet Explorer notifies the user of the restricted page and displays a dialog box prompting for the supervisor password. If the password is entered, the page is displayed. This allows parents to view material that would otherwise be restricted for their children.

Finally, the Advanced tab enables you to add additional rating systems and delete existing systems. To add a new rating system requires a file that defines the system. This file should have the .RAT extension. It should be obtained from the group or organization responsible for defining the system. Once you have this file, click the Rating Systems button. This brings up a dialog box that lists all existing systems. Click the Add button and browse the location of the .RAT file. Select the file and click the Open button. This should install the new rating system. Now click the OK button to close the Rating Systems dialog box. To change the settings for the new system, go back to the Ratings tab and select the appropriate levels. Then click OK to save and close, or Cancel to discard changes.

TIP Although it is not required, it is a good idea to place new .RAT files into the `windows\system` directory where the original RSACi file resides. This enables all such files to be similarly located and should avoid future confusion or accidental deletion of one or more of these files.

Internet Ratings API

Microsoft is currently working on an Internet Ratings API to provide developers with support for PICS-based rating systems and related services. This API is not available at the time of this writing; but when available, should do the following:

- Provide a common interface for parsing and obtaining PICS-compliant rating information.
- Eliminate the need for individual applications to define their own control systems.

The introduction of this API should encourage the development of many new applications with innovative new uses for the rating systems.

From Here...

In this chapter, you learned about the basic cryptographic technologies employed in the secure Internet communication protocols. You also saw an outline of Microsoft's Internet Security Framework, which lists the protocols that will form the basis for secure network computing on the Microsoft operating systems and how they interact with other systems on the Internet. In addition, you learned how to apply these technologies to your Internet/intranet applications utilizing the features available in Internet Information Server and Internet Explorer.

For more information on some of the topics addressed in this chapter, see the following chapters:

- To learn how to set up and administer a Web server with IIS, see Chapter 18, "Building A Web with Internet Information Server (IIS)."
- To learn more about the features of Internet Explorer and some of the other browsers available, see Chapter 19, "Web Browsers."

Part
V

Ch
25

Index

Check out Que® Books on the World Wide Web
http://www.quecorp.com

As the biggest software release in computer history, Windows 95 continues to redefine the computer industry. Click here for the latest info on our Windows 95 books

Make computing quick and easy with these products designed exclusively for new and casual users

Examine the latest releases in word processing, spreadsheets, operating systems, and suites

The Internet, The World Wide Web, CompuServe®, America Online®, Prodigy® —it's a world of ever-changing information. Don't get left behind!

Find out about new additions to our site, new bestsellers and hot topics

In-depth information on high-end topics: find the best reference books for databases, programming, networking, and client/server technologies

A recent addition to Que, Ziff-Davis Press publishes the highly-successful *How It Works* and *How to Use* series of books, as well as *PC Learning Labs Teaches* and *PC Magazine* series of book/disc packages

Stay on the cutting edge of Macintosh® technologies and visual communications

Find out which titles are making headlines

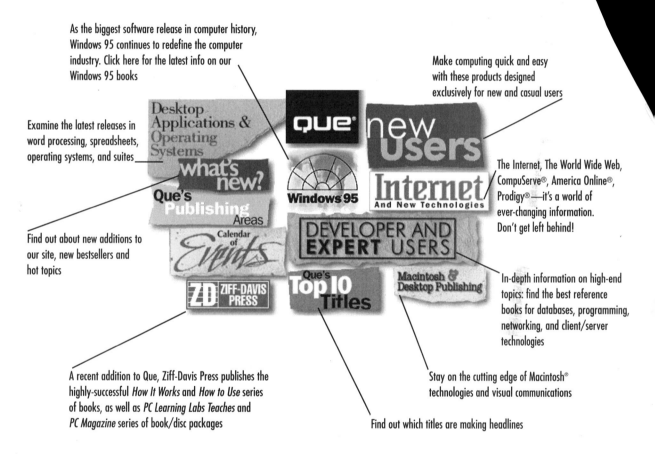

With 6 separate publishing groups, Que develops products for many specific market segments and areas of computer technology. Explore our Web Site and you'll find information on best-selling titles, newly published titles, upcoming products, authors, and much more.

- Stay informed on the latest industry trends and products available
- Visit our online bookstore for the latest information and editions
- Download software from Que's library of the best shareware and freeware

Complete and Return this Ca[rd]
for a *FREE* Computer Book C[atalog]

Thank you for purchasing this book! You have purchased a superior computer [book] expressly for your needs. To continue to provide the kind of up-to-date, pertinen[t] you've come to expect from us, we need to hear from you. Please take a minute [to] and return this self-addressed, postage-paid form. In return, we'll send you a free [catalog of] all our computer books on topics ranging from word processing to programming a[nd the] internet.

Mr. ☐ Mrs. ☐ Ms. ☐ Dr. ☐

Name (first) ☐☐☐☐☐☐☐☐☐☐☐ (M.I.) ☐ (last) ☐☐☐☐☐☐☐☐☐☐☐☐☐☐☐

Address ☐☐☐☐☐☐☐☐☐☐☐☐☐☐☐☐☐☐☐☐☐☐☐☐☐☐☐☐☐

☐☐☐☐☐☐☐☐☐☐☐☐☐☐☐☐☐☐☐☐☐☐☐☐☐☐☐☐☐

City ☐☐☐☐☐☐☐☐☐☐☐☐☐ State ☐☐ Zip ☐☐☐☐☐ ☐☐☐☐

Phone ☐☐☐ ☐☐☐ ☐☐☐☐ Fax ☐☐☐ ☐☐☐ ☐☐☐☐

Company Name ☐☐☐☐☐☐☐☐☐☐☐☐☐☐☐☐☐☐☐☐☐☐☐☐☐☐☐

E-mail address ☐☐☐☐☐☐☐☐☐☐☐☐☐☐☐☐☐☐☐☐☐☐☐☐☐☐☐

1. Please check at least (3) influencing factors for purchasing this book.

Front or back cover information on book .... ☐
Special approach to the content .... ☐
Completeness of content .... ☐
Author's reputation .... ☐
Publisher's reputation .... ☐
Book cover design or layout .... ☐
Index or table of contents of book .... ☐
Price of book .... ☐
Special effects, graphics, illustrations .... ☐
Other (Please specify): _____ ☐

2. How did you first learn about this book?

Saw in Macmillan Computer Publishing catalog .... ☐
Recommended by store personnel .... ☐
Saw the book on bookshelf at store .... ☐
Recommended by a friend .... ☐
Received advertisement in the mail .... ☐
Saw an advertisement in: _____ ☐
Read book review in: _____ ☐
Other (Please specify): _____ ☐

3. How many computer books have you purchased in the last six months?

This book only .... ☐   3 to 5 books .... ☐
2 books .... ☐   More than 5 .... ☐

4. Where did you purchase this book?

Bookstore .... ☐
Computer Store .... ☐
Consumer Electronics Store .... ☐
Department Store .... ☐
Office Club .... ☐
Warehouse Club .... ☐
Mail Order .... ☐
Direct from Publisher .... ☐
Internet site .... ☐
Other (Please specify): _____ ☐

5. How long have you been using a computer?

☐ Less than 6 months   ☐ 6 months to a year
☐ 1 to 3 years   ☐ More than 3 years

6. What is your level of experience with personal computers and with the subject of this book?

	With PCs	With subject of book
New	☐	☐
Casual	☐	☐
Accomplished	☐	☐
Expert	☐	☐

Source Code ISBN: 0-7897-1142-7

wing best describes your

stant .... ☐
... ☐
sor .... ☐
... ☐
/COO .... ☐
tor/Medical Professional .... ☐
ucator/Trainer .... ☐
Technician .... ☐
nt .... ☐
ployed/Student/Retired .... ☐
(Please specify): _____ ☐

Which of the following best describes the area of
the company your job title falls under?

Accounting .... ☐
Engineering .... ☐
Manufacturing .... ☐
Operations .... ☐
Marketing .... ☐
Sales .... ☐
Other (Please specify): _____ ☐

9. What is your age?
Under 20 .... ☐
21-29 .... ☐
30-39 .... ☐
40-49 .... ☐
50-59 .... ☐
60-over .... ☐

10. Are you:
Male .... ☐
Female .... ☐

**11. Which computer publications do you read
    regularly? (Please list)**

_____
_____
_____
_____
_____
_____
_____
_____
_____
_____

Comments: _____
_____
_____

Fold here and scotch-tape to mail.

BackOffice Solutions Don't Stop Here...

The Most Complete Reference

Volume 2

- Master expert techniques and strategies for network administrators and Internet professionals
- Master Exchange Server 5.0 and Outlook, the new client-exchange with powerful groupware features
- Use BackOffice for workgroup collaboration and groupware, document routing, and messaging
- Learn about the the new Microsoft Transaction Server

Special Edition

USING MICROSOFT

BACKOFFICE

CD-ROM includes IIS 4.0!

ISBN: 0-7897-1130-3 • PRICE: $75.00 USA

For more answers to your BackOffice questions, complete your BackOffice set with *Special Edition Using Microsoft BackOffice, Vol 2*.

Discover additional coverage of:

- Exchange Server 5.0
- Outlook 97 and its powerful new features
- Using BackOffice for collaboration, document routing, and messaging
- New Microsoft Transaction Server (MTS), code-named Viper
- Advanced features of SQL Server including replication and the Distributed Transaction Coordinator
- SMS 1.2 and SNA Server 3.0

Volume 2 also includes a power-packed CD-ROM with electronic versions of these Special Edition Using books in Que's BackOffice Library:

- Special Edition Using SQL Server 6.5, Second Edition
- Special Edition Using Exchange Server 5
- Special Edition Using System Management Server 1.2
- Special Edition Using Windows NT Server 4

Available at your local bookstore!
Or to order call 1-800-772-0477
Or visit us on the Internet at: http://www.quecorp.com

Discover The Power™ Copyright 1997 Macmillan Computer Publishing USA. A Simon & Schuster Company. The Publishing Operation of Viacom Inc.

Licensing Agreement

By opening this package, you are agreeing to be bound by the following: